THE ENCYCLOPEDIA OF
MUSIC

THE ENCYCLOPEDIA OF
MUSIC

Musical instruments and the art of music-making

M A X W A D E - M A T T H E W S & W E N D Y T H O M P S O N

LORENZ BOOKS

Publisher: Joanna Lorenz
Editorial Director: Judith Simons
Project Editor: Felicity Forster
Editor: Beverley Jollands
Photographer: John Freeman
Designers: Ian Hunt and Michael Morey
Jacket Design: Stephen Knowlden
Picture Researchers: Cathy Stastny and Daniela Marceddu
Production Controller: Ben Worley

ETHICAL TRADING POLICY
At Anness Publishing we believe that business should be conducted in an ethical and ecologically sustainable way, with respect for the environment and a proper regard to the replacement of the natural resources we employ. As a publisher, we use a lot of wood pulp in high-quality paper for printing, and that wood commonly comes from spruce trees. We are therefore currently growing more than 750,000 trees in three Scottish forest plantations: Berrymoss (130 hectares/320 acres), West Touxhill (125 hectares/305 acres) and Deveron Forest (75 hectares/185 acres). The forests we manage contain more than 3.5 times the number of trees employed each year in making paper for the books we manufacture. Because of this ongoing ecological investment programme, you, as our customer, can have the pleasure and reassurance of knowing that a tree is being cultivated on your behalf to naturally replace the materials used to make the book you are holding. Our forestry programme is run in accordance with the UK Woodland Assurance Scheme (UKWAS) and will be certified by the internationally recognized Forest Stewardship Council (FSC). The FSC is a non-government organization dedicated to promoting responsible management of the world's forests. Certification ensures forests are managed in an environmentally sustainable and socially responsible way. For further information about this scheme, go to www.annesspublishing.com/trees

Previously published as *The Encyclopedia of Music: Instruments of the Orchestra and the Great Composers*

PUBLISHER'S NOTE
Although the advice and information in this book are believed to be accurate and true at the time of going to press, neither the authors nor the publisher can accept any legal responsibility or liability for any errors or omissions that may have been made.

Contents

Preface

If music be the food of love, play on!
WILLIAM SHAKESPEARE (1564–1616), "TWELFTH NIGHT"

People have been making music for a very long time, probably beginning with the voice and proceeding to simple rhythmic drumming – hitting a log with a stick or banging a rock with a club – and blowing a blade of grass or a conch shell. Since these humble beginnings there has been an explosion in instrument-making, accompanied by the rise of the composer particularly over the past six centuries.

Musical instruments

The very earliest evidence of music is provided by the remains of instruments. Clappers, flutes and drums have survived from before the last Ice Age, and these are the ancient ancestors of the thousands of musical instruments used in the world today.

The book begins with an exploration of the *History of Music-making and the*

ABOVE: "Buffalo Dance" from George Catlin's North American Indian Portfolio of 1844. One of the dancers is keeping the rhythm with a shallow frame drum.

ABOVE: A 16th-century trio of musicians playing together from a manuscript.

Orchestra, presenting a general history of musical instruments, how they sounded and the kinds of music they were used for. The musical instruments of previous ages and different cultures have much to say, not only about music, but about social patterns, technology and skills, ritual and religion.

Even when they are not being played, musical instruments have a strong aesthetic appeal, which stems from their perfect blend of form and function. They are often lovingly made and beautifully decorated, with satisfying, rounded shapes and smooth surfaces that demand to be touched. Those who play them become deeply attached to them as the emotions expressed in music flow through them.

The *Encyclopedia of Musical Instruments* describes each family of instruments in detail: strings, woodwind and brass, percussion and

keyboards, ending with a section on the voice. As well as the standard orchestral instruments, folk instruments, traditional instruments from around the world, the precursors of modern instruments and those that have fallen into disuse are featured.

ABOVE: This Italian mosaic from the 2nd century BC shows strolling masked musicians.

ABOVE: A chamber group performing at an outdoor reception.

There are plenty of folk tales and myths that tell of instruments with supernatural powers: warning drums, magic flutes, diabolical violins and pianos that play themselves. There is no doubting the magic of music, and musical instruments have a share of it.

ABOVE: Musical instruments such as this double bass and bow have a strong aesthetic appeal.

The great composers

Owing to the invention of systems for writing down music in medieval times, scholars have added to their study of musical instruments a knowledge of composition methods and styles, and how these developed over the centuries.

Beginning with a discussion of the first written musical notation dating from the 9th century AD, *Composition through the Ages* provides a survey of the principal milestones in the history of musical invention, culminating in the new and sometimes unusual sounds of the 21st century.

Within such a long period of development and innovation, some composers have stood out as having defined or developed particular styles of composition, or have created for themselves a significant place in music history. *Lives and Works of the Great Composers* covers the lives and times of the individuals who are seen as the most pre-eminent in Western music: Bach, Haydn, Mozart, Beethoven, Tchaikovsky, Wagner and Stravinsky, to name but a few. The book ends with a look at contemporary composers, such as Philip Glass, Arvo Pärt and Thomas Adès, with the promise of many exciting new developments extending well into the future.

ABOVE: A painting from the mid 17th century by Jan Havicksz, entitled The Harpsichord Lesson. Baroque composers such as Pachelbel and Bach wrote major works for this instrument.

ABOVE: The symphony orchestra holds a central place in Western musical life.

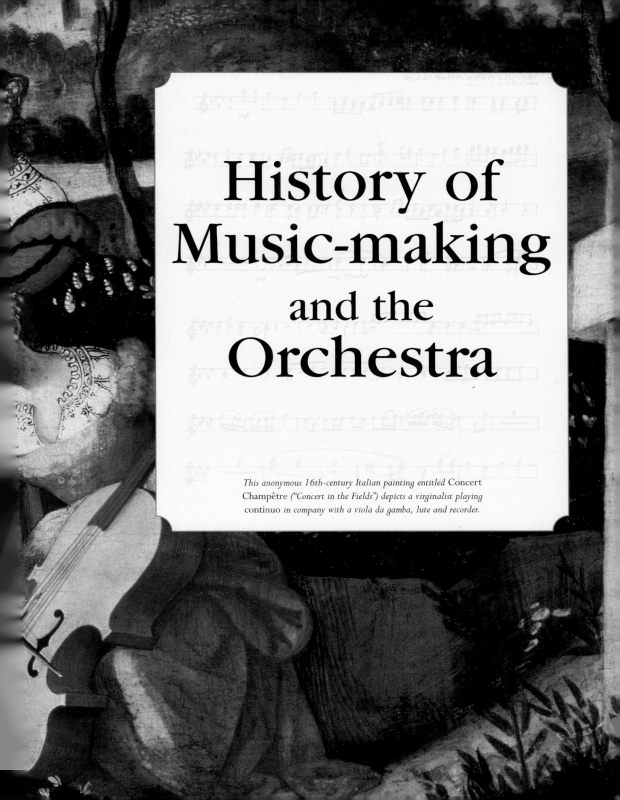

History of Music-making
and the
Orchestra

This anonymous 16th-century Italian painting entitled Concert
Champêtre *("Concert in the Fields") depicts a virginalist playing*
continuo *in company with a viola da gamba, lute and recorder.*

Introduction

Music is the universal language of mankind.

<small>Henry Wadsworth Longfellow (1807–82), "Outre-Mer"</small>

There are few people who do not react to music to some degree. The power of music is diverse and people respond in different ways. To some it is mainly an instinctive, exciting sound to which they dance or move their bodies. Other people listen for its message, or take an intellectual approach to its form and construction, appreciating its formal patterns or originality. Above all, however, there can be hardly anyone who is not moved by some kind of music. Music covers the whole gamut of emotions: it can make us feel happy or sad, nostalgic or energetic, and some music is capable of overtaking the mind until it is oblivious to all else. It works on the subconscious, creating or enhancing mood and unlocking deep memories.

ABOVE: The Amati Quartet led by Attila Balogh was one of the foremost chamber ensembles of the 1980s and early '90s. This picture, taken in 1988, shows the quartet giving one of their recitals.

Music is intimately bound up with important events in all our lives. There is hardly a ceremony, whether personal or national, that is not accompanied by music. It may be as simple as the nightly ritual of a mother singing her baby to sleep or as formal as the playing of a national anthem. It may be a spontaneous outpouring of mass emotion, such as the spectators singing before a football game, or it may be a highly wrought and carefully rehearsed performance of massed bands or choirs at a great state wedding or funeral.

The history of music is a part of the history of humanity. Ethnographic studies of ritual among primitive societies have provided plenty of evidence to show that music-making is a basic and universal instinct. Because it is not a concrete art form, we can have no knowledge of what music sounded like in the centuries before

ABOVE: Instruments that were in use in the Iberian peninsula during the 13th century included a portative organ, cornetts, double bladder pipe, bagpipes, lutes and shawm.

ABOVE: A performance of Carmen *at Blackpool Opera House in 1938. Bizet's most successful opera opened in Paris in 1875, during the last year of his short life.*

ABOVE: This painting by Anne Vallayer-Coster, entitled The Attributes of Music, *was completed in 1770, just before the French Revolution and the beginning of the Romantic period in music. The instruments (from left to right) are horn, cornemuse, lute, flute and violin.*

it began to be written down or, much later, recorded. But very early written accounts remain, as well as ancient instruments and pictures or carvings showing them in use, to convey some idea of the importance of music to ancient civilizations.

In the 20th century, there has been an unprecedented interest not only in the written remains of the music of previous generations, but in establishing how such music really sounded. As recently as the 18th century, musicians were expected to provide only new works for concert audiences, whereas modern music-lovers are avid for music from all historical periods, often performed on instruments and in styles that attempt to recreate the

effect intended by the composer. There are many ways in which we try to understand the lives of previous generations in order to set our own lives in a secure context, and music is a powerful way of evoking the past.

At the same time, musicians are constantly seeking new forms of expression. As in every other contemporary art form, originality is highly prized in music, and every new development in technology is explored by both composers and players. Recording techniques have made all forms of music instantly available to a universal audience, but have not diminished the demand for live performance, on a wider range of instruments than ever before.

ABOVE: At the far left of this 15th-century Spanish painting are three singers reading from sheet music, accompanied by a band of six musicians on the right.

What is Music?

Musick is a tonick to the saddened soul.

ROBERT BURTON (1577–1640), "ANATOMY OF MELANCHOLY"

When asked "What is music?" people will give various replies. Some will try to be scientific and say that music is a succession of sound waves. But that is also the result of scratching a blackboard with the fingernails, which most people would not describe as music.

The making of music is not restricted to human beings. Many animals, such as whales and birds, appear to use music as a means of communication. Natural music was utilized by the French composer, Olivier Messiaen, who used to go out into the countryside to transcribe birdsong, which he incorporated almost note-for-note into his orchestral and piano music. The American composer John Cage believed that the mechanical background sounds of everyday life could be described as music, and other composers have written works

ABOVE: Although birdsong is not created for a human audience, it is still music to human ears and one of the pleasures of life.

requiring all kinds of everyday objects to be used as "musical instruments".

Perhaps an easier question would be "What is not music?", though the answers would be just as varied. To some, the sounds made by a heavy metal rock band constitute music, while to others they are just highly amplified noise. Rock music of the 1950s and '60s, such as the songs of Buddy Holly, Jerry Lee Lewis, the Beatles or the Rolling Stones, was adored by its teenage fans but dismissed as unbearable noise by many of their parents. Many of Berlioz's contemporaries harked back to the "good old days" of Bach, while many early 20th-century music-lovers were none too impressed when confronted with the ground-breaking compositions of Stravinsky.

When André Previn was once asked the difference between popular and classical music, his reply was that there

was no such thing as popular or classical music, there was just good music and bad music. While there are many wonderful "classical" works, there are some that are not worth the manuscript paper upon which they were written. Conversely, as there are many popular songs that end up in the dustbin of history, there are many modern tunes that Mozart would have been proud to have written.

Beauty is in the ear, as well as the eye, of the beholder, and the

ABOVE: Drums are known to all cultures. This sculpture of a figure playing a small frame drum dates from AD 800, and is of the Peruvian Mochica culture.

ABOVE: The military drum was originally used as a means of signalling in battle, and was also beaten to set a rhythm that focused the minds of marching troops.

ABOVE: *Rattles made out of gourds are one of the oldest percussion instruments and have been found in every part of the world.*

Listening to music is a psychosomatic experience that, as well as promoting harmony and peace, holds a power for inner reassurance and satisfaction which stems from deep within the human spirit. Many people would count themselves the poorer without it. We do not have to go into the science and philosophy of music to find the answer to our question; we simply need to go into our own souls, for that is where music belongs.

appreciation of a piece of music depends to some extent on the listener's culture and upbringing. To someone born in the West, for example, the music of East Asia is mysterious and possibly difficult to listen to, because its idiom is unfamiliar. However, once its context is understood and Western preconceptions about musical conventions are set aside, it becomes more accessible. Even without understanding, all music has the power to exert an effect on the emotions.

ABOVE: *While the ringing of a single church bell might not be classified as music, a peal of three or more certainly is.*

LEFT: *The Portuguese* Quineto de Cristal *in 1882. Crystallophones were a 19th-century innovation and for a while were very popular in Europe and the United States. The glasses were arranged in five octaves and struck with small hammers. In time interest flagged, and crystallophones became historical curiosities.*

What is a Musical Instrument?

Music is the sound of universal laws promulgated.

HENRY THOREAU (1817–62)

Musical instruments and their story have always been part of human history, and the story of music begins with the story of humanity. Music, or sound, stood at the cradle of all religions. When primitive humans struck a piece of rock, stone or skin, or blew into an old bone or hollow branch, they perhaps concluded that what they heard was the voice of the object. They therefore assumed that by awakening the "voice" of the object, they could propitiate the unseen nature of which their life was a part.

The rhythmic articulation of time by means of an instrument of some kind is far older than the construction of a true musical instrument. Any objects that early humans happened to pick

up when singing or dancing could become sound-producing "musical instruments". Implements created for use exclusively as musical instruments developed only very slowly and many, if not all, early instruments (such as the pot drum) were merely adaptations

LEFT: Very early in human history it was found that a very loud sound could be produced by blowing into a conch shell.

of artefacts already invented for some other purpose. Instruments are the working tools of music; they are the practical devices by which the acoustic properties of nature are managed for the artistic purposes of music that begin with the player. The musical instrument cannot be separated from the musician. In the hands of an incompetent amateur, the finest Stradivari may as well be a block of wood. However, in the hands of a virtuoso, even a crude violin can sound heavenly.

Obviously, we do not know the world's first "tunes". The development of music predates the invention of writing by thousands of years, and there is no way of knowing what

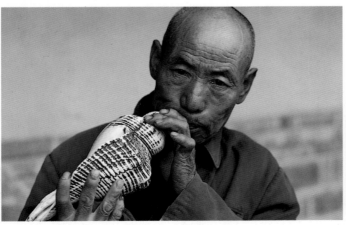

ABOVE: The conch shell is still used as a musical instrument in present-day China; at some temples the shell is blown to announce the beginning of prayers. This conch shell has been fitted with a bamboo mouthpiece.

ABOVE: Rhythm plays an important part in African music. These painted wooden rattles are from Nigeria.

The two elements — the body and the column or box of air — together form a coupled acoustic system.

Other very early instruments include hollow tubes such as reeds and bones, and conch shells, which are believed to have been used as signal instruments. It is possible that these were at first shouted into, until it was discovered that more pleasing sounds could be produced by blowing.

sounds the Neanderthals and early *Homo sapiens* enjoyed. The first "instrument" was certainly the human voice, and ritual chanting is likely to have been accompanied by rhythmic clapping or stamping. This in turn would have led to the striking of an object, such as a convenient log or stone, which could produce a different, and probably a louder, sound.

These early musical instruments, made of naturally sonorous materials, are termed "idiophones". Modern percussion instruments, such as gongs, wood blocks, cymbals and xylophones, are also examples of idiophones. Before long the early musician would have realized that the sound produced by hitting a solid log was different from that produced by a hollow log. The latter is an example of the coupled system of sound production, in which the vibrations are excited in one source with the collaboration of an associated structure — such as the air in the log. This discovery is the foundation of the design of modern wind instruments, such as the horn or oboe, and of the body and soundbox of stringed instruments, such as the violin.

ABOVE: Scrapers are some of the earliest percussion instruments and are known virtually everywhere. These examples from Laos are made from bamboo.

RIGHT: Shakers or rattles come in various shapes and sizes, such as a plastic ball, metal box, wicker basket and natural pod.

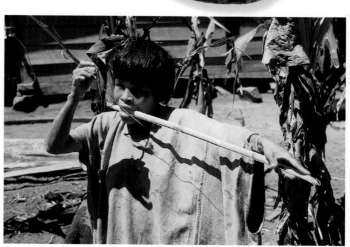

ABOVE: Musical bows are known almost all over the world. Often the mouth serves as a resonator while the string is set in vibration by either being tapped with a small stick, as in this example from Colombia, or plucked with a plectrum.

Music of Ancient Civilizations

*Provide me now a man that
can play well and bring him to me.*

1 Samuel 16:17

The earliest archaeological evidence of the use of musical instruments dates from about 3000 BC. By then, the Sumerians, an ancient society living in the fertile crescent of Mesopotamia, had assembled a range of musical instruments, including lyres, harps and reed-pipes, which may have been played as an ensemble. It is also known from written records that they practised antiphonal singing or chanting in their temples. There is no way of knowing what their music sounded like, but it is clear that it was a sophisticated part of Sumerian culture and that it had religious and ceremonial significance.

Egypt
The importance of music in ancient Egypt cannot be overestimated. Music was one of the concomitant joys of life; indeed, as a sign of this, the soundbox of the harp was sometimes fashioned to represent the sacred lotus flower in bloom.

ABOVE: This finely decorated 12th-century BC Egyptian harp is depicted on a tomb painting in Anhour Khaou's tomb in Thebes. In reality the left hand would have played the "back" of the instrument.

From the beginning of the New Kingdom in about 1550 BC, music, which was mainly performed by women, began to play a very prominent part in religious life. Many of the first musicians in the temples were the wives and daughters of priests, the more senior of whom enjoyed a high status second only to that of the king. The instrument of sacerdotal potency and ecclesiastical authority was the *sistrum*, a type of rattle with metal discs strung on a framework of wires, which symbolized divine power. Egyptian temple music was much more than just chanting and jingling. Harps, pandoras and pipes were also used to praise the gods, since it was part of the regular duties of the priest to extol the god in song, and dancing, accompanied by temple musicians, played an important part in many cults.

As time went on and the empire broadened, female slaves from captured nations were brought back to Egypt to serve as musicians. They attended academies of music where they were instructed in both singing and playing instruments. Music in Egypt was of such a high standard that even the Greeks commended it. Instrumental music was important in secular as well as religious life. Musicians played in homes as well as at feasts, in processions and at funeral ceremonies.

The earliest evidence of parallel pipes in Egypt is from about 2700 BC. Divergent pipes came into use – and in

ABOVE: A Theban tomb painting shows a musician playing double shawm pipes and another holding a lute-type instrument.

fact largely replaced the older instrument – in about 1500 BC. The divergent pipes were held with one pipe in each hand, with the proximal ends forming a V. Played exclusively by

ABOVE: This Egyptian wall painting dates from about the 15th century BC and shows a female musician playing an angular harp.

women, each pipe originally had four finger-holes, but later five or six became common. The right hand played the melody while the left pipe sounded a drone accompaniment.

The frame drum arrived in Egypt in about 1550 BC. Also played only by women, the drum accompanied many aspects of Egyptian life, ranging from the cult of Osiris to the dancing of the slaves in the Pharaonic court. Frame drums were similar in

appearance to the modern tambourine, complete with jingling metal rings, discs or pellet bells.

Israel
In ancient Israel, music had a place in almost every activity and at almost every event. The double-headed drum, in the form of the *tof*, is known to have been played in Biblical times, when women used it to accompany their songs and dances. Until about 1000 BC music was the spontaneous outpouring of the people. Later, however, with the establishment of a trained and official body of musicians to lead worship in the temple, it became more formal and more ritualized. Trumpets represented the power of God, and the cantillation of scripture was a potent reminder of the sanctity of God's word, setting it apart from the unsanctified conversation of daily life.

Pipes were also known in Biblical Israel where smaller pipes, called *halil*, were made of cane or metal. The Hebrew prophets plied their trade under the influence of music and were

often preceded by musicians playing drums, pipes and lyres. (The Latin word *praecinere*, which was used in translations of the scriptures to describe their activity, means both to prophesy and to play the pipes.)

By 200 BC the temple had an established choir of 12 men and a number of boys, who sang to the accompaniment of lyres, pipes and cymbals. Antiphonal singing, which had been a part of Sumerian religious practice and was known to the Egyptians, was adopted by the Jews for the singing of psalms.

ABOVE: This Egyptian tomb painting from Thebes, 1425 BC, depicts dancers performing to the music of a double shawm.

ABOVE: An impression of the Temple of Jerusalem, used as an illustration to a 1732 Bible, showing Solomon dedicating the Temple to the Lord. Music was a feature of the Temple life, and trained musicians were employed to lead the worship.

ABOVE: One of the oldest horns still used today is the Jewish shofar. They are made from a billy goat's horn or a ram's horn.

Classical Greece

That classical Greece was a musical Greece can be seen from the many modern musical words that owe their roots to Greek. Apart from "music" itself, they include "melody", "harmony", "symphony", "orchestra", "organ", "chorus" and "rhythm". The Greek work *mousike* embraced not only what is considered to be music today but also the text and accompanying dance. Greek poets did not just write the words, they also produced the work, trained the singers and dancers (who were mainly amateurs) and directed the accompaniment.

To the Greeks, music, singing and dancing were the main characteristics of a civilized society. They used music for many different purposes, ranging from celebration and the worship of gods to the boosting of morale. Musicians played to workers performing repetitive jobs, such as spinning and weaving, rope-making, grinding corn and treading grapes.

Music also played an important role in military exploits. An essential member of an Athenian trireme's crew was the aulete, or double-pipe player, who played to keep the rowers in time. Spartan armies marched to the sound of the aulos, which kept them at a steady pace without breaking rank. Aulos music also served as a morale booster to the troops, in much the same way as Scottish Highland regiments use the bagpipes today.

Greek contests

The notion of competition was dear to the hearts of the Greeks, and music was no exception. As a focus for competition, the art of *kitharodia* (singing to the self-accompanying of a kithara, or lyre) dates from about 670 BC. Choral contests were instituted about 50 years later, while in 580 BC the Spartans introduced aulos music into their public contests. These festivals were a magnet for performers, who came from great distances to take part.

LEFT: This Greek terracotta statuette from about 275 BC depicts a female musician playing a kithara. Held at a tilt, the Greeks used the kithara as the primary instrument of classical drama and official cults.

Kithara versus aulos

During the 5th century BC, musical styles changed radically, as traditions were ousted by new ideas. Plato (c.428–347 BC), who was suspicious of change and denounced the new style as entertaining rather than edifying, complained about the "modern music" of his day, especially the use of the versatile aulos in preference to the kithara, which had also been adapted in an attempt to imitate the aulos and now had an expanded number of strings. Such was Plato's aversion to the aulos that he banned it from his ideal republic, believing that those who could not play the kithara were lacking in education.

Ancient Rome

Music was a rich and constant presence in Roman life. The everyday life of the Romans abounded in songs concerned with all subjects, ranging from reaping to weaving, from weddings to funerals and from love to satire. In the homes of the wealthy, music was often played during dinner, while in the theatre, plays and comedies often included the music of the *tibia* (the Roman version of the aulos) or the hydraulis, or water-pipe. The hydraulis also had a place in the arena, where it was often played with brass instruments, such as the *cornu* and *tuba*, to accompany chariot fights and gladiatorial contests

ABOVE: That music played an important part in Greek cultural life can be seen from this 5th-century BC vase painting depicting a young man learning to play the lyre.

ABOVE: *This Etruscan wall painting of the early 5th century* BC *shows an ambulatory musician playing an aulos, or double pipe. The player was known as an aulete.*

ABOVE: *The Roman Colosseum, seen here as it was in 1835, was a centre of Roman entertainment, much of which was to the accompaniment of music.*

in the arena. Pantomimes, another popular Roman entertainment, regularly incorporated choral singing, instrumental music and dancing.

Cult music in Roman life ranged from elaborate festival performances to accompaniments for the ritual slaughtering of an animal, when the playing of the *tibia* drowned out the cries of the doomed creature. Roman professional musicians had their own associations, which furnished performers for both public and private entertainments: extravagant fees were not unknown for the more popular musicians. Because of their connection with the state cult, these musicians benefited from certain privileges, such as being allowed to roam the streets unhindered, even though they were masked and frequently drunk.

ABOVE: *Second-century Roman mosaic of a hydraulis, the ancestor of the modern organ. Under the pipes was a keyboard that operated perforated sliders. When a key was pressed, a slider was pushed into position to release pressurized air from the wind canal and thereby sound the note. The scene also shows a cornicin, a large and powerful circular horn.*

ABOVE: *First-century* BC *relief from Denmark depicting Celtic carnyx players. These instruments have a warlike appearance with their bells shaped like grotesque boars' heads.*

India

The origin of the classical music of northern India is shrouded in obscurity. It is a mixture of many ancient cultural influences and the result of a long process of integration of various types of music that makes it one of the world's greatest art forms. The Sanskrit hymns of the *Rig Veda*, composed between the 14th and 10th centuries BC, were – and still are – intoned, and it is possible that the style that is used today has survived virtually unchanged from the time of their composition.

Hindus believe in the power of *samgita*, which encompasses vocal music, instrumental music and dance, to influence the universe and to play a part in freeing the individual from the cycle of birth, death and rebirth.

Raga

The *raag* is the mainstay of northern Indian classical music. There are some 200 main *raga*, each with its own scale pattern and specific rules. Some are linked with specific seasons and times of day, while some are feminine and others masculine.

The performance of a *raag* always follows a set pattern. It begins with the

ABOVE: *This painting of Indian marriage celebrations in 1561 shows guests dancing to the rhythm of tambourines, tabla drums, trumpets and cymbals.*

ABOVE: *This 17th-century painting from India depicts lotus-flower dancers performing to the music of a* dhola *drum and sitar.*

alapa, a slow, meditative mood-setter that introduces the notes of the scale in free time and is unaccompanied by drums. This can last several hours, although more usually it is a matter of minutes. The next two sections are the *jorh* and the *jhala*, in which the soloist begins to introduce a rhythmic element and explore complex variations.

The final section, the *gath*, introduces the tabla, a set of two drums played with fingertips and palms. The right-hand drum is the *tabla* and the left-hand one the *bayan*.

Both drum heads are made of skin with a paste of flour and iron filings in the centre. The *tabla* body is made of wood and that of the *bayan* of metal.

Qawwali

Another type of music associated with northern India (and Pakistan) is *qawwali*, a spiritual song that is intended to transport the mystic towards union with the creator. *Qawwali* music can be traced back at least as far as the 9th century, and in its present form to the late 13th century.

A feature of modern *qawwali* is the harmonium, an instrument introduced to India by Christian missionaries around AD 1900. Although the harmonium has the advantage that it does not need constant retuning, it does not meet with universal approval and is banned from All Indian Radio because it does not conform to the traditional flexible intonation of *sruti* music, in which the "same" note can acquire different, but recognizable, pitches in ascent and descent. Neither can the glides and swings of *gamaka*

ABOVE: The young Indian prince Shri Raga listens to the music of the vina, an instrument characterized by a long string carrier and gourd resonator.

ABOVE: This Indian scene depicts the celebrations during the birth of Timur. The musicians are playing instruments such as cymbals, tabla drums and trumpets.

music be achieved on the harmonium. The celebrated musician Rabindranath Tagore once went as far as to call the harmonium "the bane of Indian music".

Indonesia

The most famous music of South-east Asia is the vibrant, thunderous gamelan, the percussion orchestra, consisting of gong-chimes, metallophones and gongs, which is played in Java and Bali. The tradition goes back well over a thousand years and is believed to predate the Hindu-Buddhist kingdom that was founded in Bali in the 7th century, when the Balinese arrived from Java, having been ousted by the arrival of Islam.

In no other country is music such an integral part of the daily life of the community. There is a greater concentration of orchestras in Bali than

anywhere else in the world. Here, however, as in the rest of the Indonesian archipelago, music does not have a particular religious significance, as it does for Hindus in India.

Spanning over five octaves, gamelan music is like a tree, with some instruments representing the trunk, some the branches and some the flowers. The various instruments of the gamelan include drums, bamboo flutes, cymbals, the *rebab* (an upright fiddle), the great gong, which can be up to 1m/3ft in diameter, and the *trompong* (a row of ten gong chimes set in a wooden frame). One group plays the core melody, while another group stresses this at regular intervals, generally one note in four. A third group expands the core melody with a range of up to three octaves, while a fourth doubles the melody an octave above. As well as these groups, various gongs provide punctuation and drums conduct the rhythmic undercurrent.

Javanese gamelan music is courtly and gentle; the players use padded mallets and the tempo is slow and serene. In Bali, the style is much brighter, louder and more exuberant, using wood or horn hammers and employing a greater dynamic range.

ABOVE: Balinese gamelan percussion orchestras go back well over a thousand years. Trompong players are shown here, with tuned gongs in the background.

ABOVE: *This 18th-century Chinese illustration depicts a man playing a* kuchin, *a form of long zither. Traditionally, all dimensions of the* kuchin *have a cosmological meaning.*

China

Chinese music dates back millennia and is one of the oldest and most highly developed of all musical systems. The Chinese concept of music theory is different from that of the West in that the emphasis is placed on the philosophical, cosmological and educational values of music.

Music played an important part in the lives of the ancient Chinese and was closely associated with matters of state and government. To the Chinese, music is part of nature and is organically integrated with the cosmological universe. The earliest Chinese musical notation dates from the 4th century BC, while two centuries earlier Confucius had compiled a book of songs.

Chinese instruments

Since ancient times, Chinese musical instruments have been classified according to their major acoustical material — metal, stone, clay, leather, silk, wood, gourd or bamboo — and how they are played.

The ch'in, or classical long zither of China, can be dated back to the T'ang dynasty (AD 618–907). Played with a curved horsehair bow, the modern instrument has no bridges and the stopping places for the ten pairs of silk strings are indicated by ivory discs inlaid into the soundboard. The Thai *chakay*, on the other hand, is played with a single plectrum, usually made of ivory, metal or tortoiseshell.

Another typical traditional Chinese instrument is the *qin*, a seven-stringed

ABOVE: *The Chinese* yün-luo *gong chimes are of Mongolian origin and consist of between 10 and 24 small bronze bowls suspended vertically in an upright frame.*

zither that has been a favourite subject of poets and painters for over a thousand years. The most delicate instrument in the Chinese repertoire, the *qin*'s ethereal harmonics are a joy to hear.

By the 8th century, the *sheng*, or reed-pipe mouth organ, had 17 pipes. This number became the norm, and today it is tuned chromatically and played polyphonically in triads. Although historically the *sheng* was played at funerals and at court, the *lu-sheng*, traditionally a dance instrument, is now a regular feature of the Chinese orchestra.

The Chinese bronze *bo* cymbal of the Hai Province differs from the Turkish cymbal in that the rim turns out slightly. Used in the Peking opera, these cymbals are about 20cm/8in wide. In the south of the country, in Canton, the cymbal of choice is the *dabo*, held by a small central knob.

Chinese temple and court

The ritual temple music of southern China lives on in the Temple of

ABOVE: *Dancers from the traditional Chinese opera in Canton. In spite of the political upheavals in China, Cantonese opera has survived.*

ABOVE: *Three female musicians playing Chinese drums and a flute painted on a vase of about 1640.*

Sublime Mysteries in Suzhou. Here the monks play a wide range of music, including pieces for silk and bamboo instruments, flutes and oboes, long trumpets and a whole battery of percussion. In orchestral, ensemble and solo instrumental court music, multipart form dominates. Four stages of court music development are most commonly heard: the introduction, the elucidation of the theme, the transition and the summing-up.

Chinese opera

Kunqu opera, which evolved in the 16th century in Kiangsa province, is a sophisticated opera based on an earlier form of literary drama. Based on written librettos, its tunes are slow-

ABOVE: *A row of Chinese Miao people playing lu-sheng mouth organs and long bamboo trumpets.*

moving, with a regular 4:4 rhythm. The principal instruments used in *kunqu* are the *titzu* and *hsiao* (the transverse and end-blown flutes).

In 1790 the visits of various acting companies to Peking, for the 80th birthday celebrations of Emperor Ch'ien-lung, introduced to the capital the operatic styles that were to go on to form the core of "Peking opera". Performed in teahouses, its characters, unlike those of Western opera, are categorized by the kind of person they represent rather than by vocal range. The four main types are: *sheng* (male), *tan* (female), *ching* (warriors and gods) and *ch'ou* (clowns).

ABOVE: *This quintet of Chinese musicans are playing (from left to right) a two-stringed* dutar, paipan *(clapper),* chettö *(flute),* sheng *(mouth organ), and* pipa *(lute).*

ABOVE: *Top row — three trumpets, drum, two* erh-hu *(fiddles),* kuchin *(zither). Middle row —* yün-luo *(gong chimes),* lo *(gongs), two* chettö *(flutes), drum. Bottom row — drum, three* pipa *(lutes),* sheng *(mouth organ).*

Japan

Japanese musical history can be divided into several stages of development. The first stage is the period up to the 6th century when the country, which had previously been ruled by a number of clans, was developing into an imperial state. Shinto became the state religion, and the music and dance associated with it became the main body of court music. The second stage, which lasted for the next three centuries, saw the introduction of continental Asian music and dance, as well as Buddhism. It was during this time that *gagaku* came into being.

Gagaku court music is the oldest surviving music in Japan and has been preserved at the imperial court and at a few temples. Nearly 20 different types of instrument are used in *gagaku*, including the *sho* (a reed-pipe mouth organ), flute, drums, gongs and chimes. The various types of *gagaku* include *kangan* (instrumental ensembles), *bagaku* (dance music) and the ritual music for Shinto ceremonies.

ABOVE: Japanese girls playing a samisen *(a guitar-like instrument with three strings) and a* koto *(a 13-stringed zither).*

The third stage in the development of Japanese music came in the period between 900 and 1573. It was then that the theatrical form called *noh* was developed. A marriage of drama, theatre, music and dance, the beauty of *noh* lies in its refined symbolism and sophistication.

The last period saw the Japanese version of the zither, the *koto*, come into fashion. The *koto*, which has 13 silk strings that pass over movable bridges, is played mainly by women, who wear three long ivory plectra on the right hand: one on the thumb, one on the index finger and the third on the middle finger. The left hand is used to dampen the strings and change the pitch. Other Japanese classical instruments of the period include the *shakuhachi* (bamboo flute) and the *biwa* (lute).

ABOVE: The shakuhachi, *a bamboo end-blown flute with five finger-holes. The instrument originated in China and was taken to Japan by Buddhist priests in AD 935.*

Korea

The music of Korea can be traced back over 5000 years and is based on two modes, the *p'yongjo* (common in court music, such as *aak*, and folk songs) and the more widely used *kyemyonjo*. The greatest period of musical development in Korea was during the reign of King Sejong (1418–50). Not only did Sejong reputedly devise the Korean alphabet,

ABOVE: A Korean musician playing the koto, *a kind of zither.*

ABOVE: A Korean musician playing the soduang, *a two-stringed instrument with a round resonating box covered with leather at one end and open at the other to admit the neck.*

but he also created an advanced system of musical notation.

Korea treasures its musical heritage, and classical Korean music is actively promoted at the Seoul National Classical Music Institute, where leading musicians are classed as national treasures.

The Korean tradition of *samulnori* drumming goes back at least a thousand years. Played by a quartet of musicians on drums and gongs, *samulnori* originated in the rural farmers' dances that are still performed by dancers wearing hats with long ribbons that swirl into spectacular shapes as the dancers move their heads.

Korea is also known for large orchestras of flutes, oboes and bronze and stone chimes that still play on the first Sunday in May at the ancestral shrine in Seoul. This is a very colourful sight: the massive frames of the chimes are richly decorated with dragons and birds, and contrast with the bold, bright costumes of the musicians.

The *kayagum*, a 12-stringed zither, provides the accompaniment to vocal music and is also played as a solo instrument accompanied by the *changgo* (an hourglass-shaped drum) and the *taegum* (a wooden flute). It has been said that the beauty of *kayagum* music is that when a melody makes a leap down it sounds like a waterfall, and when it reaches the bottom the note vibrates in the same way that water bubbles at the foot of a waterfall.

ABOVE: A Korean cholgo, *or temple drum, resting on a wooden stand shaped like a tortoise. In ancient mythology the world was deemed to rest on a tortoise.*

ABOVE: A Korean honga *orchestra playing Confucian ritual music. A feature of the orchestra is the* pyongyong *or stone chimes. Sixteen tuned stones are freely suspended in a wooden frame in two rows and are struck with a mallet made of cow horn; they continue to emit a clear sound for several minutes.*

European Music in the First Millennium

The chime of minstrel music, dulcimer, and harp with many strings,
a pleasant dinning makes to him who heareth not distinct the note.

DANTE ALIGHIERI (1265–1321)

During the first millennium there seems to have been little innovation in Western music, but an exception was the introduction of Gregorian chant in church services. This was a reshaping of the older Roman chant, in which melodies were sung to the accompaniment of a sustained note on, it is believed, a stringed instrument.

ABOVE: *Gregorian church chant from* De Harmonica Institutione *of Benedictine Abbot Regino von Prum,* AD *915.*

Pope Gregory I (AD 590–604) is said to have ordered the collection and codifying of the plainsong used in the Roman church, and his name became associated with this form. The chants were written down by monks, using a form of letter notation above the lines of text. The appearance of "neumes" in the 9th century led to a more exact method of defining pitch.

The teaching of the chant was put on an official footing in the church by Pope Vitalian (AD 657–72), who was instrumental in founding the Scola Cantorum, based on the model of the Byzantine court. It was under Charlemagne (AD 742–814) that the Gregorian chant became widely used. With the associated antiphonal psalmody (a liturgical chant that was sung in association with a psalm), it was sung all over Europe.

The chant's system of eight tones was directly related to the eight church modes. It was for unaccompanied voice for, according to St Aloysius, any form of musical instrument was a tool of the devil, while St Augustine expressed concern over the seductive "peril of pleasure" created by beautiful singing. However, in the 9th century Benedictine culture began to include the advancement of music. The monastic revival of the late 10th century saw the gradual introduction of organs into churches, although these were not originally used as an accompaniment to the singing, but rather served for signalling purposes, both to call people to worship and to denote points of the service, like the bell at the elevation of the host.

ABOVE: *This 8th-century illumination shows King David playing the crwth, accompanied by four horns and two dancers. Scribes are writing down the words.*

ABOVE: *This drawing from the late 10th century shows Pope Gregory dictating to Deacon Peter.*

Secular music

Songs were, of course, also sung outside the church, especially on long journeys such as those to the various crusades and on pilgrimages. It is known that music played a role in the building of Notre-Dame (1163–1250), when the workers sang as they worked. Indeed, at this time Paris was the musical centre of the Western world, and its university was one of the first officially to teach music.

One of the leading French musicians of the time was Léonin, who was active in Paris between 1163 and 1190. Léonin played a part in the early development of polyphony, by composing *organum* (a medieval form of part-writing) for two voices taken from the solo portions of graduals and alleluias for all the principal feasts of the ecclesiastical year. The main significance of this work was the introduction of a rational system of rhythm into polyphonic music. After Léonin's death, his work was modified by his pupil Pérotin.

This was the age of the peripatetic musician. There were two main classes: the troubadour (a cultivated travelling musician, generally of noble birth) and the minstrel (a professional entertainer, of more lowly birth). In Germany, the 12th, 13th and 14th centuries saw the heyday of the *Minnesinger*, the German equivalent of the French troubadours. All these singers were both poets and composers of their own songs, for at this time very few sang other people's music.

ABOVE: *While peripatetic minstrels were a feature of the medieval landscape, some houses retained their own musicians. This trio is playing a tabor, pipe, small harp and lute.*

ABOVE: *A group of four early 14th-century German troubadours playing the unusual combination of two trumpets, drum and bagpipes.*

Structuring Music

Music is the reaching out towards the
utmost realities by means of ordered sound.

RALPH VAUGHAN WILLIAMS (1872–1958)

The Greek mathematician Pythagoras (c.570–500 BC) carried out the earliest known acoustical experiments. Knowing that the shorter the length of a string the higher the pitch will be, Pythagoras demonstrated that pleasing intervals were sounded when a string is divided into certain ratios. When the length is halved, an octave is formed; when it is reduced to two-thirds the pitch is raised by a perfect fifth; when reduced to three-quarters it gives the perfect fourth. The same applies to the length of a column of air in a wind instrument. Over the years the remaining intervals of the scale were filled in with tones and semitones and thus began the gradual progress that culminated in the recognition of

ABOVE: The number of lines in each staff varied. This music from the Furtmeyer Missal, *written for the Archbishop of Salzburg in 1481, is on a four-line staff.*

ABOVE: The frontispiece of Franchino Gaffari's Theorica Musicæ *(1492) showing Pythagoras playing instruments such as tuned bells, musical glasses and pipes.*

tonality, or key. This concept has since remained the basis of musical composition in the West, though smaller intervals, called "microtones", occur in other musical cultures, such as in Indian music, and have been used by some experimental composers of the 20th century.

Harmonic vibrations

It was not until the 17th century that the relationship between the frequency of vibration and the length, diameter, tension and density of the string was established. It was Galileo (1564–1642) who discovered that if either the string's thickness or length is doubled, the frequency of vibration, and consequently the pitch, is halved. For this reason, bass strings can be

made thicker than treble ones – if they were all of the same thickness the lowest string in a piano would have to be about 6.5m/7 yards long.

Notation

The staff originated in medieval Europe as a means of recording plainsong. At first it was a single line around which the neumes, like small ticks, were placed to show the approximate melodic and rhythmic shape. Additional lines were added in the 11th century and the spaces, as well as the lines, were used to position the notes. By the 16th century, today's exactitude of recording pitch was arrived at when a pair of five-line staves became the norm, arranged as a "grand staff" with the top five lines

ABOVE: This 12th-century plainchant from the Missale Romanum *shows the neumatic notation of the day. There is only one line of "notes" which rise and fall.*

ABOVE: *This manuscript, entitled* Sumer is Icumen In *(c.1240), uses a six-line staff.*

Novel notation

During the 20th century, various avant-garde composers have experimented with new forms of notation, including squiggles, blobs, graphs and wiring diagrams. Only one system made an impression, albeit very minor, and that was only because a very rich man, Cornelius Pot, was behind it. Pot, a Dutchman, invented Klavarskribo in 1931. Intending it as a new method of piano notation, he even founded the Klavarskribo Institute to promote it. By 1950 he had produced some 10,000 works transcribed into Klavarskribo notation but, in spite of copies regularly turning up in second-hand music shops, no known pianist can read it.

ABOVE: *Guido d'Arezzo (991–after 1033), seen here on the left, is remembered for his development of a system of precise pitch notation through lines and spaces as well as for propagating the method of sight-singing that has evolved into the tonic solfa.*

forming the treble clef and the bottom five lines the bass clef.

The *flat* sign, which originally applied only to the B line, originated as a lower case *b*. The natural sign was a square gothic *b* that was later modified to give today's symbol. The *sharp* sign originated as a cancelled *b* with a stroke through it.

Tonic solfa

The tonic solfa had its roots in the 11th century when a monk named Guido d'Arezzo devised a way to help singers learn a new melody by relating its notes to the pitches of certain syllables associated with a well-known tune. The tune he chose was a Latin hymn in which the first syllables of the first six lines were each set one note higher than the previous one. Using the first syllable of each line as his model, he came up with Ut, Re, Mi, Fa, So, La. Apart from the change of Ut to Doh and the addition of Ti, these syllables are still used today.

Strings

*There's not a string attuned to mirth
but has its chord in melancholy.*

THOMAS HOOD (1799–1845)

If we believe Greek legend, it was the twang of a bowstring that first made the god Apollo aware of the musical properties of a vibrating string. The fundamental pitch at which a stretched string, held in tension between two points, is heard, depends upon its length, thickness, weight and tension, together with the properties of the soundbox or soundboard. The frequency at which a given string will vibrate is inversely proportional to its length, proportional to the square of its tension and inversely proportional to the square of its mass, while the amplitude varies with the energy imparted and transmitted.

Materials

A string for a musical instrument may be made of any material that can produce a musical sound when it is held under tension and plucked, bowed or struck. Although most early

ABOVE: *These two putti, one playing a small harp and the other the portative organ, are from the frieze of musical angels in the Chapel of Isotta degli Atti in Rimini.*

strings were made out of gut or silk, many other materials have also been used, such as gold wire strings found in Persia dating from the 5th century BC. More recently, nylon or steel strings have become common, and many strings are bound with fine wire.

Gut strings were made from the guts of lambs, from seven to eight months old. After cleansing and pickling in an alkaline solution, the guts were twisted together under tension before being polished with pads made of hair. The final diameter of the string was determined by the number of guts used, which ranged from two for the smallest mandolin string, up to 120 for a double bass.

Methods of string-playing

There are three ways to excite the string: plucking, bowing or striking. Although plucking excites an active range of high harmonics, they are short-lived. Plucking imparts energy by a single impulse and there is no means of maintaining the vibration. The optimum place to pluck a string is about one-seventh of its length from the end, as this will give the best selection of harmonics as well as amplitude. If the string is plucked either with the fingernails or with a plectrum, it is displaced at a sharp angle and a bright sound is produced, as opposed to the duller sound made when it is plucked with the pad of the finger or thumb.

ABOVE: *This 13th-century illustration of King David shows him playing a harp whose arching neck terminates in an open-mouthed zoomorphic head.*

ABOVE: *A mid 13th-century fiddler playing with a large arched bow. The stick extends beyond the end of the hair, the projection serving as a handle.*

A more solid sound is obtained by striking the string (as on a piano or a dulcimer). A struck string vibrates longer, giving a slower decay in the upper harmonics. However, in the stiffer and tenser lower strings of the piano the vibrations tend not to subdivide indefinitely into the shorter lengths, causing the upper harmonics to be weaker, with most of the energy going into the lower harmonics. Like the plucked string, the struck string has only a single impulse for each note sounded.

One of the more pleasing sounds achieved from a string is by using a bow, which maintains the supply of energy for vibration and thus permits the playing of sustained notes. The sound depends on the position of the bow and the width of the hair brought into operation. Different sounds can be produced by bowing slowly with the full width of the hair, bowing near the centre of the string, bowing swiftly with the edge of the hair, or bowing near the end of the string.

Types of string

TOP ROW, FROM LEFT TO RIGHT: Until the 1970s many violinists used gut strings exclusively, but as the high-tensioned E string had a tendency to break easily, it was replaced by wire.

Viola strings are usually made of gut. The lower two, or sometimes all, are wire-wound.

Harp strings are like piano strings, except that they are plucked.

Most classical guitar strings are made of nylon. They are usually sounded with the left side of the fingernails, but some players prefer to use the right side of their nails.

BOTTOM ROW, FROM LEFT TO RIGHT: Acoustic guitar strings can be made of gut or steel, played with fingers or plectrum.

Mandolin strings are laid in four courses of two. Tuned to the same pitch as the violin, the strings are played with a plectrum.

The strings of the sitar are carried over two bridges, first the "small" bridge and then the "main" bridge. Tuning is achieved by the pegs, and beads are used for fine tuning.

The strings of a piano range in thickness from very thin top strings to the thickly wound bass strings shown here.

Bows

The Devil rides upon a fiddlestick.

WILLIAM SHAKESPEARE (1564–1616), "HENRY IV PART 1"

The use of a bow as an instrumental accessory originated in the Byzantine Empire but, because of the weak tone of early bowed instruments compared with that of plucked ones, it was considered to be worthy only of the "common people". It was introduced into Europe in the 11th century by the Islamic conquerors of Spain, and within 100 years the bow had become known and was being used over most of western Europe.

Early bows

The form of the early bows, which were in the shape of fully drawn hunting bows, differed greatly from those in use today. As its name suggests, the bow originally had a convex shape, designed to hold a band of horsehair under tension so that it could be drawn across the strings of an instrument to set up a sustained vibration. In time the bowed shape became longer and more slender,

ABOVE: Early bows, as the name implies, were similar in appearance to bows used in archery, with a high arched stick.

though it was still convex. By the 12th century, bows with a curve at one end – a type still occasionally found in eastern Europe – had become popular.

The horsehair was tied directly to the stick at both ends, and the player varied the tension while using the bow, to facilitate the playing of single strings or multiple stopping (drawing the string over more than one string simultaneously). To allow for this, the bow was held in the fist and pressure was exerted on the hair with the fingers.

Early bows differed greatly in size; they could be as small as 20cm/8in. In the 16th century, the violin was becoming a popular instrument for dance music, and short bows of about 35cm/14in were adequate for this purpose. Concert bows were substantially longer, and some were more than twice the

ABOVE: Detail from Bellini's Maria with Child and Saints *(1505) showing an angel playing a large viol with a bow that shows the trend for the arch to become lower.*

size of the instrument being played. Some bows had sticks that extended well beyond the end of the hair, the projection serving as a handle.

Modern bow

In the second half of the 18th century the bow underwent a number of radical changes, principally to suit the development of the violin as a solo, virtuoso instrument. The new designs were the work of François Tourte (1747–1835) and Wilhelm Cramer (1745–99). Cramer designed a concave bow, which quickly led to the abandonment of the convex version. Tourte widened the ribbon of hair to about 1cm/⅓in, composed of 150–200 strands cut

ABOVE, FROM TOP TO BOTTOM: The ribbon of the modern violin bow is made of horsehair. The viola bow is similar to the violin bow but is slightly larger.

ABOVE: The standard length of the cello bow is about 68cm/27in.

ABOVE: The double bass bow is shorter and heavier than the cello bow, and can be held either from above or underneath.

ABOVE: The insipid tone of early bowed instruments was due to the bow stick being weak. The player could not tighten the hair and so the strings could not be firmly gripped.

from white horses' tails. He attached this to a strong, movable frog, so that the tension on the hair could be adjusted and set at the beginning of the performance. The bow could now be held lightly with the fingertips, instead of being grasped firmly in the whole hand. This allowed much greater flexibility and delicacy of playing style, which facilitated the rise of the great 18th and 19th-century violin virtuosi.

ABOVE: This illustration of 1830 shows the "old" and "new" styles of bowing the violin.

Bach bow

The Bach bow was created by Knud Vestergard of Viby, Denmark to play the Bach solo violin sonatas "precisely as written", and is associated with the violinist Telmányi. The bow has a very high arch, with as much as 10cm/4in separating the bow stick and the hair at the highest point. When playing on individual strings the bow hair can be tightened by a lever worked by the thumb. By loosening the hair the player is able to encompass all the strings, and thus sustain multiple stops continuously. The creation, however, succeeds in playing Bach's music only as imagined by the bow's 20th-century inventor — not as Bach intended or heard it.

Tourte also fixed the length of the violin bow at about 75cm/30in and the playing hair at about 65cm/25in. To make the stick he chose red Brazilian pernambuco wood for its combination of strength and lightness. These innovations in design established the form of the standard modern bow, which is sometimes referred to as the "Tourte bow".

ABOVE: Early 14th-century fiddler playing with a high arched bow. The player is gripping the bow where the stick extends beyond the end of the hair.

ABOVE: The modern bow, as used by American violinist Isaac Stern (born 1920). Stern's playing — particularly of the Barber and Bruch concertos — has thrilled audiences for over 50 years.

Reeds

There's music in the singing of a reed.

LORD BYRON (1788–1824)

The sound of a reed instrument is initiated by the vibration of the reed, which sets up the vibration of the air column in the tube of the instrument. Reed instruments fall into two main categories, according to the use of the reed: they are known as "bleating" and "free". The ancient Greek aulos was an early bleating reed-pipe and is known to date back to at least 2800 BC.

Reed preparation

In ancient Greece, cane for making aulos reeds was cut during early summer, when at its most elastic,

and laid out to season in the open. It was scraped and cleaned during the following spring, and cut into segments at the nodes: each internode furnished two reeds. Segments closer to the root were suitable for the left-hand pipe of the aulos and those closer to the tip of the stem were used for right-hand pipes. This is an indication that the left-hand pipe was the lower pitched of the two.

Today, reeds are still cut from the stem of the large semi-tropical grass *Arundo donax* or *Arundo sativa*, commonly, but inaccurately, called cane. The plants are specially cultivated in parts of Spain and southern France. They are now factory-cut, but many players learn to cut their own, a very skilled art. Various attempts to find substitutes for *Arundo donax* have been made from time to time, and materials as diverse

ABOVE: A single reed.

as silver and whalebone have been tried, but have never been successful. A recent development has been the use of manmade fibres, although the general consensus is that artificial reeds sound coarser than those made from natural cane.

Bleating reeds

A reed that beats against a surface is known as a "bleating" reed, and instruments that work on this principle can also be subdivided according to whether they use single or double reeds. The single reed, typified by that

ABOVE: A selection of different types of single reeds (from top to bottom) – clarinet, alto saxophone, tenor saxophone and baritone saxophone.

ABOVE: A selection of oboe double reeds – two baroque, classical, classical oboe d'amore, modern oboe, modern oboe d'amore, two cor anglais and bass oboe.

ABOVE: *The idea for a reed instrument must have evolved from people finding that blowing on a blade of grass produced a sound. This engraving is from Bonanni's* Gabinetto Armonico *(1723).*

ABOVE: *The various stages in making a reed. Top – the cut cane. Middle – the cane is cut in half, split and the scrape is shaped. Bottom – the final stages in shaping, trademarking and packaging the reed.*

of the clarinet, is a narrow slip cut to length, flattened on the inner side, and on the other side scraped down to a feather edge at one end. It is fastened to the mouthpiece of the instrument and vibrates against it.

The double bleating reed, typified by that of the bassoon, is made up of two slips of "cane", hollowed out on the inside until quite thin and again scooped to a feather edge on the outside. The two slips are then bound together and mounted in a short metal tube, known as the "staple".

Free reeds

The free reed is found mainly in certain organ pipes and bellows-blown instruments such as the harmonium and accordion. It is also used in the harmonica (mouth organ) as well as in the traditional Chinese *sheng*. The pitch

of the reeds, which are fastened over slots cut into the metal frame, can be lowered by filing near the fixed end, or raised by filing near the free end. A major development in the history

of the accordion was the introduction by firms such as Höhner, founded in Trossingen in 1857, of high-tempered steel reeds, which helped to ensure the instrument's popularity.

LEFT: *Although most professional oboe players make their own reeds, the process takes time and skill, and ready-made reeds are available.*

Valves

The irremediable vulgarity of the cornet's timbre
has kept it away from the symphonic orchestra.

MICHAEL BRENET

In 1815 a notice appeared in the *Allgemeine Musikalische Zeitung* that was to change the evolution of the brass instrument forever. Heinrich Stölzel, a 38-year-old horn player in the orchestra of Prince von Pless in Upper Silesia, announced that he had produced a horn on which a scale of nearly three octaves could be achieved by means of two airtight valves that were pressed down by "piano keys" and returned by springs. Although Stölzel is often regarded as the sole inventor of the valve, it is believed that he was ably assisted by his fellow musician Friedrich Blühmel.

ABOVE: An 1848 view inside Adolph Sax's factory showing brass instruments being produced.

Function of the valve

The purpose of the valve is to admit vibrating air into, or exclude it from, auxiliary tubing of sufficient length to lower the basic pitch of an instrument by a certain musical interval. The length of this tubing must be in proportion to that of the main tubing; the length for a whole tone is about one-eighth of the whole and that for

ABOVE: A trumpet has three piston valves and two finger grips.

a semitone about one-fifteenth. On a three-valved instrument the depression of the first valve lowers the pitch of the instrument a whole tone; depression of the second lowers it a semitone; and the third a whole tone plus a semitone. This combination, with different harmonics obtainable by altering the pressure of the lips, allows a complete scale to be played.

Once the valve has been depressed and released it is instantly returned by a spring; the most common method is to have the spring push the valve back up from the bottom.

Although valves are traditionally made of brass, sometimes plated with silver or nickel, other materials have been used. The Boosey "Solbron" was made of bronze while, for its

tubas, the Swiss Hirstbrunner Company produces the "Trypen" valve, which is made from a combination of brass and plastic. The most efficient valves, however, are those made from "Monel", which is a copper-nickel alloy.

Piston valve

In the years between 1820 and 1840, various experiments resulted in the production of two different types of valve: piston and rotary. In 1835 Wilhelm Wieprecht produced his robust short-stroke Berliner Pumpen

LEFT: The piston valve is returned to its open position by means of the spring, while the coquilles connect with and admit air into the additional tubes that change the pitch of the instrument.

ABOVE: Each piston valve has its own tuning slide; the further out the slide is pulled, the lower the note produced.

valves. These had horizontal passageways and were used on all types of brass instruments. In 1839 this was improved upon by Etienne-François Périnet, who made a lighter and narrower valve, in which the coquilles were positioned obliquely in the piston. The main advantage of this valve was that it could be worked faster and the air column moved around a curve instead of, as with Wieprecht's valve, around a 90° bend.

ABOVE: Tuba valves are, of necessity, bigger than trumpet valves and as such take longer to return to the open position after being depressed. This means that as a rule the tuba does not play fast music and is usually not expected to play notes shorter than semi-quavers.

ABOVE: The flugelhorn uses piston valves to produce the different pitches required.

Today, many euphoniums and tubas have four valves. The extra valve not only helps to keep the instrument in tune, but also allows the musician to play lower harmonics. Most makers place the extra valve at the back of the instrument, where it is operated by the first finger of the left hand. However, the Yamaha Company of Japan positions its four valves together, parallel with the bell, and all are operated by the fingers of the right hand.

Rotary valve

Although several people experimented with rotary valves, Joseph Riedel of Vienna produced the design that is used in modern horns. Riedel's valve, which was patented in 1832, has two passageways that pass through the rotor, one on each side of a central spindle. When the valve is operated the cylinder rotates through 90°, directing the air into the valve tube much as water flows through a tap.

ABOVE: Close-up view of the rotary valves on a French horn. Rotary valves were invented by Joseph Riedel in 1832.

Drum Heads and Sticks

The noisy drum has nothing in it, but mere air.

THOMAS FULLER (1608–61)

When a drum is struck, the membrane vibrates in both a circular and a segmental pattern, producing a fundamental tone and various harmonic overtones, the number and strength of which affect the timbre of the instrument. The timbre and apparent pitch of the drum also vary according to the type of beater used, the degree of hardness or softness of the beater and its contact area on the drum head. Hard beaters produce high overtones while light ones have virtually none.

The sound of the drum is also influenced by the place where the membrane is struck. If this is at the edge, high overtones will be elicited, while if it is hit at or near the centre, deeper tones will predominate. Percussionists get to know their instruments and know the place on the membrane (the "beating spot") that is best to strike.

Drum heads

The first drum heads were made of hide, but animal skin reacts strongly to changes in atmospheric humidity,

ABOVE: *The Indian* dhol *has two indefinitely pitched heads, each with a loud, deep sound. The drum is used to herald public announcements and to lead processions.*

RIGHT: *One of 12 musical angels painted by the Italian painter Fra Angelico in 1433. This one is playing a drum with a parchment head.*

so today artificial materials such as plastic are used. Early side drum heads were tensioned with ropes drawn into V-shapes, with leather buffs at the point of each V which were drawn to tighten the ropes and thus increase the tension. Other methods were introduced later, the most usual being rods with screw nuts. Until World War II, most drums were single-tensioned, with one screw working on both heads. However, as most players prefer to have one head tighter than the other, double-tensioning was introduced, whereby each head is separately controlled by rods that screw into blocks halfway down the shell.

Drum sticks

There are three main types of beater head: hard, medium and soft. The choice of suitable sticks or beaters depends on the tonal effects required, as different types of stick or beater will influence the sound of the drum in three ways: volume, tone and attack. The harder the head of the beater, the louder the sound will be.

All drums have a sound-spectrum: they will produce a wide range of different sounds. A thin, hard-headed stick will bring out the higher sounds, causing the drum to sound bright and clear. A soft-headed beater, on the other hand, will elicit the low tones, producing a mellow, muffled sound. Hard beaters will produce a crisp,

ABOVE: *The military side drum is covered with a head of either calfskin or plastic.*

Timpano, timbale and bass drum heads

ABOVE: A timpano with a plastic head. The timpanist tunes the head to the required pitch by means of a foot pedal, a device that was invented in 1881 by Carl Pittrich.

ABOVE: The screw-tensioned heads of timbales are made of plastic and usually tuned a certain distance apart. They are usually played in pairs with wooden sticks.

ABOVE: This military bass drum has a plastic head. Plastic, unlike organic hide, is not affected by moisture and is therefore suitable for use in military parades in wet weather.

well-defined attack, while soft beaters, which tend to have larger contact areas, will give a less distinct delivery, the sound being smothered by the spread of the beater head at each contact with the drum.

In general, hard wooden sticks are used for snare drums, while sticks with hard to medium rounded heads (of wood, woven yarn, plastic or hard rubber) are used for playing xylophones and vibraphones. Instruments such as the marimba are played with soft-headed beaters, while timpani can be played with sticks in three degrees of hardness, according to whether the core is covered with soft, medium or hard felt. Some timpani sticks are double-ended, with felt heads on one end and wooden ball-shaped heads on the other, so that the sticks can be quickly reversed as required by the music.

BELOW, FROM LEFT TO RIGHT: Sticks for the bass drum, glockenspiel, vibraphone, rototom, timpani and xylophone.

ABOVE: A percussionist may need a number of different sticks and beaters for a given performance. A selection of sticks is shown here in a container suitable for travelling.

Keyboard Keys and Hammers

Seated one day at the organ I was weary and ill at ease,
And my fingers wandered idly, Over the noisy keys.

ADELAIDE A. PROCTER (1825–64), "A LOST CHORD"

Early European keyboards were simple devices with heavy levers operated with the hands rather than the fingers. The spacing between the keys on early organs, the oldest keyboard instruments, was the same as that for the pipes, sometimes as much as 10cm/4in. Up to the 13th century keyboards were diatonic, with C as the first key. When the B flat was added, this was not intended only for the playing of melodies but also as an aid to transposition. Used solely to accompany plainsong, early keyboards had a range not exceeding two octaves – matching that of the voices of the monks. In the 14th century, with the development of polyphony, the keyboard compass began to widen, and

ABOVE: Detail from Court Concert at Prince Bishop's of Lüttich in Seraing Palace *by Paul Delcloche (1753). This finely decorated piano still lacks a pedal.*

by 1330 most of the chromatic keys that we know today had been added.

Closed-case keyboard instruments, in which the tuned strings are held taut above a sounding board, include those in which the strings are plucked, such as the harpsichord and spinet, and pianos, in which they are hammered. Since the harpsichord player cannot control the force with which the strings are plucked, larger instruments frequently have a second keyboard that can be used to add variety in weight and sound quality. Both piano and harpsichord keyboards have the keys for the diatonic notes at the front, with the keys for the other five notes of the chromatic scale (the black keys) arranged between and a little behind them. The modern full-size piano keyboard has 88 notes.

ABOVE: The piano keyboard consists of white and black keys. The white keys are the natural notes while the black ones cover the sharps and flats.

ABOVE: Detail of the strings of a grand piano made by the Berlin firm of Bechstein.

ABOVE: *The piano hammers hit the strings from underneath. Over the strings is the row of dampers that stop the sound.*

ABOVE: *The hammers of a square piano, in which the strings are arranged horizontally in a rectangular box-like case.*

ABOVE: *Interior view of an upright piano.*

Hammerheads

Several materials have been used for covering piano hammerheads. Early German pianos used buckskin, but this suffered from variations in thickness and elasticity. Early 19th-century leather-covered hammers were light, but as the mass and tension of the strings increased, makers tried to increase the weight of the hammers by loading them with lead. This, however, also increased the effort required to play the instrument and the method was quickly abandoned. In England, a coarse woollen cloth was tried, but it was clear that a softer, more durable

ABOVE: *Clavichord hammers are responsive to the force of the player's finger movements.*

material was needed and in 1826 Jean-Henri Pape patented felt hammers that were a blend of sheep's wool and rabbit fur. This material remained in contact with the string for longer before rebounding, thereby producing a fuller, rounder tone than that achieved by leather.

Bass hammerheads, which are much thicker and heavier than those that strike the treble strings, are pricked with holes to give them a softer texture. The softer the felt the more slowly it rebounds from the string, thus preventing unwanted high overtones. If the felt is untoned it produces an uneven tone, many of the notes sounding duller or brighter than their neighbours.

Piano action

In a grand piano the hammers strike the strings from underneath and fall back by gravity, the action being, therefore, more responsive than in the upright piano, which has to rely on springs to return the hammers. For this reason the quick repetition of notes on the grand piano is generally

more efficient than on the upright. Quick repetition is also facilitated by the escapement, which allows the hammer to rebound from the string and be ready for the same note to be struck again. By catching the hammer before it reaches its original position, the note can be repeated more quickly than would be possible if the hammer travelled the full distance.

ABOVE: *Interior view of a harpsichord, showing the jacks under the strings.*

Evolution of the Orchestra

Musicke is said to be the rejoycing of the heart:
Musicke comforteth the mynde and feareth the enimie.

JOHN FLORIO (1553–1625), "FIRST FRUTES"

The word "orchestra" comes from the Greek, and originally meant the place where the Greek chorus sang and danced. In the Roman theatre, this space was reserved for the seats of senators. Later it was applied to the stage itself. The term was revived in the late 17th century, and by the early 18th century it had been applied in France to the players themselves.

The roots of the modern orchestra go back to the 16th-century consorts employed in noble households, and to the groups of instrumentalists

ABOVE: Five musical angels from a triptych by Hans Memling painted in about 1480. The instruments depicted are the psaltery, tromba marine, lute, sackbut and tenor shawm.

ABOVE: Fifteenth-century Italian fresco of an angel playing a sackbut – a standard instrument in civic bands at this time.

especially assembled for important occasions such as royal weddings and funerals. During the 17th century the composition of orchestras varied from place to place: strings were preferred in Italy, France and England, whereas the German courts preferred brass ensembles.

Municipal consorts

Musicians were employed by European civic authorities from as early as the 13th century. The first town known to have availed itself of a regular musician was Brunswick, Germany, in 1227. Florence in Italy and Ypres in Belgium had civic musicians by 1291 and 1297 respectively. In Germany, town musicians were known as *Stadtpfeifer* (town pipers) and in England as waits.

The duties of these official musicians were many and varied, ranging from civic functions to church festivals and celebrations.

English waits

The word "wait" derives from either Anglo-Saxon *wacian* or Old High German *Wahta*, both meaning "watch" or "guard". In time the word began to be used for the shawm, the instrument played by the watch, which was generally dubbed the "wait pipe". Many English towns possessed waits at an early date, York (1272) and Norwich (1288) being among the first recorded. The musical part of the waits' duties grew and by the mid 14th century three waits were included in the Royal Band of Edward III. By the

15th century most towns employed waits, whose main function it was to attend the mayor on ceremonial occasions and, in some towns, to play in the streets at night.

Most bands of waits performed only in their local area, but some travelled farther afield. In 1589 Sir Francis Drake employed five Norwich waits, equipped with their shawms, trombone and recorder, to provide shipboard entertainment for his expedition to Lisbon – forming what must have been the first ship's band.

German Turmmusik

Although Germany had had *Stadtpfeifer* since the 13th century, in the 16th century a phenomenon known as *Turmmusik* (tower music) became common. This was music played from the church or town-hall tower. The repertory of these bands consisted in the main of harmonized chorales but also included occasional *Turmsonaten*, which were played by instruments such as cornetts, trombones and trumpets, in four or five-part harmony.

ABOVE: Detail from a mural The Nuremberg Town Band, *painted in about 1500 by Albrecht Dürer. Pictured are two trombones, two cornetts, two shawms and a drum. Later that century a greater variety of instruments was in use, including recorder, viol, fiddle, cornett, guitar, lute, bandora and bagpipes.*

Sixteenth-century consort

The main instrument of a medieval consort was the shawm, a double-reed woodwind instrument that was first used in western Asia for dance and ceremonial music, and was brought to Europe by returning crusaders in the 12th century. The forerunner of the oboe, it had a piercing, brilliant tone, which made it especially suited for playing outdoors. It was initially used in folk music, and much later in opera.

Like its eastern prototype, the eight-holed European shawm was made from a single, conically bored piece of hardwood, terminating in a bell.

By the beginning of the 16th century shawms were being used in consort, and several sizes were made. The type instrument was the seven-holed treble, which was about 66cm/26in long. The shrill-toned soprano shawm was tuned a fifth above the treble and was about 48cm/19in long. The alto shawm, tuned a fifth below the treble, was about 76cm/30in long. The tenor shawm, which was tuned a fifth below the alto, was 112cm/4ft long and had a long S-shaped staple on which the reed and pirouette were mounted.

The bass instrument, which was known as the "bombarde" due to its resemblance to the newly invented artillery piece, was tuned an octave below the tenor and was 1.8m/6ft long. It had two keys at the front and two at the rear. There was also a giant bass shawm of about 3m/10ft in length which when played was passed under the musician's arm with the bell resting on the floor behind him.

ABOVE: A 15th-century consort consisting of musicians playing small kettledrums, fiddle, horn, triangle, lute and bagpipes.

Baroque Orchestra (1600–1750)

*Handel's entertainments are calculated for the Quality only,
people of moderate fortunes cannot pretend to them.*

THE ENGLISHMAN'S JOURNAL, 1738

In the 17th century, instrumental music was still the privilege of the great aristocratic and royal households that had the means to employ full-time orchestras and composers. Indeed, the only way that a composer could earn a living was to be employed as a servant by some wealthy patron, either a leading church dignitary or a member of the aristocracy.

A feature of Baroque music was the *basso continuo*, or figured bass, and most music was written for strings and a harpsichord. The harpsichord shared the bass line with the cello, but also added chords that helped to thicken the harmonic texture.

Italy

One of the first orchestras resembling those of today was formed in 1607 by Claudio Monteverdi (1567–1643).

ABOVE: *Jean-Baptiste Lully (1639–87) is seen here with the score of* Armide et Renaud, *which he composed in 1686.*

Language

By the early 17th century Italian composers had begun to write expression marks into their music, which is why today Italian is still, by convention, the language of Western music. Indeed such was the influence of Italy that some 19th-century English musicians adopted Italian versions of their plain English names, believing — not without good reason — that this would impress their public. The composer John Cooper (c.1570–1627) became Giovanni Coprario, and the Irish tenor and friend of Mozart, Michael Kelly (1762–1826) called himself "Ochelli". Charles Dickens satirized this curious affectation in his story *The Dancing Academy*, in which the dancing master is a certain Signor Billsmethi.

Employed by the Duke of Mantua at one of the richest courts in Italy, Monteverdi was able to use a 40-strong band of strings, flutes, cornetts and trombones for his opera *Orfeo*. The fusion of brass and strings — as opposed to the earlier orchestration of strings and woodwind only — had been adopted by many bands in northern

Italy, particularly that of St Mark's, Venice, where Monteverdi ended his career.

This was a period when opera flourished in Naples in the hands of Alessandro Scarlatti (1660–1725). However, in Italy instrumental music also began to be played in its own right, independently of opera, and the concerto came into being. Two of the foremost Italian composers of this form were Arcangelo Corelli (1653–1713) and Antonio Vivaldi (1675–1741). Both wrote *concerti grossi*, characterized by the interplay between a large and a small group of instruments.

France

The *Vingt-quatre Violons du Roi*, which confusingly sometimes numbered 25, was set up to provide music at the court of Louis XIII (1601–43). It served as a training ground for the most brilliant players in France, as well as establishing a stylized method of playing dance music. The band, which had the reputation of decorating and embellishing everything it played, played from memory and as a result some of its performances were nothing short of disastrous. However, when Jean-Baptiste Lully became Louis XIV's *Compositeur de la Musique Instrumentale* he set up his own band, the *Petits Violons*. This band, whose members were the first to wear a uniform and to use their bows in the same direction, was greatly admired and soon became a model for the rest of Europe.

Public concerts

Although music had been banned in England during the Commonwealth (1648–60), on his return from exile in France it was not surprising that Charles II was quick to introduce French music and customs to the English court. One of the Royal violinists was John Banister who, in 1672, started organizing musical performances at his home, which an invited audience would pay to hear.

At the beginning of the 18th century, public concerts as we know them today were still unknown, and musical performances were restricted to the homes of the nobility. However, as the standard of living gradually rose, so did the mercantile class, whose new opulence stimulated a desire for novelty in all forms of artistic expression, including music. It was, however, still music by the upper classes for the upper classes.

Some of the earliest public paid-entry concerts in France were the *Concerts Spirituels*, which began in 1725 in a hall in the Tuileries, Paris.

ABOVE: The Concert *(1690) by A. D. Gabbiani shows seven Modena court musicians playing violins, cello and harpsichord.*

These were primarily performances of sacred music, sung in Latin, which took place on holy days in the church calendar (when the opera was closed). The difference between these events and those organized by Banister in England was that whereas Banister's audience consisted solely of invited guests, there were no restrictions on admission to the Paris concerts.

ABOVE: In the middle of the 18th century the rich still employed musicians to perform in their homes. This painting shows a group of patrons listening to a singer accompanied by a chamber band consisting of a harpsichord, two violins, viola and cello.

ABOVE: Johann Sebastian Bach performing on a piano before his patron Frederick the Great in May 1747.

Classical Orchestra (1750–1830)

Orchestral music is one of the glories of the world.

GEORG SOLTI (1912–97)

The love of orchestral music had become so widespread by the year 1775 that it was said that even "common servants" could be met who pretended "as much judgement of an opera tune as my Lady Duchess". It was also a period when professional performers began to make large fortunes and composers were able to make an independent living, without having to tie themselves to any one court or church. Two of the first truly independent composers were Wolfgang Amadeus Mozart (1756–91) and Ludwig van Beethoven (1770–1827).

ABOVE: London's 18th-century Vauxhall Gardens were the centre of social intercourse for the upper classes. Anybody who was anybody spent time there chatting to the background music of the house band.

Instrumentation

Mozart wrote his early symphonies for the forces he had available, namely strings, two oboes and two horns. By 1782, however, he was independent and began writing for his ideal orchestra, which included flutes, clarinets, bassoons, trumpets and kettledrums. It was, however, Joseph Haydn (1732–1809) and Beethoven who established the nucleus of the modern symphony orchestra; by 1800 the average size of the orchestra was about 40.

Mannheim

One of the first "modern" symphony orchestras was founded by Johann Stamitz (1717–57) at the court of Duke Karl Theodor at Mannheim, Germany, in 1742. The Mannheim orchestra consisted of 50 virtuoso players, making it the largest regular ensemble in Europe at that time. "Its *forte* was like thunder, its *crescendos* like mighty waterfalls, its *diminuendos* like a gentle river disappearing into the distance, its *pianos* like a breath of spring." When a long *crescendo* began it was not unknown for the audience gradually to rise from their seats. This *crescendo* became known as the "Mannheim Steamroller", while an expressive falling phrase was the

ABOVE: Mozart was one of the few musical child prodigies whose genius developed with maturity. By the age of two he was already discovering chords on the keyboard and, by the time he was five, was performing on and composing pieces for the instrument. As well as 18 masses, 21 concertos and 41 symphonies, Mozart also wrote 12 operas, two of the most popular being The Marriage of Figaro *and* The Magic Flute.

"Mannheim Sigh", and various interpolated woodwind trills and turns were "Mannheim Birdies".

Subscription concerts

By the end of the 18th century concerts were being held frequently. Although they were now public events rather than private parties held in the homes of the nobility, they remained an exclusive form of entertainment due to the high price of subscriptions, which had become established by 1760. By charging in advance in this way, promoters of concerts knew just what money was available and thus were able to hire the finest performers they could afford. It was not until the middle of the 19th century that there was a change from subscriptions to the selling of tickets at reasonable prices.

In the days of Mozart and Haydn the audience did not sit quietly as (in theory) they do today, but engaged

in many activities, including eating, drinking, chattering to their friends and falling asleep. It is said that Haydn wrote his Symphony No. 94, nicknamed the "Surprise", to wake them up.

ABOVE: The band of strings and horns at the San Beneto Teatro. The musicians are placed in two serried ranks at the side of the hall in Venice.

Music festivals

A phenomenon unique to British society during the Classical period was the music festival. Lasting two or three days, these were held in many provincial towns in aid of local charities, drawing in the famous musical names of the day to give local people a chance to hear what London audiences were able to enjoy on a regular basis. The annual *Three Choirs* festival, held in Gloucester, Worcester and Hereford, was one of the first to be founded, in 1724. Leicester held two such festivals in 1771 and 1774 and, in July 1803, just over the border in Warwickshire, Nuneaton held a two-day event. In 1823 and 1825 York held two very successful festivals and, in 1826, under royal patronage, over £2400 (US$1485) was raised in Birmingham, a town that had been holding triennial festivals since the 1790s. The forward march of

ABOVE: Beethoven, who had received his early musical education from his father, became a professional musician at the age of 11. Over the next few years he took lessons from Mozart and Haydn. Soon his aristocratic patrons recognized the worth of his work and gave him financial support for the rest of his life.

ABOVE: By the early 19th century renowned opera singers such as Giuseppe de Begnis were performing virtuoso parts full of technically difficult vocal pyrotechnics.

19th-century musical life in Britain continued in 1813 with the founding of the London Philharmonic Society, whose main aim was to perform the great orchestral works of the day.

Romantic Orchestra (1830–1910)

It is scarcely credible that a distinct Romantic school could be formed in music, which is in itself romantic.

ROBERT SCHUMANN (1810–56)

By the 1850s the orchestra was increasing in size, and by 1880 it was not unusual to see an ensemble of 100 or more instrumentalists. Composers were beginning to treat the orchestra as a homogeneous whole rather than as diverse sections, with an increasing awareness of the importance of internal balance.

One of the greatest Romantic composers was Richard Wagner (1813–83) who, unlike earlier composers, was not content simply to write for the instrumental forces already present in the orchestra. As well as introducing existing instruments to the orchestra, he even specified the making of new ones, such as the bass trumpet and the Wagner tubas for *The Ring*. Hector Berlioz (1803–69) was also an

ABOVE: A scene from the première of Wagner's Rienzi, *performed at the Dresden Hoftheater on October 20, 1842.*

ambitious composer, and in his *Requiem* he called for a chime of 16 timpani. Gustav Mahler (1860–1911) wrote on an equally grand scale, and his Eighth Symphony was written for a chorus of 500, as well as 350 children's voices, seven soloists and an augmented orchestra – not for nothing was this work nicknamed the "Symphony of a Thousand".

On June 17, 1872 the largest orchestra ever formed took part in a concert at the World Peace Jubilee in Boston, Massachusetts. The orchestra of 1000 instrumentalists and choir of 20,000 voices were conducted by Johann Strauss the younger, who was on a tour of the United States. Armed with a long illuminated baton and 100 assistant conductors, he led the band (as Strauss later recalled) in an "unholy racket" such as he had never before or since heard.

Larger orchestras meant higher overheads and, as many orchestras no longer had royal patronage, it was only through the efforts of the rich music-lovers who sponsored events that most orchestras survived. Bigger concert halls were built to accommodate the large paying audiences that were needed at concerts to make the orchestras viable.

Promenade concerts

The concept of the promenade concert originated in France, where successful concerts were mounted in Paris by Philippe Musard and Louis Antoine Jullien. The format was brought to Britain, and the first London promenade concert was held in December 1838. Unlike promenade concerts today, where the audience is static, those attending these early events literally did promenade, chatting to their friends as the concert progressed. Music was a secondary

ABOVE: Richard Wagner, one of Europe's finest Romantic composers, is seen here conducting the Siegfried Idyll *on the steps of his house as a surprise for his wife Cosima on the morning of her birthday in 1870.*

ABOVE: *The cover of the sheet music for the* Promenade Quadrille *showing the Covent Garden Orchestra in London, 1870.*

concern, as the audience used the opportunity to show off their fashions.

Orchestral tours

By the 1840s, large musical groups were beginning to tour, both nationally and internationally. This was mainly due to the advent of the railways, which were able to transport large numbers of people (and baggage) much faster than horse-drawn coaches. At last people in the provinces were able to see and hear what those in the capital cities had been enjoying for many years. This led to a resurgence of interest in music, and many towns throughout Europe formed their own amateur bands and choirs.

The music of preceding generations began to be revived. In contrast to the 18th century, when most of the music played was contemporary, during the 19th century the works of

RIGHT: *An illustration of an English orchestra from the early 19th century.*

dead composers, such as Beethoven, Mozart and Handel, found a place in almost every concert.

It was not only bands that were taking advantage of the better transportation; composers and soloists such as Franz Liszt (1811–86), Niccolò Paganini (1782–1840) and Felix Mendelssohn (1809–47) also began to make provincial tours, to the delight of those who were unable to travel to hear them play in the big cities.

ABOVE: *A scene from a performance of Wagner's* Tannhäuser *at the Bayreuth Festival of 1972.*

ABOVE: *An early 19th-century performance in London's Vauxhall Gardens. A feature of the band are the two black musicians — one with a tambourine and the other with a Turkish crescent. An important development during the 18th century was the adoption by European bands of "Turkish" or "Janissary" music. The instrumentation depended heavily on percussion, and a feature of these bands was that percussion instruments were usually played by young black men. Dressed in the most exotic manner, they performed incredible acrobatics as they played.*

Modern Symphony Orchestra

There are two golden rules for an orchestra:
start together and finish together.

THOMAS BEECHAM (1879–1961)

After World War I the cost of mounting such colossal works as Mahler's Eighth Symphony became prohibitive and composers turned their pens to smaller combinations. One such composer was William Walton (1902–83) whose *Façade* was greatly influenced by jazz, as was *The Rio Grande* by Constant Lambert (1905–51). The divide between "serious" music and jazz narrowed, with jazz idioms also coming to the fore in Walton's *Belshazzar's Feast*, in which the squeaking flute sounds like a slate pencil scraping on a hard stone wall. Another composer who used both new and old musical forms was Michael Tippett (1905–98), who

ABOVE: The modern symphony orchestra usually consists of over 90 players, requiring a large concert hall for its performances. The Philharmonia Orchestra is shown here performing at the Royal Festival Hall in London.

ABOVE: For maximum volume, modern composers may include a large choir and percussion section in their compositions. The Bournemouth Symphony Orchestra and Choir are seen here under the direction of Kees Bakels. Founded in 1893, this orchestra has become one of Britain's foremost provincial orchestras and has been conducted by many great maestros.

incorporated motifs from spirituals in *A Child of Our Time* and blues and boogie-woogie in *Songs for Dov*.

In the 1950s the idea developed among composers that each separate instrument should be distinctly audible playing its individual part, rather than hearing the orchestra as an entity, a single giant instrument. Players now had to work much harder than before to give richness or beauty of tone-colour to the music.

Conductorless orchestra

The post-revolutionary Pervyi Simfonicheskii Ansambl (First Symphonic Ensemble) was formed in the USSR in 1922. The unusual aspect of the orchestra was that, believing that in the ideal Marxist state all men are equal, its members felt that there was no need to be led by the dictatorial

baton of a conductor; instead they were led by a committee. Although it was a partial success, the principal difficulty with the concept was in changing tempo. The orchestra survived for ten years and had to be disbanded only when the individual talents began to rebel against the rigid control under which they were expected to play.

New instrumental techniques

Twentieth-century orchestral practice provided composers with a vast range of techniques. One composer who developed a remarkable effect was the Spanish composer Roberto Gerhard (1896–1970), who devised the ethereal ringing tone produced by stroking the edge of a cymbal with a double bass bow. Another novel use of the orchestra was that produced by Pierre Boulez (born 1925) in *Don* from *Pli selon Pli*, where he used the orchestra not as families of woodwind, brass and strings, but as three groups of high, medium and low-voiced instruments, irrespective of their colour.

ABOVE: A modern symphony orchestra stands to acknowledge the audience's applause.

Some composers, although writing music for the instruments of a conventional orchestra, arranged the instruments in unusual combinations. In his *Music for Strings, Percussion and Celeste*, Béla Bartók (1881–1945) divided the strings into two chamber groups placed on either side of a piano, harp, celeste and percussion section.

Another composer who experimented with new effects was Claude Debussy (1862–1918). His symphonic sketch *La Mer*, composed in 1905, was finished while he was staying at the Grand Hotel at Eastbourne in England, overlooking the sea, and is a well-known example of his impressionistic approach to composition. Although Debussy used large forces for his orchestral works, it was less to enhance volume than to create colour in his music.

Other new orchestral effects have been created by the woodwind deliberately overblowing, brass players being instructed to whisper, shout or yell into their mouthpieces, and string players being asked to produce harsh, grating sounds by bowing between the bridge and the tailpiece of their instruments. Compositions like these are set to continue breaking all the rules well into the 21st century.

ABOVE: A large symphony orchestra accompanying a group of jazz soloists.

Authentic Music

The tragedy in the interpetation of music of the past lies in the fact that it is confined to concert halls, congresses of musicology, or conservatory classes. Music needs air, sunlight and liberty to be alive.

WANDA LANDOWSKA (1877–1959)

It has recently become fashionable to perform music with an authentic orchestra, using the number and type of instruments that the composer would originally have intended. Players and scholars alike have investigated early music and instruments in an attempt to discover just what was played and on what instruments, how it sounded and how it was performed. Indeed, such is the current situation that a concert of early music is likely to attract a larger audience than one of modern music.

There are special problems confronting the performer of authentic music, and each of these must be considered before calling a performance truly "authentic". Design and colour cannot be separated. In the same way that an outline drawn by Raphael could not be coloured in with Cézanne's palette, a modern violinist will not play in the same manner as Corelli. Even if he is playing on a 300-year-old instrument, he still has to know how the music was intended to be played.

Although modern composers use instruments which, by name at least,

ABOVE: Authentic music performances can be a living history experience. In this case a Salzburg violinist is dressed in 18th-century costume to enhance the period effect.

would have been familiar to Haydn and Beethoven, the style of playing and the sounds produced are totally different. Orchestral sounds changed completely with the introduction of Boehm flutes, Triébert oboes, Klosé clarinets and Heckel bassoons, not to mention valved horns and electronic instruments.

Another factor to bear in mind is the size of the orchestra's string section in relation to the wind section. In the 18th century it was unusual for an orchestra to have more than eight violins, 12 being rare. By the time of Beethoven's death a violin section of 32 had become common. However, there was no relative increase in the woodwind section. It follows therefore

RIGHT: A modern group of musicians dressed in late 18th-century costume recreating an orchestra playing Mozart's Te Deum.

Johann Stein to tune Mozart's piano had a frequency of 422Hz – half a tone lower than modern pitch. From 1800–50 the pitch in France rose from 423 to 446Hz. In 1880 Steinways were tuning their pianos to 457Hz – a quarter-tone above the present pitch.

The first attempt to fix a standard was made in 1834, but had no success. In 1889 it was decided to stabilize the pitch at 435Hz and by international agreement in 1939 "concert pitch" was fixed at a frequency of 440Hz.

that a work by Mozart played by a modern orchestra will not sound like the sonorities Mozart heard – the wind being lost under a mountain of strings. Unless the orchestra plays with the correct numerical relationship between the strings and wind, as the composer understood it, the sound will never be "authentic".

Any instrument that is used over a period of time undergoes changes. These changes invariably alter the sound produced and, as composers score for instruments according to how they perceive the sound they make, so does the way they write for them. Elgar did not write for the horn in the same way that Beethoven or Purcell did.

LEFT: *Performers of early brass instruments playing* Turmmusik *(tower music). The narrow bore of the two trombones indicates that these instruments are related to sackbuts.*

Pitch

It is not only the instruments, but also the pitch that has altered. From 1762–89 the tuning-note (A) varied between frequencies of 377 and 428 cycles per second, or Hertz (from a minor third to half a tone below the modern standard). Apart from this variation, musicians in different regions tuned to different pitches at the same time. France preferred a low, Germany a middle and England a high pitch. The tuning fork used in 1780 by

ABOVE: *The Academy of Ancient Music was founded in 1973, and its ensemble is dedicated to giving authentic performances on period instruments of a mainly 18th-century repertoire.*

Chamber Music

*Chamber music concerns itself as a world of sound
that has external boundaries but no internal ones.*

HANS WERNER HENZE (BORN 1926)

Originally, the term "chamber music" described intimate music for small groups of solo instruments performing in a drawing room before either a small audience or with no listeners at all. Chamber music differs from other orchestral music in that generally only a single instrument performs each part, whereas in an orchestra the parts are played by groups of instruments.

Although there had been a lot of small-scale ensemble music in the Middle Ages, the medieval court was a place of public exhibition, with very little opportunity for domestic music-making. However, with the rise of instrumental music and an increasing interest in amateur vocal and instrumental music-making in the 16th century, music began to play an important part in the homes of the well-to-do.

Many great houses maintained one or more professional musicians and in 17th-century Italy some princely establishments appointed musicians who had special responsibility for the performance and composition of chamber music. Monteverdi held such a post in the household of the Duke of Mantua, and his contemporaries in similar posts included Enrico di Foggia and Sigismondo d'India.

ABOVE: A painting by Max Buri (1868–1915) showing a group of German village musicians in about 1910.

Another development of the period was the tendency to arrange vocal music for instruments. From the mid 16th century consort music for viols flourished, with compositions being circulated in manuscript copies. Some were published by composers such as Michael East (c.1580–1648) and William Byrd (1543–1623), who issued their collections in 1610 and 1611 respectively. During the 16th and 17th centuries many consorts were formed, the music of which led to the invention of new dances such as the slow, stately pavan and the quicker galliard, as well as the musical forms of *ricercare* and *canzona*, which in turn led to the development of the 17th-century sonata and fugue.

In the 17th and 18th centuries chamber music was encouraged in Germany by the flourishing *collegium musicum*, in Italy by the spread of music academies and in England by the formation of music clubs.

Eighteenth-century chamber music began to include wind instruments, especially in France where music for

ABOVE: A Musical Evening by Michel Ange (1680–1730). The painting shows a chamber ensemble (harpsichord, cello, violin and flute) performing to a group of friends.

ABOVE: This painting by Pieter Fabris shows a group of mid 18th-century chamber musicians playing in Lord Fortrose's apartment in Naples, Italy.

ABOVE: One of the finest musicians of the 20th century, Yehudi Menuhin, with his sister Hephzibah and the French cellist Maurice Gendron.

various combinations of violin, flute, oboe, bassoon and harpsichord was first published. This flexible instrumentation, much of which included a fully written-out harpsichord part, as opposed to the *continuo* required hitherto, seems to have been a development prompted by publishers rather than composers.

In the homes of the nobility regular music evenings were held, at which small groups of musicians played for the family and their guests. Some of these groups were professional musicians who were sponsored by the family. One such ensemble was the Rasumovsky Quartet in Vienna, which was founded and paid for by Count Rasumovsky, the Russian ambassador to Vienna, who played second violin in the group. It was considered one of the best in Europe and even Beethoven wrote pieces especially for it.

New instrumentation
In early 20th-century France there was a proliferation of works for combinations unknown before 1900.

There was a concentration on the flute and the harp – uncommitted instruments that suited the impressionistic age. Examples include the enchanting *Introduction and Allegro* by Maurice Ravel (1875–1937) and Debussy's trio, Sonata for Flute, Viola and Harp.

Another French chamber composer who went in for unconventional instrumentation was Pierre Boulez, who scored *Le Marteau sans maître* for flute, viola, guitar, vibraphone or xylophone and percussion. Igor Stravinsky (1882–1971) was also an innovator and his *L'Histoire d'un soldat* (1918) was scored for clarinet, bassoon, cornet, trombone, violin, double bass, three actors and a dancer.

However, it will take a lot to beat Schoenberg's scoring of *Pierrot Lunaire*

ABOVE: Florilegium *was founded in 1991 to play the music of the 17th and 18th centuries. The group is one of the most exuberant chamber ensembles in Europe.*

ABOVE: *An 18th-century string quartet playing at double music desks that are reminiscent of the double prayer desks of two centuries earlier.*

specialized individuals, and might offer little to the amateur performer, who instead takes refuge in more accessible works from earlier eras.

String quartet

This chamber group was evolved by Joseph Haydn while he was employed by the Esterházy family at Eisenstadt near Vienna in the late 1750s. For the first time, chamber music abandoned the harpsichord and the new ensemble may have been used for outdoor serenades, for which it was too much trouble to carry the harpsichord outside. Altogether, Haydn wrote over 70 quartets, most of them in sets of six.

One of the novel features of the string quartet was that all the instruments had an equal share of the tunes, and for this reason the music was fun to play.

ABOVE: *The San Francisco-based Kronos Quartet was founded in 1973 and exclusively devotes itself to playing music of the 20th century and beyond.*

in 1912. This extraordinary work was written for flute, clarinet, bass clarinet, violin, viola, cello, piano and a narrator. The inflexions of the latter's voice are included in the score.

Modern chamber music

In the 20th century a reaction against the large Romantic orchestrations of the 19th century led to a renewed interest in chamber music. This was not the chamber music of the past, such as piano trios, string quartets and quintets, but small groups with new sounds and unusual combinations of instruments, with an emphasis on mixed ensembles of wind and strings and often also with vocal as well as percussion elements.

Modern chamber music has moved from the private house to the concert hall, and organizations such as the Library of Congress and the Dutch Donemus Foundation, or wealthy

individuals such as Walter Cobbett have been, and still are, active in promoting it.

The original social function and context of chamber music has now wholly disappeared. Much modern chamber music can be both difficult to play and demanding to listen to. It is often written for highly skilled and

ABOVE: *Although piano duets using one or two pianos are common, it is most unusual for more than two to be played together. This photograph from a 1920s advertisement shows four musicians, each playing a Bechstein grand piano.*

ABOVE: *An early 19th-century quartet playing at a quadruple music desk especially designed for quartets.*

This is still the case today: the sign of a good string quartet is a sense of equality.

The string quartet (like the brass band) suffers from a lack of colour contrasts – but this can be overcome not only by the differences in tone between the instruments, but by the way they are played. For instance, the instruments can be either played with the bow (*coll'arco*) or plucked with the fingers (*pizzicato*). The violin player may play notes on the G string that would normally be played on other strings. This gives a warmer quality to the sound.

Another trick to thicken the sound is the use of double-stopping, in which more than one string is played on an instrument at the same time. Two composers who used double-stopping to great effect were Debussy and Grieg. Contrasts can also be achieved by resting instruments before bringing them all in together for a climax. Haydn, Mozart and Beethoven were all masters of the string quartet and often doubled instruments for special effects.

In the 18th century it was taken for granted that music should be composed with amateur capabilities in mind. However, if a composer writes simple music today it is sometimes frowned upon and regarded as fit only for learner musicians. Although Mozart, Beethoven and Schubert all enjoyed writing string quartets, the form died out in the 19th century, but was revived in the 20th century, notably by Bartók and Shostakovich. Other 20th-century composers who are noted for their string quartets are Schoenberg, Hindemith, Walton and Tippett, whose five quartets included influences from the 16th-century madrigal.

Chamber orchestras

After World War I, economic factors saw an end to some of the large orchestras that had been dominant at the beginning of the 20th century, and composers increasingly wrote for smaller combinations of instruments. In the decades between the two World Wars a number of chamber orchestras were founded, the best known of which was the Basle Chamber Orchestra, which was set up in 1926 and was conducted by Paul Sacher.

In London, the Boyd Neel String Orchestra was founded in 1933. In an attempt to get the best of both worlds, it adopted an 18th-century repertoire and instrumentation while at the same time encouraging contemporary composers to write new works for it. In an attempt to stimulate interest in chamber music, similar orchestras, such as the Swiss Melos Ensemble, were founded all over Europe.

ABOVE: *The English Chamber Orchestra was founded by Arnold Goldsbrough in 1948. One of its prime engagements was under Benjamin Britten at the Aldeburgh Festival.*

ABOVE: *The Austrian Alban Berg String Quartet was founded in 1971 and has won international distinction with its recordings of the complete Bach, Brahms, Berg and Webern quartets. They are seen here playing at the Royal Festival Hall, London, in 1998.*

European National Music

Tell me where you live,
and I will tell you how you compose.

ROBERT SCHUMANN (1810–1856)

The 19th century was a period of European nationalism, not just in military matters but also in the arts, including music. For two centuries, the dominant musical figures in Europe had been German – from Bach to Beethoven – but the Romantic movement, which stressed personal feelings, led to composers striving to express their own traditions, and drawing on the musical influences of their own countries.

United Kingdom
Since the death of Henry Purcell in 1695, the United Kingdom had not produced a major composer, but the successful career of Arthur Sullivan (1842–1900), composer of the Savoy Operas, revived British music and paved the way for a generation of recognizably "English" voices, notably Edward Elgar (1857–1934) in whose music a mixture of nobility and nostalgia defined the British spirit at the end of the Victorian era. Frederick Delius (1862–1934) wrote works full of pastoral lyricism, and Ralph Vaughan Williams (1872–1958) rediscovered and reworked the rich vein of English folk music.

Czechoslovakia
One of the first orchestral composers to compose works with a definite national character was Bedřich Smetana (1824–84). Although he seldom used actual folk songs in his music, unlike his close friend Antonín Dvořák

(1841–1904), Smetana's work was unmistakably Czech. Absorbing the traditions of Berlioz and Liszt, Smetana was also an excellent pianist in the style of Clara Schumann. In 1861 he was appointed head of the Department of Music in the newly formed Prague

ABOVE: Scandinavian scenery inspired composers such as Sibelius and Grieg.

Society of Arts and it was during the tenure of this office that he wrote his most famous opera, *The Bartered Bride*. After suffering for some time from a whistling in his ears, in 1874 Smetana suddenly became stone deaf, but, like Beethoven before him, went on composing, including arguably his best work, *Má Vlast* ("My Country"), a set of six musical landscapes.

Finland
Another 19th-century composer whose music is evocative of his country is the Scandinavian Jean Sibelius (1865–1957), who was born in the

ABOVE: Sir Edward Elgar was England's greatest national composer of the 20th century. His work includes such typically English compositions as the four Pomp and Circumstance marches and the Enigma Variations. A great friend of Adrian Boult, Elgar fixed a sign on his cottage gate, "Please Boult the Gate".

Finnish town of Hämeenlinna. Although intended for a legal career, he soon abandoned his law studies to devote himself entirely to music. In 1892 a performance of his first large-scale orchestral work, the *Kullervo* Symphony, created such a sensation that he soon became established as Finland's leading composer. One of his most popular works is the tone poem *Finlandia*, which he composed in 1899 and which was banned by the Tsar because it roused such nationalistic fervour. Although his inspiration was intimately connected with Finnish landscape and literature (such as *Kalevala*, the national folk epic), Sibelius's achievements lie principally in his remarkable mastery of form.

Norway
Edvard Grieg (1843–1907) turned to his native folk music for inspiration, having learnt the folk songs of Norway from his mother. One of his most popular works is his incidental music to Ibsen's play *Peer Gynt*, in which he evokes trolls, mists and mountains in a work that is unmistakably Scandinavian.

Germany
One of the most obvious examples of overt nationalism in 19th-century orchestral music must be the work of Richard Wagner (1813–83), whose love of everything Aryan was to make him the darling of the Nazis, who conveniently forgot his Semitic ancestry. Wagner drew inspiration from

ABOVE: In the 18th and 19th centuries Prague was one of the main musical capitals of Europe. This scene of the Old Square is as it was in the days when Mozart walked its streets, and would have been familiar to Czechoslovakia's two great national composers, Dvořák and Smetana.

ABOVE: The Battle of Polotsk, 18 August, 1812. One of the compositions that most brings to mind "Mother Russia" is Tchaikovsky's 1812 Overture, which describes in music the day when Napoleon's army was finally defeated. The work has many musical effects, from the roar of cannon to church bells ringing out the news of victory.

the legends and myths of Germanic folklore, producing epic operas such as *Tristan und Isolde* and *Tannhäuser,* as well as the renowned *Der Ring des Nibelungen*.

France
Camille Saint-Saëns (1835–1921), as president of the Société Nationale de Musique, declared himself in favour of the "essential French qualities of logic, reason and clarity", and imparted these qualities to his huge musical output, including operas, choral and orchestral works, organ and chamber music. Gabriel Fauré (1845–1924) was a pupil of Saint-Saëns, and composed ravishing songs and choral works of great delicacy and elegance.

Russia
Russian music is full of the sounds of "Mother Russia", from Tchaikovsky's patriotic *1812 Overture* to the folk-based compositions of musicians such as Mikhail Glinka (1804–57). Glinka was regarded as the "father" of Russian music, and inspired a group of composers, known as "The Five", who set out to develop a pure Russian style. They included Alexander Borodin (1833–87), whose opera *Prince Igor* relates the story of the 12th-century struggles of the Russians against the Polovtsy invaders, and Modest Mussorgsky (1839–81) whose masterpiece is the opera *Boris Godunov*, based on Pushkin's drama about the 16th-century Tsar.

Folk Music

*The best way to get to knowing any bunch of people
is to go and listen to their music.*

WOODY GUTHRIE (1912–67)

While most music tends to cross boundaries, folk music differs from area to area. The folk music of Northumberland is different from that of southern England; the music of Hamburg is different from that of Munich or the Tyrol; in Russia, the folk tunes in the west are different from those in the east. The workers on the American cotton plantations sang songs that were unknown in the industrial cities of Boston and New York. The words and tunes of folk songs were transmitted aurally, and might have existed in several versions in different places, as they were subtly altered over the years.

In Britain, most songs were traditionally sung only by men. Women exercised their vocal chords only while working or in the home, and were very rarely heard in public.

ABOVE: This print from the 1830s shows a party of villagers folk-dancing outside an inn in Süd Tirol, Austria, now part of northern Italy.

Work songs

Many traditional songs were about work, especially the hard conditions associated with occupations such as working in the fields, down the mines or on ships. Singing made hard work easier and many songs were of the call and response type, in which the leader or shantyman would sing out the story and the rest of the workers would join in the chorus. Another type of work song was the street cry, with which street vendors advertised their wares.

Ballads

The ballad was a song that told a story, and might be based on contemporary news events of the day, such as a battle or a mining disaster, or on legends or fictional tales. In the days before radio or television, when few working people were able to read newspapers, singing or listening to these ballads was one way to escape briefly from the

ABOVE: The composer Béla Bartók travelled extensively all over Hungary and neighbouring states, making recordings of folk songs.

daily grind. There were also many shorter songs, which might be pithy and humorous or lyrical and romantic.

Instrumental accompaniment

At work in the fields, or in the home, most folk music was sung unaccompanied. In Biblical Israel songs were sung to the accompaniment of the harp, while in classical Greece the singer was accompanied on the kithara. In medieval Europe folk songs were sung to pipe and tabor and later to the hurdy-gurdy or bagpipes. Bagpipes were purely a folk instrument, being thought to be crude and fit only for the tavern, in contrast to the viol, favoured by the more well-to-do.

Dancing

Feast days and their associated rituals have invariably included both music and dancing, such as the May Day Morris dancing of southern England and the sword dances of the north. These two very different traditions of folk-dancing reflect the Viking occupation of the north-east of Britain.

Originally, dances like these were performed only on certain occasions, and were part of religious ceremonies to celebrate the passing of the seasons and to bring good luck to the harvest. Though the original significance of these dances has been lost, they are

ABOVE: Before radio and television people made their own amusements, and one of the few pastimes available for the "labouring poor" was dancing. This print of 1804 shows a Polish man dancing before his friends.

ABOVE: One of the joys of life in the southern states of America is when the family play their instruments on the porch.

ABOVE: Morris dancing is thought to be associated with fertility. There are many groups who try to recreate England's past.

still performed on festive occasions, such as village fête days.

Some folk dances have become popularized far beyond their point of origin. The waltz originated as a peasant dance in southern Germany, but has become known – in its more refined state – all over the world. Another genre that has become popular way beyond its native shores, due both to migration and, latterly, to a film and stage show, is Irish dancing.

As with folk songs, the instruments that provided the music for these dances were small and portable, such as the fiddle. The accordion, invented in the early 19th century, became popular as an accompaniment for open-air dancing, and a 20th-century innovation in Morris sides is the inclusion of the concertina.

Contemporary folk music

In the 1960s, with the growth of the American civil rights movement and the increasing aversion of young people to America's involvement in the war in Vietnam, folk songs experienced a revival of interest as a means of political protest, sung by professional folk singers such as Joan Baez (born 1941), Pete Seeger (born 1919) and Bob Dylan (born 1941). Many of Bob Dylan's "protest" songs of the mid '60s have become folk classics, such as *Masters of War*, *The Times They are A-changin'* and *With God on our Side*. Country Joe McDonald's chorus, "And it's one, two, three, what are we fighting for?" has become the universal anti-war anthem.

ABOVE: One of the new-style folk singers of the 1960s was Bob Dylan, whose songs relate to the protest movement of that time.

Revolutionary Music of the 20th Century

Think nothing. Wait until it is absolutely still within you.
When you have attained this begin to play.

KARLHEINZ STOCKHAUSEN, INSTRUCTIONS TO PERFORMERS OF "ES"

s the 20th century dawned, some composers turned away from the hitherto accepted rules of harmony and composition and ventured out into the realms of polytonality, atonality and microtones.

Atonal music

In 1908 the Austrian composer Arnold Schoenberg (1874–1951) changed the whole basis of harmony. He abandoned

ABOVE: Arnold Schoenberg decided to abandon tonality in 1907 when he wrote his Second String Quartet, a work in which the keys are not stated but "sensed".

the idea of the central keynote and regarded every semitone of a chromatic scale as being of equal importance. One of his early atonal compositions was the opera *Expectation*, a work for soprano and orchestra. Although some listeners admired Schoenberg's work, many more found it unintelligible, preferring tonal music that was more pleasing to the ear.

Microtones

Another innovation of the 20th century was the use of microtones. Although microtones were, and still are, common in eastern music, and are found in some eastern European folk music, the smallest interval generally

used in European music was the semitone. The main promoter of microtones in Europe was the Czech composer Alois Hába (born 1893), who divided the notes of the scale into intervals of one-third, one-quarter and one-sixth of a tone. Due to the construction of European wind instruments, such music is only easily playable on strings and trombones.

Polytonal music

Polytonality is the use of two keys simultaneously. Again, to most listeners this is very grating on the ear, but the genre did find some early supporters. One of these was Charles Ives (1874–1954), an insurance salesman who wrote music in his spare time. Some of his music is very complex to perform: in its original form, his Fourth Symphony, for instance, needs four conductors to

ABOVE: Charles Ives was the first American composer to break away from the German style that had influenced most American music during the late 19th century.

By numbers

A composer who drew inspiration from unusual sources was the Russian Joseph Schillinger, who emigrated to the United States in 1930. At one concert he asked his audience which composer the new work he had just played reminded them of. Suggestions included Mozart, Bach and Beethoven; however, nobody could guess Schillinger's actual source, which had been the stock-market quotations. Schillinger had plotted the figures on a sheet of graph paper and given each a proportional musical value. Schillinger also taught music, and amongst his pupils was Glenn Miller, whose *Moonlight Serenade* was written as an exercise set by Schillinger.

ABOVE: *Dimitri Shostakovich was greatly influenced by his compatriots Rimsky-Korsakov, Tchaikovsky and Prokofiev.*

keep the players together. Another exponent of polytonality was Igor Stravinsky. His music for the ballet *The Rite of Spring* begins with a bassoon solo that is scored deliberately at the top of the instrument's range because he wanted the player to strive to reach the note to give the sound the quality of struggle. At its first performance in Paris in May 1913 the audience almost caused a riot. At one point the manager of the theatre, in an attempt to restore calm, was heard to say "Listen before you boo." When the composer Camille Saint-Saëns heard the work, he just kept repeating *"Il est fou."* Yet the work has since become an established and popular part of the orchestral repertoire.

Aleatoric music

Some of the music of Karlheinz Stockhausen (born 1928) never sounds the same twice over because it is aleatoric: it includes the improvisatory elements of chance and free choice. Stockhausen has abandoned conventional notation altogether and writes "text scores" in which he explains in words how the music should be played. In *Gold Dust*, for instance, he even suggests that the musicians should starve themselves for four days and nights before the performance.

Another composer who explored the operation of chance was John Cage (1912–92), whose *4' 33"* consists of

four minutes and 33 seconds of silence, the idea being that the music is created by the sounds provided by the natural environment at the time. This work was satirized by the musician and humorist Gerard Hoffnung, who in the mid 1950s announced that he had written a work that included three bars of silence. The first and third bars, so Hoffnung explained, were in 5:4 time, but the second bar was in 3:4 time, "thereby giving the whole work a quasi-Viennese flavour".

ABOVE: *Karlheinz Stockhausen abandoned both conventional musical notation and instrumentation, utilizing "instruments" such as iron chains and shortwave radios.*

ABOVE: *Igor Stravinsky had a rich and diverse musical output. Here he is shown conducting a 1951 rehearsal of his opera* The Rake's Progress *in Venice, Italy.*

Many of Cage's works for dance companies and concert performances exploited his invention of the "prepared piano", in which he created percussive effects by placing objects such as rubber bands and paperclips between the strings. He also wrote *HPSCHD*, a piece for seven harpsichords and 51 tape machines, and *0'00"* which was for any musician playing any instrument in any way.

ABOVE: *The composer and pianist John Cage was a pupil of Schoenberg. His music exploits a variety of percussive and novel sound effects produced by orthodox instruments, modified instruments such as the "prepared" piano, and objects such as radio receivers, chairs and even dead fish.*

Brass Bands

*The brass band contest is the one and only
successful rival to the football match.*

GEORGE MILLER

Brass bands came into existence in
England and Wales in the 1830s as
a result of the philanthropic efforts of
factory owners to enrich the lives of
their work forces. They saw brass bands
as valuable adjuncts to their works,
and in an era of increasing leisure,
the bands became a popular pastime.

Improvement in the manufacture of
brass instruments at around this time
made both fingering and blowing
easier, and the advent of the railways
made travel feasible for working
people. It was not long before bands
began to compete with one another
in friendly rivalry.

*ABOVE: Brass baritones from an Austrian town band giving an outdoor performance
in Salzburg, Austria.*

Contests

The first known brass band contest,
at which five bands took part, was
held at Burton Constable, near Hull,
in 1845. In those early days the
participating bands were restricted
to 12 players (as opposed to 25 today)
and played arrangements of works
by composers such as Weber, Rossini
and Mozart.

The most distinguished of these
early bandsmen was Enderby Jackson,
a conductor and arranger who, in
1854, established the principle that
all participating bands in a contest
should play the same test piece.

Today the British National Brass
Band Contest, held in London at the
Royal Albert Hall, is the highlight of
the British bandsman's year. Since
1978 the more ambitious British
bands have also been able to compete
with their European counterparts at the
European Brass Band Championships.

United States and beyond

Brass bands became popular in the
United States almost as early as they
did in Britain. One of the first bands to
be formed in the United States was the
Brass Band of New York, established by
Alan Dodworth in 1834. Brass band

*ABOVE: The "Besses o' th' Barn" band from Whitefield, Lancashire, was one of England's
foremost brass bands. It was founded in 1818 and is seen here during its successful tour
of France in 1905.*

concerts soon became a part of the American way of life. It was truly music for the people, with bandstand gazebos in almost every park. Some of these, such as that in New York's Central Park, were paid for by the railway company as a way of increasing fare income by transporting out-of-town concertgoers into the city. On Boston Common, concerts were so well attended that some are said to have attracted crowds of up to 10,000 people.

By 1900 the brass band movement had reached its zenith in England and Wales, with some 20,000 brass bands. Although their number declined after World War II, there was a revival of interest from the 1960s. This resurgence occurred not only in Britain, Australia, New Zealand and the United States but also in Europe, where British-style brass bands were formed in the Netherlands, Sweden, Switzerland, Norway and Belgium.

Repertoire
Brass bands play a mixture of transcriptions of orchestral works and original compositions. Notable early

ABOVE: The Durham Miners' Gala is one of the most eagerly anticipated events in the British brass bandsman's diary. Many bands take part in the event, both marching through the town and giving static concerts.

arrangers of music for bands include J. Ord Hume, Samuel Cope and William Rimmer. As well as orchestral composers such as Arthur Bliss, Gustav Holst and Sir Edward Elgar, all of whom wrote for brass band, the brass band's repertoire has been greatly enhanced by men such as Eric

Ball, Geoffrey Brand and Granville Bantock. At first, some of this new music was treated with suspicion, and it was not unknown for band conductors, unaccustomed to anything but the harmonies of marches and hymn tunes, to change "wrong notes" to their own satisfaction. It is reported that one conductor with a limited knowledge of Italian went into a music shop after receiving a new score with the intention of buying "some of those new-fangled *senza mutes*".

These days, band concerts in the park are still enjoyed by thousands of people who like nothing better than relaxing in the sunshine listening to a "good drop of music".

LEFT: The continued survival of brass bands in Britain depends on young people taking up brass instruments to fill the ranks of older musicians. The presence of so many youth bands in the country assures the future of the brass band movement.

Military Bands

Explain it as we may, a martial strain
will urge a man into the front rank of battle.

HENRY THEODORE TUCKERMAN (1813–71)

Soldiers of the world have always marched to music, even if it was only the rhythmic tread of their own feet. By 1600 BC Egyptians were marching to trumpet and drum, and a thousand years later Roman trumpeters played on the march. Trumpets were an integral part of Caesar's army and on that fateful day, while standing by the bridge crossing the Rubicon, the trumpets blew a thunderous blast. In 6th-century Persia the regiments marched to bands of drums, pipes and trumpets. Four hundred years later their descendants were still enjoying the stirring music of large bands of drums, cymbals, trumpets and other wind instruments.

European military bands
Military bands came to the attention of western Europeans during the Crusades from the 11th to 13th centuries, when they encountered Saracen bands consisting of *surnay*

(oboes), *nafir* (trumpets), *buq* (horns) and *naqqara* (kettledrums). During the late Middle Ages European armies began to copy these bands loosely, employing combinations of shawms, bagpipes, trumpets and drums. The duties of the musicians were mainly to play at tournaments and to accompany the soldiers on campaign.

Janissary bands
An important development during the 18th century was the adoption by European military bands of "Turkish" or "Janissary" music. The instrumentation of these bands included oboes, fifes, side drums, kettledrums, cymbals, triangles, Turkish crescent and bass drum. Such was the fad for this type of music that some regiments in Poland, Russia and Prussia even imported whole bands, complete with musicians, from Turkey. Today, remnants of the Janissary era live on in the leopardskin apron worn by bass drummers and the shape of the lyre glockenspiel.

The trend was reversed in the early 19th century when, in 1826, the Sultan of Turkey disbanded his corps of Janissaries and invited Giuseppe Donizetti (brother of the composer) to reorganize Turkish bands on the lines

ABOVE: *Russian horn bands were a feature of the late 18th and early 19th centuries. Such was the popularity of these combinations with the Russian nobility that they often sold them to one another – players as well as horns.*

ABOVE: For centuries, armies have used drums to keep their marching troops in step. Here an 18th-century side drummer leads a platoon of troops past the National Theatre in Prague.

ABOVE: Brightly dressed army side drummers playing at the Battle of Fontenoy in 1745.

of European ones. Persian bands followed suit and adopted Western instrumentation in about 1840.

New instruments

By the end of the 18th century military bands were increasing in size, mainly as a result of adding extra percussion instruments, which in turn made it necessary – for purposes of audibility – to increase the wind section. Clarinets, both B flat and E flat, were introduced into military bands and soon outnumbered any other instrument. Performing the same role as the violins in the symphony orchestra, there were two main reasons for the clarinet replacing the oboe in military bands. First, it is much easier for a marching musician to play the single reed clarinet than the double reed oboe and second, the softer sound of the oboe tends to become lost when playing with modern brass instruments.

American Civil War bands

During the American Civil War military bands proliferated on both sides of the conflict and were heard on all occasions, from ceremonial parades to battle marches. A good band was a source of tremendous pride and was long remembered by those fortunate enough to witness the "dawn of peace".

Sometimes Union bands played in competition with their southern counterparts. One such impromptu concert happened during a lull in the Battle of Spotsylvania in 1864. Each side brought their band to the front line where, for an hour or so, the bands played alternate tunes. The concert ended with the Confederate band bringing tears to the eyes of the battle-hardened men of both sides with their heart-rending rendition of *Home Sweet Home*.

ABOVE: Members of military bands often "double" on stringed instruments. The bands of the Austrian Empire were no exception and here Johann Strauss the Younger is seen conducting a military orchestra at a royal ball in Vienna.

History of Music-making and the Orchestra **67**

Military schools of music

A major event in the evolution of European military bands was the celebration of peace at the end of the Crimean War in 1856. Military bands of all the allied nations took part, giving the bandsmen an opportunity to hear each other play and compare standards. In the wake of the British bands' poor showing (particularly embarrassing when they played the national anthem in different keys), the Royal Military School of Music was founded at Kneller Hall in Twickenham, near London.

At this time British military bandmasters were still mainly civilian musicians and — more surprisingly — were in many cases foreign. Three examples were Francis Ptacek, a member of the Prague Conservatoire who was director of the band of the Leicestershire Militia; Herr Sawerthal,

ABOVE: Marching bands are popular in the United States, Australia and, to a lesser degree, Britain. This Sydney annual marching band festival takes place in Australia every August.

the bandmaster of the Royal Engineers; and Karl Tieke, the composer of the evergreen march *Alte Kameraden*, who was the director of the band of the Royal Irish Dragoon Guards.

It was not until 1887 that an army bandmaster, Dan Godfrey, the director of the band of the Grenadier Guards, received a commission. Today all directors of full-time military bands are of officer rank.

Civilian "military" bands

During the 19th century the term "military band" became something of a misnomer as it began to be used more loosely, referring also to civilian bands using military band instrumentation for public concerts. One of the most popular of these civilian bands was the renowned Jullien Band.

Jullien

Louis Antoine Jullien (1812–60) was the son of a military bandsman. After a period of study at the Paris Conservatoire, he began promoting concerts of dance music at the Jardin Ture, where he became known as the "Napoleon of Music".

ABOVE: Almost every school in the United States has its own band. This one is proudly playing on the steps of the Capitol building in Washington DC.

ABOVE: The drum corps of the Grenadier Guards playing at the annual "Trooping of the Colour" in London.

ABOVE: One of the best-known annual events in Germany is the Oktoberfest. *Held in Munich, this beer festival is enlivened by the many bands that perform.*

father's footsteps and became a professional trombonist, but later turned to the violin and conducting. Between 1868 and 1892 he built up a promising reputation as bandmaster of the United States Marine Corps Band. In 1892 he left the service to form his own famous band, which toured Europe several times as well as making a two-year world tour in 1910–11. Sousa, who is justly called the "March King", composed 136 marches, including *The Washington Post*, *The Stars and Stripes Forever*, *Liberty Bell*, *High School Cadets* and *El Capitan*. Sousa is also remembered for the redesigned helicon first made for his band in 1899, now known as the sousaphone.

In 1840 he moved to England, and made his debut in Drury Lane in June.

Thanks to a spotless white waistcoat, as well as his ambrosial curls, superb moustache and the magnificent air with which he wielded his baton, Jullien was the object of unsparing ridicule.

ABOVE: Jullien's concerts were always sold out well in advance. Despite this, he was never able to pay off the debts he had amassed in Paris, and he died bankrupt.

He was a devotee of Beethoven, and whenever he conducted works by that composer he would have a new pair of white gloves presented to him which he would wear while he conducted.

Each year Jullien tried to bring some novelty into his concerts. In 1849 he introduced the *monstre* ophicleide (a brass instrument later superseded by the tuba) which at that time was the largest wind instrument ever made. In 1851 he toured with a French drum corps, which appeared in full military uniform by permission of Prince Louis Napoleon. In the same year, appreciating the discomforts, if not the dangers, of passive smoking, Jullien requested that his concerts be non-smoking events.

Sousa

Another famous civilian wind band was that formed by John Philip Sousa (1854–1932) in 1892. Sousa was born in Washington DC, and from the age of six he learnt to play the violin, as well as studying various band instruments, harmony and musical theory. In 1867 he followed in his

ABOVE: Sousa was justly known as the "March King" – he composed 136 marches. His band became famous worldwide and he made a two-year world tour in 1910–11.

Country Music

You got to have smelt a lot of mule manure
before you can sing like a hillbilly.
HANK WILLIAMS (1923–53)

For many, country music is summed up as songs about orphaned children, lost mothers, betrayed lovers, train wrecks and coal-mining disasters. However, there is actually a lot more to country music than sentimentality and sickly patriotism. It is not just "hillbilly music" but has a century of tradition, with many styles evolving and co-existing over the decades. It is a blending of the two distinct traditions of the American settlers: European ballads, story songs and dance music, and African-American blues and work songs.

ABOVE: Hank Williams was America's greatest honky-tonk performer, whose early death ensured him a permanent place in country music's pantheon of stars. One of his best-known songs is Cold, Cold Heart.

The commercialization of this blend came in the mid 19th century with the minstrel shows that were created by white performers parodying black manners. These shows gave birth to two distinct forms of entertainment. In the North they evolved into vaudeville, while in the South they nurtured home-grown banjo and fiddle players.

Another seedbed for country music was the southern rural church where singing was — and still is — a central

part of the service. Although the white and black churches had different styles, they merged into a tightly harmonized music called "bluegrass". An early example of this type of music was that sung by the Carter Family from Virginia, whose songs were based on the ultimate embodiment of home and family values. Their unornamented, nasal, simple four-square harmonies were entirely white with no black influences whatsoever.

In marked contrast to the "home harmonizers", there were more progressive singers, such as Jimmie Rodgers (1897–1933), who sang a combination of jazz, blues and country. Although he recorded with many bands, his most moving performances were those in which he was accompanied only by his guitar — songs such as the autobiographical *T. B. Blues*, *T. for Texas* and *Waitin' for a Train*, which is one of the most popular train songs ever.

ABOVE: The fiddle is one of the most popular instruments with country musicians. It is used in many types of country music, from bluegrass to the sentimental tones accompanying the songs for which the genre is famous.

ABOVE: This country fiddle player is being accompanied by an accordion player.

ABOVE: *Before the advent of the electric bass guitar, every country band had a string bass. Some bass players were very versatile and were able to produce remarkable effects on their instrument.*

pianos and a strong string section, became known throughout the world. Nashville remained the bastion of country music throughout the 1960s, but remained very conservative, both artistically and politically. In the '60s and early '70s there was, for example, an unhealthy number of songs supporting America's involvement in the Vietnam War, notably Merle Haggard's *Okie from Muskogee* and *The Fightin' Side of Me*, which cemented his stardom but enraged liberals everywhere. The slushy sounds of Nashville were rejected by singers such as Waylon Jennings (who had played with Buddy Holly) and Willie Nelson. They left Nashville and went to Texas where they established what has become known as "outlaw country". During the 1980s and '90s mainstream country music has become more and more like pop, so that in many cases it is hard to spot the difference.

ABOVE: *Willie Nelson (born 1933) is one of the most influencial songwriters and singers country music has ever known. His laid-back style of singing once led one reviewer to announce that by the time Nelson had sung one line, Dolly Parton would have sung a complete song! One of Nelson's best-known albums is* Tougher than Leather, *which deals with the effects of fate on life.*

Rodgers influenced many country singers, including the legendary Hank Williams (1923–53). Williams sang in the first person and dealt head-on with issues such as adultery and alcoholism. His many songs are still part of almost every country singer's repertoire and there is hardly ever a country music concert anywhere that does not include at least one Hank Williams song.

Grand Ole Opry

Country music spread into the homes of Americans via radio programmes, in particular Chicago's *National Barn Dance*, the *Louisiana Hayride* from Shreveport, and WSM Radio's *Grand Ole Opry* from Nashville, Tennessee. In the mid 1950s Nashville became the centre of country music and the "Nashville Sound", featuring tickling

ABOVE: *Many solo country singers have teamed up with a colleague to produce duets. One of the most successful of such pairings is Dolly Parton and Kenny Rogers.*

Jazz

*If you're in jazz and more than ten people like you,
you're labelled commercial.*

HERBIE MANN (BORN 1930)

Jazz is a truly American music, being a combination of that country's two dominant cultures – African and European. As a genre it is almost unique in embodying both rural and urban sounds, as well as ranging from the raw sounds of New Orleans Dixieland bands to the sophistication of New York cool jazz groups.

New Orleans

Dixieland jazz evolved from the ragtime music of the late 19th century, which was epitomized by the work of Scott Joplin, composer of piano rags such as *The Entertainer*. Finding the steady ragtime 2:4 time monotonous, some musicians doubled the time to 4:4 and began to play the melody just a little ahead of or behind the beat, which gave an unevenness to the pulse.

ABOVE: Louis Armstrong single-handedly transformed jazz from a collective art to one of solo expression. His clear, ringing trumpet-playing was impeccable.

These subtle rhythmic changes increased the swing of the music, producing the fast, happy, high-energy music now known as traditional jazz.

One of the earliest exponents of the genre was Buddy Bolden (1877–1931), who is remembered for his blues songs, such as *Careless Love*. Another of the early traditional players was Jelly Roll Morton (1885–1941), a brilliant pianist, arranger and composer, who is best remembered for his *Tiger Rag*.

Another early New Orleans bandleader was "King" Oliver (1885–1938), who moved to Chicago in 1918 and formed his own band, the Creole Jazz Band, in 1922. One of the musicians Oliver invited to join him was Louis Armstrong (1901–71), who had started his professional life playing trumpet in the red-light district of New Orleans for 15 cents a night. Armstrong, a master of improvisation, formed his own band in 1925 and revolutionized jazz for all time. He was the first to create solo improvised melodies that complemented the basic theme, and thus established the central role of the soloist in what had previously been an ensemble form. His technical virtuosity was breathtaking – he was, for instance, able to hold high notes effortlessly for three or four bars at a time.

Chicago "traditional" jazz

Influenced by what was happening in New Orleans, the Chicago of the early 1900s was also a centre of jazz. Led by Nick LaRocca, the Original Dixieland Jazz Band – which was composed

ABOVE: When one thinks of jazz, one automatically thinks of New Orleans, a city where almost every bar and club has its own house band.

melodic improvisation is very free in cool jazz and players often use counterpoint to play two improvised melodic lines at the same time. Two of the best-known exponents of cool jazz are Miles Davis (1926–91) and the Dave Brubeck Quartet.

ABOVE: As well as being a comedian and film maker, Woody Allen is an enthusiastic jazz clarinettist, his favourite being New Orleans jazz. He is seen here guesting in a band show.

ABOVE: Thelonious Monk was one of the greatest jazz pianists. Born in New York City, he began playing at his local Baptist church. Although he had his own big band, he is better known for his jazz quartet.

solely of white musicians – made the first ever jazz recordings in 1917. One man who was inspired by the band was the legendary Bix Beiderbecke (1903–31) who, after hearing a recording by LaRocca, persuaded his parents to give him a cornet. He formed his own band – the Wolverines – in 1923, but by 1925 he had gone solo and was performing with various touring bands. Although he died at only 28, Beiderbecke was the man chiefly responsible for introducing Dixieland jazz to a white audience, and without him the genre would never have become so popular.

Bebop and cool jazz

An offshoot of classical jazz is bebop, which developed in Harlem in the early 1940s. The onomatopoeic name was coined by young musicians including Dizzy Gillespie (1917–93), Charlie Parker (1920–55) and Thelonious Monk (1917–82) to describe the style that emerged during their jam sessions, characterized by upbeat rhythms, fast tempo and improvisation. Bebop later became accepted as the nickname for the

whole wave of new jazz that exploded after World War II.

Cool jazz ("modern jazz") musicians take a more intellectual approach to their music. Disdaining any kind of showmanship, they often play with their backs to the audience. The rhythm is muted, the drummer simply keeping the beat, on which the players stay rather than syncopating. The

ABOVE: Dizzy Gillespie, trumpeter, composer and bandleader, was responsible for giving jazz a whole new style that included whole-tone scales and altered chords.

Big Bands

To swing is to affirm.

FATHER G. V. KENNARD

In the mid 1920s the move began to form larger jazz bands, which were in fact small orchestras. Two of the early dance bands of the era were those led by Paul Whiteman (1890–1967) and Fletcher Henderson (1897–1952).

Whiteman, a classically trained violinist, formed his first (all-white) small band in 1919. In 1924 he organized the first ever concert of jazz music at New York's Aeolian Hall, at which the highlight was George Gershwin playing his *Rhapsody in Blue* for the first time. Whiteman's orchestra was so successful that at one time there were no less than 28 different "Whiteman" bands touring the United States.

Fletcher Henderson, whose band consisted of all black musicians,

ABOVE: Glenn Miller formed his band in 1938, and within a year his trademark sound of soothing reeds — for example in In The Mood — *had become world famous.*

played at New York's Roseland Ballroom. However in 1923, after Louis Armstrong had played for a short time with the band, Henderson changed his style from polite dance music to swing jazz. Henderson is remembered especially for his revolutionary "call and response" arrangements, which split the band's instruments into two groups, the first group stating a melody and the second responding to it.

Instrumentation

One of the important innovations of the big band was the introduction of the saxophone. One of the first jazz saxophonists was Coleman Hawkins (1904–69), who introduced the instrument to Henderson's band in

1923. Between the 1930s and '60s, saxophones were to feature strongly in the "big band" orchestras led by people such as Glenn Miller and Duke Ellington in the United States, Henry Hall in England and Bert Kaempfert and James Last in Germany.

Big band leaders

One of the most talented jazz musicians was Duke Ellington (1899–1974). His compositions are still standard works in most bands' repertoires and include classics such as *Satin Doll* and *Mood Indigo*. Ellington, whose band was at its peak during the 1930s, introduced the "jungle style", in which growling trumpets and wailing clarinets gave the music an unmistakable African feeling.

ABOVE: George Gershwin was one of America's most versatile songwriters. With his brother Ira he wrote musical comedies, such as Funny Face *and* Tiptoes.

ABOVE: Duke Ellington: pianist, bandleader and composer.

ABOVE: *Noted especially for his minimalist piano style, which he had perfected by the end of the 1930s, Count Basie was one of the finest jazz pianists of the 20th century.*

Another jazz man to hit the scene in the 1930s was the clarinettist Benny Goodman (1909–86). Goodman was well known for his sight-reading skills and was the first white jazz musician to break the colour barrier and work with black colleagues. Goodman's band, which was noted for being the best rehearsed and most precise, played the "pop" music of its day.

Kansas City swing

Count (William) Basie (1904–84), who became the leader of Kansas City swing, began his career as pianist in the Bennie Moten band, one of the first to feature the combination of five brass, four reed and four rhythm players. After Moten's death in 1935, Basie began to build his own ensemble from the remnants of his mentor's band. He soon became one of the most successful jazz bandleaders, and led his band until his death in 1984. The band was noted for its "head arranging", in which riffs were improvised during performances, the other musicians having hastily to adjust their parts.

Western swing

Western swing is a combination of string-band music with jazz styles that developed in the late 1920s. One of the first bands to feature the new type of music was the Light Crust Doughboys, which featured the fiddler Bob Wills (1905–75). Wills soon left to form his own band, the Texas Playboys, which became the epitome of western swing. Wills incorporated old-time country fiddling, jazz, blues, boogie-woogie and the Tex-Mex sounds that became so popular in the 1960s.

ABOVE: *Although the early days of Basie's band were exhilaratingly wild, under his leadership they became the most disciplined and sleek big band of the era.*

ABOVE: *Benny Goodman, the "King of Swing", was at home in jazz and classical music.*

ABOVE: *Duke Ellington was the master of swing and endured long after the period was history. He led arguably one of the greatest swing bands of all time.*

Rock and Pop

You have to blame Thomas Edison for today's rock 'n' roll.
He invented [sic] electricity.
STAN GETZ (1927–91)

Rock music evolved from the blues. After the end of World War II many African-Americans from the Deep South moved to northern cities such as Chicago, in search of work and to escape the racialism that was — and to some extent still is — rife in the former Confederate States. Here, musicians created an urbanized rhythm that served as a foundation for pioneer rock 'n' rollers such as Little Richard and Chuck Berry.

Electric guitar

Although the first solid-body electric guitar was built by Les Paul, it was first mass-produced by Leo Fender, and became a key element in rock 'n' roll. Fender, a California-based guitar and

ABOVE: The Beatles, who began their musical career in a nightclub in Liverpool, became the world's top pop group with hit records such as She Loves You *and* A Hard Day's Night.

amplifier manufacturer, had often been asked by musicians if he could give more volume and at the same time eliminate screech and feedback from the electrified instruments of the time. He came up with the solid-body guitar that he developed just after World War II. His first model, the Broadcaster, entered mass production in 1948, and its sharpness and attack made it an instant success, especially with country musicians. In 1950 its name was changed to the Telecaster, and it was this instrument that gave the rock of that decade its distinctive sound. In 1951 Fender introduced his solid-body bass guitar and, five years later, his futuristic Stratocaster.

One of the pioneers of electric guitar-playing was Muddy Waters (1915–83), who moved up to Chicago from Mississippi. In 1944 he bought his first electric guitar, one made by Fender, and within two years had formed his first electric combo.

African-American music

The importance of African-American music cannot be overestimated. From the Motown sound of the 1960s, through soul and disco to the rap of the 1990s, the exciting sounds of black music have dominated and led the way in many popular music trends. More than anything else, rock music has helped to integrate black and white America, breaking down the racial barrier that has plagued the country.

The 1950s

Many of the young white singers of the 1950s derived their inspiration from black music, including Elvis Presley (1935–77), who became one of the most influential rock 'n' roll singers of the 20th century. Born in Tupelo, Mississippi, as a boy Elvis was always in demand for singing at church services and revival meetings, and was greatly influenced by black blues singers. Indeed, when people who did not know him heard him singing, they could not believe that he was white. Presley's romantic, suggestive ballads, which were matched by his gyrations on stage, made him one of the first mass idols of American adolescent culture (as well as getting him banned from many television stations).

ABOVE: Elvis Presley was the foremost and most influential popular singer of the 1950s and '60s. His style ranged from country to rock and mainstream.

ABOVE: *The legendary rock guitarist Jimi Hendrix, born in Seattle, had his first hit in Britain with* Hey Joe *in 1967.*

Another pioneer was Buddy Holly (1936–59), whose short career was the inspiration for many singers of the 1960s, including Mick Jagger. Holly was a shy, bespectacled youth from Texas whose life was tragically cut short in a plane crash in 1959.

Rock 'n' roll was synonymous with rebellion and no one was more rebellious than Jerry Lee Lewis (born 1935), who shocked the morality of the age by marrying his 13-year-old cousin. It was not until the mid 1960s that Lewis once again gained public approval.

ABOVE: *Abba, whose name was taken from the initial letters of the members' names, were one of the few pop groups outside America or Britain to gain international stardom.*

Pop music

The 1960s have been rightly dubbed the "Swinging Sixties", and musically they were dominated by the Beatles and the Rolling Stones. Whereas the Beatles based their music on the rock of the 1950s, the Rolling Stones were rhythm-and-blues-based. Both bands had great success, and in one way or another have influenced almost every other rock band since.

While many bands were conventional, some performers · mirrored the violence of the time (especially the United States' involvement in Vietnam). One of these was Jimi Hendrix (1942–70), who was one of the greatest guitarists of the '60s and had been a member of James Brown's backing band, the Famous Flames. His erotic stage actions, suggestive lyrics and guitar-smashing antics brought him much criticism — on one occasion he doused his guitar with lighter fuel and set it on fire. Other like-minded bands included The Who and the Sex Pistols.

ABOVE: *Frank Zappa (1940–1993) started writing music at high school, inspired by the rhythmic experimentation of the avant-garde composer Edgar Varèse.*

ABOVE: *Vanessa Mae (born 1976) became one of the youngest musicians to play with the London Philharmonic and took the music world by storm with her album* The Violin Player.

Another band of the 1960s and '70s, Frank Zappa's Mothers of Invention, was used as a vehicle for band-audience involvement. Music was only a part of the performance, which also included satire and comedy. Anything could happen, from a bag of vegetables being opened and examined to "dead air", when the band stopped and completely ignored the audience. On one occasion, when the audience had become unsettled and angry, Zappa approached the microphone saying, "It brings out the hostilities in you, doesn't it?" Zappa went on to become a film producer and classical composer, and died in 1993.

There was a respite from "heavy metal" when in 1974 a breath of fresh air entered the pop charts with Abba. This Swedish quartet, who depended more on television and radio than live concerts to build an image, achieved their breakthrough by winning that year's Eurovision Song Contest with *Waterloo*, a song that became a top-ten hit in many countries and many languages.

Famous String Players

*To play great music you must keep
your eyes on a distant star.*

YEHUDI MENUHIN (1916–99)

The idea of a stringed instrument being a virtuoso instrument emerged during the Baroque period, when composers such as Arcangelo Corelli, who was a violinist, began to exploit the strings' expressiveness in *concerti grossi* and solo sonatas. Eighteenth-century refinements in stringed instrument design allowed for increasing technical brilliance by a number of great Italian virtuosi, culminating in the talents of the violinist Niccolò Paganini (1782–1840), who confirmed the star status of the soloist. He was also an expert on the mandolin, guitar and viola.

Violin

The great violinists of the Romantic period included Rudolphe Kreutzer (1766–1831), for whom Beethoven wrote his *Kreutzer Sonata*, and Joseph Joachim (1831–1907), to whom Brahms's Violin Concerto was dedicated. Fritz Kreisler (1875–1962) showed an early talent for the violin and by the time he was 15 had

ABOVE: Yehudi Menuhin was one of the most respected musicians who has ever lived. His violin-playing inspired young players.

ABOVE: David Oistrakh coupled the technical brilliance of Heifetz with the warmth of Menuhin. He can truly be said to be one of the greatest violinists of all time.

achieved worldwide success. His playing epitomized Viennese lilt and warmth, while his almost constant vibrato made him one of the founders of the modern school of violin-playing.

As well as being the foremost composer of his generation, Paul Hindemith (1895–1963) was also an outstanding viola player, playing in the Rebner and Amar Quartets, and the Opera Orchestra in Germany from 1915–23. Also an accomplished violinist, it was said he could play every instrument in the orchestra.

Yehudi Menuhin (1916–99) began his career as a child prodigy, and was at home in all types of music, achieving a unique tone and mastery of rhythm. He will always be remembered for his playing of the Elgar Violin Concerto under the direction of the composer, and as a humanitarian for the schools he founded for musically gifted children in England and Switzerland.

David Oistrakh (1908–74) achieved national recognition in the former Soviet Union after performing Glazunov's Violin Concerto in 1927. The Soviet authorities prevented him from performing outside the USSR until the early 1950s, but from then on he took the international stage by storm. He remained a Soviet citizen all his life and was committed to contemporary Russian composers such as Prokofiev and Shostakovich.

The Israeli violinist Itzhak Perlman (born 1945), although a victim of poliomyelitis at the age of four, was giving public recitals when he was ten years old. In his subsequent career, Perlman's charismatic stage presence, combined with his instinctive directness of musical expression, brilliant technique and a concern for refinement of detail, has brought him international recognition.

ABOVE: Mstislav Rostropovich was a close friend of Benjamin Britten, who wrote several cello works for him.

ABOVE: *The charismatic Jacqueline du Pré made her debut at the age of 16.*

Cello

As the cello took a more prominent role in chamber music during the 18th century, composers such as Liugi Boccherini (1743–1805) began to recognize its potential as a solo instrument. An early British virtuoso, Robert Lindley, began playing when he was five years old. His technique was said to be so brilliant that he was able to play first violin parts on his cello. In 1794, aged 18, Lindley played before the Prince Regent and, by 1826, had become lead cello with the Italian Opera in London.

Pablo Casals (1876–1973) probably did more for the cello than any other player. Although he is mainly remembered for his masterly playing of the Bach solo cello suites, Casals was also a conductor and a member of a chamber trio, and founded an annual festival of chamber music in France. Another influential cellist of the 20th century is Mstislav Rostropovich (born 1927), who has been immensely successful in playing the works of composers such as Shostakovich, Prokofiev and Britten.

The talent of Jacqueline du Pré (1945–87) was recognized at a very early age. She launched her professional career in 1961 with a concert at London's Wigmore Hall, at which she played a cello of 1672 by Antonio Stradivari. One of the great musical icons of the 20th century, she was admired by her audiences for the love she radiated in her playing, which was noted for its instinctive feeling for style as well as its technical proficiency. In 1973 her career was suddenly interrupted by the onset of multiple sclerosis, but she continued to teach.

Harp

Nicholas Bochsa (1789–1856), though a skilful player of almost every instrument, was best known for his expertise on the harp, an instrument on which he was constantly discovering new musical effects. Harpist to Louis XVIII, in 1817 he had to leave his native France hurriedly, due to his part-time business in forged documents. One of Bochsa's favourite pieces was his *Fantasia for Harp and Violin* which he often played with

ABOVE: *Since making her London debut in 1963, Marisa Robles has become a professor at the Royal College of Music.*

ABOVE: *John Williams is a very versatile guitarist, playing classical, jazz and pop music — he founded the pop group, Sky.*

Nicholas Mori, who was said to have handled his violin as tenderly as a mother her child, but as playfully as the child its toy.

The Spanish harpist Marisa Robles (born 1937) is one of the foremost players of the 20th century, noted for the quicksilver quality of her playing.

Lute and guitar

The eminent Spanish guitarist Andrés Segovia (1893–1987) was largely self-taught, but championed the guitar as a concert instrument, commissioning many new works. One of his pupils was Julian Bream (born 1933), who also took up the lute and quickly became a leading performer on it. In 1971, Bream began giving encouragement to guitar and lute makers by inaugurating the Semley Festival in Wiltshire to promote rare chamber music.

John Williams (born 1942) also studied guitar with Segovia. As a composer, he is particularly active in crossover projects, using tapes and electronics in his music and drawing on non-Western influences.

Famous Woodwind and Brass Players

*It takes perhaps a thousand poor musicians
to produce one virtuoso.*

RALPH VAUGHAN WILLIAMS (1872–1958)

As with other orchestral instruments, the expansion of the solo repertoire for woodwind and brass went hand in hand with technological advances that enabled the instruments to be played with far greater range and expressiveness.

Flute

Although Vivaldi and Mozart wrote for the solo flute, it was neglected during the 19th century, but found favour with French impressionists such as Debussy, and many modern composers have since written for it. The virtuoso James Galway (born 1939) is widely known as a popular soloist, but also spent many years as an orchestral player, including a period as principal flautist with the Berlin Philharmonic under Herbert von Karajan. A strong advocate of contemporary music, Galway's bright tone and twinkling

vibrato has brought him thousands of fans all around the world.

Jean-Pierre Rampal (born 1922) was an all-round musician of astonishing versatility. His repertoire ranged from Baroque to contemporary, while his playing was noted for its pure tone, subtle dynamics and exquisite phrasing.

Oboe

The sweet tone and expressive playing of Leon Goossens (1897–1988) set new standards for the instrument. Principal oboe with Henry Wood by the time he was 16, Goossens's phrasing, superlative finger technique and breath control were to influence many composers to write concertos for the oboe.

Another leading 20th-century oboist is the legendary Heinz Holliger (born 1939), who is an eminent exponent of sounding chords, double trills and

ABOVE: Leon Goossens was one of the finest oboe players of the 20th century. A member of a very musical family, he was brother to the conductor Eugene and the harpists Sidonie and Marie.

glissandos. He is not shy of experimentation; his work with sounds produced by a microphone placed within the bore of his instrument encouraged composers such as Hans Werner Henze to write for the oboe.

Clarinet

One of the 20th century's finest clarinettists was Benny Goodman (1909–86), a musician who was equally at home in classical music and jazz. He formed a 12-piece jazz band in 1934, but did not forsake his classical roots, for he later recorded the Mozart Clarinet Quintet with the Budapest Quartet, as well as commissioning works from Aaron Copland and Paul Hindemith.

ABOVE: One of Ireland's most popular musicians, James Galway has entertained millions with his flute-playing, performing both classical music and popular songs.

ABOVE: Barry Tuckwell studied horn technique with the virtuoso Dennis Brain (1921–57) on his arrival in England in 1950. He was Professor of Horn at the Royal Academy of Music (1963–74), launching his solo career in 1968.

Horn

Barry Tuckwell (born 1931) began his musical career in Melbourne, Australia, at the age of 15 and played with the Sydney Symphony Orchestra. He was principal horn with the London Symphony Orchestra from 1955 to 1968, in which year he founded the Tuckwell Wind Quintet. The leading horn player of his generation, Tuckwell is famed for his outstanding ability to make light of extreme technical and musical difficulties, achieving his marvellous tone by playing a large-bore Holton double horn, rather than the lighter-toned instrument preferred by many of his contemporaries.

Trumpet

One of the finest trumpet players was Louis Armstrong (1901–71), a man who almost single-handedly transformed jazz from a collective art to one of solo expression, exemplified in a series of 1920s recordings known as the "Hot Fives" and "Hot Sevens". His clear ringing trumpet sound influenced many modern trumpet players, both jazz and classical.

The innovative player Maurice André (born 1933) has brought the trumpet to a whole new audience. One of his main contributions to trumpet-playing has been his pioneering of the small, four-valved piccolo trumpet. He has transcribed for it many Baroque compositions originally written for other wind instruments.

Another champion of modern trumpet music is Håkan Hardenberger (born 1961). He has had various works written specially for him, including Harrison Birtwistle's trumpet concerto *Endless Parade*. A master of musical effects, Hardenberger's playing combines technical brilliance with a great beauty of sound.

Wynton Marsalis (born 1961) comes from New Orleans, and is chiefly known as one of the most famous jazz trumpeters of his generation. However, such is his catholic taste that he is as much at home with Haydn's trumpet concertos as he is with the

ABOVE: Håkan Hardenberger is one of the world's top trumpet players, famous for his flawless technical ability and the beautiful quality of his tone.

ABOVE: The great jazz trumpeter Louis Armstrong in a scene from High Society.

Lincoln Center Jazz Orchestra. He is also a composer, and in 1997 won a Pulitzer Prize for his operatic piece *Blood on the Fields*.

Trombone

Many technical developments of the 20th century have been due to the influence of jazz musicians. One of the foremost jazz trombonists of the second half of the century is the German virtuoso Albert Mangelsdorff (born 1928). He played with various German jazz groups before forming his own band in 1958. In 1964, influenced by his recent tour of Asia, he started introducing eastern elements into his playing. His main claim to fame, however, is that he was the first trombonist to succeed in playing three and four-note chords on his instrument, a feat that he achieved by a skilful combination of lip and vocal sounds.

Famous Keyboard and Percussion Players

*The great pianists have nothing to show
save technique and affection.*

<small>LUDWIG VAN BEETHOVEN (1770–1827)</small>

The harpsichord had a major role in the Baroque ensemble as a continuo instrument, but other keyboard instruments, from majestic church organs to the domestic spinet, have largely been used as solo or accompanying instruments, or in chamber music. The modern piano is capable of suggesting the range and richness of an entire orchestra, and has a vast solo repertoire. It is sometimes used in modern orchestral music, but is treated like a special member of the percussion section.

Keyboard

One of the most remarkable keyboard players of the 18th century was William Crotch (1775–1847). Born in Norwich, the son of a carpenter, he was a child prodigy without parallel in the history of music. By the time he was two he was able to pick out tunes on an organ, and a year later his mother took him on a series of concert tours throughout England. As well as the piano Crotch also played the violin, which he did standing on a chair so as to be seen by his audience. In 1822 he was appointed principal of the newly established Royal Academy of Music.

Frédéric Chopin (1810–49) soon established himself as a pianist, making his public debut when he was eight years old. He arrived in Paris in 1831, where he was introduced to the artistic circle of Romantics such as Liszt, Berlioz and Bellini. Brought up on the

ABOVE: *Clara Schumann, the wife of the composer Robert Schumann, was a fine performer and teacher and became one of the foremost pianists of the late 19th century.*

music of Bach, Chopin was an intellectual who forged his own forms. His unique music is unmistakable, and he is recognized as one of the greatest composers for the piano.

Born in Hungary, Franz Liszt's (1811–86) early promise was rewarded by a subscription from five noblemen, which enabled him to study piano in Vienna. There he met Beethoven, who prophesied an excellent future for him. In 1831, on hearing Paganini's first concert in Paris, Liszt resolved there and then to become the Paganini of the piano. From 1838–47 he toured Europe, where the amazing strength of his fingers, which enabled him to execute the most rapid passages with amazing force, won him his reputation as the greatest piano virtuoso of his

ABOVE: *Franz Liszt was the most popular pianist of his day. This caricature shows him being ecstatically received by his adoring female fans.*

82 *History of Music-making and the Orchestra*

day. One of the outstanding musical personalities of the 19th century, Liszt created a brand new style that carried piano-playing technique further than ever before.

Clara Schumann (1819–96) was born in Leipzig, and was taught the piano by her father, the composer Friedrich Wieck, who also taught Robert Schumann. Clara made her musical debut in 1828, but after her marriage to Robert Schumann in 1840 she largely abandoned touring until after his death. Her playing was characterized by her seriousness and restraint, and her repertoire concentrated on Schumann, Beethoven, Chopin, Bach and Mozart. As well as editing many of her husband's works, she also composed many piano pieces of her own. She was also a famous and influential teacher.

The next generation of piano virtuosi included Ignacy Paderewski (1866–1941), who also became, briefly, prime minister of Poland in 1919; Sergei Rachmaninov (1873–1943), best known for his piano compositions in the Romantic style; and Artur Schnabel (1882–1951), an outstanding interpreter of Beethoven.

The Canadian pianist Glenn Gould (1932–82) performed on the concert

ABOVE: Evelyn Glennie, now a full-time solo percussionist, has collaborated with indigenous performers in many parts of the world to further audiences' understanding and appreciation of world music.

platform for only ten years, but was renowned for his charismatic recordings of the keyboard music of Bach. Alfred Brendel (born 1931) is known for his interpretations of Mozart, Beethoven, Schubert and Liszt. Vladimir Ashkenazy (born 1937), who was joint winner of the 1962 Tchaikovsky Piano Competition, was born in the former Soviet Union but left in 1963 and now lives in Iceland. A passionate pianist, he is equally known as a conductor.

Percussion

In Western music the percussionist has acquired virtuoso status in the 20th century, as composers have begun to use percussion more prominently and many new instruments from around the world have been added to the percussion section. The British player James Blades (1901–98) was a world-renowned orchestral player and an authority on percussion, who lectured and broadcast for many years. He influenced Evelyn Glennie (born 1965), who, although she partially lost her hearing at the age of eight,

was introduced to percussion when she was 12. Glennie made her solo debut at the Wigmore Hall in 1986. In 1989 she was the first solo percussionist to perform at the Proms. She has since toured with major orchestras and has had many pieces composed especially for her.

ABOVE: Although an infrequent piano performer, Mitsuko Uchida's inspired repertoire includes Mozart, Schoenberg, Birtwistle and Debussy.

ABOVE: Russian-born Vladimir Ashkenazy shared first prize in the Tchaikovsky Piano Competition of 1962 with the British pianist John Ogdon (1937–89).

Court Composers

*Music must be supported by the king and the princes,
for the maintenance of the arts is their duty.*

MARTIN LUTHER (1483–1546)

Before the 18th century, musicians and composers worked for princes and kings. Such was the prestige of top organists that Paul Hofhaimer (1459–1537), imperial organist to the Holy Roman Emperor Maximilian I, travelled with his royal master in his own special chariot. Maximilian's contemporary in England, Henry VIII, was also greatly interested in music and maintained a private band of 40 instrumentalists and singers.

Secular music was composed for private – not public – performance. Before 1750, professional musicians copied their music by hand, and even towards the end of the century Mozart often prevented his music from being widely circulated, as he feared it would be copied. As there was no protection of copyright or performing rights, patronage was the only way composers had of securing an income.

ABOVE: An autographed manuscript of Mozart's Symphony No. 8, written in brown ink on thick cream paper.

Lully

One of the most musically influential courts in Europe was that of Louis XIV (1643–1715). Jean-Baptiste Lully (1632–87) was born in Florence but had moved to France when he was 14, working first as a servant, then as a violinist. He entered royal service in 1652 and attained the post of Royal Composer in 1662. He developed the French operatic style, favouring short, simple songs rather than the florid arias so popular in Italy, and made a large fortune by obtaining a monopoly over French opera production.

Haydn

In 1761, Joseph Haydn (1732–1809) entered the employment of the Hungarian Count Esterházy, with whom he spent the next 30 years. Although Esterházy's musical establishment was disbanded in 1790, Haydn retained his salary when he returned to Vienna. His long service with the family gave him great scope for composition, and he earned a reputation across Europe for his symphonies and string quartets, two forms for which he established the classical style. He then spent two years in London, where he wrote the last 12 of his 104 symphonies.

ABOVE: Lully went to Paris as a servant but his musical talents soon came to the attention of Louis XIV. He transformed music from a mere court pastime into a national art.

On his return to Vienna, he gave some lessons to a young German named Beethoven. Haydn was a prolific composer, and a humble and genial man who was well loved by the musicians he directed.

Bach

Orphaned at the age of ten, Johann Sebastian Bach (1685–1750) was brought up by his older brother, who taught him to play the organ, but his musical debut was as a choirboy at Lüneburg when he was 15. In 1703 he was appointed organist at Armstadt, but displeased his employers when he immersed himself in innovative organ music while neglecting his routine duties as choirmaster.

In 1708 he was appointed Kapellmeister to the Duke of Cöthen.

ABOVE: *Signed copy of the first movement of Bach's Sonata in G Minor for solo violin.*

ABOVE: *The one certain way for musicians to make a living in the 18th century was by having a royal patron: Mozart's father introduced his son to various European courts.*

As the Duke was a Calvinist, he required little music in his religious services, and Bach was able to concentrate on secular compositions and recitals. However, as a devout Lutheran, he wished to return to church music and in 1723 he accepted a more lowly post as cantor at the

Thomasschule in Leipzig, where he remained for the rest of his life.

Bach, who once said that it was his purpose to dispel sadness and bring joy, could turn his skills to almost any kind of music, although, in his own day, he received greater recognition as an organist than as a composer. His major standing as a composer was achieved only with the 19th-century revival of interest in his works.

Handel

George Frideric Handel (1685–1759) was born in Germany, but became a naturalized English citizen and one of England's greatest composers. Although he showed an early taste for music, Handel entered the University of Halle as a law student. However, after a short period as organist at the cathedral, he gave up his studies and went to Hamburg. It was here, in 1705, that his first operas *Almira* and *Nero* were produced. Five years later he became Kapellmeister to the Elector of Hanover. His period in Hanover was short, for by 1712 he was in London and in good favour with

Queen Anne, who gave him a life pension. In 1714 Anne died and his former master, the Elector, became King George I. Without doubt, Handel's greatest work is the *Messiah*, which he wrote in three weeks. It was first produced in Dublin in 1742, with a choir of about 30.

ABOVE: *In 17th-century England the main patron of music was the king. William III was no exception and encouraged his composers.*

ABOVE: *One of the most influential English composers of the first half of the 18th century was George Frideric Handel.*

Modern Composers

My music is best understood by children and animals.

IGOR STRAVINSKY (1882–1971)

While the Romantic composers of the 19th century believed that the prime function of music was to express emotion, those of the 20th century were more likely to see it as a search for new sounds and, consequently, new instruments on which to produce them.

United States

Aaron Copland (1900–90) used American jazz and folk idioms, as well as special effects, such as the orchestral reproduction of a gunfight in *Billy the Kid*. Other works by Copland that use folk music include *Rodeo* and *Appalachian Spring*. Another 20th-century American composer is Leroy Anderson (1908–75), whose light classical music gained wide popular appeal. His music was a blend of infectious melodies, popular dance rhythms and novel effects, such as the *pizzicato* strings in *Plink, Plank, Plonk*, the percussion in *The Syncopated Clock*, and unconventional "instruments" such as a typewriter and sandpaper.

John Cage (1912–92) was as much an inventor as a composer. A pupil of Schoenberg, Cage relegated harmony and pitch to a secondary role and gave priority to rhythm and noise. He drew up large charts on which he plotted rhythmic structures to compose works such as his *Concerto for Prepared Piano*. In *Music of Changes* the progressions all depend on the tossing of a coin.

Russia

Dimitri Shostakovich (1906–75) graduated from Petrograd Conservatory in 1925. His First

ABOVE: Although Shostakovich ran foul of the Russian state in 1948, he was politically rehabilitated in 1956 and his work greatly influenced young Russian composers.

Symphony, composed while he was still a student, won international acclaim in 1926, but his Fourth was withdrawn in 1936 during rehearsal when the Stalinist authorities objected to his opera, *Lady Macbeth of the Mtsensk District*. Although he attempted to ingratiate himself with his Fifth Symphony, his relationship with the government remained uneasy, and in 1948 he was denounced for "formalism" and fired from his teaching post at the Leningrad Conservatory. He undertook to bring his work nearer to "folk art", and finally regained his job in 1960.

Shostakovich wrote 15 symphonies and several operas and ballets, as well as chamber, choral and piano music, and his work had a great influence on younger Russian composers.

ABOVE: Aaron Copland's use of the jazz and folk idioms of his native land in his music cannot fail to stir up images of the America of the late 19th and early 20th centuries.

ABOVE: In his youth Messiaen used to write down birdsong, which he included in his music. Taken prisoner by the Germans in World War II, his Quartet for the End of Time *was written in a concentration camp.*

France

Paul Dukas (1865–1935) achieved worldwide success for his orchestral work of 1897, *L'Apprenti sorcier* and, although he wrote some successful music for the stage, it is virtually by this work alone that Dukas is remembered. His severe self-criticism reached such a pitch that he refused to publish any new composition, eventually going as far as to burn everything not yet published. His surviving work includes the opera *Ariane et Barbe-bleue* (1907), *La Péri*, a ballet published in 1912, and a sonata for the piano in E minor.

One of Dukas's pupils at the Paris Conservatoire was Olivier Messiaen (1908–92). Messiaen, an organist as well as a composer, was greatly influenced by Indian and eastern music, and his orchestral compositions display great rhythmic complexity.

Electronic music

The *ondes Martenot* ("Martenot waves"), one of the earliest successful electronic instruments, was patented by the French cellist and radio engineer, Maurice Martenot (1896–1980) in 1928. Using oscillating valves as the sound source, the pitch was controlled by moving one hand along a wire, while the other hand operated a number of "expression" keys. Later a keyboard was added for pitch orientation. The *ondes Martenot* was first used in an orchestra for a performance of Messiaen's *Turangalíla* Symphony in 1947. Arthur Honegger (1892–1955) and Pierre Boulez also wrote music for the instrument.

In 1949 an electronic music studio was set up in Paris to further the work of Pierre Schaeffer (born 1910), a radio technician and the founder of *musique concrète*, a term he coined to describe a form in which pre-existing real sounds were manipulated in various ways and combined into a kind of sound collage. Other composers to use the studio included Stockhausen, Messiaen and Boulez.

Jean-Michel Jarre (born 1948) became a pupil of Schaeffer in 1968. He combines electronic music with melodic orchestration to produce commercially successful recordings such as *Oxygène* (1977) and *Equinoxe* (1978). He has mounted a series of live performances on a huge scale, culminating in a Bastille Day celebration in Paris in 1990 that was attended by 2.5 million people.

ABOVE: Boulez is a great exponent of avant-garde music. He once said that his music, like fashion, was self-destructive so that it could be replaced by a new collection.

ABOVE: Jean-Michel Jarre studied counterpoint, fugue and harmony at the Paris Conservatoire and released his first electro-acoustic recording, La Cage, *in 1969.*

Role of the Conductor

*It is better to conduct with the ear than with the arm.
The rest follows automatically.*

GEORG SOLTI (1912–97)

Although the role of the virtuoso conductor was a 19th-century phenomenon, there had always been one member of an ensemble whose duty it was to direct the others and so ensure a uniformity of performance. In ancient Greece the "giver of time beat with his stave up and down", while in Rome, time was indicated by the leader stamping his feet. In 17th-century France it was the custom to beat time loudly on the floor with a large staff – which on one occasion had fatal consequences. In 1687, while conducting a *Te Deum* to celebrate the king's recovery from sickness, Jean-Baptiste Lully brought his long staff down on his foot instead of the floor and died of the subsequent gangrene poisoning. The staff survives today both as the conductor's baton and in the mace carried by drum majors

leading military bands. During the 15th and 16th centuries some choral conductors kept time by waving a rolled-up sheet of music.

Until the 18th century it was usual for the conductor to be the composer. He generally directed the band from his seat at the harpsichord, although in France it bcame fashionable for the first violin to direct. This was also the case with the Mannheim orchestra, an ensemble that was greatly influenced by French practice.

Although Beethoven is known to have conducted his own works, his methods were far from conventional. When conducting from the piano, he bent lower to indicate that he wanted the music played softly. When the music came to a *crescendo*, he raised

LEFT: The modern conductor's baton – used for beating time and indicating expression – is a thin tapering stick about 50cm/20in long. Although first seen in the late 18th century, batons did not come into general use until the 1820s.

himself by degrees and, upon the commencement of the *forte*, would spring bolt upright. To increase the *forte* even more, he would often join in with a shout to the orchestra.

From the late 18th century music became more complex, with each instrumental section having more solo music to play. Although Carl Maria von Weber (1786–1826) conducted an orchestra with a baton in 1817, the first man to conduct an orchestra in the modern sense – moving his hands and arms without making a sound himself – was the German violinist Louis Spohr (1784–1859), leader of the orchestra of the Theater an der Wien, who conducted the Philharmonic Society of London in 1820.

In Vienna, the directors of the new waltz orchestras of the early 19th century, such as Johann Strauss the elder (1804–49) and his rival Joseph Lanner (1801–43), led while playing the violin, beating time with the bow. This custom is sometimes resurrected by the conductors at the annual New Year's concert in Vienna.

Nineteenth-century conductors took on more and more responsibility for the performance. They established the speed and helped players come in at the right time. They decided how the

ABOVE: After making his conducting debut in 1943 with the New York Philharmonic, Leonard Bernstein (1918–90) conducted many famous orchestras, including La Scala, the Vienna Philharmonic, the Israel Philharmonic and the London Symphony Orchestra.

ABOVE: *The custom in the 18th century was for the leader of a musical band to conduct from the keyboard. Here Bach is seen conducting an ensemble from the clavichord.*

music should be played and phrased. They were also more necessary because orchestras were growing larger. Although he never achieved his dream, Berlioz's ideal orchestra size was 465. Conducting soon came to be regarded as an important profession in its own right and, as the 19th century progessed, a conductor cult grew. It became usual for composers to conduct not just their own works but also those of others.

In opera it was customary for the conductor to concentrate on the singers rather than the band, and to this end he was placed immediately in front of – and facing – the stage, with the orchestra behind him, following his beat as best they could. It was not until 1897, when Gustav Mahler (1860–1911) became conductor of the Vienna State Opera, that the podium was moved to the back of the orchestra pit.

ABOVE: *Some conductors use very subtle gestures, in which even minor movements of the forearm can cause the players to respond instantly.*

Conducting with style

ABOVE AND LEFT: *Many conductors are showmen, relishing their position in the limelight, and their antics sometimes seem intended more to impress the audience than direct the orchestra. These photographs show just a few of the hundreds of gestures and instructions made by a conductor within the context of a performance.*

Famous Conductors

You must have the score in your head,
not your head in the score.

HANS VON BÜLOW (1830–94)

In his *Notes for Conductors*, Richard Strauss advises a conductor to put his left thumb in the armpit of his waistcoat and lead the orchestra with the right. It is, so Strauss advises, the audience and not the conductor who should sweat. One man who followed Strauss's advice to the extreme was Arthur Nikisch (1855–1922), who certainly allowed the baton to do all the work. He never distracted the orchestra or the audience with elaborate gestures, and conducted almost solely from the wrist down. Indeed, any minor movement of his forearm would so alarm the players that they would instantly respond with a massive *fortissimo*. Amongst Nikisch's disciples were Fritz Reiner (1888–1963) and Adrian Boult (1889–1983).

ABOVE: Arthur Nikisch, seen here with the Berlin Philharmonic Orchestra, was known for conducting the orchestra in a subtle manner, moving his arms only slightly.

ABOVE: The English conductor Sir Thomas Beecham founded the London Philharmonic Orchestra in 1932. He was especially known for his interpretations of Delius's music.

Thomas Beecham (1879–1961) never had a technique! His baton did whatever the state of the performance prompted. He disdained to be seen beating anything less complex than phrases, but at the same time he discreetly beat time by opening and closing the fingers of his left hand. He was renowned for his dry wit: during one rehearsal he remarked that the second trumpet was too loud. The embarrassed leader had to explain that the second trumpet player had telephoned to say that he would be a little late. Unperturbed, Sir Thomas replied: "Well, when he comes, tell him he is too loud."

The qualities of a conductor as a personality are always important. That some have more pleasant personalities than others is a fact of life, and some, however musical they are, leave a lot to be desired. Arturo Toscanini (1867–1957) was notoriously temperamental. At one rehearsal of Verdi's opera *Falstaff*, he threw the score at four different women soloists, alleging that they had not learnt their parts. At another rehearsal he threw his gold watch to the floor and stamped on it. His disregard for other people's feelings was legendary and on one occasion, when a red carpet was laid from the stage entrance to the podium as a mark of respect for him, Toscanini refused to enter until it was taken up, growling "*Non sono un cardinale.*"

Most great conductors have, however, been more amenable and well respected by the musicians with whom they work. The British conductor John Barbirolli (1899–1970), who succeeded Toscanini as conductor of the New York Philharmonic in 1937, was vivacious and charming. He returned to Britain in 1943 to become permanent conductor of the Hallé Orchestra in Manchester. Another well-loved figure was Malcolm Sargent (1895–1967). Particularly noted for his choral work, from 1928 he was the conductor of the Royal Choral Society. Sargent was noted not only for his

ABOVE: *The son of an émigré Italian violinist, Barbirolli became one of Britain's foremost conductors. For his services to music, he was knighted in 1949.*

immediate grasp of a complicated score and for his extraordinarily effective "stick technique", but also as a "showman". In 1950 he succeeded Adrian Boult as conductor of the BBC Symphony Orchestra. Sargent, the natural successor to Henry Wood as principal conductor of the Promenade Concerts, was equally at home with classical and modern music, and many young and inexperienced players gained much confidence by his support.

Herbert von Karajan (1908–89) was a far less accessible man and personified the image of the conductor as star. Between the 1950s and '70s he was the dominant figure in European music. While presiding over the Berlin Philharmonic for 35 years, his influence also spread over the Vienna State Opera, the Salzburg Festival, the Vienna Symphony Orchestra, the Philharmonia Orchestra in London and La Scala in Milan. Karajan was an

imperious, stubborn and demanding conductor who worked only on his own terms. Throughout his career he continued to question and rework his own musical interpretations, but his intimate knowledge of the players of the Berlin Philharmonic and his belief in their potential enabled him to turn it into one of the world's finest orchestras.

His predecessor in Berlin had been Wilhelm Furtwängler (1886–1954), whose conducting was characterized by a curious wavering beat that often confused those who were not used to him. He was particularly associated with the music of Wagner, at a time when it came to stand for the ideals of the Nazi regime in Germany. Otto Klemperer (1885–1973), on the other hand, was denounced by the Nazis and left Germany to become an American citizen. Another leading conductor of his time, his performances were notable for their attention to detail, especially in the woodwind section.

An outstanding figure of the new generation is Simon Rattle (born 1955). At the age of 16 he took lessons in conducting from Pierre Boulez, and in 1974 won first prize in the Bournemouth International Conducting Competition. In the same

ABOVE: *In 1980 the British conductor Sir Simon Rattle was appointed principal conductor of the City of Birmingham Orchestra, which he transformed into a world-class ensemble. He has a deep solidarity with his orchestras.*

year he was appointed assistant conductor of the Bournemouth Symphony Orchestra. In 1980 he became principal conductor of the City of Birmingham Symphony Orchestra, which he transformed into a world-class ensemble. In 1999 it was announced that he would replace Claudio Abbado as chief conductor of the Berlin Philharmonic in 2002.

ABOVE: *Herbert von Karajan was one of the most respected conductors of the 20th century. He was principal conductor of the Berlin Philharmonic for 35 years.*

ABOVE: *Sir Georg Solti studied under notables such as Bartók and Kodály, and was Musical Director of the Chicago Symphony Orchestra until his death in 1997.*

Famous Concert Halls and Orchestras

...For we must have music, We must have music
To drive our fears away.

NOEL COWARD (1899–1973)

Until the 18th century, public concerts as they are known today did not exist. One of the first rooms to be devoted to formal concerts was that opened in London by Thomas Hickford in 1711. From then on other custom-built concert halls and opera houses gradually started to appear all over Europe.

German patrons of music built concert halls on a grand scale. At Schwetzingen, the Elector of Palatine built a new opera house capable of holding an audience of 5000, while Duke Karl Theodor of Württemberg bankrupted his entire principality to provide sensational opera productions at Mannheim.

The Berlin Opera House was built by Frederick the Great of Prussia (1740–86). A notable flautist and patron of music, Frederick was deeply immersed in French culture and maintained a French-speaking court. Opened in 1773, the Opera House, which employed singers from Italy and dancers from France, was equipped with parking space for 1000 carriages. The staircases were so wide that sedan

ABOVE: *The Amsterdam Concertgebouw Orchestra was founded in 1888. Its hall is renowned for its magnificent acoustics.*

chairs could be carried up to the fourth tier of the boxes, and three enormous chandeliers illuminated the whole auditorium.

In London, purpose-built concert halls included Carlisle House, Soho Square (1764); the Pantheon, Oxford Street (1772); and the Hanover Square Rooms (1775). Halls were also opened in some major provincial centres, such as Bath, which, thanks to its spa, was the centre of English fashionable society in the 18th century.

Throughout the 19th century the orchestras involved in London concerts contained so many of the same players that it would be difficult to describe each orchestra as different. Players had little or no financial security and were engaged for each concert, not for the entire season. The custom of sending a deputy to the rehearsals, or even the concert, had become established, meaning that the composition of the orchestra was constantly changing.

One of the first conductors to recruit musicians for an entire season was Charles Hallé (1819–95). Hallé had made his reputation in Paris, but was driven to England by the revolution of 1848 and eventually settled in Manchester, which had an influential German community. He threw himself heartily into the town's musical life and in 1857 founded what was to become the celebrated Hallé

ABOVE: *This painting by Ludwig Edward Lutke shows the German State Opera House in Berlin, c.1845.*

ABOVE: *The New York Metropolitan Opera House was founded in 1883 but was rebuilt after a fire destroyed the original building.*

Orchestra. Its members were always present at both rehearsal and concert, making the orchestra the most disciplined and efficient band in the country. They never sounded, as did so many other orchestras, like a bunch of instrumentalists thrown together for a single event.

During the 20th century several great orchestras have been founded in London, including the London Philharmonic, which was founded in

ABOVE: *Musical events held at the Royal Albert Hall in London range from brass band contests to rock concerts.*

1932 by Thomas Beecham, and the BBC Symphony Orchestra, which was founded in 1930 and was the first orchestra to offer an annual salary and paid holidays.

As the 20th century progressed, orchestras faced the problem of financial support. The Boston Symphony Orchestra was founded in 1881 by the financier Henry Lee Higginson. He gave his conductors absolute artistic freedom and kept the orchestra at the highest level of achievement. Its financial future was assured by Higginson's creation of a body of 300 guarantors. Further south, the New York Philharmonic was founded in 1842. For the first 66 years of its existence it was run by an internal committee of musicians.

However, in 1908, due to financial difficulties, the orchestra was taken over by a syndicate.

The Berlin Philharmonic Orchestra, which acquired its high international reputation under the directorship of Herbert von Karajan, is funded by the city of Berlin, and has its home in an acoustically brilliant concert hall affectionately known as the "circus tent". Although it has a capacity of 2000, the seats virtually surround the orchestra, giving the hall a feeling of intimacy.

The audience at the Royal Albert Hall in London is seated in a vast ellipse, but had to suffer poor acoustics until they were remedied in the 1960s. The brick and glass building was built from 1867–71, and is universally known as the venue for the annual Henry Wood Promenade Concerts, which have been performed there since World War II when their former home, the Queen's Hall, was destroyed.

The Sydney Opera House on Bennelong Point is one of the city's most notable features. Designed by

ABOVE: *Kurt Masur conducting the New York Philharmonic Orchestra in 1999. Masur made his United States debut in 1974.*

Jørn Utsen, the building was largely financed by the Australian lottery and was opened in 1973. Its programme offers 16 different operas a year and there is a performance almost every night during the winter.

The world's largest opera house is the Metropolitan Opera House at the Lincoln Center in New York, completed in 1966 with an audience capacity of 4065.

ABOVE: *Looking like something that has just emerged from the sea, the main features of the Sydney Opera House in Australia are its nine flying roofs, the highest point of which is 67m/220ft above sea level.*

Encyclopedia
of
Musical
Instruments

The modern symphony orchestra consists of around 20 different
musical instruments. These can be categorized into four main groups:
strings, wind, percussion and keyboards.

Introduction

*The noise or sound which musicians make while they are tuning their instruments is
nothing pleasant to hear, but yet is a cause why the music is sweeter afterwards.*

FRANCIS BACON (1561–1626)

Musical instruments can be categorized in various ways. The most straightforward system (used in this book) is to divide them into four main groups: strings, wind, percussion and keyboards (with the voice as a fifth category, although perhaps not strictly an "instrument"). The categories are not necessarily mutually exclusive. Some instruments in the keyboard category, for example, are related to those in other groups: the piano could also find a home in the string section, while the organ, which is operated by a system of pipes, could easily fit into the wind section. To these main groups could be added electronic instruments. However, as most of these feature keyboards, they can be found in this book with the other keyboard instruments.

Musicologists classify instruments according to the way in which the sound is produced. "Idiophones" are

ABOVE: This segment of a string section shows the first and second violins in the foreground.

those in which the body of the instrument vibrates when struck to produce the sound. They include bells, rattles, cymbals and xylophones. The group called "membranophones"

consists entirely of drums, in which the skin is struck and vibrates. "Chordophones" include all stringed instruments, such as the violin, guitar and piano, and "aerophones" are wind instruments, such as the trumpet, clarinet and organ, in which a column of air vibrates. In "electrophones", such as the electric organ or synthesizer, the sound is produced electronically.

Instruments can also be listed in two groups depending on whether the musician forms a unity with his instrument, or a duality. The former group includes wind instruments that are played by combining a vibrating column of air – produced by the player's breath – with the tube of the instrument. The second group represents a slightly more advanced stage of musical development and includes stringed instruments, in which the player produces the

ABOVE: The woodwind section consists of flutes, oboes, clarinets and bassoons.

vibrations in the soundbox by exciting the strings with a bow or his fingers.

There are many musical instruments that are widely used but are not part of the standard orchestra. Some are folk instruments, such as the concertina and the bagpipes, or traditional instruments from Africa and East Asia. Others are early instruments that fell into disuse but in recent years have been revived to play the early music that was written for them.

The 17th and 18th centuries saw many improvements in musical instruments, especially in extremes of pitch, achieved by innovations in design and engineering, such as the addition of extra holes and keys. As technical advances were made, players were able to refine their technique and composers were prompted to write more challenging and expressive music. This often led, in turn, to the need for further refinements in the design of the instruments.

The industrial revolution was a springboard for sophisticated improvements in instrumental mechanics. The development of

ABOVE: Percussion sections may include a wide variety of instruments. This set-up shows xylophones, tubular bells, gong, and a collection of drums and cymbals.

the cast-iron frame turned the piano into a high-tension, high-performance instrument. Work by people such as Jakob Grundmann and Carl August Grenser, who increased the number of keys and provided alternative fingering on the oboe; Heinrich Stölzel and Adolphe Sax, who did so much work on developing valved instruments; and

ABOVE: An orchestral brass section.

the German goldsmith Theobald Boehm, who improved the flute, resulted in much greater versatility in the use of wind instruments. Yet the creations of the great 17th-century violin makers have never been equalled, and many attempts to introduce new materials have resulted in the makers returning to traditional methods that have proved unbeatable.

ABOVE: The keyboard instrument most often seen on the concert platform is the piano.

❖ Strings ❖

How Stringed Instruments Work

What can be more strange, than that the rubbing of a little hair and
cat-gut together should make such a mighty alteration in a man.

JEREMY COLLIER (1650–1726)

Although the orchestral term "strings" is used only for the violin family, there are many other stringed instruments, played with or without a bow, that come under the general term "chordophone". In every case, the mechanics are the same.

One group of stringed instruments, which includes the harp and lyre, is played with open strings – each string producing only one note. The other group, into which most other stringed instruments fall, consists of those played with "stopped" strings: each string can be held down, effectively changing its length, so that it will produce a range of notes.

Sound production

There are two distinct types of construction of stopped-string instruments, each with its own acoustic implications. The lute is a perfect example of one type, with a flat soundboard and a bowl-shaped back, with no connecting ribs or soundpost. Instruments of the second

ABOVE: Detail of two violins, showing the f-holes and parts of the bridges.

type, by far the most common, have flat soundboards and flat or moderately arched backs, joined by side ribs. In both cases the sound is produced by the vibration of the strings being transmitted into the soundbox via the bridge.

The pitch produced by a string depends not only on its length but also on its thickness, weight and tension. In most instruments it is impractical to vary only the length of the strings, as the lower strings would have to be so long as to be unwieldy, so strings of different thicknesses are used: they may then all be of the same length. The tension of the string is also important. Too slack a tension sounds

ABOVE: Unlike violins, violas and cellos, viols have frets on their fingerboards.

ABOVE: The string family (from left to right): two violins, a viola and a cello. The central motif of the stained-glass window is a lyre, a universal symbol of music.

ABOVE: A cello section performing in a modern symphony orchestra.

there was no clear demarcation between the body and the neck. Examples of such instruments are the mandora and the rebec.

The mandora evolved into the mandolin, while the rebec has survived in the form of the *lyra* of modern Greece and Crete and the Bulgarian *gadulka*. Used as a folk instrument to accompany songs and dances, the traditional *lyra* or *gadulka* has three gut strings that are played with a horsehair bow. It is held vertically while it is played, with the lower end tucked into the player's belt when standing, or held on the hip when seated.

feeble, while too thick a string is hard to get vibrating and restricts the higher harmonics. Low strings are usually wound with a fine wire on a moderate core to allow them to be held under sufficient tension without excessive mass or stiffness.

Shape of stringed instruments

Although stringed instruments come in various shapes and sizes, many have waisted bodies that allow both freedom for the bow and a more complex vibration. Stringed instruments were, however, waisted many centuries before the advent of the bow, and instruments so shaped appear in Babylonian sculptures. The shape may have been used not only for musical effect but perhaps because it had some symbolic or ritual association with the female form.

Early stringed instruments were usually carved from a solid block of wood that tapered in such a way that

RIGHT: This painting by Jean-Baptiste Mauzaisse (1784–1844) depicts the daughters of the Duke of Orleans being given a harp lesson by their tutor Mme de Genlis. The young musicians are playing pedal harps.

Violin

The true mission of the violin is to imitate the accents of the human voice, a noble mission that has earned for the violin the glory of being called the king of instruments.

CHARLES-AUGUSTE DE BÉRIOT (1802–70)

The violin is the lead voice and most numerous instrument of the modern orchestra. The average orchestra has about 35 violins, which are divided into two sections – first and second. The violin's four strings give the instrument a range of over four octaves, including all the semitones and many microtones. Its extraordinary musical versatility, coupled with its emotional appeal and agility, makes possible – depending on the skill of the player – an expression of moods ranging from the tender lyrical music of Mozart to the dramatic tones of Wagner.

Origin

Although no one knows who invented the violin, some of the earliest instruments were made by Giovan Giacoba dalla Corna and Zanetto Montichiaro, both of whom are named in Giovanni Lanfranco's *Scintille di Musica* (1533). The first "famous" violin maker, however, was Andrea Amati (1525–1611), who was born in Cremona and became the founder of the Cremonese school of violin-making.

ABOVE: The scroll and pegs of a violin.

Although the violin family (violin, viola and cello) has been the mainstay of the symphony orchestra since its rise in the 17th century, the three-stringed violin had been in existence since the early 1500s. It was certainly known in 1508, for it appears in a wall painting of that date in the Sala del Tesoro at the Palazzo di Ludovico il Moro in Ferrara. Twenty or so years later, Gaudenzio

Ferrari depicted the instrument in *The Madonna of the Orange Trees*, painted for the church of San Cristoforo in Vercelli. The same artist included violins in his fresco in the cupola of Saronno Cathedral in 1535.

These early three-stringed violins were an amalgam of two other instruments that were well known at this time – the fiddle and the rebec. The new instrument combined the

LEFT: The violin is the lead instrument in the orchestra. This one was made by Anton Kreutzinger in 20th-century Germany.

sonority and playing potential of the former with the simplicity of the latter.

Construction

Although the violin appears to be of simple construction, it is in fact made of over 80 separate parts. The soundboard is generally made of European spruce and the back and the ribs are made of maple. Maple is also used for the neck, pegbox and scroll, while the fingerboard, which runs along the neck and extends over the soundboard towards the bridge, is generally made of ebony.

Originally, all four strings were made of gut. However, from about 1700, to improve the tone, the G string was wound with silver wire. Modern instruments still have the G, D and A strings made in this fashion, while the E string is generally constructed of steel.

The mid 18th century saw some major modifications in the construction of the violin. The emergence of purpose-built concert halls and the resultant larger audiences created a demand for instruments capable of producing greater volume and brilliance of tone. To achieve this, the neck and fingerboard were

ABOVE: *This violin was made by the Italian craftsman Giuseppe Guarneri (1666–1739) in about 1695. Guarneri was the younger son of Andrea Guarneri, who had served as an apprentice to Nicola Amati and began the second great dynasty of Cremonese violin makers.*

lengthened, the bridge was made higher, the soundpost was thickened and the soundboard was made thinner.

Another modification was that the number of nails attaching the neck was reduced from four to three. The neck had to be nailed, as glue would have adversely affected the tone. Modern violins have the neck mortised into the upper block so that nails are no longer needed.

RIGHT AND BELOW: *A collection of modern violins. These instruments were made in the early 1990s by David Lipkin and Haim Algranati, London.*

Key features

TYPE: stringed

TUNING: *g, d', a', e"*

NOTABLE PLAYERS OF THE VIOLIN: Niccolò Paganini, Joseph Joachim, Eugène Ysaÿe, Jascha Heifetz, David Oistrakh, Yehudi Menuhin, Isaac Stern, Itzhak Perlman, Kyung-Wha Chung, Nigel Kennedy, Anne-Sophie Mutter.

ABOVE: *The Bavarian village of Mittenwald has been a centre of violin-making since 1684 when Matthias Klotz, who was born in the village, returned from Cremona. Johann Reiter, a craftsman of Mittenwald, is seen here working in his shop.*

ABOVE: *A depiction of a violinist on a Swedish-made carpet designed by Per Nilsson in 1781.*

The violin outside Italy

By about 1550, four strings had become standard and schools of violin-making had been established in Venice, Cremona and Brescia. The makers not only catered for Italian musicians, but also exported instruments to England, France, the Low Countries and Germany. Charles IX of France bought 12 violins from Andrea Amati of Cremona, while the English were such avid customers that they were accused of "dispeopling" Italy of violins. Even in the 16th century, large sums were being paid for fine violins; one sold by Gasparo da Salo of Brescia in 1588 fetched over four times his housemaid's annual wage.

Music for the violin

At first, the violin was used only for doubling the voice and to accompany dancing. For the former purpose, the violinist used the vocal score, while dance musicians played from memory, so no music for the violin was published until the end of the 16th century. The first music known to have been published specifically for the violin was the *Balet Comique de la Royne*, which was devised for the French court by Balthazar de Beaujoyeulx in 1582. It included two dances that were scored for ten violins in four parts. This royal patronage was a breakthrough indeed, for up to this time the violin had been looked down upon, with "virtuous people" preferring the viol, which produced

ABOVE: Known as the Emile Sauret (because it was once owned by that French violinist), this Stradivari violin was made in 1683.

greater resonance but less volume. The social status of the violin was further enhanced in 1626 when the ensemble known as the *Vingt-quatre Violons du Roi* was founded at the court of Louis XIII.

Stradivari

Without doubt, the greatest of all violin makers was Antonio Stradivari (1644–1737). Descended from an old Cremonese family, young Antonio was first apprenticed to a wood-carver. However, he soon became associated with Nicola Amati (1596–1684), the grandson of Andrea and the finest maker of the Amati family, who taught him the art of violin-making. Stradivari's earliest surviving violin is dated 1666. With the death of his master, Stradivari's fame began to spread and he soon became recognized as the finest violin maker of his day.

Stradivari's highest pinnacle was reached in 1715 when his now well-known, orange-brown coloured varnish, which dried to a light delicate elastic skin, began to appear. Although varnish cannot improve a violin's tone, it can affect it adversely. A hard varnish causes an instrument to produce a hard

ABOVE: The Japanese violinist Kyoko Takezawa playing a Stradivari violin in Munich in 1993.

sound, with little or no tone-colour. A thick oily varnish, on the other hand, inhibits the wood's vibrations and a varnish that is applied badly may well prevent the best tones from being realized. Sadly, the recipe for Stradivari's varnish is now lost.

ABOVE: Two violins made by the two greatest Cremonese violin makers. On the left is the back and front view of Stradivari's Alard *which was made in 1715 and is considered to be the finest Stradivari in existence. On the right is Guarneri's* del Gesù.

Decline of Italian violin-making

Despite the fact that the violin had become the backbone of the emergent orchestras and operas of Europe by the 18th century, this period coincided with a general decline in violin-making in Italy. By the end of the century, France had become the centre of excellence in violin-making. One of the greatest French makers was Nicolas Lupot (1788–1824) who, taking Stradivari as his model, linked French and Italian workmanship. Another French violin maker was François Tourte (1747–1835) who revolutionized and standardized the design of the bow.

ABOVE: Nigel Kennedy (born 1957) is one of England's most controversial violinists, and is shown here playing a Stradivari violin. His intense concentration, vitality and all-or-nothing approach make him one of the most likeable musicians on the stage today.

🎼 Fritz Kreisler

One of the finest violinists and composers for the violin in the 20th century, Fritz Kreisler (1875–1962) was born in Austria but became an American citizen in 1943. As well as writing numerous short pieces for the instrument, he also added cadenzas to the concertos of Beethoven and Bach. In addition, he fooled the musical world by composing many works in an archaic style that he ascribed to various 18th-century composers such as Pugnani and Francoeur. In spite of many experts — who had been misled — being angered when Kreisler admitted to the hoax in 1935, these works continue to enrich the violin repertoire.

ABOVE: This 19th-century photograph shows a Hardanger fiddle being played held against the chest. Despite its name, it is a violin and today, with the addition of a chinrest, the instrument is played in the manner of orchestral violinists.

Playing techniques

Although the violin is basically the same as it was 300 years ago, playing techniques have improved, allowing new types of music to be written. Before the invention of the chinrest — by Louis Spohr in about 1820 — the violin was played in several different ways. It was held either at the chest, at the shoulder, to the right or left of the neck, or, in the case of folk music, cradled against the left upper arm.

By the late 18th century, performance styles had changed so much that the violin needed strengthening. Heavier strings and tighter string tension were needed to produce the stronger sound required to fill the new larger concert halls.

Vibrato

One of the characteristics of modern violin-playing is vibrato. Created by a controlled rocking of the finger that is stopping the string, vibrato adds intensity to the tone. In the 18th and 19th centuries it was considered solely as ornamentation. Such is its universal acceptance, however, that whereas pre-20th-century music was marked where vibrato was required, today it is marked where it is not required. The use of vibrato seems to have become fashionable in the 1930s, due to the influence of performers such as Fritz Kreisler and Jascha Heifetz (1901–87). Some players use it all the time, and some, it is said, use it to cover up bad intonation.

Jazz violin

One of the first great jazz violinists was Eddie South (1904–62), a classically trained black musician who had already formed a popular dance band in Chicago when he toured Europe and discovered gypsy fiddling in Bucharest. He arrived back on the Chicago jazz scene in the late 1920s. South worked with the guitarist Django Reinhardt,

ABOVE: Jascha Heifetz, seen here in 1929, is remembered for his hard sound that could melt unexpectedly into the sweetest, most effortless legato. His nimble left hand and flawless bowing technique astonished all who heard him.

and his version of *Eddie's Blues* (recorded in 1937) is regarded as one of the finest of its genre; South's piteous blue slides and scoops were ably invigorated by Reinhardt's potent

ABOVE: The violin can be held in several different ways — under the chin or resting against the jaw, as shown here, or held against the chest.

guitar. Reinhardt also had a famous partnership with Stéphane Grappelli (1908–97), whose jazz violin style had been inspired by South: the two played together as principal soloists in the Quintet of the Hot Club of France from 1934–39.

Jazz is also a medium in which the electric violin is used. The electric violin has no soundbox and has a solid body, with a set of pick-ups that transmit the sound to an amplifier. It is capable of producing many new sonorities, and various avant-garde jazz players and composers have experimented with the instrument. One of the foremost electric violinists is Jean-Luc Ponty (born 1942) who, as well as working with musicians such as Frank Zappa, has produced hitherto unheard tones, some of which blare out like an electrified jazz horn.

Folk violin

The violin is used in folk music almost all over the world. Folk violinists do not follow the conventions of orchestral violinists, in that the instrument is not always held to

the chin. Country band fiddlers also often perform very skilled acrobatics with their instrument, such as playing it upside down, backwards, behind their back or even under their legs. In North American folk dance music, the violin is held against the chest or even the waist, while in North Africa the performer plays seated on the ground

LEFT: This musician is standing outside the Geigenbau, a stringed instrument museum in the southern Bavarian village of Mittenwald. Today it is a technical school, and a dozen artisans still carry on the long tradition of violin-making in the village.

with the instrument resting upright against the left knee.

Variations on the traditional violin include the single-fret *mazanki* of the Wielkopolska region of Poland. Carved out of one piece of wood, the *mazanki* is usually played in ensemble with the *dudy*, a form of bagpipe. The Hardanger fiddle, or *Hardingfele*, of western and southern Norway, was invented in about 1650, and was improved during the 18th century by Trond Isaksen (1712–72). The instrument, which includes four sympathetic strings placed below the fingerboard and playing strings, is still played today.

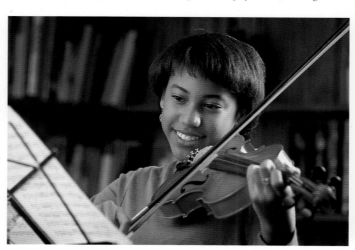

ABOVE: The violin is an extremely popular instrument among young people. Many students will learn the violin at school and carry on playing into adulthood.

ABOVE: Electric violins come in various sizes, including this MIDI of 1999.

Viola

The viola is a philosopher, sad and helpful; always ready to come to the aid of others, but reluctant to call attention to himself.

ALBERT LAVIGNAC (1846–1916)

The viola is the alto of the string section, and is pitched a fifth below the violin, whose fingering and bowing technique it shares. Fortunately, not many people share Wagner's view that it is "commonly played by infirm violinists or by decrepit wind players who were at one time acquainted with the violin". It came into being in northern Italy in the early 16th century and, by 1535, had become established as one of the three principal members of the new violin family. Known as the "instrument of the middle", the viola, with its dark, warm and rich tone, was used for both the alto and tenor registers. The strings were originally made of gut, but modern violas have

Key features

TYPE: stringed

TUNING: *c, g, d', a'*

NOTABLE PLAYERS OF THE VIOLA: Victor Lalo, Lionel Tertis, Paul Hindemith, William Primrose, Yuri Bashmet.

strings that are made of wire wound over gut or metal cores.

The main problem with the original viola was its size; some of the early models were so large that they could barely be played on the arm. The huge Andrea Amati tenor viola, for instance, had a body length of 47cm/19in. This problem was aggravated in the 19th century when some makers attempted to improve the viola's acoustics by making the body even longer. These improvements could only be effective if players had sufficiently long arms.

The perfecting of the Tourte bow, around 1785, opened a new era in string-playing. During the early 19th century the viola went through various alterations to increase string tension and carrying power, modifications that

LEFT: The viola is slightly larger than the violin, and is pitched a fifth lower.

involved the introduction of heavier strings and the lengthening of the neck.

Repertoire

Before 1740 there were no known outstanding violists and consequently, virtually no repertoire for the instrument. Although composers such as Bach, Handel and Vivaldi had given the viola important parts in fugues and concertos, it was not until the late 18th century that it began to be treated as a solo instrument.

One of the first composers to write a major part for the viola was Mozart, who, in his 1779 *Sinfonia Concertante* (K364), treated the viola and violin as equal partners. Paganini played the viola as well as the violin, and wrote caprices for the instrument. In the 20th century, mainly through the presence of outstanding players such as Lionel Tertis and Paul Hindemith, more solo viola works were written, including concertos by Walton, Bartók and the American composer

ABOVE: The composer Paul Hindemith (1895–1963) was an outstanding viola player. He had the distinction of being the first to play Walton's Viola Concerto in 1929.

Quincy Porter (1897–1967). Hindemith himself also wrote a number of works for the viola, including four concertos, four pieces for viola and piano, and two for unaccompanied viola.

Modern viola

Today's violas owe much to the work of the English viola virtuoso Lionel Tertis (1876–1975) who, in the 1940s, created an instrument that, although combining the fullness, depth and beauty of tone of a "full-size" viola, was still manageable by the player. More recently, Carleen Hutchins (born 1911), of the American Catgut Acoustical Society, has designed and built a whole new family of eight instruments acoustically scaled to the violin. Her viola, which

ABOVE: *The viola section of the London Symphony Orchestra.*

LEFT: One of the builders of the viola d'amore was Jacob Rauch who made this one in 1718.

is rescaled to a body measurement of about 53cm/21in, has a spike and is played between the knees like a cello.

Viola d'amore

An instrument related to the viola, the viola d'amore was popular during the late 17th and 18th centuries. It is unfretted with 14 strings – seven playing and seven simpathetic strings tuned an octave higher. Although it fell out of use during the 19th century, it was revived in the 20th century by composers such as Janáček, who used it in his opera *Kátya Kabanová* (1921) and Prokofiev, who included it in the score of the ballet *Romeo and Juliet* (1935).

BELOW: Despite its name, the viola da gamba is actually a viol. Unlike the viola, the viola da gamba has frets and is played between the knees like a cello.

♪ Harold in Italy

One of the most important 19th-century works for the viola was Berlioz's *Harold en Italie*, a symphony with viola obbligato, written in 1834. Although it had been commissioned by Paganini, who had just acquired a Stradivari viola, when he saw the composition he declined to play it, complaining that it did not give him enough work to do, or adequately display his talents as a virtuoso.

Cello

*The cello is like a beautiful woman who has not grown older but younger
with time, more slender, more subtle and more graceful.*

PABLO CASALS (1876–1973)

The violoncello, commonly
referred to by its
abbreviated name in English and
German, is the bass instrument
of the violin family, sounding an
octave below the viola. The instrument
originated in the 16th century. One of
the earliest makers was Andrea Amati
of Cremona, who built his *King Amati*
in 1572.

One of the disadvantages of the
original cello was its size. Early cellos
were considerably larger than those of
today, some having a body as long as
80cm/32in. This large size made it
difficult to play rapid passages and
so, in about 1660, experiments
began in Bologna to create a
smaller cello. At some time
between 1707 and 1710 Stradivari
decided on a length of about
75cm/30in, a length that has been
standard ever since.

It took some time for the cello to
become fully accepted, and it was not

*RIGHT: A view of a
cello player's bow action
and fingering technique.
This performer is using
the modern overhand
bow grip with his
right hand, while the
third finger of his left
hand has reached a
high note on the top
A string.*

until the latter half of the 17th century
that composers began to score for
it regularly. One of the earliest
composers for the instrument was the
Bolognese cellist Domenico Gabrieli
(c.1655–90) who, in 1684, published
his *Balletti, gighe, correnti, sarabande, a
due violini e violoncello con basso continuo.*

Improvements

In the 18th century various
improvements to the cello were
carried out, including lengthening and
thinning the neck and fingerboard,
raising the bridge and introducing
thinner and tauter strings, an
innovation that produced a clearer
and more responsive tone.

There were also improvements
to the bow. Until the second
half of the 18th century,
cello bows were either
straight or convex – like
those of the viol and violin –
and were gripped in the fist,

*LEFT: The cello is a large instrument,
and since it is supported by a spike and not
the left hand, the strings can be stopped
with the thumb as well as the fingers.*

Key features

TYPE: stringed

TUNING: *C, G, d, a*

**NOTABLE PLAYERS OF THE
CELLO:** Giuseppe Jacchini,
Luigi Boccherini, Alfredo
Piatti, Karl Davidov, Pablo
Casals, Paul Tortelier, Mstislav
Rostropovich, Jacqueline du Pré.

ABOVE: *A Romanian child playing a gardon by plucking the strings immediately after he has hit them with a stick.*

RIGHT: *The Portuguese cellist Guilhermina Suggia (1885–1950) played a Stradivari. She is remembered for her grace and style.*

 Cello music

While it has never been as well provided for as the violin, some notable 20th-century works have been composed for the cello, including Elgar's Cello Concerto (1919), Kodály's Sonata for Cello and Piano, Op. 4 (1910), Webern's *Drei Stücke* (1914), Villa-Lobos's *Bachianas Brasileiras* (1916), part of which is written for eight or more cellos, Britten's Cello Symphony (1963) and Mauricio Kagel's *Match* (1964), in which the two cello soloists dress as table-tennis players and perform against each other.

with the palm facing upward, as for the viol, or downward. François Tourte allowed cello players greater control when he introduced his concave bow of pernambuco wood in the 1780s, and fixed it at a length of 72cm/29in, with the playing hair between 60cm/24in and 62cm/25in.

Method of play

Early cellists either sat with their instrument resting on the floor between their legs, or stood with it leaning against their body. Sometimes it was played resting on a stool, or even in a horizontal position. By 1700, it was usual for the player to place his cello between his knees and support it with his calves. This high posture permitted the player to draw the neck back towards him, so that the left hand could approach the strings from the side, instead of from behind, thereby making the entire compass of the instrument more accessible.

In the 17th century cellos were also played in religious processions, especially in northern Italy. The peripatetic cellists cut a hole in the back of their instrument through which a strap was passed, which was hung around the player's neck, leaving him free to play with both hands – not an easy task.

Gardon

Originating from the eastern Carpathians, the gardon is a folk instrument similar to the cello, and is played as a rhythm instrument by Romanian gypsies. It used to be made out of a single block of wood, but the modern gardon has a body like that of the cello. It has three or four strings, all tuned to *d*. The player, who either sits or stands, hits the strings with a wooden stick or may slap the fingerboard. The strings may also be plucked.

ABOVE: *This painting of 1753 vividly shows the old style of playing the cello with the instrument grasped between the legs – there is no spike. The bowing technique shows the hand under the bow rather than over it, unlike the technique favoured by modern cellists.*

Double Bass

A composition without a bass
would be full of confusion and dissonance.

GIOSEFFO ZARLINO (1517–90)

The double bass is the largest and lowest-pitched stringed instrument of the orchestra. As well as being indispensable in the symphony orchestra – the average orchestra has eight – the double bass is also an essential member of jazz and dance bands, where its *pizzicato*-playing provides the rhythmical bass line. Today the bass generally has four strings, tuned in fourths, but this has not always been the case. During the 17th century five-string basses were used in Austria and Germany and in the early 18th century three-string basses were normal.

Size

The double bass has always been made in a number of sizes. The full-size instrument was used in the early Baroque period, but with the development of the overwound gut

RIGHT: On the double bass the tuning pegs jut out at the back. Because of the high tension of the strings, a cog wheel mechanism is used for tuning.

ABOVE: *A double bass player.*

string, makers were able to reduce it to more manageable dimensions. The modern orchestra generally uses a three-quarter size instrument, with a body length of about 115cm/45in, and all-steel strings are commonly used. Jazz and dance bands also use the three-quarter size, although they sometimes play the "piccolo bass", which is fitted with thin strings and tuned an octave higher than the standard bass. In the 17th century half-size basses were carried in processions, suspended by a strap over the shoulder.

At the other extreme, some gigantic basses have been built. These include Vuillaume's *octobasse*, which was built in 1849. Over 4m/13ft high and tuned an octave below the conventional bass, it was so big that it required two people to play it and the strings could only be stopped by operating a system of levers and pedals. Even larger was Paul de Wit's bass, 4.8m/16ft high, which he built for the 1889 Cincinnati Music Festival. One of the largest double basses built in Britain – if not the largest ever – was that constructed by Mr Martin, the landlord of the Blackamoor Lady in Leicester. Martin's instrument was so big that a hole had to be cut in his ceiling

ABOVE: *Vuillaume's* octobasse *(1849) was so big that the bow had to be held in place by a kind of oarlock.*

ABOVE: *Double bass strings are very long, so they vibrate well – the instrument is highly suited to playing* pizzicato.

through which the neck protruded, and it could only be tuned by going upstairs into the room above.

Virtuosi

Domenico Dragonetti (1763–1846), a Venetian, was considered the world's finest bass player of his time. He was a great friend and admirer of Beethoven and wrote several concertos and other pieces for the instrument. He freed it from doubling the cello part and assured its permanent place in the orchestra by pushing the playing technique to new heights. Such was Dragonetti's mastery over his instrument that once, while staying at a monastery, he stood in the corridor outside his room during the night and imitated a storm with his bass. The next day the main topic of the monks' conversation was the "thunderstorm" of the previous night.

Giovanni Bottesini (1822–89) extended the range of the double bass even further than Dragonetti, and was known in his day as the "Paganini of the double bass", particularly for his use of high harmonics. He toured Europe, Russia and the United States as a double bass soloist, wrote an important book on the instrument and composed a large number of works for it. A friend of Verdi, he conducted the first performance of Verdi's opera *Aida* in Cairo in 1871.

Bowing techniques

Methods of bowing for the double bass vary in different countries. Most players in Europe use the Bottesini, or "French" bow, which is shaped like a shorter, heavier cello bow and held overhand as for the cello. In central and eastern Europe, however, players prefer the "German" bow designed by Franz Simandl (1840–1912), which is derived from the old Dragonetti bow. Used underhand like a viol bow, it is also known as the "meat saw".

Bass music

It was only in the 19th century that composers started to write distinctive double bass parts. Before this time the bass player shared the cello part, usually playing an octave below the cello. By the early 19th century the bass was becoming popular as a solo instrument and composers were writing more exposed passages for the instrument, such as that in Schubert's "Trout" Quintet of 1819. In Saint-Saëns's *Le Carnaval des Animaux* (1886), the elephant is represented by the double bass. Other composers for the double bass include Hindemith, Prokofiev and Darius Milhaud.

ABOVE: *This double bass player is using the German technique, whereby the bow is held from underneath – similar to viol technique.*

Harp

His harp, the sole companion of his way.

JAMES BEATTIE (1735–1803), "THE MINSTREL"

One of the largest of all orchestral instruments, the modern harp has 46 strings with a compass of six and a half octaves. It is played tilted back against the player's right shoulder and usually has double-action pedals, which allow the player to raise the pitch of the strings by either a semitone or a tone. The harp is unique in that the strings run perpendicular to the resonator, whereas in all other stringed instruments the strings run parallel. The strings are plucked with the fingers, as was the case with early harps, although by 2000 BC the plectrum had been introduced.

The modern frame harp is descended from two basic types: the bow or arched harp, and the angular harp.

Bow or arched harp

The earliest form of harp is thought to have developed from the hunter's bow. Bow harps first appeared in western Asia in about 3000 BC, where they were played in processions and at

LEFT: A beautifully decorated modern pedal harp made by Leffler of Germany.

banquets. They had a resonator at the base from which the strings were attached to a curved neck. Many of these harps, which were just over 1m/3ft long, were decorated with a bull's head motif.

The first Egyptian harps of which we know date from the Fourth Dynasty (2625–2500 BC). They were used alone to accompany singing as well as in larger bands, and varied in size from the hand-held shoulder harp, usually played by women, to the larger instruments that were played by men. One of these, over 2m/6ft in height, is seen on a wall painting in the tomb of Rameses III (c.1150 BC). Played with the resonator resting on the floor, this instrument is decorated with a carved human head. Today the arched harp survives mainly in Africa and East Asia.

Angular harp

The earliest evidence of angular harps is to be found in three marble statuettes of seated musicians which date from about 2000 BC. Usually played by women, these instruments were in the shape of an equilateral triangle with each side some 55cm/21½in long. The strings were attached to the neck, forming a 60° angle with the resonator that rested on the player's right thigh.

Although the angular harp had been introduced into Egypt by about 1500 BC, it was several centuries

LEFT: This Egyptian mural from the tomb of Rameses III at Thebes (c.1150 BC) shows a harp with nine strings and a carved human face at the base of the resonator.

LEFT: An ancient Egyptian musician playing an arched harp. Played with the resonator resting on the floor, this six-stringed instrument is typically decorated with a carved human head.

Western Europe

The harp was known in western Europe by the 7th century. An 8th-century Anglo-Saxon manuscript depicts a frame harp, as does the 9th-century Utrecht Psalter. There is also a reference to the harp in Wace's 12th-century French poem, *Roman de Brut*. In the frame harp, the third side of the triangle, left open in the angular harp, is closed by the piece known as the pillar, so that the strings are enclosed within a frame. In early European harps, the pillar was usually curved.

before it gained full acceptance. It was played in an upright position, with the resonator held against the body and the neck resting in the player's lap.

ABOVE: This illustration of a harp player, entitled Gabinetto Armonico, *was drawn by Bonanni in the 18th century.*

Egyptian harpists evolved highly developed playing techniques, such as using the flat of the hand to dampen the strings. Another innovation was the sounding of stopped as well as open strings.

In Greece the harp never achieved the popularity of the lyre and was denounced by Plato as a "dreamy" instrument that was usually played only by women. The angular harp became popular in Imperial Rome where it was often played (again by women) in processions, sacrificial ceremonies and at the religious rites associated with the cult of Isis, which the Romans had adopted from the Egyptians.

RIGHT: A late 13th-century French illustration showing King David playing the harp.

Irish harp

The earliest evidence of the Irish harp, with its slender neck, pillar and resonator, is seen on relief carvings on 9th-century stone crosses. The instrument, which had a pronounced outward curve of the pillar, from which a low neck projected, was played held against the player's left shoulder. The harpist plucked the metal strings of the upper register with the long fingernails of his left hand. Early instruments were about 60cm/24in high and had up to 30 strings, but by the 16th century they had become larger and boasted up to 43 strings. Unlike earlier harps played with both hands, the new type was held against the body with one hand and played with the other. The Irish harp virtually died out in the late 18th century.

BELOW: A wooden Irish, or Celtic, harp. It has 22 strings with a flat soundboard on a round-backed resonator. The strings are tuned by means of pegs.

ABOVE: An Irish, or Celtic, harp decorated with gilt vine. This harp differed from other harps in that the strings were played with the fingernails instead of the fingertips.

Welsh harp

Known as the *telyn*, the Welsh harp is mentioned in poetry from the 10th century. Such was its importance that it was said to be one of the three indispensable possessions of a freeman. Unlike its Irish relation, the Welsh harp's strings, 31 or 34 in number, were made of horsehair or gut.

In the late 17th century the traditional Welsh harp was superseded by the triple harp, a chromatic instrument capable of producing all the notes in every key, and this remained the standard bardic instrument until the 19th century. Its diatonic strings were in the two outer rows, tuned in unison, allowing repeated notes to be played quickly using alternate hands. The strings in the inner row were tuned to the semitones. Held at the shoulder, the left hand generally played the treble and the right the bass strings.

Modern harp

An alternative to the chromatic harp was the hook harp, in which the pitch was raised a semitone by a series of U-shaped hooks set in the neck. The drawback with this system was that it was manually operated, so the player temporarily lost the use of one hand when tuning each string. This inconvenience was remedied in about 1720 by the invention of the pedal harp by Jakob Hochbrucker of Donauwörth and Johann Vetter of Nuremberg. The first pedal harps had five pedals that were connected to the hooks by wires passing through the hollow pillar. By depressing one of the pedals, all the strings of one note were raised by a semitone. The number of

ABOVE: An early 19th-century pedal harp player.

ABOVE: *Detail of the top area of a modern harp, showing the tuning pegs and chromatic shift mechanisms.*

to be a suitable instrument for ladies to play, and many were sold for domestic use during the 18th and 19th centuries.

One of the more notable harp makers of the 20th century is Victor Salvi (born 1921), who made his first harp in 1954. Seeking traditional Italian carving and veneering skills, Salvi moved from New York to Genoa, Italy, where he began producing harps such as the *Orchestra*. Salvi's innovations include a stainless steel linking system and nylon bearings, eliminating the need for lubrication. By the 1970s Salvi harps were available in a number of different sizes, ranging from the 164cm/65in high *Angelica* to the 188.5cm/74in high *Electra*.

ABOVE: *Although not all musical works include a part for the harp, the modern harpist is a key member of most large symphony orchestras.*

pedals was eventually increased to seven — one for each note of the diatonic scale, and this has remained the number in common use today.

Refinements to the system — replacing hooks with levers or forks — were made by the French makers Cousineau and Erard in the late 18th century. Erard created the double-action harp, with pedals that can be set in two positions to raise the pitch of each string by either a semitone or a whole tone. The harp was considered

ABOVE: *A close-up view of three harp pedals.*

Repertoire

The first symphony to include a part for the harp was Berlioz's *Symphonie Fantastique* (1830). Before this it had mainly been used orchestrally for special effects, as in the operas of Handel and Gluck. An exception was Mozart's Concerto for Flute and Harp, which he wrote in 1778 as one of a series of works commissioned by a wealthy flautist.

At the end of Wagner's *Das Rheingold*, the gods enter Valhalla accompanied by an orchestra including six harps. Both Debussy and Ravel wrote chamber music for the instrument, each having been commissioned by rival harp makers. Following the folk tradition, the modern harp is sometimes used to accompany voices, as in Benjamin Britten's 1942 *Ceremony of Carols* as well as works by Falla and Webern.

Electric harp

The first to use an amplified harp was the American harpist Lloyd Lindroth, who introduced it in 1964. He also later modified his harp to include a "wah-wah" pedal that "bent" the harp tone.

Key features

TYPE: stringed

PITCH: concert

NOTABLE PLAYERS OF THE HARP: Turlough Carolan, Nicholas Bochsa, Elias Parrish Alvars, Sidonie Goossens, Marisa Robles.

Guitar

A guitar has moonlight in it.
JAMES M. CAIN (1892–1977)

The guitar's wide appeal as a folk instrument led to its current pre-eminent role in rock and pop music. The instrument has a long history and, although as a classical instrument it has hardly figured in the orchestra, its solo repertoire is extensive.

Gittern
The modern guitar is a descendant of the gittern, a small lute-like instrument that came to Europe via Moorish Spain in the second half of the 13th century. The gittern, which had four gut strings, was popular not only among minstrels but also with the aristocracy. During the 15th century, the instrument increased in length and the number of strings changed to three courses of two, tuned to *D*, *G* and *B*, with a single chanterelle tuned to *E*. The second string of each pair doubled at the octave.

Vihuela
In Spain the gittern became transformed into the vihuela, a flat instrument curved in at the sides, with five pairs of strings and a single chanterelle. Although it was rarely found outside Spain, Henry VIII of England was known to have had four "Spanish vialles". These possibly came into his possession though his marriage to his first wife Catherine, daughter of

BELOW: The classical guitar, made famous by Andrés Segovia, a great guitarist of the 20th century.

Ferdinand of Aragon. The vihuela was an instrument of courtly society, whereas the smaller, four-course guitar was used for more popular music, and by the end of the 16th century was famous all over Europe.
By the mid 16th century music was being especially written for the guitar, and in 1586 Juan Carlos Amat brought out the first edition of his tutor, *Guitarra Española*. Within 100 years the guitar had become the instrument of choice even in Spain, and the days of the vihuela were numbered.

Renaissance guitar
The Renaissance four-course guitar appeared during the early 15th century. Played with a quill plectrum,

the strings were strung over gut frets that were tied around the neck, and passed over a movable bridge before terminating at a fixed frontal string holder. It was a much smaller instrument than we know today, combining the small size of the gittern with the body shape of the much larger vihuela. In the late 17th century a fifth course of strings was added below the other four.

Modern guitar
The playing technique was simplified by removing one string of each pair, and the modern six-string guitar, which has a wooden resonating chamber with incurved sidewalls and a flat back, began to make its appearance in the 18th century. Early instruments were much narrower and more elongated than

ABOVE: This 17th-century painting by Vermeer shows a girl playing a five-course guitar made by Vaboam, whose trademark ornamental rose sound-hole can be seen.

RIGHT: A four-stringed gittern carved with hunting scenes, grotesques and the arms of Queen Elizabeth I.

Key features

TYPE: stringed

PITCH: varies according to type of instrument

NOTABLE PLAYERS OF THE GUITAR: Niccolò Paganini, Francisco Tarrega, Andrés Segovia, Julian Bream, John Williams, Jimi Hendrix.

those of today. Eminent makers included José Pages of Cadiz, René François Lacote of Paris and the London-based Lewis Panormo.

In the 19th century the body was broadened and the internal bracing changed to a fan shape. Fixed metal frets were fitted to the neck and the bridge was raised. These innovations were largely the work of the Spanish guitar maker Antonio Torres Jurado (1817–92), who also standardized the

ABOVE: *Chuck Berry was an early rock 'n' roll singer who helped promote the popularity of the guitar. Many young people purchased a guitar to imitate their idols.*

ABOVE: *The guitar is an ideal instrument for street buskers. This unusual group from Santa Monica, California, consists of two guitars and a balalaika.*

string length to 65cm/26in. Metal screws replaced the wooden tuning pegs and, during the 20th century, further modifications were made, including lengthening the fingerboard down to the sound-hole.

The guitar in rock music

Today the guitar is most widely used by popular music bands. The electric guitar, using pick-ups to amplify the sounds of the strings, was developed in the 1930s and the solid-body guitar was invented by Les Paul in the 1940s. As an aid to rock musicians, transposition is facilitated by a *capo tasto* that is fitted over the fretboard, stopping all the strings simultaneously. Modern electric guitars are strung with metal strings and played with a plectrum.

ABOVE RIGHT: *The tres, indigenous to Cuba and the Dominican Republic, has three double courses of strings. It is often used to accompany dance.*

MIDDLE RIGHT: *The electric guitar is always played with a plectrum. The vibrations of the strings are picked up electronically so there are no sound-holes.*

RIGHT: *The bass guitar has four thick steel strings and is made in many varied shapes. It is mainly used in rock and dance bands.*

LEFT: *The acoustic guitar, still the instrument of choice for folk and classical players.*

BELOW: *The 12-string guitar has six double courses of strings. It often has gut strings for a softer tone.*

Hawaiian guitar

A modification of the Spanish guitar, the Hawaiian guitar was introduced into the islands in the 1830s. It is believed that one Joseph Kekuku was the first person to place the guitar across his knees, in the manner of a fretted folk zither, and run a comb along the strings to produce the

BELOW: The Hawaiian guitar, played across the player's knees, is best known for the glissando effect achieved by running a steel bar along its strings.

ABOVE, FROM MIDDLE TO BOTTOM: The dobro is an acoustic guitar with metal resonator discs inside the body which add volume to the sound. It is used by rock musicians – most famously by Mark Knopfler of Dire Straits – and country and bluegrass singers. The ukulele was advertised in 1916 as the most popular instrument of the day, its popularity being mainly due to its small size, light weight and low cost.

glissandos for which modern Hawaiian music has become known.

In the early 20th century the Hawaiian guitar became popular in the United States and makers began to market models for which a steel bar was sold as an accessory for slide playing – hence the American term "steel guitar". Outside Hawaii, the use of the steel guitar is now almost solely restricted to country music bands, where the doleful sound is a feature of many songs about lost love. The player holds the steel bar in one hand, while the fingers of the other wear plectra that are used to pluck the strings. In the 1950s, pedals and knee levers were introduced as an aid to rapid alteration in tuning.

Dobro

The dobro is a guitar that has one or more metal resonator discs inside the body under the bridge. It was first produced by the National String Instrument Corporation of Los Angeles in 1925 to a design by John Dopyera, the son of a Czech violin maker. Three years later Dopyera left the company to set up – with two of his brothers – the Dobro Corporation. The idea for the resonator discs came from the banjo, which sometimes had a metal resonator in its back. The dobro was originally developed in response to the growing demand for a guitar that would produce a greater volume than the conventional instrument. Although occasionally used by rock musicians, the dobro is mainly used in country and bluegrass music, where it is often played, Hawaiian-style, across the knees.

The name "Dobro" was formed by eliding the first syllables of Dopyera

ABOVE: This 19th-century painting, The Concert by Vincente Palmaroli, shows a Spanish woman playing her guitar to a small audience at home.

Brothers – though it also, helpfully, means "good" in Czech.

Ukulele

In 1879 Portuguese sailors introduced their *machete de braca*, a cross between a guitar and a mandolin, into Hawaii, where it was transformed into the ukulele, a word meaning "leaping flea". For

ABOVE: Two mandolins – English (top) and an Italian copy, both played by plucking the strings.

about 30 years the instrument remained relatively unknown outside the islands; its introduction to American popular music came in 1915 at the San Francisco Panama Pacific Exposition, where a group of Hawaiian performers enthralled the crowds with their music and in so doing created a new musical vogue.

The instrument reached a peak of popularity in the 1930s and '40s, in Britain mainly due to the music-hall artist George Formby, and in the United States due to the television

ABOVE: In Hawaii a small type of guitar is used to accompany the joyful vocal groups that are a feature of these wonderful islands.

🎼 Guitar music

The earliest surviving music for the four-course guitar is found in Alonso de Mudarra's *Tres libros de musica en cifras para vihuela*, published in 1546. In the late 16th century the Italian Melchiore de Barberis (born 1545) wrote four fantasias for guitar. Much of the music subsequently written for the classical guitar has been by Spanish and South American composers.

Francisco Tarrega (1852–1909) was the first guitarist to use the improved design of Torres, for which he both composed solo works and transcribed the works of other composers. The classical repertoire also includes works by Manuel de Falla (1876–1946), Joaquin Turina (1882–1949) and the Mexican Manuel Ponce (1882–1948).

Most popular of all is the *Concerto de Aranjuez* by Joaquin Rodrigo (born 1902), which was first performed in 1940.

star Arthur Godfrey. Its music is usually written in tablature — representing the player's finger positions rather than pitch.

Guitarillo

The Bolivian guitarillo has five double courses of gut strings and six frets. The instruments are often played in pairs by the Chipaya people to accompany

the *waynus de cordero* and *tonadas del cordero* (songs in praise of sheep and cattle) at the *k'illpa* festival.

BELOW, FROM TOP TO BOTTOM: A Gibson Stereo electric guitar and an Epiphone mandolin with four double courses of strings, usually plucked with a plectrum.

ABOVE: A guitarist in Buenos Aires playing with the aid of a capo tasto. Fitted over the fretboard, this device enables different keys to be played with the same chord positions.

Fiddles

They hadde menstrales of moch honours,
Fydelers, sytolyrs, and trompours.

THOMAS CHESTRE, "SIR LAUNFAL" (C.1400)

The first fiddles were almost as tall as their standing players. Held vertically, they had three strings and a round pegbox. Although all fiddles were generally made from a single block of wood, hollowed out and covered with a wooden soundboard, there were regional variations in shape. Three strings continued to be the norm until well into the 13th century, when five strings became general. Although gut was the usual material for strings, silk was sometimes used, and from the 13th century metal strings began to appear.

There were two distinct methods of playing the fiddle. In areas of Islamic influence it was held upright with the lower end resting against the player's knees or on the floor. The bow was held palm-up. In all other areas it was held approximately horizontally,

BELOW: The Cretan lyra *is a short-necked fiddle with three gut or wire strings. The bow was once fitted with small bells to give rhythmic accompaniment.*

sometimes supported across the chest with a strap, or vertically with the lower end against the player's chest or shoulder and the pegbox pointing down to the ground.

Kit

Used mainly by French dancing masters from the 16th to the 19th centuries, the kit was a small unfretted fiddle that was made in a great variety of shapes. When not in use the instrument was kept in a pocket in the teacher's coat-tails, a practice that gave it its nickname "pocket violin". The kit was made in four main forms: rebec,

ABOVE: A woodcut from Agricola's Musica Instrumentalis Deudsch (1529) showing four fretted viol-type fiddles: bass, tenor, alto and descant. Each instrument has not only a round sound-hole in the centre of the resonating box, but also two f-holes by the neck.

ABOVE: This 19th-century watercolour by Per Nordquist shows a man playing the nyckelharpa or keyed fiddle.

mandora, viola and violin — the last being the most common. Its name may be derived from the Greek kithara, or may be a reference to its diminutive size, like the kitten of the violin family.

Nyckelharpa

Used throughout Scandinavia for popular dance, festive and folk music, the nyckelharpa is a keyed fiddle. Fifteenth-century nyckelharpan had between seven and 12 wooden keys and from three to six strings, some of which were drones. The oldest surviving nyckelharpan date from the 16th century and are of two types. One has an elongated body in the shape of a figure eight, with a flat bottom and flat soundboard. The

LEFT: This 15th-century fresco by Fra Angelico at San Marco, Florence, depicts an angel playing a pear-shaped rebec.

century, when it was the recognized instrument of professional minstrels attached to noble households, and was played at courtly feasts and dances.

By the mid 16th century the rebec had been relegated to street musicians as people took up the increasingly popular violin. Indeed, such was the pejorative feeling against the rebec that in 1682 the French forbade musicians to exercise their trade unless they had served a six-year apprenticeship and had passed an examination; those who failed the examination were permitted to play only the rebec.

second type is pear-shaped and the soundboard and neck are made in a single piece. More recently, the shape of this type has come to resemble that of the violin family.

Rebec

An adaptation of the Byzantine lyre and the Islamic two-stringed rabab, the rebec was a plucked lute that dates back to at least the 8th century. The rebec was a bowed string instrument with a vaulted back, carved from one piece of wood that tapered in such a way that there was no clear demarcation between the body and the neck. At first the instrument had only two strings — tuned a fifth apart — with a compass of ten tones. However, by the 15th century it had anything from one to five strings, the average being three.

Although as early as the 13th century both the French and English courts employed rebec players, the heyday of the instrument was during the 15th

ABOVE: The rebec was introduced into Spain by the Arab invaders and, after undergoing various modifications, it evolved into the pear-shaped instrument of the early 11th century, which was played held propped against the shoulder.

ABOVE: When the bow reached Europe it was applied to instruments that had hitherto been plucked. For the first time, instruments such as this guitar-shaped fiddle were bowed, thus allowing them to produce a sustained sound.

Lyre

The lyre is welcome at the feasts of Jupiter.

HORACE (65–8 BC), "ODES"

The lyre is distinct from the harp in that its strings are attached to a yoke that lies in the same plane as the soundboard. There are two types of lyre: the box lyre, in which the resonator is a built-up wooden box, and the bowl type, which has a natural or artificially hollowed-out bowl as the resonator.

Origins

The lyre was played in Sumeria, since a representation of a lyre, standing higher than the seated player, has been found on a seal of about 3000 BC. Such lyres were asymmetrical, with the longer arm held away from the player. Plucked with the fingers of both hands, they had from eight to 12 strings that were fastened in a bunch on the lower left of the resonator before fanning out to the crossbar. Tuning was achieved by winding each string around a small rod tangential to the crossbar. Many lyres were carved with a bull's head and sometimes the strings emerged from a bull's body, perhaps giving a quasi-divine voice to the instrument. From Mesopotamia, the lyre passed on to Syria and Israel. The Hebrew lyre, or *kinnor*, had strings of sheep gut and

LEFT: The main type of lyre used in ancient Greece was the kithara. It had a wooden resonator and a row of gut strings attached to a bridge and crossbar, but no examples have survived. The words "guitar" and "zither" probably derive from "kithara".

was probably the "harp" of King David. The Hebrews had two methods of playing the lyre. For the dance, a plectrum was used, while for accompanying the voice, the strings were plucked with the fingers. The Israelites used the lyre only to express joy; it was considered a sacred instrument and was never used for sad music. When the Jews were in exile they suspended their "harps" on the willows, unable to "sing the Lord's song in a strange land".

Egypt and Greece

Around 1360 BC huge lyres appeared in Egypt, often decorated with a duck's head as a sign that they were associated with the god Amun. They were played with a long plectrum held in the right hand; all the strings, which varied in number from 7–15, were struck with a sweeping movement, while the left hand dampened those that were not wanted.

Lyres appeared in Crete by about 1800 BC, from where they passed to the Greek

RIGHT: An artist's impression of some of the instruments used by the ancient Egyptians and Hebrews. The blue instrument in the centre of the picture is an Egyptian lyre.

ABOVE: *A Roman woman using a plectrum on a form of lyre.*

and louder, with a wooden sound-chest and arms. Held at a tilt, the kithara was the primary instrument of Greek classical drama, contests and official cults.

Rome

From Greece the lyre migrated to Etruria, where tomb paintings of the 5th century BC show instruments with six or seven strings, a heavy bridge and a small body with long arms. Although the lyre was known to the Romans from this time, it did not play an important part in the city-state's musical life. In Roman art, Orpheus was often depicted playing his lyre to pacify lions. In the early days of Christianity, this subject was replaced by that of Christ with a flock of sheep, signifying the "Good Shepherd".

mainland, assuming a horseshoe shape. The Greeks originally made their resonators out of tortoiseshell. Later other materials were used, but were made to resemble tortoiseshell. In Greece the lyre evolved into the more sophisticated kithara, which was larger

ABOVE: *The 19th-century Italian mezzo-soprano Sofia Scalchi in Gluck's opera,* Orpheus, *holding a replica of a Greek lyre.*

ABOVE: *This painting by Madjera (c.1900) shows a Roman muse playing the lyre.*

Medieval lyre

A six-stringed lyre was the main stringed instrument of northern Europe between the 5th and 7th centuries. Substantial remains of a lyre were discovered in the excavation of the Sutton Hoo ship burial, dating from before AD 625. Early medieval lyres were usually made from a hollowed block of oak, 3–4cm/ 1¼–1½in thick, to which a thin

ABOVE: An early 19th-century painting of Elizabeth O'Neil as Melpomene the Tragic Muse leaning on a lyre. This is a medieval lyre with tuning pegs on the crossbar, rather than the Greek method of rings and rods.

soundboard of maple or other fine-grained wood was attached. Ranging in length from 40cm/16in to 80cm/ 32in, these were an improvement on the classical lyre, in that the tuning was now achieved by pegs inserted into the top, as opposed to the rings and rods

used previously. The lower ends of the strings, which numbered five, six or seven, were secured to a short projection at the bottom of the resonator. The lyre was held in front of the body, resting on the player's knee, and the strings were played with a plectrum.

Bowed lyre

By the 11th century, the four-stringed bowed lyre, or *rotte*, had evolved. Instruments that are bowed require strings to be under a greater tension than plucked ones, so the frame of the lyre had to be strengthened. The former yoke was enlarged and the open arc considerably diminished, ultimately becoming little more than a hand-hole. Of the four strings, only one was played, the others acting as drones. Bowed lyres were generally played resting against the player's chest, shoulder or, as a sign of the fiddle to come, the chin. They were also played supported by the left arm in an upward slanting position, resting on the player's right thigh.

During the early Middle Ages a "figure-of-eight" lyre evolved in central Europe; it was three times longer than it was wide, but was doomed to failure as it was not able to withstand the strain imposed upon it by the bow.

ABOVE: This painting by John Strundwick shows an angel playing a rotte, *a medieval type of lyre. In its early form it was plucked, but by the 11th century it was bowed.*

LEFT: Lyres were introduced to Ethiopia from Egypt at a very early date. They have survived to the present day almost unchanged, as can be seen from this Eritrean box lyre.

crwth was played in the violin position. In addition to the four playing strings it had two drone strings, which were set individually to the left of the fingerboard. Its unique feature was the bridge, which had two feet: a short one that rested on the soundboard and a longer one that passed through one of the small circular sound-holes and rested on the back of the body, thus serving as a soundpost to transmit the vibrations to the back.

African lyre

Forms of lyre are still played (mainly as a solo instrument to accompany the player's singing) in parts of Africa such as Ethiopia, the Sudan, Kenya and Zaire. Some have a wooden resonating bowl covered with lizard skin. In the absence of a bridge, the plucked strings create a buzzing sound when they hit the soundtable. In Kenya, where it is viewed as a ritual object with healing powers, the lyre is played at weddings, both as an entertainment and as a blessing. In Buganda it sometimes appears in consort with flute, drum and tube fiddle.

BELOW: The crwth is a form of Welsh lyre. Unlike its ancestors, the crwth has sound-holes in the resonator.

ABOVE: A 16th-century Italian depiction of a lyre, the shape of which has come to serve as a universal symbol for music in Western civilization.

Although the plectrum-played lyre died out in the early Middle Ages, the bowed version survived into the 15th century, by which time it had been replaced almost everywhere by the fiddle. It did survive, however, in parts of Wales and East Africa.

Crwth

In Wales the lyre lived on in the form of the crwth, which is about 60cm/24in long, 30cm/12in wide and 6cm/2⅓in deep, the body, arms and crossbar all being made in one piece. Still in use in the 19th century, the

Lute

The lute is the most perfect of all instruments.

GIOVANNI LANFRANCO (1490–1545), "SCINTILLE DI MUSICA"

The lute is believed to have originated in Mesopotamia; the earliest depiction of a primitive lute-like instrument, which may have either two or three strings, appears on a terracotta plaque dating from the 17th century BC, now housed in Baghdad Museum. Always played by men, the prototype lute had a small ovoid body and a long fretted neck.

Africa and Asia

The instrument soon reached Egypt where, interestingly, it was played by women. Some of these two-stringed lutes were made with a tortoiseshell body and an animal-hide belly with six sound-holes. Sometimes the end of the neck, which was about 32cm/12¾in long, was carved with the head of a goose or falcon. Played with a plectrum, contemporary paintings show lutes with ovoid bodies and fretted necks that penetrate the whole length of the body. The strings

BELOW: An Italian lute built in about 1600 by Magno Tieffenbrucher of Venice, showing the sharp angle between the pegbox and neck.

were fastened underneath the belly, through which they issued through a hole and were secured by tuning pegs at the upper end of the neck. Over 3000 years later this type of lute still survives in north-western Africa.

The long-necked lute appeared in Greece in the 4th century BC, whence it travelled to Etruria and Rome, although it never achieved popularity in any of these areas. In the 5th century AD long-necked lutes were being played in Byzantium and Libya, but did not reach India until the 10th century.

Ud

The Western lute is directly descended from the Arab ud, a short-necked instrument with four strings, played with a plectrum. The ud first appeared in Mecca during the 6th century. Tuned in fourths, the instrument was improved when a fifth string course — and subsequently a sixth — was added. Although the ud was introduced into Europe by the Moors during their occupation of Spain (711–1492), it did not appear in other parts of Europe until the 13th century.

BELOW: The saz is a long-necked fretted lute originating from Iran and Turkey. It has eight to ten metal strings.

LEFT: The kora is a long-necked, 21-stringed, plucked lute-like instrument found in Senegal and neighbouring countries.

ABOVE: The lute has survived in various forms. In Morocco, because of the country's strong historic links with the Arab world, the instrument of choice is the ud.

RIGHT: The ud is the principal instrument of the Arab world. Its name means "wood" and "tortoise", referring to the material from which it is made, or to its shape.

Structure of the lute

The medieval lute was characterized by its vaulted body and flat soundboard. The body was constructed from a number of separate ribs, usually of maple or sycamore, shaped, bent and glued together. The strings were laid along the distinct neck and the fingerboard, which was tied with four gut frets. By 1480 the frets were being made of fixed metal, and over the years their number was increased to ten. One of the most notable features of the lute is the pegbox, which is placed

Lute music

The first half of the 16th century was the golden age for lute music, with more than 400 pieces being published all over Europe. The first music specifically written for the lute was Spinaccino's *Ricercai*, composed in 1507. Much lute music developed an international character that reflected the travels of the great lutenists of the day, such as Francesco Canova da Milano (1497–1543), Alberto da Ripe and the Hungarian Bakfark.

almost at a right angle to the neck. The lute's strings are arranged in paired courses. At first, European lutes had four courses of strings, but during the 15th century a fifth course was added and, in about 1600, a sixth. By 1630, ten and even 12 courses were common. Metal strings were a German invention and first appeared in Nuremberg in 1414.

ABOVE: A 15th-century illumination showing a lute player and two men playing the anvil as a percussion instrument.

ABOVE: This early 16th-century Italian lute has five courses of strings and ten frets.

By the beginning of the 16th century the lute had attained its perfection of form. In spite of the great size of its resonance cavity, it was remarkably light, since the ribs that made up the swelling, pear-shaped body were extremely thin. The strings were tied to the bridge, which was glued to the soundboard. The bent-back pegbox was also made as light as possible. The most famous lute-making centre at this time was in Bologna, the workshop of Laux Maler (1518–52) being one of the finest. Other craftsmen worked in Venice and Padua, and, although working in Italy, nearly all were German.

ABOVE: The lute is instantly recognizable by its characteristic swelling pear-shaped body and flat belly. This lute has six courses of strings, five of which are paired.

Playing methods

The medieval lute was a melodic instrument that was played with a quill plectrum. It played one line of music, with chords at cadences and phrase endings. During the 15th century, however, it began to be played with the fingertips, a development that allowed for the playing of several parts at once. The substitution of fingers for plectrum-plucking is a sign that the lute was becoming a solo instrument with a polyphonic style of playing.

Notwithstanding its popularity, the lute was in a sense the most inefficient musical instrument ever conceived; the bulbous form of its large body made it difficult to keep in position. This was such a problem that it was not unknown for the little finger of the left hand to be "glued" to the soundboard, thereby immobilizing the entire hand. The lute was also difficult to tune and the strings were often breaking. Indeed, in 1713, it was said that an 80-year-old lutenist had spent 60 of his years just tuning his instrument.

Theorbo

Believed to have been invented by the Florentine Antonio Naldi in the late 16th century, the theorbo was longer

ABOVE: Longer than the lute, the theorbo has a separate nut and pegbox for the unstopped bass strings. When the theorbo was introduced into England (1605) it was confiscated by the customs who, remembering the recent activities of Guy Fawkes, believed it to be a device to kill the king.

ABOVE: The theorbo is still occasionally seen today and one musician who has revived the instrument is Paula Chateauneuf, who is seen here performing in 1993.

than the conventional lute and had a separate nut and pegbox for its set of unstopped bass strings, which were known as diapasons. It was popular during the 17th and 18th centuries both as a solo instrument and as an accompaniment to singing.

Archlute

During the 16th century, in response to the lutenists' requirements for additional bass strings, a new series of bass lutes came into being. They were characterized by their open bass strings secured to a separate pegbox as with the theorbo, as opposed to the conventional lute whose bass strings were always stopped. The archlute resembled a smaller version of the theorbo, but had 13 or 14 double string courses, whereas the theorbo had single courses. Used both for solos and accompaniment during the 17th

ABOVE: An engraving from Bonanni's Gabinetto Armonico of 1723 depicting an archlute player.

and early 18th centuries, the archlute was plucked using the fingernails of the right hand. One of the last composers to write for the archlute was Handel, who gave it a part in his oratorio Athalia in 1733.

Balalaika

A descendant of the 16th-century dombra, the balalaika is a lute-like folk instrument of northern and central Russia. It has a triangular

BELOW: Today the balalaika is internationally known, in no small part due to the tours in the 1960s and '70s of the former Red Army Ensemble, and its prominence in the score for the film Dr Zhivago.

body, a long neck with four or five movable frets, three rib-fastened gut strings and a simple pegdisc. It has a flat back and a thin, slightly arched soundboard made from four strips of spruce into which the small sound-hole is cut. In the later years of the 19th century the St Petersburg musician Vassil Vassilyevitch Andreyev (1861–1918) designed balalaikas in six sizes, each with three strings. Andreyev's work transformed the balalaika from the realms of folk music into a popular instrument used in bands and orchestras.

ABOVE: The balalaika is often used to accompany the hectic folk-dancing for which the Russians are famed.

ABOVE: Side and front views of a balalaika, showing the distinctive triangular ribbed shape of the body. The balalaika has only three strings, and comes in a variety of sizes.

Banjo

A long-necked lute-type instrument, the banjo originated in West Africa and was introduced into North America by African slaves as early as the 17th century. From the southern

plantations the banjo slowly moved north, where it became a feature of black-faced minstrel shows. Through the influence of white banjoists in these shows, such as Joel Sweeney (c.1810–60) and Dan Emmet (1815–1904), the composer of *I Wish I Was in Dixie*, the banjo was rapidly introduced to American white urban culture, where it was increasingly played as a parlour instrument in the 19th century. It was exported to Britain and taken up by music hall entertainers and jazz bands. It has occasionally been used in 20th-century orchestral music, such as Kurt Weill's *Mahagonny* (1927) and Gershwin's *Porgy and Bess* (1935).

The modern banjo has five steel strings, although "classical" banjo players still use gut strings. The fifth of these – the "thumb string" – is short and is secured by a peg in the side of the neck at the level of the fifth fret. It is tuned to G and plays only that note, usually being sounded between beats.

BELOW: The modern banjo's tambourine-shaped body consists of a plastic membrane stretched over a circular frame, tightened by screws.

Banjo key features

TYPE: stringed

TUNING: *g', c, g, b, d'*

NOTABLE PLAYERS OF THE BANJO: Pete Seeger, Earl Scruggs.

ABOVE: A musician sitting on his front porch in Nevada playing the banjo. The banjo became a popular instrument in the southern states of America.

Cittern

A citole in hir right hand hadde she.

GEOFFREY CHAUCER (C. 1340–1400), "THE KNIGHT'S TALE"

The cittern evolved from the citole, a plucked lute-like instrument played by 13th-century French troubadours. Made from a single piece of wood, the citole had a flat, pear-shaped body and a short neck, and was usually fitted with three single brass or steel strings that passed from a flat pegdisc to a frontal string-holder.

Shape of the citole

In different parts of Europe the citole assumed various shapes, all of which had a protuberance at the bottom to which the strings were attached. The Italian style was a "spade-fiddle" shape, with the shoulders swept upwards to form points. In France, the shoulders developed into wings and the oval sides became either straight or slightly waisted. The English and Germans preferred a citole of a "holly-leaf" shape with the

RIGHT: The flat-backed cittern was the most important plectrum-plucked instrument of the Renaissance, and its popularity is attested by numerous literary references.

ABOVE: This finely carved cittern is said to have been made by the great Italian stringed instrument maker Antonio Stradivari in 1700.

sides forming points at the intersections of concave curves.

During the 15th century a bridge was added to raise the strings off the soundboard, the pegdisc became a pegbox and the neck was fitted with 12 or more brass frets. The quill was abandoned and the four courses of strings began to be plucked with the fingers. The citole seems to have lasted longest in Spain, but by the early 16th

century it had become universally transformed into the cittern.

Early cittern

A characteristic of the cittern, which was very popular in the 16th and 17th centuries, was its unusual neck, which was half cut away from behind the fingerboard on the bass side. The resulting overlap formed a "channel", which facilitated very rapid shifts to and from the high positions that were so often required in the instrument's solo repertory.

Modifications

During its early years the cittern underwent many modifications, including increasing the number of courses of strings from five to 12. In 16th-century France and northern Europe the cittern eventually became standardized as a four-course instrument, with the top two courses of strings doubled and the other two trebled.

Towards the end of the 16th century a larger cittern with extra bass strings appeared. Called the *ceterone*, it was developed as a continuo instrument, its extra strings being secured to a separate pegbox, much like the theorbo. In the early 17th century a small English version of the cittern appeared. One person who enjoyed

ABOVE: This 18th-century engraving shows a trio of musicians, with one playing a bass cittern. It had seven courses of single strings and a set of five extra bass strings that were fixed to a separate pegboard.

ABOVE: This early 17th-century painting by Wouter Pietersz Crabeth shows a cittern (left) being played in company with a lute and flute.

ABOVE, FROM LEFT TO RIGHT: Back and front views of a bell cittern, which became popular in Germany in the 17th century. The Neapolitan mandolin is distinguished from other lute-type instruments by the pronounced increase in depth of vaulting at the body's lower end.

playing the *Englisches Zitterlein* was J. S. Bach's grandfather Veit, who, it is said, played it while working in his mill.

Demise of the cittern

By the mid 17th century in England and France, the cittern had degenerated into a barbershop instrument and was fast losing out to the increasingly popular guitar. By the mid 19th century the guitar had completely taken over and, apart from a few pockets in rural areas of Germany and Switzerland, the cittern had died out by the beginning of the 20th century.

Archcittern

During the 17th century Italian and French builders began to make larger citterns with two pegboxes. These archcitterns had from five to seven melody gut strings and six or seven off-board strings on the lines of the theorbo. Popular in the 18th century, they were about 1m/3ft long, and reportedly as loud as a harpsichord.

Hurdy-gurdy

One of the street musicians was an old lady who played upon a hurdy-gurdy.
She had been about the streets of London for upwards of forty years, and being blind,
had had during that period four guides, and worn out three instruments.

HENRY MAYHEW (1812–87), "LONDON LABOUR AND THE LONDON POOR"

Originally known as the organistrum, the hurdy-gurdy is a kind of mechanical violin able to sound two or more notes simultaneously while producing a continuous drone. Although it was built for use in churches and monastery schools to teach music and provide correct intonation for singers, by the end of the 13th century it had lost its ecclesiastical position to the newly developed portative organ.

Known from at least the 10th century, these early instruments, which had three strings, were up to 2m/6ft long. To play, they were set horizontally across two players' laps. One turned a handle to rotate the wheel that set the strings into vibration, while the other operated the keys that determined the pitch. For singers, the advantage of the organistrum over other conventional stringed instruments was that the stopping mechanism ensured an exact, invariable pitch, while the disadvantage was that only slow playing was possible.

Evolution

By 1300, the organistrum had become much smaller and was played by one musician. It now had a higher pitch, a range of over an octave, and could be played much faster than before. It became fully established as a minstrel instrument and was played suspended by a strap around the neck, in particular by blind musicians and beggars. Its use as a beggar's

BELOW: This replica of a six-stringed hurdy-gurdy clearly shows the keys and the handle.

Hurdy-gurdy music

In 18th-century Germany, marches and polonaises were written for the hurdy-gurdy, and in 1786 Haydn wrote five concertos for the instrument. Mozart scored for it in a set of minuets (K601) and four German dances (K602), while Nicolas Chédeville (1705–82) adapted Vivaldi's *Four Seasons* for the instrument. Gaetano Donizetti (1797–1848) included two Savoyard songs with hurdy-gurdy accompaniment in *Linda di Chamounix* (1842) and it is interesting to note that itinerant Savoyards were still playing the instrument in the streets of London and Paris at the end of the 19th century.

instrument continued, for in the 17th century the French were referring to it as an *instrument de truand*, while those still writing in Latin called it the *lyra mendicorum*. Its name also changed in England, the name "hurdy-gurdy" first appearing in 1749. In Italy it was known as the *lira tedesca*, possibly signifying that the instrument had been imported from Germany.

The hurdy-gurdy as a "serious" instrument

In 18th-century France, where it was known as the *symphonie* (a name that could be applied to almost any

ABOVE: A 17th-century hurdy-gurdy player in Georges de la Tour's Le Vielleur.

instrument that could emit two or more tones simultaneously) or the *vielle*, the hurdy-gurdy achieved heights not reached elsewhere when it became accepted as a fashionable court instrument during the vogue for *fêtes champêtres*. The variation favoured by the aristocracy was the *lira organizzata*, an instrument that had two ranks of organ pipes and bellows housed in its body. There were many French virtuosi of the hurdy-gurdy, and many composers wrote music for it. The most notable of them were Henri Baton (died 1728), who redesigned the *vielle*, and his son Charles (died 1754), who composed a number of suites for it and also wrote a history of the instrument in 1741. As with many other things associated with the aristocracy, the popularity of the hurdy-gurdy in France ended with the Revolution.

ABOVE: The neck of this six-stringed German hurdy-gurdy is finely decorated and is carved in the shape of a head.

ABOVE: Detail from Four Musicians, *painted in 1678 by Jacob Toorenvliet, showing a hurdy-gurdy player.*

ABOVE: The Blind Hurdy-gurdy Player *by David Vinckboons (1576–1632). Because it was easily portable, the hurdy-gurdy was widely used by travelling minstrels, pilgrims and especially by the blind, who could make a living from it even if they had learnt only a few tunes.*

Zither

It was an Abyssinian maid,
And on her dulcimer she played, Singing of Mount Abora.
SAMUEL TAYLOR COLERIDGE (1772–1834), "KUBLA KHAN"

The term "zither" is generically applied to any stringed instruments not classified as harps, lutes or lyres. It refers to instruments in which the resonator can be detached from the string-bearer without destroying the sound-producing apparatus. Evolved from instruments played over 2000 years ago, there are various forms of the instrument, ranging from the simple ground zither to the more sophisticated folk instruments that are played in southern Germany and Austria.

ABOVE: The harp zither is used by Austrian folk musicians.

Ground and trough zithers

The most primitive of the family is the ground zither, which is nothing more than a string stretched between posts in the ground, set over a bark-covered pit that acts as the resonator. The string is beaten by pieces of wood, and is used to accompany singing mainly to reinforce the rhythm of the music. Evidence of ground zithers has been found in neolithic excavations, and they are still played in parts of Africa and South-east Asia. A development of the ground zither is the trough zither, which is also found in Africa. This is usually plucked and consists of a hollowed-out piece of wood, sometimes elaborately sculpted, with a length of string laced back and forth over it.

Tube and raft zithers

The tube zither, as the name implies, is based on a wooden tube, usually cane. These are found in diverse parts of the world, ranging from New Guinea to eastern Europe. The strings are formed by detaching long fibres from the body of the tube and raising them on bridges. Several tube zithers bound together form a raft zither, which is played in parts of Africa. The Nigerian version has a gourd resonator attached to the underside. Popular in Cameroon, the harp zither has strings made of raffia that run over a tall vertical bridge.

Psaltery

An ancestor of the modern European zither is the psaltery, a development of the Turkish *qanun* that reached Europe in the 11th century. Psalteries were flat boxes of various shapes, ranging from the early square or triangular to the wing shape of the 14th and 15th centuries. They could also have incurved sides and some were even semicircular, and they were often made with finely decorated cases. The psaltery was played with quill plectra or sometimes plucked with the fingers, either resting on the lap or leaning against the chest.

ABOVE: A wood cut, Die Hackbrettspielerin, *by Tobias Stimmer (1539–84). One of a series of nine, it depicts a courtier playing a medieval trapeze-shaped zither.*

ABOVE: Unlike most of the rest of the world, in Iran the zither occupies a pre-eminent place in classical music and is never used in folk music. It is played with two hammers.

Dulcimer

The dulcimer is virtually identical to the psaltery, but is played by striking the strings with small hammers, the instrument resting either on the lap or on a table. It probably originated in Persia, and is still played in modern Iran. The Hungarian version is a large concert instrument called the *cimbalom*, which features in Kodály's opera *Háry János* (1926). The dulcimer is also played in China, where it arrived from the West around 1800. It is called *yang ch'in*, or "foreign zither".

Ch'in

The indigenous Chinese zither is a plucked instrument with seven strings and no bridges, and is one of the oldest instruments in China. As such, it is a symbol of culture and civilization and is often depicted as an attribute of the sage, especially Confucius.

Scandinavian zither

Although unfretted box zithers were in use in Europe from at least the 12th century onwards, fretted zithers seem to have been developed from the 16th century in northern Europe. The concept was probably brought back to Europe by merchants who had travelled in the East.

Alpine zither

Most modern European zithers, which are popular in Austrian and southern German folk music, are board zithers. Laid flat on the knees or on a table, they consist of a shallow wooden box either with two curved sides or one curved and one straight. Usually the body acts as a resonator, although

BELOW: The ukelin is a kind of bowed zither used in North American folk music. It has a system of hoops along the side of the instrument; by threading the bow through different hoops, chords can be played.

sometimes a supplementary resonator is added. The 45 strings, of which five are melodic and the rest accompaniment, run parallel to the body along its entire length.

Several variations of the alpine zither have been invented, and various schools of playing have developed. The most common type today is the

ABOVE: The dulcimer is now restricted to the alpine regions of Austria and Switzerland. It can be played on its own, but is more often accompanied by guitars and accordions.

Salzburg form, with a semicircular projection on one side, which can be played in one of two tunings, the "Munich" or the "Viennese".

ABOVE: The zither has been used as a folk instrument in Scandinavia since the 16th century. In Sweden it is referred to as a lǻngharpa and in Norway it is a langspil.

Sitar

*The mark of a good sitar player is the ability to improvise extensively
without abandoning the laid down set of rules defining the raga.*

JAMEELA SIDDIQI

The sitar, a large, fretted, long-necked lute, is the best-known Indian instrument. Prominent in the classical chamber music formerly played at the Muslim and Hindu courts, tradition credits the invention of the sitar to the court poet Amir Khusrav (c.1253–1325). The name is an Urdu transcription of the Persian *sihtar*, or "three-stringed", Persian being the court language of northern India between the 13th and 19th centuries. The *tambura*, a long-necked lute and near relation of the sitar, is recorded in a late 16th-century contemporary account of court musicians in the reign of Akbar.

The sitar took on the outline of its present form as a classical solo instrument in the 18th century, when the use of a gourd for the shell and the adoption of the carvel-built ribs and heavy metal frets and strings became the norm. Usually accompanied by the tabla drums, the sitar has six or seven main strings, four of

RIGHT: The characteristic sound of the sitar is derived from the shimmering echoes of the sympathetic strings and the distinctive rectangular bridge.

which are played by a plectrum, the others being drones. In addition there are anything from 11–19 sympathetic strings, fitted on to a separate bridge. To the long hollow neck are fitted 20 brass frets that can be moved easily to conform to the scale of a particular *raag*. The convex neck allows the player to alter the pitch by pulling the string sideways across the fret, thus creating the sliding *portamento* that is so characteristic of Indian music.

Although several types of sitar are made, the most common is the *tarafdar sitar* (concert sitar), which is made in two main models: the single-gourd and the double-gourd. It is made of wood with a bulging gourd segment and is based on the large sitar of the 19th century, which was standardized to a length of about 122cm/48in. The wood used is usually toonwood (from the Punjab) or teak. The neck is a large

ABOVE: An Indian shop showing a row of sitars displayed for sale.

ABOVE: Sometimes referred to as the glory of all stick zithers, the vina is a type of sitar with its strings passed between two large gourd resonators.

ABOVE: Ravi Shankar (born 1920) is the foremost player of and composer for the sitar.

As well as being one of the world's foremost players of the sitar, Ravi Shankar — who as a young man trained as a dancer as well as a musician — is also a composer for the instrument. He came to world attention in the 1960s when George Harrison of the Beatles was inspired by some of his complex, yet graceful, sitar improvisation. His mesmerizing impromptu performances introduced the West to the sophistication and beauty of Indian music.

hollowed piece of wood, rounded at the back, and about 90cm/36in long and 9cm/3½in wide.

The sitar is always played with a twisted wire plectrum worn on the right index finger. The player sits on the floor with the left leg tucked flat beneath the right and the shell supported in the hollow of the right foot. Some players sit cross-legged with the raised right thigh supporting the neck of the sitar.

Surbahar

The surbahar is a bass sitar that produces a deep, dignified sound. The neck is wider and longer than that of the sitar but its frets are fixed. The soundtable is also much larger, with a diameter of over 40cm/16in. The instrument was invented in about 1820 by the sitar player Glunlam Muhammad of Lucknow.

ABOVE: Played by both men and women, the sitar is India's most popular instrument.

Vina

The name "vina" has become a generic term for stringed instruments in southern India, and the sitar is sometimes described as one. Originally, the vina was a type of stick zither with the fingerboard stretched between two gourds, but it underwent structural changes in the 16th century. The modern instrument is a kind of lute, with a hollow neck attached to a large hollow body and a soundboard made of wood. It has seven strings, three of which are drones, and there are 24 adjustable frets along the neck. It has a softer, sweeter tone than the sitar and is the principal instrument of classical southern Indian music.

ABOVE: Illustration of a vina from Oriental Drawings (1806) by Charles Emilius Gold.

Woodwind
✦ and ✦
Brass

Harnessing the Breath

Never let the horns and woodwind out of your sight:
if you can hear them at all, they are too strong.

RICHARD STRAUSS (1864–1949)

Wind instruments can be classed in two main groups: woodwind and brass. Technically known as "aerophones", wind instruments produce sound when the column of air inside them is set into vibration by either a reed or the player's lips. They depend for their tuning on the length of their pipe; the longer the pipe, the deeper the note that is produced.

Transposing instruments

Instruments with a fundamental note other than C are described as "transposing" instruments. This means that their music is written not at the actual pitch produced, but transposed by a specific interval upwards or downwards. The result is that the player can maintain the same fingering (or harmonics, in the case of brass)

ABOVE: The woodwind section of the BBC Symphony Orchestra rehearsing in London.

ABOVE: The woodwind section consists of flutes, oboes, clarinets and bassoons.

when playing instruments of different pitch. For instance, the B flat trumpet's written part sounds a tone below that which is written – if it is to play in the key of G major its part is written in A major. Other transposing instruments include the F horn and B flat clarinet.

Woodwind

Four distinct families of instruments make up the woodwind section of the modern symphony orchestra: flutes, oboes, clarinets and bassoons. Although today some of these instruments are no longer made entirely of wood, they still keep the appellation "woodwind", and can be divided into two types depending on

the shape of the bore, which is either cylindrical or conical.

Early woodwind instruments, such as the curtal, shawm and racket, were not only difficult to play in tune but also made harsh sounds. As such they were not popular, and in the mid 17th century Lully excluded them from his band. The then leading French woodwind maker, Jean Hotteterre (c.1605–90) and the court musician Michel Danican Philidor (c.1600–59) are credited with the design and production of new-style instruments, including the transverse flute and the three-section recorder. The shawm was redesigned to create the oboe, and the bassoon was a development of the curtal. The new instruments had a

ABOVE: B flat euphoniums are really tenor tubas, and are a major feature of brass and military bands. Although they are not a standard orchestral instrument, they are sometimes used to great effect. Holst, for example, wrote a part for the euphonium in his suite The Planets (1916).

Brass

A modern orchestral brass section usually consists of four horns, two trumpets, three trombones and a tuba. Brass instruments – which were originally used in hunting, for military functions or on religious occasions – became regular members of the orchestra in the 18th century, when court orchestras called on the resources of the military bands attached to the same household.

Mouthpiece

The cup mouthpiece can be dated back at least 3000 years, having been found on northern European *lurs. Lurs* were bronze conical trumpets built in two or more detachable parts, the smallest of which had the cup mouthpiece cast with it. The Etruscans, whose civilization can be traced back beyond the 8th century BC, were noted bronze workers whose horns and trumpets – which were played with cup mouthpieces – were eventually adopted by the Romans. Etruscan horns in the shape of three-quarters of a circle are seen in tomb murals from the 5th century BC. These were carried in funeral processions on the shoulders of white-robed officials, who held them by a crossbar as they played.

refinement and flexibility that enabled them to co-exist with Lully's violin orchestra, and he accepted them back into his band.

In the 1830s the woodwind instruments were redesigned again, this time by Theobald Boehm, who developed a new system of keys.

ABOVE: Besson & Co. were the foremost manufacturers of brass instruments in the 19th and early 20th centuries. Founded in Paris in about 1838, the firm opened in London in 1851. The makers were inventors and patentees of the "Prototype" system of manufacture, assuring the exact duplication of instruments, as well as marking the birth of modern methods of musical instrument manufacture.

ABOVE: A brass section: horns, euphonium, trumpets, trombones, tubas (and saxophones).

ABOVE: The modern trombone mouthpiece is deeper than its medieval counterpart.

Flute

*The flute has now achieved such perfection and evenness of tone
that no further improvement remains to be desired.*

HECTOR BERLIOZ (1803–69)

Except for percussion, the flute is arguably the oldest musical instrument known, and ancient examples have been found all over the world, apart from Australia and New Zealand. Unlike the modern side-blown (cross or transverse) instrument, early flutes were end-blown (vertical) and were made of animal bones, such as a reindeer horn or sheep's tibia, pierced with a blow-hole and several finger-holes. The flute has been used as a decoy instrument throughout history, from the Pied Piper of medieval central European folklore to bird-catchers of the 20th century.

BELOW: The modern flute follows the improved design devised by the Bavarian goldsmith and musician Theobald Boehm in the 1830s.

Boehm's system used larger holes than hitherto; he also changed all the closed keys into open keys and cut the holes within easier control of the fingers. In 1847 he brought out an improved metal flute with 15 holes and 23 levers and keys. This system was so successful that it was adapted for the oboe, clarinet and bassoon.

Ancient Egypt

A 5000-year-old Egyptian palette from Hierakonpolis has been found that depicts a fox playing a flute, accompanying a dancing ibex and a giraffe. Egyptian flutes predating the pharaonic dynasties were made of cane or metal. Known as *m'ats*, and dating back to at least 2000 BC, they were 90–100cm/36–39in long. These early forms of flute had from two to six finger-holes and were played by being blown across the sharp top end of the tube. A descendant of the *m'at*, known as the *n'ay*, is still played today in some Islamic countries.

Early transverse flute

The transverse flute has been known in Etruria and Greece since at least the 4th century BC, since it is found depicted on Etruscan tombs and urns of that period as well as in contemporary Greek art. An early reference to the instrument and its method of playing appears in Apuleius's *Metamorphosis*, written in the 2nd century AD, which describes "tibia players who have their oblique instruments extended towards the right ear".

Western Europe

The earliest unambiguous reference to the use of the transverse flute in western Europe occurs in the mid 12th-century *Hortus deliciarum* of the Abbess Herrad of Landsberg. During the 14th century the flute spread to most parts of Europe, especially Spain, France and Flanders. The first extant

ABOVE: This painting by Dirck de Quade van Ravesteyn (c.1612) shows a woman playing a keyless cylindrical flute.

written reference to the instrument in England – "… and many flowte and lyltyng horn …" – appears in Chaucer's *House of Fame*, written from 1378–80.

Although the main material used for making flutes was boxwood, some were made of other materials such as silver, and it is possible that the *flute traversaine* mentioned in the inventory of the Duke of Anjou's property in 1360 was made of this metal rather than wood. Henry VIII had three flutes made of glass, a material that was still being used by certain French makers in the early 1800s.

As international trade grew in the 19th century, flutes began to be made of harder woods, such as South American granadilla, pallisando or rosewood, and ebony from Africa. From the 1840s artificial materials were sometimes used, such as ebonite, a substance that is still popular today for instruments intended for beginners and schoolchildren. Wood is now rarely used, as silver and even denser metals, such as gold or platinum alloys, are considered to enable the player to produce a more expressive tone.

ABOVE: *The newly fashionable one-keyed Baroque flute became a firm favourite with both professionals and amateurs, so much so that it was fashioned in the form of walking sticks. In mid 18th-century Dublin these were referred to as* German Canes. *Twenty years later Parisians were still able to buy* flûtes en forme de canne.

ABOVE: *This 1759 portrait by Gainsborough shows William Wollaston holding a one-keyed four-sectioned flute.*

ABOVE: *A depiction of a transverse flute of the early 18th century.*

The flute in the orchestra

The transverse flute is believed to have been used for the first time in the orchestra in 1681, in one of Lully's ballets for the French court. By 1691 the flute had entered the French Royal Chapel band, and over the next 50 years, coupled with the advent of public concerts in France, Germany and England, it became an indispensable member of the orchestra.

In 1702 Michel de la Barre gave the world his *Pièces pour la flûte traversière avec la basse-continue* – the first music for solo flute ever published. In 1717 the instrument received a seal of approval when J. S. Bach scored specifically for the *flauto traverso*. Hitherto he had preferred the recorder, whose dulcet tones compared favourably with the shrill sound of the flute. As well as Bach, Handel was also a prolific composer for the instrument. Handel's set of 12 *Sonates pour une traversière, un violon ou hautbois avec basse-continue* (1730) still occupies a central place in the repertoire of many modern flautists. By the end of the 18th century the position of the transverse flute was secure, and it had completely replaced the recorder in the orchestra.

Boehm flute

Always a difficult instrument to master, many people have tried to improve the mechanics of the flute. One of its more important modifiers was Theobald Boehm (1794–1881), a flautist from Munich, who in the 1830s introduced a large-holed instrument that overcame the acoustic deficiencies inherent in earlier flutes. Boehm's changes were revolutionary inasmuch as they changed the hitherto closed keys into open keys controlled by rings. By 1847 he had increased the size of the tone-holes so much that they had to be closed by padded covers, worked by keys that both operated independently and interacted with others, and it is this type of flute that is played today.

ABOVE: *The flute section of a youth band.*

BELOW: *The alto flute, a fourth lower than the concert flute, was invented by Theobald Boehm in the 1890s. It is a larger version of the standard flute, measuring 87cm/34in, and is specially adapted to allow the player to reach the more widely spaced holes.*

The alto flute was said to be Boehm's favourite instrument due to its distinctive "song style"; it produces an unmistakable, full tone with a haunting sound in all registers, and is used to beautiful effect in three famous works composed between 1912 and 1916: Ravel's Daphnis et Chloé *(1912), Stravinsky's* The Rite of Spring *(1913) and Holst's* The Planets *(1916). More recently, the alto flute has been used in Britten's works for the stage, in compositions by Boulez and Stockhausen, and in music composed for television.*

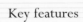

Key features

TYPE: woodwind

PITCH: C

NOTABLE PLAYERS OF THE FLUTE: Charles Nicholson, William Kincaid, Severino Gazzelloni, Jean-Pierre Rampal, James Galway, Harvey Sollberger.

LEFT: *The bass flute is pitched an octave below the flute. Its tubing is 130cm/51in long, and it is bent back on itself near the mouthpiece to make it more manageable.*

Fife

Smaller than the flute, the fife has a narrower bore and hence a louder and shriller sound. Played to accompany marching and for giving signals during battle, the fife was used in the British army until the 1890s. Fife and drum corps continue to thrive in the United States, performing early American martial music.

Alto and bass flutes

Pitched in G and a fourth lower than the concert flute, the alto flute was developed in the 1890s. It proved popular in France, where its slightly melancholic, haunting tone was used to the full by Ravel in *Daphnis et Chloé* (1912) and by Stravinsky in *The Rite of Spring* (1913). The bass — or double bass — flute in C, pitched an octave below the standard flute, is now rarely found.

Piccolo

Pitched in C and an octave higher than and half the size of the concert flute, the piccolo evolved early in the 19th century. One of the first composers to write regularly for the piccolo was Beethoven, who used it in his Fifth and Sixth Symphonies.

BELOW: *The piccolo is pitched an octave higher than the flute. Perhaps the first composer to use the piccolo to its full potential was Tchaikovsky.*

RIGHT: *The well-known 1866 painting by Edouard Manet, entitled* Le Fifre *("The Piper").*

Recorder

*Did buy a recorder, which I do intend to learn to play on, the sound
of it being, of all sounds in the world, most pleasing to me.*

SAMUEL PEPYS (1633–1703)

The recorder is a relatively simple instrument and can be traced back about a thousand years, for what looks like a duct flute with a tapering bore appears in an 11th-century French miniature. It is possible, therefore, that the Normans introduced the instrument to England, the only country, incidentally, where the instrument is called a "recorder" – mainland Europe preferring such terms as *flûte à bec* or *Schnabelflöte*. In England the name goes back to at least 1388, when the recorder is mentioned in the household accounts of the Earl of Derby, who later became Henry IV.

The recorder is relatively simple to play and was one of the most popular instruments of European Renaissance and Baroque music. A type of whistle flute with a wide tapering bore, it was originally made of a single piece of boxwood or ivory with a beaked mouthpiece. French 17th-century makers improved its construction,

*ABOVE,
FROM LEFT
TO RIGHT:
Three modern recorders
of varying pitches —
tenor, treble and descant.*

making it in three sections. Twentieth-century examples are made from many kinds of wood, or from plastic.

Early types of recorder

Until 1470, the recorder had six equidistant finger-holes and a thumb-hole. In Italy, in or about that year, an extra hole was added. Although Italian recorders continued to be built with a wide bore, in northern countries it was somewhat narrower. The two types can be clearly seen in two pictures: Caravaggio's *Lute Player* includes a wide-bore instrument in the composition, while Dürer's *The Men's*

Bath depicts a recorder with an extremely narrow bore. Another early illustration of the instrument is a woodcut of four recorders published in Sebastian Virdung's *Musica getutscht und ausgezogen* in 1511. The earliest known extant recorder was found under a 15th-century house in Dordrecht, and is presumed to be at least as old as the house.

The Renaissance recorder was built for playing in consort rather than as a solo instrument. Henry VIII was a recorder player and had many cased sets of between four and nine instruments. These would have been made together and tuned to match each other. Samuel Pepys and his wife

*ABOVE: During the 16th and 17th
centuries recorders were played in consorts
of various sizes. This picture shows the very
large, bassoon-like bass recorder.*

Recorder music

The renewed popularity
of the recorder in the
20th century led
composers such as Benjamin
Britten (*Noyes Fludde* and
A Midsummer Night's Dream)
and Hans Ulrich Staeps
(*Sieben Flötentänze*) to score
for the instrument.

ABOVE, FROM LEFT TO RIGHT: A selection of recorder-type instruments — one-keyed flute, bass recorder, double flageolet and boxwood recorder.

both played the flageolet, but he heard the recorder played at the theatre in 1668 and thought it superior.

In late 16th-century Germany recorder-like instruments, turned on a lathe, were known as *Kolomen*, while in France, by the mid 18th century, the recorder was known as the *flûte à neuf trous*. The ninth hole to which this name refers was an alternative hole for the little finger used by left-handed players of the one-piece instrument; the unused hole on the other side was sealed with a plug of wood or wax.

The recorder in the orchestra

By the 16th century recorders were being made in five different sizes: descant, treble, tenor, bass and contrabass, the latter between 2.5m/8ft and 2.8m/9ft long. In the 16th and 17th centuries they were widely played by groups of amateurs, but by the 18th century the recorder

had become an established part of the orchestra, and both Bach and Handel scored for it, the latter writing a number of sonatas for the *flûte à bec*. Around 1750, however, the recorder — which was known in France as the *flûte d'Angleterre* — was being discarded in favour of the transverse flute, which offered a greater dynamic range and better pitch control. By the 1790s the recorder had totally disappeared from the orchestra.

Twentieth-century revival

Were it not for the revival of interest by Arnold Dolmetsch (1858–1940), the recorder might now be only a museum piece. Dolmetsch pioneered the reconstruction of obsolete instruments, realizing that without them the music that had been written for them could not be heard. He made his first recorder in 1919, and presented a consort of four in a performance in 1926. His son Carl, a recorder virtuoso, made further

improvements that enabled the recorder to play effectively with a modern string orchestra.

The renewed popularity of the instrument led to the development of cheap plastic recorders which are particularly useful in schools, where the recorder is often the first musical instrument taught to children. It was first introduced into schools in the 1930s. In this way, the modern recorder has become widespread in most of Europe and the United States.

> Key features
>
>
>
> **TYPE:** aerophone woodwind
>
> **PITCH:** C or F
>
> **NOTABLE PLAYERS OF THE RECORDER:** Franz Brüggen, Rudolf Barthel, Amico Dolci, David Munrow.

RIGHT: Recorders were originally made from one piece of boxwood or ivory, rather than the three-piece instruments common today. Here we see a one-keyed flute and a boxwood recorder.

LEFT: The bass recorder, unlike its smaller counterparts, is blown via a curved metal mouthpiece called a crook. The bass recorder's sound is deep and resonating.

LEFT: This 17th-century German columnar alto recorder bears the device of two trefoils, with the stems curving to the right beneath the upper grill and on the base.

Oboe

The inimitable, charming sweet tone of the oboe.

JOHN BANISTER (1630–79)

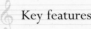

LEFT: The oboe's broad, sweet, plaintive and melancholic tone — which blends in so well with the violins — is an unmistakable feature of the modern symphony orchestra.

The English word "oboe" is a phonetic rendering of the French *hautbois*, meaning "high wood", which refers to the instrument's tone. It is not known who actually invented the oboe, but it was being played in Paris by 1670 and within ten years had spread to other European cities. It was developed as a woodwind instrument that could provide a tone quality suitable for indoor music, as opposed to the shrill sound of the shawm, which was regarded as fit only for open-air performances. Prototype oboes had two keys, and were first played in the band of Louis XIV's *Grande écurie* in 1657. One of the first compositions actually to specify a line for the oboe was Robert Cambert's opera *Pomone* (1671).

The oboe differed from the shawm in that whereas the latter was a one-piece instrument, the oboe was made in three sections connected by tenon-and-socket joints. The oboe's musical superiority over the shawm was assisted by the abolition of the pirouette, the turned wooden component into which the double reed was inserted. Instead, the reed was mounted on a staple clear of the body, facilitating a more delicate control of the reed between the lips. A greater compass was also attained by altering the size and disposition of the finger-holes to allow for a fully chromatic system of fork or cross fingerings through two octaves.

The oboe reached England in 1674, when a band of French musicians was brought over for a performance of John Crowne's masque *Calisto*. One of these instrumentalists was James Paisible (died 1721), who remained in London, entered the king's service, and became the first professional oboist in

Key features

TYPE: double-reed woodwind

PITCH: C

NOTABLE PLAYERS OF THE OBOE: Jacques Hotteterre, Giuseppe Sammartini, Johann Christian Fischer, Leon Goossens, Pierre Pierlot, Heinz Holliger.

England. The oboe soon became popular, and by 1695 the first printed tutor for the two-keyed oboe was published. One of the first to score for it was Henry Purcell (1659–95), who used it in all his larger works, including at least three obbligato parts for solo oboe.

The Horse Grenadiers adopted the instrument in 1678, and by the early 18th century almost every European band and orchestra included a pair of oboes. By the 1750s, players had begun to hold the instrument with the left hand above the right, as is standard today.

Nineteenth-century oboe

During the 19th century the original two keys were increased to eight and a speaker, or octave, key was introduced. This small aperture, which was placed above the finger-holes, greatly facilitated over-blowing, thereby giving the

ABOVE: An early 18th-century oboe as depicted by Johann Weigel.

instrument a wider compass. The two-keyed model was still being made up to the 1820s, with the four-keyed variety becoming popular in the 1830s. At about this time, the French makers began to develop the instrument in ways that differed from the simpler German and Austrian construction.

Frédéric Triébert

The most celebrated of the French oboe makers was Frédéric Triébert (1813–78). His contributions to the development of the oboe included narrowing the instrument's bore, resulting in a much more refined tone. The reed was made narrower and thinner, and the position and size of the finger-holes changed. The firm

Oboe music

An obbligato part for the oboe appears in Purcell's *Come Ye Sons of Art* (1694), and during the 18th century it became a leading solo instrument, featuring in concertos by Vivaldi and Albinoni. It was used extensively by Bach and Handel, and was particularly well understood by Mozart, who wrote an Oboe Concerto in C (K314). It was not prominent as a solo instrument in the 19th century, but in the 20th century oboe soloists came into their own with concertos by Richard Strauss, Ralph Vaughan Williams, Gustav Holst and many others. One of the major composers for the oboe is the player Heinz Holliger, whose *Siebengesang* of 1966 has an elaborate oboe part.

ABOVE: A present-day oboe player.

LEFT: The algaita *is a type of oboe played in West Africa, made from a single piece of wood covered in leather. The player presses his lips to the disc and uses his cheeks as an air reservoir so that the instrument can be blown continuously.*

of Triébert introduced both the "thumb-plate" and "Conservatoire" systems, which are still in use on modern instruments. After Triébert's death, his erstwhile foreman François Lorée continued to experiment with the instrument, developing a complicated key system known as the "plateau". Today, at least four systems of keywork are in use on the oboe.

RIGHT: The oboe is the principal instrument of the orchestra's woodwind section.

Cor anglais

The cor anglais or English horn, the tenor version of the oboe, is a misnomer, for it is neither English nor a horn, and the origin of its name is a mystery. Played with a curved brass crook that carries the reed, the fingering and keywork of the cor anglais are the same as that for the

ABOVE: The cor anglais is used only in certain passages of music. This player has his oboe by his side, ready to be taken up when the music no longer calls for the cor anglais, or tenor instrument.

RIGHT: The straight cor anglais that is played today is based on Henri Brod's model of 1839. The origin of the name is unknown, but it is known that Haydn referred to the instrument as the cor anglé ("bent horn").

oboe. The cor anglais of the mid 18th century was usually curved to a crescent or bent at an angle and covered in black leather. As the holes were of necessity farther apart than those on the conventional oboe, the curve or bend made the instrument both easier to hold and to play. The straight cor anglais that is familiar today, with its characteristic globular bell, is based on Henri Brod's *cor anglais moderne* of 1839. Brod got around the problem of reaching the widely spaced finger-holes by introducing keys with long levers.

Although the cor anglais was mainly used in French military music, both

Bach and Purcell included the instrument in their orchestral scores, as have various later composers.

Oboe d'amore

A close relation to the cor anglais is the oboe d'amore, pitched in A. Known since about 1720, the distinctive feature of the oboe d'amore is the bulbous end joint that modifies the timbre by allowing the air to expand before it is forced through a smaller aperture. It was used by J. S. Bach in his *St John Passion* (1723) and about 60 other works, in order to achieve low notes then outside the oboe's range and also because it could cope with sharp keys. Due to the difficulties of playing it in tune, the oboe d'amore did not survive much beyond the 1750s, but it was revived in 1854 when the Belgian instrument maker Victor Mahillon reconstructed one for a performance of one of Bach's works in Brussels. Since then it has rarely been used; the most notable 20th-century work requiring the oboe d'amore is Richard Strauss's *Symphonia domestica* (1904).

Baritone oboe

The earliest baritone oboe known, which was pitched one octave below the regular orchestral oboe, was that made by Charles

RIGHT: The baritone oboe.

ABOVE: The characteristic long curved brass crook that carries the reed of the cor anglais.

LEFT: The oboe d'amore, whose pitch falls between the oboe and the cor anglais, has a narrow bore and a bulbous end joint, resulting in a less strident tone.

experimentation, Heckel produced his heckelphone – however, it had taken him so long that Wagner had been dead for 20 years before the first one was produced.

Generically allied to the oboe and pitched at baritone range, the heckelphone was built in three sections, with a wide conical bore and bulbous bell, the large diameter of the instrument calling for a powerful double reed like that of a bassoon, which is carried on a curved crook. In 1905 Richard Strauss wrote an important part for the heckelphone in *Salome*, and since then its deep and powerful tone has been used freely as a substitute for the bass oboe.

RIGHT: This three-keyed fruitwood oboe with fishtail brass keys and trapezoidal covers was made by Andreas Kenisgperger.

Bizet in the 1740s, which now resides in the Paris Conservatoire de Musique. Bizet solved the problem of the excessive length of tubing by doubling the bore on itself and carrying the mouthpiece on a crook. He was also able to reduce the distance between the adjacent finger-holes by boring them obliquely through thickenings in the tube wall. Although Delius scored parts for the baritone oboe, today it is virtually a museum piece.

Heckelphone

In 1884 Richard Wagner asked the maker Wilhelm Heckel of Biebrich for a baritone double-reed instrument that would combine the character of the oboe with the soft but powerful tone of the alphorn. After much

ABOVE: The oboe section of the London Symphony Orchestra.

Clarinet

The many-keyed clarinet, which can sound so ghostly in the deep chalumeau register but higher up can gleam in silvery blossoming harmony.

THOMAS MANN (1875–1955), "DR FAUSTUS"

The clarinet was invented in the first few years of the 18th century by the renowned woodwind maker Johann Christoph Denner (1655–1707), or his son Jakob (1681–1785) of Nuremberg. It was the first reed-blown instrument to have a cylindrical rather than a conical bore. Denner's main achievement was in his practical use of the way that the scale of fundamentals could be made to sound a twelfth higher if a vent hole were pierced at the upper end of a cylinder. This hole was covered by what is now known as the speaker key.

Made of boxwood, the first clarinets were pitched in C and had six finger-holes and two keys. A third key was soon added to extend the range down a semitone and, more importantly, to make possible the playing of the "missing" *b'* at the break – even today,

ABOVE: The first mention of the clarinet was in an advertisement by the Amsterdam publishers Roger & Le Cene in 1706.

amateur clarinettists still find this note difficult to produce. The body was divided into three sections, a feature that allowed the use of interchangeable joints of varying length to facilitate playing in different keys.

The first clarinets were played with a reed about 15mm/⅝in wide, tied to the mouthpiece with twine – the barrel of the modern instrument did not appear until the 1760s. At first it was common practice to play with the reed uppermost against the top lip. The modern style of placing it on the lower lip was adopted by the Paris Conservatoire in 1831, but did not become universal for many years.

Around 1750, when the fourth (A flat and E flat) and fifth (F sharp and C sharp) keys were added and the foot joint expanded into a bell, the clarinet became more accepted into the orchestra, having previously been used chiefly as a solo instrument, but it did not become firmly established until the mid 19th century. For a time it looked

as if it might replace the oboe and, although the latter has retained its position in the symphony orchestra, the clarinet has succeeded in ousting it from military bands.

In 1790 a sixth key, invented by Jean Lefèvre, was added to give an additional C sharp and G sharp, and the pear-shaped barrel disappeared. In spite of these improvements the instrument was still beset with problems of fingering and intonation, and for these reasons clarinets were built at different pitches. Although the "type" instrument was in C, there was also a B flat clarinet for playing in flat keys and A, B and D models that could be used for sharp keys.

Modern clarinet

In 1809 Iwan Müller (1786–1854), one of the finest clarinettists of his day, brought out the prototype of his 13-keyed model pitched in B flat, which was to become the standard instrument for the next hundred years.

ABOVE: A 19th-century two-keyed clarinet.

Key features

TYPE: single-reed woodwind

PITCH: B flat or E flat

NOTABLE PLAYERS OF THE CLARINET: Anton and Johann Stadler, Heinrich Baermann, Benny Goodman, Frederick Thurston, Gervase de Peyer, Woody Herman, Jack Brymer, Alan Hacker.

In 1817 its development was refined when Müller, who was the first to use pads over the countersunk tone-holes, invented the metal ligature. His tutor was published in 1826, and dedicated to George IV. As an instrumentalist Müller performed all over Europe, his style being described as brilliant and expressive.

The final major modification of the clarinet occurred between 1839 and 1843 when the clarinettist Hyacinthe

ABOVE: *A monk playing an 18th-century two-keyed clarinet.*

Eleonore Klosé collaborated with the maker Louis-August Buffet to simplify the fingering system, using the ring-keys Boehm had developed for his flutes.

Chalumeau
The clarinet was a modification of the chalumeau, a small woodwind instrument with seven holes. Chalumeaux were difficult to play and

LEFT: *The bass clarinet has a compass from D to f". To accommodate its length and make it easier to play, it has a curved bell and has its reed mounted on a curved crook.*

were never popular. Not only was it difficult to obtain the correct embouchure (lip technique), but they were restricted to a range of just over an octave. The sound of the chalumeau was also not to the liking of all, the Hamburg musician Johann Mattheson (1681–1764) describing the instrument's tone as a "dreadful evening symphony". The lower register of the clarinet is known as the chalumeau register.

Bass clarinet
The first bass clarinet was made in 1772 when Giles Lot of Paris produced one with a range of three and a half octaves. In 1793 Carl August Grenser of Dresden presented his *Klarinettenbass*, an instrument built in the form of a bassoon with nine keys. Various other attempts followed, but were all made redundant by Adolphe Sax's bass clarinet of 1838, which resembled a saxophone, with both bell and mouthpiece bent back. Although it has not always been part of the standard woodwind section, many works call for it, including Wagner's *Ring* and Franck's Symphony in D minor.

ABOVE: *Hand positions on the bass clarinet.*

🎼 Clarinet music

One of the first composers to write for the clarinet was Jean-Philippe Rameau (1683–1764), who scored for it in *Zoroastre* (1749). Its inclusion in the Mannheim orchestra established it as an orchestral instrument, and as such it was used by Mozart, who also wrote three important works for the clarinettist Anton Stadler: the *Kegelstaff Trio* (K498), the Clarinet Quintet (K581) and the Clarinet Concerto (K622). With the improvements to the clarinet that were made in the early 19th century, composers such as Carl Maria von Weber (1786–1826) and Louis Spohr (1784–1851) began to write solos for it. One of the great works of the 20th century that features the clarinet is George Gershwin's (1898–1937) famous symphonic jazz poem, *Rhapsody in Blue*. This original work was written in 1923 in the unbelievably short space of ten days.

Saxophone

The saxophone is the embodied spirit of beer.

ARNOLD BENNETT (1867–1931)

The saxophone is characterized by a fairly wide body made from a conical tube of thin metal, commonly brass, which is expanded at the open end with a small flare. It has 18–21 tone-holes of graduated size, all of which are controlled by keys. At the mouthpiece end are two speaker keys that enable the instrument to over-blow at the octave. The mouthpiece, which is fitted with a single reed, was originally made of wood, but is now commonly of ebonite or sometimes brass.

The saxophone was patented in 1846 by Adolphe Sax (1814–94). Although Sax's combination of a single bleating reed with a conical body was not entirely new, the saxophone was the first successful instrument of this type. The idea had first been used by William Meikle, a Scotsman who in about 1825 had produced a now virtually forgotten "alto fagotto", a modified small bassoon played with a clarinet mouthpiece.

LEFT: The alto saxophone was invented in 1846 by Adolphe Sax as an attempt to introduce a more powerful group of instruments into military bands to form a link between the clarinets and tenor brasses.

The saxophone family consists of the sopranino in E flat, soprano in B flat, alto in E flat, tenor in B flat, baritone in E flat and bass in B flat. Larger saxophones are made more manageable by introducing a U-bend and tilting the bell slightly forward. From the baritone size downwards, the tubing is doubled by being folded at the upper end.

At the beginning of the 21st century many new models, with only minor differences, are still being brought out yearly. One more radical development was the plastic saxophone, in which all

but the keys and mountings are moulded from synthetic materials, but this instrument has not been enthusiastically adopted by players.

Rise in popularity

Since its introduction into French infantry music, the saxophone has steadily gained favour in military bands. Bands such as Jullien's, which introduced the instrument to England in 1850, did much to make the instrument familiar to concert audiences, as did Sousa's band half a century later in America. The saxophone, which became established as a regular member of British military bands in the 1920s, is now also an

ABOVE: One of the most important roles for the saxophone has been in jazz.

Key features

TYPE: single-reed woodwind

PITCH: B flat or E flat

NOTABLE PLAYERS OF THE SAXOPHONE: Sidney Bechet, Marcel Mule, Johnny Hodges, Coleman Hawkins, Lester Young, Charlie Parker, John Coltrane, Stan Getz.

ABOVE: One of the finest exponents of the alto sax was Charlie Parker (1920–55), whose astounding technique meant that he was idolized by jazz fans everywhere.

ABOVE: The saxophone's popularity has spread all over the world. Here a Tanzanian musician is entertaining his audience.

established part of the modern symphony orchestra. The alto instrument was the first to be so used, but Richard Strauss's *Symphonia domestica* (1902) called for a saxophone quartet.

Jazz saxophone

Since World War I the saxophone has become extremely popular in music of all kinds, and is now one of the most common wind instruments. Its playing

RIGHT: The B flat soprano saxophone.

technique is regarded as fairly simple compared with other reed instruments. Since the 1930s it has played a leading role in jazz bands, and it is in this medium that the instrument's potential has been most thoroughly exploited. Although today's jazz musicians mainly use B flat tenor

and E flat alto saxophones, between the 1930s and '60s, saxophone consorts of the four main types featured strongly in big bands, such as those led by Glenn Miller and Duke Ellington in the United States, Henry Hall in England and Bert Kaempfert and James Last in Germany.

ABOVE: The most commonly used saxophone is the tenor. This musician is playing for passengers boarding a Mississippi river boat.

Bassoon

The wedding guest here beat his breast,
For he heard the loud bassoon.

O ften described as the clown of the orchestra, the bassoon is the bass of the woodwind section. As well as solo work, the bassoon adds colour to the orchestra, as it blends in well with all the other instruments.

In France the word "bassoon" came into use in 1613 to denote the double or bass curtal. Over the next 25 years it was transformed into the separately jointed instrument that is known today as the bassoon. First provided with three swallow-tailed keys – two for the thumbs and one for the little finger – by the mid 17th century the bassoon was being made in four separate sections: the butt, wing, bass and bell. Pitched in C, and made of maple or pearwood, it formed a continuously expanding tube of 2.4m/8ft, which

LEFT: The bassoon has a compass of about three and a half octaves. The tube, which is usually made of maple, is doubled.

ABOVE:
Pitched an octave below the bassoon, the contrabassoon has a metal bell as its last section.

was doubled to make it manageable. By 1730 a fourth key had been added, and by 1800 six were common.

During the 19th century many more improvements were made to the bassoon. One of the more notable modifiers of the instrument was Charles-Joseph Sax (1791–1865), who by 1825 had introduced covered tone-

holes. Sax continued his work and in 1851, with his son Adolphe, brought out a 23-keyed metal bassoon.

Another important figure in the history of the bassoon is Carl Almenraeder (1786–1843). A performer, teacher, bandmaster and composer, in 1825 he published a treatise in which he described how, by adding certain keys and relocating others, not only could the intonation be improved, but playing in all keys could be facilitated. By 1831 he had founded his own factory in Biebrich, near Wiesbaden, where by increasing the number of keys to 15 he was able to extend the bassoon's compass to nearly four octaves. On Almenraeder's death, his partner Johann Heckel (1812–77) continued to refine the instrument, which by 1843 had 18 keys and a chromatic range of over four octaves. Successive members of the Heckel

ABOVE: The bassoon is the bass member of the woodwind section of the orchestra, with the contrabassoon, supported on a spike, playing the lowest notes.

Key features

TYPE: double-reed
woodwind

PITCH: C

NOTABLE PLAYERS OF THE BASSOON: Paolo Besozzi, Felix Rheiner, Georg Wenzel Ritter, James Mackintosh, Archie Camden, Simon Kovar.

family carried out many reforms to the bassoon, launching a famous model in the 1870s, and it is through their efforts that the instrument reached its present degree of perfection. French and Italian players tend to prefer an alternative French design by Buffet-Crampon, made in rosewood.

Music for the bassoon

An outstanding work in the bassoon's solo repertoire is Mozart's Concerto in B flat (K191) of 1774, and many chamber works for bassoon and strings were written around 1800. Hummel and Weber wrote bassoon concertos; Paganini wrote a Concertino for Bassoon and Horn. The bassoon achieved greater prominence in the 20th century, with solo works such as Elgar's *Romance* (1909) and orchestral

ABOVE: The bassoon player of the orchestra of the Paris opera in 1868.

RIGHT:
To encourage children to take up the bassoon, small faggottini *have been made. This one is seen side by side with a full-size instrument.*

parts like the opening of Stravinsky's *The Rite of Spring* (1913). Shorter compositions for the bassoon in the 20th century have often been given picturesque titles, such as Granville Bantock's *Dance of the Witches*, Gilbert Vinter's *The Playful Pachyderm* and André Bloch's *Dancing Jack*.

Curtal

In the 16th century the need for instruments of a bass register for use with choirs led to the creation of the curtal or dulcian, the immediate predecessor of the modern bassoon. More manageable than the bass shawm because of its doubled tube, the curtal

was named after a short-barrelled cannon of "curtailed" length. By 1600 curtals were being played over much of Europe, from Spain and Italy to Germany and England. Small high-pitched models were particularly popular in Austria and Spain, where they were often played in church ensembles. Court bands also included curtals, and composers such as Giovanni Gabrieli (1555–1612) began writing separate parts for them.

Curtals were made in one of two different ways. The more usual method was to bore two channels, connected to each other by a U-bend at the lower ends, into a single block of wood. The other method was to hollow out two sections of wood, then glue them together. In each case, the finished instrument was covered with leather. A slightly flared bell was fitted to the terminal end of the bore, while a short crook with a double reed was attached to the proximal end.

ABOVE: Known since at least 1559, the curtal was less strident in tone than the shawm and as such was often dubbed the dulcian. This replica was made in 1971.

Horn

The horn is perhaps the least efficient instrument of the brass family,
but it produces the most beautiful sound of all.

BARRY TUCKWELL (BORN 1931)

The horn is unique among orchestral instruments, not only in that the keys are operated with the left hand, but because it is also played backwards, with the bell facing towards the rear of the orchestra. It is the most expressive brass instrument in the orchestra, and also the most difficult to play. The normal position for the right hand is with all fingers close together against the far side of the bell and with the thumb close against them. The hand is cupped and can be straightened to sharpen various harmonics, while increased cupping of the hand flattens the harmonics.

LEFT: The learner needs a good ear, for the horn has the longest series of harmonics of any brass instrument, the number depending on the skill and lip strength of the player, who must also learn the varying degrees of hand-stopping.

Although still popularly referred to as the French horn, most horns played in orchestras today are in reality the wider bore German horn. Both, however, evolved from the long, coiled *cor de chasse* of the French hunt, and by 1900 had come to resemble the modern instrument closely. F had become the standard pitch and rotary valves were the norm.

Animal horn

The first horns were, as the name implies, made from animal horns. In Africa they were made principally from the horns of antelopes, cattle horns being a poor substitute. One of the oldest types of horn is the Jewish *shofar*, or ram's horn. Made from a ritually killed sheep or goat, the *shofar* is the only musical instrument that has survived into the 20th century in the same form it had in antiquity. The small end of the horn is pierced with a long narrow passage that connects the proximal end with the main cavity of

the bore. Two pitches are possible, and are often, but not always, a fifth apart. The *shofar's* use as a martial instrument is documented in the story of the capture of Jericho, when its powerful sound is said to have caused the city walls to fall down. It is still used today in Jewish religious ceremonies such as Rosh Hashanah (the Jewish New Year) and Yom Kippur (the day of atonement).

Hunting horn and post-horn

The horn has been a part of European hunting life since Saxon times. By the 17th century there were two types: in Germany the preference was for a curved shape, while the English hunt

ABOVE: Some horns had the tube coiled several times. This 19th-century painting shows two brothers playing horn and drum.

Key features

TYPE: brass aerophone

PITCH: F

NOTABLE PLAYERS OF THE HORN: Denis Brain, Barry Tuckwell.

ABOVE: *The* shofar *is an early type of horn still used today to mark the Jewish occasions of Rosh Hodesh (the first day of the month) and Rosh Hashanah (the New Year).*

ABOVE: *Before valves were introduced, horns were very simple instruments consisting solely of a coiled tube and a large bell into which the hand was inserted.*

preferred a straight horn, which could give a more penetrating call. When postal services began to operate in the 15th century, the courier would announce his arrival and impending departure by a distinctive call on a small brass horn.

From crooks to valves

The main problem of the early horns was that, without hand-stopping, they could play only one set of harmonics. One solution, put forward in about 1750 by the Dresden instrument maker Johann Werner, was the slide crook. As each crook was a separate coil of tubing of the correct length for each tonality, by fitting on the appropriate crook the horn could be played in all keys. Useful as this was,

the drawback was that the player had to carry a full set of up to 13 crooks, one for each key, which they had to fit as and when required. Composers allowed for this and, when the music modulated, they gave time for the horn players to change coils before they made their first entry in the new key.

In 1815 the invention of the valve revolutionized the playing of the horn. With the two valves with which the horn was originally fitted, only two extra crooks were now needed. At this time composers wrote for specific orchestras, and it is said that Beethoven wrote the horn solo in the slow movement of his Ninth Symphony for the fourth horn player in the orchestra, as he was the only one playing an instrument with valves.

Double horn

One of the perennial problems for horn players is hitting the wrong note in the high harmonics, where they lie close together. To address this problem in 1898 Fritz Krupse of Erfurt

ABOVE: *The double horn enables the player to change the pitch from F to B flat by depressing an extra valve.*

RIGHT: *An 18th-century German post-horn made in three coils of tubing.*

designed a double horn. As its name implies, this is two horns in one, each with its own set of valves but sharing the same mouthpiece and bell. It is pitched in F and B flat, the playing choosing his pitch by depressing an extra valve. The advantage of the double horn was that the twelfth harmonic in F became the ninth in B flat and was, therefore, much safer to play.

🎼 Horn music

Mozart wrote four horn concertos, which is all the more remarkable when it is remembered that in his time the horn did not have valves and that pitch depended solely on hand-stopping. Another composer who used the horn to full effect was Richard Strauss. Hindemith and Tippett both wrote sonatas for four horns, and Thea Musgrave wrote a Horn Concerto in 1971. The most ambitious of all works for the post-horn is the popular *Post-horn Galop*, which was composed in 1844 by Koenig, the principal cornettist in the famed Jullien military band.

Trumpet

The quality of tone of the trumpet is noble and brilliant.

HECTOR BERLIOZ (1803–69)

The trumpet has a narrow, mainly cylindrical bore and is lip-vibrated. Forms of the instrument are found all over the world, and with rare exceptions they have traditionally been played by men. They have often been associated with magic and ritual, and with official or military ceremonies.

ABOVE: The Greeks compared the sound of the trumpet to that of an elephant, and elephants are still said to "trumpet".

Egypt and Israel

The ancient Egyptians used metal trumpets 50–60cm/20–24in long and made of silver or bronze; they were sacred and were played only in the worship of Osiris. On their return from exile in Egypt, the Israelites adopted the Egyptian trumpet. It became part of the insignia of the Hebrew priests, who used pairs of silver trumpets to be played in certain rites of the temple.

Etruria and Rome

A forerunner of both the trumpet and the alphorn, the Etruscan *lituus* evolved from a curved animal horn attached to a slender wooden cylindrical tube terminating in an upturned bell. The Romans modified the *lituus* by discarding the bulb bell, thus creating a straight wide-bore bronze trumpet about 1.2m/4ft long. This was known as the *tuba*, and was played with a long detachable conical mouthpiece. As well as being used in the civilian arena, this instrument was also played by the cavalry, who used it bent into two folds like a modern bugle, making it easier for a mounted man to play.

Post-classical trumpet

Early post-classical trumpets were made in the same form as the straight Roman instruments with detachable mouthpieces. They were held halfway down with the right hand, while the left hand held the mouthpiece. In the 11th century, the Spanish adopted the straight-tubed Arab *nafir*, which they called the *trompeta morisca*. The crusaders took over the Saracens'

ferocious *cor sarrazinois*, calling it a *buisine*, a term that is an etymological ancestor to *Posaune*, the modern German name for the trombone. The *buisine*, made of brass, copper or silver, terminated in a wide bell.

Medieval Europe

Such was the importance attached to the trumpet in early medieval Europe that the right of owning one was restricted to the aristocracy. Later, because of its noble associations, it became the instrument of the cavalry, a branch of the army that was originally formed from the nobility, where trumpets were used both to sound military signals and to help maintain morale. One such occasion

ABOVE: This 15th-century French miniature depicts the Bible story of the fall of Jericho. The event is signalled by the trumpets of Joshua, which had very long bores.

Key features

TYPE: brass aerophone

PITCH: B flat, C or D/E flat

NOTABLE PLAYERS OF THE TRUMPET: Giovanni Pellegrino Brandi, Valentine Snow, Louis Armstrong, Dizzy Gillespie, Miles Davis, Wynton Marsalis.

was the night before the Battle of Agincourt (1415), when the opposing armies were "serenaded by the continuous sound of the trumpets".

Trumpet players were attached to the more important European courts and, as the 14th century progressed, long trumpets appeared with banners displaying the seigneurial arms suspended from the bell to the boss. Such was the prestige of the instrument that, when Charles VI entered Reims in 1380, he was preceded by over 30 trumpeters.

Slide trumpet
It was when trumpets began to be played in ensembles with other instruments that problems of pitch

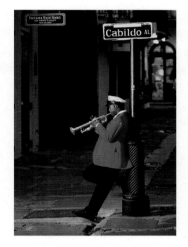

Trumpet music

Although by the 1560s trumpets were being played between acts in the theatre, they were not formally introduced into the opera band until Monteverdi scored for the instrument in *Orfeo* in 1607. By the mid 17th century they were becoming a regular part of the orchestra, used in works by Pietro Cavalli (1602–76) and Giovanni Legrenzi (1626–90). Purcell's *Dioclesian* (1690) used trumpet fanfares, while Alessandro Scarlatti (1660–1725) frequently included trumpets in his operas. The valved trumpet, developed in the 1820s, was introduced to the orchestra by Gioacchino Rossini (1792–1868), who used it to wonderful effect in *William Tell* in 1829.

arose. One solution was the slide trumpet, which not only allowed the trumpeter to adjust his pitch easily, but also gave him the first opportunity to play a chromatic scale on an instrument that was otherwise only playable in harmonics. The slide trumpet had an elongated mouthpiece, sometimes over 50cm/20in in length, that was held by the left hand, while the right hand drew the body of the instrument in and out like the slide of a trombone.

A variation on the slide trumpet was designed in the late 18th century by the English trumpeter John Hyde. Hyde's trumpet, in F, had a U-shaped slide that replaced the bend nearest the player and could be pulled out when needed and returned by a spring. Although not fully diatonic, the slide did allow the player to temper the 11th and 13th harmonics that were out of tune with the normal scale.

Keyed trumpet
The various attempts by instrument makers and players to improve the trumpet by altering the pitch with circular tuning bits and crooks only raised the pitch of the whole instrument, which still played only

LEFT: A trumpeter playing in the streets of New Orleans, Louisiana.

harmonics. There were several attempts during the 18th and early 19th centuries to create a trumpet that could play a chromatic scale.

One successful innovator was the Viennese instrument maker Joseph Felix Riedel, who made a 15-keyed trumpet to the plans of Anton Weidinger, a trumpeter at the Viennese court. Although the keyed trumpet became popular in Austrian and Italian military bands, it was soon overtaken by the valved trumpet, which began to appear in the 1820s.

Modern trumpet
Although most 19th-century trumpets were in F, military bands preferred E flat trumpets, while in the 1880s trumpets in A, B flat and C started to be produced. During the 19th century various special types of trumpet were made, such as the "Aida" trumpet and the "Bach" trumpet. Today, however, most trumpeters' instrument of choice – whether they are orchestral, jazz or pop musicians – is generally the B flat trumpet, although orchestral musicians occasionally use trumpets pitched in D.

ABOVE: A Ganter rotary valve B flat trumpet. This rotary valve trumpet has a hand protector on the tubing to protect the surface against wear while it is being held.

Trombone

The trombones are too sacred for frequent use.

FELIX MENDELSSOHN (1809–47)

The trombone, with its telescopic slide, is the most distinctive member of the orchestral brass section. Invented in the mid 15th century as an answer to the demands of late 14th and early 15th-century composers who were increasingly writing for low pitches, the first trombones were a development of the large S-shaped trumpets that were being built by Flemish makers for the Burgundian court. The instrument's first name was the *trompette-saicqueboute* – the "push-pull trumpet". Different countries abbreviated this descriptive name in various ways: in England it was called the sackbut (first recorded in 1470), in Italy the *trombone* and in Germany the *Posaune*.

These early instruments, which had a softer and mellower timbre than those in use today, were often used –

sometimes coupled with cornetts – as an accompaniment to a single voice, especially in Venetian churches.

Indeed, by the early 18th century the trombone was rarely heard outside ecclesiastical establishments. It did not become a conventional part of the orchestra until the late 18th century. The first classical composer to score for the trombone regularly was Beethoven, who used it for the first time in his Fifth Symphony in 1808.

ABOVE: A trombonist performing in a New Orleans jazz club.

Trombone variations

Although there have been various cosmetic modifications, the principle of the trombone's telescopic slide has remained virtually unchanged. By the 17th century trombones were being made in three sizes: alto in F, tenor in B flat and bass in E flat. During the 17th century various attempts were made to produce ever-larger trombones. One such, built in 1615 by Hans Schreiber, was twice as long as the tenor and consequently pitched an octave lower. Other contemporary contrabass trombones built in Germany include those of Isaac Ehe (1612) and Jan Brueghel (1620).

The double-slide trombone briefly appeared in Nuremberg in the early 17th century and re-emerged in France in the 19th century. Although the basic idea was admirable – to be able to obtain all seven positions with greater ease by diminishing by half the distance between positions – it was found

ABOVE: The trombone has seven slide positions; the farther out the slide, the lower the fundamental. The seventh position is like depressing all three trumpet valves.

BELOW, FROM LEFT TO RIGHT: Mutes for brass instruments come in a variety of sizes – trombone mute, French horn mute, trumpet mute, trumpet cup and piccolo trumpet mute.

ABOVE: *The trombone has a distinctive, large bell.*

LEFT: *Most trombonists today prefer B flat and F trombones. By depressing the thumb key, the length of tubing can be altered, minimizing slide action.*

to be impracticable as it proved impossible to make the tube airtight.

The valved trombone was first produced in Vienna in about 1818, and achieved its peak of popularity in the mid 19th century. It was, however, not able to compete with its slide counterpart, and by the end of the 20th century its use was restricted to Latin American, eastern European and Asian bands.

B flat and F trombones

The bass trombone, pitched in G, was so long that the slide had to be operated by a wooden handle.

Although it is still sometimes found in English brass bands, by the 1970s the G trombone had been virtually replaced by the B flat and F trombone, which was introduced as early as 1839 by the Leipzig maker C. F. Sattler. The F trombone consists of a B flat tenor instrument with an F attachment, made of about 1m/3ft of coiled tubing, and brought into play by a rotary valve operated by the player's left thumb.

Modern trombone

Today the trombone is made with one of three bores: France prefers

ABOVE: *The valved trombone has never been a widely popular instrument and today it is used more in novelty than serious music.*

a narrow bore, England a medium and the United States and Germany a wide bore. The wider the bore, the warmer and richer the sound. It is only necessary to compare the tone of a pre-World War II narrow bore "peashooter" with that of a modern B flat and F to appreciate the difference.

Key features

TYPE: brass aerophone
PITCH: B flat
NOTABLE PLAYERS OF THE TROMBONE: C. T. Queisser, F. A. Belcke, A. G. Dieppo, Glenn Miller, Tommy Dorsey, Albert Mangelsdorff, Christian Lindberg.

Bent Sørensen

The Danish composer Bent Sørensen (born 1958) wrote a trombone concerto for the Swedish virtuoso Christian Lindberg. The work is described as a "*pianissimo*" rather than a "roaring" concerto and is influenced, as is most of Sørensen's work, by his fascination with birds, bells and jazz. Another solo trombone composition by Sørensen is *The Bells of Vineta*, a piece that imagines the ringing bells of the church, threatened by coastal erosion, sinking into the sea.

Tuba

The tuba is certainly the most intestinal of instruments,
the very lower bowel of music.

PETER DE VRIES (BORN 1910)

The tuba is the bass of the orchestral brass section. English and German orchestras generally use a tuba in F, while those in Italy and the United States prefer the larger CC or BB flat types. In France, the instrument of choice is a very large bore six-valved tenor tuba in C, which was a development of the five-valved tuba used at the Paris Opera House between 1880 and 1892, and which Ravel included in his orchestration of Mussorgsky's *Pictures at an Exhibition* written in 1922.

The orchestral bass tuba was patented by Johann Gottfried Moritz in 1835, and Berlioz enthusiastically asked his publishers to substitute tubas for the ophicleides specified in the score of his *Symphonie fantastique* (1830). In 1832, A. G. Guichard of Paris brought out his newly invented three-valved *ophicleide à pistons* in E flat, and three years later Wilhelm Wieprecht, the bandmaster of the Prussian Dragoon Guards, introduced a five-valved bass tuba in F as a

RIGHT:
The E
flat tuba is
the bass brass
instrument.

Cerveny had began building tubas with rotary valves, a modification that soon became standard on Austrian and German instruments. In other countries, however, tuba players preferred to retain the piston valve.

Over the years, various large tubas have been produced, including Adolphe Sax's sub-bass in E flat and the sub-contrabass in B flat (1855). Among other giants was Cerveny's *Kaiserbässe*, which was 2.4m/8ft high and had a tube length of almost 13.7m/45ft.

Since World War II tuba players have improved their technique and steadily pushed the range upward. Another important influence is the rise in popularity — especially in the United States — of the brass quintet. Composers who have produced pieces for this ensemble

Key features

TYPE: brass aerophone

PITCH: F, E flat, B flat or C

NOTABLE PLAYERS OF THE TUBA: William Bell, Howard Johnson, Philip Catelinet, John Fletcher, Roger Bobo.

replacement for the bass trombone. It was not long before these early tubas had totally replaced the serpent, bass horn and ophicleide. Although today the word "tuba" refers only to the bass instrument, originally the name was applied equally to the whole range. In 1852, for instance, Schubert did not distinguish between the cornet, flugelhorn or tuba. The E flat tuba is still sometimes referred to as a "bombardon".

By the mid 19th century the Bohemian instrument maker Václav

ABOVE: Two well-worn rotary valve tubas being played in Ghana.

have treated the tuba as a tenor instrument and many write for it in the same way as for the cello.

The instrument that is known today as the B flat euphonium is really a tenor tuba and until the late 19th century it was uncommon to find anything bigger in orchestras. It was for this instrument that Holst wrote a part in *The Planets* (1916). The first true bass tubas were in F, as used in orchestras, or E flat, as used in brass bands. The BB flat, with its orchestral version in C, is now the normal brass and military band bass and was introduced into the orchestra by Wagner when he scored for a *Kontrabass* tuba in *The Ring* (1876).

Wagner tuba

Invented by Johann Moritz for use in Wagner's *Ring*, Wagner tubas were intended as a bass voice that is a cross between the horns, trumpets, trombones and bass tubas. Built in B flat and E flat with four valves, they were designed to be played by horn players; they have horn mouthpieces and are keyed using the left hand.

Helicon

As the large tubas were rather unwieldy, some builders designed

ABOVE: Two tuba players in a youth band.

them in circular form, resting the bell on the player's left shoulder with the tube passing under the left arm. Such instruments were known as helicons. The disadvantage was that due to the shape, much sound was lost when it was projected to one side. John Philip Sousa (1854–1933) modified the instrument by having the bell project forward over the player's shoulder and, through association, the instrument became widely known as the sousaphone. Today, sousaphones are often made with a fibreglass bell in an attempt to keep the weight down.

ABOVE: The euphonium is a tenor tuba and is mainly found in brass and military bands.

ABOVE: Sousaphones in a Chilean police band, showing the bells facing forwards.

Tuba music

Since World War II, composers of classical, jazz and avant-garde music have all used the unique character of the tuba, which was given a high profile in popular music with George Kleinsinger and Paul Tripp's *Tubby the Tuba* of 1948. Vaughan Williams's Tuba Concerto was written in 1955. Hindemith, Gordon Jacob, Alex Wilder and Malcolm Arnold have all written solo works, and Walter Hartley and Barney Childs have composed works for tuba ensembles.

ABOVE: An unusual view of the bell of a B flat euphonium.

BELOW, FROM LEFT TO RIGHT: These tuba and euphonium mutes are much larger than other brass mutes.

Early Valved Instruments

The two Ajax showing off with a swagger their double thorax
amid immense blasts from Sax's horns.

Jacques Offenbach (1819–80), "La Belle Hélène"

LEFT: *The cornet is the "violin" of the brass band, and a virtuoso player can truly make the instrument sing.*

The invention of the valve at the beginning of the 19th century transformed the design of brass instruments. Instead of using a set of crooks to change the key of a horn, the player could produce a full range of tones by operating a system of valves to change the length of the tubing in the instrument.

Cornet

After the horn, one of the earliest valved instruments was the cornet. In the 1820s when Jean Hilaire Asté (known as Halary) applied first two, then three valves to the little *cornet de post* – a post-horn with tuning slides and crooks in straight rather than circular form – the instrument became known as the *cornet à pistons*. In England the first manufacturers of the new instrument were Pace and Köhler of London, who called their creation the cornopeon (the "horn of triumphant songs"). By the mid 19th century, however, the usual generic term for the instrument had become "cornet". Although at first a wide variety of crooks was available, ranging from B flat down to F, by about 1850 B flat was becoming the norm.

The cornet differs from the trumpet in that it has a conical rather than a cylindrical bore. The other essential difference is in the mouthpiece: the cornet's is much deeper, which makes the instrument more flexible and less tiring to play for long periods.

Saxhorn

In 1842 the Belgian instrument maker Adolphe Sax (1814–94) moved to Paris where, under the patronage of Berlioz, he set up a brass and woodwind workshop. In the early 1840s, Sax produced a family of five conical-bore brass instruments, subsequently extended to ten. Although the principle behind the saxhorn was not entirely new, the proportions

Cornet key features

Type: brass aerophone

Pitch: B flat or E flat

Notable players of the cornet: George Macfarlane, Hermann Koenig, Jules Levy, Howard Reynolds.

ABOVE: *Cornets can be made in silver instead of brass, such as this B flat cornet.*

between an authorized military band and a smaller group, led by the inventor, playing Sax's instruments, the latter were officially adopted and Sax secured a virtual monopoly as supplier of instruments to the French army. The fury this engendered among the more established Paris instrument makers led to attacks on his business and lawsuits that resulted in Sax's financial ruin, but not before the name "saxhorn" had passed into common usage.

ABOVE: The Distin family playing the set of six coiled circular horns that Sax built for them in 1845. Sax later redesigned his horns with the bell pointing upwards.

adapted by Sax made his instruments superior. Built in upright form, they were generally pitched either in E flat or B flat and were fitted with three vertical valves on horizontal tubing. On early saxhorns these were fitted with Wieprecht's *Berliner-pumpen* valves, but later instruments were provided with slender Perinet valves.

Sax's breakthrough with the saxhorn came in 1843. After a public contest

ABOVE: The piston valves of a B flat cornet.

ABOVE: A rotary-valved flugelhorn player busking on the Paris Métro.

Distin family

The earliest performers on Sax's instruments included the Distin family. Led by John Distin, who had served at Waterloo as a member of the band of the Grenadier Guards and had subsequently been principal trumpet in the private band of King George IV, the band also included John's three surviving sons. In 1846 Distin established a music shop in London and became Sax's British agent. Four years later the Distins began to manufacture their own saxhorn-type instruments, and also started to publish *Distin's Brass Band Journal*.

Saxhorns became especially popular in British brass bands. The first group to be completely equipped with them was the Mossley Temperance band,

which achieved success in the Belle Vue Contest of 1853. The tenor saxhorn in E flat, these days known simply as the tenor horn, is still used in brass and military bands.

Over-the-shoulder horn

Introduced by Alan Dodworth, over-the-shoulder horns were especially popular during the 1850s and '60s in the United States. The advantage of this type of instrument was that the sound of the larger instruments went to the rear of the band rather than up into the air. During static performances some bands had the over-the-shoulder horn players facing backwards, so that the sound was projected in the same direction as all the other instruments.

RIGHT: Over-the-shoulder horns were popular in the mid 19th century with American bands. Today they are found only in living-history bands.

Alphorn

He that blows best, bears away the horn.

PROVERB

The alphorn, as its name implies, is an instrument found in mountainous districts, not only in the Swiss Alps, but also in the Carpathian Mountains of Poland and Romania, as well as in Lithuania and Scandinavia. The instrument is distantly related to the Etruscan *lituus*, whose name survived into the mid 19th century in the Swiss canton of Unterwalden, where the horns were called *liti*.

Construction

No matter where it is found, the alphorn is almost invariably made of wood. It has a conical bore, and the oldest form is the straight expanding tube with a slight flare at the end, while alphorns constructed

ABOVE: Brightly painted bells of a collection of Swiss alphorns.

ABOVE: A 1661 engraving of an alphorn.

in more recent years usually have an upturned bell.

Although ash, lime and hazel have been used in the manufacture of alphorns, the wood of choice was usually a young fir growing out of a mountainside and curving upwards from its roots, thereby giving a natural upturned bell. After seasoning, the long poles were longitudinally halved using an axe or saw, then hollowed out and glued back together. In Switzerland the method of making the alphorn changed in the 19th century, when the bore was formed from a single log by burning out the centre. The bell was made separately and added to the end. By about 1850 the total length of the alphorn had become standardized at about 3m/10ft, but modern Swiss instruments range from 1.5m/5ft to 4m/13ft in length and are made in two detachable sections.

Switzerland

Originally a herdsman's instrument, the Swiss alphorn can be traced back to the 14th century, when it had an average length of about 1.5m/5ft. Because of its superior carrying power, it was used as a signalling instrument to warn villagers of danger, and, in later years, to summon them to church. It is this use of the alphorn that was quoted by Beethoven at the end of his *Pastoral Symphony* in 1808. In 1826 an innovation occurred when Ferdinand Huber of Switzerland had three alphorns made of different sizes and tuned to different keys, for use in two and three-part ensemble performances.

In modern Switzerland the alphorn is now principally used to entertain tourists, if possible siting it where it will set up an echo on the opposite side of a valley. It is also used to call

cattle down from the mountains, and a traditional melody played for this purpose is known as a *ranz des vaches* (which means something like a procession of cattle). Different tunes of this type exist in each district, of which the Gruyère version is one of the most famous. The tunes are characterized by short motifs frequently repeated, giving them

a mesmerizing effect. They now have words and are sung in the manner of folk songs, but the intervals used indicate that they were originally composed for the alphorn, which can play only harmonics.

Northern Europe

In Lithuania, alphorns were used both for signalling and in folk music, and

were played in processions and at weddings. In the western Carpathians they are played only by women and children, and among the Mari people of the Urals 1.5m/5ft wooden alphorns are especially made for the spring festival. The Polish version of the alphorn is the *trombita*; made of pine, it can be up to 4m/13ft long. A feature of the instrument is that, while the bells of most alphorns rest on the ground, the bell-end of the *trombita* is supported on a post.

In Moldova and Romania the alphorn is called the *bucium*, of which there are five kinds that vary in length from 1.5m/5ft to 3m/10ft. They are either straight or curved and are bound with bark, roots or gut. Although they are usually made of wood, in the north of Romania the *bucium* is often made from metal, sometimes with the tubing coiled back on itself.

ABOVE: *What more epitomizes Switzerland than an alphorn player in his local costume, the sound resonating across the valleys?*

Pipes

Into the street the Piper stept, Smiling first a little smile,
As if he knew what magic slept, In his quiet pipe the while.

ROBERT BROWNING (1812–89), "THE PIED PIPER OF HAMELIN"

Simple blown instruments, consisting of cylindrical or conical tubes without mechanism, have evolved in many cultures and are widely played as folk instruments.

Aulos

The best-known double pipe is the aulos, an ancient Greek reed instrument that dates from at least 2800 BC. Each pipe consisted of a slender cylindrical tube made out of cane, wood or ivory, about 50cm/20in long, with from three to six tone-holes. Two pipes were played as a pair, the musician holding one in each hand.

At the proximal end of the pipe was a bulb of wood or ivory that served as the staple for the reed. As the whole reed was taken into the mouth, it is unclear from illustrations whether auloi were single or double-reed

ABOVE: A variation on the aulos was when one pipe terminated in a bell. The aulos was mentioned by Homer as an instrument of the countryside.

instruments, all the original reeds having long since disintegrated. In order to support the lips and cheeks, male players — who apparently blew harder than their female colleagues — wore a *phorbeia*, or leather mouth-band tied around their heads.

The aulos was played on many different occasions. It was part of the orgiastic cult of Dionysus, and was used to accompany choirs and at marriages and funerals, at which it was played in processions. It was also played in celebration of famous people or victorious athletes, as well as in musical contests between performers, such as those held at the Pythian games at Delphi.

LEFT: A pupil learning to play the aulos. This early 5th-century BC vase painting depicts an aulos in which the left pipe is longer than the right.

Pan-pipes

The pan-pipes consist of a set of vertical tubes of different resonating lengths joined side by side. The tubes are stopped at the lower end while the player blows across the upper ends. They are made from various materials and are found all over the world. In most societies the pan-pipes have always had a lowly status, and are often portrayed as a characteristic instrument of herdsmen.

Classical Greek pan-pipes, known as a *syrinx*, consisted of a set of tubes all of the same length; each tube was

Aulos music

Auletes competed at the Pythian games by composing and playing the Pythian *nomos*, a solo performance that was descriptive of Apollo's legendary victory over the Python of Delphi. The music was presented in five sections, which had to illustrate the different stages of the battle. The winner in 586 BC was Sacadas, who created "sounds like those of the trumpet and gnashing like that of the serpent as it grinds its teeth after being pierced by arrows".

blocked with wax to the depth necessary to give the required notes. By the Hellenistic period, however, especially in Etruria and Rome, the tubes were graded in length. The pipes were usually stuck together with wax and the assembly was reinforced by a cloth binding or a wooden frame.

ABOVE: An area where the pan-pipes are still found is South America, where they are an integral part of Bolivian and Peruvian folk music. Some of these pipes are very large.

Occasionally pan-pipes were made from a solid block of wood, ivory or other material into which the holes

RIGHT: According to the legend surrounding the pan-pipes, one day the god Pan was pursuing the nymph Syrinx who fled to the river and, in an attempt to escape from her pursuer, transformed herself into a reed. Unable to distinguish her from the other reeds, Pan cut several at random and formed them into what are now known as pan-pipes.

were bored. The pipes were held in both hands and moved from side to side as the player blew across the top.

Bladder pipe

Known from the 9th century, the bladder pipe was played by blowing through a short blowpipe into an animal bladder in which a reed was enclosed. This bladder served, like the bag of the bagpipes, as a wind reservoir. Out of the bladder came the chanter, with a varying number of finger-holes. Although the bladder pipe became virtually obsolete during the Renaissance, a descendant of the instrument survives in Poland, where it is still played in rural districts.

ABOVE: This representation of a bladder pipe is from Agricola's Musica Instrumentalis Deudsch *of 1529.*

Picco pipe

One of the more unusual musicians who toured Europe in the 1850s was Picco, a blind Sardinian minstrel who played a three-holed pipe only 8.5cm/3½in long, which he called his "pastoral tibia". Picco, who evoked "strains that would charm Apollo", played not only simple folk tunes but also variations on the *Carnival of Venice*, and was said to manage a range of three octaves. His popularity led to the commercial production of "Picco" pipes. Another person who played a small pipe in the mid 19th century was the Hungarian Kransky Baschik. Even smaller than Picco's pipe, Baschik's instrument could be played in octaves and thirds.

Cornett

The sound of the cornett is like a ray of sunshine piercing the shadows.

MARIN MERSENNE (1588–1648)

Spelt with a double "t" to differentiate it from the 19th-century valved instrument, the cornett's origin can be traced back to at least the 9th century, when holes were pierced in cow and goat horns so that tunes could be played on them. The instrument was certainly known in 14th-century France, for romances of the period mention the *cor à doigts*. It was a wooden lip-vibrated wind instrument with finger-holes and a cup-shaped mouthpiece that was customarily played at the side of the

LEFT: A late 16th-century six-holed, curved cornett.

mouth. The soft tone of the instrument made it – along with trombones – an ideal accompaniment for voices in churches, but it was also used to accompany dancing, both indoors and outdoors.

Construction

By the 13th century the cornett had five finger-holes and a bell made of animal horn. A later version had six finger-holes on the upper side and a thumb-hole on the underside. It was fitted with a separate mouthpiece, commonly made of ivory, bone or horn.

By the 16th century slender curved cornetts, which got their name from the Italian word for "little horn", were being carved from roughly shaped

blocks of hard, close-grained wood. The blocks were halved lengthways and channels gouged into each half to make a cylindrical bore when they were glued back together. Finally, black leather was glued over the wood to seal any possible leaks.

Use of the cornett

Classified as valveless trumpets, medieval cornetts were made both straight and curved. The Germans preferred the former, while most of the rest of Europe settled for the latter. There were three main sizes of cornett: the small treble (cornettino),

ABOVE: A 17th-century illustration of a cornett player by Weigel.

ABOVE: This 19th-century painting by John Spencer shows an angel playing a cornett.

the treble and the tenor. In its heyday – between 1550 and 1650 – the treble cornett was used more than any other wind instrument for virtuoso-playing.

Cornetts were used with trombones and organs to accompany choral music, especially in Venice where, in 1600, they formed the nucleus of the band led by the composer and organist Giovanni Gabrieli (c.1553–1612). Some Italian curved cornetts were very ornate, with the bell end carved in the shape of a beast's head. In England, cornetts were used to support the treble voices of the choir of the Chapel Royal, while in France cornetts and trombones were the usual instrumentation for ceremonial music up to about 1650.

RIGHT: A mid 16th-century German engraving of a woman holding a cornett.

Decline

The cornett was tiring to play and presented problems in getting a good embouchure; in spite of Mersenne's remarks, it was often not played well. The higher register was similar to that of a trumpet and the lower like a trombone, while the indistinct wailing sound of the middle register was very unattractive when played in isolation. When used with other instruments the cornett could achieve special effects, however it began to fall out of use from about 1650. It was inevitable that the finest players of the instrument would start to turn their attention to the developing oboe.

By the end of the 18th century the cornett was no more than a rare curiosity. One of the last pieces written especially for the instrument was Matthew Locke's *Music for his Majesty's Sagbutts and Cornetts* (1661), while the last composer actually to score for the cornett was Christoph Willibald Gluck (1714–87), who used it in his *Orpheus*, composed in 1762. The last bastion of the cornett was in German *Turmmusik*, in which it lasted well into the 19th century. It was revived in the 20th century by early music specialists.

ABOVE: This 15th-century painting shows three English musicians on a balcony (top right) playing cornetts to accompany a dance.

ABOVE: Replica cornetts are made for living-history groups by Otto Steinkopf of Berlin (straight cornetts) and Christopher Monk of Surrey, England (curved cornetts).

Bugle

The diabolical clamour produced by the call to arms sounded by the bugles and drums.

ALEXIS DE TOCQUEVILLE (1905–59)

The word bugle is derived from the Latin *buculus*, meaning "bullock", a reference to the fact that the first bugles were made out of short cattle horns. Originally the bugle was a hunter's instrument, but by the 15th century town watchmen and soldiers had begun to use it. Made of brass, copper or silver, the bugle retained its horn shape into the 18th century, when it began to be made with an upward-pointing bell.

In the 18th century the shape evolved into a large semicircle, which was held to the body by a leather harness. This form, called in German *Halbmond*, was introduced during the Seven Years War (1756–63) as a distinguishing instrument for the Prussian *Jäger* battalions. In the early 19th century the tubing began to be arranged in an elliptical coil, and in 1814 it was adopted as the badge of the British Light Infantry. The regular infantry B flat bugle, with twice-wound tubing and a small bell,

ABOVE: *A silver-plated bugle. As a protection against loss, the mouthpiece is attached to the instrument by a chain.*

was first authorized in 1858. In the United States this type is known as a cavalry bugle.

Keyed bugle

In the early 19th century Joseph Haliday (1772–1857), the bandmaster of the Irish Cavan Militia, transformed the bugle into a keyed instrument. Haliday subsequently sold the patent to the Dublin instrument maker Matthew Pace, who made the first keyed bugle as a compliment to the Duke of Kent, the then Commander in Chief of the British army. Henceforth the instrument became colloquially known as the Royal Kent Bugle. The earliest instruments had five keys, but a sixth was soon added and later examples had up to 12 keys.

When the keyed bugle was played by the band of the Grenadier Guards at a military review held in Paris after the battle of Waterloo in 1815, the Russian Grand Duke Konstantin was so impressed with the instrument that he

ABOVE: *A bugle major of the Royal Sappers in 1823.*

ABOVE: *The flugelhorn is a cross between the cornet and bugle. It is mainly seen in brass bands and some jazz combinations.*

ABOVE: *A 19th-century brass bugle.*

commanded John Distin, the band's chief musician, to have one of the new instruments made for him. Distin, who was later to manufacture instruments himself in London, approached the Paris instrument maker Jean Hilaire Asté (Halary). In 1821 he took out patents to cover three forms of keyed bugle: the clavi-tube, quinti-tube and ophicleide. In its various forms, the keyed bugle was the first fully melodic treble brass instrument and immediately became popular for solo work, until superseded in the middle of the century by the flugelhorn and the cornet.

Ophicleide

A much more efficient bass instrument than the serpent or bass horn, Asté's ophicleide of 1821 – named from the Greek for "keyed serpent" – was made of metal, the long tubing bending back on itself, with nine keys covering the large tone-holes. It was often unkindly called the "chromatic bullock". The first composer to score for the ophicleide was Gaspare Spontini (1774–1851), the *Generalmusikdirektor* to the king of Prussia, who used the instrument in his opera *Olimpie* in 1819. It soon entered many orchestras and bands, including the one led by the famous French bandleader Louis Jullien, who used it to augment the trombones.

With the invention of valves the construction of brass instruments was revolutionized, and in 1832 the Parisian brass instrument maker A. Guichard brought out his three-valved ophicleide, which had tuning slides for C and B flat. Although the ophicleide was eventually replaced by the tuba in the middle of the 19th century, it survived, especially in Italy, into the early 20th century.

ABOVE: This 19th-century French comical caricature shows a young boy learning to play the ophicleide, the largest wind instrument of the time.

ABOVE: A mounted bugler blowing a large-bell instrument.

Serpent

What the devil is that?

GEORGE FRIDERIC HANDEL (1685–1759), ON FIRST HEARING A SERPENT

The serpent, so named from its winding S-shape, is believed to have been invented by Canon Edmé Guillaume of Auxerre in about 1590, as an improvement on the bass cornett, to accompany plainchant in churches. Used to double men's voices, it blended perfectly, adding depth and fullness to the sound. Like the cornett, it was made of wood, with a cup-shaped ivory or horn mouthpiece mounted on a metal crook. It had a conical bore with six finger-holes but no thumb-hole.

Manufacture

There were two main methods of constructing a serpent. One was to hollow out two complete halves from

ABOVE: This 13-key serpent was made in London, c.1850.

solid blocks of wood, usually maple, and then glue them together to make a tube before covering the whole with leather. The alternative – the method preferred in England – was to build up the instrument from fairly short overlapping half-sections of wood, which were then glued together and covered with leather.

Although serpents were usually made of wood there are rare instances of metal instruments being made, such as

ABOVE: A serpent player from Bonanni's Gabinetto Armonico of 1723.

those built in about 1800 by Carl August Grenser of Dresden. Sadly, no metal serpent is known to have survived.

One of the largest serpents was that built by the Wood Brothers in about 1840. Used in York Minster, it was twice the size of conventional instruments, containing nearly 4.8m/16ft of tubing.

Upright serpent

The main problem with the serpent, which was over 2m/6ft long, was getting the finger-holes within reach of the player's hands. This was the reason for the serpentine contours of the instrument, but an alternative solution was that provided in 1788 by J. J. Régibo, a musician of the church of St Peter in Lille, who built an upright serpent with straight double tubes. Régibo's instrument, which was capable of being dismantled into three sections, also had the advantage that it was

Key features

TYPE: woodwind aerophone

PITCH: E, D or C

NOTABLE PLAYERS OF THE SERPENT: Abbé Aubert, Abbé Lunel, Louis Alexandre Frichot, André, Jepp.

louder and easier to play than conventional models. It opened the way for a number of bassoon-shaped serpents, including the later English models that are recognizable by their short overlapping sections, giving U-bends rather than the older S-curves.

The serpent in the orchestra

By the mid 17th century the serpent had left the confines of the church and was being used in secular instrumental ensembles. By 1756 it was employed in the orchestra of the Comédie Italienne and was spreading to Germany, the Low Countries and England. By the 19th century the serpent had become firmly established in orchestras, with both Mendelssohn and Wagner scoring for it. In French orchestras the serpent was often substituted for the contrabassoon. It was at about this time that the serpent was first made with keys; at first it had only three or four, but by the end of the instrument's existence 14 had become the norm.

Great skill and musicianship were required to play the serpent, since every note depended on the player's embouchure. Various fingering charts were published during the 18th and 19th centuries, all of which differed widely.

ABOVE: A Royal Marine Band of 1826. The seated musician is playing the serpent.

Military bands

In the 18th century the serpent gained a foothold in English and German military bands, where it became known as the *serpent militaire* as opposed to the ecclesiastical *serpent d'église*. The military version generally had a metal mouthpiece. One notable version of the military band serpent was the ophibaryton, which had a straight bell in the form of a painted dragon's head. Although some bands in Spain were still using the instrument as late as 1884, the serpent fell into disuse with the invention of the valved tuba in the 1830s.

RIGHT: Early serpents such as this one had finger-holes instead of keys.

ABOVE: This 17th-century drawing by Bracelli shows a sackbut on the left and a serpent on the right.

Bagpipes

*Twelve Highlanders and a bagpipe
make a rebellion.*

PROVERB

Nobody is ambiguous about bagpipes – they either love them or hate them. They probably originated in Sumeria and perhaps independently in Greece. They were known by the Romans, and Arab references to the instrument date back to the 11th century. Their main characteristic is the continuous sound that is achieved using the air reserved in the bag, so that the player can breathe while playing. To articulate the melody, and ensure that each note is not tied to the next, the piper interpolates a grace note before each note of the melody. Most bagpipes have a limited range, with a compass of about nine tones.

The bag is inflated by air from the mouth or a set of bellows operated by the player's arm. The blowpipe, reeded chanter and drones, which are usually tuned in octaves and fifths, are inserted through the sides of the bag. Early bags were made from either the whole skin of a small animal, or the stomach or bladder of a larger one. Whole skin bags usually have the chanter inserted into the natural neck and the drones and blowpipe into the forelegs. Modern bags are usually made of tanned sheepskin cut to shape.

Scottish Highland pipes

The distinctive feature of the Highland bagpipes, with their loud and

BELOW: Believed to have been introduced to Scotland by the Romans, the Highland pipes have been used as a martial instrument from at least the 15th century.

penetrating tone, is the long blowpipe that allows the player to stand erect rather than leaning forwards. There are three single-reed drones, two tenor and one bass, and a double-reed chanter. Scotland is the most active of pipe-playing countries, and Scottish pipes have been exported to France and India.

Northumbrian pipes

Although bagpipes were once common in England as well as Scotland, today they are found only in Northumberland, where the bellows-operated small-pipes, intended for

indoor use, are played seated with the drones lying across the knees. A feature of these pipes is that the chanter has a closed end, enabling the piper to play staccato and repeat a note without interpolating grace notes.

Kathryn Tickell (born 1967) is recognized as one of the leading Northumbrian pipers of the present generation, and has been appointed the official piper to the Lord Mayor of Newcastle upon Tyne.

Irish pipes

The mouth-blown Irish war-pipe fell into disuse in the 18th century when it began to be replaced by the Scottish Highland pipe, although a new version was made during the 20th century. The bellows-blown union pipes, which are played seated, were probably introduced in the early 18th century. The modern pipe, which has a double-bore chanter with two reeds, has become so complex that it is often referred to as the "Irish organ".

Musette

Originally a pastoral instrument, the French bellows-blown musette

LEFT: A 14th-century English bagpipe with a single drone and chanter. This instrument pre-dates the Northumbrian pipes — it is not bellows-operated. Instead, the player inflates the bag by means of a blowpipe.

ABOVE: The Irish union bagpipes were introduced in the 18th century and, unlike the Scottish variety, they are played in a sitting position.

In some parts of Latvia and Estonia bags were often made of sealskin or a seal's stomach, which were unaffected by dryness or damp. In the 18th century the playing of such instruments was discouraged, as it was thought that they led to disorder and crime. They did, however, survive into the 1940s and have since been revived by several folklore groups.

In south-eastern Europe the end of the chanter was sometimes carved into the shape of an animal's head. The Czech *kozial*, commonly called "wedding pipes", can be traced back to the 14th century, while the Bosnian and Croatian *diple* is played outdoors on festive occasions. The bellows-blown Hungarian *duda*, which terminates in a cow's horn, has a small finger-hole opposite the thumb-hole, which raises any note by a semitone, thereby allowing modulations.

Indian bagpipes

The traditional Hindustani *masak* is the simplest bagpipe of all. It consists of a single-reed cane pipe and a blowpipe tied into a whole goatskin. Another

ABOVE, CLOCKWISE FROM TOP LEFT: Four different types of bagpipes – Irish Uilleann pipe, French cornemuse, Italian calabrian and French musette.

Indian bagpipe, the southern Indian *bajana scuti*, was used mainly to accompany devotional music until replaced in the mid 19th century by the harmonium.

was popular in the 17th century at court, where it was used to accompany dancing. By the 18th century, with its ivory pipes inserted into a bag of matching silk and velvet, the musette had become a fashionable and delicate "toy" of the nobility and as such disappeared in the wake of the French Revolution.

Zampogna

Native to southern Italy and Sicily, the *zampogna* has two drones and two chanters arranged for playing harmony. At Christmas in the streets of Naples, two-man teams called *zampognari* serenade images of the infant Christ set up at the roadside.

Eastern European pipes

Today there are two main types of pipes in Poland: the bellows-operated *dudy*, whose drone pipe folds back on itself and terminates in a curved bell, and the *dudy zywieckie*, which is mouth-blown and played solo or with a violin.

ABOVE: The Italian single-drone bagpipe, the zampogna, *is native to southern Italy and Sicily. Both Handel and Bach alluded to the instrument.*

Mouth Organ

A cherub in a box.

ANONYMOUS

The concept behind the modern, horizontally held mouth organ came from Christian Friedrich Buschmann (1805–64) of Berlin, who realized in 1821 that melodies could be played on a set of pitch-pipes that he had made for use when tuning an organ. Various other people experimented with the idea, and the first instrument that looked like the modern harmonica was produced by Christian Messner, a young German clockmaker who began to construct similar instruments to Buschmann's, which he sold at country fairs and inns. At about the same time the first commercially produced mouth organs appeared in Vienna, one of which was Ernst Schmidt's apollolyra, with its 44 reeds controlled by keys.

Harmonica

In Tossingen, Christian Weiss and Matthias Höhner (1833–1902) started manufacturing harmonicas in the mid 1850s. Although their early models were all handmade, Höhner soon adapted the new methods and techniques of mass production and it was not long before his business had grown beyond all expectations. By 1879 he had made over 700,000 harmonicas – of which over 60 per cent had been exported to the United States.

Although harmonicas are made in various sizes and compasses, all consist of a set of free reeds mounted in a grooved metal box, which is moved from side to side in front of the player's mouth. Sounds are produced by both blowing and sucking and, if the instrument is diatonic, only one key can be played on any one model. The chromatic harmonica, which is used as a performing instrument, was first produced in the early 1920s.

Although virtuosi such as Larry Adler (1914–2000) have given the harmonica a wider appeal, the instrument has always been considered as more of a toy than a serious instrument. Since World War II, however, several symphonic composers have scored for it. In the 1960s the mouth organ became popular with folk singers such as Bob Dylan and

LEFT: A modern harmonica made by Höhner. The sound is produced by both blowing and sucking air through the rows of reeds inside the instrument.

Donovan. To keep their hands free to play the guitar, they held the mouth organ in a frame worn around the neck.

Melodica

Another type of mouth organ is the melodica, an innovative vertical form of the instrument produced from 1959. The two main types are the piano melodica, which has a miniature keyboard played with one hand, and the soprano melodica, which is operated by a series of push keys, one hand playing the diatonic and the other the chromatic tones.

ABOVE: The harmonica has always been very popular among young people. This photograph shows a class of girls being taught to play the famous Höhner harmonica.

ABOVE: The piano melodica has a miniature piano-like keyboard, which is played with one hand while blowing into the mouthpiece.

BELOW: The modern chromatic Chinese sheng *has 17 pipes and is played polyphonically in triads. It is now a regular feature of the Chinese orchestra.*

Sheng

The modern mouth organ has evolved from the classical Chinese *sheng* that dates back to the Chou dynasty (1122–221 BC), and consists of a gourd into which are inserted a short blowpipe and up to 36 bamboo pipes of varying length, each with a finger-hole and a free reed cut from a length of bamboo that vibrates when the finger-hole is closed. The pipes are arranged in an incomplete circle representing, according to popular legend, the folded wings of the mythical phoenix.

A new type of mouth organ, the *paisheng*, appeared in China in the 1960s. It is the size of a small piano, complete with keyboard, and has a range of four octaves. Used in the concert hall, the player sits in front of the instrument at the keyboard and fills the wind-chamber by blowing through a long blowpipe.

ABOVE: Bob Dylan was one of the youth idols of the 1960s. He usually wore his mouth organ in a frame around the neck so that he could play the guitar at the same time.

Didgeridoo

*The spectrum of sound which can be produced by the didgeridoo
evokes association with sounds perceived in the womb.*

Dr Wolfgang Strobel

The didgeridoo is an end-blown straight natural trumpet used by the indigenous peoples of Australia. Depending on the region, didgeridoos are made of various types of eucalyptus wood, such as yellow box gum tree, bloodwood, Red River gum, stringy bark or woollybutt. To be suitable for making a didgeridoo, the trunk or branch must have the right diameter (7.5–15cm/3–6in), length (1.2–2m/4–6ft) and, of course, have been hollowed out by termites. As the didgeridoo builder cannot see that the trees are hollow from the outside, he peels off a piece of bark and taps the tree with his knuckles. Once a tree is selected, it is chopped down and the bark is peeled off.

The next stage involves using long chisels to scrape out any layers of wood that have not been devoured by the termites. The builder then thins the end of the interior walls to a depth of 30–40cm/12–16in to make a funnel shape. Although the didgeridoo is played without a separate mouthpiece, a rim of beeswax or eucalyptus gum is sometimes fitted to the mouth end.

*LEFT: A didgeridoo is
made from a scraped-out
tree trunk or branch. By means
of circular breathing, a player
can produce a continuous sound.*

Decoration
Didgeridoos are decorated only for special occasions; generally they are plain. When they are decorated, the motifs are subject to religious taboo and are seen only by the initiated. The decoration is removed immediately after the ceremony and in some cases the didgeridoo is destroyed. On the other hand, some musicians decorate their instruments with totemic decoration, in which case the motif is down to the artist's imagination and has no religious significance.

Method of play
Didgeridoos are played by men and boys, often together with clapping sticks, to accompany singing and dancing as well as for funeral ceremonies. Although it is known for players to perform standing and sometimes moving around with the dancers and singers, the best position for playing the didgeridoo is seated with one leg bent to the side and the other stretched forward, with the foot helping to support the instrument. Sometimes, for added effect, the end is inserted into a tin-can resonator. Other performers prefer to support it off the ground between their feet. It is a very difficult instrument to play, and virtuoso players are recognized and highly valued members of society.

The pitch of the didgeridoo varies according to the length of the tube. To

ABOVE: Didgeridoos are now being mass-produced for tourists in workshops like this one.

ABOVE: *A native Australian playing a didgeridoo in Sydney, Australia.*

Gondwanaland, formed in 1978, features an electronically amplified didgeridoo whose unique rhythmical sound forms a bridge across thousands of years of musical history. The band uses no less than ten different didgeridoos played by Charlie McMahon, each of which is tuned to a different key.

McMahon has also played the didgeridoo with the London Philharmonic Orchestra, and invented an instrument that he calls the "didgeribone". As its name suggests, it is a cross between a didgeridoo and a trombone, and consists of two wooden tubes placed one inside the other. The inner tube slides in and out to create different tones, as with a trombone.

produce the characteristic continuous drone, frequent breaths are snatched though the nose while the air, which is stored in the cheeks, is continuously expelled down the tube. Although generally only one tone is available, a good player can produce another tone a fourth higher. Changes in the shape of the mouth can be made to change the timbre, and the tongue is used to give vibrato effects and achieve rhythmic patterns. Voiced sounds, which may imitate bird and animal noises, are superimposed on the fundamental drone.

Popular music

The didgeridoo is also used in pop music. The Australian band

ABOVE: *A selection of painted didgeridoos.*

ABOVE: *Today some Australian pop bands, such as the Marshall Whyler band, include a didgeridoo in their instrumentation.*

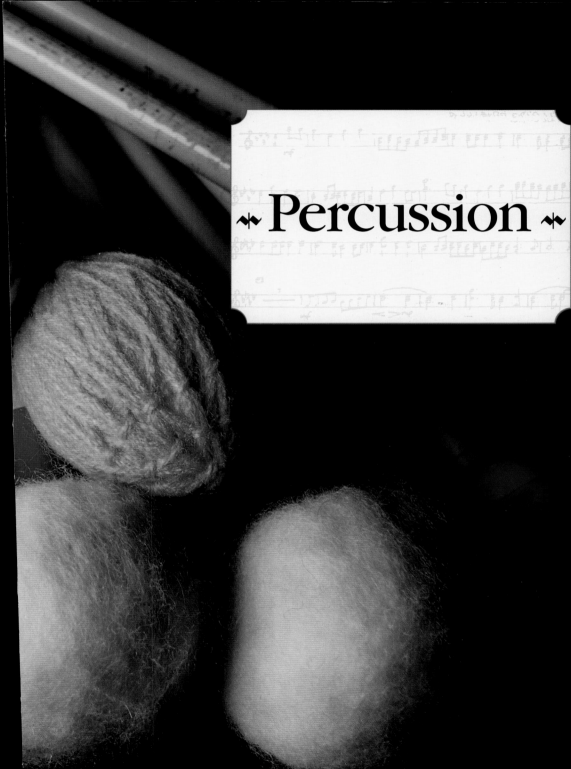

Percussion

Rhythm and Drama

The percussion acts as a central heating system.

IGOR STRAVINSKY (1882–1971)

Percussion in music is universal. There is not a country in the world that does not make percussion instruments of some kind to provide a rhythmic backbone for its music. Drums are probably the world's oldest musical instruments, but percussion is used for many effects that are not simply rhythmic: many instruments, such as cymbals, shakers and jingles, make more continuous, but exciting, noises, while a single stroke on a gong may create a dramatic climax to a musical work.

There are two main types of percussion instruments: those that are tuned to a definite pitch, such as timpani, xylophone or tubular bells, and those whose pitch is indefinite, such as the triangle, bass drum or

tambourine. Orchestral percussionists play an ever-increasing number of instruments as composers search for original musical effects, and each player may need to play ten or more instruments in a single work. To manage a large percussion section, professional players have to master a range of techniques, as well as making purely practical arrangements to enable them both to reach the instruments and read the music on the concert platform without tripping over each other. The most specialized percussionist in the orchestra is the timpanist.

Magic and myth

Long before the drum became a musical instrument, its noise-making qualities were no doubt credited with the powers of making thunder and chasing away devils, not to mention frightening the enemy. In ancient Greece soldiers beat on shields made of tightly stretched ox-hide – a custom perpetuated by Zulu warriors well into the 19th century.

Like so many other musical instruments, the earliest use of the bell was in magic and ritual. Its power to ward off evil is illustrated in the *Book*

BELOW, FROM LEFT TO RIGHT: A ridged guiro, wooden beater and wood block. The guiro can be struck or scraped and the wood block is struck to produce a short, untuned note.

of *Exodus*, written between the 9th and 5th centuries BC, when Aaron is instructed to wear bells of gold when he goes into the "holy place". Among the Bobati people of Zaire, bells were rung as a guard against evil influences entering the chief's body whenever he drank or smoked. In East Africa the Teso people wear bells around their ankles to appease the spirit of the storm, while the Bakrewi attach bells to the entrances of their houses to ward off evil.

Religious significance

Rattles often have a magical and religious significance, and a rattle or shaker is one of the accoutrements of

ABOVE: Russia is a country of large bells; these two men are erecting three bells.

BELOW, FROM LEFT TO RIGHT: The jingle stick and tambourine are two forms of the same instrument. They can be struck to produce a percussive sound, or shaken to prolong the ringing.

ABOVE, FROM LEFT TO RIGHT: *An orchestral percussion section showing timpani, congas, bass drum, gong, cymbals, claves, glockenspiel and tambourine.*

ABOVE: *The cog ratchet rattle has been used for many years and for many reasons — from scaring birds off the fields to supporting a favourite football team.*

the shaman. In China the thunder god Zin Shin was surrounded by a revolving wheel to which alternate barrel drums and kettledrums were fixed, the god striking them with a drumstick held in one hand. Ancient Japanese belief connected the playing of percussion with the invention of music, the myth being that the gods beat the measure upon "the mother of all the castanets".

Ever since their invention, drums have been used in rituals. Some were classed as sacred objects, while others were status symbols and emblems of royalty. In ancient Mesopotamia the hide of a sacred bull was used as the drum head, while a seal of the third millennium BC shows the goddess Ishtar standing before an altar that looks like an upturned hourglass drum. The practice of using the drum as an altar has been carried into modern times, with soldiers in the field using an upturned drum as the focus of acts of worship.

Ancient scrapers were made from animal bones or ridged gourds, and have survived into modern times in folk instruments such as the guiro of Venezuela, a hollow gourd with a serrated surface. Related to the scraper is the cog rattle or ratchet, which was used in medieval religious ceremonies during Holy Week. Ratchet rattles are still used in some German festivals, particularly in the South. The cog rattle's tribal attributes re-emerged in the mid 20th century when it was taken up by football supporters.

ABOVE: *Maracas are hollow gourds filled with seeds. They are used in Latin American dance music, shaken to provide the rhythms.*

ABOVE: *A rainstick is a wooden or plastic tube containing pellets that make the sound of rain when the tube is turned over.*

ABOVE: *A selection of hand shakers. At the top are a ganza and a multi-guiro, and at the bottom is a torpedo. They can be struck with beaters as well as being shaken.*

ABOVE: *A native American shaman beating an octagonal buffalo-hide frame drum in the fields of Washington State.*

Timpani

When drums speak out, laws hold their tongues.

THOMAS FULLER (1608–61)

The timpani are the most important members of the Western orchestral percussion section. They can uniquely be tuned to a definite pitch and are used both as rhythmic and as melodic instruments.

Early kettledrums

Large kettledrums were developed during the 14th and 15th centuries in Germany. They were played as a pair, slung on either side of a horse. Such was the prestige of owning kettledrums in Germany and Sweden that they became the preserve of the aristocracy; no one under the rank of baron was permitted to own them. Kettledrums entered certain cavalry regiments that were owned

and to a large extent manned by the nobility. By the early 1600s they had followed the trumpet into church music and shortly thereafter into the orchestra.

Tuning

Before the military kettledrum was able to play a full part in the modern orchestra, it had to undergo various radical changes. Early kettledrums were expected only to contribute the tonic and the dominant of a tonality, which rarely changed. However, from the late 18th century composers such as Beethoven wrote music that expected the drummer to modulate right in the middle of a piece of music, a process that even for the most experienced players took one or two minutes.

LEFT: Pedal-operated timpani are a main feature of the symphony orchestra. Pedals can change the tuning much faster than the old system of hand-tuning screws or taps.

At this time the instruments were tensioned using square-topped screws turned with a loose key. The first advance was to replace the screws with taps. They were quicker and quieter to operate, but the timpanist still had to stop playing to re-tune, and the composer had to allow for this each time his score called for a key change.

There were various other attempts to make the life of the timpanist easier. These ranged from Gerhard Cramer's central screw (1812), which operated all the other tuning screws simultaneously to a method of rotating the barrel of

ABOVE: This 17th-century engraving by Weigel shows a pair of early kettledrums from Germany being played with two wooden sticks in an outdoor setting.

ABOVE: A 19th-century kettledrummer of the French Lancers. Carried on either side of the horse, the drums are dressed with banners bearing the regimental crest.

the drum itself, devised in 1821 by J. Stumpff of Amsterdam.

Adolphe Sax endeavoured to build a kettledrum with holes of different sizes in the shell. These were covered by keys that could be opened to produce different pitches. Sax also tried doing away with the shell altogether. Although this was intended to reduce the weight of the drums, the resulting framework was so heavy that the instruments weighed more than ordinary ones!

Pedal system

Modern orchestral timpani are tuned by a pedal that acts on a central screw, allowing the drummer to change tonality while continuing to play with both hands. This method was developed in the early 1880s by Carl Pittrich, a player in the Dresden Orchestra. Although Pittrich was not the first to produce pedal timpani, his were the first successful models. The Americans William Ludwig and Robert C. Danly brought out their balanced-action mechanism, with the pedal held by a spring, in 1925. Pedal timpani are known as "machine drums", and they have allowed composers like Bartók to include *glissandos* in their timpani parts.

Even with machine drums, a separate drum is needed for each different note when they follow each other in quick succession. The modern orchestral set consists of at least five pedal timpani in graduated sizes, giving a range of about two octaves. The large bowl-shaped resonating chambers are made from copper. Fibreglass is a much lighter, cheaper alternative, but gives an inferior tone. Plastic heads have now replaced calfskin.

India

Kettledrums in India are chiefly used in the *nahabat*, the noisy band that plays at state ceremonies and in processions. These bands often include a pair of silver kettledrums over 150cm/5ft in diameter and weighing about 205kg/450lb, which are mounted on an elephant. Each drum has its own player, who strikes the drum head with a silver stick. The small pairs of hand drums called *tabla* and *bayan* are miniature versions of the kettledrums.

Nakers

An early form of kettledrum is the nakers, a pair of small drums up to 25cm/10in in diameter, one pitched higher than the other. They were adapted from the Arab *naqqara* during the crusades of the 13th century. In Europe, these portable drums were used both for military music and in consort with trumpets and pipes.

ABOVE: *Drums are known in every part of the world. In India there are many types of folk drum, including the small kettledrum that is played strung around the neck.*

ABOVE: *The 15th-century Italian musician on the left is playing the nakers — small drums with barrel-shaped wooden, metal or clay bodies covered with animal skins.*

ABOVE: *A set of modern pedal-operated orchestral timpani with plastic heads.*

Side Drum

*There is no instrument the sound of which proclaims
such vast internal satisfaction as the drums.*

GEORGE MEREDITH (1828–1909)

The side drum gets its name from its playing position in military bands, where it is slung from the shoulder and worn on an angle at the player's side. It consists of a cylindrical shell of wood or metal covered at each end with a head of calfskin or plastic. Although the depth of the shell varies according to the purpose of the instrument, modern marching-band side drums usually have a depth of about 30cm/12in.

The orchestral side drum or snare drum is 10–30cm/4–12in deep with a diameter of 35–40cm/14–16in. In the 19th century, however, it was much deeper, at about 50cm/20in. It is played with wooden sticks, usually of hickory or ebony, with slim, rounded heads known as "acorns".

*RIGHT:
Although
the side drum is generally
played with wooden sticks,
for special, softer effects
orchestral and jazz drummers
sometimes use wire brushes
instead. Evocative names
for particular rhythmic
ornamentations include
"paradiddle",
"flamadiddle" and
"ratamacue".*

picks up sympathetic vibrations from other instruments, which can cause the snares to buzz very audibly. To resolve this, a quick-release lever allows the drummer to release the snares almost instantaneously when the drum is not being played. Playing the side drum with the snares released gives a tom-tom effect.

Tabor

An early version of the side drum was the 12th-century French tabor. This was a small and light cylinder drum, which was buckled on to the chest or left arm. The outside of the upper membrane was fitted with a snare, and it was this that was hit rather than — as is customary now — the membrane itself. Tabors,

*ABOVE: This 15th-century Italian painting
shows an angel playing the side drum by
hitting the snare head.*

Snares

Giving the drum its characteristic timbre, the snares consist of eight or more strings of gut or thin wire coiled on a silk core, stretched across the lower head. Today an open coil of wire is often used, particularly by jazz players, which instead of producing a sharp rhythm adds a buzz to the sound. The snares must be at the right tension to produce the best sound and are tightened by screw devices.

One problem with snares in the orchestra is that the side drum easily

*RIGHT:
The tabor
was played
to accompany
dancing, and
would have been
accompanied
by bagpipes.*

ABOVE: A regimental side drummer of the Fifteenth Kings Regiment of Light Dragoons ("The Hussars") in 1768.

which were used to keep time for dancing, were beaten by musicians who usually simultaneously played a three-holed pipe.

The name "tabor" is also given to a long, narrow drum, with or without snares, which is sometimes used in orchestral music and is otherwise known as a tambourin.

Military side drum

The side drum came into fashion in the late 18th century when Janissary bands, which imitated the Turkish music played by the Ottoman sultan's bodyguard, became popular in Europe. A feature of these bands, which says more about the moral values of the day than about musical taste, was that side drums were usually played by young black men, who dressed in the most exotic manner and performed incredible acrobatic feats with their drumsticks as they played.

Playing technique

The main difficulty of playing the side drum is that the initial sound is of short duration. A longer sound is obtained by the roll, which is a rapid reiteration of strokes. This is a very skilled act and it requires a great deal of practice to produce an even roll with two strokes from each hand. It is much easier to play a roll on a drum with modern snares, as the traditional type make a snap rather than the contemporary buzz.

ABOVE: This side drum has been turned upside down to show its wire snare.

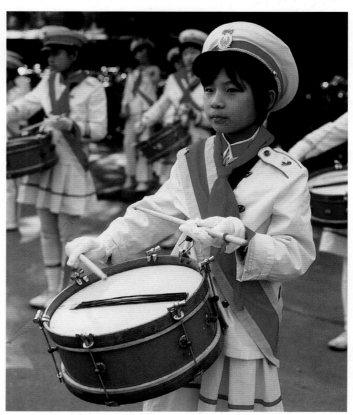

ABOVE: A member of a Chinese girls' band playing a shallow side drum in Beijing.

Bass Drum

A drum is a woman.

SMALL-CAPS: DUKE ELLINGTON (1899–1974)

The bass drum, the largest orchestral drum of indefinite pitch, remained a rarity in Europe until the 18th century, when it became well known through the Turkish Janissary bands that were fashionable at the time. The orchestral bass drum is played from a standing position, supported on a stand or a swivel frame which can be adjusted to suit the percussionist. It is struck with a large felt-headed stick, and the usual technique is to strike the drum with a glancing blow midway between the centre and the rim. Sometimes a double-headed beater is used, played with a rapid oscillatory movement of the wrist. This technique is called for in Dukas's *L'Apprenti sorcier* (1897) and Stravinsky's *The Firebird* (1910) to produce a bass drum roll.

LEFT: A rod-tensioned orchestral bass drum. The instrument is struck with a felt-covered beater and damped with the other hand.

Davul

The bass drum played in the modern orchestra is a descendant of the 14th-century Turkish davul. Introduced into Europe in the 18th century with other Janissary instruments, the davul was played with two different beaters: a heavy, spoon-shaped club and a light stick. The davul is still played, accompanied by a shawm, by buskers in modern Istanbul. In Europe it was first played in military bands, and was beaten on one head with a solid club and on the other with a switch of birch twigs in imitation of the Turkish style. It was introduced into the orchestra by Michael Haydn (1737–1806) in his *Turkish Suite* (1777) and was also used in Mozart's *Die Entführung aus dem Serail* (1782) and in Joseph Haydn's *Military Symphony* (Symphony No. 100) of 1794. In the scores for these works, the use of the two different beaters was distinguished by the direction of the stems of the notes. Today, this distinction is lost if felt-headed or lambswool beaters are used for both heads.

Military bass drum

The military bass drum, which consists of a cylindrical shell of wood or, more commonly today, metal or laminated wood, has a diameter at least twice as great as its depth. The average parade bass drum has a depth of about

ABOVE: The orchestral bass drum is often supported on a tilted stand facing the performer.

ABOVE: *An orchestral bass drum, seen from the player's perspective.*

ABOVE: *Rock and pop groups, such as this 1950s band, often include a drum kit with a bass drum that is struck with a foot pedal.*

Giant bass drum

The British firm of Distin & Son built a giant bass drum with a diameter of 240cm/8ft for the 1857 Crystal Palace Handel Festival. It was broken up in the late 1950s. One of the largest bass drums in existence today is in Disneyland in California. Built in 1961 by the Remo Company, it has a diameter of 320cm/10½ft, but it is never played.

30cm/12in and a diameter of about 70cm/28in. It is carried with the shell resting against the player's chest and the two heads facing sideways, and is played with hard felt beaters. The heads, which were originally of calfskin, are now more commonly made of plastic, which avoids the problems formerly experienced by drummers when marching in wet weather. The heads are lapped on to hoops placed over the open ends of the shell and secured by counter hoops. The tension of the heads is adjusted by thumbscrews, rods or rope.

The military bass drum player sets and maintains the marching tempo, as well as signalling to the rest of the band to stop playing using two fast successive beats called a "double tap".

Gong drum

Orchestras used to have their own kind of bass drum known as the gong drum. The advantage of this over the double-headed bass drum was that as it had a single head, so it was easier to stop vibrations and thus play short notes. On the other hand, as single-headed drums have a definite pitch, it had to have a very large head. Today the gong drum has largely been abandoned in favour of a double-headed drum with a diameter of about 150cm/5ft and a depth of about 50cm/20in.

ABOVE: *A band bass drum with a royal crest painted on the shell.*

Other Drums

*You're not supposed to rape the drums,
you make love to them.*

BILLY HIGGINS (1936–2001)

A drum can be any hollow body over which a membrane, or head, is stretched. When the head is hit, the ensuing vibrations are amplified by the body. Thousands of different drums – both pitched and unpitched – have evolved all over the world, to provide a rhythmic foundation for music and dance, to send signals, work magic or stir up emotions in battle.

ABOVE: *A trio of Cuban conga players.*

Tambourine

This ancient instrument, which has remained virtually unchanged since Roman times, consists of a shallow hoop, usually covered with a parchment head. Circular metal jingles set into the hoop sound continuously when shaken or briefly when the head is struck or rubbed with the thumb.

Tom-toms

Unsnared small drums with wooden shells and double heads, tom-toms are usually double-tensioned. The smaller ones are clamped together in pairs, and the drums are supported on legs or attached to the bass drum of a drum kit. Although tom-toms are usually of indefinite pitch, they can be tuned roughly within the range of E to B flat. Sets of chromatic tom-toms are now made.

ABOVE: *The tambourine is an instrument of the dance and has been so since at least the 17th century when it was played by the singer and dancer Barbara Campanine.*

Bongos

Usually played in pairs, bongos are found in most Latin American countries. In Cuba they are made from short sections of hollow tree trunks with drum skins nailed over the larger ends, then held near a source of heat so that they become taut. Factory-manufactured bongos are made in pairs and are held between the knees. There is usually an interval of about a fourth between the two small drums. Bongos are the highest-pitched hand drums of Latin America, and are widely used in popular music.

ABOVE: *Congas are made in a wide variety of sizes; this one is a medium conga.*

Congas

Conga drums or "tumbas" are the lowest-pitched Latin American drums. They are single-headed drums with a long tapering wooden shell. Like the bongo, the conga has a depressed rim that leaves the head free for finger-style playing.

RIGHT: *Although bongos are authentically played with the fingers or hands, wooden sticks can be used for a louder sound.*

Timbales

Built with shallow shells made of brass or copper, single-headed timbales are supported on an adjustable stand and are played in pairs with thin wooden sticks. They are of Latin American origin. Although each one of a pair is of the same depth, they each have a different diameter that can range from 23cm/9in to 36cm/14in. Timbales give a bright, penetrating sound that is metallic with a pronounced ring.

ABOVE: The timbale drum is predominantly used in Latin American dance music.

Tabla

The Indian tabla is an instrument consisting of two small, single-headed hand drums, the *tabla* and the *bayan*.

*ABOVE: The Indian tabla player uses every joint and knuckle of his fingers and thumbs to produce a wide variety of sounds on the two drums (*tabla* and* bayan*).*

They produce a mellow, round sound of well-defined pitch. The *tabla* is the higher-pitched of the two, with a wooden shell and a diameter of about 15cm/6in. The head is made of three layers of skin, with a central black patch of a paste of flour and iron filings made according to an ancient recipe. The *bayan*, the bass drum, has a metal shell and a diameter of about 23cm/9in. It also has a black patch on the head.

There is also an Arabic drum called a tabla, which has an egg-cup shape and is made variously out of wood, earthenware or metal. It is either laid horizontally across the left knee or held under the left arm, and is beaten with the hands.

RIGHT: Steel drum pans can be played on the march, hung around the neck, or, as in this case, resting on a stand.

Steel drums

Originating in Trinidad in the 1930s and '40s, steel drums were first developed as instruments for use in processional and carnival bands, and were originally made by cutting down

RIGHT, CLOCKWISE FROM TOP LEFT: The drum kit consists of a ride cymbal, floor tom, two toms, snare drum, crash cymbal, hi-hat cymbal and bass drum.

ABOVE: Steel drum bands take part in many festivals. Here a band in the Virgin Islands is seen playing at an Easter sunrise service.

oil drums. A steel drum usually has a range of two octaves, and there are five steps in tuning it. First the head is pounded into a concave shape, after which the units are marked out by grooving with a steel punch. It is then tempered by burning, and the barrel is cut to the required length. Finally, the drum is tuned using a small hammer. Struck with a rubber-headed panstick, the tenor, or "ping-pong", plays the tune while the rhythm, guitar and bass pans provide the rhythm.

Drum kit

Dance, pop and jazz-band drummers generally sit at a drum kit that includes a variety of percussion instruments, including a bass drum of about 60cm/24in diameter that is played with a foot pedal. Other parts of the drum kit, such as the snare drum, cymbals and blocks, are played with sticks or brushes.

Cymbals and Gongs

*One single cymbal clash by Bruckner is worth all
the four symphonies of Brahms with the serenades thrown in.*

HUGO WOLF (1860–1903)

The cymbals are possibly the most spectacular percussion instruments of the orchestra. Generally made from copper or brass concave plates, the dramatic activities of the extrovert cymbalist never fail to attract the audience's attention.

Ancient cymbals

Cymbals were known in ancient Israel, where they were played during the dedication of the Ark. In Egypt small cymbals, only about 15cm/6in in diameter, were used from about the 8th century BC. From there the cymbals travelled to Greece, where they were originally used as a ritual instrument associated with the cult of the goddess Kybele. They passed into

ABOVE: Orchestral cymbals are held in the centre by leather hand-grips that pass through holes in the circular plates.

martial use and subsequently into the Greek theatre. The Greek *kymbala*, from which the modern name is derived, spread to Etruria, and so on to Rome and its empire.

Orchestral cymbals

The cymbals were almost forgotten in the West until the introduction of "Turkish" music in the second half of the 18th century. So unusual were cymbals at this time that when the French composer André Grétry (1741–1813) scored for them in his *L'Amitié à l'épreuve* (1770), it had to be explained to the performers how they were to be played. Nine years later Christoph Willibald Gluck used cymbals in *Iphigénie en Tauride* while, in the last quarter of the 18th century, the "clashpans" found their way into European military bands.

Cymbals began to be used regularly in orchestras in the early 19th century. Some composers used them simply as noisemakers, but others realized their full potential. One such composer was Berlioz, whose *Grande Messe des Morts* (1837) required ten cymbals, while his symphony *Roméo et Juliette* (1839) called for two "antique cymbals" tuned a fifth apart. Made of thick bronze and copied initially from those discovered in the ruins of Pompeii, antique cymbals or *crotales* are capable of being tuned to a definite pitch. They are sometimes arranged in a chromatic series and played with sticks. Other composers who have used the antique cymbals include Claude Debussy in *Prélude à l'après-midi d'un faune* (1892) and Igor Stravinsky in *The Rite of Spring* (1913).

Special effects

Cymbals are not just clashed together, but are capable of achieving many

ABOVE: This 15th-century painting shows a player holding a pair of cymbals vertically by their handles, the prevailing mode of playing in the West.

ABOVE: As well as being crashed together loudly, cymbals can be slid lightly across each other to produce a soft note, or struck with a drum stick.

in pairs to the thumb and forefinger or middle finger of each hand, are played in many countries, especially Egypt. Finger cymbals of a different type, like thimbles, are worn by Chinese dancers on the thumb and middle finger of each hand. Both kinds are also widely used in Western orchestral music.

ABOVE: Orchestral cymbals are heavy, and care is needed when preparing for an entrance.

ABOVE: Finger cymbals are attached in pairs to the thumb and forefinger or middle finger of each hand. These are still played in many countries, including Egypt and Greece, where the dancers prefer the two to be about a semitone apart.

effects. In the "slide", the edge of one cymbal is slid across the other, giving a quiet, sustained effect. The faces of the two cymbals can also be scraped together in a "roll *a due*". In his Five Orchestral Pieces (1909) Schoenberg asks that a cello bow be drawn over the edge of the cymbal, while Bartók's Sonata for Two Pianos and Percussion (1937) calls on the percussionist to stroke the edge of the cymbal with the blade of a penknife. In Debussy's *La Mer* (1905), a coin is scraped across the surface of the cymbal.

Modern cymbals

Since World War II, orchestras have come to prefer thinner cymbals with a lighter sound than the 19th-century instruments. Modern cymbals, made of an alloy of copper and tin, are usually considerably larger than earlier ones, and range between 30cm/12in and 65cm/26in in diameter, the most common being about 40cm/16in.

Finger cymbals

Usually made of brass or silver, finger cymbals originated in Asia as dancers' accoutrements, and they are still used this way. Miniature cymbals, attached

ABOVE: Bangladeshi dancers performing a traditional Manipur dance using small cymbals.

Hi-hats

Sometimes the cymbals are operated by a foot pedal. Originally, pedal cymbals were merely a pair of matched plates attached to wooden jaws held open with a spring, the player clashing the two together with the foot. Today, however, pedal cymbals – which are known as hi-hats (in dance bands) or choke cymbals (in orchestras) – are mounted on top of a stand so that they can be either played with the foot or clashed with a stick. They are occasionally found in the orchestra, but are a more common feature of small bands.

Jazz and pop bands

Since the 1920s, jazz bands have preferred Chinese-made cymbals because they make a louder clash with a shorter period of resonance. They have an upturned rim and a squared-off central section. Pop bands use various types of cymbals, such as the snap cymbal (which produces a quick splash of sound), the sizzle cymbal (which produces a sizzling sound due to the loose rivets inserted into the rim) and the ride cymbal (in which a constant reiteration of strokes does not build up into an echoing roar).

Indian cymbals

Various types of cymbals are used in India. The *cakva* of Maharashtra are about 9cm/3½in in diameter. Held by

ABOVE: Hi-hat cymbals are played mounted on a column and either struck with a stick or clashed together by a foot pedal.

ABOVE: In the 18th and early 19th centuries regimental bands often gave the cymbals to black musicians in the belief that they added "colour" to the band.

cloth handles, they are used in dancing and folk-singing. The *bartal*, on the other hand, is a large and heavy metal cymbal native to Assam. When clashed, the deep resonant tone of the *bartal* can be heard for over 15 seconds.

Another type of Indian cymbal is the *ilatalam*, which is mainly used in temple music, dance dramas and shadow-puppet plays. Found in the Kerala region, these flat instruments, made of brass and 12–15cm/5–6in in diameter, are played in two distinct ways. One method is to clash a pair horizontally together and then slip the edge of one against the rim of the other to obtain a prolonged ringing sound. The other method is to hold them vertically in the hollow of one hand and clash them by contracting the fingers towards the palm.

ABOVE: Cymbals are an important part of the modern drum kit.

also be made of silver (Tibet), iron (Africa) or bell metal (India). They are found in various sizes. Those that are bossed have a definite pitch, while those that are unbossed have indefinite pitch. In the orchestra the unpitched gong, or tam-tam, needs to be at least 100cm/39in in diameter to produce a deep enough fundamental.

Apart from the *chempung* of Sumatra, which is played resting on a bed of banana leaves, gongs are generally freely suspended and are struck in the centre with either a beater or the fist.

ABOVE: The tam-tam is a shallow suspended bronze gong with a long and colourful reverberation. Those with a shallow rim are from China, while those with a deeper rim come from Burma.

ABOVE: Detail of a traditional Chinese gong, showing the mallet striking the centre of the instrument.

Gong

For those of a certain age the gong will forever be associated with the opening credits of Rank films, in which a gigantic gong is struck by a muscular man. The player on the soundtrack of this famous sequence was the eminent percussionist James Blades.

Gongs are usually made of thin bronze with a turned edge, but may

Gong chimes

The Chinese *yun lo* is a set of small bronze gongs suspended vertically in an upright frame in three rows of three, with a single one at the top. Although they are all of the same diameter, they vary considerably in thickness. Originally they were Confucian and Buddhist cult instruments. Today, however, their

use is restricted to funeral processions. Sets of tuned gongs are also made in the West for orchestral use, with a range of up to four and a half octaves.

ABOVE: The gong plays an important role in many religions. Here a monk is about to strike a gong suspended in a Chinese temple.

ABOVE: A tam-tam mallet.

RIGHT: The gong is an Asian instrument with its origin in 6th-century China, where it was used to ward off evil spirits. Until the beginning of the 20th century Chinese servants preceded their masters and mistresses beating a single gong, the rank of the personage being indicated by the number of strokes.

Castanets

*My feet were alright
but I could not manage the castanets.*

MIKHAIL GLINKA (1804—57)

Castanets are percussion instruments of indefinite pitch that are either clicked rhythmically or sounded in a sustained roll. The name of the instrument comes from the Latin *castanea*, meaning chestnut, the wood out of which they were traditionally made. Today, however, other hardwoods, such as boxwood or walnut, are preferred. Each castanet is made from a single piece of wood, cut in half and hollowed out in the centre to form a hemispheric cavity. The two halves are united by a cord that is looped over the thumb for playing.

LEFT: Castanets have been used to accompany dancing from the earliest times. They came to Spain with the Arabs, but did not spread to the rest of Europe until the 16th century.

Ancient castanets

Clappers have been known for over 5000 years; in their most primitive form they were simply two sticks beaten together. Examples have been found made of wood, ivory or metal, and clappers originated both as a substitute for hand-clapping to accompany dance and as a noise to dispel devils. Hinged clappers, operated by one hand, have been traced back to the early third millennium when they were used by dancing girls in Sumer.

Vessel clappers, made from materials such as hippopotamus teeth, began to appear in Egypt from about 2000 BC. In some of these instruments the natural hollow inherent in the material formed the vessel, but in others the cavity was enlarged to increase the volume of sound. A hole was pierced in each shank to tie a pair together. Such instruments were always played by women to accompany dancing. These clappers evolved into prototype castanets, which made their first appearance — even though they were much longer than today's — in popular music-making in Greece and Egypt in about 500 BC. In a modified form they are still used by Copts in religious services. Castanets are also known to have been used in ancient Rome.

Spain

In Europe the castanets are primarily a dance instrument associated with flamenco in Spain, where they are believed to have been introduced while it was a Phoenician colony. Certainly a popular folk instrument, the castanets have virtually become Spain's national instrument. Although they are traditionally made of wood, it is recorded that during the Roman occupation the dancers of Cadiz played castanets made from metal.

Often used with a guitar to accompany dances — especially the

RIGHT: What would a Spanish dance be without the rhythmic sound of the dancers' castanets?

saraband — Spanish castanets consist of two almost circular discs, hollowed in the centre of the striking side and connected by an ornamental cord. The two castanets of a pair are of different pitches. The lower-pitched one (the *macho*, or "male") is held in the left hand, while the higher-pitched one (the *hembra*, or "female") is held in the right hand. The cups are held downwards and are manipulated by the fingers, using the middle two fingers of the left hand and all four fingers of the right hand. By 1588 both the dance

LEFT: *Of all national dances, the Spanish flamenco must rank as the most difficult to perform; the dancer not only has to concentrate on his or her steps, but also has to keep time with the castanets.*

RIGHT: *Orchestral castanets are attached to a handle. The player shakes the handle, striking the shells on the free hand.*

and the instrument had spread northwards into France, for in that year it is reported that the Duc de Richelieu, with castanets on his fingers and bells on his shoes, danced the saraband at a court ballet.

Orchestral castanets

True castanets are difficult to master and most modern orchestras use pairs, sometimes made of Bakelite, attached to long handles for ease in clicking. Many composers have scored for castanets in their Hispanic works, such as Georges Bizet's ever-popular opera *Carmen* (1873), Emmanuel Chabrier's *España* (1883) and Jules Massenet's *Le Cid* (1885).

Other composers have used the castanets to create special effects. Richard Wagner used them to create a great emotional impact in the lead-in to the "Venusberg" music in *Tannhäuser* (1845). Richard Strauss scored for them in the "Dance of the Seven Veils" from *Salome* (1905), and Benjamin Britten used them to imitate the sound of a night bird in *Let's Make an Opera!* (1949). The *castagnettes de fer*, for which Darius Milhaud scored in *Les Choëphores* in 1915, sounded like small cymbals or clappers.

LEFT: *Castanets are not the sole preserve of Spanish folk music. As this lithograph of 1840 shows, they are also found in Italy.*

Triangle

*Triangles and similar non-musical instruments
are forbidden to cornettists, be they master or apprentice.*

STUTTGART REGULATION OF 1721

The triangle was originally used as a folk instrument, and its value as an orchestral instrument was first realized in 1710 when it was employed by the Hamburg Opera. Seven years later it had entered the Dresden Opera. In both cases it was probably used to accompany folk-dancing.

Ancient triangle
The triangle is a descendant of the Egyptian *sistrum*, which was used in the worship of Hathor and Isis, and to ward off evil spirits. There were two main forms of the *sistrum*: the metal arched version and the faience "shrine" *sistrum*, which had as a central feature a head of the goddess Hathor. The metal version was shaped like an inverted U and was often made of silver with

ABOVE: The method of playing a triangle was described by Jacques Cellier: the triangle hung from the left thumb and was struck by a steel stick held in the right hand.

a straight wooden handle protruding from the bottom. Loose-fitting metal rods or wires jingled when shaken, and small loose metal discs were hung on the rods to create additional sounds.

European folk triangle
In medieval Europe triangles were used for religious purposes and dance music. In northern Europe these early instruments, larger than they are today, were of trapezoid form and usually had a series of loose rings, or jingles, threaded on to the lower bar. Before 1660 three rings were standard, whereas after this date as many as five appeared. By the 19th century the rings had disappeared completely. Italy and Bohemia favoured a stirrup shape devoid of rings.

For many years the "lowly" triangle was frowned upon and considered a

beggar's instrument, chiefly in use among vagrants and gypsies. Such was the musical snobbery of the early 18th century that cornett players in Stuttgart were actually forbidden to play the "paltry instrument".

The triangle in the orchestra
As an orchestral instrument the triangle was first scored for in about 1750 in an overture by Johann Friedrich Fasch (1688–1758). When the fashion for Janissary music arose in the mid 18th century, the triangle was substituted in the orchestra for the Turkish crescent, or bell tree (otherwise known as a "jingling Johnny"), which was used by military bands to create exotic effects with the cymbals and bass drum. Mozart scored for it in *Die Entführung aus dem Serail* (1782), Haydn

ABOVE: This 18th-century English scene shows a small boy playing the triangle, accompanied by a tambourine and flute.

ABOVE: So that it is always in reach, the orchestral triangle is usually suspended over one of the side drums.

in his *Military Symphony* (1794), and
Beethoven in his Ninth Symphony
(1823). Originally used only to
provide rhythm, in the mid 19th
century the triangle claimed its place
as an indispensable member of the
orchestra when Liszt raised it to the
rank of a solo instrument in his Piano
Concerto in E flat of 1853.

Many composers have since used the
triangle to great effect, but none more
picturesquely than Edward Elgar. In
the eleventh of his *Enigma Variations*
(1899) it is used to depict the tinkle of
the medal on the collar of the bulldog
Dan as he shakes himself after a plunge
into the River Wye.

Construction

The modern triangle is a steel rod bent
in the shape of an equilateral triangle,
left open where the ends meet so as to
allow the whole length to vibrate. It is
usually suspended by a thin thread or
wrist strap, so as not to interfere with
the vibrations. The triangle is beaten
with a rod of the same material.
Although the sound it makes is not
loud, because of its enharmonic
overtones its indefinite pitch can be
heard above the full orchestra. Were
the gap closed to make a complete
triangle, it would have a definite pitch.
Orchestral percussionists generally use
a range of triangles in different sizes.

ABOVE: *The blurred beater in this picture indicates that this orchestral performer is playing a rapid trill on the triangle.*

ABOVE: *Although the triangle is traditionally struck on the bottom bar, for special effects it can be struck almost anywhere.*

ABOVE: *This late 15th-century painting shows angels playing open tambourine and triangle.*

Xylophone

I must own that the skill of Michael Guzikow [Polish xylophonist] beats everything
that I would have imagined, for with his wooden sticks resting on straw
he produces all that is possible with the most perfect instrument.

FELIX MENDELSSOHN (1809–47)

The xylophone was introduced into the orchestra in 1874 when the French composer Camille Saint-Saëns scored for it in *Danse Macabre*, intending it to represent the rattling bones of the dead. Although little original orchestral music has been written for the xylophone, it has a small but useful solo repertoire.

ABOVE: The xylophone has tuned wooden bars with tubular resonators suspended underneath, and is played with wooden, rubber or plastic beaters.

The xylophone is a set of tuned wooden percussion blocks, which are laid in a row parallel to one another and are played by being hit with sticks or knobbed beaters. Tuning is achieved by reducing the length of the block to raise the pitch, or filing the underside at the centre of the block to lower it. As no vibrations occur at the ends of the blocks, they are either placed on straw ropes or pierced and fixed to a frame, without impairment of tone. Up to the 1920s xylophones in Germany were built using the former method, a feature that caused them to be called *Strohfiedel* ("straw fiddles").

The modern xylophone owes much to the work of Hermann Winterhof who, in 1927, invented the "arcuate notch". This is an arc cut on the underside of each key, both to improve the quality of tone and to give greater definition of pitch. Modern instruments are built in various sizes capable of playing up to four octaves, with rosewood keys arranged in two rows like those on a piano keyboard. Suspended under each key is a tubular metal resonator that gives the instrument its characteristic sound.

Europe

The xylophone has been known since at least the early 16th century, when Hans Holbein painted his *Dance of Death* showing Death carrying a xylophone suspended horizontally, like a tray, from a cord around his neck. However, the instrument did not become popular until the 1830s, when the Polish xylophonist Michael Joseph Gusikow brought it to the attention of the public with his concerts. Gusikow gave the instrument an enduring popularity in folk music.

Asia

The xylophone is believed to have originated in South-east Asia. One Asian version is the *mokkin* of Japan,

ABOVE: The marimba was developed in the United States around 1910. It is similar to the xylophone but is pitched an octave deeper, giving it a characteristic mellow sound.

ABOVE: *The marimba can be played with four beaters instead of two. Playing in this way produces soft, deep chords.*

ABOVE: *The* rang nat *is a type of metallic xylophone – known as a "metallophone" in Java and Bali – used in Javanese Gamelan bands. Also seen in this photograph are some gong chimes, or* khong vong yai.

which, although it has between 13 and 16 keys, is used as a rhythm rather than a melody instrument, chiefly in *kabuki* music. In Burma the *pattala* has up to 23 keys, which are finely tuned by fixing wax pellets to the undersides. The xylophones and metallophones of Indonesian percussion orchestras are many and varied, ranging from single-octave models to large multi-octave instruments that are played using two beaters. As early as the 7th century, Balinese *gambang* players were using four beaters, two in each hand, held to form a V.

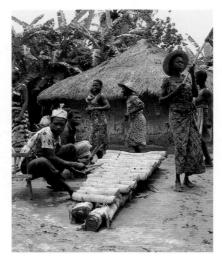

ABOVE: *In Zaire and other central African countries, xylophones are made by placing logs sliced into increasing sizes over a base of two long logs.*

Africa

From Asia the xylophone migrated to Africa. Here the simplest form is the pit or ground xylophone which, as the name implies, is a pit in the ground over which the ends of wooden bars are placed on bundles of grass. This primitive instrument is still played in parts of the continent, an example being the eight-keyed *ndara* of Uganda. The log xylophone, found in East and West Africa, as well as in Indonesia and Papua New Guinea, is composed of a few keys placed across the outstretched legs of the player. In a more developed form, gourds are suspended from the keys to augment the sound. In Nigeria a small portable version has ox-horn resonators.

Bells

Gay bells or sad, they bring you memories
of half forgotten innocent old places.

W. B. YEATS (1865–1939)

In one form or another, bells are known all over the world. Ancient Egyptian priests wore small closed silver bells as protective amulets when they were in the temple, a practice continued in the Christian church: as late as the 11th century, Archbishop Lanfranc of Canterbury wore a cope edged with 51 bells.

The practice of fitting animals with bells to ward off evil dates back to at least 520 BC, when they are mentioned in the *Book of Zachariah*. In Siberia small bells are still fitted on to the yokes of horse-drawn vehicles to scare off wolves and devils.

Ancient Greek soldiers attached bronze bells to their shields in an effort to terrify the enemy. It must have been an awesome sound for, owing to the density of bronze, their bells would have clanged rather than emitting the clear ringing tone that is expected today. The Greeks also issued bells to watchmen and sentinels for use in alerting the population in times of danger.

The custom of ringing a "passing bell", with the object of keeping evil spirits away from the dead, dates back to at least the 8th century. The Bayeux Tapestry, made in the late 11th century, clearly shows two boys, each carrying a pair of hand bells, accompanying the coffin of Edward the Confessor for exactly this reason.

Casting

Early bells were cast using the *cire perdue* or "lost wax" method. A clay or brick model of the inside surface of the

ABOVE: A late 7th-century BC bronze bell found in Bologna, Italy.

bell was made. Over this, a layer of wax was built up to the shape and thickness of the finished bell. Once the wax had set, it was covered by another layer of clay and the entire mould was thoroughly baked. As the clay hardened the wax melted and drained away, leaving a vacant space into which the bell metal was poured to form the actual bell. The Whitechapel Bell Foundry in London, which still casts church bells and a five-octave range of hand bells, was founded in 1420.

Some early bells were not cast but made from thin iron plates hammered into circular or rectangular sheets and riveted together before being dipped into molten copper to seal the joints.

ABOVE: The bells of the Church of San Francisco in Córdoba, Spain. Bells are traditionally hung high in church towers so that they can be heard over great distances.

Church bells

Early church bells were of a long, thin beehive shape. During the 12th and 13th centuries, however, the form of the bell evolved into a slightly conical sugar-loaf shape, which by the beginning of the 14th century had reached the fatter, wider appearance that is familiar today.

One of the earliest references to ringing church bells in England is found in Rutland. Here, in the church of St Andrew in Stoke Dry on the early 12th-century south pillar of the Romanesque chancel arch, is depicted a man pulling on a bell rope. Although it was not until the 16th century that bells regularly began to carry inscriptions, at Littleborough, Nottinghamshire there is a bell made in about 1170 that bears the inscription "Santa Maria".

The mechanics of the church bell are relatively simple. The crown of each bell is fixed to a headstick of metal, which is in turn attached to a large wheel. The rim of the wheel is grooved to hold the bell rope which, when pulled, raises the bell, causing it to swing until its mouth is high enough for the clapper to strike it.

Change-ringing

Britain differs from the rest of Europe in that church bells are rung in changes. A change is the ringing of a set of bells in all possible combinations. Thus a set of three bells contains six changes (123, 231, 213, 321, 312 and 132). Each set of changes constitutes a peal. A peal of three bells consists of six changes, while a peal of four bells contains 24, one of eight bells contains 40,320 and so on.

ABOVE: *The custom of fitting animals, such as horses and cows, with bells was originally to ward off evil, although on a more practical level it is also useful for the farmer to be able to hear them moving around.*

ABOVE: *The earliest known carving (12th-century) of church bell ringers.*

ABOVE: *An engraving of an 18th-century French bell foundry showing a bell being hoisted from its casting mould.*

Hand bells

Hand bells, as the name implies, are relatively small bells fitted with a handle that enables them to be held in the hand for ringing. The oldest known hand bells come from China and date from about 1600 BC. Chinese hand bells were, however, in existence before this, for there are earlier written references to their use in religious music. In 9th-century Japan small hand bells struck with hammers were used to accompany the singing of *goeka*, a kind of Buddhist plainsong. This tradition lives on, and at the beginning of the 21st century there are many enthusiasts who form several thousand *goeka* societies in Japan, and hold regular conventions.

Modern Western hand bells are normally made in sets numbering between six and 60, covering a range of up to five octaves, and are usually rung by groups of between four and 15 ringers. Generally each player holds one or two bells in each hand. Sometimes, however, the bells are laid on a table and are lifted and rung as they are required.

By the mid 19th century almost every village in England had its own hand-bell team that played at local fairs, entertainments and during the Christmas season. In the 20th century, hand-bell ringing again became popular, this time in the United States. In 1954 the American Guild of English

ABOVE: A modern handmade set of bell chimes.

Hand-bell Ringers was founded and today there are more than a thousand teams representing over 10,000 ringers.

Bell wheel

One of the earliest ecclesiastical uses of small bells is the bell wheel, or *Zimbelstern*, examples of which are recorded from the 10th century. Mainly found in France, Germany and Spain, and to a lesser extent in Britain, this contraption consisted of a number of small silver bells attached to a large wheel. The wheel was originally revolved by means of either a rope or a hand-crank, but by the 13th century clockwork was also used, and some were attached to the church organ and operated by a stop.

One of the finest bell wheels was the "Star" of Fulda Cathedral in Germany. This wonderful creation, which was suspended from the nave ceiling, was 7.3m/24ft in diameter and had no less than 350 bells attached to its 14 rays. In 1781 tragedy struck when its rope broke, causing it to crash down upon the assembled congregation. Since its restoration, it still has 150 of its bells and is operated by a treadmill.

Bell chimes

Although tuned sets of bell chimes have been in existence for at least 3000 years, it was not until the 11th century that they reached Europe. The first depiction of the instrument, in an illustrated Bible of about 1070, shows a musician hammering a seven-bell chime with one hand while tapping a frame drum with the other hand. During the 13th century some chimes, which were connected to town clocks, were mechanized, the time being sounded by bells that were struck by hammers operated by a cogwheel.

LEFT: Hand-bell groups were very popular in the 19th century. One such band that toured extensively was the "Swedish Bell Ringers".

Carillon

The art of making bell chimes was perfected in the Low Countries and northern France, where the bells were suspended from a framework inside a tower. Hammers were automatically released by iron pegs set into a large wooden barrel (later a metal cylinder) that was turned by weights and pulleys. As the barrel revolved, the pegs tripped levers that were in turn connected to the hammers by wires.

ABOVE: *The carillon at the church of Corneille sur Risle, France.*

ABOVE: *A 13th-century illumination depicting a man playing a bell chime with crudely made hammers. By his side is another musician playing a viol in the style of the period.*

Two of the earliest town clocks fitted with bells were the one in Mons (1328) and the astronomical clock in Strasbourg Cathedral (1354). The latter's pegs were fitted in such a way that the bells could play several tunes.

From about 1500 a keyboard was added to the Antwerp carillon, making it possible to play the bells manually. During the 16th century the compass of the carillons extended downwards, involving larger, heavier bells. As these were impossible to play by hand, a pedal board was added. The number of bells continued to increase and, by 1612, St Paul's church in Liège boasted a carillon of 24 bells.

As the popularity of the carillon grew, so did the demand for longer and more varied tunes. Once the cylinder had made a single complete revolution all its music had been played, so to accommodate longer tunes larger cylinders were made, some reaching over 2m/6ft in diameter.

The most famous carillon builders of the 17th century were the Van der Gheyn family and the Hemony brothers, Pierre and François, who came from Lorraine but worked in Amsterdam. In 1655 Pierre Hemony built the largest carillon yet, a machine containing 52 bells. He was such a perfectionist that he required his bells to contain the overtones of three octaves, two fifths, a major third and a minor third.

Today the world's foremost builder of carillons is the British bell foundry Taylor & Co., in Loughborough. Their creations have been installed in bell towers all over the world, including their home town, where a 47-bell carillon was built in 1923 as a memorial to those men of the town who died in World War I.

ABOVE: *These traditional Swiss cow bells are accompanying a procession of alpine singers.*

Bells in the orchestra

Bells have been used in orchestras since the 18th century. One outstanding use of bells took place in 1882 at the first performance of Tchaikovsky's *1812 Overture*. Although the ambitious Tchaikovsky had wanted to have all the church bells of Moscow peal out in the grand finale, the city fathers deemed the idea impractical so the composer had to be content with the bells of Uspensky Cathedral, in which the concert took place.

Many 19th-century composers, however, preferred to use other instruments to imitate the sound of the bell. Rimsky-Korsakov, for instance, used a combination of triangle, cymbal and gong combined with *pizzicato* and sustained chords from the strings and wind in his *Russian Easter Festival*

LEFT: Orchestral sleigh bells recreate the sound of the bells placed around the necks of sleigh-pulling Russian horses.

overture in 1888. Generally, however, modern orchestras use tubular bells, but since the 1970s synthesizers and other electronic instruments have been increasingly used to imitate bells.

Tubular bells

Tubular bells originated in South-east Asia. When they became known in Europe the chimes were at first made of bell metal, but this proved expensive. In 1886, after various experiments, a British instrument maker, John Hampton of Coventry, produced tubular bells made of bronze. Today chimes are usually made of brass. Ordered in graduated lengths to give a range of up to two octaves, they all have the same diameter and are suspended from a frame.

ABOVE: Modern orchestral tubular bells.

ABOVE: Tubular bells mallets.

ABOVE: By the 16th century some bell chimes were connected to a keyboard, thereby making it possible to play the bells manually.

ABOVE: Tubular bells are sounded by being hit at the top with hard mallets. A foot pedal operates a felted damper to stop the sound when required.

Glockenspiel

The European concept of the glockenspiel originated in the Netherlands, where it was introduced from Indonesia in the second half of the 17th century. The European instrument was originally a miniature carillon, and its earliest known use was in 1739 when Handel used one in a production of *Saul*. Today it is more commonly made of a series of graduated steel bars, arranged in two rows like the black and white keys of a piano, and played with moderately hard beaters.

ABOVE: *The modern glockenspiel has steel bars covering two and a half octaves.*

The keyed glockenspiel, in which small metal hammers strike the bars from below, arrived in the orchestra before what is now the standard instrument took its place in the mid 19th century, and Mozart, Tchaikovsky, Saint-Saëns and many other composers included it in their scores. Nearly all these parts are now played on the conventional glockenspiel, which has a superior tone and dynamic range.

Bell-lyra

The portable glockenspiel was designed in the 19th century specifically for German marching bands. Originally a single row of metal cups, it is now made with a series of metal bars arranged like a piano keyboard that are hung in a lyre-shaped frame set on a wooden handle. Tapped with a metal beater, it is carried in front of the player, level with the head.

Celesta

Similar to the keyed glockenspiel, the celesta resembles an upright piano. The metal bars are struck by felt-covered hammers activated by a simple piano mechanism, and there is a sustaining pedal. It was invented by Auguste

Mustel of Paris in 1886 as an improvement on the "dulcitone", an instrument consisting of a series of tuning forks operated by a keyboard, which he had constructed some 20 years earlier.

According to legend, Tchaikovsky was walking down a street in Paris when he heard a celesta being played. He was so enchanted by the sound that he used it to represent the Sugar-plum Fairy in *The Nutcracker* (1892). Béla Bartók scored for the celesta in his *Music for Strings, Percussion and Celesta*, which was published in 1936.

ABOVE: *The celesta is played like a piano but has a bell-like sound. Although mainly used in classical orchestras, it is also occasionally used in popular music.*

Vibraphone

The vibraphone is a cross between the glockenspiel and the xylophone, and was invented in the United States in 1921. Beneath the alloy bars are tubular resonators fitted with resonating lids that are made to vibrate by means of an electric motor. The vibraphone produces a bell-like sound and has been scored for by composers such as Benjamin Britten and Luigi Dallapiccola (1904–75). It quickly became popular as a jazz instrument, first played by its leading exponent Lionel Hampton (1909–2002).

ABOVE: *The vibraphone has a foot pedal that opens and closes the resonating tubes.*

Bells music

Among the earliest composers to score for bells were Nicholas Dalayrac (1753–1809) in his opera *Camille* (1791), and Luigi Cherubini (1760–1842) in *Elisa* (1794). Rossini called for a bell in the second act of *William Tell* (1829), and Giacomo Meyerbeer (1791–1864) demanded a specially made large bell for *Les Huguenots* (1836).

❦ Keyboards ❦

Striking Chords

*The most difficult things written by one perfectly versed in the difficulties of the keyboard
are far easier to play than the easiest things conceived by an amateur.*

ROBERT SCHUMANN (1810–56)

Early keyboards had only natural notes (the "white" notes) identified by the first seven letters of the alphabet (A–G), which were often marked on the appropriate keys to allow the player to differentiate between otherwise identical keys. In time a B flat was inserted between the A and B keys, which were cut away for the purpose. In Germany the B flat is still referred to as B, while the B is known as H. By the 15th century the keyboard had become fully chromatic, with the five raised sharp and flat notes forming an upper row as they do today. The oldest surviving chromatic keyboard dates from 1361 and is found on the organ of Halberstadt Cathedral in Germany.

With the introduction of sharps and flats to the keyboard, the old modal system — which had been built around the different notes of the diatonic

ABOVE: *This painting is from the cover of a virginal. It shows a band of musicians in the
midst of the autumnal wine-making festivities. Built by Paul Wissmayr for Lucas Behaim
in 1619, Behaim himself is seen playing the bass viol.*

ABOVE: *The keys of the harpsichord differ
from those of other keyboards in that the
"naturals" are black and the "accidentals"
are white.*

"natural" scales — slowly died out and its place was taken by the familiar major and minor scales that were better suited to harmony. In the Middle Ages there had been six modes, but now there were just two, each available in 12 keys.

Although Pythagoras's natural intervals had been adequate for the simple melodies and harmonies of the modal system, based on a handful of common chords, they caused problems when the chromatic keyboard was introduced. The reasons for this are found in mathematics. On a seven-octave keyboard there are 12 fifths. Pythagoras showed that the frequency ratio of an octave to its fundamental was 2:1 and that of a fifth was 3:2.

To cover the seven octaves, $(2:1)^7$ could be expected to equal $(3:2)^{12}$. However, $(2:1)^7$ produces 128 and $(3:2)^{12}$ gives 129.75.

Mean-tone temperament

A partial solution was adopted in the 16th century when mean-tone temperament was developed by Francisco Salinas (1513–90), a music theorist at the University of Salamanca, to "temper" or adjust the intervals of fixed-pitch instruments to fit them for practical performance. The system was founded on the accuracy of the major third. Taking C' as the fundamental, the fourth fifth reaches e. However, this e did not make an exact major third with the c immediately below it.

Mean-tone temperament flattened the *e* so that an exact major third was formed, and in so doing the four fifths that had been passed through were also slightly flattened. This method of tuning was fine for the major scales of A, G, D, C, F and B flat, and the relative minors of the last three, but not for other scales, because it made the distance between the semitones unequal, so that a passage played in one key sounded discordant when played in another. Keyboard composers before the 18th century therefore wrote in comparatively few keys and used very little modulation.

Equal temperament

The problem was solved by dividing the octave into 12 equal semitones, creating equal temperament. In so doing, each semitone was slightly adjusted from its natural position. By this means, for example, D sharp and E flat became identical, although

ABOVE: A 1920s rosewood baby grand piano with ivory keys, made by Steinway.

according to "natural" tuning they differ slightly. When fixed-pitch instruments were tuned in this way, they could be played in any key, and modulation into any other key was possible.

This system had originally been suggested as early as the 16th century, but was not adopted until the 18th, when it was still opposed as an impure compromise. Bach's 48 Preludes and Fugues, published in two books in 1722 and 1744 as *The Well-tempered Clavier*, were written in all the major and minor keys as an endorsement of the system of equal temperament.

ABOVE: The organ at the Royal Festival Hall in London was built with meticulous workmanship by Harrison & Harrison and was inaugurated in 1954.

ABOVE: The grand piano is an important orchestral and solo instrument.

Clavichord

Who dislikes noise, raging and fuming, whose heart bursts in sweet feelings,
neglects both the harpsichord and the piano and chooses the clavichord.

CHRISTIAN SCHUBART (1739–91)

The clavichord is of deceptively simple construction, consisting of a small shallow box without stand or legs. Behind the keyboard, the strings are attached to hitch-pins at the left of the box, then pass across the back halves of the keys and over the bridge to the tuning pins on the right. When a key is depressed the tangent (a small upright brass blade set directly in the key) gently touches the corresponding string, making a vibration node at the point of contact; to the right of this strike point the string crosses the bridge that transmits the vibrations to the soundboard. The superfluous section of the string to the left is deadened by a strip of felt that is woven between the strings.

The loudness of the tone depends directly on the force used by the player on the key, and the tangent remains in contact with the string while it is sounding. The loudest possible sound is produced by depressing a key quickly, but at its loudest the

LEFT: This clavichord was built by Georg Schmahl of Ulm in 1807. Although not as ornate as some of this maker's earlier creations, the natural keys are covered in plumwood.

clavichord is too quiet to be anything other than a solo instrument. Its soft, ethereal tone is, however, ideal for domestic use in small rooms.

Fretted clavichord

Until the early 18th century all clavichords were "fretted": each string was struck by the tangents of several keys. An individual string for each note was unnecessary, as notes as close as a tone or a semitone apart were rarely played together in the predominantly melodic music of the time. In the bass octave each of the notes usually had its own string; two or three keys shared a string in the middle register, while the treble strings were shared by two, three or four keys.

Key features

TYPE: keyboard
PITCH: concert
RANGE: *E' to e"*

ABOVE: This finely detailed painting, executed by the Dutch master Jan Muyckens in 1648, shows a gentleman seated at a clavichord. The instrument is resting on a table and the lid has been raised to show the action.

The first clavichords had a compass of two and a half octaves, but by the 17th century this had risen to four, with a short octave in the bass in which no keys were provided for unnecessary chromatic notes as a device to save space. Essentially domestic instruments, clavichords were also used by organists when practising.

Unfretted clavichord

In the early 18th century German clavichords began to appear unfretted, that is with a separate string for each note. Larger clavichords with a five or six-octave compass were built, and superb examples of decorated casework were made. Although this would appear to have been an improvement, it did not prove popular, for more strings meant a larger, heavier and therefore more expensive instrument.

Germany

Although the clavichord gave way to virginals and spinets throughout much of Europe in the 16th and 17th centuries, it remained popular in Germany, Scandinavia and Spain. By 1650 northern Germany was the centre of clavichord-making and manufacturers were building clavichords that cost about one-quarter

ABOVE: A 17th-century Dutch painting by Gerrit Dou of a woman at the clavichord.

of the price of a harpsichord. By the mid 1700s the German clavichord had become a symbol of the *Empfindsame Zeitalter*, standing for noble simplicity as a bastion against the encroaching ostentation of the piano.

Germany also developed its own style of playing. As the tangent remains in contact with the string, a slight variation of finger pressure on the key

ABOVE: This simple line drawing is said to date from about 1440 and shows a musician playing the clavichord at a table.

can alter the tension of the string. By caressing the key a *bebung* effect was produced that gave warmth and feeling to the note in much the same way as the violinist uses vibrato.

Even in Germany, however, the clavichord finally had to give way to the piano, and by 1820 it was virtually extinct, until it was recreated in the 20th century for the playing of early music.

Clavichord music

Sixteenth-century music composed for the clavichord usually consisted of dances such as Hugh Aston's *Hornepype*, the *Quatorze gaillards* published by Pierre Attaingnant in 1531, and the *Intavolatura nova di varie sorte de balli* issued in Venice by Gardane in 1551. Music was still being composed for the clavichord in the 18th century by composers such as C. P. E. Bach (1714–88), Christian Neefe (1748–98) and Friedrich Rust (1739–96), who wrote pieces that included special effects for the instrument such as strumming and drumming on the strings.

RIGHT: An unfretted clavichord made by the Bavarian instrument maker Christian Gottlob Hubert in the late 18th century.

Harpsichord

One should have an easy manner at the harpsichord and
avoid either staring fixedly at any object, or looking too vague.

FRANÇOIS COUPERIN (1668–1733), "L'ART DE TOUCHER LE CLAVECIN"

The harpsichord can be dated back to at least 1397, when there is a record in Padua of the invention of an instrument called a *clavicymbalum*, a name that was translated as "virginal" in England. It did not become known as the harpsichord, from the Italian *arpicordo*, until 1607. The new instrument was the first to use a mechanical plucking action to activate the strings; this system was also used in the virginal and the spinet.

LEFT: A harpsichord made in 1756 by Jacob Kirckman of London. The interior surfaces are decorated with holly and walnut marquetry, while the case is veneered with burr walnut.

stops modify the sounds in other ways, such as the "harp" stop that mutes some strings to give a *pizzicato* effect, or the "lute" stop that operates extra jacks nearer the ends of the strings to give a nasal sound.

Mechanism

The harpsichord is a mechanized version of the psaltery. Each key operates a wooden rod, or "jack", on which is mounted a quill plectrum. As the key is depressed, the jack rises and the plectrum plucks the string. The jack is so constructed that on its way down, when the key is released, the plectrum is pivoted back and avoids the string. As the jack descends a felt damper quietens the string.

Because the strings run at right angles to the keyboard, it is possible to mount more than one jack on each key, and more than one string to each note, each with its own jack. Each set of strings is called a "choir". By moving the jacks to one side, using a stop, one or more choirs can be left unplucked, so that the volume of sound produced is reduced. Apart from this facility, the player has no control over the level of sound, as the string is always plucked in the same way. However, additional

Two-manual harpsichord

From the 1670s, the development of double manuals allowed performers to change from louder to softer passages without interrupting their playing. The lower manual worked two choirs, while the upper manual worked a single choir for quiet passages. In French harpsichords, the two mechanisms could be coupled to operate all three choirs together for maximum volume.

ABOVE: A beautifully decorated harpsichord.

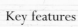

Key features

TYPE: keyboard

PITCH: concert

RANGE: *c'* to *c''''*

NOTABLE PLAYERS OF THE HARPSICHORD: Wanda Landowska, Arnold Dolmetsch, Thurston Dart, Christopher Hogwood.

Styles

The earliest surviving instruments are Italian, including one dated 1515. They have single manuals and separate outer cases, and may have had only a single set of strings.

Flemish harpsichords, principally made by the Ruckers family of Antwerp from the mid 16th to late 17th centuries, were played all over Europe. They were beautifully decorated with printed papers, and in some instruments the paintings inside the lid were by Rubens. Many Ruckers harpsichords were later rebuilt for the French market by Pascal Taskin, who inherited the French firm of Blanchet, the royal harpsichord makers.

The major English makers of the 18th century were Burkat Shudi (1702–73), who was joined in 1761 by John Broadwood (1732–1812) and Jacob Kirckman (1710–92). While French instruments were elaborately painted and gilded, English harpsichord cases were relatively austere, but were finely veneered in walnut and sycamore or, later, in satinwood and mahogany.

ABOVE: *Harpsichords are often beautifully decorated, with gold panelling and painted scenes.*

Innovations

During the 18th century there were many attempts to modify and improve the harpsichord. Jean Marius's *clavecin brisé*, or folding harpsichord of 1700, was made in three hinged sections. The century also saw ever-larger harpsichords with three and even four registers, together with a complex system of stops to provide different tone-colours. In 1769 Shudi patented the "Venetian swell", a device that opened and shut like a Venetian blind over the strings and soundboard, to produce *crescendos* and *diminuendos*. The quill plectrum was replaced by one made of hard leather.

Decline

In 1768 Johann Christian Bach's London recital made the piano instantly fashionable and ended the supremacy of the harpsichord. Although the harpsichord was still being built in Dublin as late as 1824, it was soon overtaken by the new, more expressive instrument. By 1837 it was almost extinct, for when in that year the pianist Ignaz Moscheles gave a "historical" recital in London, he had difficulty in finding a harpsichord on which to perform.

The modern revival began in the 1880s, when the French piano makers Erard and Pleyel built copies of 18th-century harpsichords, and in London Arnold Dolmetsch began to present recitals of Renaissance and Baroque music on antique instruments.

ABOVE: *Detail of a modern harpsichord keyboard built by Colin Booth in 1993.*

Virginal

*To teach men's daughters on the virginal is
as harmless a calling as any man can follow.*

SOLOMON ECCLES (1618–83)

Although virginals were the most popular keyboard instruments in Elizabethan households, the name is not, as many believe, a compliment to the "Virgin Queen". Descended from the psaltery, the instrument has been known since at least 1460, 50 years before Elizabeth's birth. The etymology of the word "virginals" (like "scissors", it is often used in the plural) is uncertain. It may be from the Latin *virga*, meaning "rod" or

ABOVE: A 16th-century engraving showing a woman playing a virginal.

ABOVE: A 1976 replica of a 1623 Ruckers virginal from Antwerp. Apart from their musical quality, instruments from Antwerp are notable for the elaborate decoration of their interiors with printed paper and painting.

"jack", or may even be a reference to the young ladies who most commonly played the instrument.

By 1500 virginals were being played throughout Europe. They are mentioned in a proverb that was inscribed on the walls of Manor House, Leckingfield, Yorkshire, in about 1500, while on the other side of Europe the court organist at Buda played the virginal to entertain the prince at mealtimes in 1501. Henry VIII is known to have purchased five virginals in 1530, while in 1549 the Innsbruck court bought an instrument made by an organ builder from Königsberg. Virginals were extremely popular as domestic instruments in the Low Countries, England, Austria and Germany. In England they eventually gave way to the spinet and in Germany to the clavichord.

Shape

Strung with 32 metal strings lying parallel with the keyboard, the virginal had the form of a clavichord coupled with the sound of a harpsichord, since the strings were plucked. Each string was longer than that of its neighbour, forming a triangle inside the case, with the long bass strings at the front. In Flemish virginals the keyboard was placed either to the right or left of the centre of the long side, a feature that determined the timbre of the instrument. When it was placed to the right, the strings were plucked nearer their centre, and this produced a nasal tone that was described as "grunting

ABOVE: Detail of the inside of a virginal with delicately painted flowers and embellishments. The highest standards of craftsmanship went into the lavish decoration of the domestic instruments.

without a lid. Flemish virginals, which were chiefly made in Antwerp, had recessed keyboards made of thicker softwood and were furnished with a lid. English virginals, all surviving examples of which were made between 1640 and 1680, combined features of both the Italian and Flemish styles. They were exceptionally deep and featured a vaulted lid.

Double virginal

An extremely popular form was the double virginal, invented in Antwerp. Nicknamed the "mother and child", it combined a large keyboard cheek by jowl with a smaller one half the size. The smaller one was set in a recess between the soundboard and the bottom of the case, usually to the left of the larger keyboard. Although it could also be played on its own, during performance the "child" could be withdrawn and placed on top of the "mother" so that the latter's keyboard played both instruments, the "child" sounding an octave above the "mother". These were built in the late 16th century, and in 1584 a Leipzig musical instrument dealer named Krause had in his stock *"I neu Instrument mit 2 Clavieren"* ("one new instrument with two keyboards").

like pigs". This form was called a *muselar*. With the keyboard to the left, in the form called a *spinett*, the sound was brighter.

There were three main centres of virginal-making: Italy, Belgium and England. Italian-made virginals, which were characterized by a projecting keyboard like the contemporary Italian spinet, were made of cypress wood

Spinet

*Called upon one Haward, that makes virginalls, and did there like of a little espinette, and will
have him finish it for me: for I had a mind to a small harpsichon, but this takes up less room.*

SAMUEL PEPYS (1633–1703)

The spinet, a small version of the harpsichord, is believed to have got its name from either the Italian word *spina* or the French *épinette* ("thorn"), both references to the plectra with which the instrument's strings are plucked. Another theory is that it is named after one of the early builders of the instrument, the Venetian Giovanni Spinetti, one of whose surviving instruments is dated 1503.

The spinet has the same action as the harpsichord, but is built on a smaller, domestic scale. It was popular in France from the late 15th century. As well as being mentioned in an Avignon contract of 1503, the instrument is also included in the household accounts of the Countess of Angoulême in the mid 1490s. Although early instruments were built of thin cypress wood, without a lid, by the 18th century the cases were being made of thicker wood, such as Brazil or pine, and were complete with lids. Smaller spinets, termed "spinettinos", were also made.

LEFT: A typical early English example of a bentside spinet built in London in about 1770. This compact harpsichord, whose keyboard occupies much of the case, is made of walnut, with Italian-style interior trim in cypress.

The spinet was not introduced into England until Charles II's return from France at the Restoration in 1660. It soon proved very popular, and by the end of the century an English school of spinet-building had developed, and the instrument was beginning to replace the virginal. Most English spinets had a compass starting with G, whereas continental spinets tended to begin on F.

For those who could not afford a harpsichord or did not have room for one, the spinet was the next best thing. It flourished longer in England than anywhere else, only disappearing when it was replaced by the square piano in the early 19th century.

Shape

The spinet's single set of strings is arranged across the instrument (in

Key features

TYPE: keyboard

PITCH: concert

RANGE: *c' to c''''*

ABOVE: This finely decorated 16th-century polygonal spinet was built by the Italian maker Annibale dei Rossi. He and his son Ferrante were recorded in 1595 as improvers and modernizers of clavichords.

contrast to the harpsichord where the strings are set at right angles to the keyboard). The oblique stringing of the early models produced a trapezoid shape, while the characteristic Italian spinet of the 16th and 17th centuries was five or six-sided, with a keyboard projecting from the long side.

Small spinets of the Italian pattern were most popular in France in the 16th and 17th centuries. These were usually about 80cm/32in (tuned to an octave above concert pitch) or 102cm/40in long (tuned to a fourth above concert pitch).

In Germany there were rare cases of wing-shaped spinets being made with two manuals for use by organists and teachers.

In 1631 Girolamo Zenti invented the bentside or "leg of mutton" spinet, a development that achieved great popularity in England. So named because of its wing shape, it was made in the shape of a triangle with unequal sides, with the keyboard set into one of the shorter sides. It was a conveniently compact shape, being both shorter and narrower than a harpsichord of equal range.

ABOVE: An engraving entitled Dame am Spinett *by Johann Sartorius.*

Double-strung spinet

As a rule the spinet was not capable of changes of tone-colour or volume. An attempt to rectify this was the double-strung spinet. Examples of this rare type are the two-manual octave spinet built by Israel Gellinger, and Cristofori's *"cembelo traverso"*. Variations were obtained in these instruments by moving the keyboard in or out, so that both or only one set of jacks would be lifted when the keys were depressed.

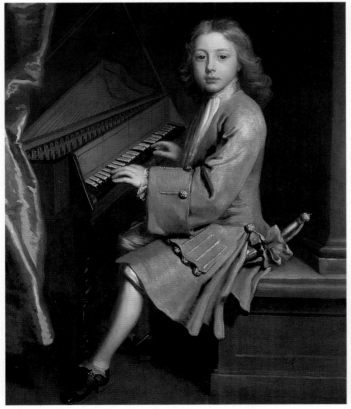

ABOVE: An 18th-century painting of a young man playing the spinet by Jonathan Richardson (1665–1745). Like the harpsichord, the "natural" keys of the spinet are black and the "accidentals" are white.

ABOVE: This spinet was made by one of the main English keyboard makers of the 18th century, Thomas Hitchcock of London.

Piano

The pianoforte is the most perfect of all musical instruments: its invention was to music what the invention of printing was to poetry.

GEORGE BERNARD SHAW (1856–1950)

The months of May and June 1768 saw the turning point in the history of the piano. On May 19, Henry Walsh gave the world's first public performace for solo piano in Dublin; two weeks later, on June 2, at the Thatched House, St James's Square, London, Johann Christian Bach (1735–82) – J. S. Bach's youngest son – performed on a square piano. These were not the first occasions that the instrument had been heard in public, for a year earlier Charles Dibdin had used a piano to accompany a song sung during the interval of a production of *The Beggar's Opera* at Covent Garden, London. However, the kudos given to the piano by Bach's recital made the instrument fashionable overnight.

Bartolomeo Cristofori

The pianoforte was invented around 1709 by Bartolomeo Cristofori (1655–1731), a harpsichord builder and keeper of the royal musical instruments in Florence. The early Cristofori pianos, which looked and sounded like contemporary harpsichords, had a range of four octaves, half that of a modern grand. Indeed the very name, *gravicembalo col piano e forte*, implied that it was considered merely as another type of harpsichord, there being no real desire at the time to create an entirely new instrument. Surviving Cristofori pianos, with their thin strings and

LEFT: An ornate 19th-century grand piano built by Joseph Schneider.

hard hammers, do in fact sound very like harpsichords.

The main difference between the piano and the harpsichord was that the strings of the former were struck

ABOVE: This sturdy grand piano was presented to Ludwig van Beethoven by the London firm of John Broadwood & Sons in 1817.

by hammers rather than being plucked by quills, as in the harpsichord. When the piano key was pressed, the hammer struck the string and immediately came away, allowing the string to vibrate and sound until the key was released, activating a damper to silence it. The earliest music published specifically for the piano was a sonata composed by Lodovico Giustini in 1732, the year after Cristofori's death.

Square piano

Actually an oblong shape similar to the clavichord, the square piano was first made in 1742 by Johann Sacher, a Bavarian instrument maker. Although these instruments took up less space and were cheaper to produce than grand pianos, the main problem was that the bass strings had to be short and were therefore weak in tone as well as volume.

In Britain, square pianos were made by Johannes Zumpe from 1760, and it was one of his instruments on which J. C. Bach gave his London recital. An early French builder of square pianos was Sébastien Erard (1752–1831) who introduced various improvements to the Zumpe design including the *agraffe* in 1808, a device that improved the tension of the strings, and, in 1821, the double escapement action that

ABOVE: *Franz Liszt playing a piano built by Ludwig Bösendorfer.*

ABOVE: *This 1726 Cristofori piano represents the climax of the Italian's work. It is double-strung and has a four-octave compass as well as a synchronized damper.*

ABOVE: *This square piano built by Adam Beyer of London in 1777 is decorated with two sorts of mahogany.*

increased the speed at which notes could be repeated.

Although upright pianos gradually became more popular in European homes during the 19th century, square pianos survived for many years, particularly in the United States, where they grew large and elaborate.

The piano in the home

By the end of the 18th century the piano had become more than just a fashionable toy, and was a living force

Frédéric Chopin

Without doubt one of the greatest composers for the piano who ever lived was Frédéric Chopin (1810–49), the son of a French father and a Polish mother, who moved to Paris in 1831. His music was a kaleidoscope of three distinct traditions: German classicism, Italian *bel canto* and Polish folk music, and he composed almost exclusively for the piano. No other composer has enjoyed such lasting and continuous-popularity with so many people, and his music is still found on almost every piano in the world. Chopin can truly be said to have dipped his pen in moonbeams and flooded the world with melodies.

in culture and entertainment in the homes of the wealthy. As a sign of the piano's increased popularity as a domestic instrument, in 1797 James Harrison launched his *Piano-Forte Magazine*. Each issue included a note, signed by Harrison, promising a new piano to any reader who purchased the entire 250 numbers and could produce the signed certificates that were included in each issue.

ABOVE: *The First Piano Lesson by Jules Alexis Meunier (1863–1942) depicts an early 19th-century young lady receiving piano tuition from her teacher.*

Upright piano

Larger than harpsichords, early horizontally strung pianos took up a lot of floor space, and to address this problem Domenico del Mela of Gagliano built the first vertical piano in 1739. The piano was simply turned upright on a stand, with the strings and soundboard towering above the keyboard. About 1800 it was realized that the soundboard could be dropped towards the floor, placing most of the string length behind the keyboard in front of the player's knees, thereby decreasing the overall height of the instrument. The strings were tuned at the top and the hammers arranged to strike from the front. In 1811 the "cottage" piano appeared in London. It was just over 1m/3ft tall, with diagonally arranged strings.

In the 1830s the problem of the short bass strings was solved with the invention of the overstrung piano, in which the shorter strings ran vertically and the bass strings crossed obliquely over them allowing for greater length. This method of stringing soon became the norm for all pianos and is the method still used today.

ABOVE: Der Appollosaal, Berlin, is one of the centres in the reinstated German capital where piano recitals are given on a fairly regular basis.

Sound

As the 19th century dawned, there were two distinct piano sounds. There was the light action and sensuous tone of German and Austrian instruments, on which musicians such as Mozart had performed, and there was the firmer action and stronger tone of English instruments, particularly those made by John Broadwood. It was one of the latter that Beethoven used, for as his deafness increased he could no longer hear what he was playing on a Viennese instrument.

Pedals

In 1759 Weltmann in France had invented a piano-harpsichord combination with knee levers that were used to effect registration, but pedals were introduced by John

LEFT: This small upright piano was built by the renowned firm of Clementi of London in 1825. The instrument is veneered in rosewood with pleated silk panels in the front.

ABOVE: Upright pianos have two pedals. The left one is the "soft" pedal and the right the "sustaining" pedal.

Broadwood, the pre-eminent British maker, in 1783. There were usually two pedals to operate two stops, *forte* and *una corda*, but many experiments were made with other devices to modify the tone. Some pianos had as many as four extra pedals. The *forte* or sustaining pedal lifted the dampers so that the sound was sustained after the key had fallen back, while the *una corda* or "soft" pedal shifted the action sideways so that the hammers struck only one string for each note. One special stop created a bassoon effect

with a strip of parchment passed through the strings, and in deference to the craze for "Turkish music" some pianos were built with small drums, bells, cymbals and triangles inside the case, all controlled by pedals.

Strings

The instrument on which J. C. Bach had played in 1768 sounded very different from a modern piano. Beethoven and Mozart would not recognize their music now, as the "modern" piano sound did not begin to appear until about 1850. The strings of early 19th-century pianos were still quite light and thin and at much lower tension than today's models, in which the strings are so rigid and tense that they behave more like bars. This thinness gave the instruments more harmonic overtones than a modern piano, a characteristic that gives early pianos an "out-of-tune" tone quality, reminiscent of ragtime pianos of the 1920s. To increase the volume of sound, makers increased the thickness of the strings. This meant that the tension also had to be increased to maintain them at the same pitch.

ABOVE: *Instruments by Erard, one of the great makers of pianos (and harps) were used by players from Beethoven to Ravel. Built in 1866, this is an early example, veneered in costly Amboyna wood.*

ABOVE: *Piano fingering is very important, both to reach the notes and to interpret the music. There are nearly one hundred keys but only ten fingers to play them with.*

Frame

Added tension in the strings meant that the frame had to be reinforced. Although the first iron frame appeared as early as 1800, it was not until 1828 that Adolphus Babcock of Boston produced the first square piano with a full iron frame, cast in a single piece. The first iron frame for a grand piano was made in Boston in 1843 by Jonas Chickering. In the 1860s Steinway's cast iron frames were first seen in Europe, and almost all makers followed suit.

♪ Unusual sounds

During the 20th century many new sounds and colours were brought out of the piano. Erik Satie (1866–1925) put sheets of paper between the strings for a performance of *La Piège de Meduse* in 1914. John Cage altered the tone of the piano by attaching objects such as paper, nails and milk bottles to the strings. One composer, David Bedford (born 1937), asked a performer to scream inside the piano to make the strings vibrate, while La Monte Young (born 1935), for reasons best known to himself, asked the pianist to bring a bale of hay and a bucket of water on to the stage for the piano to eat and drink.

ABOVE: *An inside view of a modern Steinway grand piano.*

ABOVE: *By the end of the 19th century there was a piano in almost every middle-class home. Singing around the piano was an enjoyable family activity.*

Organ

When the full Organ joins the tuneful Quire
Th' Immortal Pow'rs incline their Ear.

ALEXANDER POPE (1688–1744)

The organ is without doubt capable of producing the greatest effects, and is truly worthy of Mozart's praise as the king of instruments. Devised in Alexandria in the 3rd century BC, by the 2nd century AD the organ had become one of the main instruments of Rome and was heard in almost all aspects of Roman entertainment, including the theatre, games, gladiatorial contests, circus and banquets. Even Nero is believed to have played the organ.

Water organ

The direct ancestor of the modern pipe organ is the hydraulis, or water organ, believed to have been invented by Ctesibius, an Alexandrian engineer who is also credited with the invention of the water-pump, water-clock and water-powered artificial singing birds.

Although water was not the motive force in the hydraulis, it acted to maintain an even pressure of air, which was supplied by a hand-pump. The sound was produced through a set of bronze pipes, graded in length like the contemporary pan-pipes; indeed, the hydraulis was sometimes described as a *syrinx* played with the hands. Originally there was only one row of pipes, but by the 3rd century AD the instrument was being built with four, six or even eight ranks of pipes. It was said to be so loud that hydraulis players had to plug their ears. Ctesibius can truly be called the "Father of the Organ", for his basic conception of the provision

of a continuous wind supply to an array of tuned pipes controlled from a keyboard remains unchanged to this day.

The main drawback of the water organ was that it required precision engineering and needed constant

LEFT: This beautifully painted positive organ was built in about 1600.

maintenance, as it was prone to corrosion. By AD 200 the water tank had been eliminated in favour of a windbag inflated by bellows and compressed air.

Church organ

The European "organ revival" of the 10th century came about because the instrument was reintroduced from Byzantium. Between the 10th and 13th centuries the organ became almost exclusively a church instrument in western Europe. Organs were erected in places such as Cologne Cathedral (AD 950), where one was used "for purposes of teaching the

LEFT: A 4th-century illustration of a water organ, or hydraulis. The player stood at the keyboard while his assistant operated the long lever that worked the pump. Under the pipes was a keyboard that operated perforated sliders. When a key was pressed, a slider was pushed into position to release pressurized air from the wind canal and thereby sound the note. When the key was released, a spring pulled the slider back, shutting off the air supply and stopping the note.

science of music", and the Benedictine Abbey in Bagas, Spain (AD 972), where the instrument was placed near the entrance. At the consecration of the Bagas organ special mention was made of the fact that it could be "heard from afar", which has led to the theory that it was used for summoning the congregation, much like modern church bells. In England, an organ was built at Winchester in about AD 990.

By the 10th century, foot-operated bellows began to appear and the sliders, which all looked the same and therefore had the name of each note written on them, terminated in handles. For several centuries these relatively small organs constituted the typical church organ. By the 13th century all instruments other than organs were excluded from various churches in Spain, Italy and France. In the 15th century many new churches were built, most with an organ as part of the regular furniture.

ABOVE: *The beautiful and ornate organ in Roskilde cathedral, Denmark, was built in 1554. This is an organ of the type known as "swallow nests", because they were suspended against a church wall.*

ABOVE: *Grinling Gibbons decorated the interior of the church of St James, Piccadilly, in London in the 1680s. One example of his craftsmanship is the gilded organ case that is surmounted by musical angels.*

During the 13th century the sliders began to be replaced by keys. The early keyboards had wide keys that decreased in width from the wide bass keys to the narrower treble keys.

During the 14th century, with full chromaticism and larger compass, the keyboard began to take on its modern appearance, with the accidentals (the "black" notes) in an upper row.

In the 14th century the organ compass, which hitherto had not exceeded two octaves, increased until a chromatic compass of three octaves was achieved. By now, organs were becoming common and were no longer restricted to the major churches. By the end of the century some of the larger and more important churches, such as Meaux, Leyden and Westminster, had two organs: a great organ in the west end and a smaller positive organ in the choir.

Classical organ

Two manuals began to appear in the 14th century, enabling the same organist to control both the main organ and the small positive organ. This led to the rapid development of the organ and its performing potential, which ensured its pre-eminence in Europe until the mid 18th century.

A large organ may have thousands of pipes, divided into groups, or stops, each of which is brought into play by pulling out a knob on the console. Each pipe produces a characteristic sound, depending on its shape, whether it is made of wood, tin or an alloy, and whether it is a flue or reed-pipe. In early organs all the pipes were open flues but during the 16th century reed pipes, with resonators of brass or wood, came into use. Various types of reed are used to create distinctive sounds, some imitating orchestral instruments or the human voice.

RIGHT: Built by John Byfield of London in 1766, this is an outstanding example of an almost unaltered English house organ, with original glass doors and superb limewood carvings. The case is solid mahogany.

A series of up to five five-octave manuals and a 32-note pedalboard control valves that release air from the wind-chest into the various sets of pipes. The sets and their relative manuals are usually known as the Choir, Great, Swell, Solo and Echo.

Noted organ builders

During the late Renaissance, organ-building reached new heights of refinement. Organs were sumptuously decorated with inlaid wood, ivory and gold. The organ in the palace of Frederiksborg in Denmark, built in 1612 by Esaias Compenius, has solid silver stops shaped like human faces.

In Britain the period of the Commonwealth (1642–60) saw the Puritans execute the "speedy demolition of all organs". At the Restoration an influx of Dutch and émigré English builders arrived. The most noteworthy was Father Bernard Schmidt (died 1708) who introduced the "echo" organ in 1684. It was Schmidt who built London's Temple Church organ (1682–84), an instrument that was regarded as "a luxury unique in England", as well as organs for Westminster Abbey and St Paul's Cathedral. John Snetzler arrived in Britain from Switzerland around 1740. His work includes the organ used in Dublin for the first performance of Handel's *Messiah* in 1742, and that for the Lutheran Savoy Chapel in London.

Gottfried Silbermann (1683–1753) was a friend of J. S. Bach. He was influenced by Casparini, who had built organs in northern Italy, especially Venice, and he also trained in Paris. He built a total of 45 organs in Saxony, all carefully sited for the best acoustical effect, and they remain unsurpassed. Silbermann's organs have a distinctive silvery sound, praised by Mozart as "magnificent beyond measure".

Portative organ

Emerging in the 13th century, the small portative organ was used mainly for secular purposes but also found its way into religious processions, in which it was carried suspended from a strap around the neck. It was positioned at right angles to the body for playing, allowing the player to operate the bellows with the left hand and the keys with the right. Like many "folk" instruments of its time the portative organ was fitted with drones – two tall pipes (bourdons) at the treble end.

ABOVE: Detail of the pipes of the English house organ pictured above right.

ABOVE: *This marble relief depicts, among others, a putto playing a portative organ; the right hand plays the keys and the left hand operates the bellows.*

Positive organ

By 1425 the positive organ was being used in churches that either could not afford a large fixed organ or needed an additional chamber-size organ for occasional use such as for a service in a side chapel. It was distinct from the portative organ in that it was "moveable" rather than portable. It usually had two rows of flue pipes, a single manual and no pedalboard. An assistant was needed to operate the bellows while it was played.

Fairground organ

Gavioli of Paris started building fairground organs around 1870 to imitate a military band. One of the largest ever built had 104 keys, with large figures on each end of the front operating a bass drum and a side drum. Made by Charles Marenghi of Paris, this monstrous construction was said to reproduce the sounds of over 1200 instruments and was illuminated by hundreds of varicoloured electric lamps.

Cinema organ

Organs built by the American Wurlitzer Company in the early 20th century were designed to replace a small orchestra and to provide the perfect accompaniment to silent films. Every possible percussion instrument was imitated, including drums, telephone bells, surf, horses' hooves and even police sirens. In the United States the cinema organ died out with the advent of sound films, but in Britain it was retained and used to give short recitals before the films began.

BELOW: *An elaborate Dutch fairground organ, still a feature of many carnivals.*

In the 19th century many old organs were enlarged and improved. In France, Aristide Cavaillé-Coll, who pioneered electrically powered pneumatic tracker action, created flexible and expressive organs that inspired French composers to write a flood of large-scale secular works for solo organ.

The organ symphony originated with Charles Widor (1844–1937), professor of organ at the Paris Conservatoire and organist at Ste Sulpice (1869–1933). César Franck (1822–90) was another leading figure in the French organ world and Widor's predecessor at the Conservatoire. He was organist at Ste Clotilde (1859–90) and wrote several pieces for the instrument, including *Six Pièces* (1862), *Trois Pièces* (1878) and *Trois Chorales* (1896). Franck's style is easily recognizable through its harmonic idiom and method of construction.

ABOVE: *A three-manual Wurlitzer cinema organ, looking like the deck of a jet aeroplane. The hands are kept busy with the stops and the feet have to master all the pedals.*

Accordion

*The accordion is an instrument with
the sentiments of an assassin.*

AMBROSE BIERCE (1842–1914)

The accordion is a hand-
held free-reed aerophone,
in which the sound is
produced by tempered steel
reeds that vibrate when
air is forced through
them by a set of
bellows. On one side of
the bellows there are rows
of buttons or a keyboard
on which the melody is
played, while on the other
side there are buttons for
the bass notes and chords.

*LEFT: The long rows of buttons for
the right hand of the accordion
produce the melody, and the
buttons for the left hand play
the bass notes and chords.*

accompaniments in all keys,
the piano accordion was still an
instrument of the people, its use
being restricted to popular and
rural entertainment in cafés, dance
halls and music halls. By 1931,
however, the accordion was
beginning to be taken seriously,
for in that year a music school for
accordionists was established in the
German town of Trossingen, a
location chosen for its vicinity to the
famous Höhner accordion factory.
The British College of Accordionists
was founded in 1936.

Early accordions

In 1821, Christian Buschmann
(1805–64) of Berlin patented his

Handäoline, an instrument
that was worked by lever-like keys.
Seven years later, Cyrillus Demian
(1772–1847), a Viennese musician,
brought out his *Akkordion* (German for
"harmony"), which, although similar in
principle to Buschmann's instrument,
had accompanying chords. Made in
rosewood with inlays of
ivory and mother-of-pearl,
the instrument was copied by
various other musicians, who,
not being able to use the
copyrighted name, referred to
their versions by the generic term
Handharmonikas. One of the most
important advances in the history of
the accordion occurred in 1852 when
Monsieur Busson of Paris introduced
piano-type keys to the instrument.

Piano accordion

Although by the beginning of the 20th
century the bass keyboard had been
sufficiently developed to provide

*ABOVE: The piano accordion has become a
folk instrument in most of Europe. Sweden
is no exception.*

*ABOVE: In 1852 Monsieur
Busson of Paris introduced piano-type keys
to the accordion. The advantage of the new
instrument was that it could be played
informally by ambulant performers. This
diminutive instrument is one of Busson's
first and does not have the chord and bass
keys of the more developed types.*

ABOVE: A busker playing a piano accordion in Prague's Golden Lane.

Modern accordion
Today's instruments have up to 140 basses actuated by seven rows of buttons and a keyboard compass ranging from two to four octaves. The usual 120-button Stradella fixed-bass keyboard, first developed by the Italian Mariano Dallape in 1876, consists of two rows of bass notes and four rows of chord buttons. Some models have a converter switch that enables chords to be played in any inversion. In Italy, a small variant of the accordion, the *organetto*, has almost replaced the *zampogna*, a type of bagpipe whose repertoire it shares.

Bandoneon
In Argentina, Uruguay and Brazil, South American tango bands often feature the bandoneon, a double-action square-shaped type of accordion. Invented in the 19th century by

ABOVE: The double-action bandoneon is used in the tango bands of Latin America. This example was made by Wilhelm König in 1914.

Accordion music
In 1948, when the Trossingen school became an official state academy, the first principal was Hugo Herrmann who, in 1927, had written *Sieben Neue Spielmusiker*, the first original composition for the solo accordion. Although the accordion is mainly played as a solo instrument or as part of the instrumental line-up in folk bands, many major composers have scored for it.

These include Sergei Prokofiev (1891–1953) in *Cantata for the 20th Anniversary of the October Revolution* and Paul Dessau (1894–1979) in *Die Verurteilung des Lukullus*. Roberto Gerhard (1896–1970) also used the accordion in various works such as his Nonet and Concerto for Eight.

Heinrich Band of Krefeld, Germany, the early models had more than 88 notes. Today's instruments, however, are usually restricted to 71.

Concertina
Based on much the same principle as the accordion, the concertina, invented by Charles Whetstone (1802–72) in 1829, consists of two hexagonal casings, each containing a small button keyboard. The casings are connected by bellows that, when extended or contracted, cause a flow of air to activate the free reeds of the instrument when one of the keys is pressed.

There are two main types of concertina: the English, in which there

ABOVE: The concertina is unusual in that it has 14 keys to the octave and is tuned to mean rather than equal temperament.

is a uniform tone – the same note being sounded on both extension and contraction of the bellows – and the German, which sounds different notes on extension and compression.

Although it was played by people such as Giulio Regondi (1822–72), a guitarist and player of the *mélophone*, and Richard Blagrave (1826–95) whose playing was once described as a "first-rate workman on a miserable tool", the concertina was never a popular instrument and its use today is almost solely restricted to folk music, although composers such as Charles Ives (1874–1954) and Percy Grainger (1882–1961) did occasionally score for the instrument.

ABOVE: South America has many accordion aficionados. This young man is playing at the Vallanato Festival in Colombia.

Harmonium

It is astonishing what an effect the sound of some simple air played on an harmonium on a Sunday evening has on the loiterers in the streets.

MUSICAL OPINION, JUNE 1905

The harmonium, which resembles a small organ, was often used as a substitute for its big brother in small churches and chapels, as well as being popular as a household instrument. A distant relation of the mouth organ, it consists of a series of free reeds operated by a keyboard and activated by a wind supply from foot-operated compression bellows.

LEFT: Built by the leading firm of Alexandre of Paris in 1859, this harmonium was widely used both in homes and churches.

Early French harmonium

The harmonium evolved from Gabriel Grenié's *orgue expressif*, a free-reed keyboard instrument of about 1810. The register of Grenié's instrument was supplied by bellows worked by two pedals. The "expression" was a stop that enabled direct contact between the bellows and the wind-reservoir by means of the pedals, thereby permitting dynamic gradations for the first time in the history of the organ.

In 1834 an improved version by the eminent French organ builder Aristide Cavaillé-Coll was exhibited at the Paris exposition. Built in the form of a small, square piano, Cavaillé-Coll's instrument, which was called the *poïkilorgue*, had a range of one and a half octaves. In 1843 Grenié's pupil Théodore-Achille Muller patented a portable model that could be folded up into a rectangular box.

Although the French were the leaders in making and perfecting the harmonium, experiments were also being carried out in Bavaria. Here, in 1815, Bernhard Eschenbach devised a free-reed keyboard instrument that was capable of "expression", which he called an *Aoline*.

Improvements

The harmonium achieved its ultimate popularity in the form patented by the Parisian Alexandre-François Debain (1809–77) in 1842. Debain's harmonium incorporated a three-octave keyboard with sets of reeds of different thicknesses and widths. One of the new features was that each key controlled a valve that regulated the amount of wind produced by the compression bellows. This made possible, for the first time, the production of different tones. Further improvements, added by Debain in 1848, included the shifting keyboard, a device that permitted transposition by any interval, while playing the music as noted. In 1854 Victor Mustel added a divided expression stop worked by knee-levers.

Experimental harmoniums

Because of its ability to sustain a constant tone, the harmonium was well suited for acoustical experiments

ABOVE: The popularity of the harmonium in the 19th century was mainly due to its price. This New Cottage Harmonium cost seven guineas, a fraction of that of a piano.

and demonstrations of different tuning systems. The best known of these experimental harmoniums was that designed by Shohé Tanka and built by Johann Kewitsch of Berlin in 1889. Such was the accuracy of Tanka's instrument that it was tuned to pure intervals, with no less than 20 keys to the octave. This, however, was child's play compared with Banquet's experimental harmonium, which was constructed to produce 53 microtones to the octave.

India

The harmonium was introduced into India by missionaries around the mid 19th century to accompany hymn-singing. Since the 1920s small portable harmoniums have been made in India and Pakistan; Palitana in Gujarat is the centre of manufacture of the reeds. Harmoniums are very popular, and many homes have one. They are widely used to accompany devotional music, to the dismay of aficionados of traditional Indian music, as their fixed pitch is at odds with the flexible intonation of Indian vocal and instrumental music They have also led to the demise of indigenous instruments such as the *bajona sruti*, or Indian bagpipe.

As is common with Indian musicians, the harmonium player sits on the floor, playing the keyboard with one hand and operating the bellows with the other. Harmoniums are, however, now giving way in their turn to the ubiquitous electronic keyboard.

Indian harmoniums

LEFT, BELOW AND RIGHT: Small portable harmoniums have been very popular in India, with many homes owning one. The musician usually sits on the floor, playing the keyboard with one hand and operating the bellows with the other.

Mechanical Instruments

*A good melody is such a one as would grind
about the streets upon the organ.*

THOMAS ARNE (1710–78)

In the years before recording and broadcasting, instruments that played pre-set tunes became popular. When no musician was available, turning a handle could provide music, whether at home, for street entertainment, dancing, or for church services.

Barrel organ

The barrel organ made its appearance in Italy in the early 1700s. One of the first makers of the instrument was Giovanni Barbieri of Modena; his name was perpetuated by the French, who called the Italian's invention *orgue de Barbarie*. However, by 1774 many had obviously forgotten the Italian's pioneer work, for in that year an advertisement appeared offering for sale *"Un veritable orgue de barbarie fait par les sauvages."*

These early constructions were small enough to rest on the player's left hip

LEFT: This 19th-century English barrel organ has three barrels. Two play dance music and popular songs, while the third provides hymn tunes.

while the right hand turned the handle. The barrel organ's mechanism consisted of two or more ranks of organ pipes placed above a set of bellows in an enclosed cabinet, while the music was supplied by a pinned cylinder or barrel that was mounted on a metal spindle. Each pin raised a trigger-shaped key that opened a pallet, allowing wind to enter the required pipe. Each tune required one complete rotation of the barrel.

In the 19th century, with the demand for longer and more complicated music, barrel organs became larger and larger. In 1887 Michael Welte patented an instrument in which the barrels were pegged spirally and rotated 12 times during one piece of music, making it possible for quite long compositions to be played.

Street organ

In the early 19th century an Italian named Gavioli, who was established in Paris, started making portable organs in which the barrel was replaced by perforated cardboard strips, concertina-folded and based on the

THE STREET ORGAN.

LEFT: The organ grinder was once a familiar sight in the streets of most European towns, surrounded by children. The music made a welcome break in an otherwise monotonous day.

card patterns used by jacquard weavers. Gavioli's organs were often mounted on handcarts and wheeled about by "organ grinders", who were invariably accompanied by little monkeys. These organs were very successful and were seen on the streets of most European cities until well into the 20th century.

Church barrel organ

Until the introduction of the harmonium, many small churches and chapels used a "barrel and finger organ" as a substitute for a conventional organ. These were so-called because they had a conventional keyboard at the front and a barrel movement at the back. The barrels were pegged with hymns, chants, psalms and even voluntaries so that if no organist was available for a service, music could still be produced by turning the handle.

ABOVE: Early barrel pianos, operated by turning a handle, were quite small domestic instruments.

ABOVE: An orchestrion or "orchestral organ", showing the internal mechanisms, including the pipes and barrel.

Orchestrion

The main drawback of the barrel organ was its monotonous sound, and in an attempt to rectify this the orchestrion was invented. Intended for indoor use in wealthy households, the orchestrion was composed of ranks of organ pipes of differing timbres that were constructed to imitate the sounds of orchestral instruments. It was an elaborate assembly with refined cabinet work and had as many as eight ranks of pipes with a chromatic compass of over five octaves, plus percussion instruments such as cymbals, drums and triangles.

One of the first successful orchestrions was built in Holland in 1789. Said to be capable of imitating a whole orchestra, it was encased in a 3m/10ft cube and was complete with four manuals and a pedalboard for obtaining *crescendos* and *diminuendos*. The componium, a Dutch invention of 1821, could compose variations on a theme, using two movable barrels.

Apollonicon

In 1817, Flight & Robson of London exhibited their massive apollonicon, which had been constructed the previous year. No less than 7.2m/24ft in height and 6m/20ft wide and deep, it had nearly 2000 pipes, disposed in 46 registers. It had five manuals that could be played either mechanically or, when detached from the main body, manually by five performers, all facing the public. It was displayed and operated in the window of the company's London showroom for some years, but was not a financial success and was dismantled in 1840.

Music box

Small musical movements were first made in the late 18th century for snuff boxes. By the 1830s the music box was established in its standard form, with tuning combs that had as many as 250 teeth covering a range of about six octaves. Many of these boxes were finely decorated and embellished with marquetry and mother-of-pearl. The early combs were fitted to cylinders, but by the 1890s disc-operated boxes were appearing, with discs up to 85cm/34in in diameter. They were eclipsed by the arrival of the gramophone.

ABOVE: This internal view of a music box built in the last year of the 19th century in Sainte-Croix, Switzerland, shows the steel comb whose tuned tongues are plucked by pins on the clockwork-driven cylinder, as well as the bells and drum.

Electronic Keyboards and Computers

The synthesizer is no more inhuman than the piano.

MILTON BABBITT (BORN 1916)

O ne of the first electronic instruments was Thaddeus Cahill's keyboard-operated "dynamophone" or "telharmonium", the first full-size version of which was completed in 1906. It supplied current to telephone receivers fitted with cardboard horns, and was used for daily concerts. Although the aim of the instrument was "to generate music electrically with tones of good quality", Cahill's pioneer work was too far ahead of its time and his invention was eventually sold for scrap, but his ideas were the basis of later developments during the 1920s and '30s.

Theremin

The Russian scientist Lev Theremin invented the theremin in 1924. Its signals were produced by oscillators, and were modified by the position of the player's hands. Volume was controlled by the proximity of one hand to a metal loop, and pitch by moving the other hand towards or away from an antenna protruding vertically out of the instrument. Although some musicians were able to demonstrate its vocal qualities, it was very difficult to play and as such did not become widely used. The radical composer Edgard Varèse (1885–1965) used two theremins in *Ecuatorial* (1934) but later replaced them with the more reliable *ondes Martenot*.

LEFT: The electronic keyboard has become one of the most important instruments in many small bands. The sound of almost every instrument of the orchestra — and other sounds — can be achieved.

Ondes Martenot

The *ondes Martenot*, invented by the French musician and engineer Maurice Martenot (1896–1980), was produced in 1928. Although its oscillating valves are similar to those of the theremin, it is very much easier to control the pitch produced, as the player is guided by a five-octave keyboard. A substantial number of works have been written for it, and it produces haunting sounds.

Hammond organ

The American Laurens Hammond invented the Hammond organ in 1935, with the intention of replacing the pipe organ for both church and domestic use. Like the conventional organ, it has two small manuals and a pedalboard, but produces sounds electronically. This versatile organ became very popular in the 1960s,

RIGHT: The eponymous Hammond organ, with its ability to produce (albeit limited) special effects, was a forerunner of the modern electronic keyboard.

especially with rock musicians. Special stops and tabs control the manuals and produce effects such as "wah-wahs", *glissandos* and arpeggios.

Synthesizer

The first synthesizer of major importance was the RCA Mark II, which was acquired in 1959 by the Columbia-Princeton Electronic Music Center in New York. It had been developed at the Sarnoff Research Center, New Jersey, from the Mark I of 1955 by Harry Olsen and Herbert

ABOVE: Composing music has come a long way from the quill pen of Purcell to the MIDI keyboard and computer of the modern composer.

ABOVE: A mixing desk is standard equipment in the modern recording studio.

Belar. Using transistors instead of valves, it was much smaller than the Mark I, a colossal machine that almost filled a room with controls for the multitude of oscillators, mixers, filters and amplifier.

Since 1966 much smaller synthesizers have been made available commercially, including the Moog Sonic Six and the Buchla. Originally developed for producing tapes for recordings, by the mid 1960s synthesizers had reached the concert platform as chordal instruments for live performances, and were especially popular with rock bands.

Although the synthesizer keyboard looks like that of a piano, it behaves in a different way: it controls not only the pitch of a note (which may not be the same as that on a piano), but also its length. Some keyboards are touch-sensitive so that, depending on the way the keys are depressed or released, different functions may be performed.

Some modern synthesizers, such as the Kawai CP150, have dummy keyboards to give the performer the feeling of playing a "real" piano. The

Kawai CP150 has a unique weighted action with wooden keys that simulate a hammer action by using a dummy hammer within the mechanism. The effect is so natural that in time the action beds down and settles in, just like a real piano keyboard.

Digital revolution

Today almost every recording studio has an abundance of computer-related equipment. The music is digitally saved on to a hard disk and then edited on a mixing desk using sophisticated

software before the final version is mastered on to digital audio tape. This Musical Instrument Digital Interface (MIDI) deals with all aspects of the performance, including pitch, velocity and duration. As well as the MIDI keyboard, there are conventional MIDI instruments that connect electronically with the mixing desk. Even acoustic instruments can have tiny microphones attached to convert analogue pitch into digital information. Such is modern technology that it is almost possible to play a flute concerto on a kazoo.

ABOVE: This mixing desk, a Virtua Digital Console, has eliminated the need for long rows of buttons and dials.

ABOVE: The computer combines all the functions of a mixing desk and multi-track tape machine to create a "virtual studio".

The Voice

The Human Instrument

Song is man's sweetest joy.
ARISTOTLE (384–322 BC)

The fundamental musical instrument is the human voice. Singing is the most natural and spontaneous mode of musical expression, and since it is almost always linked to a text it can unambiguously express thought as well as emotion. As the singer is his or her own instrument, the voice is never altogether distanced from the personality. However, a good voice does not make a singer unless it is combined with accurate rhythm, good sense of pitch and enunciation. As in other instruments, the sound of the voice is the result of amplified vibrations. The vibrations of the

ABOVE: Boys' choirs have been a feature of Christian ritual for a thousand years. As women were banned from taking part in the service, when polytonal music developed it was the youthful soprano voices that sang the top line of the music, while men sang the alto and baritone lines.

ABOVE: Diana Ross was a founder member of the Supremes, one of the singing groups that emerged from Detroit in the 1960s.

vocal cords resonate in the cavities of both the chest (in the lower register) and the head (in the upper register). The singer automatically adjusts the shapes and sizes of these cavities to produce the required notes.

Vocal ranges

When men and women sing together, men usually sing an octave lower: the normal range of women's voices is in the treble clef, and the men's is in the bass clef. Each voice has its own natural range of pitch. The highest woman's voice is the soprano, and the lowest the contralto, or alto, with

the mezzo-soprano lying between the two extremes. These pitches are also within the range of boys' voices (known as trebles).

The lowest male voice is the bass and the highest is usually the tenor, with the baritone between them. Some male singers have a natural extension at the top of their range which allows them to sing in the alto, or countertenor, range.

Madrigals

The early church forbade women to participate in services, so treble parts were sung by boys and countertenors.

Until the 15th century most music was written for high voices, but with the expansion of polyphony, songs began to feature two parts below the tenor and the qualities of the bass voice became better appreciated.

By the 16th century all secular music used vocal ranges that were comfortable for male voices, with countertenor parts never going above *d"*. When women joined singing groups, madrigals with parts as high as *g"* appeared. Madrigal singers and composers became increasingly interested in secular music and the ornamentation – forbidden in church music – that could be added to it.

Opera

The birth of opera between 1575 and 1625 resulted in an entirely new kind of singer. The madrigal singer had a relatively limited range, rarely exceeding an octave and a half. Opera singers began to extend their range, both up and down, to accommodate the composers who were experimenting in new forms of vocal music, just as instrument makers were experimenting in the construction of musical instruments.

Voice production

Singing styles and techniques before the advent of sound recordings are even harder to study than instrumental playing styles, as once the singer has died their voice is forever lost. There is no surviving instrument to help with research into the lost sound.

Although styles of singing changed, the Italian method of voice production, known as *bel canto* ("beautiful singing"), remained the same from the time of Monteverdi to that of Rossini. The main characteristic of *bel canto* voice production is the forward-placing of the voice, with a concentration of resonance in the nasal cavities to give a light, florid effect.

ABOVE: The music of a cathedral choir is a joy to hear in a candlelit setting.

ABOVE: The British mezzo-soprano Anne Murray (born 1949) was especially praised for her Covent Garden performance of the title role in Handel's Xerxes *in 1985.*

In the 20th century there were two main developments in singing. One is the *verismo*, or realistic style, as perfected by Enrico Caruso (1872–1921). Operatic composers around 1900 – particularly Italians such as Pietro Mascagni (1863–1945) and Giacomo Puccini (1858–1924) – began to write operas with more contemporary, realistic plots, for which the artifice of the traditional *bel canto* vocal style was unsuitable.

The second development was due to the invention of electronic amplification. Until the 1920s there was little difference between classical and popular singing. However, as popular singers began to use microphones, new singing styles developed. There was now no need to project the voice as before. Because it was easier for sound engineers to amplify a soft voice, early radio performers who sang with light, intimate voices were preferred.

ABOVE: The London Philharmonic Choir in rehearsal.

Choirs

Let the pealing organ blow To the full-voiced quire below
In service high and anthems clear.

JOHN MILTON (1608–74)

Organized choral singing has been known for at least 3000 years, since it is mentioned in Homer's *Iliad*, composed in about 850 BC. The ancient Greek chorus, from which choirs derive, included dancers as well as singers, and participated as a group in religious festivals. Some of these groups were very large, and could comprise up to 600 people. In Greek drama, the chorus provided a moral commentary on the action. Tragedies had a chorus of between 12 and 15 people, while comedies had from 24–50.

Polyphony

Choral music, in the form of plainsong, was an essential component of services in the early church. Early medieval choirs were small: they usually consisted of from four to eight boys and from 10 to 18 men, women being absolutely excluded from church services. One of the largest choirs of the 12th and 13th centuries was that of Notre-Dame in Paris, which consisted of almost 30 singers.

As polyphonic composition gradually replaced unharmonized chant, the range of voices widened. The earliest surviving mass, by Guillaume de Machaut (c.1300–77) is written in four parts. Antiphonal music, which was developed at St Mark's in Venice by Andrea and Giovanni Gabrieli, involved a solo voice and a choir, or two or more contrasting choirs, who sang verses and responses from different parts of the church. The increasing richness and complexity

ABOVE: A 14th-century French church choir. These singers are sharing a single manuscript copy of their text and musical line.

Vienna Boys Choir

The Hofmusikkapelle, which evolved into the world-famous Wiener Sängerknaben (the Vienna Boys Choir), was founded in 1498 by the Holy Roman Emperor Maximilian I. Its original purpose was to provide musical training for the choir of the Hofburg in Vienna. Now, however, it is a private boarding school. The 150 boys are divided into four choirs, each of which tours Europe and the United States for three months of the year.

ABOVE: The world-famous Vienna Boys Choir.

ABOVE: *To say that the Welsh love singing is like saying that fish like swimming. Almost every village has its own choir, an institution that binds the communities together.*

century, choral singing has been an important focal activity of the *eisteddfod* since it was first introduced in 1825. For many years virtually the only songs the singers knew were hymns, but by the second half of the 19th century cantatas, oratorios and works by contemporary Welsh composers such as Joseph Parry (1841–1903) and David Jenkins (1849–1915) were added to the repertoire.

During the 20th century many outstanding choirs were formed, and choral festivals have included Harlech (1867–1934), Cardiff (1892–1910) and the Three Valleys Festival (1930–39). Since 1947 choral singers from all over the world have flocked to Llangollen for the annual International Eisteddfod.

ABOVE: *A girls' choir performing at a concert.*

of polyphony culminated in works by the Roman school, led by Giovanni Pierluigi da Palestrina (1525–94).

Church choir

The sung mass became one of the most important forms of church music. Composers of all periods have written settings of it, and choral singing has a central role in almost every religious service. Renaissance choirs sang in a minimum of four parts, often six, eight or more. The choirs grew larger, and were accompanied by instrumental groups. After the Reformation, Protestant choirs were modelled on the Catholic pattern, and women therefore continued to be excluded, preserving the tradition of using boys' voices. This tradition is only gradually being challenged.

Choral societies

The overwhelming popularity of Handel's oratorios in late 18th-century Britain – especially *The Messiah* (1742) – led to the formation of new choral societies, which did include women, in almost every town. At first only religious music was sung, including, as well as Handel, Haydn's *Creation* (1799) and later Mendelssohn's *Elijah* (1846), but secular music eventually crept in, such as the popular songs of Gilbert and Sullivan's Savoy Operas.

Choral singing reached extraordinarily high standards in Germany, where choral societies grew up in the industrial towns, a movement that was fostered by numerous choral festivals, such as those held at Frankenhausen, Mannheim, Magdeburg and Halle. Excellent folk choirs still flourish today.

Male voice choir

One country synonymous with choral singing is Wales. Growing up with the enormous rise in the urban population in the early 19th

ABOVE: *The choir of St John's College Chapel, Cambridge.*

Soloists

The earliest solo singers were poet-composers who sang their own songs, and few singers were famous as soloists before the mid 16th century. However, they acquired greater importance as secular music became more highly ornamented. At the same time, women began to perform as singers, and a preference for the soprano voice was established. The birth of opera, which drew its earliest performers from the ranks of popular court singers of madrigals, eventually led to the rise of the professional opera star. Although many singers restrict their singing to one medium, such as opera or recital work, some have made a name for themselves in both.

ABOVE: Jenny Lind, "The Swedish Nightingale", was the pop idol of the mid 19th century. She was in such demand that tickets for her concerts were usually sold out within hours of being put on sale.

Male voices

One of the best examples of operatic singers "going solo" is the outstanding success of Luciano Pavarotti (born 1935), José Carreras (born 1946) and Plácido Domingo (born 1941) – three men whose successes in opera have been equalled if not excelled by their appearance as "The Three Tenors" at concerts held in conjunction with the three football World Cup finals in Italy (1990), the United States (1994) and France (1998).

Without doubt the most popular tenor of his generation, Pavarotti, with his trademark white handkerchief in his left hand, has brought operatic arias to enormous audiences. His recording of *Nessun dorma*, an aria from Puccini's *Turandot* that was used as the theme song of Italia '90, hit the pop charts worldwide. Many people who had hitherto felt alienated from opera realized the beauties of the music they had so long resisted.

Some classically trained male singers have deliberately pursued a solo career rather than performing in opera. These include the Austrian Richard Tauber (1892–1948), the Irish singer Josef Locke (1917–99) and the German Ivan Rebroff, whose fantastic voice ranges from the ultra bass, which must be one of the deepest known, to a high falsetto.

Female voices

One of the most popular singers of the 19th century was Jenny Lind (1820–87), known as the "Swedish Nightingale", whose appearances often caused more excitement than a royal visit. On more than one occasion when Lind was singing in London the House of Commons was unable to continue business as there were not enough MPs present to constitute a quorum – they were all at her concert. Her singing was so pure that her audiences could hardly believe that such powers existed in the human voice. She was married to the conductor Otto Goldschmidt, who often accompanied her on the

ABOVE: Adelina Patti was famous for her wealth and for never attending rehearsals, but was a great actress.

piano. Another factor that endeared
her to the public was her custom of
donating part of her salary to a
charitable institution in whichever
town she performed.

Another 19th-century diva was
the *coloratura* soprano Adelina Patti
(1843–1919), who began her career
as a child prodigy in the United States.
Hearing her voice so affected Rossini
that he rewrote the role of Rosina in
The Barber of Seville for her. He once
said to her: "Madam, I have cried
twice in my life. Once when I dropped
a wing of chicken into Lake Como,
and once when for the first time
I heard you sing."

Joan Sutherland (born 1926) is
arguably the 20th century's finest
coloratura soprano, and made many of
the great roles of Delibes, Massenet,
Rossini, Donizetti and Bellini her own.
She conquered the world in 1959 with

*LEFT: Joan Sutherland
studied singing in
Sydney and London,
and was created a Dame
in 1979. One of her
many successes was in
1974 when she sang all
four soprano roles in
Offenbach's* Tales of
Hoffmann.

her performance in Donizetti's *Lucia di
Lammermoor*, her rich and agile voice
making her one of the most popular
singers of the time. She gave her

farewell performance
on New Year's Eve
1990, in a guest
appearance with the
American mezzo-
soprano Marilyn
Horne and Luciano
Pavarotti in the
Covent Garden production of Johann
Strauss's operetta *Die Fledermaus*.

Kiri Te Kanawa (born 1944) had
begun her recording career by the time
she was 20. One of the most famous
sopranos of modern times, she made
her debut as the Countess in *Le nozze
di Figaro* at Covent Garden in 1971.

ABOVE: *One of the most remarkable "discoveries" of the 1990s was "The Three Tenors". The
trio of Plácido Domingo, José Carreras and Luciano Pavarotti brought opera to enormous
audiences worldwide, especially at the three football World Cup finals in Italy (1990), the
United States (1994) and France (1998).*

ABOVE: *Kiri Te Kanawa has become one
of the most famous sopranos in the world.
She is seen here giving one of her popular
solo concerts.*

Other Voices

God giveth speech to all, song to the few.

WALTER CHALMERS SMITH

Many composers, particularly in modern times, have sought to use the voice as an instrument in new and unusual ways, whether by extending its range outside the normal compass or by incorporating vocal sounds other than singing into their music. The style called *Sprechgesang* that Schoenberg used in *Pierrot Lunaire* (1912) falls between singing and speaking. Humming is a device that is often used in choral works, and sometimes in solos: Villa-Lobos's *Bachianas Brasileiras No. 5* uses a solo soprano voice humming a soaring tune, accompanied by cellos. Speech and shouting add new colours to choral writing, and the use of the microphone has opened up many new possibilities for vocal effects, in rock and pop as well as serious music.

ABOVE: The castrato Carlo Broschi Farinelli (1705–82) sang all over Europe, including a three-year stay in London.

Castrati

The castrato, whose voice was prevented from breaking by castration in childhood, first appeared in church choirs to sing the high parts that women, who were banned from the church, supplied in secular music. In the late 16th and early 17th century castrati found a role in the new medium of opera, and opera composers began to write special parts for them.

Some castrati achieved great wealth. One of the most famous of the 18th century was the Italian Carlo Broschi Farinelli, whose voice, it was claimed, was able to reach and sustain seven or eight notes above any other singer of the period. Farinelli's artistry was such that when King Philip V of Spain heard him he was so impressed that he commissioned the Italian to sing him four arias a night for the rest of his life. When Philip died, his successor Ferdinand VI awarded Farinelli the rank of prince and a generous pension.

The barbaric practice of castration for artistic purposes eventually died out, and castrati were banned from the papal chapel in 1903. The last castrato, Alessandro Moreschi, who had been musical director of the Sistine Chapel, died in 1922, aged 66.

Jazz singing

An oratorical style of singing that exploits the contours and cadences of speech, jazz singing is concerned with emphasizing the text rather than the tone. Because jazz singers usually follow the dynamics of speech rather than of the melody, their voices tend to be low-pitched; soprano jazz singers are very rare.

In some jazz styles the interest lies in musical effect rather than emotional content, a prime example being scat singing. This is a wordless performance, usually improvised, that uses the voice like an instrument. Although many jazz singers include scat singing in their acts, not many are capable of keeping it up for more than 32 bars. Louis Armstrong's solos in the 1920s and '30s began a vogue for the style.

ABOVE: Jazz singing has arisen from the traditions of blues singing and popular songs. It usually involves improvisation to fit the lyrics to the music.

LEFT: *The musical is the modern-day version of operetta. The Phantom of the Opera (music by Andrew Lloyd Webber, lyrics by Charles Hart) is one of the most successful ever staged. Sarah Brightman and Michael Crawford performed with the original cast.*

Human voice orchestra

In the 19th century there were various choral groups that sang not words but sounds. One such was Hoffmann's Organophonic Band or "human voice orchestra". Wearing military uniform, the 12 members, who imitated by voice alone a complete orchestra of instruments, were popular over most of Europe. This type of wordless singing was revived in the 1960s by the Swingle Singers.

Yodelling

Yodelling is the sudden change from chest voice to falsetto head voice and back again in rapid alternation. It originated in the Swiss mountains where it was, and still is, intended to be a joyful sound. In the 1930s yodelling entered American blues music where, instead of being a happy sound, it was turned into a lonesome and sad expression, first typified by Jimmy Rodgers and copied by many others since.

ABOVE: The French-Canadian singer Celine Dion (born 1967) made the transition from child star to French-language chanteuse to an internationally acclaimed ballad singer.

RIGHT: A Tyrolean yodelling party in national costume.

tem ad te uenio non rogo ut tollas eos de mundo sed ut ser

ues eos a malo ac v ia ac v ia

In die
ascen
sionis

ir galilei quid admira mini aspicientes

in celum ac v ia quemadmodum uidistis eum ascenden

tem in ce lum ita ueniet ac v ia ac v ia ac v ia po

tunieq metuerentur in celum euntem illum ecce duo uiri as

Om nes gentes plaudite manibus iubilate

deo in uoce exul ta cio nis

stiterunt iuxta illos in uestib; albis qui & dixerunt

Ascendit de us in iubila cio ne

et dominus in uoce tu be

v ia

v ia

Composition

through

the Ages

A beautiful example of a medieval choirbook emanating from Germany, now in the State Library in Gdańsk, Poland. The pages illustrated show the beginning of the plainsong chant for the antiphon Rorate coeli, *used in the liturgy for the Ascension season.*

Music as a Language

We — are we not formed, as notes of music are,
For one another, though dissimilar?

PERCY BYSSHE SHELLEY (1792–1822), "EPIPSYCHIDION"

Musical composition is one of the most mysterious of all art forms. People who can easily come to terms with a work of literature or a painting are still often baffled by the process by which a piece of music – appearing in material form as notation – must then be translated back into sound through the medium of a third party – the performer. Unlike a painting, a musical composition cannot be owned (except by its creator); and although a score may be published, like a book, it may remain incomprehensible to the general public until it is performed. Although a piece may be played thousands of times, each repetition is entirely individual, and interpretations by different players may vary widely.

ABOVE: *An early example of neumatic notation, from a German illustrated liturgical manuscript.*

Origins of musical notation

The earliest musical compositions were circumscribed by the range of the human voice. People from all cultures have always sung, or used primitive instruments to make sounds. Notation, or the writing down of music, developed to enable performers to remember what they had improvised, to preserve what they had created, and to facilitate interaction between more than one performer. Musical notation, like language, has ancient origins, dating back to the Middle East in the third millennium BC. The ancient Greeks appear to have been the first to try to represent variations of musical pitch through the medium of the alphabet, and successive civilizations all over the world attempted to formulate similar systems of recognizable musical notation.

Neumatic notation

The earliest surviving Western European notational system was called "neumatic notation" – a system of symbols which attempted to portray the rise and fall of a melodic line. These date back to the 9th century AD, and were associated with the performance of sacred music – particularly plainsong – in monastic institutions. Several early manuscript

ABOVE: *An early example of musical notation, a 3rd-century BC Greek song. The letters above the text indicate the notes.*

254 *Composition through the Ages*

ABOVE: *Guido d'Arezzo (c.977–1050), who devised the hexachord. His statue stands outside the Uffizi Gallery in Florence.*

sources contain sacred texts with accompanying notation, although there was no standard system. The first appearance of staff notation, in which pitch was indicated by noteheads on or between lines with a symbol called a clef at the beginning to fix the pitch of one note, was in the 9th-century French treatise *Musica enchiriadis*. At the same time, music for instruments (particularly organ and lute) was beginning to be written down in diagrammatic form known as tablature, which indicated the positions of the player's fingers.

Guido d'Arezzo

The 11th-century Italian monk Guido d'Arezzo invented the "solmization" system – the precursor of "tonic solfa" – in which various syllables were used to indicate pitches in a musical scale. He also invented the "Guidonian Hand", in which the tips and joints of the five fingers

were used as an aid to remembering the various notes. At the same time, attempts were being made to indicate rhythm in performance, by varying the length and angle of the tails of the neumes, and the earliest polyphony (the simultaneous performance of more than one melodic line) was being explored.

The modal system

From around 400 BC until AD 1500, European music was built on modes. In the 4th century BC, the Greek mathematician Pythagoras worked out a scale roughly corresponding to the (modern-day) white keys of the piano, and two centuries later this scale was being used by the Greeks in seven different ways. The early Christian church adopted four so-called "authentic" modes (corresponding to white-note scales beginning on D, E, F and G), and under the 6th-century Pope Gregory, four more modes were added for the performance of plainsong.

ABOVE: *Pope Gregory (c.540–604), who gave his name to "Gregorian" plainsong melodies for liturgical use.*

ABOVE: *The so-called "Guidonian Hand", Guido d'Arezzo's device for showing the notes of the scale.*

In 1547, the Swiss monk Henricus Glareanus postulated the theory of 12 modes, giving them somewhat inauthentic Greek names:

Dorian (range D–D)
HypoDorian (range A–A)
Phrygian (range E–E)
HypoPhrygian (range B–B)
Lydian (range F–F)
HypoLydian (range C–C)
Mixolydian (range G–G)
HypoMixolydian (range D–D)
Aeolian (range A–A)
HypoAeolian (range E–E)
Ionian (range C–C)
HypoIonian (range G–G)

Of these, the Aeolian and Ionian modes later became the basis of the minor and major scales respectively, which have since underpinned Western European music. The modes finally gave way to the keys we know today with the development of harmony in the late Renaissance period.

Emergence of Composers

Lovely forms do flow
From conceit divinely framed;
Heaven is music.

THOMAS CAMPION (1567–1620), "OBSERVATIONS IN THE ART OF ENGLISH POESIE"

Much medieval music survives in manuscript anthologies, some copied by monks for a particular monastery, others — often exquisitely illuminated — commissioned by an aristocratic patron. The earliest surviving ones date from the 10th century. Among the most famous manuscripts are two 15th-century English sources, the Old Hall Manuscript and the Eton College Choirbook. There are also two French sources dating from around 1470, the beautiful heart-shaped *Chansonnier cordiforme* and the *Mellon chansonnier*. Many pieces in these manuscripts are anonymous, but some were attributed to individual composers.

Ars antiqua

The Parisian composers Léonin and Pérotin were among the finest exponents of the style called *ars antiqua*, or "ancient style", a method of harmonizing plainsong melodies by adding between one and three secondary voices to the main vocal line, moving in parallel motion. This was known as *conductus*, and was an early form of polyphony — a compositional technique in which several melodic lines are combined, moving independently (as opposed to

ABOVE: An example of the ars antiqua — *a page from the* Jeu de Robin et Marion *by Adam de la Halle (1230–c.1288).*

homophony, in which the voices move together, forming blocks of harmony). European music was dominated by the polyphonic principle from the 13th to the 16th centuries.

By the 13th century, musical notation had become more sophisticated and standardized, with only the finer points of rhythmic

notation still open to interpretation. *Conductus* was gradually superseded by a new form known as the motet, a sacred Latin song, usually with a Biblical text, in which other voices moved in counterpoint to the main tune. The motet has remained a standard form of liturgical music.

Ars nova

At the same time, secular songs, such as those sung by French troubadours and *trouvères*, were being written down. Their flexibility and tunefulness led to the development of a new style (*ars nova*) in the 14th century, initiated by the theorist Philippe de Vitry. The music of the *ars nova*, which flourished particularly in France and Italy, had greater rhythmic vitality, and composers such as Guillaume de Machaut began to experiment with new techniques such as isorhythm, in which the same rhythmic pattern appears in successive repetitions of the melody, but not necessarily using notes of the same value. Many motets of the period were based on this technique, and on a *cantus firmus* — a familiar tune (either a plainsong melody or a folk song) which underpinned a polyphonic composition

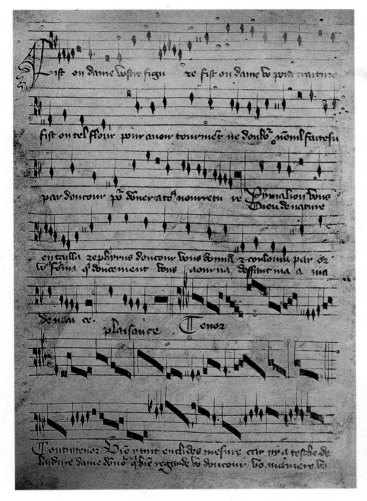

increasing sophistication of musical instruments. This was the invention of "monody", a new style in which the old principle of equal voices moving in counterpoint gave way to a single vocal line accompanied by instruments. While the tenor line still carried the main tune of a composition, it was now underpinned by a "ground bass", or *basso continuo* — a strong bass line played on keyboard and reinforced by cello and other bass instruments, which provided a harmonic foundation. The new style — the basis of all Baroque music — originated in Florence, where the composer Giulio Caccini published a famous collection of monodies, *Nuove musiche*, in 1602. The invention of monody coincided with the birth of a new secular musical genre, opera. The concept of a drama set to music, performed by costumed singers with instrumental accompaniment, originated in Florence with early examples by Peri and Caccini. Its greatest early exponent was Claudio Monteverdi.

ABOVE: An example of ars nova *notation — an anonymous 14th-century French virelai (song). Note the increasing complexity of the notation.*

by appearing throughout, usually in the tenor line.

By 1500 the system of Western European musical notation had become largely standardized, and from then onwards it became increasingly sophisticated and refined. The 16th century (the High Renaissance) was dominated by the principle of polyphony, brought to a height of perfection by composers such as Palestrina in Italy, Lassus in Germany, Victoria in Spain, and William Byrd in England.

Radical change of style

Around 1600, a musical sea-change occurred, partly as a reaction against polyphony, partly as a result of the secularization of society, and the

ABOVE: An exquisitely illuminated page from the 15th-century Squarcialupi *codex showing Francesco Landini (c.1325–97) with the score of his madrigal* Musica son.

Baroque Forms

[Opera is] one of the most magnificent and expenseful diversions the wit of man can invent.

JOHN EVELYN (1620–1706), DIARY, 1645

Music in the Baroque era (c.1600–1750) was dominated by an insatiable demand for recreational art-forms. The great aristocratic and royal households, which could support their own orchestras, also employed composers to supply a constant need for new works. In 18th-century Europe, the growing size and wealth of the new middle classes led to a gradual democratization of musical appreciation and the advent of public performances in new concert halls and opera houses.

ABOVE: A sumptuous court entertainment of 1747 in the Teatro Argentina in Rome to celebrate the marriage of the son of Louis XV.

Music and drama

Opera became a favourite entertainment at the many princely courts which dotted Europe; the first public opera house opened in Venice in 1637, followed by others in major European cities. New musical forms were developed to suit the genre, including recitative and aria: the recitative allowed the singer (accompanied only by keyboard) to advance the story rapidly; while the aria, accompanied by the orchestra, allowed for expansive and lyrical reflection on a given situation or emotion.

The Baroque era was dominated by *opera seria*, based on plots drawn from ancient mythology, legend or history, with heroic characters fulfilling their destinies according to approved behavioural concepts. The most prolific 17th-century opera composers included

Alessandro Scarlatti and Antonio Vivaldi in Italy, Reinhard Keiser in Germany, and Jean-Baptiste Lully in France.

But by far the greatest exponent of Italian *opera seria* was Handel, who managed to make his characters express real human emotions. His operas have survived, while works by his contemporaries have been consigned to history. *Opera seria* lasted into Mozart's time, but by then audiences were demanding a lighter, more naturalistic type of drama, often dealing with comic subject-matter, which flowered in the hands of Gluck and especially Mozart.

Oratorio

Despite initial resistance, not even the church could remain unaffected by these new developments. A sacred — and normally unstaged — type of musical drama called oratorio, using the same musical forms as opera, but based on biblical stories, came into

being. Most opera composers (such as Scarlatti and Vivaldi) also wrote oratorios, but again it was Handel's fine examples which have survived to the present day. Bach's *St John* and *St Matthew Passions*, relating the story of Christ's death according to the Gospels, belong to this genre.

Instrumental forms

A growing demand for purely instrumental music led to the development of other new forms, such as the sonata. This was conceived both as a form suitable for church performance — the *sonata da chiesa*, which the Italian composer Corelli developed as a standard four-movement form — and its lighter counterpart the *sonata da camera*, which had an unspecified number of dance-like movements. Dance types — gavotte, minuet, courante, allemande, gigue — found their way into instrumental compositions, and their enormous variety formed the basis of the Baroque suite, perfected by Bach and Handel.

Another new form was the concerto, a genre pioneered by Giovanni Gabrieli in the late 1500s, in which a small group of instruments (later one solo instrument) is contrasted with the main body of the orchestra (the earlier form is known as a *concerto grosso*). While Renaissance music had exalted the principle of equality, Baroque music thrived on contrast.

Transition to Classicism

The still, sad music of humanity.

WILLIAM WORDSWORTH (1770–1850), "TINTERN ABBEY"

Baroque music reached its zenith in the works of Bach and Handel. Bach concentrated on sacred music, notably in his many cantatas — dramatic works for voices and instruments intended for church performance; Handel worked in both secular and sacred genres, writing Italian operas and English oratorios. The opening instrumental overtures, or "sinfonias", of such pieces gradually expanded into the 18th-century symphony, which eventually settled into a standard four-movement form with an opening fast movement, a lyrical slow movement, a short dance movement (usually a minuet and trio) and a fast finale. This was the form which Joseph Haydn perfected in over 100 examples, together with another new instrumental genre, the string quartet, written for two violins, viola and cello.

Sonata form

These works, together with the Classical sonata itself, were dominated by the structural principle of "sonata form", in which an opening exposition, usually presenting two main, contrasting themes, is succeeded by a central "development" section, in which the themes are subjected to a variety of treatments. Then comes

ABOVE: *A group of musicians playing stringed and keyboard instruments at the court of the Duke of Modena in the late 17th century, painted by Antonio Gabbiani (1652–1726).*

a "recapitulation", in which the opening themes are repeated (often in shortened or slightly varied form),

followed by a short "coda" to round off the movement.

Haydn's great Viennese contemporaries Mozart and Beethoven consolidated and developed the symphony and string quartet, as well as the solo concerto — which was now becoming primarily a vehicle for one virtuoso performer. As the 18th-century harpsichord gave way to the more powerful and reliable pianoforte, the piano concerto — and the solo piano sonata — became favoured forms from Mozart's time onwards.

ABOVE: *An 18th-century concert with wind, string and keyboard players held at a private Italian palazzo (probably in Venice).*

The Romantic Heyday

There is nothing stable in the world; uproar's your only music.

JOHN KEATS (1795–1821)

While Napoleon Bonaparte swept across Europe, toppling the decadent aristocratic rulers of the *ancien régime*, Beethoven's powerful musical vision heralded a new age of individualism. His massive *Eroica* Symphony (No. 3) pushed Classical symphonic form to its limits, while his Sixth (*Pastoral*) Symphony showed how music could be used to illustrate humanity's relationship with nature (a favourite concept of the Romantic era, as illustrated in the art and literature of the period). Meanwhile, as aristocratic patronage declined, the burgeoning middle classes began to demand music on a domestic scale for private enjoyment – a market filled by the music of

ABOVE: One of the seminal literary works of Romanticism — an artist's impression of Goethe's Faust in his study, painted in 1829.

Schubert, Schumann, Chopin, Mendelssohn and Brahms, who produced songs with piano accompaniment, chamber music (for combinations of string and wind instruments) and solo piano pieces.

The rapid expansion of the orchestra during this period, together with the invention of new instruments such as the clarinet and the improvement of existing ones, particularly woodwind and brass, led to the creation of much larger ensembles with increased power, colour and tonal range. These demanded new types of music on a vastly expanded scale. In line with the expansionist vision of the 19th century, the symphonic canvases of Schumann, Brahms, Bruckner and Mahler became

ABOVE: A typical Romantic seascape: Moonrise over the Sea, *by Caspar David Friedrich (1774–1840).*

ABOVE: An impression of Wotan from Wagner's massive operatic cycle Der Ring des Nibelungen *(1853–74).*

ABOVE: The Russian composer Nikolay Rimsky-Korsakov was the most prominent member of "The Mighty Handful". His nationalistic works include Voskresenaya *(Russian Easter Festival Overture) and the opera* Sadko, *a setting of Russian folk legends.*

ever more inflated; while Wagner's massive "music-dramas", culminating in the epic saga *Der Ring des Nibelungen*, first performed complete in 1876, pointed the way forward to the "music of the future".

Rise of nationalism
While Germany led the musical world in symphonic terms, composers such as Smetana and Dvořák in Bohemia, Glinka, Borodin and Rimsky-Korsakov in Russia, Grieg in Norway and Chopin in Poland were beginning to discover an individual musical culture by introducing the colourful inflections of their native folk music into standard musical genres. Liszt, the Hungarian composer and virtuoso pianist, tackled the symphony from a different angle, inventing the one-movement symphonic "tone-poem" (usually inspired by a poetic, artistic or literary idea); this form was later adopted by Richard Strauss.

ABOVE: A poster advertising three operas by Gilbert and Sullivan – The Gondoliers, The Mikado *and* The Yeomen of the Guard *– produced by the D'Oyly Carte Opera Company.*

For much of the 19th century, England languished as "the land without music" until it was rescued from oblivion on the one hand by the enchantingly witty "Savoy Operas" of Gilbert and Sullivan, and on the other by the genius of Edward Elgar, the first major British composer since Purcell. Italy, however, continued to consolidate its reputation as the operatic centre of the world, with masterpieces by Rossini, Donizetti, Bellini, Verdi and Puccini.

Dawn of a New Age

Music should not decorate, it should be truthful.

ARNOLD SCHOENBERG (1874–1951)

The harmonic tonal framework established during the Baroque and Classical eras remained common musical currency until the turn of the 20th century, when the fluid, impressionistic style of the French composer Claude Debussy began to loosen the hold of tonality. At the same time, the German Expressionist composer Arnold Schoenberg was working independently on a completely new harmonic system, based on the principle of the equality of the 12 notes of the Western scale. Schoenberg's 12-note system, which destroyed the traditional ascendancy of traditional harmony, had many detractors, and he is still considered a "difficult" composer even today, but it had enormous influence on future composers, such as his followers Berg and Webern, and the French composers Boulez and Messiaen.

The innovations of both Debussy and Schoenberg, combined with the raw, exotic harmonies and rhythms of Russian folk music, melded in the works of Stravinsky, the dominant figure of 20th-century music. From his early scores for Diaghilev's Ballets Russes – *The Firebird, Petrushka* and *The Rite of Spring* – to the 12-note music written towards the end of his long life, Stravinsky produced a string of original masterpieces, constantly re-inventing his style to accommodate changing tastes. His compatriots Prokofiev and Shostakovich made significant contributions to 20th-century music – Prokofiev in the fields of ballet, opera and the concerto;

ABOVE: An example of Expressionist art – The Dream *by Franz Marc (1880–1916).*

Shostakovich most notably in his 15 symphonies and 15 string quartets.

Central Europe produced two other major 20th-century figures, both continuing their respective countries' nationalist traditions: the Hungarian Béla Bartók (who was not only a composer, but a major folk song collector), and the Czech Leoš Janáček, whose operas are now acclaimed as masterpieces.

Political events in Europe in the mid 20th century drove many fine composers (including Schoenberg and Bartók) into exile in America. But the USA had its own home-grown innovators: while Aaron Copland and Leonard Bernstein celebrated mainstream American culture in their

hugely popular and accessible works, composers such as Charles Ives and John Cage experimented with new compositional techniques, ranging from aleatory music (which depends on chance) to polytonality (music played in different keys at the same time), and even to complete silence.

As new instruments, including electronic ones, have evolved, new systems of notation have developed to cope with them. In the final decade of the 20th century, many composers abandoned traditional methods of writing music with pen and paper in favour of computer-generated scores, enabling them to produce both scores and parts rapidly and efficiently.

Music of the Future

What we need is a music of the earth, everyday music...
music one can live in like a house.

JEAN COCTEAU (1889–1963), "LE COQ ET L'ARLEQUIN"

The dawn of the 21st century finds so-called "classical" music with many questions to answer. There is no longer any one "system" to follow: the forms and musical styles of previous generations, which formed the bedrock of every composer's vocabulary, have been discarded. Composers now have to either re-invent them, or find an entirely original voice. Some – Harrison Birtwistle, Peter Maxwell Davies, George Benjamin and Thomas Adès in Britain; Steve Reich and John Adams in the USA; Hans Werner Henze in Germany; Luciano Berio in Italy; Sofia Gubaidulina in Russia – are succeeding; others are now seen as derivative or of fringe interest only.

ABOVE: Composition 21st century-style, using midi-keyboard and a computer.

Since the 1950s a chasm has opened between "serious" composers and their public. The vast majority of people listen to rock music and other popular forms, and regard classical music as an exclusive and élitist genre, of which they know nothing; while even lovers of classical music often find themselves bewildered by the new sounds produced by contemporary composers, and prefer the music of previous eras. But the 20th century certainly produced its fair share of composers whose music will endure and perhaps in time will become more popular, while young, exciting talents are still bursting on to the scene. And not all new music is inaccessible: as Schoenberg himself remarked, "There is still plenty of good music to be written in C major!"

ABOVE: The British composer Michael Nyman at a 1991 recording session in London.

ABOVE: A scene from Steve Reich's music-theatre work The Cave *(1989–93). Reich's music has connections with pop and rock music, a factor that contributes to its popularity.*

Lives and Works of the Great Composers

The Ride of the Valkyries, *inspired by an episode from Act III of* Die Walküre
by Richard Wagner, painted by William T. Maud (1865–1903).

Introduction

I would rather write 10,000 notes than one letter of the alphabet.

LUDWIG VAN BEETHOVEN (1770–1827)

For the past six centuries, Western classical music has been largely defined by the role of the composer, and this section presents a historical survey of the exceptional figures whose imagination and skill has shaped its development. The invention of notation meant that music could be preserved and musicians were no longer limited by the number of notes they could memorize. The music could become far more ambitious and complex in scope, and the act of composition became distinct from the performance of the work: the role of the composer began to evolve.

Improvisation, however, remained an important part of music. Until the 18th century, notation provided little more than the bare bones of a piece of music. Couperin wrote that "we write one thing and play another", and

ABOVE: Vienna has been a major centre for composers and musicians since the Baroque era. This painting depicts a court banquet in the Great Antechamber of the Hofburg Palace.

descants, ornaments, figured basses and cadenzas were extemporized by the performers. During the 19th century, written music became more prescriptive, but since the 1950s composers have returned to improvisatory techniques, using graphic notation to stimulate the creativity of the performer, and introducing elements of chance.

Composers may use improvisation themselves, as a way of finding their way into a piece of music. Even though Mozart was said to write his scores without revision, he liked to compose at a keyboard so that he could try out his ideas, while Tippett found it satisfying to feel his music coming through his fingers on to the keys before he committed it to paper. Haydn liked to "extemporize, sadly or joyously, gravely or playfully, as I happen to be feeling, until I lay hold of an idea."

Composition means "putting together", and various elements are involved: the composer's intrinsic talent, technical skill and the rules that have evolved to frame the music –

ABOVE: This beautifully illustrated French manuscript dates from the 13th century, when composers such as Léonin and Pérotin were working at Notre-Dame in Paris.

ABOVE: Joseph Haydn spent his career in the service of a single aristocratic family. He practically invented the Classical forms of symphony, concerto, string quartet and sonata.

ABOVE: Beethoven was a revolutionary composer who expanded musical forms and brought new levels of emotion into his compositions. This manuscript shows an excerpt from Egmont *(1809–10), Beethoven's music to Goethe's five-act play about the Count of Egmont.*

which are there not only to be followed but also to be broken or changed. Debussy's teacher, perplexed by his work, asked what rules of harmony he was following. "Mon plaisir," answered Debussy. And yet, as the old rules were stretched to their limit by the Expressionists of the early 20th century, Schoenberg sensed the need for a new musical framework, and developed the 12-note system.

As the stories of the great composers are told and put into context, the connections between them become clear: most were not isolated artists, but teachers and pupils, fathers and sons, friends or, indeed, enemies. Many were drawn to congregate in centres of excellence such as Paris and Vienna, while others – like Wagner – took an individual course.

Just as music is subject to external influences, from the expertise of performers and instrument makers to political upheaval, the prevailing religious climate and fashions in entertainment, it is also the product of personal experience. While a piece of great music has the power to move the listener regardless of the circumstances in which it was written, it is fascinating to learn more about its background. We might expect episodes of depression, bereavement or political oppression to result in sombre music, and happy romances to produce lyrical song-cycles, but even more interesting are the examples of composers who have been able to transmute their personal misery or disappointments into music of inspiring beauty.

ABOVE: Tchaikovsky's ballet, The Nutcracker *(1891–2). Despite the death of his mother and an unhappy marriage, Tchaikovsky was able to write inspiring, romantic music.*

Lives and Works of the Great Composers **267**

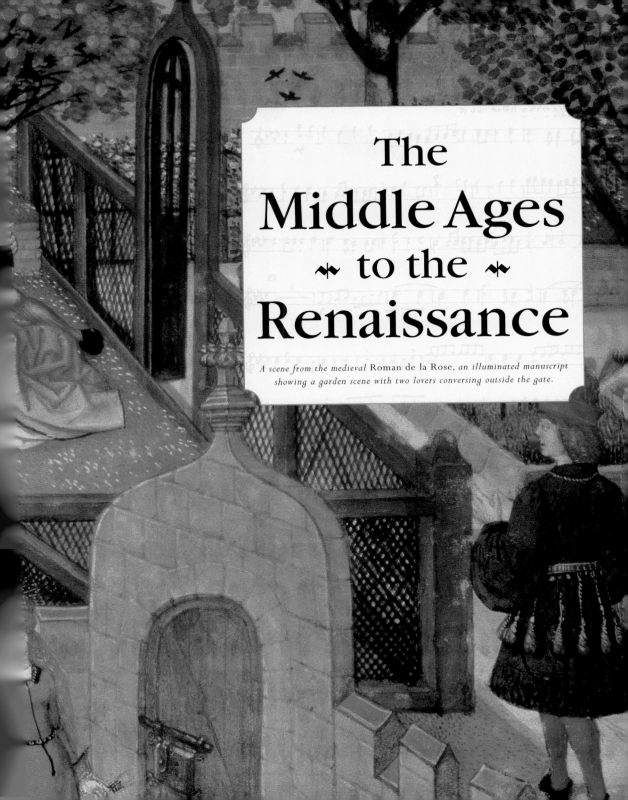

The Middle Ages
❧ to the ❧
Renaissance

A scene from the medieval Roman de la Rose, *an illuminated manuscript showing a garden scene with two lovers conversing outside the gate.*

Medieval and Polyphonic Music

The sound of the cornet, flute, harp, sackbut, psaltery, dulcimer,
and all kinds of music.

DANIEL, 3:3

Until the 20th century, there was a general perception that the history of music began with Bach. Only with the huge growth in musical research and scholarship, together with the explosion of the "early music movement" in the later decades of the 20th century, did many lost masterpieces of the medieval and Renaissance periods come to light, prompting a re-evaluation of their composers' achievements.

Sacred music

Music in the Middle Ages was largely the preserve of the church. Surviving medieval sources were mostly produced by monastic scribes, and kept in monastery libraries. While secular music existed, much of it was improvised,

ABOVE: *A page from an illuminated Flemish medieval psalter dating from c.1470.*

so the earliest music to survive was generally intended for sacred use.

The names of individual composers become scarcer the further back into history we travel. Among the earliest musicians who may be singled out from the 12th and early 13th centuries are the French composers Léonin and Pérotin, who were associated with the newly built cathedral of Notre-Dame in Paris. A spate of enormously popular recordings has recently revealed the visionary music of the 12th-century nun Hildegard of Bingen, who not only has the distinction of being one of the

earliest known composers, but was also a woman working in a field where women have traditionally not been prominent. She is now something of a feminist icon. Performances and recordings by early music groups have also uncovered a wealth of music by unnamed composers derived from medieval manuscript sources, such as the 13th-century Spanish *Cantigas* of Alfonso X.

Polyphony

The French composer Guillaume de Machaut was the single most important musical figure of the 14th century. His many innovations included being the first to compose a complete setting of the Ordinary of the Mass, the first to write music in four parts (which became the

ABOVE: *A heart-shaped score, in red and black ink, of a three-part French chanson* Belle, bonne *by Baude Cordier (fl.1390s).*

ABOVE: *French church singers dating from the 14th century, the time of the innovative composer Guillaume de Machaut.*

such as Filippo Brunelleschi (1377–1446), evident in Florentine churches such as San Lorenzo and Santo Spirito, or the wonderful ducal palace at Urbino, found a musical counterpart in Renaissance polyphony. Music, too, acquired new depth and perspective. While three Flemish composers had dominated the 15th century, the polyphonic art of the High Renaissance was perfected by a trio of musicians – Palestrina from Italy, Lassus from Flanders, and Victoria from Spain – who all spent long periods in Italy.

The polyphonic principle continued to dominate 16th-century music, from the Masses and motets written for performance in the great Catholic churches of France, Italy, Spain and southern Germany, to the equivalent settings of both Catholic and Protestant liturgies by the English composers Tallis and Byrd, and the enchanting secular partsongs of the Elizabethan madrigal school. Meanwhile the plangent songs and solo lute music of Dowland looked forward to a new age of individualism.

ABOVE: An illumination from a 15th-century manuscript showing secular musicians playing a variety of instruments – crumhorn, fiddle, lute, bagpipes, nakers (drums) and triangle.

standard polyphonic combination), and one of the first to set the typical secular poetic forms of his day: *ballade*, *rondeau* and *virelay*.

For the next century, the musical centres of gravity remained the courts and churches of northern France and Flanders, which produced the sacred and secular works of the Flemish composers associated with the court of the dukes of Burgundy: Dufay, Ockeghem, Josquin des Prez and their contemporaries. However, many drew inspiration from prolonged visits to Italy, where musical activity flourished at important courts such as those of Ferrara and Mantua.

The harmonious exercises in perspective of Renaissance architects

ABOVE: The nave and choir of the church of Santo Spirito in Florence, designed by Filippo Brunelleschi in the mid 15th century. This church is a classic Renaissance masterpiece of perspective.

Hildegard of Bingen

A feather on the breath of God.

HILDEGARD

This remarkable woman was one of the earliest known composers. A contemporary of the famous medieval lovers Abélard and Héloïse, who also ended their lives in monastic institutions, Hildegard was born into a noble German family. As the tenth child she was considered a tithe and therefore due to the church, and was dedicated to religious service. When she was eight years old, she was sent as a novice to the Benedictine monastery of Disibodenberg.

In 1136 Hildegard became an abbess in her own right, and around the age of 50 she founded a nunnery near Bingen in the Rhine Valley. She died at the advanced age of 81, and her name was

ABOVE: An illustrated 13th-century manuscript depicting The Vision of St Hildegard, *compiled 50 years after her death in 1179.*

ABOVE: A modern plaque in the German town of Bingen commemorating its famous Abbess, Hildegard of Bingen.

put forward by several popes as a candidate for canonization. Though never formally canonized, she is often referred to as a saint, and has a feast-day which is particularly celebrated in Germany.

Mysticism and music

Hildegard was a visionary, and soon gained a widespread reputation as a prophetess. Popes, emperors, monarchs, archbishops and clergymen of all kinds flocked to Bingen to consult this "Sybil of the Rhine". Between 1141 and 1170 she recorded her mystical experiences; she also wrote two important works on natural history and medicine, and a great deal

of lyric and dramatic poetry, collected together in a volume called *Symphonia armonie celestium revelationum*.

Most of her poetry is liturgical, including antiphons, sequences and hymns designed for performance on the feast-days of particular saints. Among her work is the earliest known surviving morality play, *Ordo virtutum*, which describes the 16 Virtues battling with the Devil for a human soul. This and many of her poems have music attached, written in German neumatic notation. Unlike much music of this period, Hildegard's melodies are not drawn from monastic plainsong, but are strikingly original, and sometimes highly complex and decorative.

Many of her works have been performed and recorded during the recent revival of interest in early music: the album released under the title *A Feather on the Breath of God* (1984) has enjoyed huge popularity.

Life and works

NATIONALITY: German

BORN: Böckelheim, 1098;
DIED: Bingen, 1179

SPECIALIST GENRES: Plainsong settings of her own poetry.

MAJOR WORK: *Ordo virtutum; Symphonia armonie celestium revelationum.*

The Notre-Dame School

Who could retain a grievance against the man
with whom he had joined in singing before God?

St Ambrose (c.339–97)

Léonin and Pérotin – sometimes referred to as Master Leoninus and Master Perotinus – were the best-known of a group of composers who worked in medieval Paris in the late 12th and early 13th centuries. This was the age of King Philippe-Auguste (Philippe II), during whose reign, from 1180 to 1223, the medieval kingdom of France was consolidated. Little is known of the lives of Léonin and Pérotin, but both are associated with the cathedral of Notre-Dame de Paris, whose foundations were laid in the mid 1160s, and its high altar consecrated in 1182.

ABOVE: An initial letter from an illuminated French psalter dating from the 13th century – the time of Léonin and Pérotin.

scholars have suggested that he may have worked at the royal parish church of St Germain-l'Auxerrois, near the Tuileries Palace, since there is no direct evidence that he worked at Notre-Dame.

Pérotin was active in the creation of the four-voice motet, an ecclesiastical musical form which survives to the present day. His contribution towards the development of three- and four-voice polyphony was one of the most important steps forward in musical history. Of his works, two graduals in four voices for the Christmas season survive, as do about a dozen liturgical works in three voices, and about 160 *clausulae* – polyphonic passages written for insertion into liturgical plainsong to vary the texture.

Léonin

The major work attributed to Léonin was the *Magnus liber* ("great book") designed for use by the choir of the new cathedral. He is mentioned by an anonymous 13th-century theorist as "the best composer of organum for the

amplification of divine service", suggesting that he wrote polyphonic settings for two independent voices of parts of the liturgy intended for performance on the main feast-days of the church's year. Léonin may also have been among the first to indicate rhythm as well as pitch in his musical notation. His vocal writing was imaginative, free-flowing and improvisatory in style.

Pérotin

Some time after Léonin's death, Pérotin, who may have been his pupil, seems to have revised and shortened the *Magnus liber*. Pérotin remains a shadowy figure. He may have been born around 1160, and died some time between 1205 and 1225. Some

ABOVE: A view of medieval Paris showing the cathedral of Notre-Dame, where Léonin and Pérotin worked, from the 15th-century Book of Hours of Etienne Chevalier.

Lives and works

Nationality: French

Active: Léonin, c.1163–90; Pérotin, c.1200

Specialist genres: Early polyphonic sacred music.

Major works: *Magnus liber*, motets and graduals.

Guillaume de Machaut

*...the morning star of song, who made
his music heard below.*

ALFRED, LORD TENNYSON (1809–92), "A DREAM OF FAIR WOMEN"

A near contemporary of Geoffrey Chaucer (c.1340–1400), whose poetry he influenced, Guillaume de Machaut was one of the most important composers of the 14th century. Not only did he compose more than anyone else of his period, but his works are enormously varied in style and form.

He seems to have spent much of his life in Rheims, in northern France, where he died. He entered the service of John, King of Bohemia, around 1323, and in the manner of a courtier of the time, travelled around Europe in the royal retinue until the king was killed at the Battle of Crécy in 1346. Meanwhile, however, John's patronage had enabled Machaut to procure

ABOVE: A contemporary portrait of Guillaume de Machaut (1300–77), one of the earliest surviving portraits of a composer.

several lucrative canonries at major northern French cathedrals. After John's death, Machaut continued to serve the French nobility, including the future King Charles V (for whose coronation he composed a Mass) and John, Duke of Berry.

Ars nova

Machaut's output is equally divided between sacred and secular music. His most famous piece is the *Notre-Dame Mass*, and he wrote over 20 motets, but also a large quantity of secular songs — ballades, rondeaux and virelays, which were the principal vocal types of the time. His works are representative of the French *ars nova*, or new style, and are often very rhythmically complex.

ABOVE: A joust, watched by ladies. Many of Machaut's songs dealt with courtly love.

ABOVE: The score of a Machaut motet, an example of the 14th-century ars nova style.

Life and works

NATIONALITY: French

BORN: Machaut, c.1300;
DIED: Rheims, 1377

SPECIALIST GENRES: Sacred and secular vocal music of the *ars nova*.

MAJOR WORKS: *Notre-Dame Mass*; motets; secular songs.

Guillaume Dufay

L'homme armé doibt on doubter. (Fear the armed man.)

ANONYMOUS, 15TH-CENTURY FOLK SONG

The pre-eminence of northern France and Flanders in the development of compositional technique continued into the 15th century, in the person of Guillaume Dufay. Born near Brussels around the turn of the century, the illegitimate son of a priest, he became a choirboy at Cambrai Cathedral and, around 1420, he entered the service of the powerful Italian Malatesta family. He seems to have returned from Italy to hold posts in several churches in and around Cambrai in the mid 1420s, but in 1428 he became a singer in the papal choir in Rome. While in Italy, he evidently worked for several other noble families, including the Este family of Ferrara and the dukes of Savoy. He returned north to Cambrai around 1436, when he became a canon at the cathedral, but he maintained his ties with Italy, spending seven years in Savoy in the 1450s. He died at Cambrai and was buried in a chapel in the cathedral.

ABOVE: Guillaume Dufay depicted in a French manuscript dating from 1440 called Le champion des dames.

Cantus firmus

Dufay was the most celebrated composer of his time: other budding composers flocked to Cambrai to seek his advice. His surviving compositions — about 200 in all — show his absolute mastery of the major forms of his time, together with an attractive and fluent talent for melody. Many of his works are harmonizations of liturgical chants, but eight complete Masses survive, along with Mass fragments, hymns, antiphons and motets. Many of his works are based on a *cantus firmus* — either a plainsong melody or a popular secular tune, such as the folk song *L'homme armé* (*The Armed Man*), on which Dufay based his most famous Mass. (The same tune was used in this way by many other composers of the 15th, 16th and 17th centuries.) Dufay also wrote over 80 songs — probably for his Italian patrons — for voices accompanied by instruments. He was apparently the first to write a Requiem Mass, completed just four years before his own death, but the manuscript of this work has been lost.

Life and works

NATIONALITY: Flemish

BORN: near Brussels, 1397; **DIED:** Cambrai, 1474

SPECIALIST GENRES: Polyphonic sacred and secular forms.

MAJOR WORKS: Motets; Masses; songs.

ABOVE: A Dance of the Shepherds *depicted in a 15th-century Book of Hours (of Charles d'Angoulême), now held in the Bibliothèque Nationale in Paris.*

Johannes Ockeghem

He alone of all singers is free from all vice and abounds in all virtues.

FRANCESCO FLORI (DIED 1588)

Among the composers who visited Dufay at Cambrai was the Franco-Flemish composer Johannes (or Jean d') Ockeghem, then aged around 50, and destined to succeed Dufay as the most celebrated composer of his period.

Ockeghem's early life, and even his birthplace and date, are shrouded in obscurity. The earliest mention of him is as a singer at Notre-Dame in Antwerp in 1443; shortly afterwards he entered the service of Charles I, Duke of Bourbon, at Moulins in France. In the early 1450s he was employed by Charles VII of France as a chaplain, and probably remained in the royal service until his death. He died at an advanced age in Tours, where he had been for many years, and by royal appointment, treasurer of St Martin's Church. He appears to have been admired as much for the kindness and generosity of his character as for the "extraordinary sweetness and beauty" of his music, and his death was mourned in flowery verbal and musical tributes from fellow musicians and poets.

ABOVE: Johannes Ockeghem directing a choir of monks in the Gloria of one of his Masses.

Contrapuntal innovation

Relatively few of Ockeghem's compositions have survived, among them 14 Masses, a polyphonic Requiem Mass (which is the earliest surviving example), nine motets and a handful of secular chansons. His Masses are the most important of their time. The earlier ones are based, like Dufay's, on an existing melody, either sacred or secular; but the later ones are more experimental. Instead of keeping the *cantus firmus* in the tenor part, Ockeghem shares it between the voices, producing a texture of great contrapuntal complexity. He was also the first composer known to have used the melodies of his own songs as the *cantus firmus* of a Mass setting (a technique known as "parody mass", used in his Masses *Fors seulement*, *Au travail suis* and *Ma maistresse*). Several of his works, notably the *Missa prolationum*, do not rely on a *cantus firmus*, but are freely constructed from an intricate combination of rhythmic and melodic fragments.

ABOVE: Ockeghem's last royal patron, Charles VIII of France (reigned 1477–98). He had worked for three French kings.

Life and works

NATIONALITY: Flemish

BORN: ?Dender, c.1410;
DIED: Tours, 1497

SPECIALIST GENRES:
Polyphonic sacred works.

MAJOR WORKS: 14 Masses.

Josquin des Prez

Josquin is master of the notes; others are mastered by them.

MARTIN LUTHER (1483–1546)

Among the tributes paid to
Ockeghem was the beautiful elegy
Nymphes des bois, written by the final
member of the great 15th-century trio
of Franco-Flemish composers.
Josquin des Prez, who may have been
Ockeghem's pupil, can lay claim to
being the finest composer of the High
Renaissance. Possibly born in Picardy,
he may have begun his career as a
choirboy in the collegiate church at
St Quentin, but then went to Milan,
where he sang in the cathedral choir
and also worked for the Sforza family.

In the late 1480s he was a member
of the papal choir. Around 1500 he was
working both for the French court and
for the dukes of Ferrara, but when
plague broke out in Ferrara in 1503 he
fled north, becoming provost of the
church of Notre-Dame in Condé. He
died there in August 1521 and was

ABOVE: *A woodcut of Josquin des Prez
(c.1440–1521).*

commemorated by a flood of verbal
and musical homages. Josquin's fame
as a composer during his lifetime
is attested by three individual
publications of his Masses in the

early 1500s by the Venetian printer
Petrucci. Publications devoted to
the works of one composer were
extremely rare at the time.

Matching music to words

Like Mozart some three centuries
later, Josquin took the common
musical currency of his time and
refined it into pure gold. He was one
of the first composers to relate his
music closely to the text: his word-
setting is infinitely sensitive, dramatic
and highly expressive, while his use of
complex musical techniques is handled
in a masterly but unobtrusive way. His
early Masses were based on *cantus
firmus* techniques, but the later ones,
such as *Ave Maris Stella*, *L'homme armé*
and *Pange lingua*, use a variety of
unifying devices including parody
technique and motto themes.

Life and works

NATIONALITY: Flemish

BORN: ?Picardy, c.1440;
DIED: Condé, 1521

SPECIALIST GENRES:
Polyphonic sacred
works and secular
songs.

MAJOR WORKS:
19 Masses, including
Pange lingua and
De beata virgine.

ABOVE: *A page from a 16th-century missal showing part of Josquin's Mass* Pange lingua
(Sing, my tongue).

Giovanni Pierluigi da Palestrina

*The most frivolous and gallant words are set to exactly the same music as those of the Bible…
the truth is that he could not write any other kind of music.*

HECTOR BERLIOZ (1803–69), "MEMOIRS"

Palestrina's name has become synonymous with textbook perfection in the field of harmony and counterpoint, and his reputation long outlived him. He began his career in Rome as organist and choir-master.

In 1552, under the patronage of his former bishop, now Pope Julius III, Palestrina became choir-master at the Julian Chapel, the training school for the Sistine Choir. After three years he was dismissed by a new pope because he was married, but in the same year he succeeded Lassus as choir-master of the church of St John Lateran. He resigned after a dispute over money matters in 1560, and returned to S. Maria Maggiore, but during the last two decades of his life he worked once more at the Julian Chapel.

In the 1570s Palestrina lost his brother, two of his sons, and finally his wife in plague epidemics, which led him to consider entering the

ABOVE: A contemporary painting of Giovanni Pierluigi da Palestrina, who worked mostly in Rome.

priesthood. However, in 1581, just eight months after his first wife's death, he married a wealthy widow, who assured his financial security.

Masses and motets

Palestrina worked against the background of the Counter-Reformation. The Council of Trent had initiated ecclesiastical reforms, which decreed that sacred music should be kept simple so that the words could be heard clearly. Elaborate polyphony and the extensive use of instrumental accompaniment was discouraged. Palestrina's Masses and motets are all constructed with an ear to clarity of textual declamation: the vocal lines flow freely and the intertwining parts create their own beauty, enhancing rather than obscuring the meaning of the words.

Over 100 of Palestrina's Masses survive, including the famous *Missa Papae Marcelli*, together with about 375 motets for between four and 12 voices and many other liturgical works, including Magnificat and Lamentation settings. However, as his career demonstrates, he achieved a balance between the sacred and the secular. While much of his music was written to the glory of God, some is based on secular models; and his many published collections include two books of madrigals.

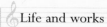

Life and works

NATIONALITY: Italian

BORN: Palestrina, c.1525;
DIED: Rome, 1594

SPECIALIST GENRES:
Polyphonic sacred music.

MAJOR WORKS: *Missa Papae Marcelli* (1567); *Missa Assumpta est Maria* (1567); *Missa brevis* (1570); Stabat Mater (1590).

ABOVE: An artist's impression of Palestrina at work, composing one of his many Masses.

Orlande de Lassus

Orlandissimo Lassissimo amorevolissimo.

LASSUS'S SIGNATURE ON A LETTER TO DUKE WILHELM V, C.1575

The Flemish composer Orlande de Lassus (sometimes known by the Italian form of his name, Orlando di Lasso) was a contemporary of Palestrina: they died in the same year. Lassus spent his early years travelling in Sicily and Italy attached to the households of various Italian nobles. His earliest collections of compositions – madrigals, songs and motets – were published in Antwerp and Venice when he was in his early 20s, and in 1556 he joined the court of Duke Albrecht V of Bavaria in Munich, as a singer in the ducal chapel.

Court music

By 1563 Lassus had risen to become the duke's *maestro di cappella*, a position he held until his death. His duties

ABOVE: *The Flemish composer Orlande de Lassus (c.1532–94), painted in 1580 by Johann von Achen.*

included providing sacred music for the chapel's services, and secular music for the court's entertainment on occasions such as state visits, banquets and hunting parties. In 1569 he provided the music for the sumptuous festivities surrounding the marriage of Duke Wilhelm V of Bavaria to Renée of Lorraine. Lassus continued to travel widely, particularly in France and Italy, but his base remained Munich for the last 34 years of his life, towards the end of which he suffered from

depression and became preoccupied with sacred works. Two of his sons became musicians. His own fame had spread far and wide, and he was one of the most respected and prolific composers of his time. About 2000 of his compositions survive.

His supreme mastery of the art of polyphony is demonstrated in his Masses, motets, settings of the Passions and other liturgical works, including the fine *Psalmi Davidis poenitentiales* (*Seven Penitential Psalms of David*) published in 1584 but written around 1563. He was equally skilled in the lighter, more lyrical style, exemplified in his Italianate madrigals and French chansons.

Life and works

NATIONALITY: Flemish

BORN: Mons, c.1532;
DIED: Munich, 1594

SPECIALIST GENRES:
Polyphonic sacred and lyrical secular music.

MAJOR WORKS: *Psalmi Davidis poenitentiales* (1584); "Tristis est anima mea" (1568); "Adoremus te, Christe" (1604) and many other motets.

ABOVE: *The Royal Chapel in Munich, c.1565, where Lassus worked as* maestro di cappella. *He is the bearded figure dressed in yellow.*

Tomás Luis de Victoria

...in solemn beauty like slow old tunes of Spain.

JOHN MASEFIELD (1878–1967)

Victoria (also known as Tommaso Ludovico da Vittoria) stands beside Palestrina and Lassus as one of the finest composers of the 16th century. He was born into a distinguished family in Ávila, where he was a choirboy at the cathedral (one of his uncles was a canon there), and attended a highly regarded Jesuit school. In 1563 he was sent to the Jesuit Collegio Germanico in Rome, where he may have studied composition with Palestrina. Eight years later he himself became a music teacher there, finally leaving in early 1577, by which time he had been

ABOVE: *The title page of a book of Tomás Luis de Victoria's motets, published in 1589 as* Cantiones sacrae (Sacred Songs)*.*

ordained as a priest. He took up a chaplaincy at San Girolamo della Carità, but also drew income from five benefices back in Spain, granted to him by Pope Gregory XIII.

Madrid

In the early 1580s Victoria decided that he wanted to return to Spain, and King Philip II appointed him chaplain to his sister, the Dowager Empress Maria, at the Madrid convent where she lived. Victoria served the empress from 1587 until her death in 1603, and subsequently remained at the convent until his own death, refusing many tempting offers from other Spanish cathedrals. From 1592–5 he revisited Rome to supervise the printing of a book of Masses, and also attended Palestrina's funeral.

Though Victoria wrote only sacred music, as befitted his priestly vocation, his works are far from solemn, revealing a naturally sunny disposition. His 20 Masses were all published in his lifetime: many of them are based on his own motets, antiphons and psalms, while the *Missa pro victoria* is a battle Mass based on a popular French chanson called *La guerre* (*The War*). There are also 16 extant Magnificat settings, many other shorter liturgical works, and a much-admired sequence of music for Holy Week, including nine expressive Lamentations.

ABOVE: *King Philip II of Spain (1527–98), painted c.1575.*

Life and works

NATIONALITY: Spanish

BORN: Ávila, c.1548;
DIED: Madrid, 1611

SPECIALIST GENRES:
Richly polyphonic
sacred works.

MAJOR WORK:
Requiem Mass for the
Dowager Empress Maria
(1603); 20 Masses;
16 Magnificats.

Thomas Tallis

As he did live, so also did he die,
In mild and quiet sort (O! happy man)

TALLIS'S EPITAPH

During his long and productive lifetime, the English composer Thomas Tallis served four monarchs: Henry VIII, Edward VI, Mary Tudor and Elizabeth I. Though born a Catholic, he managed to survive an extremely dangerous age of religious upheaval and persecution, mainly by adapting his musical style to suit the circumstances, and by keeping a low personal profile.

Royal monopoly

Probably a native of Kent, Tallis's first recorded post was as organist of the Benedictine Priory in Dover. He then joined the choir of Waltham Abbey, near London, around 1538. The Abbey was dissolved in 1540, during Henry VIII's reign, and Tallis became a lay clerk at Canterbury Cathedral. From around 1572 until his death he shared the position of organist and composer to the Chapel Royal with his pupil, William Byrd.

ABOVE: *Thomas Tallis shared with Byrd the right to print music and music paper.*

In 1575 Tallis and Byrd received a patent from Elizabeth I granting them a 21-year monopoly on printing music and music paper in England. Their first publication was a joint collection of 34 *Cantiones sacrae* (sacred songs) in five and six parts.

Textual clarity

Tallis is chiefly remembered for his church music, setting text in both Latin and English, depending on the prevailing religious climate. One notable feature of his style was a move away from florid, elaborate counterpoint towards simpler, syllabic declamation in which the text could be clearly heard: in this respect he was pointing the way forward to the Baroque era.

His mastery of contrapuntal techniques is amply demonstrated in his breathtaking 40-part motet *Spem in alium*, which opens in 20-part imitation. The hymn tune known as "Tallis's Canon" (later set as a hymn tune to the words "Glory to thee, my God, this night") was written for Archbishop Parker's *Metrical Psalter* of 1567, and another tune was used by Vaughan Williams as the basis for his *Fantasia on a Theme of Thomas Tallis* (1910).

LEFT: *Queen Elizabeth I, by George Gower (1540–96). During the Elizabethan period (1558–1603) Tallis wrote his later works, such as the Whitsuntide anthem* O Lord give Thy Holy Spirit.

Life and works

NATIONALITY: English

BORN: ?Kent, c.1505;
DIED: Greenwich, 1585

SPECIALIST GENRES: Polyphonic motets in Latin and English.

MAJOR WORKS: Motet *Spem in alium* (c.1570); *Lamentations of Jeremiah*; *Cantiones sacrae*.

William Byrd

How daintily this Byrd his notes doth vary,
As if he were the Nightingale's own brother.

ANONYMOUS, FROM THE PREFACE TO "PARTHENIA", 1613

Apart from Tallis, the other giant of 16th-century English music was his pupil, William Byrd. In 1563, aged about 20, Byrd was appointed organist and master of the choristers at Lincoln Cathedral. He married in 1568 and had several children. In 1570 he became a Gentleman of the Chapel Royal in London, while also making the acquaintance of various powerful nobles, to whom he dedicated compositions.

Catholicism

His noble patrons undoubtedly helped to protect Byrd through difficult times, when he became known as a Roman Catholic recusant and continued to risk prosecution by writing Masses for undercover use by prominent Catholic families. His three fine Latin Masses, in four, three and five parts respectively, were published openly in the 1590s, but after his publication between

ABOVE: William Byrd was a Catholic composer who managed to survive persecution at the time of Elizabeth I.

1605–10 of the *Gradualia* (a huge collection of music for use with the Catholic liturgy), possession of the volume became a criminal offence.

Songs and instrumental music

Between 1588 and 1611, Byrd published three collections of *Psalmes, Songs and Sonnets*, miscellaneous collections of English anthems, secular partsongs, madrigals and pieces for viol consort. His instrumental music was particularly fine: he was a master of the art of consort music (particularly fantasias for viols), and of keyboard music, especially the pavans and galliards so much loved by Queen Elizabeth I and her court. His keyboard music

appeared in various collections intended for aristocratic use, including the *Fitzwilliam Virginal Book, My Lady Nevell's Book* and *Parthenia*, a printed collection issued in 1613 jointly with John Bull (1563–1628) and Orlando Gibbons (1583–1625).

Byrd's later years were spent at an Essex mansion, where he died. His Latin church music lay forgotten until the mid 19th century, although his Anglican anthems remained constantly popular. His madrigals and lively keyboard music were rediscovered in the early 20th century. At least two of the English madrigalists were his pupils, and his influence on English music was profound.

Life and works

NATIONALITY: English

BORN: ?Lincoln, c.1543;
DIED: Stonden Massey, Essex, 1623

SPECIALIST GENRES: Sacred music, songs, madrigals, keyboard works, consort pieces for viols.

MAJOR WORKS: Masses, three Latin and one English; *Cantiones sacrae* (1575); 140 keyboard pieces, including *The Queenes Alman* and *Wolsey's Wilde*.

ABOVE: A magnificently inlaid virginal, once owned by Queen Elizabeth I. Byrd wrote a great deal of virginal music.

Carlo Gesualdo

...music oft hath such a charm
To make bad good, and good provoke to harm.

WILLIAM SHAKESPEARE (1564–1616), "MEASURE FOR MEASURE"

Gesualdo, Prince of Venosa, occupies a unique place in the history of music: he was both a composer (albeit an amateur one) and a murderer. He came of an aristocratic Neapolitan family: his mother was a niece of Pope Pius IV and the sister of a prominent cardinal, and his uncle was Archbishop of Naples — a potent and dangerous brew of religion and politics which characterized the highest levels of contemporary Italian society.

Scandal
In 1586, after the death of his elder brother left Gesualdo heir to the family title, he married his beautiful cousin Maria d'Avalos, daughter of the Marquis of Pescara. Four years later he caught his wife with her aristocratic lover and had them both stabbed to death. The double murder caused a storm of protest, and Gesualdo retired to his country estates, and devoted himself to composition.

ABOVE: Carlo Gesualdo, Prince of Venosa (kneeling), with his uncle, Carlo Borromeo, Archbishop of Naples.

In 1594 he visited Ferrara, where he married Leonora d'Este, the niece of Alfonso, Duke of Ferrara. This second marriage also proved unsuccessful.

Leonora soon tired of her gloomy husband's introspective and melancholy nature, and after their only son died in childhood, Gesualdo increasingly withdrew from the world. He died on the edge of madness, a lonely and embittered man.

Harmony and dissonance
Gesualdo's place in musical history is assured by his six collections of madrigals. Many of these illustrate dolorous texts (containing many references to pain, death and sorrow) with extraordinarily advanced chromatic harmony — perhaps reflecting his tortured mental state. Four centuries later, Gesualdo's love of dissonant harmony excited the interest of Stravinsky; but he had little immediate influence, being seen as an extreme example of the "mannerist" style in music. Nevertheless, he is one of the composers who bridged the divide between Renaissance and Baroque.

Life and works

NATIONALITY: Italian

BORN: Naples, c.1560;
DIED: Naples, 1613

SPECIALIST GENRES:
Secular vocal
music.

MAJOR WORKS: Six
books of madrigals.

ABOVE: A painting showing the view of the shoreline at Naples, by Gaspar van Wittel (1653–1736), now in the Palazzo Pitti in Florence.

English Madrigal School

He would sing of her with falls
Used in lovely madrigals.

ELIZABETH BARRETT BROWNING (1806–61), "A PORTRAIT"

The madrigal – a setting of a (usually secular) text for several voices – developed in Italy towards the end of the 13th century, but flowered some 300 years later in the hands of both Flemish and Italian composers, including Gesualdo and Luca Marenzio (1553–99). During the reign of Elizabeth I (1558–1603) this immensely popular form was imported to England by Italian composers working at the English court. The publication in 1588 of the Italian collection *Musica transalpina* inspired native composers to follow the Italian example.

ABOVE: An English masque at the time of Elizabeth I, with musicians playing lute, viols, gittern and flute, and singing madrigals.

Thomas Morley

Among these was Byrd's pupil, Thomas Morley (1557–1602), who may have been a friend of Shakespeare (his famous setting of "It was a Lover and his Lass" was probably written for the original production of *As You Like It* in 1599). In 1601 Morley edited *The Triumphs of Oriana*, a celebrated anthology of madrigals by the best composers of the time in honour of the Queen, to which he himself contributed "Arise, Awake" and "Hard by a Crystal Fountain".

Thomas Weelkes

Morley's friend Thomas Weelkes (c.1576–1623) was another contributor to the same anthology (with the madrigal "As Vesta was from Latmos Hill Descending"). He was an organist and composer, who published three books of madrigals between 1597 and 1600. His accomplished compositions include "O Care, Thou Wilt Despatch Me", "Thule, the Period of Cosmography" and "Like Two Proud Armies", as well as some fine church music.

John Wilbye

Wilbye (1574–1638) published two madrigal collections in 1598 and 1614; he is regarded as one of the greatest exponents of the genre. His madrigals include the powerfully expressive "Draw on, Sweet Night", "Sweet Honey-sucking Bees" and "Weep, Weep, Mine Eyes".

John Dowland

At the same time, the solo song with lute accompaniment was coming into its own in England. Dowland (c.1563–1626), its finest exponent, was the royal lutenist to the court of James I. Among his greatest works are the affecting songs "Flow my Tears", "Sweet, Stay Awhile" and "In Darkness Let Me Dwell", together with his 1604 collection of lute pieces *Lachrimae* (*Tears*).

ABOVE: One of John Dowland's songs, from The First Booke of Songes or Ayres of Foure Partes, *with tablature for the lute (1597).*

Other Composers of the Era

Modern church music is so constructed that
the congregation cannot hear one distinct word.

DESIDERIUS ERASMUS (1466–1536)

Many composers made outstanding contributions to the development and vitality of polyphonic music during this period. Notable for his chansons and motets, Gilles Binchois (c.1400–60) was organist at Mons Cathedral, and a member of the Burgundian court chapel from 1430. He may also have served as a soldier, fighting with the occupying English army at the time of Joan of Arc. His death was lamented in works by both Ockeghem and Dufay (in a rondeau – a form much cultivated by Binchois). His secular songs embody the courtly tradition of the time, and his sacred music represents a consolidation of the Burgundian style.

Binchois's contemporary, John Dunstable (c.1390–1453), was the leading English composer of his time. Also an astrologer and mathematician,

ABOVE: *Gilles Binchois (right) with his great contemporary and fellow composer Guillaume Dufay, c.1440.*

Dunstable travelled widely in Europe in the service of his aristocratic patrons, and enjoyed an international reputation. He was a master of isorhythmic technique, and his Masses and motets greatly influenced Dufay.

The 15th-century Flemish composer Jacob Obrecht (c.1451–1505) divided his time between the Netherlands and Ferrara, where he died of the plague. He often used secular tunes as the basis for his Masses and motets (a technique he bequeathed to Josquin des Prez), and was one of the first known composers to employ number symbolism in his music.

Antiphony

Another Flemish-born composer, Adriaan Willaert (c.1490–1562), played a significant role in the transition between Renaissance and

Baroque styles. One of the earliest madrigal composers, he became choir-master at St Mark's in Venice in 1527, where he established the principle of writing antiphonal music for double choirs, a form well suited to the special acoustic properties of the Byzantine-style basilica.

Willaert's work greatly influenced Giovanni Gabrieli (1557–1612), who became organist at St Mark's in 1585, inheriting the post from his uncle Andrea (c.1510–86), who had been Willaert's pupil. Giovanni initiated the tradition of writing Venetian motets with instrumental accompaniment. He perfected antiphonal technique both in his motets and his purely instrumental music. The first set of his *Sacrae symphoniae*, 1597, contains the famous *Sonata pian' e forte* for groups of brass instruments.

ABOVE: *The English Agincourt Song, celebrating Henry V's victory at Agincourt (1415), dating from the time of Dunstable.*

ABOVE: *The Flemish composer Adriaan Willaert, who served as music director at St Mark's Cathedral, Venice, for over 30 years.*

The Baroque **✦ Era ✦**

A concert given to the Procurators of Venice by the girls of an 18th-century Venetian orphanage. Vivaldi taught at such an institution.

Harmony and Ornament

Architecture in general is frozen music.

FRIEDRICH VON SCHELLING (1775–1854)

The term "Baroque", which is derived from *barroco*, the Portuguese word for a misshapen pearl, was originally used – in a pejorative sense – to describe the flamboyant, ornate architecture found in German, Austrian and Italian churches of the 17th century, which were designed as a reaction to the cool classicism of Renaissance architecture. One of the most prominent Baroque architects was the Italian sculptor Gianlorenzo Bernini (1598–1680), who worked principally in Rome. His work exhibits the fluid, dynamic shapes, theatricality and illusion that characterize the style.

In music, the Baroque period covers the years from c.1600–1750, during which Renaissance polyphony gave way to a new, highly ornamental style with a strong harmonic basis. Most Baroque music – from operatic arias to *concerti*

ABOVE: *Baroque flamboyance at its height – the interior of St Peter's Basilica in Rome in 1730.*

grossi for groups of instruments – was supported by a *basso continuo*, a firm bass line played on keyboard and reinforced on cello or bass, which provided a harmonic foundation.

Opera

The Baroque period saw the introduction of several new forms, mostly developed in Italy. In the late 16th century, a group of poets and musicians formed an association in Florence called the Camerata, and several of their members – the poet Ottavio Rinuccini (1562–1621) and the composers Jacopo Peri (1561–1633) and Giulio Caccini (c.1550–1618) – collaborated to produce

the earliest music-dramas, or operas. The new form was taken up and transformed by the genius of Claudio Monteverdi, whose three surviving operas are the earliest still to be regularly performed today.

Opera spread like wildfire, with demand coming not only from aristocratic patrons, but also from newly opened public opera houses. Monteverdi's pioneering work was carried on by composers such as Vivaldi and Alessandro Scarlatti in Italy, Hasse in Germany, Lully, Charpentier and Rameau in France, and the German-born Handel in England. Alongside secular operas (usually based on plots derived from ancient history or mythology), a similar sacred form – oratorio – developed, using the same forms and styles as opera, but based on biblical stories. Oratorio flourished both in the Catholic South and the

ABOVE: *An opera theatre in Munich, Germany, in 1665.*

ABOVE: *A realistic depiction of an 18th-century private concert against an allegorical background, one of a set of four Fine Arts designs by Giuseppe Zocchi (1711–67).*

Bach and Handel

In musical terms, the Baroque era reached its height in the works of Bach and Handel. Both were reared in the German Protestant tradition, but their careers took very different paths.

Bach concentrated on church music, whether for voices and instruments (in the form of the church cantata, a kind of unstaged mini-drama performed during the Sunday services), or for instruments alone (particularly solo organ). His Passion settings brought a German tradition to its peak, and his monumental Mass in B minor took the form to an unprecedented level.

Handel flourished in a more cosmopolitan environment, first in Italy and then in England, where he stepped neatly into the void left by the early death of Henry Purcell. Handel's many Italian operas, written for London theatres, have recently resumed their place in the repertoire, while his English oratorios have always been a well-loved feature of the British choral tradition.

Protestant North, where Heinrich Schütz pioneered it in Germany, paving the way for the great sacred works of J. S. Bach. It reached its apogee in the works of Handel, written in English, of which *Messiah* has been the most frequently performed.

Instrumental forms

The Baroque period also saw a huge demand for instrumental music, particularly concertos, *concerti grossi*, sonatas and suites, and almost all major composers worked in these new forms. Again, they flourished in Italy in the hands of Corelli, Vivaldi and Alessandro Scarlatti, but were equally popular in Germany. Bach's *Brandenburg Concertos* and Handel's sets of *concerti grossi* brought the genre to its peak, while the solo concerto and solo sonata underwent further metamorphosis in the Classical era. Meanwhile Alessandro Scarlatti's son Domenico, an exact contemporary of Bach and Handel, defied convention by removing to the Portuguese and Spanish courts, where he developed his own highly individual form of keyboard sonata.

ABOVE: The Rehearsal, *with viols, flute, oboe and voice, by Etienne Jeaurat (1699–1789).*

Claudio Monteverdi

Claudio Monteverdi, in moving the affections...
becomes the most pleasant tyrant of human minds.

AQUILINO COPPINI, 1608

Monteverdi was a composer of enormous significance in the history of music. Like his contemporary Heinrich Schütz in Germany, he bridged the worlds of the High Renaissance and the Baroque era. He can also be compared to Stravinsky: during the course of long lives both men showed an endless capacity to re-invent and adapt their musical styles according to changing tastes.

Early years

Monteverdi began his career as a chorister at the cathedral in his birthplace, Cremona. By the age of 16 — already a fine instrumentalist — he had published a volume of three-part motets and a book of sacred madrigals. In 1587 he published his first volume of secular madrigals, followed by a second volume in 1590. Around that time he found a job as a string player at the ducal court in Mantua, and by the

ABOVE: Claudio Monteverdi (1567–1643), painted around 1640 by Bernardo Strozzi.

time his third madrigal collection appeared in 1592 his fame as a composer was spreading rapidly. He married in 1599 and had three

children, of whom two sons survived: the elder became a musician, the younger a doctor.

Triumph and tragedy

In 1601 Monteverdi became *maestro di cappella* at the Mantuan court, where he published two more madrigal collections over the next four years. In 1607 he made his first foray into the new genre of opera with *L'Orfeo*, which was performed in Mantua in February. Seven months later his wife died after a long illness, leaving Monteverdi a grief-stricken widower with two small children.

He was obliged to pull himself together enough to finish his second opera, *L'Arianna*, which was performed in May 1608 to celebrate the marriage of the Gonzaga heir, Francesco, to Margaret of Savoy. (Only one aria from this opera has survived.) During rehearsals another tragedy struck when Caterina Martinelli, the young principal singer and a close friend of Monteverdi, died of smallpox. Monteverdi then suffered a complete collapse, although his glorious setting for voices and instruments of the *Vespro della beata vergine* (*Vespers of the Blessed Virgin*, 1610) dates from this unhappy period.

Venice

After making several attempts to leave the service of the Gonzagas, Monteverdi was finally dismissed in

ABOVE: The interior of the Teatro Olimpico in Vicenza, designed by Andrea Palladio (1508–80).

ABOVE: A scene from a 1975 production of Monteverdi's L'incoronazione di Poppea *(1642), shortly after its re-introduction to modern audiences.*

1612, and in 1613 became *maestro di cappella* at St Mark's Cathedral in Venice, where he remained for the rest of his life. He also continued to write ballets and operas for the Mantuan court, but many of his scores were destroyed when Austrian troops sacked the palace in 1630. In the same year Venice was ravaged by plague, and shortly afterwards Monteverdi renounced the world and took holy orders.

In 1637, after the first public opera house opened in Venice, he was commissioned to write several operas. The two that survive – *Il ritorno d'Ulisse in patria* (The Return of Ulysses)

ABOVE: The sinfonia da guerra *(Battle Sinfonia) from the score of Monteverdi's* Il ritorno d'Ulisse in patria *(1640).*

and *L'incoronazione di Poppea* (The Coronation of Poppea) – are masterpieces of the genre in their superb characterization and instinctive feel for dramatic effect. The final scene of *L'incoronazione di Poppea*, despite celebrating the union of two ambitious and deeply unpleasant people, contains one of the most intensely passionate love duets in all opera.

The works of Monteverdi's Venetian years include three more madrigal collections. Book 8 of 1638, entitled *Madrigali guerrieri et amorosi* (Songs of War and Love), contains substantial dramatic works such as *Il ballo delle ingrate*, and the famous *Combattimento di Tancredi e Clorinda*, a graphic description of a duel between the Christian knight Tancred and the pagan Clorinda, who is disguised as a man. As a whole, the madrigal collections show Monteverdi moving with the times, from typically Renaissance polyphonic pieces in the earlier volumes (one of the most beautiful and frequently performed of these is the five-voice *Zefiro torna*, a setting of words by Petrarch), to highly expressive dramatic works for

solo voices with instrumental accompaniment in the later ones. All his music, early or late, is characterized by qualities of emotional intensity, depth of expression and understanding of human nature comparable with those that inform the works of Shakespeare.

ABOVE: The title page of a collection of poetical tributes in commemoration of Monteverdi's death, published in 1644.

Heinrich Schütz

The most spiritual musician the world has ever seen.

ALFRED EINSTEIN (1880–1952)

The achievements of J. S. Bach would not have been possible without the ground-breaking work of his illustrious predecessor, Heinrich Schütz. Born into a middle-class family of innkeepers in Saxony, Schütz became the most esteemed German composer of the 17th century. During two prolonged visits to Italy – the first, made while he was still a law student, enabling him to study in Venice with Giovanni Gabrieli – Schütz absorbed the Italian style, which he then amalgamated with the very different musical tradition of his native Germany.

Dresden *Kapellmeister*

On his return from Italy in 1613 after Gabrieli's death, Schütz became organist and then *Kapellmeister* at the electoral

ABOVE: A portrait of Heinrich Schütz (1585–1672), by his contemporary Christoph Spetner.

court in Dresden, the most important musical centre in Protestant Germany. He published his first important compositions in 1619. These were a collection of settings for voices (some with instrumental interludes in the Venetian style) of the Psalms of David, described as "various motets and concertos". In the same year he married Magdalena Wildeck, daughter of a court official. Their happy union, which produced two daughters, was tragically brief: Magdalena died in 1625, and the grief-stricken composer never remarried. He outlived both his children: the elder died at the age of 16, and the younger in 1655, aged 31.

Schütz's court duties included writing music for official events, such as weddings and funerals. For the wedding of the elector's daughter to the Landgrave of Hessen-Darmstadt in 1627, he wrote the first German opera, setting the same libretto (*Dafne*) which the Italian composer Jacopo Peri had set 30 years earlier. Unfortunately the music has not survived.

In 1628 Schütz paid a second visit to Italy, where he met Monteverdi. This contact with recent musical developments bore fruit in a second published collection of vocal and instrumental music, *Symphoniae sacrae*. But there were troubles at home: Germany had entered the Thirty Years

ABOVE: Schütz's birthplace in Bad Köstritz, Germany. The building is now a museum devoted to the composer.

292 *The Baroque Era*

War, and the Elector of Dresden found himself unable to pay his employees. Schütz escaped for two years to the court of the Crown Prince of Denmark, for whose wedding festivities he provided elaborate musical entertainments. But despite constant financial problems, he remained in the service of the Dresden court (apart from two more visits to Denmark) until 1657, when he was pensioned off. After his retirement he continued to write works for the electoral chapel until his death at the age of 87.

Schütz's music

Although Schütz was an enormously prolific composer, many of his manuscripts were destroyed by fire or the ravages of war. Even so, some 500 works survive. *Die Geburt unsers Herren Jesu Christi* (*The History of the Birth of Jesus Christ*), performed at Christmas Vespers at the Dresden court in 1660,

ABOVE: Gondolas moored near the Rialto Bridge in Venice, where Schütz studied with Giovanni Gabrieli.

is the earliest known German setting of the Nativity story in which the words of the Evangelist – or Narrator – are sung in recitative, rather than chanted as in earlier settings. His settings of the four Passions, together with innumerable psalm and motet settings and Italianate madrigals, influenced later composers such as Bach. Although Schütz's music fell out of fashion fairly rapidly, it was rediscovered in the 20th century, and championed by performers such as Roger Norrington in Britain, who founded first the amateur Heinrich Schütz Choir in 1962, and then the professional Schütz Choir of London.

Life and works

NATIONALITY: German

BORN: Köstritz, 1585; **DIED:** Dresden, 1672

SPECIALIST GENRES: Sacred vocal and instrumental music, including oratorios and Passions.

MAJOR WORKS: *Psalmen Davids* (1619); *Cantiones sacrae* (1625); opera *Dafne* (1627); *Symphoniae sacrae* (1629, 1647, 1650); *Sieben Worte Jesu Christi am Kreuz* (*Seven Words of Christ on the Cross*, 1645); *Christmas Oratorio* (1660); Passions according to Matthew, Mark, Luke and John (1664–6).

ABOVE: The title page of Schütz's Psalmen Davids, *settings of the Psalms for voices and instruments published in 1619.*

Jean-Baptiste Lully

The musician is to follow the poet's direction, only in my opinion, Lully is to be exempted,
who knows the passions and enters further into the heart of man than the authors themselves.

SEIGNEUR DE SAINT-EVREMOND (1610–1703)

The founder of French opera owed his success partly to his exceptional talent, and partly to his ruthless, ambitious nature – only Wagner has rivalled Lully in sheer single-mindedness of purpose and grandiose vision. His career mirrored that of his patron, the "Sun King" Louis XIV (1643–1715), perhaps the greatest European monarch of his age, who saw his own glory reflected in the sumptuous entertainments devised by his clever court composer.

King and composer enjoyed a close, symbiotic relationship: indeed Lully's death, in 1687 at the age of only 55, marked the zenith of the Sun King's reign. Thereafter it was a long, slow story of royal decline, marked by personal misfortunes and military defeats.

ABOVE: Louis XIV's court composer,
Jean-Baptiste Lully (1632–87).

The ambitious page

The son of a humble Florentine miller, Lully's singing voice was spotted at the age of 13 and he was taken to Paris and employed as a pageboy to a distant member of the royal family. Having perfected his own talents for dancing and playing the violin, he applied himself to social climbing, and quickly got his first royal appointment. His job was to write music for the lavish court ballets, and to drill the orchestra which accompanied them, the *Vingt-quatre violons du roi*. He soon established himself as a strict disciplinarian with a quick temper – later in life, as director of the opera house in Paris, he allegedly punched his pregnant leading lady in the stomach, causing her to miscarry, rather than jeopardize his productions.

ABOVE: The courtyard of Louis XIV's palace at Versailles, the envy of many other European
monarchs. Many of Lully's court ballets and comedy-ballets were performed here.

ABOVE: A 17th-century engraving of Lully
in his role as director of the royal orchestra.

ABOVE: *An original stage design by Jean Berain for Lully's* tragédie-lyrique, Armide, *first performed at the Académie Royale de Musique in Paris in 1686.*

Lully's ruthless nature suited his purposes well. He made an expedient marriage in order to disguise his homosexuality – a predilection which the king (a great lover of women) abhorred – and consolidated his position at court by choosing as his bride the daughter of the court composer, Michael Lambert. Meanwhile he cultivated the playwright Molière (1622–73), with whom he collaborated on several *comédies-ballets* (a hybrid form – half play, half ballet) for the entertainment of the court. The most famous of these was *Le bourgeois gentilhomme* (1670).

Opera at Versailles and Paris

Lully's next move, in 1672, was to take advantage of the bankruptcy of a fellow musician who had obtained a royal licence to import Italian opera. Lully seized the licence for himself, and while continuing to supply music for lavish court entertainments at the magnificent new palace of Versailles, he established a virtual monopoly over operatic productions, opening his own opera house in a disused tennis court

ABOVE: *A costume design for a character in* Armide, *regarded as Lully's masterpiece.*

in Paris. The following year he turned his old friend Molière's troupe of actors out of their centrally sited theatre in the Palais Royal, and took it over, with the king's permission, rent-free.

Over the next 14 years, Lully and the poet Philippe Quinault (1635–88) produced a succession of brilliant operas in an entirely new and original style. These "lyric tragedies" were based on subjects drawn from mythology and legend (such as *Isis, Thésée, Phaëton* and *Armide*), worked into plots which subtly flattered Louis XIV – his victories, his devotion to duty and his personal concept of glory. Audiences of the time loved them – as did the king. Lully had struck gold, and made a huge fortune.

A bizarre end

Lully's court position required him to compose sacred music for the royal chapel, and while conducting a Te Deum written to celebrate Louis XIV's recovery from illness, he accidentally struck his foot with the heavy stick he used to mark the beat by banging it on the floor. Gangrene set in, but Lully refused to have the toe amputated.

As he lay dying, he was visited by a priest. In a final dramatic gesture to mark his penitence, Lully threw his last opera manuscript on to the fire, and received absolution. After the priest had gone, a horrified friend asked Lully why he had wantonly destroyed his last great work. "Don't worry," whispered the dying man, "I've got another copy!"

Arcangelo Corelli

I never met with any man that suffered his passions to hurry him away so much whilst he was playing on the violin as the famous Arcangelo Corelli, whose eyes will sometimes turn as red as fire.

FRANÇOIS RAGUENET (C.1660–1722)

While 17th-century German composers were bringing the art of organ-playing to a peak of perfection, Italy remained pre-eminent for nurturing the art of the violin. With the products of an unsurpassed school of instrument-makers – the Amati and Guarneri families, Stradivari, Gasparò da Salo and Maggini – at their disposal, Italian performers could hardly fail to establish a European reputation as masters of their art. One of the most influential of these – both in terms of violin technique and musical style – was Arcangelo Corelli.

Success as a performer
Corelli came from Fusignano, a town between Bologna and Ravenna. He took music lessons from a priest in nearby Faenza, and in 1666 arrived in Bologna, where he studied the violin

ABOVE: Arcangelo Corelli, probably painted by the Flemish artist Jan Frans van Douven around 1700.

with several fine players. By 1675 he had made his professional debut in Rome where, over the next few years, he established himself as a brilliant performer, taking part in the elaborate church performances commissioned by Rome's decadent but artistically inclined prelates, and in secular performances at the theatres. In 1679 he became chamber musician to the exiled Queen Christina of Sweden, to whom he dedicated his first compositions, a set of 12 *sonate da chiesa*.

Before long, the ambitious violinist had decided to replace his patron with a more influential one: Cardinal Pamphili, one of the richest men in Rome. From 1684 onwards Corelli began to play regularly at musical events organized by Pamphili, while introducing his own works — including a set of chamber trios

LEFT: A highly romanticized impression (1913) of the violin maker Antonio Stradivari in his workshop at Cremona, by Edgar Bundy (1862–1922).

RIGHT:
The Hellier
Stradivarius,
made in 1679.

him two Roman players since he distrusted the abilities of the Neapolitans. To his surprise, he found that the despised southerners could actually play quite well, while he himself had embarrassing difficulty with a particular passage that his hosts managed fluently.

In 1707 Corelli met Handel (who was working in Rome), and played in a performance of an early Handel oratorio. Shortly afterwards he retired from playing to devote himself to composition. His health deteriorated, and he died early in 1713. He was buried in the Pantheon. His reputation both as performer and composer long outlived him: his compositions were reprinted many times and sold all over Europe. They were particularly popular in England and Germany, where they influenced many later composers, including Handel, Telemann and Bach.

dedicated to Pamphili – at the musical academies held on Sunday afternoons at the cardinal's sumptuous palazzo. His social climbing bore fruit, and in July 1687 he was formally engaged as the cardinal's music master, and given a suite of rooms in the palace.

Orchestral compositions

In 1690 Pamphili moved to Bologna, but Corelli declined to follow him. Instead, he was engaged by a rival cardinal, the young Pietro Ottoboni, nephew of Pope Alexander VIII, another ostentatious patron of the arts. Corelli and Ottoboni became good friends, and Corelli dedicated a second set of chamber trios to him in 1694. He also began to write orchestral works (sinfonias and concertos), which attracted much attention. He was described as "the famous violinist...the Orpheus of our time," whose works were "prized and esteemed".

In 1702, however, his self-esteem was shaken when he visited Naples to play in the opera orchestra, taking with

ABOVE: *Queen Christina holding court. She is talking with the French philosopher René Descartes (painting by Dumesnil the Younger, 1698–1781).*

Henry Purcell

*Mr Purcell, in whose person we have at length found
an Englishman equal with the best abroad.*

JOHN DRYDEN (1631–1700)

Unlike some European countries, which enjoyed a strong and continuing musical tradition from the Renaissance onwards, England – while strong on literature – has suffered from a distinctly patchy musical heritage. After the Elizabethan flowering, only a few distinctive figures emerged in the early 17th century – notably the Lawes brothers, Henry (1596–1662) and William (1602–45), and later John Blow (1649–1708); but England produced no composer of European stature until the brilliant but tragically short-lived Henry Purcell.

Occasional music

Purcell began his career as a chorister in the Chapel Royal; in 1679 he succeeded Blow as organist of Westminster Abbey. He seems to have married around 1680, and had several children, of whom a son and a daughter survived him. In 1682 he was appointed an organist of the Chapel Royal, and a year later became organ-maker and keeper of the king's instruments.

His court appointments were renewed after Charles II's death, and he continued to produce many odes and welcome songs (cantata-like compositions) for occasions such as royal birthdays, marriages and New Year's Day. Most of these "occasional" works are now among the least known of his output, but the 1692 Ode for St Cecilia's Day, *Hail, Bright Cecilia*, is one of his best-loved works.

*ABOVE:
A 19th-century lithograph of Henry Purcell by Alfred Lemoine (1824–81).*

LEFT: William III (1650–1702) and his wife Mary II (1662–94), who reigned jointly as King and Queen of England from 1689.

Life and works

NATIONALITY: English

BORN: London, 1659;
DIED: London, 1695

SPECIALIST GENRES: Opera and incidental music for the stage, odes, anthems, instrumental music.

MAJOR WORKS: *Dido and Aeneas* (1689); *King Arthur* (1691); *The Fairy Queen* (1692); *Hail, Bright Cecilia* (1692); *Come, Ye Sons of Art* (1694); Te Deum and Jubilate in D (1694); Funeral music for Queen Mary (1695).

LEFT: *The opening of Purcell's* Golden Sonata *for two violins and* basso continuo.

RIGHT: *The frontispiece to the text of Purcell's 1683 Ode to St Cecilia,* Welcome to all the pleasures.

A
Muſical Entertainment
PERFORM'D
On NOVEMBER XXII. 1683.
IT BEING THE
Feſtival of St. CECILIA, a great Patroneſs of Muſic;
WHOSE
MEMORY is ANNUALLY honour'd by a public Feaſt made on that Day by the MASTERS and LOVERS of Muſic, as well in England as in Foreign Parts.

LONDON,
Printed by J. Playford Junior, and are to be ſold by John Playford near the Temple Church, and John Carr at the Middle-Temple Gate, 1684.

Stage works

During the last decade of his life, Purcell combined his court duties with writing music for the stage. Opera as such did not exist in England at the time, but between 1690 and 1695 Purcell provided incidental music for five major "semi-operas" put on at London theatres: Betterton's *Dioclesian, King Arthur* and *The Indian Queen* (with texts by John Dryden), *The Fairy Queen* and *The Tempest* (both loosely based on Shakespeare).

Purcell's most famous stage work, however, is the opera *Dido and Aeneas*, long thought to have been written around 1689 for a girls' school in Chelsea, but possibly dating from several years earlier. He also provided individual musical items for over 40 other plays by the most notable playwrights of the time. The Rondeau from his music for Aphra Behn's 1695 play *Abdelazer* was used by Benjamin Britten as the theme of his *Young Person's Guide to the Orchestra* (1946).

Purcell's legacy

Apart from his dramatic music, Purcell wrote many exquisite anthems, a Magnificat and a Te Deum, a vast number of solo songs and partsongs (some with extremely bawdy texts which have only recently been

permitted to surface), instrumental music including fantasias for viol consort, a set of 12 trio sonatas for two violins and continuo, a set of 10 sonatas "in four parts", clearly influenced by Corelli, and some charming keyboard music, including eight suites. Among his last works was the moving Funeral Music for Queen Mary, written for the young and much-mourned queen: within a short

ABOVE: *The choir of Westminster Abbey, where Purcell was buried at the foot of the organ.*

while Purcell had followed her to the grave at the age of only 36. The music he had written for the queen was played at his own funeral.

Purcell's genius lay in his unique response to the setting of English words, whether sacred or secular, his gift for appealing melody, his assimilation of elements from both Italian and French music – notably Corelli's violin writing, and Lully's unusual effects (the "Frost Scene" from *King Arthur*, in which each note is sung with a shiver, was borrowed from a similar scene in Lully's opera *Isis*) – and his forward-looking treatment of the orchestra, particularly the strings.

Though regarded as a "one-off" genius, the end of a tradition rather than an initiator, Purcell is still held in high esteem. *Dido and Aeneas* is often performed, and in the last decade of the 20th century, particularly during the tercentenary celebration of his death, most of his music was made widely available through high-quality performances and recordings.

Antonio Vivaldi

He is an old man, who has a prodigious fury for composition. I heard him undertake to compose a concerto, with all the parts, with greater despatch than a copyist can copy it.

CHARLES DE BROSSES, 1739

For many people, the name Vivaldi is associated with just one piece of music – *Le quattro stagioni* (*The Four Seasons*) – which has been recorded countless times. But many other gems of Vivaldi's output are worth exploring: he was one of the most prolific and influential composers of his time, and without his contribution to the development of concerto form, the instrumental music of later composers such as Bach would have been the poorer.

The Red Priest

Vivaldi was born (during a minor earthquake) in Venice, to a baker turned professional violinist,

ABOVE: *The violinist and composer Antonio Vivaldi (1678–1741), painted in 1723 by François Morellon La Cave.*

with whom the young Antonio studied. In 1693 he began to train for the priesthood, while still living at home and continuing his violin studies. He was ordained in 1703, and his startling red hair earned him the nickname of *il prete rosso* (the Red Priest), but the ecclesiastical life did not entirely suit him, and several times he found himself at odds with the church authorities.

In the year of his ordination, Vivaldi was appointed violin teacher at the Conservatorio dell'Ospedale della Pietà, a Venetian orphanage which housed and educated young girls. Music was held in high esteem there,

and its reputation was such that many leading performers took part in its concerts. Vivaldi was required to teach and rehearse the students and to maintain the instruments. His initial appointment lasted six years, during which time he published a set of 12 trio *sonate da camera* and a set of solo violin sonatas. He had already begun to write concertos, which became his favourite medium.

Vivaldi's concertos

In all Vivaldi wrote well over 200 violin concertos, around 27 cello concertos, around a dozen for flute, three for

ABOVE: *Vivaldi's family home on the Fondamenta del Dose in Venice.*

ABOVE: *A page from the cello part of Vivaldi's collection of concertos* L'estro armonico.

piccolo, 20 for oboe, 37 for bassoon (an instrument for which few other composers have written concertos), and many more double and multiple concertos, of which the E minor concerto for four violins, Op. 3 No. 4, is very well known.

The fanciful titles of some of his concertos gave Vivaldi plenty of opportunity for descriptive writing. As well as the famous *Four Seasons*, programmatically depicting seasonal activities such as skating on the ice (winter), hunting (autumn), and listening to birdsong (spring), their titles include *La tempestà di mare* (*Storm at Sea*), *L'amoroso* (*The Lover*), *La caccia* (*The Hunt*) and *Il corneto di posta* (*The Posthorn*).

A set of 12 concertos for one, two or four solo violins was published in Amsterdam in 1711 under the title *L'estro armonico*, and instantly sold all over Europe (Bach made keyboard transcriptions of five of them). Another set of 12 (*La stravaganza*) appeared in 1714, and from then on Vivaldi's music was much in demand (the collection

ABOVE: *The title page of Vivaldi's* L'estro armonico, *published 1711 with a dedication to the Grand Duke of Tuscany.*

containing *The Four Seasons* was published in 1725). He also wrote around 60 *concerti grossi* for strings and bass.

In 1711 Vivaldi returned to the Pietà, where he took the opportunity to write sacred as well as instrumental music. His cheerful *Gloria* is still much

performed today. He was associated with the institution until his death, although his frequent absences were not popular. He also began to write operas (about 45 in all) for various Italian courts and opera houses, including Mantua, Venice and Rome. Several have recently been revived, although interest still tends to be academic.

Fall from grace

Vivaldi spent much of the last two decades of his life on the move. Around 1725 he became involved with his singing pupil, Anna Giraud. The church authorities cannot have been pleased with the whiff of scandal surrounding the "Red Priest" and in 1737 he was censured for unpriestly conduct. In 1741 Vivaldi undertook a mysterious journey to Vienna (perhaps connected with Anna's work as an opera singer). He arrived on 28 June, and a month later he was dead, apparently of unknown causes. His arrogance and egotism had made many enemies, but his posthumous influence was immense.

Life and works

NATIONALITY: Italian

BORN: Venice, 1678; **DIED:** Vienna, 1741

SPECIALIST GENRES: Instrumental music, especially violin concertos.

MAJOR WORKS: Over 400 concertos published in sets, including *L'estro armonico* (1711); *Il cimento dell'armonia e dell'inventione* (1725 – 12 concertos of which the first four are *Le quattro stagioni*).

ABOVE: *The Piazza San Marco in Venice, painted in 1723 during Vivaldi's lifetime by the Italian artist Canaletto.*

Johann Pachelbel

A perfect and rare virtuoso.

DANIEL EBERLIN (1647–C.1715)

Johann Pachelbel, an important predecessor of J. S. Bach, is remembered today chiefly for a single composition, known as "Pachelbel's Canon" (of which many versions – including rock – now exist). But in his day he was much admired for his contribution to German Protestant church music, particularly for the organ.

Born in Nuremberg, he began his career as organist at St Stephen's Cathedral in Vienna. In 1677 he became organist at Bach's birthplace, the Thuringian town of Eisenach, but a year later he moved a few miles east to Erfurt,

ABOVE: The title page of Pachelbel's Hexachordum Apollinis, *printed in Nuremberg in 1699, six "arias" for organ or harpsichord, with variations.*

where for the next 12 years he was organist at the Predigerkirche. There he came into contact with members of the Bach family (he was godfather to one of J. S. Bach's sisters, and taught his elder brother Johann Christoph, who in turn taught Johann Sebastian).

While at Erfurt, Pachelbel married, only to lose his wife and their baby son two years later in a plague epidemic. He remarried in 1684, and raised a family of seven children. He then spent two years as court organist at Stuttgart, and three as town organist at Gotha, before finally moving back to his own birthplace as organist of St Sebald's Church.

Pachelbel's music

The organ chorales composed by Pachelbel – complex polyphonic pieces based on Protestant hymn tunes – had

enormous influence on those of Bach. He was also a master of various other keyboard genres of the time, including toccatas, *ricercari*, fantasias, chaconnes and variations – his *Hexachordum Apollinis* (1699) is a group of six arias with variations for organ or harpsichord, each in one of five keys making up a perfect fifth.

Pachelbel also wrote six suites for two violins and keyboard, the masterly and justly famous Canon (a set of 28 canonic variations originally scored for three violins and bass), motets, sacred concertos and 11 fine settings of the Magnificat for chorus and instruments, intended for the Vesper services in Nuremberg.

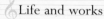

Life and works

NATIONALITY: German

BORN: Nuremberg, 1653;
DIED: Nuremberg, 1706

SPECIALIST GENRES: Organ music.

MAJOR WORKS: Canon and Gigue in D major; six suites for two violins; organ chorales.

ABOVE: A 1732 engraving of a concert with organ, strings, wind and brass instruments. Pachelbel specialized in organ church music.

Dietrich Buxtehude

*I should place an organist who is master of his instrument
at the very head of all virtuosi.*

LUDWIG VAN BEETHOVEN (1770–1827)

The Danish organist and composer Dietrich Buxtehude was an almost exact contemporary of Pachelbel, and like him, proved a formative influence on J. S. Bach. Probably of German origin, he was born some time around 1637 in the duchy of Holstein, where his father was a schoolmaster and organist. In 1668 Buxtehude himself became organist at St Mary's Church in Lübeck, in north Germany. This appointment was one of the most important and lucrative in Germany, and competition was fierce (even though one of the stranger conditions attached to it was that the successful

ABOVE: A painting by Johannes Voorhout depicting the friendship between Dietrich Buxtehude and his colleague J. A. Reincken (at the harpsichord).

candidate should marry a daughter of his predecessor). This Buxtehude did – although Handel apparently declined an offer of the post nearly 40 years later when confronted with the necessity of marrying Buxtehude's own ageing daughter.

Buxtehude remained at Lübeck for the rest of his life. His duties at St Mary's required him to play and compose music for the main services, but he also reinstated an old tradition of giving substantial concerts in the church on the five Sundays before Christmas, just after the afternoon service. These *Abendmusiken*, as they were called, became famous, as was Buxtehude's extraordinarily accomplished organ-playing. In the winter of 1705–6, the young J. S. Bach is reputed to have walked from Thuringia to Lübeck just to hear the great man play.

ABOVE: St Mary's Church in Lübeck, where Buxtehude was organist for nearly 40 years, and where Bach heard him play.

Buxtehude's music

Buxtehude left a substantial body of compositions, including cantatas, several oratorio-like works intended for the *Abendmusiken*, many organ works including chorale preludes, fantasias, fugues and variations based on chorale themes, as well as some lighter chamber and keyboard music. His organ works, which had enormous influence on Bach, exploit the characteristic range of tone-colour of north German organs of the period, and liberate the pedal from its traditional role as harmonic foundation – some of Buxtehude's pedal parts require virtuoso footwork in their own right.

Life and works

NATIONALITY: Danish

BORN: Oldesloe, c.1637;
DIED: Lübeck, 1707

SPECIALIST GENRES: Organ music, cantatas for the German Protestant liturgy.

MAJOR WORKS: 120 sacred cantatas and other vocal pieces; many organ works; chamber and keyboard music.

Johann Sebastian Bach

Johann Sebastian Bach has done everything completely,
he was a man through and through.

FRANZ SCHUBERT (1797–1828)

For many music-lovers, the music of J. S. Bach fulfils a profound spiritual need: it has a timeless, other-worldly quality which could only come from a composer who felt himself close to God. Just as Bach's birthplace was over-shadowed by the Wartburg mountain, topped by the fortress in which Martin Luther hammered out the fundamental principles of Protestant theology, so his life was dominated by his devotion to the Lutheran faith, and his music was dedicated to its service.

Early years

Unlike many of his more cosmopolitan contemporaries, Bach spent his entire career in Germany – mostly in the central regions of Thuringia and Saxony. He was born

into a long dynasty of Thuringian organists and composers who worked as church organists and choir-masters, municipal musicians, and at the many small princely or ducal courts which flourished in the region. Bach's father, Ambrosius, was himself employed as a musician by the town council of Eisenach, where Johann Sebastian was born on 21 March 1685.

After losing both parents by the age of ten, Bach was sent to live at Ohrdruf with his married elder brother, Johann Christoph, who was organist there. It seems likely that Johann Christoph helped with his young brother's musical training, but once Johann Sebastian reached the age of 15, there was no longer room for him in the Ohrdruf household, and he obtained a free place at St Michael's

ABOVE: Johann Sebastian Bach, four years before his death, in a painting by E. G. Haussmann.

RIGHT: A room in Bach's probable birthplace, containing contemporary instruments.

ABOVE: The house where Bach is believed to have been born in the Rittergasse in Eisenach, Thuringia, now a Bach museum.

LEFT: A view of Eisenach, with the Wartburg Castle on the hill behind.

RIGHT: Thomaskirche in Leipzig, where Bach was an organist and choir-master, and where he was subsequently interred.

School in Lüneburg, 320km (200 miles) away in north Germany. There he benefited from a solid musical education and sang in the choir, but his formal education came to an end in 1702.

Arnstadt and Mühlhausen

At the age of 17, Bach returned to his native Thuringia to look for a job. After a temporary spell as a violinist at the Weimar ducal court, he was appointed organist at the New Church in Arnstadt, not far from Weimar. There he started to compose in earnest, and in the winter of 1705–6 he made his legendary pilgrimage (allegedly on foot) to Lübeck, 420km (260 miles) to the north, to hear the celebrated organist Dietrich Buxtehude.

After his return to Arnstadt, Bach's relationship with the church council deteriorated (he had a stubborn and at times arrogant streak, which caused problems with all his employers), and in the summer of 1707 he left to take up a new post as organist at the imperial free city of Mühlhausen, some 58km (36 miles) to the north-west. His salary was now such that he felt able to marry his second cousin, Maria Barbara Bach. But although his personal life had settled down, Bach quickly became dissatisfied with conditions at Mühlhausen, and in 1708 he moved again, this time to the ducal court at Weimar.

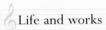 Life and works

NATIONALITY: German

BORN: Eisenach, 1685; **DIED:** Leipzig, 1750

SPECIALIST GENRES: Sacred music for the German Protestant liturgy, especially cantatas, instrumental and keyboard music.

MAJOR WORKS: *Brandenburg Concertos* (1721); 4 orchestral suites; 7 harpsichord concertos; 3 violin concertos; *Goldberg Variations* (1722); *The Well-Tempered Clavier* (1722–44); over 200 cantatas; *St John Passion* (1723); *St Matthew Passion* (1729); *Christmas Oratorio* (1734); *Italian Concerto* (1735); *The Musical Offering* (1747); Mass in B minor (1749); *The Art of Fugue* (1750).

ABOVE: Bach directing a concert in 1714 at the Court Chapel in Weimar, where he worked from 1708 until 1717.

Weimar

In the early 18th century Weimar was just another small, provincial town – its period of glory was to come some 80 years later, when its residents would include Goethe, Wieland and Schiller. Bach's job was as organist at the ducal chapel in the castle, but six of his children – including the future composers Wilhelm Friedemann (1710–84) and Carl Philipp Emmanuel (1714–88) – were christened at the City Church of St Peter and Paul during the Weimar years.

It was here that Bach began composing cantatas in earnest for performance at court, and he also provided instrumental music for the court orchestra. His early years at Weimar were happy and productive but, after 1713, relations with his employer, Duke Wilhelm Ernst, began to deteriorate and in 1717 Bach accepted

ABOVE: A romanticized artist's impression of Bach's visit to Frederick the Great at the palace of Sans Souci in Potsdam, May 1747.

with concertos for violin (including the famous Double Concerto in D minor), orchestral suites, sonatas for harpsichord, violin, and flute, the suites for solo cello and the sonatas and partitas for solo violin. These works show that Bach had thoroughly absorbed the Italian style, through intensive study of works by Corelli and Vivaldi.

Remarriage

In May 1720, while Bach was away at a spa with his employer, Maria Barbara died suddenly. Bach remarried the next year: his bride, Anna Magdalena Wilcken (1701–60), proved a great asset to her husband, both domestically and professionally (the daughter of a musician, she was a singer, harpsichordist and music copyist). She inherited Bach's four surviving

ABOVE: Bach's eldest son, Wilhelm Friedemann (1710–84), painted around 1760. Like his father, he was a composer.

the job of *Kapellmeister* to the court of Prince Leopold of Anhalt-Cöthen. The duke was so reluctant to let him go that he placed him under house arrest for a month. Eventually, in December 1717, the Bach family was allowed to leave.

Cöthen

While most of Bach's compositions up to 1717 had been organ works and sacred cantatas, he now exploited the instrumental resources available to him at the Cöthen court. Most of his work there was secular, since the Calvinist Prince Leopold required little sacred music. Among the works he composed during this period were the six *Brandenburg Concertos* for various instrumental combinations, together

ABOVE: The trumpeter Gottfried Reiche (1667–1734), who played the high clarino parts in Bach's works in Leipzig.

children, to whom she added another 13, including another future composer, Johann Christian (1735–82), later known as the "English Bach", since he spent much of his career there. Shortly after their marriage Bach began to compile two *Clavierbüchlein* (*Little Keyboard Books*) for his wife, which contain, among other works, the 15 Inventions and Sinfonias and several preludes and fugues, which were later assembled with others as *Das wohltemperierte Clavier* (*The Well-Tempered Clavier*).

In 1721 Prince Leopold of Anhalt-Cöthen married his cousin, and life changed irrevocably at the Cöthen court. The frivolous new princess was uninterested in music, and Bach soon felt obliged to move on – probably with some regret. In June 1722 the post of Kantor of the Thomasschule in Leipzig became vacant. The town council wanted Telemann, but he could not be released from his job at Hamburg, and so, after much deliberation, they appointed Bach. On 22 May 1723 he moved into his new quarters in the Thomasschule, where he stayed until his death 27 years later.

Leipzig

Bach's years at Leipzig, where he was required not only to teach, but to supply music for the town's two principal churches, St Thomas and St Nicholas, were relatively uneventful, but were punctuated by acrimonious disagreements with the council over pay and conditions. Nonetheless, they were amazingly fruitful. One of his principal jobs was to write, rehearse and direct cantatas for the Sunday services at the two churches, and his output included around 250 of these substantial works for voices, chorus

ABOVE: A page from the manuscript score of Bach's St Matthew Passion, *first performed in Leipzig on Good Friday in 1729.*

and orchestra, mostly based on well-known Protestant chorale tunes.

In addition, he produced two magnificent settings of the Passion story, according to St Matthew and St John, the Mass in B minor, the *Christmas Oratorio*, and other major sacred works, into which he poured all the resources of vocal and instrumental writing available to him. Towards the end of his life, several books of keyboard music were published, but Bach's fame remained local. Among his last major

works were the *Goldberg Variations* for harpsichord, allegedly written for an aristocratic insomniac; *Das musicalisches Opfer* (*The Musical Offering*, based on a fugue subject devised by Frederick the Great when Bach visited him at Potsdam in 1747), and the almost visionary *Kunst der Fuge* (*The Art of Fugue*), a complex series of canons on which Bach worked during the last years of his life, when his sight began to fail. He was almost totally blind when he died, leaving his widow in dire financial straits.

By the time of Bach's death, musical fashions were fast changing, and his music was perceived as antiquated. During his lifetime he had been more celebrated as an organist than as a composer. Unlike Mozart or Beethoven, he had little posthumous influence until Mendelssohn rediscovered his choral masterpieces in the 19th century, and his works began to be performed once more. He is now revered as one of the greatest of all composers.

ABOVE: A romanticized 19th-century impression of the Bach family at their morning prayers.

George Frideric Handel

Handel understands effect better than any of us —
when he chooses, he strikes like a thunderbolt.

WOLFGANG AMADEUS MOZART (1756–91)

Handel and Bach were born in the same year, in much the same area of central Germany — Halle, Handel's birthplace in Saxony, is about 160km (100 miles) north of Thuringia. Both men lived to a reasonable old age, and both had lost their sight when they died. But their respective careers could not have been more different.

Early years

While Bach was content to live and work within the musical tradition of his family, Handel had to struggle to make a career in music. His father wanted his son to study law, and tried to stifle the boy's interest in music. But Handel persisted, and was eventually allowed to study music as part of his general education. Only after his father's death did he take it up full-time and in 1703, aged 18, he set out for Hamburg in search of employment.

ABOVE: George Frideric Handel (1685–1759). He never appeared in public without his voluminous wig.

Hamburg

One of Hamburg's attractions was as a flourishing centre of opera. Germany's first commercial opera house had opened there in 1678, and had scraped along financially under a succession of entrepreneurial directors with flair but no money. Here Handel found an ideal proving-ground for his early attempts at the genre which would dominate his life. But he refused the offer of a permanent post, and instead departed for Italy — the birthplace of opera.

The Italian experience

Handel travelled to Italy under the patronage of Prince Ferdinando de'Medici, and in 1707 his first mature opera, *Rodrigo*, was produced at a Florentine theatre. It was a success, earning Handel the favours of the grand duke's mistress, the singer Vittoria Tarquini. Perhaps wisely, Handel quickly departed for Rome, where he found employment at the court of Cardinal Pietro Ottoboni, the immensely wealthy papal vice-chancellor. There he met celebrated musicians including Corelli and the Scarlattis, and tried his hand at music for the unfamiliar Catholic liturgy, including a setting of the Vespers. His first oratorio, a setting of the Resurrection story, was performed with great splendour on Easter Sunday 1708 at the Palazzo Bonelli.

From Rome Handel travelled on to Naples and then to Venice, where his opera *Agrippina* was performed during

ABOVE: An anonymous painting of Hamburg, one of the most important of the Hanseatic ports, in 1700.

ABOVE: *The square in front of St Peter's Basilica in Rome, painted in 1754 by G. P. Pannini.*

ABOVE: *A romantic impression depicting Handel making music at the keyboard with his friends.*

the 1710 carnival season. Then, ever eager for new experiences, he returned north to Hanover, to be appointed *Kapellmeister* to the elector at a good salary and with the promise of a year's sabbatical leave. He took it immediately, and promptly left with an invitation to London. His transformation from a German to an English composer had begun.

England

In Queen Anne's England, Handel stepped into a musical vacuum left by the deaths of John Blow and his gifted pupil Henry Purcell. He decided to fill it by satisfying the growing middle-class demand for opera. His opera *Rinaldo* scored a huge success at the Queen's Theatre in London, both musically and dramatically. Audiences were particularly intrigued by a dramatic masterstroke – the release of a flock of sparrows onstage to lend verisimilitude to the aria "Augelletti" ("Little Birds"). But Handel was under an obligation to return to Hanover, where he spent some 15 months

perfecting his instrumental compositions – overtures and *concerti grossi*.

In the autumn of 1712 Handel obtained another period of leave from the indulgent Elector of Hanover, and

returned to London, where his next opera, *Il pastor fido* (*The Faithful Shepherd*), was put on at the Haymarket Theatre. This time the public was disappointed. As one critic put it: "The habits [costumes] were old. The opera short." Handel immediately hit back with a full-length, five-act opera, based on the Greek myth of Theseus. At the same time he began to fulfil royal commissions, supplying royal odes and a triumphantly received Te Deum and Jubilate to celebrate the Treaty of Utrecht, which ended the War of the Spanish Succession.

Life under a new king

Handel had absented himself from his duties in Hanover for two years when in 1714 he received a rude shock: Queen Anne died childless, and the English throne passed to his neglected former employer the Elector of Hanover, now George I of England. It is said that the famous *Water Music*, written to accompany the king's triumphal procession up the Thames, was composed as a peace-offering (although it was probably written three

ABOVE: Handel playing one of his organ concertos at the Covent Garden Theatre in London.

Radamisto, Rodelinda, Admeto, Giulio Cesare and *Tamerlano*, and engaged some of the finest European singers to perform them. These included the great castrato Senesino, a man possessed of a "powerful, clear, equal and sweet contralto voice", and the sopranos Francesca Cuzzoni and Faustina Bordoni, all engaged at astronomical salaries. Apart from the entertainment of the operas themselves, London society was soon treated to the diverting spectacle of the two rival divas fighting on stage while Senesino spent his time sulking in the background.

Change to oratorio

George I died in 1727. For his successor, George II's, coronation Handel provided four anthems (including *Zadok the Priest*, which has been sung at British coronations ever since). By this time the Academy was in deep financial trouble, and Handel's own financial losses — combined with waning public enthusiasm for this "exotic and irrational entertainment", the unexpected popularity of John Gay's satirical *Beggar's Opera* in 1728, and a complete breakdown in health — prompted a change of direction. He was already

years after George's accession). In any case, Handel was quickly forgiven, and remained a favoured royal composer for the rest of his life. He also acquired a new patron, the Duke of Chandos, for whose magnificent estate in Edgware Handel wrote the 11 *Chandos Anthems*, a Te Deum, the masque *Acis and Galatea*, and his first attempt at an English oratorio, *Esther*.

The Royal Academy

In 1719 the grandly named Royal Academy of Music came into being. This institution, supported by a group of 62 royal and noble subscribers, aimed to establish a regular opera company in London, with Handel as its composer-in-residence. Over the next eight years he supplied some 14 Italian operas for the company, including

LEFT: The aria "How beautiful are the feet" from Handel's autograph score of Messiah.

RIGHT: Handel's choir singing an oratorio by Willem de Fesch, as drawn by Hogarth in 1731.

writing instrumental music, especially organ concertos, for the London pleasure gardens, but although he continued to write Italian operas, including *Ariodante* and *Serse*, until 1740, he needed a new genre. He found it in the English oratorio, beginning with *Deborah*, *Athaliah*, *Saul* and *Israel in Egypt* in the 1730s, but reaching its apogee in *Messiah*, written for performance in Dublin in 1742.

In setting these Biblical stories, Handel adapted elements from Italian opera, particularly the recitative-aria format; but reduced the soloists' importance in order to give more prominence to the chorus and orchestra. This clever ploy ensured the survival of his oratorios as a mainstay of the repertoire of British choral societies. *Messiah* was followed by some 15 further oratorios, including *Samson* (1741–2), *Semele* (1743), which is more of an opera than an oratorio, *Judas Maccabaeus* (1746), *Alexander Balue* and *Joshua* (1747), *Solomon* (1748) and *Jephtha* (1751), all of which are still regularly performed.

ABOVE: *Handel's memorial in Westminster Abbey, London.*

Last years
Handel's fortunes were mixed in the last years of his life. He had amassed considerable wealth despite his losses, and used some of it to support philanthropic causes, such as the Foundling Hospital. In April 1749 he fulfilled his last royal commission:

music to accompany a grand firework display in London's Green Park to mark the Peace of Aix-la-Chapelle – an occasion marred when the firework pavilion burnt to the ground. But Handel's *Music for the Royal Fireworks* ranks with the *Water Music* among his most popular instrumental compositions.

Two years later his sight was failing. A painful operation to cure cataracts proved useless, and for the last seven years of his life he was totally blind. But the people of his adopted land had taken him to their hearts, and while Bach's death went largely unremarked, Handel was buried with full honours in Westminster Abbey. His epitaph summed up his extraordinary achievement:

The most Excellent Musician
any Age ever produced:
Whose Compositions were
a Sentimental Language
rather than mere Sounds;
And surpassed the Power of Words
In Expressing the various Passions
of the Human Heart.

ABOVE: *A contemporary artist's view of the structure erected in Green Park for the 1749 firework display celebrating the Peace of Aix-la-Chapelle.*

ABOVE: *The Handel Centenary Commemoration concert (1785) in Westminster Abbey.*

Domenico Scarlatti

Scarlatti frequently told M. L'Augier that he was sensible
he had broke through all the rules of composition...
CHARLES BURNEY (1726–1814), "GENERAL HISTORY OF MUSIC"

The son of the composer Alessandro Scarlatti, Domenico probably began his musical training with his father. At the age of 16 he was appointed organist in the Neapolitan royal chapel, where his father was *maestro di cappella,* but in the spring of 1705 Alessandro ordered his son to seek his fortune in the northern Italian cities of Florence and Venice, describing him in a letter of recommendation as "a young eagle whose wings are grown: he must not remain idle in the nest, and I must not hinder his flight". In fact, Alessandro continued to interfere with his son's career until Domenico obtained legal independence in 1717, at the advanced age of 32.

In 1709 Domenico entered the service of the exiled Polish Queen Maria Casimira in Rome, where he encountered other up-and-coming musicians, including his contemporary,

Handel. After a spell as *maestro di cappella* at the Julian Chapel in the Vatican, he decided to leave Italy for Portugal, and from 1719 until 1728 he worked in Lisbon.

Keyboard sonatas

Scarlatti's duties in Lisbon included teaching the king's musical daughter Maria Barbara. When the princess married the Crown Prince of Spain and moved to Madrid in 1728, Scarlatti accompanied her. He remained in her service for the rest of his life, and it was for her that he wrote the 550 or so one-movement keyboard sonatas on which his fame rests.

These sonatas are unique in the keyboard repertoire. Apart from their unusual binary format, they explore new playing techniques, including hand-crossing and rapid note repetition. Each sonata, which Scarlatti himself described as "an ingenious jesting with art", focuses on a particular technical problem, and many incorporate special effects in imitation of Spanish idioms, such as the thrumming of guitars and the clicking of castanets.

ABOVE:
A contemporary
portrait in oil of
Domenico Scarlatti
by Antonio de Velasco.

LEFT: The Harpsichordist, *by Edith Hipkins (1885), now in the Royal Academy of Music in London.*

 ## Life and works

NATIONALITY: Italian

BORN: Naples, 1685;
DIED: Madrid, 1757

SPECIALIST GENRES:
Virtuoso harpsichord music.

MAJOR WORKS:
550 keyboard sonatas.

Jean-Philippe Rameau

The expression of thought, of sentiment, of the passions,
must be the true aim of music.

RAMEAU

The French composer Jean-Philippe Rameau is now chiefly remembered for his operas, but like Janáček, he was a late starter in the operatic field. Born two years before the great Bach-Handel-Scarlatti triumvirate, he spent the earlier part of his career working as an organist, moving between various major towns in central France and Paris, where he eventually settled in 1722. In that year he published a textbook on harmony, *Traité de l'harmonie*, which established him as one of the most innovative and controversial musical theorists of his age.

Over the next 25 years or so Rameau worked principally as a harpsichord teacher, and his volumes of enchanting "character" pieces for keyboard in the tradition of François Couperin became very popular. In 1730 he found a wealthy patron, the tax-collector Le Riche de

ABOVE: Jean-Philippe Rameau with his violin, a famous portrait by Joseph Aved (1702–66).

ABOVE: Sophie Arnould (1740–1802), one of the most celebrated French opera singers of Rameau's time.

la Pouplinière, who introduced him to the playwright Abbé Simon-Joseph Pellegrin. Rameau's first opera, *Hippolyte et Aricie,* to a libretto by Pellegrin, was produced at the Paris Opéra in October 1733. It established the composer as a worthy successor to Lully in the operatic field.

Rameau went on to write some 30 stage works – full-blown *tragédies-lyriques* in the Lullian mould such as *Castor et Pollux, Dardanus* and *Les boréades;* opera-ballets (operas with a substantial dance element, often written to celebrate royal victories or marriages), such as *La princesse de Navarre, Les fêtes de Polymnie* and *Zaïs;* and straightforward ballets such as *Pygmalion.* All are characterized by

sensitive handling of the text, whether comic, sentimental or tragic; colourful and innovative use of the orchestra (especially evident in the many brilliant and lively dances); and expressive and powerful choral writing.

War of the Buffoons

In the early 1750s Rameau (or rather his supporters) became embroiled in the celebrated *"Querelle des bouffons"* – a war of words between admirers of Rameau's traditional French style, and those of the newly imported Italian style of Pergolesi. In the long run, the Italians won, and Rameau's operas finally dropped out of fashion. They were resurrected some 200 years later by William Christie's *Les arts florissants* in France and the British conductors John Eliot Gardiner and Nicholas Kraemer.

Life and works

NATIONALITY: French

BORN: Dijon, 1683;
DIED: Paris, 1764

SPECIALIST GENRES: Opera and opera-ballets in the French style.

MAJOR WORKS: *Les Indes galantes* (*The Courtly Indies*, 1735); *Castor et Pollux* (1737); *Pièces de clavecin* (1741).

Other Composers of the Era

*The Italian style and the French style have for long divided
the Republic of Music in France.*

FRANÇOIS COUPERIN (C.1626–61)

The Baroque era produced a plethora of minor composers, many of whom are remembered today only for a handful of works.

Italy

Among these was the Italian priest and singer Gregorio Allegri (1582–1652), who worked at the Sistine Chapel in Rome. His chief claim to fame is the nine-part Miserere which he wrote for the exclusive use of the chapel, and which was jealously guarded until the young prodigy Mozart wrote it out from memory after hearing it twice on a visit in 1770.

Giacomo Carissimi (1605–74), who worked in Rome as choir-master to Queen Christina of Sweden, adapted Monteverdi's operatic style to the sacred oratorio, of which he wrote

ABOVE: *Gregorio Allegri (1582–1652), noted particularly for his nine-part* Miserere.

over a dozen, together with many motets and cantatas. He was the last composer to use the ancient folk tune "L'homme armé" as the musical basis for a Mass setting.

Carissimi's pupil Alessandro Scarlatti (1660–1725) also worked for Queen Christina, and spent his life moving between Rome and Naples in the service of court and church. More than half of his 115 operas survive, but only a handful, including *La Griselda* (1721), have been revived. Scarlatti invented the *da capo* aria, with its long introduction and closing orchestral *ritornello*. He is credited with introducing recitative accompanied by orchestra rather than keyboard, and invented the "Italian overture", a two-part slow-fast orchestral introduction

to a dramatic work, which later developed into the symphony. He also wrote a large volume of sacred music, and around 700 chamber cantatas.

The Venetian composer Tomaso Albinoni (1671–1751) is now more famous for one work which he did not compose – the Adagio for organ and strings constructed from musical fragments by Remo Giazotto in 1945 – than for his genuine 81 operas, 99 sonatas, 59 concertos and nine sinfonias. His solo concertos for oboe (the earliest known) and trumpet, and some of his *concerti grossi*, are now back in the repertoire.

Giovanni Battista Pergolesi (1710–36) died of tuberculosis at the age of only 26. Many of his works were lost, but he is remembered for a brilliant comic opera, *La serva padrona*

ABOVE: *Alessandro Scarlatti (1660–1725), father of Domenico, and a noted composer in his own right.*

ABOVE: *Giovanni Battista Pergolesi (1710–36), a highly talented composer who died young of tuberculosis.*

ABOVE: *An atmospheric contemporary portrait of the great Italian violinist and composer Giuseppe Tartini (1692–1770).*

(*The Maid as Mistress*, 1733), a Stabat Mater (1736), and for tunes he probably did not write (but which were ascribed to him after his death because of his popularity) which Stravinsky recycled in his ballet *Pulcinella* (1920).

Like Corelli, Giuseppe Tartini (1692–1770) is remembered for his daringly original violin music. A brilliant virtuoso, he wrote 42 violin

sonatas of immense technical difficulty (the most famous is the *Devil's Trill*, said to have been played to him in a dream by the Devil), 135 violin concertos, and many other instrumental pieces.

France

In France, the vacuum left by Lully's death in 1687 was filled by Marc-Antoine Charpentier (c.1645–1704), who began his career as music master and court singer to the Duchesse de Guise. From 1672 until 1686 he was also associated with Molière's troupe, writing music for the original production of *Le malade imaginaire*, among other works. He wrote a great deal of fine sacred music: 10 Magnificats, 37 antiphons, 84 psalms, over 200 motets and four Te Deums (one of which is now often performed) for Sainte-Chapelle on the Ile de Paris. Among his many fine stage works, *Les arts florissants* (1685–6) has lent its name to one of the foremost modern French ensembles playing music of the Baroque period.

Another French composer, François Couperin (c.1626–61), worked for the courts of Louis XIV and Louis XV. Born into a famous musical dynasty (his uncle Louis was a fine composer for organ and harpsichord), François became organist at the royal chapel. His harpsichord works (four published volumes contain around 230 pieces) are masterpieces of delicacy and musical description; many have enigmatic titles. He also wrote several instrumental suites in the fashionable style of Corelli.

Germany

The composer Johann Hasse (1699–1783) concentrated on opera, becoming director of the Dresden court opera. In 1763 he moved to Vienna, where he continued to write *opere serie* on texts by Metastasio, even though fashions were changing.

ABOVE: *François Couperin, known as "Le grand" ("the Great"), one of the finest composers of keyboard music of his time.*

Georg Philipp Telemann (1681–1767) spent most of his career as music director to the Hamburg churches. Probably the most prolific composer in the history of music (his output includes 600 overtures, 40 operas, 44 Passion settings and a huge quantity of instrumental music), he was in his day more highly regarded than Bach. His instrumental music is still popular today.

ABOVE: *Johann Hasse (1699–1783), upon hearing the 15-year-old Mozart, remarked "This boy will cause us all to be forgotten."*

ABOVE: *Georg Philipp Telemann (1681–1767) holds the record as the most prolific composer of all time.*

The Classical * Period *

A painting by J. F. Greipel (1720–98) of the 1765 performance of Gluck's
one-act "theatrical serenata" Il parnaso confuso (Parnassus in Confusion).

Music of the Enlightenment

Dust as we are, the immortal spirit grows
Like harmony in music.

WILLIAM WORDSWORTH (1770–1850), "THE PRELUDE"

By classical music, most people today mean serious music of any period, as opposed to jazz, pop, rock or other similar genres. But the term Classical is strictly applied to music written between about 1750–1830, corresponding to a period of classicism in art and architecture.

Classical style

During this period, the flamboyant, heavily ornate Baroque style of architecture (exemplified by the interior of the church of St Nicholas in Prague's Old Town, where Mozart played the organ on one of his visits) gave way to a cooler, more restrained style, based on the serene proportions of the ancient world. The 18th century was the age of the Grand Tour, when upper-class young men were despatched to Italy to study Greek and Roman

ABOVE: The building which inspired much 17th- and 18th-century neo-classical architecture – the Parthenon (Temple of Athena) on the Acropolis in Athens, built between 447 and 422 BC.

architecture, as revealed through recent archaeological excavations.

Contemporary architects such as Robert Adam designed grand country houses with Classical façades, while the furniture designed by Sheraton and his colleagues took on a graceful, delicate look. In England, the fashion for the

ABOVE: A fine example of 18th-century neo-classical architecture – designs for Home House in Portman Square, London, by Robert Adam (1728–92).

ABOVE: Vienna in the 18th century – a view of one of its main streets, the Kohlmarkt. St Michael's Church can be seen on the right.

Classical look reached its height around the turn of the 19th century (the age of Jane Austen), continuing into the Regency period (1811–20). In France, particularly, there was a short period of transition between the Baroque and Classical styles known as Rococo, characterized by delicate but elaborate ornamentation, as seen in French furniture of the mid 18th century, and the paintings of artists such as Antoine Watteau (1684–1721) and François Boucher (1703–70).

Classical style in music

Musical tastes inevitably followed the decorative arts, and the florid, ornamental, technically intricate styles of late Baroque composers gave way to a new emphasis on clarity, order and balance, exemplified by the Classical symphony, string quartet and solo sonata. A few composers fitted the Rococo label, including C. P. E. Bach, François Couperin, the English composer William Boyce (1710–79), and Gluck and Rameau — both primarily opera composers — in some of their works. But generally speaking, the Classical period in musical history is dominated by four giants, all associated with Vienna, and sometimes collectively known as the First Viennese School. They were Haydn, Mozart, Beethoven and Schubert. Their works are still part of the core repertoire of classical music as a whole.

Music's place in society

The late 18th century was a period of great social upheaval. The breakdown of the old social order reached its culmination in the French Revolution (1789–99), and music ceased to be the exclusive preserve of pampered aristocrats or prelates. This radical social shift is reflected in the careers of the four great Classical composers.

Haydn, the oldest, spent his long career in the service of a single

ABOVE: A charming example of 18th-century Rococo art — The Dance (c.1719) by Antoine Watteau (1684–1721), a favourite artist at the French court.

aristocratic family, who regarded him as a valued servant. Mozart began his career in a similar way, in the employment of the Archbishop of Salzburg, but when more lucrative court appointments eluded him, he took the radical step of trying a freelance existence, which allowed

ABOVE: Private music-making — The Lost Chord by Stephen Lewin (fl.1890–1910).

him personal liberty, but failed to provide sufficient financial security.

Beethoven, in a similar situation, enjoyed the friendship and patronage of several wealthy noblemen, but he was not so fettered by 18th-century convention as Mozart. He understood his own worth as an individual, and his patrons played to his tune, not the other way round. Beethoven was one of the first composers to free himself from the idea of musician as servant, and to produce powerfully individualistic music which he himself promoted to an audience of the rising middle class.

Schubert, a native of Vienna, never tried to obtain a permanent job. A composer who stood on the threshold of the Romantic age, he wrote music out of personal choice, aimed at people like himself (he had a close circle of musically inclined friends). Much of his music — particularly his songs and chamber music — was intended for a domestic market, and none of his symphonies was professionally performed during his lifetime.

Christoph Willibald Gluck

Hearing "Iphigénie" I forget that I am in an opera house
and think I am hearing a Greek tragedy.

Gluck's career overlapped with that of Rameau, his senior by over 30 years, and like Rameau, he worked during the transitional period between Baroque and Classical styles, often known as the Rococo age. Born into a German family of foresters who lived in Upper Bohemia, he escaped being coerced into the family profession by running away from home when he was about 13. He went to Prague, and then to Vienna, where he was attached to a nobleman's household. When the nobleman moved to Milan, Gluck went with him, and it was in Italy that he realized his true profession — that of opera composer.

By 1744 eight of his operas had been produced in Italy, many based on

ABOVE: Christoph Willibald Gluck, painted by Duplessis in 1775, when Gluck was alternating between Vienna and Paris.

libretti by the great Italian dramatist Pietro Metastasio. In 1745 Gluck went to London, where he found himself in competition with Handel (who is said to have remarked that "Gluck knows no more of counterpoint than my cook", though in fact he liked Gluck and arranged a concert with him). After leaving London, Gluck spent several peripatetic years travelling around Europe with an Italian opera company, before making an advantageous marriage and settling in Vienna. In 1754 the Empress Maria Theresa appointed him composer to the court theatre.

"Reform" operas

Over the next few years Gluck evolved the operatic style which would make him famous. It was clear that *opera seria*, and its French equivalent, the *tragédie-lyrique*, had run their course. Audiences were beginning to demand different types of entertainment, portraying real people in real-life situations rather than cardboard-cutout ancient heroes. To Gluck's mind, opera had been taken over by the often absurd demands of star singers, who felt able to dictate their wishes to librettists and composers, usually in defiance of dramatic reason. In collaboration with the poet Raniero de Calzabigi (1714–95), and with the active encouragement of the Intendant of

ABOVE: Gluck at the keyboard, by the French artist Eugène Delacroix.

ABOVE: The opening of Act II of Gluck's "azione teatrale", Orfeo ed Euridice.

320 *The Classical Period*

ABOVE: A design by V. D. Polenov (1844–1927) for Act I of Gluck's opera Orfeo ed
Euridice, *for a performance of the French version in Moscow, 1897.*

the court theatres, Count Giacomo Durazzo, Gluck set out to "reform" operatic convention.

He began by writing a series of comic operas in the French style, including *La fausse esclave* and *L'île de Merlin* (1758), but his first major collaboration with Calzabigi and the choreographer Gasparo Angiolini was the ballet *Don Juan* (1761), a work of great dramatic force which influenced Mozart's opera *Don Giovanni* (1787). It was followed in 1762 by the opera *Orfeo ed Euridice* – the most expressive setting of this tragic love story since Monteverdi. Orfeo's aria "Che farò senza Euridice" is one of the most affecting operatic laments, while the scenes in Hades and Elysium (especially the famous "Dance of the Blessed Spirits") gave Gluck ample opportunity for dramatic instrumental and vocal effects, backed up by innovative staging.

In 1767, Gluck and Calzabigi produced the second of their "reform" operas, *Alceste*. In a famous preface to the score, Gluck laid out the principles of this new type of opera, free of the abuses "which have so long disfigured Italian opera and made of the most splendid and beautiful of spectacles the most ridiculous and wearisome". Gluck aimed to "restrict music to its true

ABOVE: The title page of the first edition of the score of Orfeo ed Euridice, *published in Paris in 1764.*

office of serving the poetry by means of expression and by following the situations of the story", seeking "a beautiful simplicity", free of unnecessary vocal display at the whims of individual singers. He also tried to make the overture an integral part of the drama. These principles governed his next Viennese opera, *Paride ed Elena* (*Paris and Helen*, 1770).

In 1774 Gluck moved to Paris, where over the next six years he wrote three new operas (two based on the story of Iphigenia, and *Echo et Narcisse*), as well as revisions (in French) of *Orfeo* and *Alceste*. He also found himself drawn into competition with the Italian composer Niccolò Piccinni (1728–1800). After *Echo et Narcisse* failed to please, Gluck returned to Vienna, where he died of the last of a series of strokes incurred, it was said, after drinking an after-dinner liqueur in defiance of his doctor's instructions.

Joseph Haydn

So far as genius can exist in a man who is merely virtuous,
Haydn had it.

FRIEDRICH NIETZSCHE (1844—1900)

Joseph Haydn was the eldest and longest lived of the four great composers of the so-called "First Viennese School". Born when Bach and Handel were at the height of their fame, he outlived his friend Mozart by 18 years, and saw his former pupil Beethoven well established in his own career. It was Haydn who practically invented the Classical musical forms of symphony, concerto, string quartet and sonata. Mozart, Beethoven and Schubert all owed an incalculable debt to their genial, hard-working predecessor.

Haydn's life spanned a period of great social change. He was one of the last major musicians to work for a single aristocratic patron — in his case, the Hungarian Esterházy family, whose seat was the castle of Eisenstadt, some 80km (50 miles) from Vienna.

ABOVE: Joseph Haydn at the keyboard (c.1795) with the score of his penultimate symphony — the Drumroll *(No. 103).*

The arrangement worked quite well for Haydn — his employers treated him fairly — but in their eyes he was no better than a servant. His life-long desire for freedom was granted only towards the end of his long career, when he was effectively pensioned off and was able to travel and enjoy his spreading European reputation.

Early years

Haydn was one of 12 children born to the village wheelwright in Rohrau, about 50km (30 miles) south-east of Vienna. When he was only six, his budding musical talent was noticed by his family and neighbours, and a relative in Hainburg, who was a schoolmaster, offered to take the child as a boarder and begin his musical education. Shortly after his eighth birthday, Haydn was taken on as a choirboy at St Stephen's

LEFT:
Prince Nikolaus Esterházy ("the Magnificent"), Haydn's patron and employer from 1762–90.

RIGHT:
The courtyard of the Esterházy family palace at Eisenstadt, near Vienna, where Haydn worked.

ABOVE: A performance in 1775 of Haydn's opera L'incontro improviso (The Unforeseen Encounter), *in the theatre at Eszterháza. The composer is playing the harpsichord.*

🎼 Life and works

NATIONALITY: Austrian

BORN: Rohrau, 1732;
DIED: Vienna, 1809

SPECIALIST GENRES:
Symphonies, string quartets,
opera, oratorios, Masses.

MAJOR WORKS:
15 surviving operas;
104 symphonies; violin and
keyboard concertos;
string quartets; keyboard
sonatas; chamber music
and songs; 12 Masses; Stabat
Mater (1767); *Die Schöpfung*
(1797–8); *Die Jahreszeiten*
(1798–1801).

Cathedral in Vienna, under the harsh regime of the choir-master Karl Georg Reutter. Haydn said later in life: "I never had a proper teacher. I started with the practical side…I listened more than I studied, and tried to turn to good account all the things that impressed me."

Haydn left the choir in 1749, and for the next decade he eked out a meagre living in Vienna as a music teacher. His major breakthrough came when Prince Paul Anton Esterházy happened to hear a symphony of Haydn's and immediately offered the young composer a job. Haydn accepted, but first he took the disastrous step of getting married. His first love had become a nun, and perhaps out of a mistaken sense of duty to her father, Haydn agreed to marry her elder sister, Maria Anna Keller. His wife turned out to be bad-tempered,

unattractive, and didn't care "whether her husband was a cobbler or an artist". She was also apparently unable to have children. During the years ahead Haydn found consolation with other women, but by the time his wife died in 1800 he was too old to think of remarriage.

ABOVE: The exquisite mirrored concert room at the summer palace of Eszterháza, built in the mid 1760s.

LEFT: A 19th-century edition of Haydn's Symphony No. 84 in E flat, first published as the fourth of the set of six Paris Symphonies.

RIGHT: A 19th-century artist's impression of Haydn and friends playing string quartets. Haydn was a good violinist.

Eisenstadt

In May 1761 Haydn took up his new post. His duties included training the choir and orchestra at Eisenstadt, maintaining all the instruments and music, and keeping discipline. He was also required to compose to order. Among the first works that Haydn wrote for his new patron were three symphonies called *Morning*, *Noon* and *Evening*, possibly intended to be played by the prince himself.

Less than a year later, Prince Paul Anton died. His successor, his brother Prince Nikolaus, was far more socially ambitious (he acquired the nickname "the Magnificent"), and soon Haydn found himself turning out a stream of music for his patron's entertainment: symphonies, concertos, string quartets, trios, and a vast quantity of chamber music for the prince's own instrument, the archaic, six-stringed baryton (similar to the viola d'amore).

Move to Eszterháza

In 1764 Nikolaus decided that Eisenstadt was no longer equal to his pretensions. He ordered the construction of a new summer palace – fit for a prince – on the shores of Lake Neusiedler. It had 126 lavishly decorated guest rooms, an art gallery, a concert hall, a ballroom and a 400-seat theatre. The Empress Maria Theresa attended a performance of one of Haydn's operas there in 1775, and declared: "If I want to hear a good opera, I go to Eszterháza." All in all, Haydn wrote some 25 operas for Eszterháza, including *L'infedeltà delusa* (*Infidelity Deluded*, 1773), *Il mondo della luna* (*The World on the Moon*, 1777) and *Atmida* (1783).

While Haydn enjoyed the isolation of Eszterháza, where there was no one to bother him, and he was, as he said, "forced to become original", the other musicians hated it. Each year Prince Nikolaus found it harder to tear himself away from his fairy-tale palace, and he and his courtiers spent as little time at Eisenstadt as possible. But many of the court musicians had families in Vienna, and they begged Haydn to intercede with the prince.

ABOVE: A romantic impression of Haydn walking in the streets of Vienna carrying one of his scores under his arm.

His witty answer was the *Farewell* Symphony (No. 45), written in November 1772, in which one by one the musicians left the stage, packing up their instruments and blowing out their candles, until only two violins were left playing. The prince apparently took the hint.

The *Farewell* Symphony is one of a group of distinctive symphonies written during the 1770s in the fashionable, literary-influenced style known as *Sturm und Drang* ("storm and stress"). Many are in unusual keys, and exhibit a wide variety of moods. The same emotional style also influenced Haydn's other work of the period, including his highly original string quartets – of which he wrote 68 – and piano sonatas.

ABOVE: Haydn's last public appearance, at a performance of his oratorio The Creation *in the Great Hall of the University of Vienna on 27 March 1808, in honour of his 76th birthday.*

International fame

By the 1780s, Haydn's international reputation was spreading rapidly, and he managed to negotiate a new contract with his employer which

ABOVE: A romantic impression of Haydn crossing the English Channel in the 1790s.

allowed him to compose for other patrons, and to have his works published. In 1785 he became a Freemason, and around the same time he was commissioned to write several symphonies by a Parisian masonic lodge. The result was the "Paris" symphonies (Nos. 82–7) – several of which carry nicknames such as *The Bear*, *The Hen* and *The Queen* (a tribute to Marie Antoinette). Their success helped to consolidate his fame abroad.

After the death of Prince Nikolaus Esterházy in 1790, Haydn was free to travel for the first time. He was persuaded by the impresario Johann Peter Salomon to visit London, where he was – to his surprise – fêted by the court and high society. In July 1791 Oxford University honoured him with the degree of Doctor of Music. His twelve "London" symphonies (Nos. 93–104, some again with nicknames including *The Surprise*, *The Miracle*, *The Military* and *The Clock*) met with great public enthusiasm. Haydn made a further trip to England in 1794–5, but resisted King George III's invitation to stay permanently.

Last years

Haydn returned to Vienna as *Kapellmeister* to a new Esterházy prince, Nikolaus II, who in contrast to his predecessors required only sacred music for his newly austere court. Between 1796 and 1802 Haydn produced six fine masses, including the *Missa in tempore belli* (*Mass in Time of War*) and the *Missa in Angustiis* (*Nelson Mass*), both reflecting the political turmoil of the Napoleonic wars. He also wrote two Handelian oratorios, *Die Schöpfung* (*The Creation*, 1798) and *Die Jahreszeiten* (*The Seasons*, 1801). These, his last major works, teem with vibrant detail and an undimmed creative impulse.

The increasingly frail composer made his last public appearance at a performance of *The Creation* at Vienna University in honour of his 76th birthday, and died at the end of May 1809, during the Napoleonic occupation of Vienna. The whole art-loving world of Vienna attended his memorial service, which included a performance of Mozart's Requiem. Eleven years later his remains were reinterred in the chapel at Eisenstadt.

Wolfgang Amadeus Mozart

Mozart is sunshine.

Antonín Dvořák (1841–1904)

The works of Mozart and Beethoven stand at the heart of Western art music. Until the mid 20th century, Beethoven was perhaps the more revered as a heroic figure, battling against personal misfortune to produce his visionary and powerfully original music; while Mozart's music tended to be dismissed as "galant" and superficial. But over the past half-century, the re-evaluation of Mozart, together with the performance and recording of many of his lesser-known works, has revealed a composer of inestimable profundity and infinite variety, whose music has enriched the lives of performers and listeners alike.

Family background

The "miracle whom God let be born in Salzburg" made his appearance on 27 January 1756, the last of seven children born to Leopold Mozart and his wife

ABOVE: Wolfgang Amadeus Mozart, painted nearly three decades after his death by Barbara Krafft.

Anna Maria, and one of only two to survive infancy. Leopold Mozart – a talented violinist, and the author of a successful treatise on violin technique – played in the court orchestra of the Archbishop of Salzburg, one of the most powerful prelates in Austria.

Mozart's relationship with his father was central to his life. Leopold Mozart has been vilified as the archetypal domineering father, dragging his prodigiously talented son around the courts of Europe at an early age, not only subjecting him to the rigours of prolonged travel, but forcing him to display his skills on the keyboard to any bored aristocrat who would pay money to listen; then hectoring him when he grew older, trying to obstruct him from leaving a miserable existence in Salzburg for the excitements of Vienna, and interfering in his personal life. In fact, there is no evidence to suggest that Leopold was motivated by anything other than love and solicitude for his son. The Mozart family was

LEFT: Mozart's birthplace on the Getreidegasse in Salzburg, where the family lived from 1747 until 1773.

RIGHT: Mozart's father Leopold (1719–87), painted in 1756 – the year of his son's birth.

ABOVE: Mozart at the age of six in court dress, painted by P. A. Lorenzoni.

Childhood

At the age of four, Wolfgang began to study keyboard and composition with his father. Wolfgang's elder sister Maria Anna (Nannerl) was also a talented pianist, though once she reached adulthood, the conventions of the time obliged her to confine her talents to the domestic sphere. Leopold saw it as his duty to exhibit his exceptional children to the world. When they were six and 11 respectively, he took them to perform before the Elector of Bavaria at Munich, and the Empress Maria Theresa in Vienna.

In 1763 the whole family undertook a trip to Paris and London, where Wolfgang played to both French and English monarchs. By this time he was already composing: four early keyboard sonatas were published in Paris, and he wrote his first symphonies in London. The family arrived back in Salzburg in November 1766. A further trip to Vienna failed to result in a hoped-for opera commission, but on returning home Mozart wrote one anyway, and *La finta semplice* (*The Pretend Simpleton*) was performed at the Archbishop's palace in May 1769.

very close, and their voluminous correspondence is full of protestations of affection. Leopold's only concern was for Wolfgang's well-being and success. He was one of the few people who fully recognized his son's unique gift, and he took every step to prevent it being squandered.

🎼 Life and works

NATIONALITY: Austrian

BORN: Salzburg, 1756;
DIED: Vienna, 1791

SPECIALIST GENRES:
Opera, symphonies, piano concertos, string quartets, church music.

MAJOR WORKS: *Le nozze di Figaro* (1786); *Don Giovanni* (1787); *Così fan tutte* (1790); *Die Zauberflöte* (1791); 21 piano concertos; five violin concertos; concertos for clarinet and other wind instruments; 41 symphonies; 24 string quartets and other chamber music; 17 Masses.

ABOVE: A concert given by the young Mozart in the Redoutensaal (ballroom) of the Schönbrunn Palace in Vienna.

ABOVE: *Leopold Mozart and his two talented children, Maria Anna and Wolfgang, 1763.*

ABOVE: *The young Mozart (aged six) being presented by Joseph II to his wife, the Empress Maria Theresa, at Schönbrunn Palace on 13 October 1762.*

Years of travel

In December 1769 Leopold took Wolfgang to Italy for the first time. After visits to Milan, Florence, Rome and Naples, Mozart received his first opera commission. *Mitridate, rè di ponto* was performed at Christmas 1770 at the Milanese court; but although both it and a further opera, *Lucio Silla*, were well received, Mozart's request for a job was turned down.

Back in Salzburg, Mozart settled down reluctantly as *Konzertmeister* to the court orchestra of a new (and less tolerant) Archbishop, and continued to compose. In January 1775 he and his father travelled together for the last time, to Munich, for the performance of Mozart's comic opera, *La finta giardiniera* (*The Pretend Gardener*). Two years later he asked for another period of leave, for an extended trip to Paris. The Archbishop promptly dismissed him, and Leopold, realizing that his own position was now in jeopardy, decided not to go. Mozart set out with his mother as chaperone.

The trip was a disaster. After a prolonged stay in Mannheim, where

Wolfgang fell madly in love with a young singer called Aloysia Weber, he was peremptorily ordered by Leopold on to Paris. There he found the sophisticated French capital totally uninterested in an unknown provincial composer, now too old to be

ABOVE: *A romantic artist's impression of Mozart composing, painted around 1880 by Josef Büche.*

interesting as a prodigy. Although the Paris experience did produce some fine works — the *Paris* Symphony (No. 31) and a concerto for flute and harp (both fashionable French instruments) — there was no financial gain and a severe loss, when Mozart's mother died suddenly. Saddened and disillusioned, Mozart returned home.

Idomeneo

For the next 18 months he buried himself in his official court duties, writing sacred music for the Salzburg court, as well as symphonies, serenades, the Sinfonia Concertante for violin and viola (inspired by the French model) and a double piano concerto for himself and Nannerl. Then, in the summer of 1780, he was commissioned to write a new opera for Munich, on the subject of Idomeneus, king of Crete. *Idomeneo* is Mozart's first great opera — the first in which he demonstrated his extraordinary talent for bringing characters to life, allowing them to express real human emotions through the medium of music.

Vienna: early years

After being fêted in Munich, Mozart felt stifled by the petty humiliations of life in Salzburg. In March 1781 he was summoned to Vienna in the Archbishop's retinue, and took advantage of the rising antagonism between himself and his employer to engineer his own dismissal – albeit "with a box on the ear and a kick on the backside".

To Leopold's dismay, Mozart announced his intention of remaining in Vienna, where he would teach, compose, and give concerts. It was a bold idea, but ultimately an unsuccessful one. Austria was at war with the Turkish Empire, money was short, and fashions ephemeral, but for a few years, Mozart's novelty value paid dividends.

During his first year in Vienna he composed a group of three new piano concertos to play at his own subscription concerts, three magnificent wind serenades, and a new opera, *Die Entführung aus dem Serail* (*The Abduction from the Seraglio*), with a German text and spoken dialogue (a type known as a *Singspiel*). Its success

ABOVE: Mozart's first-floor apartment (with bay-window, second from right) in Vienna. He composed The Marriage of Figaro *there.*

was marred only by the laconic remark of the emperor that it seemed to have "too many notes".

Mozart also got married, much against his father's wishes. His bride, Constanze Weber, was the younger sister of his first love, Aloysia, who had turned him down. Constanze was an amateur singer: Mozart described her as "kind-natured…not ugly, but no beauty either". She has often been accused of ruining her husband's life by her bad housekeeping, but the accusation seems to have been unfounded, and the marriage – which produced two surviving sons (four other children died in infancy) – was very happy. When Leopold Mozart finally visited his son in 1785, he was much impressed with Wolfgang's fine apartment and high standard of living.

Vienna: middle years

For several years Mozart's new career proved successful. He had a busy teaching and concert programme, for which he turned out a string of piano concertos, raising the genre to new heights of virtuosity, passion and expression. Among these may be singled out the Concerto in D minor (K466), a highly emotional work in the *Sturm und Drang* ("storm and stress") style; and its companion in C major (K467), whose exquisite slow movement featured in the 1967 film *Elvira Madigan*.

ABOVE: Mozart's wife Constanze (1763–1842), painted by Hans Hansen in 1802, 11 years after Mozart's death. She remarried in 1809.

ABOVE: The final page from Mozart's own thematic catalogue of his works, which he kept from 1784 until his death. This page shows entries for the operas Die Zauberflöte *and* La clemenza di Tito, *the Clarinet Concerto and a Masonic cantata, finished in November 1791.*

ABOVE: *Stage set for* The Magic Flute, *designed by Simon Quadligo for a performance in Munich on 27 November 1818.*

Mozart's first love, however, was for opera – the genre which could make or break a composer – and in 1785 he began work on a daring new operatic venture, based on Pierre Beaumarchais's notorious French play *La folle journée, ou le mariage de Figaro*, which had been produced the previous year. This attack on aristocratic morals, disguised as a comedy, had already been banned in Vienna. Mozart's literary collaborator was the Italian adventurer, ex-priest and poet Lorenzo Da Ponte (1749–1838), with whom Mozart also worked on two later operas, *Don Giovanni* and *Così fan tutte*.

Le nozze di Figaro (*The Marriage of Figaro*) is one of the great monuments of Western art – a masterpiece of characterization, quicksilver wit and emotional depth. But Vienna failed to appreciate it. By this time, Mozart's arrogance had made him many enemies, including the powerful court composer, Antonio Salieri. Salieri and his friends were intensely jealous of

Mozart's abundant talent, and did all they could to sabotage the opera's production. (Salieri may not literally have poisoned Mozart, as some later claimed, but he certainly stifled his rival's career.) However, the music-lovers of Prague, where Figaro was

ABOVE: *A seduction scene from Mozart's opera* Don Giovanni (1787).

produced in 1787, took the opera to their hearts (the city went "Figaro-mad"), and immediately commissioned a new opera, *Don Giovanni*. Mozart's visit to Prague also produced a new symphony (No. 38), known as the *Prague*.

Vienna: last years

The final years of Mozart's brief life were a dismal catalogue of financial worry, constant moves to cheaper apartments, and failing health. He finally achieved his desire of a court appointment, but only as chamber composer, writing dance music for court balls, for a meagre salary. By June 1788 he was writing begging letters to his fellow Freemasons, asking for loans. *Don Giovanni* had been performed with even less success than *Figaro*.

In the summer of 1788, Mozart wrote his last three symphonies, including the *Jupiter* (No. 41), in the space of a few weeks; it is not known

ABOVE: *A scene from Act II Scene 3 of the original 1791 production of* The Magic Flute *at the Theater auf der Wieden in Vienna.*

if he ever heard them performed. A third opera written with Da Ponte, *Così fan tutte* (literally, "so do all women"), was premièred in the autumn of 1789, but the emperor died shortly afterwards and all theatres were closed. Two trips to Berlin and Frankfurt to give concerts failed to make any money, and by the end of 1790 Mozart was deeply depressed.

In the spring of 1791, he busied himself with dance music and pieces for mechanical organ and glass harmonica, several works for clarinet, including a fine concerto and quintet, and also with the serious and beautiful Piano Concerto in B flat (K595), a work tinged with melancholy. He also began work on another *Singspiel*, written for an actor-manager friend who ran a small suburban theatre. On the surface, *Die Zauberflöte* (*The Magic Flute*) appears to be an amusing pantomime with glorious music attached. But closer inspection reveals that the piece is infused with Masonic symbolism, including thinly disguised versions of Masonic rites and initiation ceremonies. Mozart was taking an

enormous risk, and it has been suggested – probably wrongly – that he paid for his presumption with his life.

While working on *The Magic Flute*, he received two more commissions, one for an *opera seria*, *La clemenza di Tito* (*The Clemency of Titus*), which was produced in Prague in September 1791 and was to be the last major work of this type, and another for a Requiem Mass. The latter was commissioned anonymously, via an emissary dressed in grey, by a Viennese nobleman whose young wife had died. Mozart's own health was failing by this time, and as he worked on the Requiem, he became obsessed by the idea that it would be his own, and that he was being poisoned. In fact he had advanced kidney disease. He died on the morning of 5 December in his wife's arms. Because he left little money, he was given the cheapest possible funeral in an unmarked grave. Few mourners accompanied the cortège. The unfinished Requiem was completed after his death by Franz Süssmayr, one of his pupils.

ABOVE: *A 19th-century artist's impression of Mozart's last hours, by Henry O'Neil (1817–80). The composer died in his wife's arms, aged 35.*

Ludwig van Beethoven

Nature would burst should she attempt to produce nothing save Beethovens.

ROBERT SCHUMANN (1810–56)

Mozart died in Vienna in the late autumn of 1791, a victim of the stifling class conventions of the *ancien régime*. A year later, a 20-year-old named Ludwig van Beethoven arrived in Vienna, keen to make his name as a musician. By this time, the face of European society was changing fast. The French Revolution was in full swing, and Austria — horrified at the treatment meted out to the French monarchs, particularly Queen Marie Antoinette, a former Austrian archduchess — had declared war on France. For more than two decades, Europe would be ripped apart by war. While Mozart's life had remained largely unaffected by international politics, Beethoven's revolutionary artistic vision was shaped by the ideology and volcanic social change of the turbulent times in which he lived.

ABOVE: Ludwig van Beethoven (1770–1827), painted in 1823 by Ferdinand Georg Waldmüller.

Early years

Beethoven was born into a musical family. His grandfather had been music director to the Archbishop-Elector of Cologne, and his father was also employed at the electoral court, though in the lowlier position of singer and instrumentalist. As with the Mozart family, the majority of the seven children born to Johann van Beethoven and his wife died in infancy. Three boys survived: Ludwig, born on 16 or 17 December 1770, and two younger brothers, Caspar Carl and Nikolaus.

Johann van Beethoven, an alcoholic bully, was determined that his eldest son should follow in the young Mozart's footsteps as a child prodigy. But Johann lacked Leopold Mozart's abilities as a teacher, and forced his son to practise the keyboard constantly at the expense of his general education. From around 1780 Beethoven received more kindly and sympathetic instruction from the court composer and organist Christian Neefe, who organized the publication of his pupil's first compositions — a set of keyboard variations. In 1783 a set of three piano sonatas appeared in print with a dedication to the elector, whose successor appointed Beethoven second court organist the following year.

In 1787 Neefe suggested that Beethoven should travel to Vienna to take lessons from Mozart, who was much impressed with the young man's talent. But Beethoven's trip was curtailed by news of his mother's serious illness: she died of tuberculosis in the summer of that year, leaving him to cope with his father's violence and alcoholism. At the age of 18 Beethoven assumed responsibility for the family affairs, being granted half his father's court salary as well as his own. He also found an influential patron, Count Ferdinand Waldstein, who persuaded the elector to allow Beethoven leave to study with Haydn in Vienna. The

ABOVE: Beethoven's birthplace in Bonn. He was born in the third-floor attic.

he had an apartment), and despite
his unprepossessing appearance –
stocky, swarthy, with an ugly, red,
pockmarked face – and rather boorish
manners, he found himself tolerated
by fashionable society.

He gave his first public concert,
playing a new piano concerto of his
own, at the Burgtheater on 29 March
1795, astonishing the audience with his
fiery virtuosity and establishing a
pattern which would continue for
several years. By 1796 he had
published a set of piano trios and three
piano sonatas (a genre he would
develop far beyond the Classical
"galant" style of Mozart and Haydn),
and had earned enough money to set
himself up in his own apartment.
Over the next four years he went
on occasional concert tours, gave
subscription concerts in Vienna, and
issued his chamber works in print –
sonatas for piano (including the
magnificent *Pathétique* Sonata No. 8 in
C minor), violin and cello, and the
Op. 16 Quintet for piano and wind.

All these works show Beethoven's
desire to push at the boundaries of
conventional compositional technique,
to expand sonata form, and to infuse
his work with unheard-of drama
and passion.

These principles were already
evident in the first of his nine
symphonies (written in 1800), which,
while conforming to the standard
Classical four-movement format,
relies not so much on lyrical themes
as on rhythmic dynamism and the
development of short melodic
fragments, or motifs. Clearly, the
old courtly "minuet and trio" which
traditionally constituted the third
movement of a symphony had outlived
its purpose: from the Second
Symphony onwards Beethoven
replaced it with a faster, more dynamic
and rhythmically propelled scherzo,
while retaining a tripartite structure
with a slower, more lyrical central
section. "There is something
revolutionary about that music,"
remarked the emperor.

elector agreed, and in 1792 Beethoven
arrived in Vienna, the city which
became his permanent home.

Vienna

Beethoven found that his lessons with
Haydn were not a great success, but
he quickly began to make a name as a
pianist, with a formidable reputation
for improvisation. "He is greatly
admired for the velocity of his playing,
and astounds everybody by the way he
can master the greatest difficulties with
ease," a local paper reported. He also
found a new and powerful patron,
Prince Lichnowsky (in whose mansion

ABOVE: Beethoven, aged 17, playing to Mozart. Mozart declared that the young genius would "soon astonish the world".

The Classical Period **333**

ABOVE: A view of rural Heiligenstadt, where Beethoven escaped from city life to compose and recuperate, and where he wrote the "Heiligenstadt Testament".

The Heiligenstadt crisis

Around the turn of Beethoven's 30th year, just as his career seemed to be soaring, he was struck by an appalling personal crisis. He was forced to acknowledge the fact that he was going deaf. For several years he had tried to hide his hearing problems for both professional and social reasons, but it became clear that the affliction was incurable.

In the summer of 1802 he reached a nadir of despair, while staying at the country retreat of Heiligenstadt, just outside Vienna. He wrote a long letter (known as the "Heiligenstadt Testament") to his brothers, in which he described his utter misery: "For me there can be no pleasure in human society, no intelligent conversation, no mutual confidences. I must live like an outcast." But though he had contemplated suicide, Beethoven concluded that he must henceforth live for his art: "It seemed impossible to leave the world before I had accomplished all I was destined to do." The letter was never sent, and was found among his effects after his death.

Years of struggle

Beethoven's inner struggle is reflected in the titanic works of the next few years. These included the massive *Eroica* Symphony (No. 3), originally dedicated to Napoleon, nearly twice as long as a conventional symphony, with a powerful and tragic funeral march as its slow movement; the Triple Concerto for piano, violin and cello; two piano sonatas (No. 21, the *Waldstein* and No. 23, the *Appassionata*); and his only opera, *Fidelio*.

The opera's plot was based on a French Revolutionary tale of a wife's heroic efforts to save her imprisoned husband. (For political reasons, Beethoven was obliged to move the action to 18th-century Spain.) By the time of the opera's production, in 1805, Napoleon's army had occupied Vienna and *Fidelio* received only two performances. It remains a lone masterpiece of its kind in Beethoven's output, perhaps lacking the innate sense of theatre of Mozart's mature operas, but containing memorable dramatic moments such as Leonora's great "Abscheulicher" aria, the quartet "Mir ist so wunderbar" and the moving chorus when the prisoners are brought from their cells and greet the light of day.

ABOVE: The "Heiligenstadt Testament", a letter written in 1802, in which Beethoven expressed his suicidal despair at his deafness.

ABOVE: Napoleon Bonaparte (1769– 1821), the original dedicatee of Beethoven's Symphony No. 3 (the Eroica), but whom Beethoven despised when he proclaimed himself Emperor of France.

ABOVE: The première of Beethoven's opera Fidelio *at the Theater an der Wien in Vienna, 1805. The opera was not an immediate success, owing to the French occupation.*

Disillusioned after *Fidelio*'s failure, Beethoven concentrated on instrumental pieces, producing a set of three string quartets dedicated to the Russian ambassador to Austria, Count Andreas Razumovsky, the Fourth Symphony, the Violin Concerto (again a lone masterpiece), and his Fourth Piano Concerto. Just before Christmas 1808 the Fifth and Sixth Symphonies, both revolutionary in concept, were premièred at the same concert. The Fifth, with its progression from tragedy to hope, has been interpreted as representing Beethoven's own struggle against adversity, and is one of the first symphonic works to recycle thematic material between movements. The Sixth (the *Pastoral*) is a harbinger of Romanticism. One of the earliest symphonic examples of "tone-painting", it illustrates scenes of Austrian country life, including a realistic thunderstorm, birdsong and a village festival.

By this time, Beethoven was enjoying a measure of financial security through the support of several wealthy patrons, including the Archduke Rudolph (to whom Beethoven dedicated his Fifth Piano Concerto, known as *The Emperor*). When Napoleon's troops invaded Vienna in 1809, the imperial family fled to safety: Beethoven celebrated their return from exile in 1810 with the Piano Sonata No. 26, *Das Lebewohl* (*The Farewell*). Seven years later Rudolph also received the dedication of the *Hammerklavier* Sonata (No. 29).

Disappointment in love

Apart from his deafness, Beethoven's life was marred by his failure to find a partner: the objects of his affection were usually either married, or else above him in social station (such as Countess Giulietta Guicciardi, the dedicatee of the *Moonlight* Sonata). An unsent letter written in 1812 reveals a deep attachment to an unspecified

ABOVE: The triumphant entrance of Napoleon's army into Vienna in 1805. The French occupation caused hardship for Viennese citizens.

ABOVE: Countess Giulietta Guicciardi, to whom the Moonlight *Sonata was dedicated.*

ABOVE: *A 19th-century artist's impression of Beethoven (in later life) composing in his Viennese apartment. He was notably untidy.*

woman, "the immortal beloved", who may possibly have been Antonie Brentano, the wife of a Frankfurt businessman. She and Beethoven never met in later life, but many years later he dedicated to her his last work for piano, the *Diabelli Variations*.

Beethoven seems to have despised women of a lower social class: an attitude which led to acrimonious rows with his brothers over their "unsuitable" choice of wives. In 1820, after a long legal battle begun after his brother's death in 1815, he became sole guardian of his nephew Karl, perhaps fulfilling his own frustrated desire for an heir. Their relationship, however, proved a stormy one, and overshadowed the later years of Beethoven's life.

Last years

In 1813 Beethoven celebrated Napoleon's defeat on the Iberian Peninsula with his *Battle Symphony*. Originally written for a mechanical instrument called the "panharmonicon", the piece is far inferior to the contemporary Seventh and Eighth

ABOVE: *Beethoven's ear-trumpet lying on the manuscript of his* Eroica Symphony.

ABOVE: *The opening of the Theater in der Josefstadt in Vienna, 1822, for which Beethoven wrote the overture* The Consecration of the House.

ABOVE: *The Kärntnertor Theatre in Vienna, where the première of Beethoven's Ninth Symphony took place on 7 May 1824.*

Symphonies. By this time Beethoven had more or less abandoned public performance, and by 1818 he was stone deaf.

He became increasingly withdrawn and anti-social, but continued to compose. Sacred music had never figured largely in his output, but in 1822 he completed the *Missa solemnis*, originally intended to celebrate Archduke Rudolph's enthronement as Archbishop of Olmütz. This great work, written "from the heart to the heart", ranks with Bach's B minor Mass as one of the crowning achievements of its composer's career. Sections of it were performed in May 1824 at a concert which included the première of the Ninth Symphony, the result of Beethoven's desire to write a "choral symphony with voices". Within a traditional symphonic framework (except that the scherzo is placed second), Beethoven burst the bonds of convention by introducing into the finale a setting for solo voices and chorus of Schiller's *An die Freude* (*Ode to Joy*), with its ecstatic vision of an international brotherhood of man.

Beethoven's last instrumental compositions – the last three piano sonatas and the late string quartets (including the six-movement Op. 130, with its immense fugal finale) – have always been regarded as embodying

Western musical art at a peak of perfection. They are introspective works, not intended to be "understood" or applauded in the conventional sense. They are the work of a man who had withdrawn into an inner life, which could only be expressed through the medium of pure, abstract music.

In 1826 Beethoven's nephew Karl attempted suicide. By this time the composer (a heavy drinker) was already mortally ill with liver disease. After months of suffering, Beethoven died on 26 March 1827. In contrast to Mozart's low-key burial, 10,000 people are estimated to have watched Beethoven's funeral procession. The poet Franz Grillparzer delivered the funeral oration, in honour of "the man who inherited and enriched the immortal fame of Handel and Bach, of Haydn and Mozart... Until his death he preserved a father's heart for mankind. Thus he was, thus he died, thus he will live to the end of time."

ABOVE: *A contemporary watercolour of Beethoven's funeral procession leaving the "House of the Black Spaniard", his last residence (to the right of the church).*

Franz Schubert

If you go to see him during the day, he says "Hello, how are you? — Good!"
and goes on working, whereupon you go away.

FRANZ VON SCHOBER (1798–1882)

On 29 March 1827, Beethoven was buried in the village cemetery of Währing, just outside Vienna. Among the torch-bearers in the funeral procession was a dark-haired, bespectacled young man of 30. His name was Franz Schubert, and he was paying homage to the member of his own profession he most revered. Less than two years later, Schubert's own body would be interred in the same cemetery, close to Beethoven's grave.

Unlike Beethoven, whose fame during his lifetime had spread all over Europe, Schubert's reputation was largely local. His composing career was short – a mere 15 years – and although he worked in the same genres as his three great predecessors, it was not his operas, or even his symphonies, but his more intimate works, particularly the songs and chamber music, which posthumously ensured his unique place in musical history.

By the time war in Europe ended with the Congress of Vienna (1815), European society had changed dramatically. A new generation of middle-class, independently minded citizens had sprung up, but conservative politicians, such as Prince Metternich in Vienna, attempted to maintain the status quo of the ruling classes and banish "subversive and revolutionary tendencies" by keeping the populace firmly under control through censorship and political repression.

ABOVE: Franz Schubert (1797–1828), aged about 28, painted by Wilhelm August Rieder around 1825.

People sought relief through social activity. Balls and parties became fashionable for the rich, while the less well-off built up a network of like-minded friends, meeting in private homes or at the local coffee houses. This was Schubert's social milieu.

Youth
Vienna was the centre of Schubert's universe. He was born on 31 January 1797 to a suburban schoolmaster, who taught all his children to play musical instruments. Franz learned the viola, and together with his father and brothers made up a string quartet. In 1808 he won a scholarship to the imperial seminary, where he had daily music lessons and played in the school orchestra. He also made several formative friendships, one with Joseph von Spaun, an ex-pupil and law student. By the time Schubert left school at the age of 16, he had already written a substantial quantity of music.

Schubert and Goethe
After his mother's death and his father's remarriage, Schubert spent some time as a teacher at his father's school. He also fell in love with a young singer named Therese

ABOVE: The great writer Johann Wolfgang von Goethe (1749–1832), the father of German Romanticism, painted c.1790.

Grob, who performed in his F major Mass in the autumn of 1814. Perhaps as a result of unrequited love, he began composing songs. His first efforts marked the beginning of a lifelong involvement with the poetry of Europe's most celebrated writer and the "father" of Romanticism, Johann Wolfgang von Goethe (1749–1832). Among these early songs was "Gretchen am Spinnrade" ("Gretchen at the Spinning Wheel"), from Goethe's *Faust*, a masterly characterization of the abandoned Margaret's distress.

The next year produced a huge crop of some 150 songs, many of them settings of Goethe's texts, such as the delicate ballad "Heidenröslein" ("Briar-rose"), and the stormy "Erlkönig" ("The Elf-king"), depicting a father's wild ride through the night to save his sick child from the grasp of Death. In spring 1816 Schubert's friend Spaun sent 28 Goethe settings to the poet, asking permission to dedicate them to him. Goethe, who loathed musical settings of his work, returned the volume without comment. Fortunately undeterred, Schubert went on to add another 100 songs – including the immortal settings of Goethe's "Nur wer die Sehnsucht kennt" ("Only he who knows yearning") and "Kennst du das Land" ("Do you know the country where lemon trees blossom?") – to his canon before the end of the year. In his 20th year he completed his Fourth and Fifth Symphonies, both very much in the Classical mould, for private performance by amateur orchestras.

Maturity

Schubert finally left the family home in December 1816, at the prompting of another close friend, Franz von Schober. A wealthy law student, Schober persuaded Schubert to abandon the drudgery of teaching and concentrate on composition (the song "An die Musik" – "To Music" – is a setting

ABOVE: The autograph manuscript of Schubert's setting of Goethe's poem "Heidenröslein" ("Briar-rose"), one of his best-known early songs.

of a Schober poem). He also introduced Schubert to the singer Johann Michael Vogl, who became the leading interpreter of his songs. These continued to pour out throughout 1817, together with seven piano sonatas, heavily influenced by Beethoven.

🎼 Life and works

NATIONALITY: Austrian

BORN: Vienna, 1797; **DIED:** Vienna, 1828

SPECIALIST GENRES: Songs, piano music, symphonies, chamber music.

MAJOR WORKS: Symphonies No. 8 (*Unfinished*, 1822) and No. 9 (*The Great*, 1828); String Quintet in C (1828); Piano Quintet in A (*The Trout*, 1819); Octet in F (1824); String Quartet No. 14 in D minor (*Death and the Maiden*, 1824); Fantasy in C major for piano (*The Wanderer*, 1822); Fantasy in F minor for piano duet (1828); over 600 songs; song-cycles *Die schöne Müllerin* (1823) and *Winterreise* (1827).

ABOVE: A view of a Viennese square in Schubert's time. Schubert spent all of his short life in Vienna.

ABOVE: *An idealized portrait of the composer on his balcony, painted in 1917.*

In 1818 Schubert's Sixth Symphony – a substantial work which shows Beethoven's influence – was performed (again by an amateur orchestra), and he spent five happy months on a Hungarian aristocratic estate as music teacher to the daughters of Count Esterházy of Galanta, concentrating on piano music for his young pupils. "I live and compose like a god", he told a friend.

Life in Vienna

The change of scene encouraged Schubert to broaden his horizons, and the next summer he and Vogl took a holiday in Steyr, where Schubert completed another piano sonata and the *Trout* Quintet, based on his own song "Die Forelle". From then onwards, Schubert's life took a regular shape. In Vienna, he was the focus of a close-knit group of talented young people — writers, poets and students — who enjoyed a happy and carefree existence, meeting at cafés, at parties in each other's homes or, in the summer, at a country estate owned by Schober's uncle. These informal gatherings, with games of charades, poetry readings and performances of Schubert's music, became known as "Schubertiaden". In the summers, Schubert and Vogl went on long walking tours of Upper Austria, where Schubert drew inspiration from the dramatic landscape.

The early 1820s brought mixed fortune. Vogl's performance of "Der Erlkönig" at a concert in the Burgtheater in 1821 brought public recognition for the as yet unpublished composer, but he had no experience of

ABOVE: *Schubert playing the piano during an evening at Joseph von Spaun's.*

business matters, and when demand for his work rose, he rashly sold the copyrights of ten volumes of songs to the publisher Diabelli. And by 1823 it was clear that Schubert's operatic ambitions would never be realized. Of his 17 stage works, none achieved success, and only the charming and popular incidental music to *Rosamunde* has survived.

Tragedy

The same year – 1823 – brought disaster. Schubert's hedonistic existence had left him suffering from syphilis, then a potentially fatal disease. At the height of his illness, he composed the two-movement *Unfinished* Symphony, restless and tragic in mood, as well as the great *Wanderer* Fantasy and the A minor Sonata, both for piano. He also composed his first song-cycle, a new genre consisting of a set of thematically linked songs based on a sequence of poems, telling a story. *Die schöne Müllerin* (*The Fair Maid of the Mill*) is a quintessentially Romantic tale of rejected love and death by drowning.

The last four years of Schubert's life were a constant struggle against

ABOVE: *An excursion of the "Schubertians" from Atzenbrugg to Aumuhl, painted by Schubert's friend Leopold Kupelwieser. Schubert (wearing a top-hat) is walking behind the carriage.*

ABOVE: A "Schubertiad" (Schubert evening) in a Viennese salon. Schubert at the piano is accompanying the singer Johann Michael Vogl.

depression and illness, interspersed with frantic creative activity. As well as the Ninth Symphony (a work of Beethovenian proportions and unstoppable rhythmic impulse, which a Viennese orchestra declared "unplayable"), the works of these years included a great deal of chamber music: the Octet for wind and strings, string quartets in A minor and D minor (*Death and the Maiden*), two massive piano trios, and the three last piano sonatas (which Schumann memorably described as "purely and simply thunderstorms breaking forth with Romantic rainbows over slumbering worlds").

Last months

Schubert continued to compose songs until the end of his life. Some, such as the radiant "Ständchen" ("Serenade"),

express a passionate delight in life; others — such as the bleak song-cycle *Winterreise* (*Winter Journey*), based on

ABOVE: Schubert's spectacles lying on the manuscripts of some of his last works.

poems by Wilhelm Müller — plumb the depths of despair. Among the last was "Der Doppelgänger" — a terrifying setting of a poem by Heinrich Heine in which a young man sees his "double", foretelling his own death. It was a prophetic vision.

By September 1828, Schubert's health had worsened, and he moved in with his brother. That month he completed the sublime String Quintet in C major, followed in October by his last major work, *Der Hirt auf dem Felsen* (*The Shepherd on the Rock*), for soprano and piano with clarinet obbligato. He died of typhus on 19 November, aged 31, leaving only an unsurpassed musical legacy. His tombstone in the Währing cemetery carries the telling epitaph by Grillparzer: "The art of music has buried here a rich possession, but still fairer hopes."

Other Composers of the Era

Classicism is health, romanticism is sickness.

JOHANN WOLFGANG VON GOETHE (1749–1832)

Two sons of J. S. Bach bridged the gap between the Baroque and the Classical eras. Carl Philipp Emmanuel Bach (1714–88), born in Weimar, decided to follow a musical career, and in 1738 became keyboard player to the future Frederick the Great of Prussia. He remained in Berlin until 1767, when he succeeded Telemann as director of music at Hamburg. He is chiefly remembered for his inventive keyboard sonatas (of which he wrote over 200, for both "connoisseurs and amateurs"), which played a major role in the development of sonata form. His sinfonias, concertos and flute sonatas are also still performed today.

C. P. E. Bach taught the harpsichord to his younger brother Johann Christian Bach (1735–82). Bach's

ABOVE: Thomas Augustine Arne (1710–78), the composer of "Rule, Britannia!"

youngest son continued his studies in Italy, where he began a career as an opera composer, but moved to London in 1762 and remained there until his death, becoming known as "the English Bach". He was initially composer to the King's Theatre in London, and was later appointed music master to Queen Charlotte. His later operas were not very successful, but his instrumental works – particularly his skilfully crafted sinfonias and 40 or so piano concertos – had great influence on Haydn, Beethoven, and particularly Mozart, who met Bach when he visited London at the age of eight.

While British music in the 18th century was largely dominated by European imports, Thomas Arne (1710–78) was a notable home-grown

exception. Arne's output was largely theatrical, including masques and operas (his 1740 masque *Alfred* contained the song "Rule, Britannia!"), but he also wrote some charming symphonies, keyboard concertos and sonatas, and songs, including "The British Grenadiers".

Muzio Clementi (1752–1832) was born in Rome, but lived mostly in England. A brilliant pianist, who later went into publishing and piano-making, he toured Europe as a virtuoso from 1781–83, but then settled in London, where he became a much sought-after teacher (his pupils included John Field). Clementi's own compositions, which include sonatas, sonatinas and studies for piano, are still used as teaching pieces.

ABOVE: Carl Philipp Emmanuel Bach (1714–88), J. S. Bach's third son, who was an influential composer.

ABOVE: J. S. Bach's youngest son, Johann Christian Bach (1735–82), "the English Bach", who worked mostly in London.

ABOVE: Luigi Boccherini (1743–1805), who worked in Vienna and Madrid. He was a fine cellist.

Muzio Clementi's German contemporary, Johann Nepomuk Hummel (1778–1837), studied the piano with Mozart, and also worked for Haydn's employer Prince Esterházy. From 1819–37 he was

ABOVE: The Italian Domenico Cimarosa (1749–1801), court composer in St Petersburg and Vienna, playing the clavichord.

Kapellmeister to the Weimar court. His fluent, tuneful works were very popular: his Trumpet Concerto (1803) is still much performed, as are his *Septet militaire* (1829) and a Piano Quintet of 1802. His piano concertos and sonatas influenced Chopin.

While the Classical period was dominated by the four Viennese giants, Italy continued to produce its fair share of talented composers. Among them was Luigi Boccherini (1743–1805), whose music is similar in style to Haydn's. He worked in Vienna from 1757–64, but in 1769 moved to Madrid as composer to the Spanish court. An enormously prolific composer, Boccherini left a vast output of chamber music, including 91 string quartets, 154 quintets and 60 trios, as well as symphonies, concertos and church music. His famous Minuet (featured in the 1955 British film *The Ladykillers*) comes from his String Quintet in E, Op. 13, No. 5.

Mozart's rival Antonio Salieri (1750–1825) worked principally in Vienna, where he was first an opera composer, and then court conductor. His operas, unlike Mozart's, have not survived, but he was an influential teacher; Beethoven, Schubert and Liszt were among his pupils.

Domenico Cimarosa (1749–1801) spent some time in St Petersburg as court composer to Catherine the Great of Russia, before succeeding Salieri as court *Kapellmeister* in Vienna. After 1792 he returned to his native Naples. Most of his 65 operas have been forgotten, with the single exception of the comic opera *Il matrimonio segreto* (*The Secret Marriage*, 1792). He also wrote an oboe concerto, around 30 keyboard sonatas, and other instrumental works.

His rival and contemporary Giovanni Paisiello (1740–1816) also worked in St Petersburg and Naples, producing

ABOVE: The title page of a comic opera by Antonio Salieri, produced a few months after Mozart's Marriage of Figaro, *in 1785.*

over 100 operas as well as symphonies and piano concertos. His 1782 opera *Il barbiere di Siviglia* (*The Barber of Seville*), written when he was court composer to Catherine the Great, was at first more popular than Rossini's later version.

ABOVE: Giovanni Paisiello (1740–1816), one of the most successful opera composers of his time, painted by Elisabeth Vigée-Lebrun.

The Romantic ❧ Era ❧

Dancers at a court ball at the Hofburg Palace in Vienna in the late
19th century, painted by Wilhelm Gause.

Drama and Poetry in Music

Music, moody food
Of us that trade in love.

WILLIAM SHAKESPEARE (1564–1616), "ANTONY AND CLEOPATRA"

Schubert represented a turning-point in musical history. He inherited the Classical forms of his predecessors, but while his own musical style was essentially Classical, his inspiration looked forward to the age of Romanticism. One of the key features of Romantic music is its strong association with other art-forms, particularly literature or painting. Schubert responded instinctively to the poetry and drama of the great literary figures of his time: Goethe, Friedrich Schiller, Friedrich Rückert, Friedrich Klopstock, and Ludwig Hölty. Their writings, even when dealing with historical figures or events, expressed ordinary human emotions — love, happiness, sorrow — and the beauty of the natural world. One of the most potent examples of literary Romanticism was Goethe's epistolary novel *Die Leiden des jungen Werthers* (*The Sorrows of Young Werther*), published in 1774. It was inspired by Goethe's own unrequited love for a friend's fiancée, and the news of another friend's suicide as a result of disappointed love. *Werthers* had an enormous influence on European youth, and the theme of frustrated passion became a common one in the literature of the period.

Untamed nature

The other great Romantic theme was a response to nature, especially in its wilder aspects. Earlier generations had sought to tame and cultivate the landscape; but in the late 18th century artists and writers — spurred on by Jean-Jacques Rousseau (1712–78) and his rejection of rationalism — reacted against the artificial moral code of Classical writers and philosophers, who believed in a neatly ordered world. Artists such as Théodore Géricault, J. M. W. Turner and Caspar David Friedrich began to depict the puny, helpless nature of human beings when pitted against terrifying natural phenomena such as avalanches or storms; while writers such as Lord Byron, William Wordsworth, Percy Bysshe Shelley and Sir Walter Scott identified human emotions with the turbulent moods of nature, and drew

ABOVE: *This dramatic snow-capped landscape entitled* Near Chamonix *was painted by James Stormont in the 19th century. Views such as this inspired many Romantic composers to write music that celebrated the beauty and ruggedness of nature.*

ABOVE: A caricature by Gustave Doré of Berlioz conducting at the Jardin d'Hiver (Winter Garden) in Paris, 1850.

orchestral masterpiece, the *Symphonie fantastique*, in which a young opium addict dreams he has killed his beloved and is led to the guillotine; while Mendelssohn's orchestral music records his vivid impressions of visits to Italy and Scotland. Much of Schumann's music was inspired by literary models; like Schubert, he had an immediate and passionate response to literature. At the same time, Liszt's newly invented "tone-poem" proved an ideal vehicle for musical responses to literature or art.

Virtuoso performers

The other hallmark of musical Romanticism was its emphasis on the individual – either the composer, fighting a lonely battle against incomprehension and intolerance, or the performer. The 19th century saw the rise of the star performer, and with it a division between creator and executant which became progressively more marked in the 20th century. Many 19th-century composers

ABOVE: A poster advertising Massenet's opera Werther (1887), based on Goethe's novel The Sorrows of Young Werther.

(Chopin, Liszt, Brahms, Paganini) carried on the tradition followed by Mozart and Beethoven in writing music for themselves to perform, but they also began to write for other virtuoso executants, such as the pianists Clara Schumann (1819–96), Eugen d'Albert (1864–1932) and his wife Teresa Carreño (1853–1917); the violinists Joseph Joachim (1831–1907), dedicatee of concertos by Brahms and Bruch, Ferdinand David (1810–73), for whom Mendelssohn wrote his concerto, and Pablo de Sarasate (1844–1908), for whom Lalo, Bruch and Saint-Saëns wrote concertos; and the clarinettist Richard Mühlfeld (1856–1907), for whom Brahms wrote his great chamber works for that instrument.

inspiration from the rugged landscapes of northern Europe, especially Scotland, or from the remoter, brigand-infested parts of Italy and Greece.

Portrayal of emotion

This was the climate which produced the great musical masterpieces of early Romanticism. Among these are Schubert's song-cycles *Die schöne Müllerin*, in which the brook (represented in the piano accompaniment) becomes an equal partner in a drama of rejection and suicide; and *Winterreise* (*Winter Journey*), in which both singer and accompanist paint a vivid picture of wintry desolation, mirroring the bleak emptiness in the betrayed protagonist's soul.

Berlioz left no listeners in any doubt about the "programme" behind his

ABOVE: A painting by Edgar Degas (1876) of the divertissement in Meyerbeer's 1831 opera Robert le diable, *seen from the viewpoint of the orchestra.*

Gioacchino Rossini

Rossini, in music, is the genius of sheer animal spirits.

LEIGH HUNT (1784–1859)

Towards the end of the 18th century, Italy was producing many composers of entertaining, accomplished, but undeniably ephemeral operas. Composers such as Giovanni Paisiello and Domenico Cimarosa wrote dozens of stage works, but very few survived for more than a season, and none could match the Italian masterpieces of Mozart. Opera in Italy had become stereotypical, subject to the tyrannical demands of audiences for a constant stream of hurriedly composed new works, and of singers for arias to show off their vocal technique, in defiance of dramatic exigencies. Italy needed an outstanding opera composer, and found one in the person of Gioacchino Rossini.

Rossini was the son of a horn player and a singer, and began to compose as a child. In 1806 he went to study at the Liceo Musicale in Bologna, and at the age of 15 was commissioned to write his first opera, *Demetrio e Polibio*. Further commissions followed, including several from the Teatro San Moïse in Venice for a series of one-act *farse* including *La scala di seta* (*The Silken Ladder*, 1811) and *Il Signor Bruschino* (1813).

Productive years

Rossini was able to work at high speed, and between 1810 and 1822 he turned out a steady flow of works, both comic and serious, for production in Venice, Milan, Naples and Rome, none of which took him more than a few weeks to write.

ABOVE:
A portrait of Gioacchino Rossini (1792–1868), now in the Liceo Musicale in Bologna where he studied.

LEFT:
The interior of the Teatro San Carlo in Naples, where several of Rossini's operas were first performed.

Life and works

NATIONALITY: Italian

BORN: Pesaro, 1792;
DIED: Paris, 1868

SPECIALIST GENRES: Opera (both "serious" and comic).

MAJOR WORKS: *Il barbiere di Siviglia* (1816); *La cenerentola* (1817); *Semiramide* (1823); *Guillaume Tell* (1829); Stabat Mater (1832–41); *Petite messe solennelle* (1863).

Among them were the serious operas *Tancredi*, *Elisabetta, Regina d'Inghilterra* and *Otello* (based on Shakespeare's play), and the comic operas *L'italiana in Algeri* (*The Italian Girl in Algiers*), *Il barbiere di Siviglia* (*The Barber of Seville* – Rossini's comic masterpiece), *La cenerentola* (*Cinderella*), and *La gazza ladra* (*The Thieving Magpie*). Of these, *The Barber of Seville* (based on Beaumarchais's prequel to *The Marriage of Figaro*) was a disappointing failure at its Roman première in 1816, thanks to a catalogue of onstage disasters, though by its third performance it had recovered from its initial setback. In one version of a famous story about Rossini, who was a notorious gourmet, he was asked by a journalist whether it was true that he had cried in public only twice in his life – the first time after the première of *The Barber*, and

ABOVE: A set for an 1830 production of Rossini's opera Le siège de Corinthe (The Siege of Corinth) at the Berlin State Opera.

the second when a particularly delicious piece of turkey stuffed with truffles had fallen in the river during a picnic. Rossini pondered, and then answered: "No, only once, and that was when the turkey fell in the river."

Rossini's greatest *opere serie* were written for the Teatro San Carlo in Naples between 1817 and 1823: they included *Mosè in Egitto* (*Moses in Egypt*), *La donna del lago* (based on Walter Scott's *The Lady of the Lake*), *Maometto II*, and *Semiramide*, the last of his Italian operas. In 1822 he married the singer Isabella Colbran, who had created the soprano roles in many of his operas, and after trips to Vienna and London, he settled in Paris as director of the Théâtre-Italien. He was still only 31 years old, rich and famous, with 34 operas to his credit.

Later life

Over the next six years he wrote several more operas for Paris, but after *Guillaume Tell* (*William Tell*), arguably his finest work, he effectively retired. In 1836 he returned to Italy, where he suffered prolonged periods of ill-health, but finally settled in Paris again with his second wife Olympe Pélissier, devoting himself to entertaining friends and eating (he invented, among other dishes, *tournedos Rossini*). The

only musical products of his later life are the delightful series of salon pieces which he called "the sins of my old age", and two sacred works, a Stabat Mater and the *Petite messe solennelle*.

Rossini's music

In the operatic field, Rossini's innovations included the replacement of keyboard-accompanied recitative by orchestral accompaniment, the expansion of the chorus and its dramatic integration, the development of the coloratura aria, and the revitalization of *opera buffa*; his characters, such as Figaro and the delightful Rosina, are real people with whom audiences of all ages can identify. His brilliant opera overtures (characterized by their famous, whipped-up *crescendo* endings) are still often performed in the concert repertoire today.

ABOVE: The title page of the fifth edition of the vocal score of Rossini's last opera, Guillaume Tell, published in Paris.

ABOVE: An 1829 cartoon by A. E. Chalon of the character of Figaro, the hero of Rossini's Il barbiere di Siviglia.

Gaetano Donizetti

I wallowed in rapture.

MIKHAIL GLINKA (1804–57), ON HEARING "ANNA BOLENA"

Italian opera in the early 19th century was dominated by three composers: Rossini, who gave up composing in 1829; Bellini, who died at the early age of 33 in 1835; and Donizetti. These three laid the foundations for the work of Giuseppe Verdi.

Donizetti was born to a poor Bergamo family, but was fortunate to be able to attend a free music school in Bergamo founded and run by the opera composer and local *maestro di cappella* Johann Mayr (1763–1845). After two years of further study in Bologna, he began composing with astonishing speed and fluency. In 1822 he wrote a successful opera for production at the Teatro Argentina in Rome, and then moved to Naples, where over the next few years he turned out up to five operas

ABOVE: A portrait of Gaetano Donizetti, now in the Liceo Musicale in Bologna.

a year. In 1828 he married Virginia Vasselli, a lawyer's daughter who died during a cholera epidemic nine years later – a tragedy from which Donizetti never recovered.

Maturity

In 1830 Donizetti achieved his first major international success with *Anna Bolena*. From then on he wrote for other operatic centres, including Milan, where he composed the enchanting comedy *L'elisir d'amore* (*The Love Philtre*), and the tragedy *Lucrezia Borgia*, performed at La Scala in December 1833. It was followed two years later by *Maria Stuarda*, based on Schiller's play about the Queen of Scots. Scotland also provided the

impetus for Donizetti's greatest success, *Lucia di Lammermoor*, based on Walter Scott's tragic novel, which opened at the Teatro San Carlo, Naples, in 1835. (The heroine's famous "mad" scene was parodied over 50 years later by Gilbert and Sullivan in *Ruddigore*.)

In 1838 Donizetti moved to Paris, where his new works – including *La fille du régiment*, *Les martyrs* and *La favorite* – were hugely successful. But he was suffering from syphilis, and both his physical and mental faculties were in decline. In 1842 he was appointed *Kapellmeister* to the Austrian court, but his last operatic masterpiece, *Don Pasquale*, was produced at the Théâtre-Italien in Paris in 1843. He was eventually committed to a lunatic asylum, before being taken home to die in Bergamo.

ABOVE: The "Swedish Nightingale" Jenny Lind as Marie, the heroine of Donizetti's La fille du régiment, *in an 1847 production.*

Life and works

NATIONALITY: Italian

BORN: Bergamo, 1797;
DIED: Bergamo, 1848

SPECIALIST GENRES:
Bel canto opera.

MAJOR WORKS:
L'elisir d'amore (1832);
Lucrezia Borgia (1833);
Lucia di Lammermoor (1835);
La fille du régiment
(1840); *Don Pasquale*
(1843).

Vincenzo Bellini

Long, long melodies, such as no one has ever written before.

GIUSEPPE VERDI (1813–1901)

Vincenzo Bellini was the youngest member of the trio of early Romantic Italian opera composers. He was taught from an early age by his father and grandfather, both musicians, and at 18 went to study at the Royal Music Conservatory in Naples. The first of his ten operas was performed there in 1825, leading to further opera commissions from Naples and Milan.

Bellini achieved more or less instant success with *Il pirata*, produced at La Scala in 1827. It was written in collaboration with the librettist Felice Romani, who went on to supply the texts for six more Bellini operas, including *I Capuleti ed i Montecchi* (*The Capulets and the Montagues*, Venice, 1830), *La sonnambula* (*The Sleepwalker*) and *Norma* (both Milan, 1831), and *Beatrice di Tenda* (Venice, 1833). The failure of this last opera coincided with a rift with Romani, and the termination of a long-standing love affair with a married woman.

In the spring of 1833 Bellini visited London and Paris, where he was fêted, and made many valuable social contacts. The Théâtre-Italien in Paris commissioned his last opera, *I puritani* (*The Puritans*, based on Walter Scott's

Old Mortality), which was performed with huge success in January 1835. Eight months later the composer was dead, after a violent attack of gastro-enteritis, less than two months short of his 34th birthday.

Coloratura

The hallmarks of Bellini's mellifluous, essentially lyrical art are expressive declamation and the close relationship of music and words. "Bellini's music comes from the heart and it is intimately bound up with the text," said Wagner. His operas, like those of Rossini and Donizetti, were written for the great voices of his time. They fell out of favour after the art of *bel canto* declined in the late 19th century, but enjoyed a revival in the 20th century with the emergence of a new breed of coloratura sopranos, such as Maria Callas (1923–77) and Joan Sutherland (born 1926). The aria "Casta diva" from *Norma* became one of Callas's showpieces.

ABOVE:
Vincenzo Bellini (1801–35), a portrait now in the library of La Scala, Milan.

LEFT:
The interior of La Scala (1819), where Bellini's Il pirata *was produced in 1827.*

Life and works

NATIONALITY: Italian

BORN: Catania, Sicily, 1801;
DIED: Puteaux, near Paris, 1835

SPECIALIST GENRES:
Bel canto opera.

MAJOR WORKS:
La sonnambula (1830); *Norma* (1831); *I puritani* (1835).

Carl Maria von Weber

Weber, who seems to whisper in my ear like a familiar spirit,
inhabiting a happy sphere where he awaits to console me.

HECTOR BERLIOZ (1803–69)

Carl Maria von Weber, a leading pioneer of the German Romantic and nationalist movement, is chiefly remembered today for his opera *Der Freischütz (The Free Shooter)*, the sparkling piano piece *Aufforderung zum Tanz (Invitation to the Dance)* which was orchestrated by Berlioz, the *Konzertstück* for piano and orchestra, and his brilliant works for clarinet.

Weber was born into a musical family in northern Germany, the son of a theatrical impresario and a singer. He took music lessons as a boy with Joseph Haydn's brother Michael in Salzburg, and by the age of 14 had already written his first opera. He completed his musical education in Vienna, and then spent over a

ABOVE: A portrait of Carl Maria von Weber (1786–1826) by Caroline Bardua.

A new German opera

On Christmas Day 1816 Weber was appointed to the prestigious post of *Kapellmeister* at the Dresden court. His brief was to establish a national German opera to rival the current dominance of the Italians, and throughout his time at Dresden he had to contend with the overt hostility of the royal *Kapellmeister* (an Italian), as well as with the early symptoms of tuberculosis. Nevertheless he persevered with building up his opera company, and with the composition of his German opera *Der Freischütz*.

The première of *Der Freischütz* in Berlin on 18 June 1821 was

Life and works

NATIONALITY: German

BORN: Eutin, near Lübeck, 1786; **DIED:** London, 1826

SPECIALIST GENRES: German Romantic opera, works for clarinet.

MAJOR WORKS: Two clarinet concertos; Clarinet Quintet (1814); *Grand Duo Concertant* (1816); *Aufforderung zum Tanz* (1819); *Konzertstück* in F minor (1821); *Der Freischütz* (1821); *Euryanthe* (1823); *Oberon* (1826).

ABOVE: Costume designs for villains Samiel and Caspar in Der Freischütz *(1821).*

decade working at various courts and municipal theatres in Germany (during which time he wrote many of his instrumental pieces) before being appointed director at the Prague Opera in 1813. During his tenure there he fell in love with the singer Caroline Brandt, but their tempestuous courtship lasted for four years before they were married.

ABOVE: Berlin in Weber's time — a view of the Brandenburg Gate and the Pariser Platz.

Last performances

Oberon, commissioned by the manager of the Covent Garden Theatre in London, was scheduled for performance in the spring of 1826. By the end of 1825 Weber knew that he was dying. Although his wife and friends tried to dissuade him from travelling to London to conduct the opera, Weber was so worried about making financial provision for his young family that he insisted on making the journey.

He managed to conduct the première of *Oberon* on 12 April 1826, also undertaking many other concert engagements, but he was failing fast. He died at his lodgings in Great Portland Street in London on 5 June, aged only 39. Eighteen years later, Wagner, whose own early operas in the German Romantic style owed an enormous debt to Weber's pioneering work, had his predecessor's remains taken back to Dresden.

a triumph. Compared with the stuffy court operas of the period, it was entirely fresh and riveting, based on a story drawn from German folklore, and with music strongly influenced by German folk song idioms – the music of the people. It is based on the tale of a young forester who tries to win the hand of his beloved by selling his soul to the Devil in return for seven magic bullets which cannot fail to hit their targets. This gave Weber the opportunity for a marvellous supernatural scene in the "Wolf's Glen", a gift to designers and producers, with spine-chilling music to match.

Although *Der Freischütz* went on to take Europe by storm, Weber's next two operas were less successful. Both *Euryanthe* and *Oberon*, while containing marvellous individual numbers (the overture to *Oberon* is a masterpiece), suffered from muddled, incomprehensible plots and little sense of drama. *Euryanthe* opened in Vienna in 1823, but was given only 20 performances.

ABOVE: The "Wolf's Glen" scene from Der Freischütz *— the 1982 production of Weber's famous opera performed at the Royal Opera House in Covent Garden, London.*

Giacomo Meyerbeer

Meyerbeer feels as Michelangelo felt.

GEORGES BIZET (1838–75)

While the operas of Rossini, Donizetti, Bellini and Weber have all to some extent held their place in the repertoire, those of Giacomo Meyerbeer have been revived only occasionally over the past century. In his own time, however, Meyerbeer was one of the most successful opera composers and one of the richest men in Europe. This inevitably provoked envious sniping from his less fortunate colleagues – particularly Wagner, who launched a vitriolic attack on Meyerbeer in his anti-Semitic pamphlet *Das Judenthum in der Musik* (1850).

Child prodigy

Meyerbeer was a truly cosmopolitan figure. Born in Berlin, into the same affluent, cultured, Jewish milieu as his younger contemporary Mendelssohn, Jakob Liebmann Beer (as he was originally called) showed early promise

ABOVE: Giacomo Meyerbeer (1791–1864), creator of French "grand opera". He and Berlioz shared a taste for the "monumental".

as a pianist, appearing as soloist in a performance of a Mozart concerto at the age of 11. He began writing German operas while still in his teens.

From 1816 he spent nine years in Italy, where he wrote six operas in the style of Rossini. The last of these, *Il crociato in Egitto* (*The Crusader in Egypt*, 1824), was subsequently staged with equal success in London and Paris, where Meyerbeer met the librettist Eugène Scribe (1791–1861). From then onwards, Paris became the focus of Meyerbeer's activities, although he never lived there permanently. In the 1840s he was appointed *Generalmusikdirektor* in Berlin, where he wrote a *Singspiel* for the Swedish soprano Jenny Lind (1820–87).

Grand opera

Meyerbeer's reputation rests on the "grand operas" he created for the Paris Opéra in collaboration with Scribe, beginning with *Robert le diable* (*Robert the Devil*) in 1831, continuing with *Les Huguenots* and *Le prophète*, and ending with *L'Africaine* (premièred posthumously in 1865). All were staged with spectacular and innovative effects, such as storms, ships sinking on stage and massive crowd scenes.

Unlike Rossini, Meyerbeer was not a fast worker, and his productions were eagerly awaited. He wrote with specific voices in mind, and was always searching for new vocal and orchestral timbres.

ABOVE: Costume for the role of Marguerite de Navarre, worn at the première of Les Huguenots *in Paris on 29 February 1836.*

🎼 Life and works

NATIONALITY: German

BORN: Vogelsdorf, near Berlin, 1791; **DIED:** Paris, 1864

SPECIALIST GENRES: French grand opera.

MAJOR WORKS: *Robert le diable* (1831); *Les Huguenots* (1836); *Le prophète* (1849); *L'Africaine* (1865).

Niccolò Paganini

Paganini is the turning-point in the history of virtuosity.

The Italian violinist and composer Niccolò Paganini is still revered as the greatest virtuoso of all – a true "wizard of the violin" whose technical mastery has never been equalled. His brilliant Twenty-four Caprices for solo violin have spawned many imitations, and his concertos and variations are still part of the violin repertoire.

Born into a poor Genoese family, he was forced as a small child to practise the violin constantly by his bullying father. In 1795 he spent a year studying in Parma, and at 18 was appointed leader of the orchestra (and then solo violinist to the court) in Lucca. At one of his court concerts he improvised a musical "love scene" using only

ABOVE: The legendary violinist Niccolò Paganini inspired composers and performers, including Schumann, Liszt and Chopin.

two strings of the violin, and he also wrote and performed a sonata entirely on the G string, demanding outstanding dexterity and accuracy.

From 1810 onwards, Paganini travelled Europe as a freelance virtuoso. After his 1813 debut concert at La Scala, Milan, a critic wrote: "He is without question the foremost and greatest violinist in the world. His playing is truly inconceivable. He performs certain passage-work, leaps, and double stops that have never been heard from any violinist…"

Pact with the Devil

The astonishing virtuosity of Paganini's playing, combined with his bizarre appearance – he was lean and gaunt, with a shock of long black hair, and very long, thin fingers – caused rumours that he was in league with the Devil. He never married, but a four-year relationship with a singer, Antonia Bianchi, produced one son, Achille, to whom he was devoted.

Between 1828 and 1834 Paganini's career as a touring virtuoso was at its height: he was acclaimed in Vienna, Berlin, Warsaw, Paris and London, but deteriorating health precipitated his retirement to Italy in 1834. Six years later he died of cancer of the larynx, but the church, having denounced him as a heretic, refused to allow his burial in consecrated ground. In 1845 his remains were transferred from the French Riviera to a private burial-ground in Parma, and were re-interred in Parma Cemetery in 1876. His Guarneri violin is preserved in the municipal museum in Genoa.

Paganini had enormous influence, both on composers (including Schumann), and performers: not only violinists, but also pianists. Both Liszt and Chopin were encouraged by his example to extend the frontiers of keyboard technique. Liszt's *Transcendental Studies* were directly inspired by Paganini's Caprices.

Life and works

NATIONALITY: Italian

BORN: Genoa, 1782;
DIED: Nice, 1840

SPECIALIST GENRES:
Virtuoso violin music.

MAJOR WORKS:
24 Caprices for unaccompanied violin (1820); violin concertos and shorter works, including *Le streghe* (*Witches' Dance*) and *Moto perpetuo* (*Perpetual Motion*).

Hector Berlioz

*Berlioz composes by splashing his pen over the manuscript
and leaving the issue to chance.*

FRÉDÉRIC CHOPIN (1810–49)

Like Schumann and Chopin, Berlioz is regarded as an archetypal "Romantic" artist, both for the nature of his work and for the colourful events of his life, which are documented in his entertaining *Memoirs*.

The son of a provincial French doctor, he intended to pursue a medical career, but the grisly scenes of carnage he encountered at medical school in Paris put him off. Instead he began music lessons, first privately and then at the Paris Conservatoire.

ABOVE: Hector Berlioz composing his opera
Les Troyens *(The Trojans).*

Sensitive, passionate and impulsive by nature, Berlioz was prone to violent emotions. In 1827 he saw an English theatre company performing *Hamlet* at the Odéon Theatre, and was immediately stricken with wild admiration, both for Shakespeare and for Harriet Smithson, the attractive Irish actress who played Ophelia. His unrequited passion found an outlet in 1830 in the extraordinary, programmatic *Symphonie fantastique*, subtitled "Episodes in the life of an artist". In the first three of its five movements, "the beloved" appears in various transformations as a melodic motif (which Berlioz called the *idée fixe*), whether in "passions and dreams", at a ball, or during a pastoral idyll (which owes much to Beethoven). In the fourth movement, "March to the

Scaffold", the artist dreams that he has murdered his beloved and is being led to the guillotine; in the last, a grotesque witches' sabbath, the beloved has been transformed into a hag, her theme obscenely distorted.

In 1832 Berlioz finally persuaded Harriet Smithson to marry him. But proximity to the Beloved proved less appealing than worship from afar. Although he never divorced Harriet (who died of alcoholism in 1854), he formed a liaison from 1841 onwards with the

*ABOVE: A cartoon of Berlioz conducting,
surrounded by some of the bizarre instruments
he deployed — including a cannon!*

*ABOVE: Harriet Smithson as Ophelia. Berlioz
became obsessed with her and eventually
married her, with disastrous consequences.*

Life and works

NATIONALITY: French

BORN: La-Côte-Saint-André, near Grenoble, 1803; **DIED:** Paris, 1869

SPECIALIST GENRES: Romantic orchestral and choral works, large-scale opera.

MAJOR WORKS: *Symphonie fantastique* (1830); *Harold en Italie* (1834); *Grande messe des morts* (1837); *Roméo et Juliette* (1838–9); overtures *Le corsaire* (1831) and *Le carnaval romain* (1844); *La damnation de Faust* (1846); *Te Deum* (1849); *Les Troyens* (1856–8).

singer Marie Recio, who later became his second wife.

During the 1830s Berlioz produced some of his finest works, including the symphony with obbligato viola, *Harold en Italie*. This work was commissioned by Paganini, who paid the struggling composer 20,000 francs for the piece, although he never played the solo part because he said it did not adequately display his talents as a virtuoso.

Large-scale works

Berlioz's predilection for the monumental led him to compose enormous scores for huge orchestral forces (although he himself played only the guitar, he was a master of orchestration and wrote an influential treatise on the subject). His colossal works for chorus and orchestra included a Requiem (1837), the dramatic symphony *Roméo et Juliette* (1838–9), the *Grande symphonie funèbre et triomphale* (1840), and the

operas *Benvenuto Cellini* (1834–7), and *Les Troyens* (*The Trojans*, 1856–8).

Berlioz never had enough money. He was forced to supplement his income by working as a music critic, and by touring Europe as a conductor. In 1846 *La damnation de Faust*, a "dramatic cantata" based on the play by Goethe – whom Berlioz declared, together with Shakespeare, the guiding influence of his life – failed to attract attention in Paris, though it scored a great success in Russia. But his oratorio *L'enfance du Christ* (*The Childhood of Christ*) achieved a modest success in 1854, and the exquisite "Shepherds' Farewell" scene has always remained a popular favourite.

Les Troyens finally reached the stage in 1863, when the second part only, *Les Troyens à Carthage*, was performed in Paris. Its failure broke Berlioz's heart, and his last years were clouded by depression and ill-health. (The opera was not staged in its entirety in French until 1969.) In the early 1860s he completed his last work, the

sparkling Shakespearean opera *Béatrice et Bénédict*, but thereafter wrote little until his death.

Re-evaluation

While his large-scale works are still performed relatively infrequently because they are so expensive to mount, the *Symphonie fantastique* and the concert overtures (especially *Les francs-juges*, the Byronic *Le corsaire* and *Le carnaval romain*) have remained popular, as has the delicately scored orchestral song-cycle, *Les nuits d'été* (*Summer Nights*, 1841), based on a series of poems by Théophile Gautier.

Berlioz is still perceived as an "oddball" composer, and his originality has been derided as incompetence. But the persuasive advocacy of writers such as David Cairns and conductors such as Colin Davis and Roger Norrington have restored some previously neglected masterpieces, such as *Les Troyens*, to the repertoire, and affirmed Berlioz's importance as one of the foremost 19th-century composers.

ABOVE: Caricature of Berlioz conducting, by Georges Tiret-Bognet (born 1855).

Felix Mendelssohn

A romantic who felt at ease within the mould of classicism.

PABLO CASALS (1876–1973)

Felix Mendelssohn was born into a wealthy and cultured Jewish family. His grandfather Moses was a liberal philosopher, and his father, Abraham, a prominent banker who fled from Hamburg (where Felix and his sister Fanny were born) to Berlin, to escape Napoleon's marauding troops. The Mendelssohn family enjoyed a privileged middle-class existence in Berlin, where the children (two girls and two boys) were baptized as Christians, and their father became a town councillor.

At the family home, the young Felix encountered many well-known philosophers, actors, artists, writers and musicians, and showed precocious talent in music, drawing and poetry. By the age of 13 he was already an accomplished composer, and in 1821 he was introduced by his teacher Karl Zelter to Goethe. A strong friendship

ABOVE: Felix Mendelssohn (1809–47), painted by Gustav Zerner.

based on shared interests developed between the literary giant (then aged 70) and the talented boy. Mendelssohn dedicated his Third Piano Quartet to Goethe, who greatly appreciated the young man's frequent visits to his home in Weimar.

Musical impressions

Mendelssohn travelled a great deal as a young man, visiting Switzerland, Italy and Britain. He responded passionately both to literature and to impressions of people and landscapes encountered on his travels, both of which influenced his essays in the Classical musical forms of his day — symphony, overture, concerto, sonata and quartet. At the age of 16 he composed the brilliant Octet for strings, whose scherzo was inspired by the "Witches' Sabbath" scene in Goethe's *Faust*; two early overtures were inspired

LEFT: The Leipzig Conservatory of Music, founded by Mendelssohn in 1843.

RIGHT:

The autograph score of the first of Mendelssohn's six Songs Without Words *for piano (1829).*

respectively by Shakespeare (*A
Midsummer Night's Dream*) and Goethe
(*Calm Sea and Prosperous Voyage*). Two
of his five mature symphonies – the
Scottish (No. 3, dedicated to Queen
Victoria) and the *Italian* (No. 4) –
reflect his impressions of landscapes.
His 1829 tour of Scotland also inspired
the famous *Hebrides* overture, written
after a visit to Fingal's Cave on the Isle
of Staffa.

Classical style

In Mendelssohn's two piano concertos,
the much-loved Violin Concerto and
the *Scottish* Symphony, he made
original experiments in form, such as
the recycling of thematic material and
the linking of movements, which later
became a feature of much Romantic
music. Yet, for all his Romantic traits,
he was a worthy successor to
Beethoven and Schubert in his
fluent handling of musical material.
Schumann called him "the Mozart of
the 19th century – the one who sees

most clearly through the contradictions
of the period and for the first time
reconciles them".

Mendelssohn's musical legacy

Through his tireless work as
adminstrator and conductor, especially
of the Lower Rhine Music Festival in
Düsseldorf and the Leipzig Gewandhaus
Orchestra, Mendelssohn was responsible
for resurrecting buried treasures such
as Bach's Passions and B minor Mass,
and Handel's oratorios (on which he
modelled his own *St Paul* and *Elijah*).
He also helped to establish the role of
the conductor, and raise standards of
choral and orchestral performance.

In addition, Mendelssohn promoted
the careers of other composers and
performers, including Robert and
Clara Schumann, Berlioz, the violinists
Joseph Joachim, Ferdinand David
(1810–73) and Henri Vieuxtemps
(1820–81), and the pianist and
composer Anton Rubinstein
(1829–94). Many of his protégés
were invited by Mendelssohn to join
the staff of the newly opened Leipzig
Conservatory (inaugurated in 1843),
which under his direction became one
of the most respected musical
institutions in Europe.

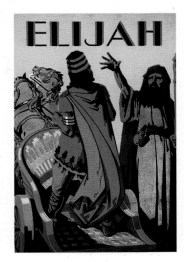

*ABOVE: An Art Deco programme cover for
a dramatized pageant performance in
London in 1936 of the oratorio* Elijah
by Mendelssohn.

In 1837 he married Cécile
Jeanrenaud, daughter of a Lutheran
pastor. They had five children and their
marriage was happy but all too short:
Mendelssohn died of overwork and
grief in November 1847, aged only 38,
shortly after hearing of the death of his
beloved sister Fanny.

ABOVE: An annotated drawing made by Mendelssohn during his 1829 tour of Scotland.

Frédéric Chopin

*After playing Chopin, I feel as if I had been weeping over sins that I had never committed,
and mourning over tragedies that were not my own.*

OSCAR WILDE (1854–1900), "THE CRITIC AS ARTIST"

Chopin epitomizes the figure of the "Romantic artist": withdrawn, temperamental, talented and doomed to a premature death from tuberculosis. Like Paganini, he was both composer and performer (although his concert-giving was actually very limited), but his music established the piano as the 19th century's most popular instrument. He was also an important figure in the early nationalist movement, drawing inspiration from the folk idioms of his native Poland.

Born of mixed French and Polish parentage, Chopin began to compose before he was seven, and made his first public appearances as a pianist. On leaving school at 16 he enrolled at the Warsaw Conservatory, where he began to compose in earnest, and on graduating three years later he decided to seek his fortune abroad. In August

ABOVE: Frédéric Chopin (1810–49), painted by Albert Graefle.

1829 he made his debut in Vienna, playing two of his own piano works, including the set of Variations, Op. 2, whose publication Robert Schumann greeted with the immortal words, "Hats off, gentlemen, a genius!"

Polish themes

Chopin then returned to Warsaw, intending to leave soon afterwards on a European concert tour, but the tour was postponed owing to the volatile political situation and, meanwhile, Chopin fell in love. While he dallied in Warsaw, unwilling to leave, he worked simultaneously on two piano concertos. From his early youth he had been fascinated by the rhythms and melodic vitality of Polish folk music, and the finales of both concertos are strongly influenced by Polish dances — particularly the mazurka. After giving their premières with great success,

LEFT: An artist's impression of Chopin at the piano, composing his Preludes.

RIGHT: The monastery of Valldemosa on the island of Majorca, where Chopin and George Sand took refuge in 1838.

Chopin left Poland for Paris. On the way, he composed the great *Revolutionary* Study, in response to the devastating news that the Russians had captured Warsaw.

Paris

Chopin gave his first concert in Paris in February 1832. Although he was not a great success with the public, he was introduced to Parisian *salon* society, where his music was a triumph. From then onwards – although he rarely played in public – he became an instant celebrity. He was a sought-after teacher, consorted with the wealthy and powerful, and enjoyed the friendship of fellow composers (Liszt, Berlioz, Bellini and Meyerbeer), writers such as Heinrich Heine and Honoré de Balzac, and artists such as Eugène Delacroix.

Chopin also found lovers in this talented milieu – first the aristocratic singer Delfina Potocka, and then the writer Aurore Dudevant (George Sand), whom he met in 1836 at the home of Liszt's mistress. Their intense relationship lasted for nine years. They

ABOVE: Chopin playing the piano in Prince Radziwill's salon in Paris, painted in 1887 by Hendrik Siemiradzki.

spent the winter of 1838 in Majorca, hoping to reap the benefits of peace and a warm climate; but inclement weather and local hostility forced them to take refuge in the derelict monastery of Valldemosa. There Chopin finished his Twenty-four Preludes and other works, including the C sharp minor Scherzo. From then on he spent the winters in Paris and the summers at George Sand's country estate, but the affair finally fizzled out in 1847. By this time Chopin was seriously ill with consumption.

In 1848, Chopin was persuaded to visit England, where he played privately for fashionable social occasions. His last public appearance was at a charity concert for the benefit of Polish refugees. He died at his Paris home on 17 October 1849.

Chopin's music

Apart from the concertos and a handful of pieces for cello and flute, Chopin's output is all for solo piano. He borrowed the Irish composer John Field's new form, the nocturne, and raised it to fresh heights of subtle expression. His *études*, preludes, waltzes, impromptus and mazurkas were written to exploit and develop

piano technique; while the later polonaises, the *fantaisies*, the scherzos, ballades, the Barcarolle and the two sonatas, were all virtuoso works.

Contemporaries praised the "exquisite delicacy and liquid mellowness" of his tone, and the "pearly roundness of his passages of rapid articulation". These are still the hallmarks of great Chopin interpretation.

ABOVE: The writer Aurore Dudevant, alias George Sand (1804–76), Chopin's lover during the 1840s.

🎼 Life and works

NATIONALITY: Polish

BORN: Zelazowa Wola, near Warsaw, 1810;
DIED: Paris, 1849

SPECIALIST GENRES: Solo piano music.

MAJOR WORKS: Two piano concertos; three sonatas; four scherzos; 25 preludes; 27 *études*; 19 nocturnes; 44 waltzes; ten polonaises; 56 mazurkas; four ballades.

Robert Schumann

To me, Schumann's memory is holy.
The noble, pure artist forever remains my ideal.

JOHANNES BRAHMS (1833–97)

Just as Mozart and Beethoven dominated the musical scene in the late 18th and early 19th centuries, Mendelssohn and Schumann were the standard-bearers until 1850. Schumann's personality and career exemplify musical Romanticism: his moody nature, fluctuating between exuberance and deep depression; his prolonged struggle to win the hand of his adored Clara; his receptiveness to literary stimuli, his obsession with numerology and secret ciphers, and finally his collapse into madness and early death, possibly as a result of syphilis (which, together with tuberculosis, put a premature end to many a flourishing Romantic talent).

Literary influences

Schumann was the youngest child of a bookseller, whose interest in literature

ABOVE: Robert Schumann (1810–56), painted by Gustav Zerner.

he clearly inherited. While still a schoolboy he began to compose music, and also to write articles and drama. He formed a society for the study of German literature, and in the novels of Jean Paul (pseudonym of Johann Paul Richter, 1763–1825) he found a role model for the two conflicting sides of his own personality, which he later characterized as Florestan (extrovert and impetuous) and Eusebius (dreamy, melancholic, introverted).

While studying law in Leipzig he began to take piano lessons with Friedrich Wieck, whose nine-year-old daughter Clara was showing extraordinarily precocious talent as a pianist. By now Schumann had decided to follow a career in music, but a hand injury (possibly a result of muscular weakness caused by mercury treatment

ABOVE: The market-place at Zwickau, where Schumann was born.

ABOVE: Schumann's study at his home in Zwickau.

for syphilis) put paid to his hopes of becoming a concert pianist. Instead, he decided to concentrate on composition and criticism.

Early works

By 1832 Schumann had published two major piano pieces: the *Abegg* Variations, based on a waltz theme derived from the name of a girl who had taken his fancy, and *Papillons* (*Butterflies*), a set of pieces linked by events at a masked ball described in a novel by Jean Paul. He also began work on a symphony.

In 1834 he founded the influential music periodical *Neue Leipziger Zeitschrift für Musik*, which he used to promote new musical talent, including Brahms and Chopin. He also used its pages to fight artistic philistinism by way of an imaginary society, the Davidsbund, or "League of David" (named after the vanquisher of

ABOVE: A romantic lithograph of Schumann composing his song-cycle Dichterliebe (A Poet's Love).

Goliath), whose members were given fanciful names: Schumann himself was either Florestan or Eusebius; Clara Wieck was Chiara or Chiarina; her father was Master Raro, and Mendelssohn was Felix Meritis. These names appeared in Schumann's set of 18 "characteristic pieces" for piano, *Davidsbündlertanze* (*Dances of the League of David*, 1837).

Marriage to Clara

In 1834 Schumann fell in love with Ernestine von Fricken, to whom he became secretly engaged (and for whom he wrote the set of piano pieces later titled *Carnaval*). When he discovered that she was only the illegitimate daughter of a Baron, he broke off the engagement and

RIGHT: Schumann composing at his piano. He had hoped to be a pianist, but was overshadowed by his more accomplished wife, Clara.

ABOVE: Clara and Robert Schumann. Their marriage in 1840 marked the beginning of a partnership that was rare for its time.

which overshadowed his own reputation as a composer), Clara stimulated her husband's creative imagination, acting as muse, confidant and critic.

Productive years

From 1840 onwards, almost in regular annual cycles, Schumann poured out song-cycles – including *Myrthen* (*Bridal Wreath*), his wedding present to Clara, *Liederkreis* ("song-cycle"), *Frauenliebe und -leben* (*Woman's Love and Life*), and *Dichterliebe* (*A Poet's Love*) – chamber music (including a piano quartet and quintet, and three piano trios), and a body of piano music unsurpassed by any other contemporary composer. It was Clara who encouraged Robert to try his hand at larger-scale works. These included concertos for piano (the popular A minor Concerto was written for her), violin and cello; four symphonies, and other symphonic works including the exuberant *Konzertstück* for four horns and orchestra and the *Manfred* overture, inspired by Byron.

Schumann's orchestral music has been criticized for heavy-handed orchestration (partly the result of his

ABOVE: Clara Schumann (1819–96), photographed in middle age. She outlived her husband by 40 years.

transferred his affections to Clara Wieck, by now a delicate, dark-haired beauty of 15. Clara's father, who guarded his daughter jealously, was furious, and forbade Schumann to contact Clara. Then began an acrimonious six-year battle between Wieck – who made outrageous allegations against Schumann's character – and the lovers. Finally, in 1840, a court ruling paved the way for Schumann's marriage to Clara, which took place on 12 September.

Thus began one of the most remarkable musical marriages –

a partnership far ahead of its time – in which both husband and wife tried to combine family life with successful, independent careers. Clara Schumann (1819–96) was one of the most extraordinary women of her time. Her fragile appearance belied a steely inner strength, which enabled her to continue her demanding schedule of concert appearances all over Europe (she was one of the finest pianists of her age) while also coping with repeated pregnancies and child-rearing. While the marriage was not without its strains (Schumann resented his wife's success,

ABOVE: *An illustration to "Du bist wie eine Blume" ("You are Like a Flower") from* Myrthen, *Schumann's wedding present to Clara.*

Mörike (1804–75) and Joseph von Eichendorff (1788–1857), but his settings of Heinrich Heine (1797–1856), particularly the *Dichterliebe* cycle and some of the *Romanzen und Balladen*, are unsurpassed for their subtlety and lyricism.

Final years

In 1843 the Schumanns were reconciled with Friedrich Wieck, no doubt anxious to see his first grandchild. After a concert tour of Russia the following year they moved from Leipzig to Dresden. Schumann had always been prone to fits of deep depression and ill-health, and in 1846 he was so beset by nerves and chronic illness that he composed very little. By 1849 (when a revolutionary insurrection forced the family temporarily to flee Dresden), Schumann was becoming disillusioned by his failure to find a real job, and in 1850 he accepted an offer to become municipal music director in Düsseldorf.

His years in Düsseldorf were marked by failing health and mental instability, which adversely affected his abilities as

ABOVE: *An illustration to Schumann's song "Der Nussbaum" ("The Walnut Tree"), No. 3 in the song-cycle* Myrthen.

own ineptitude as a conductor), but any defects are amply compensated for by its melodic charm and ingenious construction. Schumann's innovations include the recurring use of motto themes and other cyclical devices: in the D minor Symphony (No. 4), he directed that the thematically linked movements should be played without a break.

His large-scale vocal works include the secular oratorio *Das Paradies und die Peri* (1843), one opera, *Genoveva* (1850) and choral music including *Scenes from Goethe's "Faust"* (1853). As a composer of songs and piano music, he proved himself a worthy successor to Schubert. His piano music encapsulates an enigmatic private world, full of literary and musical allusions, autobiographical references and cryptograms: many of the piano pieces are built around references to Clara, such as the musical equivalents of the letters of her name. His songs include settings of Goethe, Adelbert von Chamisso (1781–1838), Eduard

ABOVE: *A page from the autograph manuscript of Schumann's Piano Sonata No. 3 in F minor, Op. 14, signed by the composer.*

a conductor and caused increasing problems with his employers. He became obsessed with phenomena such as table-turning, and suffered aural and cerebral disturbances. Among the highlights of his later years were his meetings with the young Johannes Brahms, whom Schumann hailed in his magazine as a musician of the future, and the violinist Joachim, for whom Schumann wrote his Fantaisie for violin and orchestra and the Violin Concerto. Among his last compositions were the charming *Phantasiestücke* (*Fairy-tales*, 1849) for clarinet, viola and piano, and five Romances (1853) for cello and piano.

Schumann's mental faculties finally gave way completely in February 1854, and he began to experience hallucinations. After a failed suicide attempt, he was committed to an asylum. During the two and a half years in which he was incarcerated there, he was not allowed to see Clara. She was finally summoned to his bedside two days before his death on 29 July 1856.

Franz Liszt

I have not seen any musician in whom musical feeling ran, as in Liszt,
into the very tips of the fingers and there streamed out immediately.

FELIX MENDELSSOHN (1809–47)

As a composer, Liszt tends to stand on the sidelines of music history, partly because he does not fall neatly into the German symphonic tradition, stretching from Beethoven and Schubert, through Schumann and Mendelssohn, to Brahms and Bruckner. But his influence on 19th-century music was enormous: he was a superlative performer (the pianistic equivalent of Paganini), an outstanding teacher, and a dedicated champion of the "music of the future", expressed both in his own innovative and highly individual work, and in his promotion of Wagner.

Liszt was the son of an official at the Hungarian court of Haydn's employer, Prince Nikolaus Esterházy. He showed prodigious talent as a pianist, giving his first piano recital at the age of nine, and Prince Nikolaus funded his education in Vienna, where he moved from an early age in aristocratic circles.

ABOVE: A portrait of Franz Liszt in old age, when he styled himself the "abbé Liszt" (Liszt the abbot).

Paris

In the 1820s the flamboyant young virtuoso began to cause a sensation in Paris (where his family moved) and London, where he played for King George IV. Back in Paris in the early 1830s he met Berlioz and Paganini, and made piano transcriptions of some of their works, including Paganini's Caprices, which in Liszt's version became the *Grandes études de Paganini*. He was also greatly influenced by Chopin's Romantic style.

In 1834 he began a liaison with the Countess Marie d'Agoult, which produced three children (their second daughter Cosima later married Wagner). They began a peripatetic existence in Switzerland and Italy, during which time Liszt compiled his *Années de pèlerinage* (*Years of Pilgrimage*) for piano, and the *Album d'un voyageur*.

LEFT: Liszt's summer residence on the corner of the Ilm Park in Weimar.

RIGHT: Title page of the score of Liszt's Hungarian Rhapsody No. 11.

EDITION SCHOTT
EINZEL-AUSGABE
~ 06427 ~
FR. LISZT
UNGARISCHE RHAPSODIE No. 11
NEU-AUSGABE VON
EUGEN D'ALBERT
KLAVIER
Jede Nummer 30 Pfennig

By 1839 the relationship was under strain, and Liszt resumed his touring career as a virtuoso. He and the countess finally separated in 1844, and Liszt began a period of wild womanizing, which contrasted oddly with his secret desire to become a priest. In 1848 he became music director to the ducal court at Weimar, where he eventually settled with his new companion, Princess Carolyne Sayn-Wittgenstein (who was trying to obtain a divorce from her husband). She shared Liszt's interest in religion and mysticism, and encouraged him to write his most ambitious works.

Weimar

The Weimar years (1848–59) represent the zenith of Liszt's composing career. Most of his major works date from this period. They include two pieces inspired by the Faust legend – the *Faust* Symphony (based on Goethe) and

ABOVE: Liszt playing at a Parisian salon in 1840, painted by Joseph Danhauser. Listening (from left to right) are Alexandre Dumas, Victor Hugo, George Sand, Niccolò Paganini, Gioacchino Rossini and Countess Marie d'Agoult, Liszt's mistress.

 Life and works

NATIONALITY: Hungarian

BORN: Raiding, 1811; DIED: Bayreuth, 1886

SPECIALIST GENRES: Tone-poems, programme symphonies, piano works.

MAJOR WORKS: *Années de pèlerinage* (1836–77); 19 *Hungarian Rhapsodies* (1846–85); piano concertos; *Funérailles* for solo piano (1849); tone-poems *Mazeppa, Tasso, Les préludes* and *Orpheus* (1851–4); Piano Sonata in B minor (1853); *Dante* Symphony (1856); *Faust* Symphony (1857); *Mephisto Waltz* No. 1 (1861).

Episodes from Lenau's "Faust" – the *Dante* Symphony; over a dozen symphonic poems inspired by literary or pictorial models, including *Tasso, Les préludes* (after a poem by Alphonse de Lamartine), *Mazeppa, Hamlet* and *Hunnenschlacht (The Battle of the Huns)*; the E flat Piano Concerto, the *Totentanz (Dance of Death)* for piano and orchestra, and piano works including the Transcendental Studies, the B minor Sonata, many of the Hungarian Rhapsodies, and the *Harmonies poétiques et religieuses*. In addition, Liszt championed works by other up-and-coming composers, giving the premières of operas by Wagner, Schumann, Berlioz, Verdi and Donizetti, among others. During his tenure, Weimar became known as the haven of the "New German School".

Holy orders

By 1860, however, Liszt had fallen out with conservative Weimar society (which disapproved of his open affair with Carolyne Sayn-Wittgenstein, and his promotion of "avant-garde" music).

He spent most of his later life in Rome, separated from the princess (who was never granted her divorce), and in 1865 he took minor holy orders.

A historian who saw him at the time described him as "Mephistopheles disguised as an abbé": his "diabolical" qualities, like Paganini's, were enhanced by his excessively tall, thin appearance, with long hair, originally blond, now white. He was still much sought-after as a teacher.

Liszt's later compositions are mostly sacred, and include the oratorios *Die Legende von der heilige Elisabeth (Legend of St Elisabeth*, 1857–62) and *Christus* (1862–7). However, they also include the Second and Third *Mephisto Waltzes*, one for orchestra (1880) and one for piano (1883). Among his last works – which became increasingly impressionistic in style – was *La lugubre gondola*, inspired by a premonition of his son-in-law Richard Wagner's death in Venice in 1882. Liszt himself died of pneumonia four years later in Bayreuth, having travelled there to attend the music festival.

Charles Gounod

A man has only a certain number of virtues, and all of Gounod's are concentrated on his art.

GEORGES BIZET (1838–75)

Gounod is remembered today chiefly for his opera *Faust*, based on Goethe's drama; and for the song "Ave Maria", an arrangement of his Meditation for violin on Bach's Prelude No. 1 in C. In fact, he was a prolific composer whose music was influential in both France and England.

Gounod's father was a painter and his mother a pianist. Like Berlioz, he studied at the Paris Conservatoire, winning the Prix de Rome in 1839. In Italy he fell under the spell of 16th-century polyphonic music, and began to write sacred music of his own (he also seriously considered becoming a priest). But he also met two influential women – the singer Pauline Viardot-Garcia (1821–1910), who introduced Gounod to the theatrical world, and Fanny Hensel (1805–47), who introduced him to her brother Felix Mendelssohn.

ABOVE: A scene from Goethe's Faust *– Faust tempted by Mephistopheles, painted in the mid 1820s by Eugène Delacroix.*

ABOVE: Charles Gounod (1818–93). His operas influenced Bizet and Tchaikovsky.

In 1843 Gounod visited the Mendelssohns in Leipzig, where he heard the famous Gewandhaus Orchestra, and music by Bach (then rarely performed).

Opera

On returning to Paris Gounod began to write grand operas in the currently fashionable style of Meyerbeer, together with elaborate masses and other church music. His opera *Faust* was performed at the Théâtre-Lyrique in 1859, and was an instant success: Gounod's gift for memorable tunes (such as the "Soldier's Chorus" and Marguerite's "Jewel Song"), and his subtle musical characterization of the doomed lovers, appealed to a Parisian

audience growing weary of Meyerbeerian bombast. None of his other operas (even *Roméo et Juliette*, 1867) was ever quite as successful.

England

Between 1870 and 1875 Gounod took refuge from the Franco-Prussian War in England, where his music appealed to Victorian sentimentality. Here, he acquired a ferocious English mistress, Georgina Weldon (he was chronically unfaithful), and founded the Gounod Choir, which eventually became the Royal Choral Society. In the 1880s he was preoccupied with composing oratorios (two of which were written for the Birmingham and Norwich festivals). Apart from the popular *Petite symphonie* for 10 wind instruments (1885), few of his later works have survived the test of time.

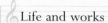

Life and works

NATIONALITY: French

BORN: Paris, 1818;
DIED: Paris, 1893

SPECIALIST GENRES: French grand opera, oratorios.

MAJOR WORKS: *Faust* (1859); *Roméo et Juliette* (1867); *La rédemption* (1881); *Mors et vita* (1884).

Georges Bizet

*I am not made for the symphony; I need the theatre,
I can do nothing without it.*

BIZET

*ABOVE: Georges Bizet (1838–75), composer
of the highly popular opera* Carmen, *the
tragic story of the life, loves and death of a
gypsy. Bizet wrote* Carmen *towards the end
of his short life.*

Bizet's fame rests largely on just one
work – the opera *Carmen* – but
although his output was primarily
operatic, several of his instrumental
works, particularly the early
Symphony in C, the suite *Jeux
d'enfants* (*Children's Games*) and
the incidental music to Alphonse
Daudet's play *L'Arlésienne* (*The
Girl from Arles*), have found a
regular place in the repertoire.

Bizet studied at the Paris
Conservatoire, winning many
prizes, including the coveted Prix
de Rome in 1857. Among his
teachers was the opera composer
Jacques Halévy, whose daughter he
later married. The coolly classical
Symphony in C was written at the age
of 17, and in 1857 Bizet's one-act
opera *Le docteur miracle* won joint first
prize in a composition competition.
He spent the years 1858–60 in Rome,
where he picked up the chronic throat
complaint which eventually killed him.

Life and works

NATIONALITY: French

BORN: Paris, 1838;
DIED: Bougival, 1875

SPECIALIST GENRES: Opera.

MAJOR WORKS: Symphony
in C (1855); *Les pêcheurs de
perles* (1863); *Jeux d'enfants*
(1871); *Carmen* (1874).

Early set-backs
In 1863 Bizet's first important opera,
Les pêcheurs de perles (*The Pearl-fishers*),
was put on at the Théâtre-Lyrique in
Paris. It failed, although the famous
duet from Act 1, "Au fond du temple
saint", has always been a popular
favourite. Afterwards Bizet was obliged
to take up hack work from publishers
in order to survive financially.
Meanwhile he worked on several more
operatic projects, none of which
achieved success. The colourful
Provençal background of Daudet's play
L'Arlésienne, for which Bizet provided

incidental music in 1872, inspired him
to find his true métier, and it was the
similarly exotic setting and tragic
story of Prosper Mérimée's *Carmen*
which finally fired his imagination.

Carmen
Bizet's great opera was produced
at the Opéra-Comique on 3 March
1875. It met with initial hostility,
but within the next four years
critics and audiences had come to
appreciate the subtlety, power and
originality of this vibrant score,
and it was being performed all over
Europe and in America. Bizet did not
live to see its success. He died of a
heart attack brought on by rheumatic
fever on the night of its 33rd
performance, just after the singer
playing Carmen had fainted during the
famous card-scene in which the gypsy
heroine foretells her own death.

*ABOVE: Célestine Galli-Marié, the first
Carmen, who fainted on stage in the fortune-
telling scene on the night Bizet died.*

Other Composers of the Era

Sounds overflow the listener's brain
So sweet, that joy is almost pain.

PERCY BYSSHE SHELLEY (1792–1822)

Although the main focus of early Romantic opera lay in Italy, France did not lag far behind. One of the most influential figures was Luigi Cherubini (1760–1842), who straddled the transitional period between Classicism and Romanticism. He began his career in his native Italy, where several of his early operas were produced, and then settled in Paris just before the Revolution. During the early Napoleonic era, Cherubini produced his most influential operas in Paris, including *Médée* (*Medea*, 1797), *Les deux journées* (*The Two Days*, also known as *The Water-carrier*, 1800) and *Anacréon* (1803). He then fell out with Napoleon, and in 1805 went to Vienna, where he met Haydn and Beethoven

ABOVE: *Luigi Cherubini (1760–1842), in front of an Italian painting. This portrait was done in the year of his death by Ingres.*

ABOVE: *Daniel-François-Esprit Auber (1782–1871), a pupil of Cherubini and a successful opera composer.*

(whose *Fidelio* owes much to *The Water-carrier*). In 1816 Cherubini became a professor (later, from 1822, director) of the Paris Conservatoire, where his influence as a teacher was far-reaching.

Among Cherubini's pupils was Daniel Auber (1782–1871), who in 1842 succeeded his teacher as director of the Paris Conservatoire. He wrote nearly 50 operas, many in collaboration with the dramatist Eugène Scribe, of which the most famous are *La muette de Portici* (*The Dumb Girl of Portici*, 1828, which ends with a dramatic earthquake), *Fra diavolo* (*Brother Devil*, 1830), *Le domino noir* (*The Black Mask*, 1837) and *Manon Lescaut* (1856, a subject later tackled by Massenet and Puccini).

Bizet's teacher, Jacques Halévy (1799–1862), was another pupil of

ABOVE: *Costume designs for an 1827 German production of Daniel Auber's opera* Le maçon (The Mason), *a musical drama written in the style of French* opéra comique.

Cherubini and also taught at the Paris Conservatoire from 1827 onwards. He was the principal singing coach at the Paris Opéra, 1829–45. Of his 30 or so operas, only *La Juive* (*The Jewess*, 1835) is occasionally revived.

Opera in Germany

Several German contemporaries of Weber advanced the cause of German Romantic opera, including Albert Lortzing (1801–51), one of the few composers who actually starved to death (he needed money so badly that he sold the valuable copyrights in his successful operas for a pittance). These included *Zar und Zimmermann* (*Tsar and Carpenter*, 1837), *Der Wildschütz* (*The Poacher*, 1842) and *Undine* (1845), based on Friedrich la Motte Fouqué's Romantic fairy-tale of 1811. This story had previously been adapted by the composer and writer Ernst Theodore Amadeus Hoffmann (1776–1822) for his 1816 opera of the same name.

Heinrich August Marschner (1795–1861), Weber's co-conductor at Dresden in the 1820s, was also influenced by the Romanticism of Hoffmann. He fared better than Lortzing, although his earlier operas — including the Gothic horror opera *Der Vampyr* (Leipzig, 1828), *Der Templar und die Jüdin* (*The Templar and the Jewess*, based on Scott's *Ivanhoe*, 1828) and *Hans Heiling* (Berlin, 1833) — achieved far greater success than his later works. He stands midway between Weber and Wagner as a pioneer of German Romantic opera.

Instrumental music

In the instrumental field, the violinist, conductor and composer Louis Spohr (1784–1859) scored great success in Germany, Vienna (where he led the orchestra at the Theater an der Wien) and London, where there was a considerable vogue for his work. From 1822 he was court conductor and later music director at the German court of Hesse-Kassel. He was one of the first conductors to use a baton. Spohr's operas have not survived, but his instrumental pieces are still played. They include 10 symphonies, 18 violin

concertos, 4 clarinet concertos, and a quantity of chamber music, including string quartets and quintets, an octet for strings and wind, a fine nonet for strings and wind, and a quintet for piano and wind.

His Swedish contemporary Franz Berwald (1796–1868) was an amateur composer. He ran an orthopaedic institute in Berlin, and then managed a glassworks in Sweden, before being appointed Professor of Composition at the Swedish Royal Academy of Music shortly before his death. Berwald is now remembered for his *Symphonie singulière* (No. 3, 1845), and for his charming *Grand septet* in B flat for wind and strings.

The Irish composer John Field (1782–1837) studied with Clementi in London, and went on to enjoy a successful European career as a virtuoso pianist, from his base in St Petersburg. He invented the short piano piece known as the "nocturne", a form and style borrowed by Chopin. Field's 19 examples are still in the solo piano repertoire.

The Rise
✦ of ✦
Nationalism

A traditional Catalan festival held on Ash Wednesday to celebrate the beginning of Lent, painted in 1907 by Xavier Nogues (1873–1940).

The Nationalist Movement

The art of music above all other arts is the expression of the soul of a nation.

RALPH VAUGHAN WILLIAMS (1872–1958)

Up to the 19th century, music had been perceived as a common international language. Italian opera held sway in all European countries, as popular in Vienna, Stockholm, Madrid or London as in Venice or Rome; while the German symphonic style of Haydn, Mozart and Beethoven was adopted and copied by all European composers of their time. Only towards the middle of the 19th century did composers start to become aware of cultural differences between nations, an awareness prompted partly by political events, and partly through the Romantic cult of individualism, celebrating the unique qualities of both individuals and nations.

Revolutions of 1848

The nationalist movement took root in central Europe, where in the 1830s a wave of nationalist sentiment swept through Germany, Poland, Belgium and northern Italy (at that time ruled

ABOVE: A Bohemian Landscape with Shepherds, *painted in 1841 by Ludwig Richter.*

by Austria). Over the next decade, the desire of autonomous states for political independence from the mighty empires that ruled them coincided with the democratic urge to replace monarchies with republican governments more in tune with the needs of ordinary citizens. This

unstoppable force flared into violence in the year 1848, when patriotic sentiment and revolutionary fervour spread across France, Italy, Germany and central Europe. Although the revolutions failed, and autocratic rule tottered on in some countries until World War I, a new spirit of

LEFT: The Old Market-place in Prague, painted in 1865.

RIGHT: Mlle Eglantine's Dancing Girls — *a poster of the Belle Epoque in Paris, by Henri de Toulouse-Lautrec (1864–1901).*

nationalistic patriotism informed European politics from this time onwards, spreading into culture and the arts.

Folk music

In music, this patriotic fervour encouraged composers to seek inspiration in their national roots, particularly folk culture (often viciously suppressed by the ruling authorities). In beleaguered Poland, carved up by neighbouring powers after the Congress of Vienna, Chopin indicated his revolutionary sympathies by his use of Polish folk dances, especially the polonaise and the mazurka.

The nationalist movement was particularly strong in Russia (where Italian music – and Italian composers – had long reigned supreme at the cosmopolitan court in St Petersburg). Glinka was the first composer to draw inspiration from the distinctive melodic patterns and rhythms of Russian folk songs and dances, and his example was taken up with proselytizing zeal by Balakirev and his disciples, known as "The Mighty Handful", or "The Five". They in turn influenced Tchaikovsky, whose music, while not consciously "nationalistic", is still recognizably Russian in inspiration, drawing on folk legends and idioms, and epic tales from Russian history.

Landscape and people

The central European areas of Bohemia, Slovakia and Hungary, whose native culture had been suppressed by centuries of foreign domination, were particularly receptive to the new spirit of nationalism. The Bohemian composer Smetana was the first to celebrate the rich history and characteristic landscape of his native land in a series of tone-poems entitled *Má vlast* (*My Homeland*), and in a series

ABOVE: Spanish gypsy flamenco dancers, painted in 1898 by Ricardo Canals y Llambi (1876–1931).

of operas based on Czech subjects, from historical or mythical figures such as Libuše, to contemporary peasant life in *The Bartered Bride*. He in turn

ABOVE: The colourful costumes of 19th-century Russian ballet dancers.

influenced his pupil Dvořák, who effortlessly incorporated Czech song and dance idioms into European symphonic structures.

Nationalism was by no means confined to central Europe. Edvard Grieg, Norway's greatest composer, was trained in the German musical tradition, but his music draws plentifully on the folk idioms which he picked up on walking excursions into the Norwegian mountains.

In Spain, Albéniz and Granados exploited the colourful characteristics of Moorish-derived flamenco in their piano and orchestral works; in Austria, the talented Strauss family turned Vienna into the waltz capital of the world, and in England, then languishing under a dearth of native talent, the quintessentially "English" Savoy Operas of W. S. Gilbert and Arthur Sullivan exploited a rich vein of satirical English humour.

Mikhail Glinka

I should like to unite in legitimate bonds the Russian popular song with the good old Western fugue.

GLINKA

Mikhail Glinka is regarded as the founding father of Russian nationalism in music. A contemporary of the Romantic poet Alexander Pushkin (1799–1837), he spent his early childhood with his grandmother, in whose care he first came into contact with the real music of Russia – the folk songs, pealing bells and ecclesiastical chants which would later inform his own music.

Glinka encountered Western music for the first time in his early teens, after he was sent to school in St Petersburg, where he studied violin and piano (including some lessons with John Field). On leaving school he became a minor civil servant, a job

ABOVE: Mikhail Glinka (1804–57) working on his opera Ruslan and Lyudmila, *painted by Ilya Repin.*

which left him plenty of time to indulge his passion for music as an enthusiastic amateur singer and pianist.

Opera

He began to compose songs and chamber music in the 1820s, but a prolonged trip to Italy in the early 1830s left him with a passionate interest in opera. His own first opera, *A Life for the Tsar* – based on the patriotic story of a heroic Russian peasant who saves the tsar's life at the cost of his own – was written after his return to Russia, and proved hugely successful on its première in 1836.

Glinka found himself acclaimed as Russia's leading composer (although, to be fair, there was little competition), and encouraged by his success he immediately embarked on his next

opera, *Ruslan and Lyudmila*. Unlike his earlier work, *Ruslan* was not well received. Its plot, based on Pushkin's fairy-tale (and involving such staging nightmares as a gigantic talking head), was cumbersome and ill-suited to the stage, and Glinka composed the score piecemeal. But its musical content – an appealing blend of elements drawn from Russian folk music, exotic orientalism and touches of "grotesquerie" – proved a rich legacy for all later Russian composers, as did his enthusiasm for the music of Spain (evinced in his two Spanish Overtures). Although Glinka died relatively young, his influence stretched far into the 20th century.

ABOVE: A cartoon of Mikhail Glinka by V. Samoilov (1853).

Life and works

NATIONALITY: Russian

BORN: Smolensk, 1804; **DIED:** Berlin, 1857

SPECIALIST GENRES: Opera and orchestral works in Russian nationalist style.

MAJOR WORKS: *Ivan Susanin* (*A Life for the Tsar*, 1836); *Ruslan and Lyudmila* (1842); Spanish overtures *Jota Aragonesa* (1845) and *Night in Madrid* (1848).

"The Mighty Handful"

Show me a people who have more songs!
NIKOLAY GOGOL (1809–52), "THE CONTEMPORARY"

This curious crowd of dedicated drinkers, who were largely amateur composers, was given its nickname ("moguchaya kuchka") by the critic Vladimir Stasov in 1867. Their self-styled leader was Balakirev, while Borodin worked as a chemist, Rimsky-Korsakov was a naval officer and César Cui was a military engineer, and the most gifted, Mussorgsky, was a civil servant whom the rest regarded with a certain contempt. Nevertheless, their influence on Russian music in the late 19th century was immense.

Mily Balakirev

Balakirev began piano lessons with his mother as a young child and

became a proficient pianist. While still quite young he came into contact with the music of Mikhail Glinka — one of his own earliest compositions was a piano fantasy on Glinka's opera *A Life for the Tsar*. Glinka imbued Balakirev with a strong sense of the importance of Russian nationalism, especially in music.

In the early 1860s Balakirev began to assemble a small band of like-minded disciples around him, and also played a major role in founding the Free School of Music in St Petersburg (he became its director in 1868). From this period date the beginnings of Balakirev's twin obsessions — collecting Russian folk music from far-flung regions and editing the works of other composers.

Balakirev was prone to fits of chronic illness and depression, and he was never a prolific composer. His single most frequently performed work is the ferociously difficult "oriental fantasy" for piano, *Islamey*. His main reputation was as an uncompromising critic of other composers' works. Tchaikovsky, among others, fell victim to Balakirev's stinging criticisms.

Of Balakirev's disciples, César Cui (1835–1918) was the least important. He wrote some 15 operas and other stage works, all of which have now disappeared from the repertoire.

Life and works

NATIONALITY: Russian

BORN: Nizny-Novgorod, 1837; **DIED:** St Petersburg, 1910

SPECIALIST GENRES: Romantic orchestral and piano works using Russian idioms.

MAJOR WORKS: *Overtures on Russian Themes* (1858, 1864); two symphonies; *Islamey* (1869); many other works for piano; symphonic poem *Tamara* (1882).

ABOVE:
Mily Balakirev (1837–1910), the driving force behind Russian musical nationalism.

RIGHT: The statue of Peter the Great in front of the Cathedral in St Petersburg (1844).

Alexander Borodin

Borodin wrote only one opera, but music from it is still a concert favourite. The illegitimate son of an elderly Russian prince, Borodin was brought up by his gentle, cultured mother, and showed an early interest in music. But his chief love was science, and he became a distinguished professor of chemistry, founding a School of Medicine for Women.

In 1862 Borodin met Balakirev, and immediately began work on a symphony. It was performed in 1867 with great success, and he started work on his second. Shortly afterwards, in 1870, he began work on the opera *Prince Igor*, whose composition dragged on over the next 17 years, and remained unfinished at his death. Although it was subsequently completed by Rimsky-Korsakov, it is rarely performed, but the exotic "Polovtsian Dances" which end Act II (in Rimsky-Korsakov's orchestration) have always been highly popular, as have the Second Symphony in B minor

ABOVE: Alexander Borodin (1833–87), the composer of Prince Igor, *one of the most colourful Russian nationalist operas.*

and the languorous Nocturne from the Second String Quartet. Many of Borodin's most famous tunes formed the basis of the 1953 musical *Kismet*.

Modest Mussorgsky

Arguably the most original composer of "The Five", Mussorgsky was bedevilled by mental instability, exacerbated by his heavy drinking. He showed an early talent for music, becoming a proficient pianist, but was destined for an army career. He completed his training and enlisted in the élite Preobrazhensky Regiment, but resigned his commission within two years. By then he had met Balakirev, with whom he began to study music seriously.

Financial difficulties then forced him to take a job in the civil service, while he continued to struggle with his first opera, *Salammbô*, based on Flaubert's novel. Although he started various projects with great enthusiasm, he finished few of them, and his three great operas — *Boris Godunov*, *Khovanshchina (The Khovansky Affair)* and *Sorochinskaya yarmarka (Sorochintsy Fair)* — were all left incomplete at his death (from alcoholic epilepsy), just after his 42nd birthday. He is also remembered

ABOVE: Russian folk dancers. All five composers in "The Mighty Handful" drew inspiration from their native folk music.

ABOVE: *Modest Petrovich Mussorgsky (1839–81), painted in the year of his death by Ilya Repin.*

and his talent for orchestral colour, combined with exotic, oriental-sounding harmonies, produced many rich and glowing works including the *Capriccio espagnol* (*Spanish Caprice*), the symphonic suite *Sheherazade*, inspired by tales from the *Thousand and One Nights*, and the *Voskresenaya* (*Russian Easter Festival Overture*). This heady blend of Russian folk material and orientalism also informed the scores of many of his 15 operas.

Rimsky-Korsakov devoted as much time to his friends' work as to his own. He was responsible for orchestrating and completing, among others, Borodin's *Prince Igor*, and several works by Mussorgsky, including *Night on the Bare Mountain* and the operas *Boris Godunov* and *Khovanshchina*. Naturally he applied his own ripe orchestral palette to these works, and the modern trend in performance is to return as far as possible to the originals.

ABOVE: *Nikolay Rimsky-Korsakov (1844–1908), one of the most popular Russian composers of his day.*

for his orchestral piece *Ivanova noch na Lisoi gore* (*Night on the Bare Mountain*), inspired by a witches' sabbath, the famous *Kartinki s vistavki* (*Pictures at an Exhibition*) for piano, later orchestrated by Ravel, and his affecting song-cycles *Detskaya* (*The Nursery*, 1870), *Bez solntsa* (*Sunless*, 1874) and *Piesni i plyaski smerti* (*Songs and Dances of Death*, 1875–7).

Nikolay Rimsky-Korsakov

The most active and prominent of "The Mighty Handful" (and the youngest), Rimsky-Korsakov was born into a well-to-do naval and military family. He managed to combine a career as a naval officer with a productive sideline in composition. In 1871 he became professor of composition and instrumentation at the St Petersburg Conservatory.

Like his musical colleagues, he was deeply influenced by the nationalist work of Glinka, and he too fell under Balakirev's spell. Orchestration was Rimsky-Korsakov's great strength,

ABOVE: *Sheherazade and the Sultan — a scene from the Russian Ballet version of Rimsky-Korsakov's* Sheherazade.

Life and works

NATIONALITY: Russian

BORN: Tikhvin, near Novgorod, 1844; **DIED:** Liubensk, near St Petersburg, 1908

SPECIALIST GENRES: Operas based on Russian fairy-tales.

MAJOR WORKS: *Snegurochka* (*The Snow Maiden*, 1881); *Capriccio espagnol* (1887); *Sheherazade* Suite (1888); *Voskresenaya* Overture (1888); *Sadko* (1898); *Tsar Saltan* (1900); *Skazkanie o nevidimom gradie Kitezhe* (*The Tale of the Invisible City of Kitezh*, 1903–4); *Zolotoy Petushok* (*The Golden Cockerel*, 1906–7).

Pyotr Ilyich Tchaikovsky

Music is not illusion, but revelation.

TCHAIKOVSKY (ATTRIB.)

Tchaikovsky could claim to be the world's most popular "classical" composer. His music has always held a special appeal, for its passion, lyricism, extravagant emotionalism, and glowing orchestral colour. It reflects the extremes of temperament of its composer — a moody, melancholy character, prone to fits of depression, but also of heightened optimism.

Throughout his life, Tchaikovsky was torn between his desire for a "normal" family life, and his homosexual nature. This constant, unhappy struggle was reflected in his music, particularly the later symphonies. Although associated with "The Mighty Handful", Tchaikovsky was never a member of that nationalist group. Much of his own work, however, draws on a rich vein of Russian folk culture, which he successfully fused with the Western symphonic tradition. He wrote: "As far as the Russian element in my music is

ABOVE: *Pyotr Ilyich Tchaikovsky (1840–93), arguably the greatest and most popular Russian composer of the 19th century.*

concerned, this is because I grew up in the provinces, imbued from earliest childhood with the indescribable beauty of the characteristic features of Russian folk music."

Early life

Tchaikovsky was the son of a mining engineer, and was born near the Urals. From his delicate, epileptic, French mother he inherited his hypersensitive nature and a tendency to hypochondria.

When he was eight, the family moved to St Petersburg, where Tchaikovsky enrolled in the junior department of the School of Jurisprudence, a training-ground for the civil service. By this time, he had acquired twin younger brothers, Anatoly and Modest. He was exceptionally close to his mother, and her shocking death in a cholera epidemic when Tchaikovsky was 14 was a trauma from which he never really recovered.

LEFT:
Tchaikovsky's father, Ilya Petrovich, with his twin sons Anatoly and Modest.

RIGHT: *The square in front of the Mariinsky Theatre in St Petersburg in 1812.*

Tchaikovsky graduated from the School of Jurisprudence in 1859, but found life in the civil service uncongenial. When a new music conservatory opened in St Petersburg in 1862, he enrolled as a student. He graduated in 1866, and found a job as a harmony teacher at the Moscow Conservatory, which had just been established by his mentor, the pianist and composer Nikolay Rubinstein (1835–81). The successful performance of an early overture in March 1866 encouraged him to start work on a symphony, entitled *Winter Daydreams*, which was performed under Rubinstein's baton in 1868. Modelled on Mendelssohn's *Italian* and *Scottish* Symphonies, it uses melodies influenced by Russian folk tunes.

Music for the stage

Meanwhile Tchaikovsky was working on his first opera, *Voyevoda*, which was performed at the Bolshoy Theatre in Moscow in February 1869. Shortly afterwards Tchaikovsky met Balakirev, who recognized a major new talent and

ABOVE: A page from the autograph piano reduction of Tchaikovsky's ballet Swan Lake *(1877). The score is a masterpiece and the ballet is a major part of the dance repertoire.*

encouraged Tchaikovsky to tackle the tone-poem *Romeo and Juliet*. Its subject-matter, dealing with the favourite Russian themes of love and death, fired the composer's imagination, and it quickly became one of his most popular works.

In May 1872, while staying at the country estate of his beloved sister Alexandra and her family, Tchaikovsky wrote his Second Symphony, known as the *Little Russian*, which incorporates genuine Ukrainian folk tunes into its musical fabric. It was well received, but he still wanted to achieve operatic success. This eluded him until after his first venture into the world of ballet, with *Lebedino ozero* (*Swan Lake*), written for the Imperial Ballet in Moscow. Though its first production in 1877 was a disaster, it was the first of his three great ballet scores – the others are *Spyashchaya krasavitsa* (*The Sleeping Beauty*) and *Shchelkunchik* (*The Nutcracker*) – which are still the cornerstones of the classical ballet repertoire.

In 1874 Tchaikovsky's confidence received another severe dent when Nikolay Rubinstein contemptuously

rejected his First Piano Concerto as "worthless and unplayable". Tchaikovsky rightly ignored the criticism, and refused to alter the score. After Hans von Bülow gave its première in Boston, USA, the following year with great success, Rubinstein was forced to admit his

ABOVE: The Swan Princess *by M. A. Vrubel (1867–1910), inspired by the heroine of* Swan Lake.

Life and works

NATIONALITY: Russian

BORN: Kamsko-Votkinsk, 1840; **DIED:** St Petersburg, 1893

SPECIALIST GENRES: Symphonies, ballets, opera.

MAJOR WORKS: Symphonies No. 1–6; Piano Concerto No. 1; *Swan Lake* (1877); Violin Concerto (1878); *Eugene Onegin* (1879); *Manfred* Symphony (1886); *The Sleeping Beauty* (1889); *The Queen of Spades* (1890); *The Nutcracker* (1891–2).

ABOVE: A scene from the 1993 Royal Ballet production of The Nutcracker.

1896, three years after his death, she was declared insane and spent the rest of her life in an asylum.

Fatalism

In the immediate aftermath of his disastrous marriage, Tchaikovsky composed his Fourth Symphony, dedicated to Madame von Meck. He told her, "There is a programme to our symphony…the introduction is the seed of the whole work…this is Fate, the fatal force which prevents the realization of our hopes of happiness."

From then onwards, his work became increasingly dominated by the idea of Fate. It pervades his opera *Eugene Onegin*, based on Pushkin's verse novel, a powerful emotional drama set against the colourful background of Russian country life. The opera had uncanny parallels with Tchaikovsky's own situation, particularly in the ardent letter written by the heroine, Tatyana, to the insensitive Onegin, who fails to appreciate her true worth until many years later.

The same sense of predestination dominates the Fifth Symphony (1888), whose famous opening theme represents "complete resignation before Fate", while the second

mistake. Meanwhile Tchaikovsky – who spent as much time as possible travelling outside Russia – saw Bizet's *Carmen* in Paris, and Wagner's *Ring* at the opening of the Bayreuth Festival Opera. Under these twin influences he composed his tone-poem *Francesca da Rimini* (1876), based on the famous episode in Dante's *Inferno*, and, in complete contrast, the classically poised *Rococo Variations* for cello and orchestra.

Marriage

Around the same time, he began his long association with the multi-millionairess Nadezhda von Meck, the widow of a railway tycoon, who befriended the composer, commissioned his works and supported him financially, on condition they should never meet. Her patronage enabled Tchaikovsky to concentrate on composition, and rescued him from the emotional chaos caused by his hasty and imprudent marriage in 1877 to a mentally unbalanced music student, Antonina Milyukova, who had pestered him with love-letters.

Tchaikovsky had evidently hoped that marriage would bring "normality" to his life, but found himself unable to reconcile his wife's physical demands with his homosexuality. An attempt at reconciliation brought him to the brink of suicide, and within weeks of the wedding he fled to the safety of his brother's house in St Petersburg. Tchaikovsky never saw his wife again, though they were never divorced. In

ABOVE: The Mariinsky Theatre in St Petersburg. Many operas and ballets by Tchaikovsky, including The Sleeping Beauty *and* The Nutcracker*, were first performed there.*

ABOVE: *Tchaikovsky with his favourite nephew, "Bob" Davidov, son of the composer's beloved sister Alexandra.*

prompted him to compose the Byronic *Manfred* Symphony), but lost another when, in October 1890, his substitute mother-figure Madame von Meck abruptly discontinued their 14-year relationship.

Last years

The death of his sister in 1891 overshadowed an otherwise triumphant visit to the USA, and by the end of 1892 Tchaikovsky was beset by morbid fears. His last symphony, dubbed the *Pathétique* by his brother Modest, represents his final confrontation with the Fate that had dogged him. Tchaikovsky said that the symphony's "ultimate essence is Life", but that the anguished finale (marked *Adagio lamentoso*) represented Death. A week after its first performance on 28 October 1893, Tchaikovsky was dead, at 53.

The circumstances of his death remain a mystery. He is said to have died (like his mother) of cholera, after drinking a glass of unboiled water. Some scholars believe that

ABOVE: *A scene from the English National Ballet's 1999 production of* Swan Lake, *with Tamara Rojo and Patrick Armand.*

he committed suicide, either by drinking contaminated water deliberately or by taking arsenic, to avoid becoming embroiled in a homosexual scandal over a relationship with a public figure.

movement, with its exquisite opening horn solo, is a radiant love-song. Both Fate and Pushkin provided the scenario for Tchaikovsky's last successful opera *Pikovaya dama* (*The Queen of Spades*), a chilling supernatural tale of the death and destruction wrought by a gambler's obsession.

In 1878 Tchaikovsky resigned his teaching job at the Moscow Conservatory. From then onwards he spent much time abroad, in Switzerland, where he completed the Violin Concerto (another work strongly influenced by Russian folk themes), and in Italy (the inspiration of the *Capriccio italien* and the *Souvenir de Florence*). In 1880 he commemorated the historic defeat of Napoleon's army with the brash but ever-popular *1812* Overture, which he described as "loud and noisy…and probably artistically worthless".

By 1884 Tchaikovsky felt the need to settle down, and found himself a country house near Klin, outside Moscow. He renewed one acquaintance, with Balakirev (who

ABOVE: The Retreat from Moscow *by the Polish artist Jan van Chelminski (1851–1925). Napoleon's rout by the Russian army inspired Tchaikovsky's 1812 Overture.*

Bedřich Smetana

*Here is a composer with a genuine Czech heart,
an artist by the Grace of God!*

FRANZ LISZT (1811–86)

Nationalist feeling was particularly strong in 19th-century Bohemia, where Czech customs, culture, and even language were suppressed by its German-speaking Austrian rulers. Smetana was the first Czech composer openly to draw inspiration from national legends, history and landscape, and to incorporate the melodic patterns and rhythms of folk music into his work.

The son of a German-speaking master brewer, Smetana showed early promise as a pianist, and having studied in Prague and Plzen despite parental opposition, he decided to make music his career. He began by making a precarious living as a concert pianist and teacher, during which time he met the Schumanns and Liszt. In 1848 he took an active role in the unsuccessful Prague Revolution, helping to man the street barricades, and the following year he married a fellow pianist, Kateřina Kolářová.

ABOVE: Bedřich Smetana, influential in the central European nationalist movement.

Of their four daughters, three died in childhood, followed by the consumptive Kateřina herself in 1858. The family had spent much of the previous two years in Göteborg, Sweden, where Smetana had opened a music school, and where he had begun to compose symphonic tone-poems modelled on the works of Liszt, including *Richard III* and *Wallensteins Lager*, based on Schiller's play.

Czech nationalism

A few months after his wife's death, Smetana became engaged to his brother's sister-in-law, whom he married in 1860. He returned to Sweden that year, but events in his homeland were changing fast. The Austrians had suffered heavy defeats at the hands of Napoleon III's armies, and the time was ripe for a resurgence of Czech national feeling.

Smetana returned home early in 1861, hoping to become conductor

ABOVE: The Bohemian town of Litomyšl, where Smetana was born in 1824. Bohemia was part of the Austrian Empire at this time.

ABOVE: A view of Prague, showing the banks of the river Vltava, the inspiration for one of the movements in Má vlast (My Homeland).

of the new Prague Provisional Theatre, which had just opened for the performance of opera and drama, but having been raised as a German-speaker it took time to convince the authorities of his ambitions for Czech music. His first opera, *Braniboři v Čechách* (*The Brandenburgers in Bohemia*), with a libretto by the nationalist poet Karel Sabina, was produced there in January 1866 to great enthusiasm. It was quickly followed by *Prodaná nevěsta* (*The Bartered Bride*), which, with its appealing blend of rustic lyricism and the skilful incorporation of Czech dances, became Smetana's most popular opera.

Prague Provisional Theatre
In the autumn of 1866 Smetana was finally appointed conductor to the Provisional Theatre, where he introduced many major works to the repertoire, among them his own *Dalibor* (1868), based on a legendary Czech hero, and *Dvě vdovy* (*The Two Widows*, 1874). His most overtly patriotic work, *Libuše* (dealing with the legendary founder of the Czech ruling dynasty), was composed

ABOVE: Smetana at his piano, composing the opera The Bartered Bride *(1866).*

Life and works

NATIONALITY: Czech

BORN: Litomyšl, 1824; **DIED:** Prague, 1884

SPECIALIST GENRES: Nationalistic Czech operatic and orchestral music.

MAJOR WORKS: *The Bartered Bride* (1866); *Má vlast* (1872–9); String Quartet No. 1 in E minor *From My Life* (1876); *The Kiss* (1876).

between 1869 and 1872, but had to wait until June 1881 for its première, at the triumphant opening of the National Theatre.

During the composition of *Libuše*, Smetana also worked on his great cycle of symphonic poems celebrating Czech history, legend and topography, entitled *Má vlast* (*My Homeland*). The most popular individual item has always been *Vltava*, a portrait of the river that runs through Prague.

Deafness and disability
In the early 1870s Smetana became aware that his health was deteriorating: he complained of giddiness and hearing problems (the result of syphilis). In October 1874 he went completely deaf in one ear. He was also suffering from financial problems, but nevertheless managed to complete a new opera, *Hubička* (*The Kiss*), in 1876. At the same time he wrote his E minor String Quartet, subtitled "From My Life",

whose last movement is dominated in the coda by a sustained high note representing the shrill whistling sound which Smetana suffered permanently as a result of his deafness.

Like Beethoven, Smetana continued to compose in spite of his disability. A seventh opera, *Tajemství* (*The Secret*, 1878), was followed by two new patriotic symphonic poems, *Tábor* (1878) and *Blaník* (1879), both inspired by episodes from Czech history. (*Tábor* is built around an early 15th-century Hussite chorale, effectively the Czech national anthem.)

Smetana's last opera, *Čertova stěna* (*The Devil's Wall*, 1882), took three years to write, during which time he complained of feeling as if he were standing "under a huge waterfall". He completed his Second String Quartet in March 1883, but his condition deteriorated and a year later he was taken to the Prague lunatic asylum, where he died on 12 May 1884.

Antonín Dvořák

*I should be glad if something occurred to me
as a main idea that occurs to Dvořák only by the way.*

JOHANNES BRAHMS (1833–97)

Dvořák stands at the heart of the Czech nationalist musical movement. Like his contemporary Tchaikovsky, he succeeded in fusing folk idioms (the inflections of folk melodies and the characteristic rhythms of Czech dances such as the "furiant") with the symphonic techniques of his predecessors Beethoven and Brahms. His symphonies (particularly the three later ones), tone-poems, chamber and piano music are all part of the mainstream repertoire, and his operas (especially *Rusalka*, 1900) are becoming more widely known through frequent revivals.

Dvořák's father was the village butcher, and wanted his son to follow the same trade, but Antonín began to learn the violin at an early age and was eventually allowed to study music. He attended the Prague Organ School, and began his career as principal viola in the orchestra of the Provisional Theatre. He also began to compose and teach. He fell in love with a pupil, Josefina Čermáková, but when she rejected him he married her younger sister, Anna, in 1873.

By 1874 Dvořák had already completed four symphonies and two operas. That year he achieved his first real breakthrough when he entered several compositions in a competition intended to help struggling young artists. The jury included Brahms, who recognized Dvořák's talent, awarded him first prize, and took a fatherly interest in promoting his career.

ABOVE: *Antonín Dvořák, the most famous Czech composer of his time. He was equally popular in England and the USA.*

Brahms recommended Dvořák to his own publisher, who in 1878 commissioned a set of eight orchestral *Slavonic Dances* and within a year had published them, together with three *Slavonic Rhapsodies*, a Serenade for wind instruments, a String Sextet and Quartet, songs and piano duets. The infectiously tuneful *Slavonic Dances* in particular were a huge success, and assured Dvořák's international reputation.

England

From then on, Dvořák's works were performed as far afield as London and New York. In 1882 August Manns conducted the Sixth Symphony at the Crystal Palace in London, and the Stabat Mater was performed with great success in London the following year.

In 1884 Dvořák visited England for the first time, conducting some of his own works, including the Sixth Symphony and the *Scherzo capriccioso* for orchestra. He was immediately invited to write a new symphony (the Seventh, in D minor) for the Royal Philharmonic Society, and two large-scale choral works for the Birmingham and Leeds Festivals: the dramatic cantata *The Spectre's Bride* for Birmingham, and the oratorio *St Ludmila* for Leeds.

Life and works

NATIONALITY: Czech

BORN: Nelahozeves, 1841;
DIED: Prague, 1904

SPECIALIST GENRES: Opera, symphonies, tone-poems, chamber music.

MAJOR WORKS: Nine symphonies, including No. 9 *From the New World* (1893); Serenade for strings (1875); Stabat Mater (1877); *Slavonic Dances* (1878 and 1886); Requiem (1890); Cello Concerto in B minor (1895); operas; chamber music; piano music; songs.

London also saw the performance in 1887 of the *Symphonic Variations*, conducted by Hans Richter, and, in 1890, of the Eighth Symphony – often known as the *English*, although it is a thoroughly "Bohemian" work. The next year Dvořák received an honorary doctorate from Cambridge University.

America

In 1891 he was invited to become director of the new National Conservatory of Music in New York, at a very attractive salary. Dvořák spent five months touring Bohemia with several new works – including the Dumky Piano Trio and a cycle of three overtures, *V přírodě* (*In Nature's Realm*), *Carnaval* and *Othello* – before sailing for New York in spring 1892.

He spent three years there, teaching, conducting and composing. The Ninth Symphony (*From the New World*), the *American* String Quartet and Quintet, the Cello Concerto (whose coda reflects Dvořák's grief at hearing of the death of his sister-in-law Josefina), and the charming Violin Sonatina (dedicated to his six children) were all composed there. Several of these works show the influence of American folk music, especially the negro spiritual.

ABOVE: The National Theatre in Prague, opened on 18 November 1883. Dvořák's opera The Jacobin *was premièred there six years later.*

Return to Prague

The lure of his native Bohemia eventually proved too strong, and after 1895 Dvořák decided not to return to America. Instead he resumed teaching at the Prague Conservatory, and spent time with his family. The last decade of his life produced many new works, including two string quartets, four symphonic poems based on Czech folk tales – *Vodník* (*The Water Goblin*), *Zlatý kolovrat* (*The Golden Spinning-wheel*), *Polednice* (*The Noonday Witch*) and *Holoubek* (*The Wild Dove*), 1896–7 – and his two best-known operas, *Čert a Káča* (*Kate and the Devil*, 1899) and *Rusalka* (1900), both based on fairy-tales. He died on 1 May 1904, and had a state funeral.

LEFT: Dvořák with his wife and children, photographed shortly after their arrival in New York, 1892.

RIGHT: Dvořák conducting at the Chicago World Fair in 1893. The programme included the Eighth Symphony and three of the Slavonic Dances.

Edvard Grieg

I am sure my music has a taste of codfish in it.

GRIEG

Grieg was Dvořák's Scandinavian equivalent: a composer working outside the mainstream European symphonic tradition, though trained within it, who brought to his music a warmth and natural melodic facility that owed much to the folk music of his native land.

Grieg's father, Alexander, was a prosperous merchant of Scottish descent (the family name was originally Greig), who held the post of British Consul to the Norwegian port of Bergen. His mother, Gesine Hagerup, was an excellent pianist who undertook the musical education of her fourth child, Edvard, instilling in him a love for the music of Mozart, Weber and Chopin.

In 1858 the Grieg family was visited by the charismatic violinist Ole Bull, one of the pioneers of the fledgling Norwegian nationalist movement. Bull

ABOVE: *A portrait of Edvard Grieg (1843–1907), whose music epitomizes the scenic beauty of Norway.*

persuaded Grieg's parents to send him to the Leipzig Conservatory, where he studied piano with the composer and pianist Ignaz Moscheles (1794–1870) and composition with Carl Reinecke (1824–1910). He also heard Clara Schumann play her husband's Piano Concerto, which had an enormous influence on his own future concerto.

Norwegian music

Grieg began his career in Bergen, then went to Copenhagen. There he met his cousin and future wife, the singer Nina Hagerup, for whom he wrote many of his songs. His growing sympathy with the Norwegian nationalist movement dates from this period, when he met the young nationalist composer Rikard Nordraak. The two of them planned to found a society for the promotion of Norwegian music, but Nordraak died of tuberculosis. During the winter of

ABOVE: *Grieg with his wife Nina – the chief interpreter of his songs – photographed in 1906, not long before his death.*

ABOVE: *The autograph manuscript of Grieg's song* Fyremaal *(1880). Grieg often drew on Norwegian folk music for inspiration.*

388 *The Rise of Nationalism*

1865–6 Grieg also visited Rome, where he met the playwright Henrik Ibsen. He married Nina in June 1867: their long partnership survived the death in infancy of their only child, Alexandra, and Grieg's later infidelities.

Grieg had already begun to write piano pieces with a national tinge (including the first of many sets of *Lyric Pieces*), but in 1868 his enthusiasm was aroused by his discovery of a volume of Norwegian folk songs. The influence of these mountain melodies spilled over into the Piano Concerto, which Liszt played through at sight when the Griegs visited him in Italy in 1869. On returning to Norway, and with Liszt's encouragement, Grieg determined to make a name for himself. He gave a concert of his own works (songs, piano pieces, and sonatas for piano and violin), and established an Academy of Music in the Norwegian capital, Christiania (now Oslo).

Peer Gynt

Grieg also began to collaborate with the playwright and poet Bjørnstjerne Bjørnson, director of the Christiania Theatre, on incidental music for his play *Sigurd Jorsalfar* (1872) and a

ABOVE: A Norwegian folk dance. The distinctive idioms of these dances, and the sounds made by Norwegian folk instruments, permeated all of Grieg's music.

potential opera. But it was Ibsen's request for incidental music to his play *Peer Gynt* in 1874 which fired Grieg's creative imagination. The resulting music, which includes "Morning", "In the Hall of the Mountain King" and "Solveig's Song", is well known from two orchestral suites, and rivals the Piano Concerto in popularity.

Troldhaugen

From the mid 1870s Grieg combined long European concert tours as a conductor and pianist with increasing periods of time spent in reflection and composition amid the beauty of the Norwegian mountains. He was particularly fond of the Hardanger district, where he composed in a small wooden hut by a lake. On frequent walking expeditions into the mountains he heard and collected folk songs and dances, whose idioms infuse his own piano pieces and songs, including the cycle *Haugtussa* (The Mountain Maid).

In 1884, the year he completed the anachronistic *Holberg* Suite for strings, based on 17th-century dances, he had a house built at Troldhaugen, above the Hardanger fjord near Bergen, where he entertained friends such as Percy Grainger. His much-loved home is celebrated in "Wedding Day at

Troldhaugen", included in the eighth book of *Lyric Pieces*, 1896.

By 1900 Grieg was suffering increasingly from lung disease. He was still much in demand internationally, and retained his life-long interest in his national folk music (his last works include a piano arrangement of Norwegian peasant fiddle tunes, called *Slåtter*). He died on the point of leaving for England on another concert tour, and his ashes were buried at Troldhaugen, in the side of the cliff overlooking the fjord.

ABOVE: The great Norwegian playwright Henrik Ibsen (1828–1906). At Ibsen's request, Grieg wrote incidental music for his play Peer Gynt *(1874).*

Life and works

NATIONALITY: Norwegian

BORN: Bergen, 1843;
DIED: Bergen, 1907

SPECIALIST GENRES:
Songs, piano music.

MAJOR WORKS: Piano Concerto in A minor (1868); *Peer Gynt* Suites (1874–5); *Holberg* Suite (1884); 66 *Lyric Pieces* for piano (1867–1901); 140 songs.

Isaac Albéniz

Everything is possible on the piano.
Ferruccio Busoni (1866–1924)

While French and Russian composers such as Bizet, Lalo and Rimsky-Korsakov were flirting with Spanish idioms, Albéniz was the first genuinely Spanish composer of international reputation. Born in Catalonia, he was a child prodigy, making his public debut as a pianist at the age of four. He made his first concert tour at eight, and then enrolled as a student at the Madrid Conservatory, but a year later, still aged only ten, he ran away to Castile, where he went round various cities earning enough to live on by playing the piano as a vaudeville act.

ABOVE: *The Spanish composer Isaac Albéniz (1860–1909), one of the masters of atmospheric piano music.*

From then onwards, he suffered from incurable wanderlust. In 1872 he took off once more, this time as a stowaway on a boat bound for South America. He returned to Spain in 1873, but then left for England and then Leipzig, where he continued his studies. A scholarship enabled him to study composition and piano in Brussels, after which he spent several years trailing around Europe in the wake of Liszt.

In 1883 Albéniz settled briefly in Barcelona, where he married and had three children. Around 1890 he finally gave up his concert career, but still flitted between London (where he was commissioned to write three operas based on librettos written by a wealthy patron) and Paris, where he taught piano and made friends with other notable composers. From 1903 onwards he lived near Nice, moving to Cambo-les-Bains in the Pyrenees shortly before his death. His last years were spent working on the four books of piano pieces collectively called *Iberia*, tonal portraits of Spain which were orchestrated by Fernandez Arbós (1863–1939) and other composers after Albéniz's death.

Albéniz's most important works are for solo piano. All are underpinned by the rhythms and timbres of Spanish folk music. The 12 pieces that make up the *Iberia* Suite are extraordinarily forward-looking, almost impressionistic in style: they influenced both Debussy and Ravel.

ABOVE: *An Andalucian folk dance. The bell-tower of Seville Cathedral is in the distance.*

Life and works

NATIONALITY: Spanish

BORN: Camprodón, 1860;
DIED: Cambo-les-Bains, 1909

SPECIALIST GENRES:
Virtuoso piano music.

MAJOR WORKS: *Iberia* (1906–9); Piano Concerto (c.1887); *Rapsodia española* for piano and orchestra (1887).

Enrique Granados

I am not a musician but an artist.

GRANADOS

Albéniz's compatriot Enrique Granados was also from Catalonia. He was born seven years after Albéniz, and also became known as a brilliant pianist. In 1887 he went to Paris to study the piano, returning to Barcelona two years later, and making his debut there in 1890. In 1898 his comic opera *Maria del Carmen* was produced in Madrid, winning its composer a royal commendation. From then onwards Granados divided his time between composing, teaching and performing, either as a solo pianist, or in company with musicians such as the French violinist Jacques Thibaud (1880–1953) and the Spanish cellist Pablo Casals (1876–1973).

Granados went on to write several more stage works inspired by Spanish themes, but his greatest success lay in his solo piano music. This included a set of 12 Spanish dances, and the piano

ABOVE: Enrique Granados (1867–1916). Like Albéniz, his works were influenced by Spanish folk idioms.

suite *Goyescas*, a set of six highly original pieces each inspired by a painting by Goya (the most famous is "Quejas, o la Maja y el ruiseñor" – "The Maiden and the Nightingale").

The huge success of *Goyescas*, both in Spain and France, led indirectly to his death. Before leaving Paris, he had proposed to turn the suite into an opera. But the Paris Opéra prevaricated over the commission, partly as a result of the outbreak of war, and instead, Granados offered the work to the Metropolitan Opera in New York. In January 1916 he and his wife crossed the Atlantic to attend the opera's première. They returned in March, via Liverpool, from where they embarked on the liner *Sussex*, bound for Dieppe. The ship was torpedoed in the English Channel by a German submarine, and Granados drowned trying in vain to save his wife.

Life and works

NATIONALITY: Spanish

BORN: Lérida, 1867;
DIED: English Channel, 1916

SPECIALIST GENRES:
Piano music incorporating Spanish idioms.

MAJOR WORKS: 12 *Danzas españolas* for piano (1892–1900); *Goyescas* Suite for piano (1911).

ABOVE: The Clothed Maja, *a typical painting by Francisco Goya (1746–1828), now in the Prado in Madrid. Goya's paintings inspired several works by Granados.*

Arthur Sullivan

You ought to write a grand opera, Sir Arthur, you would do it so well.

QUEEN VICTORIA (1819–1901)

Arthur Sullivan was one of the most talented English composers of the 19th century, but he can only be described as a "nationalist" by default. In fact, he was impeccably trained in the German tradition. The son of a bandmaster, he won the first Mendelssohn Scholarship to the Royal Academy of Music in London, and went on to study at the Leipzig Conservatory, where he met Liszt and Grieg, before returning to England in 1861 to become a church organist. He was appointed Professor of Composition at the Royal Academy in 1866.

Savoy Operas

Sullivan was determined to succeed as a composer of serious and worthy music, particularly oratorio. But it was his meeting in 1871 with the

ABOVE: *Sir Arthur Sullivan (1842–1900). He could never take his brilliantly successful "Savoy Operas" seriously.*

playwright William Schwenk Gilbert (1836–1911) that ensured his lasting fame. Their first collaboration, *Thespis*, was a failure. But their second, *Trial by Jury* (1875), written at the instigation of the theatrical impresario Richard D'Oyly Carte, was a triumphant success. It was the first of a brilliant sequence known as the "Savoy Operas", operettas produced mostly at the Savoy Theatre in the Strand, London (which D'Oyly Carte – scenting huge profits – leased specially). Nearly all Gilbert and Sullivan's collaborations were resounding successes, *HMS Pinafore* running for 700 nights.

Composer and librettist were perfectly suited. Gilbert's hilariously witty librettos, parodying eminent British institutions such as the law, the

ABOVE: *The cover of a piano arrangement by Bucalossi of songs from* The Mikado, *inspired by the vogue for Orientalism.*

House of Commons, the police, the women's movement, the "Aesthetic" movement led by Oscar Wilde, and recognizable figures in public life, were perfectly matched by Sullivan's incomparable gift for musical parody (of Handel, Donizetti, Wagner, Verdi and others), allied with a gift for fluent melody and apt orchestration.

The partnership came under strain during *The Gondoliers*, and their last two operas, *Utopia Limited* (1893) and *The Grand Duke* (1896), were less successful. Sadly, Sullivan disparaged his own talents, rating his serious music, such as the grand opera *Ivanhoe*, much more highly. His assessment proved mistaken: the Savoy Operas have never lost their immense popularity, while the "serious" works have sunk without trace.

Life and works

NATIONALITY: British

BORN: London, 1842;
DIED: London, 1900

SPECIALIST GENRES: Operetta.

MAJOR WORKS: *The Sorcerer* (1877); *HMS Pinafore* (1878); *The Pirates of Penzance* (1879); *Patience* (1881); *Iolanthe* (1882); *Princess Ida* (1884); *The Mikado* (1885); *Ruddigore* (1887); *The Yeomen of the Guard* (1888); *The Gondoliers* (1889).

Jacques Offenbach

The opéra-bouffe is simply the sexual instinct expressed in melody.

NEW YORK TIMES, 1876

While the "Savoy Operas" of Gilbert and Sullivan took a wry look at Victorian England, France found its equivalent in the sparkling operettas of Jacques Offenbach.

Offenbach's German-Jewish family took their name from their home town of Offenbach-am-Main. His father Isaac was a cantor at a Cologne synagogue, who in 1833 took two of his sons, Julius and Jacques (by then a promising cellist), to Paris. Jacques was enrolled at the Conservatoire, but left after a year, and found a job in the orchestra at the Opéra-Comique. He also began to play in Paris salons, for which he wrote many pieces for cello and piano. During the 1840s he earned a living chiefly as a performer, and in 1850 he was appointed conductor at

ABOVE: Jacques Offenbach (1819–80). His operettas took Paris by storm in the late 1800s.

Life and works

NATIONALITY: German

BORN: Cologne, 1819;
DIED: Paris, 1880

SPECIALIST GENRES: French operetta and opéra-bouffe.

MAJOR WORKS: *Orphée aux enfers* (Orpheus in the Underworld, 1858); *Geneviève de Brabant* (1859); *La belle Hélène* (1864); *La vie parisienne* (1866); *La grande duchesse de Gérolstein* (1867); *La périchole* (1868); *Les contes d'Hoffmann* (1881).

the Théâtre Français. In 1855 he rented the small Marigny theatre in the Champs-Elysées, where he put on a summer programme of short comic pieces. The success of this venture encouraged him to move to a more permanent venue at the Théâtre Comte, which he renamed the Bouffes-Parisiens.

Burlesque opera

Over the next 25 years Offenbach turned out over 90 stage works. His witty, light-hearted operettas satirized composers such as Wagner and Meyerbeer and captured the prevailing hedonistic spirit of Second Empire Paris, with its passion for music-hall dances and its relentless debunking of the Establishment.

In the mid 1870s his audiences began to tire of his productions and a run of expensive failures left him bankrupt, just at the time that Johann Strauss, whom Offenbach had encouraged to write operetta, was enjoying his greatest success with *Die Fledermaus*. Offenbach turned to a different kind of opera.

The Tales of Hoffmann

Offenbach's reputation also rests on his one more serious work, *Les contes d'Hoffmann*, which was left unfinished at his death. His supreme lyrical gift informs this tale of thwarted love, based on three stories by the Romantic author E. T. A. Hoffmann which are treated as episodes from his life. The "Giulietta" act, set in Venice, contains the "Barcarolle" which, together with the "Can-can" from *Orpheus*, ranks among the world's most famous melodies.

ABOVE: A can-can dance from Offenbach's La vie parisienne, 1866. Rossini called Offenbach "the Mozart of the Champs-Elysées".

"The Waltz Kings"

Where he fiddles, all dance — dance they must…

IGNAZ MOSCHELES (1794–1870)

If Sullivan personified Victorian England and Offenbach Second Empire Paris, 19th-century Vienna belonged to the Strauss family. Johann Strauss and his sons took the Austrian capital by storm with a torrent of light music – polkas, galops, quadrilles, marches, and particularly waltzes. In their hands the waltz, a sophisticated form of the Austrian *Ländler,* superseded its humble peasant origins to become the favoured dance of working-class dance halls and aristocratic ballrooms alike.

Johann Strauss the elder

The composer, conductor and violinist Johann Strauss (1804–49) was the son of an innkeeper of Hungarian-Jewish origin. A talented

ABOVE: Johann Strauss II, painted at the height of his fame in 1888 by August Eisenmenger (1830–1907).

violinist, he started out as the friend and partner of Josef Lanner, director of a popular dance orchestra. In 1825 they parted company and Strauss formed his own ensemble, which soon began playing at popular Viennese taverns. Within a few years the Strauss orchestra had been engaged to play in the dance hall at the fashionable Sperl Inn in the suburb of Leopoldstadt, a popular venue which attracted distinguished foreign visitors including Chopin, the young Richard Wagner, and the writer Hans Christian Andersen.

The repertoire of the Strauss orchestra ranged from dances, such as Strauss's own *Champagne Waltz* and *Sperl*

Festival Waltz, to fantasies on popular operatic airs of the time by Bellini, Auber, Rossini, Meyerbeer and others. Of Strauss's vast output, perhaps the best-known piece is the *Radetsky March* (1848).

From 1833 onwards the Strauss orchestra began to travel abroad, not only throughout Austria and Germany, but also to Paris and London, where it took part in Queen Victoria's coronation celebrations. Back in Vienna, Strauss was created Imperial Director of Court Dance Music. He had six children with his wife Anna (three of their

ABOVE: Johann Strauss I (1804–49) with his colleagues playing at a ball in Vienna.

ABOVE: The cover of a piano reduction of Strauss II's Promenade Quadrille.

ABOVE: *Josef Strauss (1827–80), one of Johann II's younger brothers, also a talented musician.*

sons carried on the family tradition), before leaving her to live with a mistress who bore him another seven offspring. He died, aged 45, of scarlet fever caught from one of his children.

Johann Strauss II

NATIONALITY: Austrian

BORN: Vienna, 1825;
DIED: Vienna, 1899

SPECIALIST GENRES: Viennese dance music and operetta.

MAJOR WORKS: *Die Fledermaus* (1874); *Der Zigeunerbaron* (1885); waltzes, including *Morgenblätter* (*Morning Newspapers*, 1864), *An der schönen blauen Donau* (*The Blue Danube*, 1867), *Geschichten aus dem Wienerwald* (*Tales from the Vienna Woods*, 1868) and *Wein, Weib und Gesang* (*Wine, Woman and Song*, 1869); polkas, including *Tritsch-Tratsch* (1858) and *Unter Donner und Blitzen* (*Thunder and Lightning*, 1868).

Johann Strauss the younger

Strauss's eldest son, Johann, was known as "The Waltz King". He learnt the violin against his father's wishes, and in 1844 set up a rival orchestra that merged with the original Strauss band after the death of Johann I. Between 1856 and 1886 Strauss and his orchestra toured Europe, finding particular favour in St Petersburg, and also visited America.

His own compositions – waltzes, polkas, quadrilles and marches – were even more wildly acclaimed than his father's, and many of his waltzes are almost symphonic in scope. His works captured the hedonistic spirit of the Austro-Hungarian Empire at the height of its glory before World War I.

Strauss was also a talented composer for the theatre. Of his 18 light operas and ballets, the two outstanding works are *Die Fledermaus* (*The Bat*), an irresistible blend of Offenbachian wit and Viennese suavity; and *Der Zigeunerbaron* (*The Gypsy Baron*), in which Viennese Romanticism is spiced with Hungarian gypsy idioms. Both are still often performed.

Johann's younger brothers Josef (1827–80) and Eduard (1835–1916)

ABOVE: *Eduard Strauss (1835–1916), the youngest of the Strauss brothers, pictured by a* Vanity Fair *cartoonist in 1895.*

both shared in the direction of the Strauss family orchestra, and both wrote dance music of a similar kind, though neither achieved the same immense popularity as their father and elder brother.

ABOVE: **The Viennese Ball** *by Wilhelm Gause (1853–1916). The dance music of the Strauss family was the staple musical fare for such occasions.*

Other Nationalistic Composers

Art must be parochial in the beginning to be cosmopolitan in the end.

GEORGE MOORE (1852–1933), "HAIL AND FAREWELL"

Many minor French composers flourished during the 19th century, among them Léo Delibes (1836–91), a composer and organist who, like Offenbach, became noted for his operettas. His posthumous fame rests on two ballet scores for the Paris Opéra – *Coppélia* (1870, based on a story by E. T. A. Hoffmann) and *Sylvia* (1876) – and three operas. These include *Lakmé* (1883), based on a popular oriental subject. It contains the challenging coloratura "Bell Song" and the seductive "Flower Duet" for women's voices, "Dôme épais de jasmin".

Delibes's younger contemporary Jules Massenet (1842–1912)

ABOVE: Emmanuel Chabrier (1841–94), painted in 1881 by Edouard Manet.

specialized in opera and oratorio: he excelled at erotic suggestion (particularly if it involved a penitent prostitute), whether in a biblical or secular context. His most famous operas include *Hérodiade* (1881, based on the story of Salome), *Manon* (1884, based on the story by Abbé Prévost later tackled by Puccini), *Werther* (1892, based on Goethe's famous early novel), *Thaïs* (1894, which contains the famous "Meditation" for solo violin), *Cendrillon* (*Cinderella*, 1899), and *Don Quichotte* (1910, based on Cervantes's *Don Quixote*). Massenet's operas were enormously popular in his day; audiences today find them rather sickly and over-sentimental, but *Manon* and *Werther* are still in the repertoire.

Emmanuel Chabrier (1841–94) was a civil servant who decided to turn to music after hearing Wagner's *Tristan und Isolde*. His operas include *L'étoile* (1877), *Gwendoline* (1886) and *Le roi malgré lui* (*King despite himself*, 1887), all of which have had occasional revivals, but his most famous piece is the sparkling, Iberian-sounding orchestral rhapsody *España* (1883).

Edouard Lalo (1823–92) also drew inspiration from south of the Pyrenees, in his *Symphonie espagnole* (1874) for violin and orchestra, which he followed with a *Fantaisie norvégienne* (1880) for the same combination. He wrote several operas and ballets, of which *Le roi d'Ys* (*The King of Ys*, 1888) was the only success.

Apart from Grieg, Norway produced two more composers of note. Johan Svendsen (1840–1911) spent some

ABOVE: A painting entitled Norwegian Landscape: Evening *(c.1904) by Walter Leistikow. Many composers took inspiration from the wild Norwegian scenery.*

ABOVE: *The French composer Edouard Lalo (1823–92), who drew inspiration from the landscapes of Spain and Norway.*

ABOVE: *Johan Svendsen (1840–1911), a fellow countryman of Grieg, whose works include a set of* Norwegian Rhapsodies.

ABOVE: *Christian Sinding (1856–1941), a Norwegian composer chiefly remembered for the piano piece* Rustle of Spring.

time in Paris, and became a close friend of Wagner before returning to Norway as a teacher and conductor. His works include two symphonies, concertos for cello and violin, a Romance for violin and orchestra, and a set of *Norwegian Rhapsodies*.

Christian Sinding (1856–1941) spent most of his life in Oslo. Like Svendsen, he was principally noted for instrumental works, which included four symphonies, three violin concertos and a piano concerto, chamber music, songs, and many piano pieces, of which *Rustle of Spring* (1909) is still much played.

In Bohemia, Dvořák's pupil and son-in-law Josef Suk (1874–1935) carried on the tradition of Smetana and Dvořák, but without the overt use of Czech national idioms. He was also a brilliant violinist, who from 1892–1933 played in the Bohemian String Quartet. His grandson, the violinist also called Josef Suk (born 1929), carries on the family tradition. Suk's most important works were for orchestra. They include an early

Serenade for strings (1892), *Pohádka* (*Fairy-tales*, 1900), and the huge *Asrael* Symphony (1905–6), written after Suk lost both his father-in-law and his young wife. This work marked the first phase of a vast symphonic cycle, whose other components were *Pohádka léta* (*A Summer's Tale*, 1907–9), *Zrání* (The

Ripening, 1912–17), and *Epilog* (1920–9). All represent Suk's personal attempt to come to terms with the central tragedy of his life. Although much of Suk's music is not directly inspired by Czech folk music, his last work was a Czech dance (*Sousedska*, 1935) for chamber ensemble.

ABOVE: *The violinist Josef Suk (born 1929), Dvořák's great-grandson, who carries on the family musical tradition. In 1961 he became leader of the Czech Philharmonic Orchestra.*

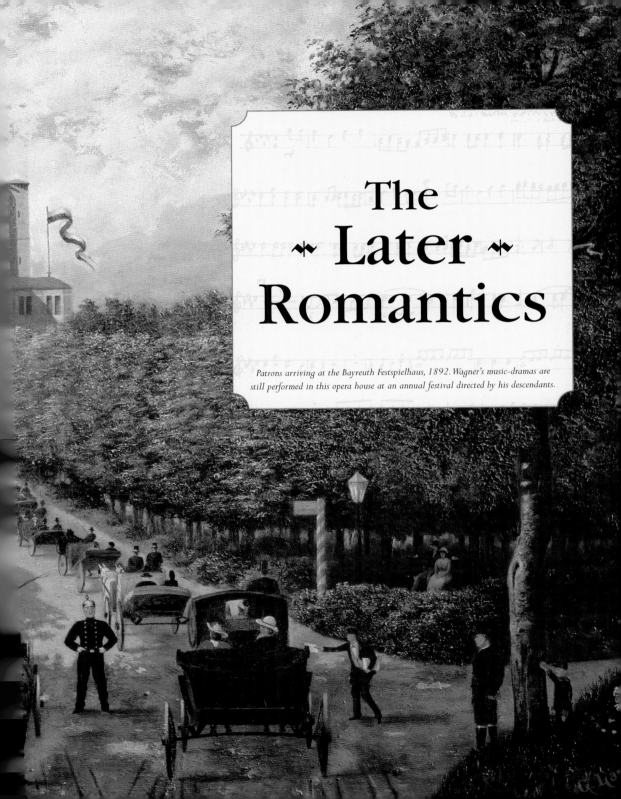

The
✦ Later ✦
Romantics

Patrons arriving at the Bayreuth Festspielhaus, 1892. Wagner's music-dramas are still performed in this opera house at an annual festival directed by his descendants.

Music on the Grand Scale

We are the music makers,
We are the dreamers of dreams.

ARTHUR O'SHAUGHNESSY (1844–81)

Two musical giants dominated the second half of the 19th century, each with a very different approach to composition. Johannes Brahms saw himself as belonging to the mainstream German symphonic tradition. Although overawed by the legacy of Beethoven, he — even more than Schumann or Mendelssohn — continued and expanded the Beethovenian principle of motivic construction. Brahms's four symphonies represent "pure", abstract music: unusually for a Romantic composer, they are unaffected by external influences such as literature or landscape. Brahms was primarily an instrumental composer. He wrote no opera, and his preferred media were orchestral, chamber and solo piano music. Yet, as his choral music and his many superb songs demonstrate, he was by no means indifferent to the power of words.

At the opposite pole stood the extraordinary figure of Richard

Wagner, whose works are almost entirely operatic. One of the most forceful and influential characters in music history, Wagner was highly receptive to influences of all descriptions — literature, myth,

drama, poetry, painting, politics and philosophy. These combined to produce his "music of the future" — a vision of *Gesamtkunstwerk*, a "total art work", which would unite music, drama, poetry and the visual arts, and which he strove to achieve in his gigantic later operas, particularly the four constituents of the *Ring* cycle, *Tristan und Isolde*, *Parsifal* and *Die Meistersinger von Nürnberg*.

The operas and tone-poems of Richard Strauss owe an enormous debt to Wagner, as do the symphonies of Bruckner and Mahler (although both were equally influenced by Brahms). Wagner's influence was inescapable, and his genius so persuasive that the more unpleasant aspects of his personality — particularly the virulent anti-Semitism expressed in his polemical writings, which certainly contributed to the climate of opinion

ABOVE: The interior of the Teatro alla Scala, Milan; an aquatint from 1819. La Scala is one of the world's greatest opera houses.

LEFT: A snowy Finnish landscape — the inspiration for symphonies by Sibelius.

in Germany that led to Hitler's National Socialism – tend to have been overlooked.

Italian opera

Meanwhile, as in the early part of the century, Italian music continued to be dominated by opera, but in a very un-Wagnerian style. Giuseppe Verdi took on the mantle of Rossini, producing a sequence of 26 operas over some 57 years which have since remained the backbone of the international repertoire. Verdi was Wagner's only real rival in the operatic field, but his works are firmly based in the Italian *bel canto* tradition.

His successor, Giacomo Puccini, wrote far fewer works but almost all have held their place in the operatic canon. Puccini owed his success to an unerring sense of theatre and a persuasive melodic gift, allied to a taste for sentimental plots which still reduce

ABOVE: *The Leipzig Opera House in the Augustusplatz, built between 1864 and 1867 (destroyed in World War II).*

audiences to tears. In the hands of less talented composers, this taste for melodrama degenerated into the *verismo* school of sex and violence, which nonetheless produced two isolated masterpieces: the one-act *Cavalleria rusticana* (*Rustic Chivalry*, 1890) by Pietro Mascagni (1863–1945) and *I pagliacci* (*The Clowns*, 1892) by Ruggero Leoncavallo (1858–1919), which are usually performed together in a double-bill.

Nationalism

By the second half of the 19th century nationalism was in full swing and few composers remained untouched by an awareness of their national culture. Mahler in Austria, Sibelius in Finland, Fauré and Saint-Saëns in France, Elgar in England and Rachmaninov in Russia all made original contributions to the musical literature of their respective countries, broadly working with the language of late Romanticism.

All except Fauré were important symphonic writers, particularly Mahler and Sibelius. Elgar occupies a special place in British music as the most gifted English composer since Purcell. His music distilled the essence of Edwardian England, while Rachmaninov inherited Tchaikovsky's ability to write superb tunes, expressed with a passion that seems essentially "Russian".

ABOVE: *The cover of* The International Quadrille *by Charles d'Albert, showing the opening of the Crystal Palace in London in 1862. It became a favourite concert venue.*

ABOVE: *Outside the Bayreuth Festspielhaus, 1892. The theatre was built in the 1870s specifically for performances of Wagner's music-dramas.*

Johannes Brahms

I believe Johannes to be the true Apostle, who will also write Revelations.

ROBERT SCHUMANN (1810–56), IN A LETTER TO JOACHIM

One of the greatest symphonic composers of the 19th century, Brahms came from a relatively humble background. His father, Johann Jakob, played the double bass in the Hamburg city orchestra. His mother, who was 17 years older than her husband, came from a middle-class family who had fallen upon hard times: she had been Johann Brahms's housekeeper. Their second child Johannes was born on 7 May 1833.

Early years

Brahms learnt the piano from the age of seven, and from 1846 onwards he also studied composition. In 1848 he gave his first public recital, and that

ABOVE: *Johannes Brahms (1833–97), painted by N. Piontkovsky.*

year he also met the Hungarian violinist Eduard Reményi (1830–98), a refugee from Austrian oppression in his homeland. Five years later Reményi and Brahms set off on a concert tour, during which they met another Hungarian violinist, Joseph Joachim, and stayed at Weimar with Liszt. Brahms also travelled to Düsseldorf to visit Robert and Clara Schumann, who were both deeply impressed with the pianistic and compositional talents of this "young eagle", as Schumann described him.

Shortly after their meeting, Schumann suffered a complete breakdown, and in 1854 Brahms

returned to Düsseldorf to help Clara, with whom he fell deeply in love. Their relationship – whether physically consummated or not – was central to Brahms's life, and may have affected his attitude to other women: though he had close female friends, he never married. During her long widowhood, Clara acted as mentor to the young composer, encouraging him – as she had done with Schumann – to push his art to the limits.

In 1857 Brahms spent some months in Detmold, where he tried out his first orchestral works (two serenades) with the court orchestra. Two years later he settled back in

ABOVE: *The influential Hungarian violinist Joseph Joachim (1831–1907), the dedicatee of Brahms's Violin Concerto.*

ABOVE: *A drawing of Brahms (aged 20) done at the request of Robert Schumann by Laurens, 1853.*

Hamburg, where he founded a
women's choir and began to write
choral music. In the meantime he had
completed his First Piano Concerto,
begun at the time he met the

Schumanns. Brahms himself gave
the première of this huge work in
Hanover, where it met with success;
but five days later, in Leipzig, the
audience greeted it coolly. By this time
Brahms was making himself unpopular
by publicly dissociating himself from
Liszt and the "New German School".
His uncompromising stance probably
caused the Leipzig publisher Breitkopf
& Härtel to reject his manuscripts,
including the Piano Concerto.

Vienna

In 1862, with several more
compositions completed (including
the Sextet in B flat, and sets of piano
variations on themes by Handel and
Schumann), Brahms left Hamburg
for Vienna. Six months later he was
appointed director of the Vienna
Singakademie, where he indulged his
awakening interest in early music,
but he soon found the administrative
burden of the new job tiresome, and
resigned after a few months.

*ABOVE: Brahms in 1867, shortly before he
decided to move to Vienna, and one year
before he wrote the* German Requiem.

In 1864 he returned home on
hearing that his parents' marriage was
in trouble — his mother was ill and
his father resented having to look after
her. Their separation, followed by his

ABOVE: A Viennese street scene during the time of Brahms: the Fruit Market on the quayside near the Maria Theresa Bridge, 1895.

mother's death in January 1865, was a bitter blow (Brahms commemorated her death in the slow movement of his powerful Horn Trio).

In 1868 Brahms decided to settle permanently in Vienna, but continued playing his own works on frequent concert tours. In 1872 he became conductor of the Vienna Gesellschaftskonzerte, but held the post for only three years. A new breed of professional virtuoso conductors such as Hans Richter (1843–1916), Hans von Bülow (1830–94), and Hermann Levi (1839–1900) had arrived on the scene, and Brahms wisely realized his own limitations. In 1869 he had already had a taste of critical vitriol when Wagner (fearing a new and talented rival) had viciously

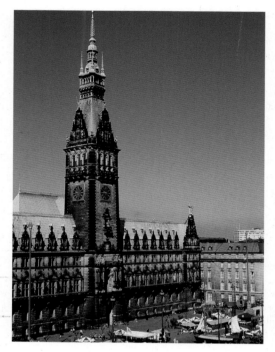

ABOVE: *The Town Hall in Hamburg, the city where Brahms was born in 1833.*

attacked him in an article entitled "On Conducting". From then onwards, Brahms devoted himself to composition.

After many years of work, in 1868, Brahms had completed *Ein Deutsches Requiem* (*A German Requiem*) for soloists, chorus and orchestra — a deeply felt response to biblical passages on the subject of death, mourning and consolation — and during the Franco-Prussian War he was hailed as a "patriot", having used material from the Lutheran Bible rather than the traditional Latin text of the Catholic liturgy. He responded by composing the *Triumphlied* (*Song of Triumph*) in the summer of 1871 to celebrate Germany's victory. By 1873, when he finished his popular *St Anthony Variations* (*Variations on a*

Theme of Haydn) for orchestra, he was earning enough to be able to live on the income from his concerts and publications, and felt sufficiently secure to turn down a lifelong contract offered by the publisher Fritz Simrock (he also rejected an honorary doctorate offered by Cambridge University).

Symphonic success

Three years later, with Clara Schumann's constant encouragement, Brahms finally completed his First Symphony in C minor, begun over 20 years earlier. Its long gestation had been haunted by the ghost of Beethoven, and by Brahms's fear that the work would be rejected because it was not "programmatic". But the Viennese public received it with enthusiasm, and

ABOVE: *The opening page of the autograph score of Brahms's Double Concerto for violin and cello (1887).*

ABOVE: *Brahms (centre) on the day of Clara Schumann's funeral, 20 May 1896. He had loved her ever since their first meeting.*

Brahms immediately began work on a second symphony.

In the late 1870s he adopted the habit of spending the summers in the Austrian countryside, at Pörtschach on Lake Wörther in Carinthia. There he completed the Second Symphony in D, the brilliant Violin Concerto (whose gypsy finale pays homage to Joachim, its Hungarian dedicatee), the G major Violin Sonata, the two Rhapsodies, Op. 79, and the eight Piano Pieces, Op. 76. From 1880 onwards he found another summer refuge at Bad Ischl, where he wrote the Piano Trio in C, the Quintets in F and G, the Three Motets, Op. 110, and many of his late chamber and vocal works.

In 1881 Brahms conducted his satirical *Akademische Festouvertüre* (*Academic Festival Overture*), based on students' songs, in Breslau, where the University had awarded him a doctorate. He did not care for honours, and failed to attend the degree ceremony. That year he completed the Second Piano Concerto in B flat – a *tour de force* of power and vitality, and a milestone of pianistic virtuosity. He also had a major disagreement with Joachim, who was intending to divorce his wife. Brahms took Frau Joachim's side, and the violinist broke off all relations with Brahms. (They were eventually reconciled in 1887, when Brahms wrote the Double Concerto for Joachim and the cellist Robert Hausmann.)

Also from 1881, the conductor Hans von Bülow – a great admirer of Brahms – offered the composer the use of the Meiningen court orchestra to try out his new works. These included the Third and Fourth Symphonies. The Third, in F,

ABOVE: Brahms at the piano – a posthumous sketch by Beckerath, 1899. Brahms had always been a fine pianist, having played since the age of seven.

was written in Wiesbaden in 1883, and the Fourth, in E minor, during two summer holidays in southern Austria, and performed on a European tour with the Meiningen Orchestra in the autumn of 1885. In its *passacaglia* finale, Brahms paid homage to another lifelong influence, that of J. S. Bach.

Last works

Brahms spent the following three summers at Hofstetten on Lake Thun, where he wrote his Second Cello Sonata in F major, two more violin sonatas, and the C minor Trio. By 1890 he had resolved to stop composing, but broke his resolution to write four clarinet works inspired by the brilliant playing of Richard Mühlfeld (1856–1907), principal clarinettist with the Meiningen Orchestra: the Clarinet Trio and Quintet and two clarinet sonatas. Clara Schumann's death in May 1896 prompted one final work – the *Vier ernste Gesänge* (*Four Serious Songs*) – but by then Brahms himself was mortally ill from liver cancer. He died on 3 April 1897, and was buried in Vienna's central cemetery.

ABOVE: The sixth book of Brahms's Collected Songs.

Anton Bruckner

Bruckner! He is my man!

RICHARD WAGNER (1813–83)

Bruckner's name is often coupled with Mahler's – but for no other reason than that both were Austrian and both wrote important, large-scale symphonies. In all other respects they were very different.

Bruckner's father was the village schoolmaster and organist at Ansfelden in central Austria. Anton, the eldest of five surviving children, was taught by his father, and by the age of ten was already a proficient organist. He also came into contact with the Catholic musical tradition at the nearby monastery of St Florian, where he enrolled as a chorister at the age of 13, after his father's death. St Florian was to remain the focus of Bruckner's life, and he chose to be buried there, beneath the organ.

Bruckner began his career as an ordinary schoolmaster in two provincial villages. Eventually, in 1845, he returned as a teacher and then as organist to St Florian. His first important compositions, including a Requiem Mass and the *Missa solemnis* in B flat, date from his early years there.

By 1855 Bruckner had decided he wanted to become a professional musician. While working as organist at Linz Cathedral, he enrolled on a correspondence course in harmony and counterpoint at the Vienna Conservatory. He graduated in 1861 at the advanced age of 37, with glowing references. But he still felt he lacked musical knowledge, and sought further tuition in symphonic form and orchestration with the principal cellist and conductor at the Linz municipal theatre, who engaged him in a thorough study of Beethoven and Mendelssohn.

ABOVE: The Austrian composer Anton Bruckner – a portrait by H. Kaulback.

LEFT: A page from Bruckner's Ninth Symphony, left unfinished at his death.

RIGHT: The organ at the Abbey Church of St Florian. Bruckner was a chorister and then organist there, and is buried beneath the organ.

ABOVE: The Graben, one of the principal streets in Vienna, in Bruckner's time. Bruckner lived in Vienna from 1868 until his death.

The impact of Wagner

Up to this point, Bruckner had been competent but characterless as a composer. Then, in 1863, he heard Wagner's *Tannhäuser*, and the experience changed his life. Overwhelmed by Wagner's genius, Bruckner immediately began to try his own hand at symphonic composition. During the mid 1860s he attended many performances of Wagner's music, and even met the great man, while his budding confidence led to the composition of three masses and the Symphony No. 1 in C minor (1865–6).

After suffering a nervous breakdown brought on by intense overwork, Bruckner was eventually persuaded to apply for a professorship at the Vienna Conservatory, to which he was appointed in 1868. He also became organist at the Imperial Chapel in Vienna, and received a government grant to allow him to compose. He lived in Vienna until his death, leaving for occasional visits to Paris and London, where his organ recitals were greeted with huge acclaim.

In Vienna (where he was appointed a lecturer at the University in 1875) he devoted much of his energy to composing symphonies. Between 1871 and his death, he turned out eight more (No. 9 remained unfinished).

Despite Bruckner's growing fame, he encountered enormous opposition and hostility from two anti-Wagnerite sources. The Vienna Philharmonic Orchestra either rejected his symphonies as "unplayable" or deliberately sabotaged their performances, and the influential critic Eduard Hanslick – a supporter of

ABOVE: The beginning of the Gloria from Bruckner's Mass in D minor (1864), a page from the autograph score.

Brahms – took every opportunity to denounce Bruckner's symphonies, especially the Third (which Bruckner, in an enthusiastic fit of hero-worship, had unwisely dubbed his *Wagner* Symphony). Diffident by nature and fatally lacking in self-esteem, Bruckner also suffered from the interference of well-meaning but misguided "friends" who persuaded him to make cuts and alterations to the scores of his symphonies, in the interests of "accessibility". Many still exist in various hybrid versions.

Bruckner's first real success came at the age of 60, with the Leipzig première of his Seventh Symphony in 1884. He had finally found critical acceptance, although he continued to revise his scores obsessively. Official honours came his way during the last decade of his life. A simple, pious, old-fashioned man, he never married, although he proposed to a succession of astonished young women. He had a morbid obsession with dead bodies, and left instructions that his own should be embalmed.

Giuseppe Verdi

It may be a good thing to copy reality;
but to invent reality is much, much better.

VERDI, 1876

Verdi was the greatest Italian opera composer of the 19th century. Unlike Wagner, who strove to create a new type of music-drama, Verdi worked within the Italian tradition of his predecessors, but throughout his long career his technique became ever more fluent, his characterizations more rounded and expressive, and his response to the text increasingly refined.

His masterpieces are the Shakespearean operas *Otello* (1887) and *Falstaff* (1893), written when he was in his 70s, but works from all periods of his life form the backbone of the present-day operatic repertoire.

ABOVE: Giuseppe Verdi (1813–1901), the greatest Italian opera composer of the 19th century.

Early years

Verdi was born in Lombardy, at a small village in the vicinity of Parma. He began to play the keyboard when he was three, and at ten he was sent to study in Busseto. In 1831 he became the protégé of a music-loving merchant, Antonio Barezzi, who financed his further musical education privately in Milan, Verdi having been rejected by the Milan Conservatory. Verdi then returned to Busseto as the town's music director. In 1836, aged 22, he married Barezzi's daughter Margherita. They had two children, who both died in infancy.

In 1838 Verdi began work on his first opera, *Oberto*. He, his wife and baby son moved to Milan, where the opera had been accepted for production at La Scala. It was premièred in November 1839, a few weeks after his son's death, and in June 1840 Verdi's wife also died. During this sad period, Verdi was working on a new opera, the comedy *Un giorno di regno* (*King for a Day*), which failed utterly at its première at La Scala in September 1840.

Verdi was so discouraged that he almost gave up composing, but a friend persuaded him to begin work on *Nabucco*, based on the biblical story of Nebuchadnezzar. This — his earliest well-known work, famous for its chorus of Hebrew slaves "Va, pensiero" — was a triumphant

ABOVE: The French dramatic soprano Rose Caron as Desdemona in Verdi's Otello. *She created the role in 1894.*

ABOVE: Arturo Toscanini, one of the great Verdi interpreters, conducting the orchestra of La Scala Opera House in May 1946.

ABOVE: A set design (c.1862) by Carlo Ferrario for Verdi's grand opera La forza del destino *(The Force of Destiny).*

ABOVE: A scene from a performance of Verdi's Aida *at the 1991 Savonlinna Opera Festival in Finland.*

success, and was soon being performed all over Europe. Before long, Verdi's name was being linked with the emerging nationalist movement in Italy, as choruses such as "Va, pensiero" and the Scottish exiles' lament from *Macbeth* (1847) were interpreted as coded rallying-cries for the oppressed Italian nation.

Galley years

With *Ernani* (1844), Verdi entered on a period he later called his "galley years", producing a string of operas for Rome, Milan, Naples, Venice, Florence, Trieste, and even London (*I masnadieri* – The Brigands, 1847). His early operas, up to *La battaglia di Legnano* (*The Battle of Legnano*, 1849), were still influenced by Rossini, and generally dealt with historical subjects (including the Shakespearean opera *Macbeth*).

Luisa Miller (1849) was the first of a series of works in which the subject-matter became more personal and intimate. The finest operas of this period are *Rigoletto* – the tragic tale of a hunchbacked court jester who seeks to avenge his daughter's seduction but inadvertently causes her death; *Il trovatore* (*The Troubadour*), another tragedy with the motif of revenge at its heart; and *La traviata* (*The Woman Gone Astray*), Verdi's version of *La dame aux camélias* by Alexandre Dumas. The

story of the courtesan who finds true love, sacrifices it for her lover's honour, and dies of consumption, is one of the most popular operas ever written.

Grand opera

Verdi's third period began with *Les vêpres siciliennes* (*The Sicilian Vespers*, Paris, 1855), and includes *Simon Boccanegra*, *Un ballo in maschera* (*A Masked Ball*), *La forza del destino* (*The Force of Destiny*, produced in

St Petersburg in 1862), *Don Carlos* (Paris) and *Aida* (Cairo). During this period he spent much time on the country estate he had bought near his birthplace, with his second wife, the soprano Giuseppina Strepponi (1815–97).

In 1861, after the Italian War of Independence, Verdi was elected to the new Italian parliament, and for the next four years mixed politics with composition. After *Aida*, he wrote little except his dramatic Requiem commemorating the death of the Italian nationalist poet Alessandro Manzoni (1785–1873).

Last works

The huge success of the Requiem prompted Verdi's publisher, Ricordi, to suggest a collaboration with the composer-librettist Arrigo Boito (1842–1918), on an opera based on Shakespeare's *Othello*. It took Verdi another decade to begin work on *Otello*, which with *Falstaff* marked the culmination of his career. His last work, in 1898, was a set of *Quatro pezzi sacri* (*Four Sacred Pieces*), including a Te Deum and Stabat Mater. By then Verdi had lost his beloved second wife, he was over 80 and worn out. He died in Milan in January 1901, leaving his fortune to a home for aged musicians which he had built in Milan, and which he regarded as "his greatest work".

Richard Wagner

Wagner's opera style recognizes only superlatives.

EDUARD HANSLICK (1825–1904)

The figure of Richard Wagner straddles the 19th century like a colossus. Composer, critic, polemicist, his abundant energy allowed him to a pursue a vision with a ruthless single-mindedness beyond the comprehension of ordinary mortals.

His operas, rooted in the German Romantic tradition, remain (like Verdi's) the cornerstones of the modern repertoire, but they require performers of extraordinary power and stamina. There are still few sopranos and tenors able to do justice to roles such as Siegfried, Brünnhilde, Tristan and Isolde, and many singers have burnt out their voices in the attempt.

ABOVE: A costume design by Franz Gaul for the 1873 production of Wagner's early opera Rienzi *at the State Theatre in Brunswick.*

ABOVE: An evocative portrait of Richard Wagner (1813–83), by Lenbach. Wagner was much given to striking romantic poses.

Early years

Friedrich Wagner died of typhus soon after his son Richard was born, and his mother Johanna married Ludwig Meyer, who introduced his stepson to the world of the theatre and music. The family moved to Dresden, where the young Wagner came into contact with Weber, then conductor at the Royal Theatre. According to Wagner, it was Weber who instilled in him "a passion for music". After his stepfather's death the family returned to Wagner's birthplace, Leipzig, where he completed his education at school and university. By now he was passionately interested in the theatre, and in 1832 he began work on his first, abortive, opera. He realized from the start that he would only ever be able to work with his own librettos.

He began his theatrical career as a chorus-master in Würzburg, where he completed his first opera *Die Feen* (*The Fairies*). It remained unperformed, but already Wagner was showing a dogged determination to succeed. He began work on a third opera, *Das Liebesverbot* (*Love's Interdict*), based on Shakespeare's *Measure for Measure*, and joined a travelling theatre company as music director. *Das Liebesverbot* had a single performance in Magdeburg in 1836, before the company went bankrupt.

ABOVE: Senta leaps to her death — an Art Nouveau illustration of the final scene of The Flying Dutchman.

ABOVE: A domestic vision of Wagner at home with his second wife Cosima, daughter of Franz Liszt.

ABOVE: A scene from the last act of Rienzi, premièred at the Dresden Hoftheater on 20 October 1842.

By this time Wagner had fallen in love with the actress Minna Planer, whom he married on 24 November. Six months later Minna ran off with another man, but was reconciled with her husband in October 1837. Their relationship remained stormy.

Paris

Wagner was working at Riga (now in Latvia) when he began *Rienzi*. By March 1839, when his contract ended, he was heavily in debt (a *Leitmotif* of his career). He, Minna and their huge dog were obliged to flee from his creditors by ship to London.

In September they arrived in Paris, where Wagner hoped to establish himself as a composer. Instead he found himself trying to make ends meet from journalism, while financial problems landed him in a debtors' prison. He did, however, come into contact with a great deal of new music, and with literature, especially the Germanic legends of Tannhäuser and Lohengrin. His Paris period thus laid the foundations of several future operas, including *Der fliegende Holländer* (*The Flying Dutchman*), which he finished in 1841. The famous, storm-tossed overture to this dramatic tale,

of a restless ghost who is finally redeemed by faithful love, was inspired by Wagner's own experiences on the ship from Riga.

Dresden

In 1842 *Rienzi* was finally performed, with considerable success, at the Dresden court theatre, which agreed to mount *The Flying Dutchman* in January 1843. Although Wagner was

Life and works

NATIONALITY: German

BORN: Leipzig, 1813;
DIED: Venice, 1883

SPECIALIST GENRES: German Romantic opera and music-dramas.

MAJOR WORKS: *Der fliegende Holländer* (1841); *Tannhäuser* (1843); *Lohengrin* (1848); *Tristan und Isolde* (1859); *Die Meistersinger von Nürnberg* (1867); *Der Ring des Nibelungen* (1853–74); *Parsifal* (1882).

disappointed with the latter's reception, his career was finally launched, and he was offered the post of conductor in Dresden. In April 1843 he completed *Tannhäuser*, based on the legend of the knight – seduced from his duties by the pleasures of Venus – who is redeemed by a divine miracle. *Tannhäuser* was premièred in Dresden in October 1845.

Wagner began work on *Lohengrin*, which was finished in 1848, the year of revolution in Europe. Wagner's pro-revolutionary sympathies implicated him (by default) in the Dresden uprising of May 1849, and in fear of his life he escaped to Switzerland. He settled in Zurich, where he worked on his creative manifesto, *Opera and Drama*, and also began work on the texts of a new project, based on the ancient Nordic saga of the Nibelungs. *Lohengrin* could not now be produced in Dresden, so Wagner sent the score to Liszt, who had sufficient confidence in it to risk censure by mounting a production in Weimar in August 1850. It eventually became an outstanding success, although Wagner himself was unable to attend a performance until 1861.

ABOVE: A Romantic impression of Wagner composing his epic saga Der Ring des Nibelungen, *a cycle of four operas completed in 1874.*

Music of the future

Lohengrin – another legendary tale of knightly chivalry with a strong magical element – marked the end of Wagner's involvement with conventional German Romantic opera. In *Opera and Drama* he set out his visionary ideal of the "music of the future", in which music and drama became indivisible. The last 30 years of his life were dedicated to realizing this ideal.

By 1852 Wagner was again chronically in debt. He was helped by the merchant Otto Wesendonk, with whose wife, Mathilde, he fell in love. Their affair inspired the opera *Tristan und Isolde*, which Wagner began in 1857. This passionate portrayal of an adulterous love which can find fulfilment only in death is one of the supreme achievements of Western art. In it, Wagner pushed chromatic harmony to its limits, from the unresolved, "yearning" motif of the Prelude to the ecstatic dignity of Isolde's "Liebestod" ("love-death")

in which she is finally united with Tristan as the strained "Tristan chord" achieves its radiant resolution.

Munich

Wagner's personal troubles continued. His wife discovered his liaison with Mathilde Wesendonk, and Wagner fled to Venice. With the police at his heels he moved on to Lucerne (where he finished *Tristan*) and then to Paris,

where performances of *Tannhäuser* in 1861 were disrupted by an organized and noisy claque.

A political amnesty of 1860 allowed Wagner to return to Germany, but he spent the next three years travelling from city to city dodging his creditors, until a knight in shining armour appeared in the person of the "mad" King Ludwig II of Bavaria. Ludwig paid off Wagner's debts and offered him sanctuary in Munich, where *Tristan und Isolde* was first performed on 10 June 1865, under the baton of Hans von Bülow. Wagner repaid Bülow by beginning an affair with his wife Cosima (daughter of Liszt and the Countess Marie d'Agoult), who bore him two daughters, Isolde and Eva.

Wagner now had to leave Germany again in the face of Bavarian opposition to his powerful influence over the king and the vast sums of money that were being lavished on him from the public purse. Minna Wagner having died in 1866, Cosima von Bülow moved in with Wagner at his new home – financed by Ludwig – at Tribschen, outside Lucerne, where their son Siegfried was born in 1869. (This event inspired Wagner to compose the *Siegfried Idyll*, rehearsed in secret and played as a surprise for Cosima on Christmas morning.) After Cosima's divorce from Bülow, she and Wagner were married in 1870.

ABOVE: The Festspielhaus at Bayreuth, built to Wagner's specifications by Gottfried Semper between 1871 and 1876 for the performance of Wagnerian music-dramas.

Cosima – a formidable woman – kept Wagner on a short leash throughout their marriage, but protected his interests, and enabled him to compose in peace.

Bayreuth

In June 1868 *Die Meistersinger von Nürnberg* – a blend of comedy, philosophy, radiant young love and wisdom as embodied in the person of Hans Sachs the cobbler – had been premièred in Munich. At the same time, Wagner continued working on his *Ring* cycle, but realized that no existing theatre was suitable for such a large project. With King Ludwig's help, he raised the money to build a dedicated "Festival Theatre" at Bayreuth, where his operas are still performed at an annual festival directed by members of the Wagner family. The new theatre was inaugurated in August 1876 with three complete performances of the *Ring* cycle of four works – *Das Rheingold,*

ABOVE: A 1914 stage set for the "Garden of Enchantment" in Parsifal, *designed by Thomas Edwin Mostyn (1864–1930).*

Die Walküre, Siegfried and *Götterdämmerung* (*The Twilight of the Gods*).

Der Ring des Nibelungen – which contains over 12 hours of music – is held together by a complex system of musical references called *Leitmotifs*, in which characters and situations are identified by individual musical motifs, such as the joyous horn call associated with the hero Siegfried. By now Wagner's musical language had

succeeded in merging voices and orchestra into one continuous texture, at the opposite end of the spectrum from the Italianate concept of opera as separate arias, ensembles and choruses. This complex, endlessly evolving web of sound proved an ideal vehicle for the grandiose Nibelung drama, which reaches its shattering conclusion as Valhalla burns and the world ends.

In 1882 Wagner finished his last opera, *Parsifal*, based on the quasi-religious myth of the quest for the Holy Grail, with its miraculous powers of healing. It was performed at Bayreuth in the summer of 1882, conducted by Hermann Levi. Wagner himself conducted the last scene of the final performance. Two weeks later, suffering from a heart condition, he took his family to Venice, where he died of a heart attack on 13 February 1883.

LEFT: Brünnhilde, from Arthur Rackham's 1910 watercolour illustrations to The Rhinegold *and* The Valkyrie.

RIGHT: The "Good Friday" scene from a 1950s Bayreuth production of Parsifal, *produced by Wagner's grandson Wieland.*

Gustav Mahler

To write a symphony is, for me, to construct a world.

MAHLER

Mahler was a transitional figure. A contemporary of Sigmund Freud and the painter Gustav Klimt, his massive orchestral works are rooted in the 19th-century Austro-German symphonic tradition and speak in a rich, late-Romantic idiom inflected with folk idioms, yet look forward to 20th-century preoccupations such as neurosis and mysticism. His most important works are his ten symphonies and his songs with orchestral accompaniment, which influenced them. Four of the symphonies – Nos. 2, 3, 4 and 8 – have substantial vocal and choral parts, which has tended to limit their performance potential, and for almost five decades after Mahler's death his works were largely neglected, admired

ABOVE: *Gustav Mahler in the loggia of the Vienna Court Opera House, where he was conductor from 1897 until 1907.*

only by a small band of devotees, until the advocacy of conductors such as Bruno Walter, Georg Solti and Rafael Kubelík in Europe, Leonard Bernstein in America and Norman del Mar in Britain, restored them to the repertoire.

Conducting

Mahler was born into a Jewish family and, although he later converted to Catholicism, his career was to some extent blighted by the anti-Semitic attitude of the Austrian establishment.

He showed musical promise as a child, and studied at the Vienna Conservatory from 1875–8, where he wrote the cantata *Das klagende Lied* (*The Song of Sorrow*). From 1880 onwards he made his living as a conductor at provincial theatres in Upper Austria, Slovenia, Bohemia, and then at Kassel in Germany, where he composed the song-cycle *Lieder eines fahrenden Gesellen* (*Songs of a Wayfarer*), and started his First Symphony.

In 1885 Mahler spent a year in Prague, and then moved to Leipzig. There he met the Weber family, who introduced him to the folk poetry collection *Des Knaben Wunderhorn* (*The Youth's Magic Horn*, published in 1805–8). From 1887 onwards he began to set some of the

ABOVE: *A page from the autograph score of Mahler's Sixth Symphony (1903–6).*

ABOVE: *Mahler's wife Alma with their daughters Maria and Anna, c.1906–7.*

ABOVE: Mahler rehearsing his Eighth Symphony (Symphony of a Thousand). The huge choir extends all around the auditorium.

Wunderhorn poems, which were reworked in his earlier symphonies. Between 1888 and 1891 he worked as conductor of the Royal Opera in Budapest, before moving to the Stadttheater in Hamburg, where he conducted Wagner's *Tristan* in May 1891. By 1892 he had completed his First Symphony (first performed at Weimar in 1894), and had begun work on a second (the *Resurrection*). By then he had established a working pattern of conducting during the winter seasons, and retreating to the mountains to compose in the summer. The Third Symphony was finished in this way at Steinbach in the Salzkammergut.

Vienna

In 1897 Mahler was appointed conductor at the Vienna State Opera (one of his first productions there was Wagner's *Ring* cycle). He remained at Vienna for ten years, as one of the Opera's most distinguished music directors. In 1901 he found a new lakeside retreat at Maiernigg in Carinthia, where over the next few summers he composed the Fourth, Fifth,

Sixth and Seventh Symphonies, the *Rückert-Lieder*, the *Kindertotenlieder* (*Songs on the Death of Children*) and other works. The glorious *Adagietto* of the Fifth Symphony was an expression of his love for Alma Schindler, stepdaughter of the Viennese artist Carl Moll, whom Mahler married in 1902. Contrary to popular belief, the deeply affecting *Kindertotenlieder* pre-dated the death from scarlet fever of the couple's elder daughter Maria in 1907, although Alma believed that the cycle had "tempted providence".

ABOVE: The Metropolitan Opera House, New York, in the early 20th century. Mahler was appointed conductor there in 1908.

Mahler's Eighth Symphony (*Symphony of a Thousand*) dates from 1906–7. It was based on the text of a medieval hymn and the closing scene of Goethe's *Faust*, Part II. Mahler thought it "the greatest work I have yet composed". At the end of 1907, the victim of a vicious press campaign, he was obliged to resign his Vienna post, and also discovered that he had a potentially fatal heart condition. He was appointed conductor at the Metropolitan Opera House, New York, from January 1908, but continued to spend the summers in Europe, where he composed *Das Lied von der Erde* (*The Song of the Earth*), based on Chinese poems about the transience of life. He also completed his Ninth Symphony and began a Tenth.

In February 1911 Mahler became seriously ill, and died in Austria, aged 50. *Das Lied von der Erde* and the Ninth Symphony were given posthumous performances; the Tenth was completed in the 1960s by the British scholar Deryck Cooke.

Edward Elgar

Look out for this man's music;
he has something to say and knows how to say it.

HUBERT PARRY (1848–1918)

Like Arthur Sullivan (another composer knighted for his services to British music), Edward Elgar transcended the class barriers of his age, rising from humble origins to epitomize — in musical terms — Britain at the height of her Imperial glory.

Early life

He was born within sight of the Malvern Hills near Worcester, where his father ran a music shop and was organist at St George's Catholic Church. Edward's first job on leaving school was to help his father in both capacities, and he also began to play the violin in local orchestras and chamber groups. In the early 1880s he began to make a living as a freelance

ABOVE: *Edward Elgar revived British music almost single-handedly.*

Creative period

By the mid 1890s Elgar was becoming known for the cantatas he had composed for provincial festivals, including *The Black Knight* (1893) and *King Olaf* (1896), and in 1897 he finally achieved a breakthrough in London with the *Imperial March* for Queen Victoria's Diamond Jubilee.

In 1899 his first truly original composition, the orchestral *Enigma Variations*, was performed at St James's Hall in London. The Variations — each a

ABOVE: *Elgar conducting in the studio in 1919, the year he wrote his Cello Concerto.*

player, teacher, conductor and self-taught composer with instrumental groups in the Malvern area. His composing ambitions were stimulated by his marriage in 1889 to his piano pupil Alice Roberts, daughter of a retired major-general. Alice, who was 40 when she married the 31-year-old Elgar, had social pretensions, and she persuaded her husband to move to London, where their only daughter, Carice, was born in September 1890.

Success as a composer at first eluded Elgar, and the following year the family moved back to Malvern, where he resumed his teaching activities and strove to overcome a sense of social inferiority. His persistence paid off when his overture *Froissart* was published.

Life and works

NATIONALITY: English

BORN: Broadheath, near Worcester, 1857; **DIED:** Worcester, 1934

SPECIALIST GENRES: Orchestral music, oratorios.

MAJOR WORKS: Symphonies No. 1 and 2; *Enigma Variations* (1899); *Sea Pictures* (1899); *Pomp and Circumstance* Marches (1901–30); *The Dream of Gerontius* (1900); Introduction and Allegro for string orchestra (1905); Violin Concerto (1910); *Falstaff* (1913); Cello Concerto (1919).

thinly disguised character portrait of a friend (including Elgar himself and his wife) – were recognized as a work of genius, while the underlying "enigma" – an unnamed tune which Elgar said "goes through and over the whole set" – has never been positively identified. The Variations encapsulate Elgar's musical style: noble, expansive, but tinged with plangent nostalgia for the English countryside.

In the autumn of 1899 the contralto Clara Butt sang Elgar's orchestral song-cycle *Sea Pictures* at the Norwich Festival, and he was commissioned to write an oratorio for the 1900 Birmingham Festival. The result was *The Dream of Gerontius*, based on a metaphysical Catholic text by Cardinal Henry Newman. Elgar was bitterly disappointed by the initial failure of this great work (which has since been recognized as a masterpiece), but the same year he was awarded an honorary doctorate by Cambridge University. His orchestral works were becoming popular, including the overture *Cockaigne*, inspired by London, and the first two *Pomp and Circumstance* Marches, of which the trio section from the first was later allied to the words of the verse "Land of Hope and Glory" written by A. C. Benson for the coronation of Edward VII. In 1904 Elgar was knighted.

The same year, the Elgars moved to a large house in Hereford, where over the next few years he wrote another oratorio (*The Kingdom*), the Introduction and Allegro for string orchestra (1905), and two symphonies. In 1910 Fritz Kreisler gave the première of Elgar's Violin Concerto,

ABOVE: *The programme for a gala performance at the Royal Opera House, 1902, in the presence of the new King Edward VII and Queen Alexandra, at which Elgar's* Coronation Ode *was performed.*

an eloquent work which bears an enigmatic dedication in Spanish: "Herein is enshrined the soul of…" This soul may have been that of John Everett Millais's daughter, Alice Stuart-Wortley, to whom Elgar seems to have been deeply attached.

In 1912 Elgar returned to London, to a grand house in Hampstead, where he wrote the cantata *The Music Makers* (1912) and the symphonic poem *Falstaff* (1913). He was greatly distressed by World War I, which he saw destroying the society in which his works were rooted, and his personal response was the elegiac Cello Concerto and three chamber works – a violin sonata, a string quartet and a piano quintet (all 1919). These were to be his last major works.

Post-war years

After Lady Elgar's death in 1920, Elgar wrote little more. He was created Master of the King's Music in 1924, and in 1932, the year the young Yehudi Menuhin made his historic recording of the Violin Concerto, the BBC commissioned a third symphony. Elgar was still working on it when he died of cancer on 23 February 1934. His wish that no one should "tinker" with it was respected for over 60 years, until it was completed by Anthony Payne (born 1936) and performed in 1997.

ABOVE: *Yehudi Menuhin (aged 16) recording Elgar's Violin Concerto in 1932, with the composer conducting.*

Jean Sibelius

Give me the loneliness either of the Finnish forest or of a big city.

SIBELIUS

The careers of Jean Sibelius and Edward Elgar have many parallels, although Sibelius, eight years Elgar's junior, outlived the English composer by more than 20 years. Each was responsible for a musical renaissance in his native land, and each developed a highly distinctive idiom, inspired to a certain extent by the musical characteristics of his native culture. Both composers lapsed into creative silence after middle age.

Sibelius was born into a Swedish-speaking family. His father, a doctor, died of cholera when Jean – who gallicized his given name, Johan – was still an infant, and the boy was brought up by his mother and grandmother. He was a promising violinist (he hoped to become a soloist), and was composing by the age of ten. From an early age he was much influenced by the *Kalevala*, the Finnish national epic, which – allied to an intense response to landscape and nature – was to provide the impetus for his own work.

ABOVE: *A coloured drawing from 1904 of the Finnish composer Jean Sibelius (1865–1957) by Albert Edelfelt.*

After leaving school Sibelius originally intended to study law, but gave it up in favour of music. In the 1880s he studied first in Helsinki,

and then in Berlin and Vienna, where he made many influential contacts, but also began the heavy drinking and financial irresponsibility which were to mar his later life.

Nationalism

Sibelius returned to Finland in 1891, where he worked on *Kullervo*, a symphonic poem for soprano, baritone, chorus and orchestra based on the *Kalevala*. Its immediate success established him as Finland's leading composer. In June 1892 he married the daughter of a Finnish nationalist general, thereby cementing his own identification with the nationalist movement (Finland was at that time part of the Russian Empire).

Although Sibelius never used actual folk tunes, his works of the 1890s are all distinctively Finnish. They include the four tone-poems based on the exploits of the legendary hero Lemminkäinen, of which the third is *Tuonelan joutsen* (*The Swan of Tuonela*); two more tone-poems –

ABOVE: *A panoramic photograph of Helsinki, the capital of Finland, c.1910. Sibelius studied music at Helsinki's Conservatoire from 1886–8, where he became friends with the Italian/German composer Ferruccio Busoni (1866–1924) who was a member of the teaching staff.*

ABOVE: *A photograph of Sibelius taken when he was a student in Vienna in his early 20s.*

En saga and *Skogsrået* (*The Wood-nymph*) – and the incidental music to *Karelia* (from which Sibelius made an orchestral suite). All these show the characteristic features of Sibelius's musical style, especially his liking for short motifs which are spun out symphonically, his use of *ostinato* patterns, and his effective handling of orchestration, with woodwind highlighted against an atmospheric string background, giving the impression of wind-blown open spaces.

Symphonies

In 1897 Sibelius – who was constantly in debt – was awarded a state pension which allowed him to concentrate on composing. Two years later he completed the tone-poem *Finlandia* and his First Symphony, clearly influenced by Tchaikovsky. It was followed

by six more symphonies, written between 1902 and 1924, each of which is highly individual. The Second (1902) and the Fifth (1915) are perhaps the most popular (like Beethoven's, the Fifth is a "heroic" work); while the Fourth (1911) is compact and austere in tone, the Sixth more pastoral, and the short Seventh (originally called *Fantasia sinfonica*) is in a single movement. An Eighth Symphony was written, but immediately destroyed.

During the early years of the 20th century, Sibelius travelled extensively, visiting England, Bohemia and Italy. The Violin Concerto dates from 1903, a period in which Sibelius's drinking and debt put his marriage under strain. In 1904 he built himself a villa outside Helsinki, where he lived for the rest of his life. The tone-poems *Pohjolan tytär* (*Pohjola's Daughter*) and *Oinen ratsastus ja auringonnousu* (*Night-ride and Sunrise*) date from this period, as does the

ABOVE: *An impressionistic illustration of Sibelius's tone-poem* The Swan of Tuonela *(1893–7) by I. J. Belmont.*

incidental music to Maurice Maeterlinck's *Pelléas et Mélisande* (a play which Debussy used as the basis for his opera) and *Belsazars gästabud* (*Belshazzar's Feast*, a Biblical episode later set by William Walton).

Silence

In 1908 Sibelius underwent an operation for suspected throat cancer, and his later works have an intensified bleakness. He continued to travel throughout Europe and to America to conduct his works until the outbreak of World War I, an event which virtually ended his creative life. After the war he wrote only four more major pieces, including incidental music for Shakespeare's *The Tempest* (1925), and his last symphonic poem, *Tapiola* (1926). For the remaining 31 years of his life, he composed nothing, disliked talking about his music and became increasingly reclusive.

Camille Saint-Saëns

There is nothing more difficult than talking about music.

SAINT-SAËNS

popular *Danse macabre*, and *La jeunesse d'Hercule* (*Hercules' Youth*). In 1871 he was a founder-member of the Société Nationale de Musique, set up to promote performances of works by younger French composers.

The French composer Camille Saint-Saëns was, like Mozart and Mendelssohn, a child prodigy. His father died just after he was born, and he was brought up by his mother and an aunt who began to teach him the piano when he was two. He was composing by the age of three, and played concertos by Mozart and Beethoven when he was ten. He also showed a keen interest in other intellectual pursuits, particularly archaeology, geology, astronomy and philosophy.

Saint-Saëns studied at the Paris Conservatoire, and was organist at the Madeleine church in Paris from 1857–76. After hearing him improvise, Liszt declared him the greatest organist in the world. In return, Saint-Saëns acknowledged Liszt's influence on his own symphonic poems of the 1870s: *Le rouet d'Omphale* (*Omphale's Spinning Wheel*), *Phaëton*, the enormously

Saint-Saëns was much attached to his mother but, much to her disapproval, when he was 40 he married a girl half his age. Their two young sons died tragically within six weeks of each other, and after just six years of marriage, Saint-Saëns walked out on his wife. After his mother's death in 1888 he spent much time abroad, especially in North Africa, and many of his works, such as the Fifth Piano Concerto, make use of exotic harmonies.

His most famous and enduring works include the opera *Samson et Dalila*, the First Cello Concerto, the Introduction and Rondo Capriccioso for violin and orchestra, the five piano concertos, the Organ Symphony (No. 3), and *Le carnaval des animaux* (*The Carnival of the Animals*), written as a private joke for performance by friends.

ABOVE: Camille Saint-Saëns (1835–1921). He was an amazingly prolific composer – "I compose music as a tree produces apples", he said.

LEFT: The entrance to the Paris Conservatoire de Musique et de Déclamation in the rue Bergère, where Saint-Saëns studied.

Life and works

NATIONALITY: French

BORN: Paris, 1835;
DIED: Algiers, 1921

SPECIALIST GENRES:
Tone-poems, piano concertos.

MAJOR WORKS: Piano Concerto No. 2 (1868); Cello Concerto No. 1 (1873); *Danse macabre* (1874); *Samson et Dalila* (1877); Symphony No. 3 (1886); *Le carnaval des animaux* (1886).

Gabriel Fauré

For me…music exists to elevate us as far as possible above everyday existence.

FAURÉ, IN A LETTER TO HIS SON PHILIPPE, 1908

Fauré was Saint-Saëns' favourite pupil at the Ecole Niedermeyer in Paris. Like his teacher, he was a gifted pianist and organist, and began his career as an organist in Rennes. In 1871 he became organist at Ste Sulpice in Paris, and was also active in the foundation of the Société Nationale de Musique, where many of his own works were given their premières.

Fauré's engagement to Marianne Viardot (the daughter of a famous singer) produced three fine chamber works: the First Violin Sonata, the First Piano Quartet, and the Ballade for piano. In 1882, five years after Marianne broke off the engagement, he married Marie Fremiet, the daughter of a sculptor. The marriage, which produced two sons, was unhappy, and Fauré found consolation with other women, including Emma Bardac (the

ABOVE: Gabriel Fauré (1845–1924), aged 18. He studied with Saint-Saëns, and later taught at the Paris Conservatoire.

second Mme Debussy), for whom he wrote the tender song-cycle *La bonne chanson*, and for whose daughter Hélène (nicknamed Dolly) he wrote the *Dolly* Suite for piano duet.

Fauré continued to earn a living as organist, choir-master and teacher, and was able to compose only in his spare time. He was happiest with small-scale genres such as songs, piano and chamber music: many of his delicate, elusive songs are settings of texts by the Symbolist poet Paul Verlaine. His famous Requiem — probably his best-known work — took over 20 years to finish. In the late 1890s he was appointed principal organist of the Madeleine church in Paris, and also

became a professor of composition at the Paris Conservatoire, where his pupils included Ravel. He became director of the Conservatoire in 1905.

By the age of 50 Fauré was well-known in Parisian society (his friends included Marcel Proust). By this time he was attempting larger-scale works, including the incidental music to Maeterlinck's play *Pelléas et Mélisande* (which also inspired Debussy and Sibelius), the orchestral suite in 18th-century style *Masques et bergamasques* (1919) and the stage works *Prométhée* and *Pénélope*.

He retired from the Conservatoire in 1920, and was finally able to devote himself to composition, although by this time he was losing his hearing. His late works were mostly for chamber combinations, including a Piano Trio and Piano Quintet.

ABOVE: Fauré playing the organ at the Church of the Madeleine in Paris, where he was principal organist for many years.

Life and works

NATIONALITY: French

BORN: Pamiers, Ariège, 1845; **DIED:** Paris, 1924

SPECIALIST GENRES: Songs, piano and chamber music.

MAJOR WORKS: Songs and song-cycles; piano music, including *Dolly* Suite (1897); *Pavane* (1887); Requiem (1888); *Pelléas et Mélisande* (1892); *Pénélope* (1913).

Giacomo Puccini

*I shall feel it [the story of Manon] as an Italian,
with desperate passion.*

PUCCINI

Puccini was the last great exponent
of Italian Romantic opera. His
operas have always held a special place
in the affections of audiences, and rival
Verdi's in popularity. He was born into
a dynasty of musicians who since the
18th century had been organists at
the church of San Martino in Lucca.
It had been intended that Puccini
should follow the family tradition,
but seeing a performance of Verdi's
Aida at Pisa made him decide to
become an opera composer.

Milan

In 1880 a scholarship enabled Puccini
to enrol at the Milan Conservatory.
He graduated in the summer of 1883,
having entered a one-act opera, *Le
villi* (*The Witches*), in a competition
sponsored by a music publisher. It
came nowhere, but the next year
Puccini played it through at a party
attended by Verdi's publisher Ricordi.
Le villi was staged in 1884, and

*ABOVE: A portrait of Giacomo Puccini
(1858–1924) painted in Paris in 1899,
three years after he wrote his highly popular
opera* La Bohème.

Ricordi immediately commissioned
another opera, *Edgar*, from the young
composer, and signed him up.

Edgar was performed at La Scala in
Milan in 1889, but was not well
received (the composer himself
described it as a "mistake"). But his
next opera, *Manon Lescaut* (based,
like Massenet's opera *Manon*, on the
novel by Abbé Prévost), was a huge
success at its Turin première in
1893. Puccini had found a winning
formula: that of the young, doomed
heroine whose flawed character leads
to an affecting early death. He
repeated it with *La Bohème* (*The
Bohemian Girl*), first performed at Turin
in 1896 under Toscanini; but it took
some time for this romantic drama of
love and death in a Montmartre garret
– now one of the world's most popular
operas – to catch the public's imagination.

Puccini's next opera, *Tosca*, performed
in Rome in 1900, was an excursion
into the brutal world of *verismo*. Its

*ABOVE: Puccini at home in the music-room of his villa at Torre del
Lago, near Lucca.*

ABOVE: A stage set for Act I of Puccini's Tosca, *set in the Roman
church of S Andrea delle Valle.*

"body count" – an attempted rape, a murder, a faked execution by firing squad which turns out to be real, and a final, dramatic suicide – has rarely been surpassed. Critics have always been snooty about *Tosca* (one described it memorably as "a shabby little shocker"), but Puccini's marvellous melodic gift and innate sense of drama save it from mere sensationalism.

Based on a real-life incident, as related in David Belasco's play, *Madama Butterfly* (La Scala, 1904) returned to the "weepie" genre. The tragic tale of a Japanese geisha, betrayed and abandoned by the American naval lieutenant she believes to be her husband, took the operatic world by storm after Puccini revised it into three acts. Another Belasco play, *The Girl of the Golden West*, provided the subject-matter for Puccini's next opera, *La fanciulla del West*, premièred at the New York Metropolitan Opera in December 1910 with Enrico Caruso and Emmy Destinn in the leading roles.

Puccini made a political mistake with his next opera, accepting a commission from the directors of a Viennese theatre instead of an Italian one,

ABOVE: A poster for the original 1904 production of Madama Butterfly. *Butterfly is shown bidding farewell to her child before killing herself.*

drawing accusations of treachery. The little-known *La rondine* (*The Swallow*) was first performed during World War I, though in Monte Carlo rather than Vienna. Puccini worked simultaneously on a "Grand Guignol" triptych of one-act operas: the horrific *Il tabarro* (*The Cloak*), the sentimental tragedy *Suor Angelica* and his one comedy, *Gianni Schicchi*, the most successful of the three. The triptych was premièred in New York in December 1918.

"Nessun dorma"

Puccini had lived since 1891 at his villa at Torre del Lago outside Lucca, with his wife Elvira (his married mistress until 1904). In 1909 their servant girl committed suicide when unjustly accused by the jealous Elvira of having an affair with Puccini. This tragedy may have inspired the character of Liù, the gentle, lovable slave girl in Puccini's last opera *Turandot*, based on an oriental fairy-tale. The work includes the aria "Nessun dorma", popularized by the "Three Tenors" at a concert staged in conjunction with the 1990

football World Cup in Italy. *Turandot* was destined to have a happy ending, when the cruel princess Turandot is outwitted by Prince Calaf and finally succumbs to love. But Puccini died of a heart attack during treatment for throat cancer in November 1924, leaving the final love duet unfinished.

ABOVE: A page from the manuscript score of La Bohème *(1896). Puccini has indicated Mimi's death with a skull and crossbones in the margin.*

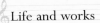

Life and works

NATIONALITY: Italian

BORN: Lucca, 1858;
DIED: Brussels, 1924

SPECIALIST GENRES:
Italian opera.

MAJOR WORKS:
Manon Lescaut (1893);
La Bohème (1896);
Tosca (1900);
Madama Butterfly (1904);
Turandot (1926).

Richard Strauss

*From time to time the cruellest discords are succeeded by exquisite suavities,
that caress the ear with delight.*

CAMILLE SAINT-SAËNS (1835–1921), OF "SALOME"

Richard Strauss, like Rachmaninov, was a composer who outlived his era. Elgar and Sibelius stopped composing shortly after World War I, perhaps realizing that the spirit of the age contradicted their personal artistic visions; but their contemporaries Strauss and Rachmaninov enjoyed a late Romantic Indian summer, oblivious to stylistic change.

Strauss was born in 1864, the son of the principal horn player in the Munich court orchestra. His father Franz played horn solos in the premières of Wagner's *Tristan und Isolde* (1865) and *Die Meistersinger von Nürnberg* (1868), but the young Richard first encountered Wagner's operas a few years later. A precociously gifted child, he had learnt the piano from the age of four and the violin from eight.

Strauss's first important work, the *Serenade* for wind instruments, was performed in Berlin in 1882 by

ABOVE: A portrait of the young Richard Strauss (1864–1949), probably dating from the 1890s.

members of the famous Meiningen Orchestra, whose conductor Hans von Bülow commissioned the young composer's Suite in B flat. During this period Strauss also wrote his First Horn Concerto, a cello sonata, a symphony (No. 2, premièred in New York), and several song settings. In the summer of 1885 Strauss became von Bülow's assistant at Meiningen, and took over from von Bülow a month later. From then on, his career was divided between conducting and composing.

Tone-poems

In 1886 Strauss moved on to the Munich court opera, where he became interested in the theories of Wagner and Arthur Schopenhauer, and in Liszt's tone-poems. His own first venture into this genre, *Aus Italien*, dates from 1886. Between 1889,

LEFT: Strauss directing an opera from the pit, 1929, by Wilhelm Viktor Krausz.

RIGHT: The frontispiece to the original piano score of Elektra *(1909), designed by Louis Corinth.*

when he moved to Weimar as assistant conductor to the court opera, and 1898, when he became chief conductor of the Royal Opera in Berlin, he wrote a sequence of seven magnificent tone-poems: *Don Juan, Macbeth, Tod und Verklärung (Death and Transfiguration), Till Eulenspiegels lustige Streiche (Till Eulenspiegel's Merry Pranks), Also sprach Zarathustra (Thus Spake Zarathustra), Don Quixote* and *Ein Heldenleben (A Hero's Life)*. Together with the *Symphonia domestica* (1902–4) and *Ein Alpensinfonie* (1911–15), they represent Strauss's most important orchestral works.

Opera

However, it was in the field of opera that Strauss achieved fame. Inspired by his marriage in 1893 to the soprano Pauline de Ahna, he began his long love affair with the voice – especially the female voice. His first opera, *Guntram*

ABOVE: *The Dresden Court Opera House, where many of Strauss's operas were performed.*

(1894), was a failure, and his second, *Feuersnot* (Fire Famine, 1901), is rarely performed; but from *Salome* (1905) onwards he created a series of magnificent and individual works which are rarely out of the repertoire. *Salome* (based on Oscar Wilde's scandalous play) and *Elektra* (based on Sophocles' drama) caused international sensations owing to Strauss's explicit treatment of their subjects. Musically, both owe much to Wagner; *Salome* in particular is a masterpiece of sensuous, overblown late Romanticism. The royalties from *Salome* alone enabled Strauss to build himself a luxurious villa at Garmisch.

The librettist of *Elektra*, Hugo von Hofmannsthal (1874–1929), worked with Strauss over the next two decades: their most successful collaboration was the Mozartian comedy *Der Rosenkavalier*. With Hofmannsthal, Strauss went on to create *Ariadne auf Naxos, Die Frau ohne Schatten (The Woman without a Shadow, 1914–17), Die ägyptische Helena (The Egyptian Helen, 1923–7)* and *Arabella* (1929–32), completed after Hofmannsthal's death. Strauss's librettist for his next opera, *Die*

schweigsame Frau (The Silent Woman, 1933–4) was the Jewish Stefan Zweig, but the prevailing political climate in Germany required Strauss to choose an Austrian librettist, Joseph Gregor, for his subsequent operas: *Friedenstag (Peace Day, 1935–6), Daphne* (1936–7) and *Die Liebe der Danaë (Danaë's Love, 1938–40)*.

Strauss's political naivety led to his exploitation by the Nazi Reichsmusik-kammer, which appointed him its president in 1933 but removed him two years later (his daughter-in-law was Jewish). He spent the war years in Vienna (where he wrote his last opera, *Capriccio*, in 1940–1), but afterwards moved to Switzerland while he was investigated – and eventually cleared of Nazi affiliations – by the denazification tribunal.

Strauss's last works are mainly instrumental: they include *Metamorphosen* for 23 solo strings (1945, a lament for the devastation of Germany), the Second Horn Concerto, the Oboe Concerto, sonatinas for wind instruments, and the radiant *Vier letzte Lieder (Four Last Songs,* 1948) for voice and orchestra. He died at his home in Garmisch, aged 85.

Life and works

NATIONALITY: German

BORN: Munich, 1864; **DIED:** Garmisch, 1949

SPECIALIST GENRES: Late Romantic tone-poems, Wagnerian-style opera.

MAJOR WORKS: Tone-poems *Macbeth* (1886–8), *Don Juan* (1888–9), *Tod und Verklärung* (1888–9), *Till Eulenspiegels lustige Streiche* (1894–5), *Also sprach Zarathustra* (1895–6), *Don Quixote* (1896–7) and *Ein Heldenleben* (1897–8); operas *Salome* (1905), *Elektra* (1909), *Der Rosenkavalier* (1911) and *Ariadne auf Naxos* (1911–12); *Capriccio* (1940–1); *Four Last Songs* (1948).

Sergei Rachmaninov

I feel like a ghost wandering in a world grown alien.
I cannot cast out the old way of writing and I cannot acquire the new.

RACHMANINOV

Rachmaninov was the last of a tradition of great pianist-composers, and the last of the Russian Romantics. The dramatic sweep of his music, combined with a haunting Russian melancholy, holds a powerful appeal. His three symphonies and four piano concertos are much loved.

He had his earliest piano lessons from his mother, a trained pianist. In 1882 his family moved to St Petersburg, where Rachmaninov entered the Conservatory. But when his parents separated, he transferred to Moscow, where he studied with the strict teacher Nikolay Zverev, and from 1888 onwards, with Alexander Ziloti (1863–1945) for piano and Anton Arensky (1861–1906) for composition. He graduated from the piano class of the Moscow Conservatory in the summer of 1891, completing his First Piano Concerto at the same time. The next year, his one-

ABOVE: *Sergei Rachmaninov, painted in 1925 while he was living in the USA, by Konstantin Andreyevich Somov.*

act opera *Aleko* won him the Conservatory's highest award for composition and, shortly after graduating, he wrote one of his most popular pieces, the Prelude in C sharp minor for piano.

In 1897, Rachmaninov's good luck changed when his First Symphony, in D minor, was performed at a Russian Symphony Concert, conducted by Alexander Glazunov. The performance was a disaster (Glazunov was rumoured to be drunk), and the critic César Cui described the piece as "a programme symphony on the Seven Plagues of Egypt". It was not

performed again until 1945. Rachmaninov suffered a nervous breakdown, and could not compose anything for three years. In due course he underwent a successful course of hypnotic treatment with a Dr Nikolay Dahl, which restored his confidence and enabled him to start work on the Second Piano Concerto, the theme of whose slow movement was used to memorable effect in David Lean's 1945 film *Brief Encounter*.

Rachmaninov gave the première of his new concerto, dedicated to Dr Dahl, on 9 November 1901, and a few months later, after finishing his cantata *Spring*, he married his cousin Natalya Satina. Over the next few years he occupied himself with opera composition, until the illness of his daughter Irina obliged the family to move to Dresden in 1906. There he completed his Second Symphony (the

ABOVE: *Rachmaninov had unusually large hands, able to cope with big stretches — an advantage for a virtuoso pianist.*

ABOVE: *Alexander Glazunov is reputed to have ruined the première of Rachmaninov's First Symphony by conducting while drunk.*

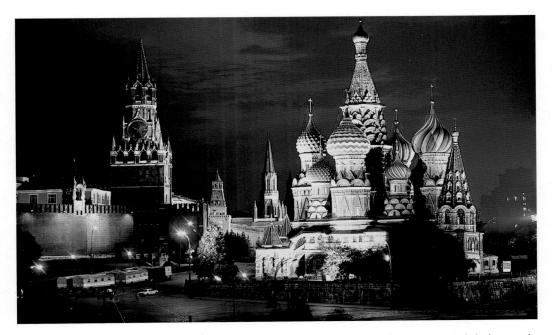

ABOVE: Red Square in Moscow, with St Basil's Cathedral illuminated. Rachmaninov drew inspiration from the Russian Orthodox liturgy, and wrote some fine sacred vocal music.

slow movement with its long-breathed clarinet solo is a masterly piece of writing), the First Piano Sonata, and the symphonic poem *The Isle of the Dead*, inspired by a painting by the Swiss artist Arnold Böcklin.

In 1909 Rachmaninov made his first visit to America, where he toured with a new work, the Third Piano Concerto. Over the next few years he spent the summers on his country estate, where he wrote the 13 Preludes for piano, Op. 13 (1910), the Liturgy of St John Chrysostom (1910), the *Etudes-tableaux* for piano, Op. 33 (1911), the 14 Songs, Op. 34, and the Second Piano Sonata (1913). During the winters he toured as a pianist, a routine that continued until the outbreak of World War I. His other major compositions of this period include the choral symphony *The Bells* (1913) and the *All-night Vigil* for unaccompanied choir (1915).

America

In 1917, the dangerous political situation in Russia forced Rachmaninov and his family into exile, first in Sweden, and then in America, where he remained for the rest of his life. From 1918 onwards he wrote little, spending most of his time performing. The Fourth Piano Concerto was written in 1926, but when it failed to achieve the success of its predecessors Rachmaninov was forced to revise and shorten it.

In 1931 he composed his last solo piano work, the *Variations on a Theme of Corelli*, followed by the brilliant *Rhapsody on a Theme of Paganini* for piano and orchestra (1934), the Third Symphony (1935–8), and the Symphonic Dances, his last work (1940). By early 1943 he was exhausted and ill, but he continued to tour. He died of cancer at his home in Beverly Hills on 28 March 1943, four days before his 70th birthday.

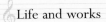
Life and works

NATIONALITY: Russian

BORN: Semyonovo, 1873; **DIED:** Beverly Hills, 1943

SPECIALIST GENRES: Piano concertos, solo piano music.

MAJOR WORKS: Four piano concertos; three symphonies; 24 Preludes for piano (1892–1910); *Rhapsody on a Theme of Paganini* (1934).

Other Composers of the Era

...some world far from ours
Where music and moonlight and feeling
Are one.

PERCY BYSSHE SHELLEY (1792–1822)

Like Rachmaninov, Alexander Glazunov (1865–1936) was among the late Russian Romantic composers. A pupil of Rimsky-Korsakov, he wrote his First Symphony at the age of only 16, and became a protégé of Balakirev. From the 1880s onwards he travelled widely, meeting Liszt in Weimar, and conducting in Paris and London. In 1905 he became director of the St Petersburg Conservatory. He suffered great hardship during the Russian Revolution, and in 1928 left Russia altogether, eventually settling in Paris. His works, which are more cosmopolitan than nationalist, include nine symphonies, two piano concertos, a popular Violin Concerto, a late Saxophone Concerto (1931), seven string quartets, and a ballet, *The Seasons* (1899).

ABOVE: Alexander Glazunov (1865–1936). Like Rachmaninov, Stravinsky and Prokofiev he left Russia after the Revolution.

ABOVE: The Polish composer Karol Szymanowski (1882–1937), director of the Warsaw Conservatory.

The Polish composer Karol Szymanowski (1882–1937) spent much of his early life in the Ukraine, but between 1905 and 1908 he lived in Berlin, where he wrote his first symphony. His Russian home was destroyed during the Revolution, and in 1920 he moved to Warsaw, where he became director of the Conservatory (later the Academy). He died of tuberculosis. His piano music was championed by Polish pianists including Artur Rubinstein, while his two violin concertos were premièred by the Polish violinist Paul Kochansky. His Stabat Mater (1925–6) is highly regarded.

Mahler's exact contemporary Hugo Wolf (1860–1903) was also his fellow pupil at the Vienna Conservatory. An enthusiastic Wagnerite, he antagonized many people with his critical attacks on Brahms. He is remembered for his exquisite songs – the worthy successors of Schubert and Schumann. They include 53 settings of poems by Mörike, 20 by Eichendorff, 51 by Goethe, 44 songs in the *Spanisches Liederbuch* (*Spanish Songbook*, 1891), a total of 46 in the two volumes of the *Italienisches Liederbuch* (*Italian Songbook*, 1892–6) and three poems by Michelangelo (1898). Apart from songs, his best-known work is the *Italian Serenade* (1892) for string orchestra (originally for quartet). In 1897, a victim of syphilis, he went mad and was confined to an asylum.

The German composer Max Bruch (1838–1920) worked as a conductor in Berlin, Bonn, Liverpool, Breslau and Scotland, and became a professor of composition at the Berlin Hochschule. An enormously prolific composer, he is remembered today chiefly for three

ABOVE: The Austrian composer Hugo Wolf (1860–1903). A brilliant composer of Lieder, he contracted syphilis and died insane.

ABOVE: *Max Bruch (1838–1920) never quite lived up to his early promise, but his Violin Concerto in G minor is much played.*

ABOVE: *Vincent d'Indy (1851–1931), who founded the Schola Cantorum in Paris in the 1890s.*

ABOVE: *Paul Dukas (1865–1935). A contemporary of Debussy, he is remembered chiefly for* The Sorcerer's Apprentice.

works, the G minor Violin Concerto (1868), the *Scottish Fantasy* for violin and orchestra (1880), and *Kol Nidrei* (1881), an *adagio* on a Hebrew melody for cello and orchestra.

France

The Belgian-born César Franck (1822–90) became organ professor at the Paris Conservatoire in 1872. An outstanding organist, he wrote a great deal of sacred music, but is chiefly

ABOVE: *Sir Hubert Parry (1848–1918), chiefly remembered for his setting of Blake's* Jerusalem *and for the six* Songs of Farewell.

remembered for his Organ Symphony in D minor (1886–8), the Symphonic Variations for piano and orchestra (1885), the Piano Quintet (1878–9), the Violin Sonata (1886) and *Panis angelicus* (1872, for tenor, organ, harp, cello and double bass).

His pupil Vincent D'Indy (1851–1931), an admirer of Wagner like his teacher, was a founder of the Schola Cantorum in Paris in 1894, originally for the study of church music but, from 1900 onwards, a general music school. He wrote several operas, but his best-known work is probably the *Symphonie sur un chant montagnard français* (*Symphony on a French Mountaineer's Song*, 1886).

Wagner also influenced the works of Paul Dukas (1865–1935), whose first major success, *L'apprenti sorcier* (*The Sorcerer's Apprentice*, 1897, based on a story by Goethe), is still much performed. Dukas wrote a fine opera based on a play by Maeterlinck, *Ariane et Barbe-bleue* (*Ariadne and Bluebeard*, 1907), similar in atmosphere to Debussy's *Pelléas et Mélisande*, but his strict self-criticism meant that he published only a few of his compositions and destroyed much of his work before he died.

Britain

In late Victorian England, Hubert Parry (1848–1918) and Charles Villiers Stanford (1852–1924) – both professors at the Royal College of Music, London – had enormous influence on a younger generation of British composers, whom they numbered among their many pupils. Parry taught at Oxford University; Stanford, the composer of seven symphonies, taught at Cambridge.

ABOVE: *Sir Charles Villiers Stanford (1852–1924) portrayed in a 1905 Vanity Fair cartoon.*

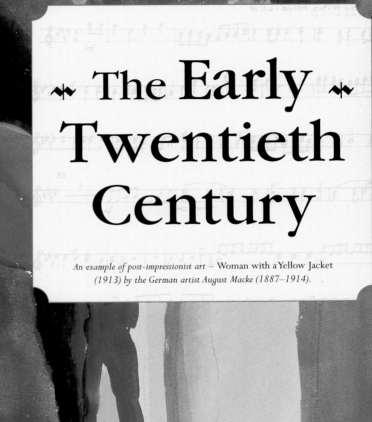

The Early Twentieth Century

An example of post-impressionist art — Woman with a Yellow Jacket
(1913) by the German artist August Macke (1887–1914).

Music in a New Framework

*Musical innovation is full of danger to the state, for when modes of music change,
the laws of the state always change with them.*

PLATO (C.428–347 BC)

ABOVE: Around the Piano *(1885) by Henri Fantin-Latour (1836–1904).*

By the closing years of the 19th century, it was clear that Romanticism had run its course. New trends were apparent in literature and art: in the Symbolist poems of Paul Verlaine, Charles Baudelaire and Stéphane Mallarmé and the plays of Maurice Maeterlinck; in the impressionist paintings of Claude Monet, Camille Pissarro and Edouard Manet, in which representational art gave way to blurred outlines and emphasis on the shifting play of light.

As the 20th century dawned, Impressionism was succeeded by post-Impressionism, and by a bewildering array of new artistic movements: the Fauves, with their bold outlines and brash colours, the Expressionist art of Edvard Munch and Wasily Kandinsky, the cubism of Pablo Picasso, the stark lines of Bauhaus art and architecture. Music, as ever, followed behind, when the focus of new trends moved decisively from central Europe to Paris.

ABOVE: An Allegory of Happiness *by
Julio Romero de Torres (1880–1930).*

Impressionism in music

In musical terms, composers realized that they need no longer be subject to the tyranny of traditional tonality – a system which had lasted for 400 years. One of the pioneers of the "music of the future" was the Frenchman Claude Debussy, whose fluid structures, built out of the repetition of tiny motifs with colouristic instrumental effects, were likened to impressionist techniques in painting. Little of Debussy's mature music could be said to be in a "key"; instead, its gravitational centre constantly shifts as a result of his use of chromatic harmony.

Atonality

Meanwhile, the Austrian composer Arnold Schoenberg began writing in a lush, late-Romantic style, but in the first decade of the 20th century he pushed chromatic harmony to its limits, experimenting first with atonality, in which the 12 notes of the chromatic scale are treated equally, and then with an original method of musical organization called the "12-note system". This method – in which musical building-blocks are created from "tone-rows" consisting of all 12 notes of the scale – influenced many succeeding composers, including Berg

and Webern (who were Schoenberg's pupils), Stravinsky, Messaien, Boulez and Stockhausen. They used it in various ingenious ways and adapted it to their own particular ends.

Nationalism

Meanwhile, musical nationalism continued to flourish: in England in the works of Ralph Vaughan Williams, Frederick Delius and Gustav Holst; in Denmark in the works of Carl Nielsen; in central Europe in the works of the Hungarians Béla Bartók and Zoltán Kodály and the Czech composer Leoš Janáček, the spiritual descendant of Dvořák. All these composers were ardent collectors of their national folk songs, first by transcribing them manually, and then, when phonographic equipment became available, recording them.

The USA — still a relatively young nation — acquired its first major composer in the form of the highly original Charles Ives, quickly followed

ABOVE: Dancing in Vienna shown in a post-World War I painting entitled Once upon a Time.

by others: Samuel Barber, George Gershwin (a populist master), and Aaron Copland, who deliberately set out to create distinctively "American" music.

Music and politics

The political upheavals of the 20th century, particularly the two world wars, had a profound effect on music, as on other art forms. During the economic depression which followed World War I, composers were forced to pare down their musical resources. Works that had required huge and expensive symphony orchestras gave way to small chamber ensembles, evident in the post-war works of Igor Stravinsky and the eclectic group of mainly French composers known as "Les Six".

Another noticeable influence during the 1920s and '30s was that of jazz, exported to Europe from the USA, and taken up with enthusiasm in England, France and Germany (especially in the works of Kurt Weill).

The rise of Nazi Germany in the 1930s struck a grievous blow. The works of "decadent" composers such as Weill were banned, and central Europe was emptied of Jewish musicians, both composers and performers, and of "non-conformist" Aryans. Some — including Schoenberg, Hindemith and Weill — fled to Britain and the USA (where they greatly enriched the musical lives of their adopted nations), while others were murdered. Apart from the aged Richard Strauss, Germany lost most of its finest composers: perhaps the best-known composer who stayed was Carl Orff, remembered only for his popular cantata *Carmina burana*, and for an influential teaching method.

Similarly, in Soviet Russia, Stalin's purges struck fear into all serious composers. The two finest Russian composers of the 20th century, Prokofiev and Shostakovich, both survived, but suffered severely under a tyrannical regime driven by political dogma and opposed to artistic innovation.

ABOVE: L'homme au violon *(The Man with the Violin), painted in 1918 by the Spanish artist Juan Gris (1887–1927).*

ABOVE: This drawing on the cover of The Theatre World *review journal shows Spanish dancers in the 1920s.*

Claude Debussy

It's music on the points of needles.

CÉSAR FRANCK (1822–90)

From the late Baroque period to around 1890, mainstream Western music was firmly rooted in Germany and Austria. Not until the late 19th and early 20th centuries did the line of succession stretching from Bach to Mahler begin to branch out, with major composers emerging from Russia, Bohemia, England, Scandinavia and the USA. It was a Frenchman, Claude Debussy, who broke the German monopoly, revitalizing French music with his uniquely subtle art, and opening up a new sound-world for the 20th century. His music explored "the mysterious relationship between Nature and Imagination".

Debussy's life centred on Paris, which was fast becoming the hub of European culture. He was born on 22 August 1862 in the suburb of St Germain-en-Laye, where his parents ran a china shop. The young Claude

ABOVE: Claude Achille Debussy (1862–1918). His unique sound-world opened the door to a new century.

Achille and his siblings were often packed off to their Aunt Clémentine in Cannes, where Debussy began to learn the piano with a former pupil of Chopin. At the age of ten he entered the Paris Conservatoire, where he unnerved his teachers with experimental harmonic improvisations at the keyboard.

Despite his unorthodox tendencies, he won the coveted Prix de Rome in 1884 with his cantata *L'enfant prodigue*, but his sojourn in Rome was not a happy one, and he returned to Paris – where he had been conducting a love affair with a married woman – in the spring of 1887. The same year he became intoxicated with Wagner's music and in 1888 visited Bayreuth. Although Debussy later described Wagner's music as "a beautiful sunset that was mistaken for a dawn", it held a life-long fascination for him. He even began work on a Wagnerian opera, but

LEFT: Entrance to the Exposition Universelle (1889) by Jean Beraud (1849–1936).

RIGHT: Debussy with his daughter Chou-Chou. He was already gravely ill with cancer when this photograph was taken in 1916.

ABOVE: A drawing by René Bull illustrating Debussy's Prélude à "L'après-midi d'un faune" *dating from 1913, the year after Nijinsky's scandalous choreographic version for the Ballets Russes.*

abandoned it when he realized that his own music needed to be "flexible and adaptable to fantasies and dreams".

Impressionism

Debussy had already found inspiration in the elusive works of the Symbolist poets, including Verlaine, whose verses he had begun to match with delicate, ethereal settings. At the same time he began to experiment with new piano sonorities, and with a scale based on whole tones, without a firm key centre. Among his early piano works are a pair of Arabesques and the *Petite suite* for piano duet.

The Javanese gamelan music Debussy heard at the 1889 Paris Exposition left a lasting impression, when he realized that economy of means – a single, shrill clarinet or a gong – could

Life and works

NATIONALITY: French

BORN: St Germain-en-Laye, 1862; DIED: Paris, 1918

SPECIALIST GENRES: Orchestral and piano music.

MAJOR WORKS: *Prélude à "L'après-midi d'un faune"* (1892–4); *Pelléas et Mélisande* (1893–1902); *Nocturnes* (1899); *La mer* (1905); *Images* (1905–7); Preludes for piano (1910, 1913); *Jeux* (1913).

ABOVE: The Great Wave of Kanagawa *(1831) by the Japanese artist Katsushika Hokusai (1760–1849). This print inspired Debussy's symphonic seascape* La mer.

ABOVE: *A piece of 17th-century Chinese embroidery. Debussy loved Oriental art, and drew inspiration from it for some of his piano pieces.*

be just as effective as a full-blown symphony orchestra. The influence of Art Nouveau, then all the rage in Paris, resulted in his cantata *La damoiselle élue* (*The Blessed Damozel*, 1888), based on a poem by the Pre-Raphaelite artist and writer Dante Gabriel Rossetti.

In the early 1890s Debussy found a tiny apartment in Montmartre, then the centre of artistic "bohemian" life. Surrounded by the artists, writers, fellow musicians, laundresses and prostitutes who constituted the district's lively residents, he set up house with his girlfriend Gabrielle Dupont and embarked on a period of penniless squalor but artistic creativity. During this period he developed his characteristic style, capturing in subtle, shifting harmonies and fragments of melody the essence of a breath of wind, the rustle of leaves, or a shaft of moonlight.

Sometimes his inspiration came from an antique dream-world peopled by masked Harlequins and Columbines playing mandolins and dancing sarabands. These visions sprang to life in the *Suite bergamasque* (1890) for

piano, of which the third piece is the haunting "Clair de lune", the suite *Pour le piano* (1894–1901), and in the Verlaine settings called *Fêtes galantes* (1891 and 1904). From the same period dates the String Quartet

ABOVE: *The Scottish soprano Mary Garden (1874–1967) as Mélisande, the heroine of Debussy's* Pelléas et Mélisande. *She created the role at the Paris Opera in 1902.*

(1893), and his most famous orchestral piece, the *Prélude à "L'après-midi d'un faune"* (*Prelude to "The Afternoon of a Faun"*, 1894). Based on an erotic monologue by Mallarmé about a faun lying in the grass one hot summer's afternoon in ancient Greece, dreaming of making love to two beautiful but elusive nymphs, the piece – turned into a scandalous ballet in 1912 by the dancer Nijinsky – was a triumphant success. According to the conductor and composer Pierre Boulez, from the first languid notes of the faun's flute, "music began to beat with a new pulse".

In the mid 1890s Debussy worked on the opera *Pelléas et Mélisande*, based on a Symbolist drama by the Belgian writer Maurice Maeterlinck. His infinitely subtle music, economically scored, and using silence as "perhaps the only way of throwing the emotional weight of a phrase into relief", perfectly complemented Maeterlinck's perplexing play, in which the characters seem to lack normal motivation. It took nine years for *Pelléas* to reach the stage, when it was greeted with incomprehension and hostility. It is now recognized as a masterpiece.

During this period, Debussy had lived off a small annual allowance from a publisher. Constant lack of money caused friction between him and Gaby, and the couple finally separated in 1898, just as Debussy finished another orchestral work, the three *Nocturnes*. These poetic evocations of a cloudy day over the river Seine, a Parisian carnival complete with brass band, and a delicate seascape with mermaids singing, are among his most "impressionistic" pieces, as are the contemporary set of *Estampes* (*Prints*) for piano, consisting of the pseudo-oriental *Pagodes*, *Soirée dans Grenade* (*Evening in Granada*, a languid Spanish habanera), and the virtuosic *Jardins sous la pluie* (*Gardens in the rain*).

ABOVE: *A page from the autograph score of Act I of* Pelléas et Mélisande.

Marriage

In 1899 Debussy – whose dark, Mephistophelean looks made him immensely attractive to women – replaced Gaby with a pretty bottle-blonde model called Lilly Texier. Ill-educated and tubercular, Lilly proved an entirely unsuitable wife. In 1903 Debussy met Emma Bardac, Fauré's ex-mistress, now the wife of a banker. They fell passionately in love and eloped to Jersey (where he wrote the piano piece *L'île joyeuse*). Lilly Debussy tried to shoot herself and Debussy was ostracized by his friends, but he and Emma set up house together in the fashionable Avenue du Bois de Boulogne, where their adored daughter Claude-Emma (Chou-Chou) was born in 1905. For the rest of his life Debussy attempted to keep Emma in the style to which she had become accustomed, often with great difficulty, and their ten-year marriage was frequently under strain, especially when he was obliged to leave on long conducting tours.

In 1905 Debussy completed his symphonic seascape *La mer*, a vivid example of his ability to create, through a mosaic of melody and delicate touches of instrumentation,

an impression of the interplay between light and water. Over the next few years he also completed two sets of *Images* for piano, the delightful *Children's Corner* (1906–8) for his daughter, two books of piano Preludes, and a set of orchestral *Images*: *Rondes de printemps* (*Dances of Spring*), *Iberia* and *Gigues*. In 1911 he tried his hand at ballet music in *Khamma*, written for the Canadian dancer Maud Allan, and in 1913, in the masterly score *Jeux* (*Games*), written for Diaghilev's Ballets Russes and choreographed by Nijinsky.

Last works

By 1914 Debussy knew that he was mortally ill with cancer of the colon. Deeply distressed by the carnage of World War I, he worked feverishly to finish two sets of piano studies, inspired by Chopin's, and three pieces for two pianos, *En blanc et noir* (1915), each dedicated to a friend killed in action. His last works were three out of a projected set of six sonatas – abstract music in a new, austere style

ABOVE: *The Russian impresario Sergei Diaghilev, the driving force behind the Ballets Russes. He commissioned Debussy's* Jeux.

– for cello and piano, violin and piano, and flute, viola and harp. He did not live to write the other three, dying during a German bombardment on 25 March 1918. His sonatas were published with the simple inscription: "Claude Debussy: musicien français".

ABOVE: *An impressionist seascape –* Storm at Agay, *1895, by Jean Baptiste Guillaumin (1841–1927).*

Maurice Ravel

All the same, he had talent, that Ravel.

RAVEL

Debussy and his younger contemporary Ravel are often classed together as "impressionist" composers, and in life they sometimes found themselves in unintentional rivalry. In fact, the music of each was quite individual.

Ravel was the son of an engineer of Swiss origin and his Basque wife. When he was a baby the family moved to Paris, where Ravel spent the rest of his life. Like Debussy, he showed early promise as a pianist, and when he was 14 he entered the Paris Conservatoire. During his student days he came into contact with Javanese gamelan music (at the 1889 Paris Exposition), Russian music and Wagner, all of which indirectly influenced his own work.

Having graduated from the piano class in 1895, Ravel returned two years

ABOVE: *The French composer Maurice Ravel (1875–1937), painted as a young man by Henri-Charles Manguin.*

later to study composition with Fauré. An interest in Renaissance literature encouraged him to set poems by Clément Marot (c.1497–1544), and to write the *Menuet antique* (1895) and the *Pavane pour une infante défunte* (*Pavan for a Dead Infanta*, 1899) for piano; the latter became one of his most popular works. However, his outstandingly original talent disconcerted the Conservatoire's staid establishment, and he failed to win the Prix de Rome five times. Indeed, when he was eliminated in the first round in 1905, having already composed the virtuoso piano piece *Jeux d'eau* (1901), the String Quartet (1902–3), and the ravishing orchestral song-cycle *Shéhérazade* (1903), a huge public row forced the resignation of the Conservatoire's director.

LEFT: *Ravel at the piano. He was a brilliant pianist, and often performed his own music.*

RIGHT: *Ravel's villa, Le Belvedere, at Montfort-l'Amaury, near Paris.*

Les Apaches

By now Ravel was a member of the artistic circle of poets, musicians, critics and painters known as "Les Apaches". His tiny stature, his addiction to elegant clothes and his impeccable toilette ensured his social popularity. His sexual proclivities are still unclear, but he never married and remained deeply attached to his mother. With the "*affaire* Ravel" at the Conservatoire behind him, he concentrated on composition, including the *Sonatine* (1903–5) and *Miroirs* (1904–5) for piano, the Introduction and Allegro for harp and chamber ensemble, the song-cycle *Histoires naturelles* (1906), and the evocative orchestral *Rapsodie espagnole* (1907–8). He also began work on his first opera, *L'heure espagnole* (1907–9), influenced by his Basque origins, and in 1911 turned his piano suite *Ma mère l'oye* (Mother Goose), originally written

ABOVE: *A design by Leon Bakst (1866–1924) for Act I of the Russian Ballet production of Ravel's* Daphnis et Chloé *in Paris, 1912.*

for two children, into a ballet score. From the same period dates his most famous ballet, *Daphnis et Chloé* (1909–12), which was commissioned by Diaghilev.

War years

At the outbreak of World War I, Ravel was working on his Piano Trio. Turned down for military service on the grounds of his size, he became an ambulance driver on the Western Front until his health broke down. The death of his mother in 1916 was a cruel blow. His creative response to tragedy was *Le tombeau de Couperin* (1917), an anachronistic keyboard suite commemorating fallen friends, and the post-war *La valse*, a savage vision of a ghostly waltz to destruction. In 1921 Ravel moved to a small villa at Montfort-l'Amaury near Paris, which he filled with cats, toys and delicate *objets d'art*. His love of children was reflected in his next opera, *L'enfant et les sortilèges* (The Child and the Magic Spells, 1925), in which he used a libretto by Colette (1873–1954) to recreate an enchanted childhood world peopled by talking toys and animals. He commemorated Debussy's early death with his Duo for violin and cello, composed the song-cycle *Chansons*

ABOVE: *Spanish flamenco dancing. Ravel's* Boléro *pays homage to his lifelong love of Spain.*

madécasses (1925–6) for the American patroness Elizabeth Sprague Coolidge, and began work on two violin works, *Tzigane* (1924) and the Sonata (1923–7).

Last works

In 1928, the year he visited America, Ravel composed the ballet *Boléro*, whose success came to haunt him. His two brilliant piano concertos (one for the left hand, in F, for the pianist Paul Wittgenstein, who had lost his right arm during World War I) appeared soon after this. His last work was the set of songs *Don Quichotte à Dulcinée* (1932–3), written for a film based on Cervantes' novel.

For the last five years of his life Ravel suffered from Pick's disease, an illness accelerated by brain damage sustained in a car crash. He died in 1937.

Life and works

NATIONALITY: French

BORN: Ciboure, Basses-Pyrénées, 1875; **DIED:** Paris, 1937

SPECIALIST GENRES: Virtuoso piano music, orchestral works.

MAJOR WORKS: *Pavane pour une infante défunte* (1899); *Jeux d'eau* (1901); *Miroirs* (1904–5); *Gaspard de la nuit* (1908); *Daphnis et Chloé* (1909–12); *Le tombeau de Couperin* (1917); *L'enfant et les sortilèges* (1925); *Boléro* (1928); two piano concertos (1929–31).

Erik Satie

My brother was always difficult to understand.
He doesn't seem to have been quite normal.

OLGA SATIE

A contemporary of Debussy and Ravel, Erik Satie was a pioneer of the avant-garde. His satirical, anti-bourgeois attitudes and eccentric demeanour anticipated Dadaism and Surrealism, while his spare, whimsical musical style was the antithesis of late Romanticism. He had enormous influence on the group of composers known as "Les Six", as well as on later figures such as John Cage.

The son of a French father and a Scottish mother, he was born in Honfleur on the Normandy coast, and moved to Paris in 1878. He studied at the Paris Conservatoire, but achieved little success. His early works for piano include *Sarabandes* (1887), the hypnotic *Gymnopédies* (1888) and the exotic-sounding *Gnossiennes* (1890). For several years he earned a meagre living playing the piano in Montmartre bars and cabarets, and also became involved

ABOVE: *Erik Satie (1866–1925), one of the great eccentrics.*

with the occult Rosicrucian sect, "founding" the Metropolitan Church of the Art of Jesus the Conductor.

Around 1890 Satie met Debussy, beginning a 25-year friendship in which Debussy was very much the superior partner, with Satie as his court jester. During this period Satie had a tempestuous love affair with the painter Suzanne Valadon (the mother of Utrillo), and became known for eccentric gestures, such as buying 12 identical grey velvet suits. In 1898 he left Montmartre for the grim suburb of Arcueil-Cachan, where he lived in one small, bare room.

Satie's later compositions often have deliberately obscure titles, such as *Trois véritables préludes flasques (pour un chien)* (*Three flabby preludes for a dog*), *Choses vues à droite et à gauche (sans lunettes)*

(*Things seen from the right and left without spectacles*) and *Trois morceaux en forme de poire* (*Three pear-shaped pieces*), though there are actually seven.

During World War I Satie collaborated with the writer Jean Cocteau (1889–1963), the choreographer Leonid Massine and the painter Pablo Picasso on the 1917 ballet *Parade* for Diaghilev's Ballets Russes. The work set out to introduce the principles of Cubism to the stage, and Satie's jazz-influenced score — including parts for typewriter, whistle and siren — caused a scandal. In complete contrast was the cantata *Socrate* (1919), which he wanted to be "white and pure like antiquity". Subsequent collaborations with Massine and Picasso, and with Francis Picabia and Réné Clair, produced the ballets *Mercure* and *Relâche* (*No Show*, 1924). By then Satie had become a recluse. A heavy drinker, he died of sclerosis of the liver in July 1925.

ABOVE: *An anonymous drawing of Satie in chalk, dated 1890 and inscribed "A mon ami Erik Satie" ("To my friend Erik Satie").*

Life and works

NATIONALITY: French

BORN: Honfleur, 1866;
DIED: Paris, 1925

SPECIALIST GENRES:
Minimalist piano music.

MAJOR WORKS:
Many piano works, including *Trois gymnopédies* (1888) and *Trois gnossiennes* (1890); ballet *Parade* (1917); cantata *Socrate* (1919).

Alexander Scriabin

It was like a bath of ice; cocaine and rainbows.

HENRY MILLER (1891–1980), "NEXUS"

Alexander Scriabin's early career has many parallels with Rachmaninov's. Like Rachmaninov, he was equally gifted as a composer and as a pianist. His mother (who died just over a year after he was born) had been a fine pianist, and he was brought up by female relatives.

Scriabin began his piano studies in Moscow with Nikolay Zverev – who also taught Rachmaninov – before entering the Conservatory in 1888, the same year as Rachmaninov. Shortly after graduating in 1892 with the second gold medal (Rachmaninov won the first), Scriabin came to the attention of the Russian millionaire publisher and philanthropist Belyayev, who began to publish his early works (including a set of 12 Studies), and sent him off on a European tour, playing his own music. From this period date several sets of piano Preludes, the Second Piano Sonata, and the Piano Concerto, which Scriabin composed on his return to Moscow.

In 1897 he married the young pianist Vera Isaakovich, with whom he had four children. But his intensely egotistical nature caused him to abandon her seven years later for another young admirer, his former pupil Tatiana Schloezer. At the same time, Scriabin gave up his teaching post at the Moscow Conservatory, and settled in Switzerland.

By 1903 he had already begun to compose orchestral music, including two symphonies, and was becoming increasingly involved in mysticism, dabbling in Nietzschean theories and

ABOVE: The Russian pianist and composer Alexander Scriabin (1872–1915), a portrait in oils by A.Y. Golovin.

the occult teachings of Madame Blavatsky, the founder of the Theosophical Society. Philosophical and mystical ideas began to influence his work from the Third Symphony (*Le divin poème*) onwards, particularly the sensuous *Poème de l'extase* (*Poem of Ecstasy*), and *Prométhée*, subtitled *Le poème du feu* (*The Poem of Fire*), in

which Scriabin developed the theory of synaesthesia, according to which art that appealed to all the senses would trigger a cataclysmic effect. To this end, different keys were associated with specific colours, demonstrated in performance by the use of coloured lighting. His Seventh and Ninth Piano Sonatas (1911 and 1912–13) are subtitled respectively *Messe blanche* and *Messe noire*.

In 1908 Scriabin returned to Russia, where his works were received with enormous enthusiasm. His later music, mostly for piano, is highly chromatic. In 1914 he visited London for a concert of his works conducted by Henry Wood, and during his stay he developed an ulcer on his lip which would not heal. He died of septicaemia on 27 April 1915.

Life and works

NATIONALITY: Russian

BORN: Moscow, 1872;
DIED: Moscow, 1915

SPECIALIST GENRES: Piano and orchestral music influenced by mysticism.

MAJOR WORKS: Ten sonatas and 85 preludes for piano; Piano Concerto (1896); *Le poème de l'extase* (1905–8); *Prométhée* (1910).

Ferruccio Busoni

I want to attain the unknown!

BUSONI, 1905

Like Scriabin, the pianist and composer Ferruccio Busoni was a maverick, important in his own right, but not profoundly influential. Italian by birth, he spent much of his career in Germany and Austria. His father was an Italian clarinettist, and his mother, a pianist of German origin. Busoni's parents began his musical education, and he gave his first public piano recital at the age of eight.

In 1876 the family moved to Graz, where Busoni conducted a performance of his own Stabat Mater (now lost), at the age of 12. He then moved to Vienna, where he met Brahms and dedicated to him the set of six Studies for piano, and an *Etude en forme de variation*. Brahms recommended that Busoni should move to Leipzig, where he met many eminent musicians, and wrote his Second String Quartet. He also began to make arrangements of organ works by Bach, re-composing them in contemporary style.

In 1890 Busoni married the daughter of a Swedish sculptor, whom he had met in Helsinki (one of their sons became a painter). He taught briefly in Moscow, but then decided to resume his career as a concert pianist in the USA. In 1894 he settled in Berlin, where he promoted orchestral concerts of the most avant-garde music, including works by Debussy, Bartók, Delius and Fauré.

Busoni also began to make daring harmonic experiments – similar to Schoenberg's although with a different approach – in his own music, especially in the set of Six Sonatinas for piano (1910–20). His orchestral music includes an extraordinary five-movement Piano Concerto which incorporates a male-voice chorus, and a more conventional Concertino for clarinet and chamber orchestra. Towards the end of his life he was preoccupied with stage works, including the operas *Die Brautwahl* (*The Bridal Choice*, after E. T. A. Hoffmann, 1912), and *Doktor Faust* (after Marlowe), which was left unfinished at his death.

ABOVE: The Italian / German composer Ferruccio Busoni (1866–1924).

LEFT: A scene from the 1999 Salzburg Festival production of Doktor Faust, *Busoni's last opera, with Thomas Hampson as Faust and Chris Merritt as Mephistopheles.*

Life and works

NATIONALITY: Italian

BORN: Empoli, near Florence, 1866; **DIED:** Berlin, 1924

SPECIALIST GENRES: Virtuoso piano works, opera.

MAJOR WORKS: Piano Concerto (1904); *Arlecchino* (1914–16); *Doktor Faust* (1916–24).

Ralph Vaughan Williams

What we want in England is real music, even if it be only a music-hall song.

VAUGHAN WILLIAMS, "THE VOCALIST" (1902)

Vaughan Williams was one of a group of composers who contributed to the renaissance of English music in the 20th century. Born in Gloucestershire, he studied music at Cambridge University and the Royal College of Music, London, where his teachers included Parry and Stanford. (In later years, he also studied with Bruch and Ravel.) He began his career as a church organist in London and, with his friend Gustav Holst, initiated a systematic study and collection of English folk songs, which – together with his interest in Tudor music – profoundly influenced his own compositions.

In 1906 Vaughan Williams was appointed musical editor of *The English Hymnal*, for which he wrote some famous hymn tunes, such as "For All the Saints" (*Sine nomine*). He also became director of the amateur Leith Hill Music Festival in Dorking, Surrey, from 1905 until his death. From 1919 until 1939 he was a professor of composition at the Royal College of Music. He married twice, the first time in 1897; after his wife's death in 1951 he married the poet and librettist Ursula Wood.

Vaughan Williams' musical style has a distinctively "English" quality, derived from his use of the modality of folk song, tinged with an elusive mysticism. He was drawn to the mystical poetry of Walt Whitman, whose verses he set in *A Sea Symphony* (1903–9) and *Toward*

ABOVE: *A photograph of Ralph Vaughan Williams (1872–1958), taken in 1952 – the year of his 80th birthday.*

the Unknown Region (1905–6). Other early works included the *Fantasia on a Theme of Thomas Tallis* for double string orchestra and the settings of poems by A. E. Housman, *On Wenlock Edge* (1908), for voice and string quartet, as well as the ever-popular part-song "Linden Lea" (1901) and the *Songs of Travel* (1901–4), based on Robert Louis Stevenson's poems.

Altogether Vaughan Williams wrote nine symphonies, including No. 2 (*A London Symphony*, 1912–13), No. 3 (*Pastoral*, 1916–21), No. 5 (1938–43, which with the gritty No. 6 of 1944–7 was perceived as the composer's response to war), and the *Sinfonia*

antarctica (1949–52, based on his score for the 1948 film *Scott of the Antarctic*). His orchestral music also includes *The Lark Ascending* (a rhapsody for violin and orchestra), concertos for violin, oboe and tuba, *A Norfolk Rhapsody*, the Fantasia on "Greensleeves" (1934) and the overture *The Wasps* (1909).

Vaughan Williams wrote in many genres, including stage and film music. His six operas are relatively infrequently revived, but his ballet score *Job: A Masque for Dancing* has remained in the orchestral repertoire.

Life and works

NATIONALITY: English

BORN: Down Ampney, 1872; **DIED**: London, 1958

SPECIALIST GENRES: Symphonies, stage works influenced by English folk song.

MAJOR WORKS: Nine symphonies; *Fantasia on a Theme of Thomas Tallis* (1910); *The Lark Ascending* (1914); *Serenade to Music* (1938); operas *Hugh the Drover* (1910–14), *Sir John in Love* (1924–8), *Riders to the Sea* (1925–32) and *The Pilgrim's Progress* (1949); ballet *Job* (1927–30).

Gustav Holst

Never compose anything unless the not composing of it
becomes a positive nuisance to you.

HOLST, 1921

Holst was born into a less privileged background than his friend Vaughan Williams, whom he met as a fellow student at the Royal College of Music in London in the 1890s. His family was of Swedish descent, and his father was an organist and piano teacher in Cheltenham.

Holst earned a living first as a trombonist, and then as a teacher in London. From 1903–20 he taught music at a girls' school in Dulwich and in 1905 he was appointed director of music at St Paul's School for Girls in Hammersmith, where he remained until his death. He was also music director at Morley College, South London, from 1907–24, professor of music at Reading University, and a teacher at the Royal College of Music.

ABOVE: The British composer of Swedish origin Gustav Holst (1874–1934), photographed in 1925.

ABOVE: The planets inspired Holst's most famous orchestral work.

He lived in Richmond (where his daughter Imogen, who also became a composer, was born in 1907) and then had a riverside house in Barnes, but composed in his room in St Paul's School at weekends and during school holidays.

Like Vaughan Williams, Holst was strongly influenced by English folk song, which informed many of his works, including *A Somerset Rhapsody* (1906–7), the Suites for military band (1909–11), the *St Paul's* and *Brook Green* suites for strings (1913 and 1933), *A Moorside Suite* for brass band (1928) and the scherzo *Hammersmith* for military band or orchestra (1930–1).

Holst's interest in mysticism and Eastern religion also permeated his music. He learned Sanskrit in order to translate hymns from the Rig Veda,

which he set for chorus and orchestra in 1908; his first major work, *The Mystic Trumpeter*, was performed at the Queen's Hall in 1905, and oriental philosophy underpins his opera *Sāvitri*. His most popular work is undoubtedly the orchestral suite *The Planets*, of which "Mars" is a terrifying vision of approaching war. The lyrical central section of "Jupiter" was later used to set the patriotic hymn "I Vow to Thee, My Country".

Towards the end of his life, Holst's style became more austere. His later works included the Hardy-inspired tone-poem *Egdon Heath* (1927), the Concerto for two violins (1929), the operas *At the Boar's Head* and *The Wandering Scholar* and the Choral Fantasia (1931). He died in 1934, following surgery for haemorrhagic gastritis.

Life and works

NATIONALITY: English

BORN: Cheltenham, 1874;
DIED: London, 1934

SPECIALIST GENRES:
Orchestral and stage works influenced by mysticism and native folk song.

MAJOR WORKS: *The Planets* (1914–16); operas *Sāvitri* (1908), *The Perfect Fool* (1922), *At the Boar's Head* (1924) and *The Wandering Scholar* (1929–30).

Frederick Delius

It is only that which cannot be expressed otherwise that is worth expressing in music.

DELIUS, "AT THE CROSSROADS" (1920)

A contemporary of Debussy, Delius was born in northern England but lived in France for much of his life. His musical style was an amalgam of English lyrical nostalgia, the Impressionism of Debussy, and Mahlerian post-Romanticism.

The son of a German-born wool merchant, Delius was brought up in Bradford, Yorkshire. His father attempted to dissuade him from considering a musical career and packed him off to Florida to manage an orange plantation, but while in America he studied music theory with an organist, Thomas Ward, and his father relented. In 1886 he was allowed to study music in Leipzig, where he befriended Grieg, but soon left to settle in Paris, where he became friends with the painters Paul Gauguin and Edvard Munch. From his Paris years date the operas *Irmelin* (1890) and *Koanga* (1895–7), the Piano Concerto (1897) and the tone-poem *Paris, the Song of a Great City* (1899).

In 1897 Delius married the Norwegian artist Jelka Rosen and settled in Grez-sur-Loing near Fontainebleau. However, his bohemian lifestyle in Paris had left him with the grim legacy of syphilis, which eventually killed him. His most famous opera, *A Village Romeo and Juliet* – a tragic *Tristan and Isolde*-like tale of young love doomed by parental enmity – was written between 1899 and 1901. From this period also date the distinctive works of his maturity, including *Brigg Fair* (1907, a set of variations on an English folk song), the cantata *Sea Drift* (a setting

ABOVE: Frederick Delius was born in Yorkshire but spent most of his life in France.

of Walt Whitman's poem), *A Mass of Life* (not a religious mass, but a setting of text from Nietzsche's *Also sprach Zarathustra*), the *Songs of Sunset* (1906–8), the First Dance Rhapsody for orchestra (1908) and the opera *Fennimore and Gerda* (1908–10).

Delius continued to compose prolifically through the second decade of the 20th century. The quintessentially "English"-sounding orchestral mood pictures *On Hearing the First Cuckoo in Spring* and *Summer Night on the River*, together with the *Song of the High Hills* for chorus and orchestra, date from 1911. During World War I he returned temporarily to England, where he wrote the Second Dance Rhapsody, sonatas for violin and cello, two concertos and his secular Requiem commemorating the war dead.

Although he spent very little of his life in England, his music still has a very "English", pastoral feel, enhanced by his fondness for triplet rhythmic patterns.

From 1922 onwards, as he became increasingly paralysed and his sight began to fail, he ceased to compose, but in 1928 he enlisted the help of the young Yorkshire musician Eric Fenby as his amanuensis. Among his later works are the *Songs of Farewell*, *A Song of Summer* for orchestra (1930), a third violin sonata, and the *Idyll* for soprano, baritone and orchestra (1930–2). He died at Grez in 1934, but was re-interred in Surrey a year later.

Life and works

NATIONALITY: English

BORN: Bradford, 1862; **DIED:** Grez-sur-Loing, near Fontainebleau, 1934

SPECIALIST GENRES: Orchestral and choral music.

MAJOR WORKS: *A Village Romeo and Juliet* (1899–1901); *Appalachia* (1898–1903); *Sea Drift* (1903–4); *A Mass of Life* (1904–5); *Brigg Fair* (1907); Requiem (1914–16); Double Concerto (1915–16); Violin Concerto (1916); Cello Concerto (1921); *Songs of Farewell* (1930).

Leoš Janáček

I want to gather the sun's rays into my hands, I want to plunge myself in shadow,
I want to pour out my longings to the full: all directly.

JANÁČEK, 1927

Born in 1854, the Czech composer Leoš Janáček might have belonged to the late 19th-century nationalist tradition, the successor to Smetana, Dvořák and Suk. But in fact, most of his music dates from the last 30 years of his long life, and he is therefore regarded as a 20th-century composer. His reputation rests largely on the extraordinary series of late operas which, until the 1960s, were largely unknown outside Europe. The efforts of conductors such as Charles Mackerras brought them to the attention of British and American audiences, and they are now regarded as masterpieces.

Born in rural Moravia, the son of a schoolmaster, Janáček studied music in Brno, the capital of Moravia, and Prague. He then returned to Brno as a music teacher, founding an organ school there in 1881. The same year he married his pretty 15-year-old pupil, Zdenka Schulzová. Although the

ABOVE: Leoš Janáček's work embodied the spirit of Czech nationalism, expressed in a moving and distinctive musical language.

marriage was never formally dissolved, it was deeply unhappy almost from the start. The patriotic Janáček resented the fact that his wife was German-speaking, and they appear to have been

sexually incompatible. Two children were born: their son Vladimir died at the age of two, and their daughter Olga at the age of 20, in 1903.

Folk songs

Janáček's early compositions include many choral pieces, for both mixed and male-voice choirs. While working on his first opera, *Šárka* (1887–8), he began to collect and edit Moravian folk songs, whose characteristic idioms – based on the flexible rhythms of speech – influenced his own compositions, giving them an entirely distinctive sound. His first important opera, *Jenůfa*, has a Moravian folk setting. This powerful tale of a young peasant girl's betrayal by her faithless lover, resulting in the murder of her newborn baby by her distraught foster-mother, was completed in 1903. It was first performed in Brno in January 1904, just before Janáček's 50th birthday.

LEFT: Janáček with his young wife Zdenka Schulzová, photographed around the time of their ill-fated marriage.

RIGHT: Janáček's cottage at his birthplace, Hukvaldy. He was there with his great love Kamila Stösslová when he was taken fatally ill.

Neither of his next two operas, *Osud* (*Fate*, 1903–7) and *Výlety páně Broučkovy* (*The Adventures of Mr Brouček*, 1908–18), based on a satirical novel by Svatopluk Čech, were notably successful. For the first two decades of the 20th century Janáček concentrated on piano music, notably the Sonata (1905), *Po zarostlém Chodníčku* (*On an Overgrown Path*, 1901–8) and *V mlhách* (*In the Mists*, 1912), chamber music and male-voice choruses. Up to this point he had written little orchestral music, but the tone-poem *Šumařovo dítě* (*The Fiddler's Child*) dates from 1912. *Taras Bulba*, an orchestral piece inspired by the heroic exploits of a Cossack leader, was written during World War I, and after the Czech Republic declared its independence in 1918, Janáček commemorated the event with *The Ballad of Blaník* (1920).

ABOVE: *Costume design for the Vixen Bystrouška by Josef Capek (1887–1945) for the Prague première of* The Cunning Little Vixen *on 18 May 1925.*

Late flowering

In May 1916 *Jenůfa* finally received its Prague première. Around the same time, the 62-year-old composer met Kamila Stösslová, the young wife of a Jewish antique-dealer. Despite the 38-year age gap between them, Janáček became infatuated with Kamila, and his passion for her inspired the radiant, life-affirming works of his old age. The first of these was *Zápisník zmizelého* (*The Diary of One who Disappeared*, 1917–19), a song-cycle dealing with a young man's love for a gypsy girl (Janáček constantly likened the dark-haired Kamila to a gypsy). This was followed by a stream of operas: the tragic *Katya Kabanová*, the life-enhancing *Příhody lišky bystroušky* (*The Cunning Little Vixen*), *Věc Makropulos* (*The Makropulos Case*), with its icy but fatally attractive heroine, and *Z mrtvého domu* (*From the House of the Dead*), based on Dostoyevsky's grim novel about life in a Siberian prison camp. Kamila appears in various guises in all these,

and she also inspired his two string quartets, *Kreutzer Sonata* (1923), based on Tolstoy's tale of adultery and revenge, and *Listy důvěrné* (*Intimate Letters*, 1928), as well as the wind sextet *Mládí* (*Youth*, 1924).

By now, Janáček was famous both at home and abroad. He visited England in 1926, shortly after writing the extrovert Sinfonietta, his best-known orchestral work. The same year he also completed the Glagolitic Mass, to an Orthodox text, and the Capriccio for piano (left hand) and chamber ensemble.

During the last seven years of his life, he worked mainly at his cottage at Hukvaldy, to which he often invited Kamila and her children. He was taken ill there in August 1928, and died in hospital of pneumonia. Kamila died seven years later; Janáček's wife, Zdenka, died in 1938.

ABOVE: *A woman dressed in Moravian national costume, from the Brno area. Janáček loved to see Kamila wearing national dress.*

Life and works

NATIONALITY: Czech

BORN: Hukvaldy, Moravia, 1854; **DIED:** Ostava, 1928

SPECIALIST GENRES: Czech opera, orchestral works, part-songs.

MAJOR WORKS: Operas *Jenůfa* (1894–1903), *Katya Kabanová* (1919–21), *The Cunning Little Vixen* (1921–3), *The Makropulos Case* (1923–5) and *From the House of the Dead* (1927–8); *Taras Bulba* (1915–18); Sinfonietta (1926); Glagolitic Mass (1926).

Béla Bartók

*Bartók's name…stands for the principle and the demand for regeneration
stemming from the people, both in art and in politics.*

ZOLTÁN KODÁLY (1882–1967)

Bartók was the greatest Hungarian composer since Liszt. He and Kodály put Hungary on the international musical map.

Both Bartók's parents were musical, and he was taught the piano by his mother. He began to compose at the age of nine, and made his pianistic debut at 11. In 1903 he emerged from his studies at the Budapest Academy as a virtuoso pianist and a promising composer.

From the start, Bartók immersed himself in the idioms of Hungarian folk music. His first folk song collection was published in 1906, and in 1907 he became a piano professor at the Budapest Academy, a post which enabled him to pursue systematic research into folk music from Hungary, Romania, Slovakia and Transylvania. From this time onwards he began to publish folk song anthologies for voice and piano, and arrangements of

ABOVE: *An evocative portrait by Roboz of the Hungarian pianist and composer Béla Bartók (1881–1945).*

folk songs, such as *For Children* (1908–9). The Ten Easy Pieces, the 14 Bagatelles (both 1908) and the ferocious *Allegro barbaro* for piano (1911) are also strongly Hungarian in idiom. Another new influence, the atmospheric music of Debussy, informed Bartók's works from the First String Quartet (1908).

Works for the stage

In 1909 Bartók married his pupil Márta Ziegler, who gave birth to a son in 1910. The next year Bartók completed his one-act opera *A kékszakállú herceg vára (Duke Bluebeard's Castle)*. This masterly score, based on a psychological interpretation of the Bluebeard legend, was not performed until 1918, after his ballet *A fából faragott királyfi (The Wooden Prince)* had been successfully staged in Budapest. Up to that point, Bartók's compositions had been largely neglected in his own country, but growing recognition of his talent prompted a second ballet, *A csodálatos mandarin (The Miraculous Mandarin*, 1918–19), whose sordid subject-matter caused outrage at its Cologne première in 1926. (The mandarin is lured into a robbers' den by a prostitute, but though stabbed and hanged by the men he refuses to die until he has had sex with her.)

During the post-war years Bartók began to tour widely as a pianist. In 1923 — when his Dance Suite, celebrating the 50th anniversary of the union of Buda and Pest, was premièred — he divorced Márta and married another young piano pupil, Ditta

ABOVE: *The opening manuscript page of Bartók's Hungarian folk song arrangements* Székely dalok *(Székely Songs) for six male voices (1932).*

ABOVE: Bartók listening to his folk song recordings on a phonogram in 1915. He was one of the major folk song collectors.

ABOVE: Bartók giving a piano concerto performance in Budapest in 1938. His second wife, Ditta Pásztory, is sitting behind him.

Pásztory. A second son was born in 1924.

Meanwhile, Bartók continued his dual career as pianist and composer. Many of his piano works – such as the First and Second Concertos (1926 and 1930–1), the Sonata, the Suite *Out of Doors*, and the Nine Little Pieces (all 1926) – were written for himself to play. His Third and Fourth String Quartets date from the late 1920s, as do the two Rhapsodies for violin and piano, both written for Hungarian virtuosi. The *Cantata profana* (1930) – a paean to the brotherhood of nations – was premièred in London in 1934, the year Bartók finally relinquished his teaching duties at the Budapest Academy to concentrate on his ethnomusicological work.

New musical structures

The late '30s – a period during which Bartók was preoccupied with musical structure, especially arch forms and constructions based on mathematical rules – produced some of his finest compositions, including the Fifth and Sixth String Quartets. He was equally concerned with timbre, exploiting the innovative sounds produced on conventional instruments, in works such as the *Music for Strings, Percussion and Celesta* and the 1939 Divertimento for strings. The Sonata for two pianos and percussion (1937) was premièred by Bartók and his wife; the Second Violin Concerto (1937–8) was written for Zoltán Székely and *Contrasts* for the violinist Joseph Szigeti and the clarinettist Benny Goodman. During the 1930s Bartók also published *Microkosmos*, six books of piano teaching pieces.

America

In 1940, alarmed by the threat of fascism, the Bartóks left for America, where they settled in New York.

The last five years of Bartók's life were clouded by public neglect, financial worries and declining health. In 1943 he was diagnosed as suffering from a rare form of cancer. He completed his most popular work, the Concerto for Orchestra (premièred by Serge Koussevitsky and the Boston Symphony Orchestra), in the summer of 1943, and the solo Violin Sonata, written for Yehudi Menuhin, the following March. His last works were the Third Piano Concerto (1945), written for his wife, and the Viola Concerto for the Scottish-born player William Primrose, which was left unfinished at his death in September 1945.

ABOVE: The anti-hero of Duke Bluebeard's Castle, *portrayed by Janos Kass.*

🎼 Life and works

NATIONALITY: Hungarian

BORN: Nagyszentmiklos (now in Romania), 1881; **DIED:** New York, 1945

SPECIALIST GENRES: Orchestral and piano music influenced by central European folk idioms.

MAJOR WORKS: Six string quartets (1908–39); *Duke Bluebeard's Castle* (1911–18); *The Miraculous Mandarin* (1919); *Microkosmos* (1926–39); three piano concertos (1926–45); *Music for Strings, Percussion and Celesta* (1936); *Contrasts* (1938); Concerto for Orchestra (1943).

Zoltán Kodály

Some day the ringing tower of Hungarian music is going to stand.

Like his friend and collaborator Bartók, Kodály raised the international profile of Hungarian music by fertilizing Western styles with Magyar folk idioms. An authority on folk music, he was also an important teacher, producing a vast body of musical educational material.

The son of a stationmaster, he spent his childhood and youth in the countryside, before enrolling at Budapest University to read languages. He simultaneously began to study composition at the Budapest Academy, where he was awarded a doctorate for his study of Hungarian folk song. From 1905 onwards he began to collect and record folk songs, often collaborating with Bartók, with whom he shared a vision of "an educated Hungary, reborn from the people". Like Bartók, Kodály devoted much of his life to the

ABOVE: Zoltán Kodály, photographed towards the end of his long life.

publication of folk song anthologies and arrangements.

In 1906 he received a travelling scholarship to study in Berlin and Paris, where he came into contact with Debussy's music. On his return he was appointed a professor at the Budapest Academy, becoming its deputy director in 1919. But his tenure of that post was abruptly curtailed by political intrigue, and his career was only rescued after the triumphant 1923 première of his oratorio *Psalmus hungaricus*, written — like Bartók's Dance Suite — to celebrate the 50th anniversary of the union of Buda and Pest. A performance in Zurich in 1926 marked the beginning of his international fame.

The same year (1926), Kodály's opera *Háry János* was performed in Budapest, and world-famous

conductors such as Arturo Toscanini, Rudolf Mengelberg and Wilhelm Furtwängler began to include the orchestral suite taken from it (which includes a prominent part for the cimbalom, a Hungarian dulcimer) in their repertoires. It was followed by other major orchestral works: the *Dances of Marosszek* (1930), the *Dances of Galánta* (1933), the *Peacock* Variations, based on a Hungarian folk tune (1939, written for the Amsterdam Concertgebouw Orchestra), and the Concerto for Orchestra (1939–40, for the Chicago Symphony). Like Bartók, Kodály opposed fascism, but he remained in Hungary when it came under Nazi rule. After the war he supervised the publication of the folk material he had collected, and continued to write educational works. In later life he was showered with honours.

ABOVE: The Liszt Academy of Music in Budapest, where Kodály studied composition, and where he later became deputy director.

Life and works

NATIONALITY: Hungarian

BORN: Kecskemét, 1882;
DIED: Budapest, 1967

SPECIALIST GENRES:
Orchestral and choral music influenced by folk music.

MAJOR WORKS: *Psalmus hungaricus* (1923); *Háry János* (1925–6); *Dances of Galánta* (1933); Concerto for Orchestra (1939–40).

Carl Nielsen

Music is life, and, like it, inextinguishable.

NIELSEN, MOTTO OF THE FOURTH SYMPHONY (1916)

Nielsen was the Danish equivalent of Grieg or Sibelius. Born into an impoverished family (his father was a painter), he began to scrape out melodies as a child on an instrument made from firewood. He started learning the violin at six and began playing in his father's folk band. In the mid 1880s he studied at the Copenhagen Conservatory, and first achieved success with his Little Suite for strings, performed at Tivoli in 1888.

The next year Nielsen became a violinist in the royal chapel, where he was able to broaden his musical outlook. During a trip to Paris in 1891 he met and married a sculptress, and on his return finished the first of a sequence of six symphonies, on which his reputation largely rests. No. 1 is an early example of "progressive tonality", beginning in one key and ending in another, while No. 2 (*The Four Temperaments*, 1901–2) uses the technique of thematic variation.

At much the same time Nielsen completed his first opera, *Saul og David*, followed a few years later by the comic opera *Maskarade*.

From 1908 until 1914 Nielsen combined composing with a position at the Royal Theatre, and then with teaching at the Copenhagen Conservatory, whose director he became in 1931, just before his death. He consolidated his foremost position in Danish musical life with three more symphonies (No. 3, *Sinfonia espansiva*, 1910–11; No. 4, *The Inextinguishable*, 1914–16; and No. 5, 1921–2), the Violin Concerto (1911), piano works including the Chaconne and the Theme and Variations, the tone-poem *Pan and Syrinx* (1917–18) and the exotic, colourfully scored incidental music to the play *Aladdin* (1918–19). His Fourth and Fifth Symphonies are imaginatively constructed, with innovative use of percussion (in a passage in the Fifth, the side-drum is instructed to improvise "in order to try to destroy the music").

Between 1914 and 1925 Nielsen published many volumes of Danish folk song arrangements, and his later works are mostly for chamber combinations or smaller orchestra. He died of heart disease in 1931.

Life and works

NATIONALITY: Danish

BORN: Nørre-Lyndelse, near Odense, 1865; **DIED:** Copenhagen, 1931

SPECIALIST GENRES: Symphonies.

MAJOR WORKS: Six symphonies; *Saul og David* (1898– 1901); *Maskarade* (1904–6).

ABOVE: The Danish composer Carl Nielsen (1865–1931), photographed as a young man.

RIGHT: The Royal Theatre in Copenhagen, where Nielsen's operas were performed, and where he worked from 1908–14.

Percy Grainger

I object to jazz and vaudeville having all the best instruments.

GRAINGER, 1930

The Australian composer and pianist Percy Grainger was brought up by his mother (to whom he was devoted) in Melbourne. In 1895 he left Australia for Europe, where he entered the Conservatory in Frankfurt; and in 1901 he settled in London to begin his career as a concert pianist, using it as a base for concert tours throughout Europe. He often visited Scandinavia, where he became a close friend of Grieg and a notable interpreter of his Piano Concerto; he was also a friend of Delius from 1907 onwards (Delius's orchestral rhapsody *Brigg Fair* is based on a Lincolnshire folk tune collected by Grainger).

In 1905 Grainger joined the English Folk Song Society, becoming an ardent folk song collector in company with

ABOVE: The Australian-born pianist and composer Percy Grainger (1882–1961).

Cecil Sharp, Holst and Vaughan Williams. Folk song infused much of his work, from piano arrangements such as the ever-popular *Country Gardens*, *Green Bushes*, *Molly on the Shore* and *Shepherds' Hey*, to arrangements for wind band, and original orchestral works such as *Mock Morris*. Much of his vocal music is now out of fashion, since he often set jingoistic verses by Kipling and other colonial writers. His original large-scale works, which include *The Warriors* for three pianos, orchestra and tuned percussion, have also fallen out of favour, with the exception of *Handel in the Strand* (1932) for strings, based

on Handel's *Harmonious Blacksmith* Variations treated in music-hall style.

In 1914 Grainger moved to the USA, where he became a US citizen, and settled in White Plains, New York State. His mother committed suicide in 1922, and over the next six years Grainger spent much time in Denmark, collecting Danish folk songs, and returned twice to Australia. In 1928 he married a Swedish artist, who was presumably willing to put up with his sado-masochistic sexual practices and other eccentricities — their wedding took place before a huge audience in the Hollywood Bowl. The rest of his life was a long creative decline, although he spent his last years experimenting with "free music", dispensing with the conventions of harmony, form and instrumentation.

ABOVE: Grainger at the piano with his adored (and domineering) mother, Rose, in the music room of their American home in 1921.

Life and works

NATIONALITY: Australian

BORN: Melbourne, 1882;
DIED: White Plains,
New York, 1961

SPECIALIST GENRES: Folk song settings and original works using ingenious instrumental combinations.

MAJOR WORKS: *The Warriors* (1912–16); *Handel in the Strand* (1932); Suite *A Lincolnshire Posy* (1940).

Charles Ives

This fascinating composer…was exploring the 1960s during the heyday of Strauss and Debussy.

IGOR STRAVINSKY (1882–1971)

Charles Ives, one of the most innovative figures in music history, was America's first major composer. His father was a town bandmaster with a most original musical mind. His experiments with acoustics and pitch, using quarter-tones, polytonality, tone clusters and simultaneously playing pieces in different keys, intrigued his young son. Ives later incorporated the unusual sounds of his childhood experiences into his own music.

In 1894 Charles went to Yale University, where he studied composition and wrote the first of his four symphonies. After graduating he moved to New York, where he worked in insurance, and by 1906 he and his partner, Julian Myrick, had set up their own very successful insurance agency

ABOVE: *Charles Ives (1874–1954), an essentially amateur composer who gave American music an individual identity.*

which made them millionaires. Ives married Harmony Twichell in a union of lasting happiness, but long hours of work combined with spare-time composing undermined his health, and in 1918 he had a heart attack. During a year's convalescence he embarked on the publication of his music. He retired from the insurance business in 1930.

Most of Ives's major compositions were written before 1920. Many were inspired by "American" landscapes, festivals, traditions, or historical events. They include four numbered symphonies (the Fourth introduces a chorus into the finale); the *Holidays Symphony* (1904–13), in which the movements are "Washington's Birthday", "Decoration Day", "Fourth of July" and "Thanksgiving Day"; *Central Park in the Dark* (1906); and three Sets for

orchestra, of which No. 1 is entitled *Three Places in New England*. He also wrote several psalm settings for various vocal combinations and organ or orchestra; over 20 Studies for piano, of which several describe stages of a baseball game; the huge *Concord* Sonata for piano, with optional parts for viola and flute; the epigrammatic three-page Sonata (1905) and the early *Variations on "America"* for organ.

Ives was a Satie-like figure, who often used punning titles (such as *Five Take-offs* or *Six Protests*). In *The Unanswered Question* (1906) for chamber ensemble, a solo trumpet asks "the question", to which a woodwind choir frantically attempts to find an answer. His innovative musical style had enormous influence on later American composers.

ABOVE: *Yale University in New Haven, USA, where Ives studied in the 1890s. He was an enthusiastic member of the baseball team.*

Life and works

NATIONALITY: American

BORN: Danbury, Connecticut, 1874; **DIED:** New York, 1954

SPECIALIST GENRES: Orchestral and piano music, often on American themes.

MAJOR WORKS: Five symphonies; *Variations on "America"* (1891); *Three Places in New England* (1904); Piano Sonata No. 2 *Concord* (1910–15); 114 songs.

Arnold Schoenberg

I am a conservative who was forced to become a revolutionary.

SCHOENBERG

Schoenberg was one of the seminal figures of 20th-century music. He loosened the grip of traditional tonality and explored new ways of working with the 12 notes of the chromatic scale. Although his own music is still generally misunderstood and has never achieved great popularity with audiences, his influence on other composers was immense.

He was born in Vienna, into an orthodox Jewish family, and began to learn the violin at eight. His father died when he was 15, and he was forced to leave school and take a job as a bank clerk. In the evenings he studied music, philosophy and literature, and taught himself to play the cello. His first composition lessons came from Alexander Zemlinsky, whose sister Mathilde he married in 1901. By that time he had written a string quartet, the string sextet *Verklärte Nacht* (*Transfigured Night*), and *Gurrelieder* (*Songs of Gurra*),

ABOVE: *The Austrian composer Arnold Schoenberg (1874–1951), painted by Richard Gerstl (1883–1908).*

for five voices, narrator, choir and orchestra. At that time Schoenberg was writing in a post-Romantic, Mahlerian style, but his works met with incomprehension from the start.

Berlin

At the end of 1901 Schoenberg moved to Berlin, where he supported his family (including his daughter Gertrud, born in 1902) first by providing and arranging music for a cabaret, and then by teaching at the Stern Conservatory. He spent the next 30 years see-sawing between Berlin and Vienna, where he moved back in 1903 as a private teacher (his most notable pupils were Alban Berg and Anton Webern). His son Georg was born in Vienna in 1906.

By 1907–8 Schoenberg was experimenting with atonality and free dissonance, in works such as the First and Second Quartets, the song anthology *Das Buch der hängenden Gärten* (*The Book of the Hanging Gardens*), and the Three Piano Pieces, Op. 11, and in his major works of 1909 — the dramatic monologue *Erwartung* (*Awaiting*) and the Five Orchestral

ABOVE: *The Reichstag (Parliament) building in Berlin in Schoenberg's time. He moved to Berlin in 1901 and taught at the Stern Conservatory.*

ABOVE: *A drawing by B. F. Dolbin of Schoenberg directing a performance of his* Pierrot lunaire *on 17 November 1940.*

ABOVE: A view of modern-day Los Angeles. In 1936 Schoenberg was appointed Professor of Music at the University of Southern California, Los Angeles. He became an American citizen in 1941 and remained on the West Coast of the United States until his death in 1951, aged 76.

Pieces, Op. 16. They were greeted with outright hostility by the conservative Viennese, and when Schoenberg applied for a professorship at the Vienna Academy of Music and Dramatic Art, he encountered virulent anti-Semitism.

As a result, in 1911 he moved back to Berlin, where his *Pierrot lunaire* (*Moonstruck Pierrot*, 1912) for voice and

chamber ensemble was well received. The work represents the first use of a technique Schoenberg called *Sprechstimme* ("speaking voice"), also known as *Sprechgesang* ("speech song"), in which the singer "speaks" rather than sings each note, starting on the pitch indicated but immediately leaving it in a rise or fall. Meanwhile, in 1912, the long-delayed orchestral version of *Gurrelieder* was applauded in Vienna, much to Schoenberg's disgust. Nonetheless he moved back to Vienna in 1915, when he briefly enlisted in the army but was discharged owing to poor health.

New tonality

After the war Schoenberg founded the Society for Private Musical Performances, which until 1921 gave some 350 performances of new music by himself, his pupils and colleagues. His works of the early 1920s laid the foundation of his revolutionary "12-note" style in the Five Piano Pieces, Op. 23, the Serenade and the Piano Suite. His wife died in 1923, but less than a year later he married Gertrud, sister of the violinist Rudolf Kolisch. He had three more children, including two sons born after he emigrated to the USA.

From 1925 until 1933 Schoenberg taught at the Prussian Academy of Arts

in Berlin, where he wrote several major works including the Variations for Orchestra, and the operas *Von heute auf morgen* (*From One Day to the Next*, 1928–9) and *Moses und Aron* (1930–2; the title was deliberately spelt this way by Schoenberg to avoid the unlucky number of 13 letters). In 1933 Hitler's anti-Semitic legislation robbed him of his job and forced him to leave Germany for good, despite the fact that he had been baptized a Christian in 1898.

America

The family spent the summer in France, where Schoenberg re-converted to Judaism, and then sailed for America, where he began teaching in New York and Boston. A lifelong sufferer from asthma, he moved for the sake of his health to the West Coast, where he taught at the University of Southern California. His late works include concertos for violin and piano, the Fourth String Quartet (1936) and the String Trio (1946), the *Ode to Napoleon Buonaparte* (1942) and several pieces inspired by his faith, including *Kol nidre* (*All Vows*, 1938), his setting of the prayer for Yom Kippur, and *A Survivor from Warsaw* (1947). A deeply superstitious man, Schoenberg foretold his own death from heart failure on 13 July 1951.

Alban Berg

The best music always results from ecstasies of logic.

BERG, IN "NEW YORK TIMES"

While Schoenberg's music is still an acquired taste, that of his pupil Alban Berg has always been more accessible to a wider audience. His two operas and his Violin Concerto are among the finest 20th-century works.

Like Webern, Berg spent most of his working life in Vienna, taking summer holidays in the Carinthian mountains where his family had an estate, and where he later bought a villa on the shores of Lake Wörther. He grew up surrounded by creative people – artists such as Gustav Klimt and Oskar Kokoschka, writers such as Peter Altenberg and Stefan Zweig – who formed a close-knit circle rather like the Schubertians of a century earlier. Around 1904 Berg began to study with Schoenberg: his first works include the beautiful Seven Early Songs (1905–8), which are clearly in the German Romantic tradition. But within a few

ABOVE: *Alban Berg, the most accessible composer of the "Second Viennese School".*

years, by the time he wrote the Four Songs, Op. 2, Berg was already beginning to push traditional tonality

to its limits, and the String Quartet, Op. 3 (1910), is a strikingly original piece, based around the whole-tone scale. The highly compressed *Altenberg-Lieder* of 1912 drew criticism from Schoenberg, who perhaps found them too original for his liking.

In 1911 Berg married Helene Nahowski after a four-year courtship. Until the 1970s their marriage was carefully portrayed (especially by the widowed Helene) as idyllically happy. But in 1977 a copy of the score of Berg's *Lyrische Suite* for string quartet (1925–6) came to light, heavily annotated by the composer, which left no doubt that this major work owed its existence to Berg's clandestine love-affair with a married woman, Hanna Fuchs-Robettin. The musical equivalents of her initials are interwoven with Berg's own to produce the underlying motif of the work.

LEFT: Adele Bloch-Bauer *by Gustav Klimt (1862–1918), an exponent of decadent, Symbolist art featuring* femmes fatales *like Berg's* Lulu.

ABOVE: *A stage design by Vladislav Hofman for the last act of Berg's* Wozzeck, *for the Prague première in 1926, one year after the opera's debut in Berlin.*

Life and works

NATIONALITY: Austrian

BORN: Vienna, 1885;
DIED: Vienna, 1935

SPECIALIST GENRES: Opera, orchestral and chamber music in atonal style with serial elements.

MAJOR WORKS: String Quartet (1910); *Lyric Suite* (1925–6); *Wozzeck* (1917–22); *Lulu* (1929–35); Violin Concerto (1935).

ABOVE: Wozzeck murders Marie in the last act of the 1990 English National Opera production of Wozzeck.

In September 1914 Berg sent Schoenberg two of his Three Orchestral Pieces, Op. 6, evidently hoping to heal the rift between them. Among Berg's most accessible orchestral works, the Three Pieces revert to a Mahlerian style, using traditional forms – "Prelude", "Round Dance" (with elements of Viennese dances, the waltz and the *Ländler*) and "March".

Operas

At the same time, Berg began work on the first of his two operas. He had seen the Viennese première of the 19th-century play *Wozzeck* by Georg Büchner (1813–37), and "at once decided to set it to music". But the war (during which he served in the Austrian army) intervened, and *Wozzeck* the opera was not completed until 1922, by which time Berg had had ample experience of the privations of a soldier's life at first hand.

Wozzeck is a masterpiece, both for its sympathetic portrayal of the main protagonists – the downtrodden, exploited soldier, and the faithless mistress whom he eventually murders – and for its complex, innovative structure. A carefully constructed

sequence of scenes is grouped into three acts, with Acts I and III framing the pivotal central act; the five scenes in Act I are described as "character pieces", each relating Wozzeck to another character in the drama. Berg described Act II as a "symphony in five movements", focusing on Wozzeck's disintegrating relationship with Marie.

ABOVE: Manon Gropius, the daughter of Mahler's widow Alma and her second husband Walter Gropius.

Act III consists of five inventions, each based on an *ostinato* rhythmic pattern or theme. But Berg's genius ensured that the audience's attention is focused not on such compositional wizardry, but on the drama itself.

Similar structural complexities underpin his last opera, *Lulu*, based on Frank Wedekind's two plays *Erdgeist* (*Earth Spirit*) and *Die Büchse der Pandora* (*Pandora's Box*). Again, the drama pivots around the large-scale rondo structure of Act II, with Lulu's Act III clients (after her descent into prostitution) paralleling – dramatically and musically – her lovers in Act I. Her last, fatal, encounter is with Jack the Ripper.

Lulu remained incomplete at Berg's death, and there is evidence that his widow obstructed its completion and performance during her lifetime. Berg's work on the opera had been interrupted by the composition of his last completed work, the elegiac Violin Concerto, written as a Requiem for Manon Gropius (daughter of Mahler's widow Alma and her second husband, the architect Walter Gropius), who died at 18 from polio. Shortly after completing it in August 1935 Berg suffered an insect sting which turned septic. He died of septicaemia four months later, aged 50.

Anton Webern

He shook the foundation of sound as discourse in favour of sound as sound.

JOHN CAGE (1912–92)

Webern produced perhaps the most compressed output of any composer in history: his complete works – some of which last only a few seconds in performance – have been recorded on to three CDs. He adopted the serial (12-note) technique of his teacher Schoenberg, and pursued it with ruthless concentration, paring it down to its essence.

Webern grew up in Vienna, Graz and Klagenfurt (his aristocratic family had a summer estate in Carinthia, where he developed a life-long love of walking, botany and geology). He was taught the piano by his mother, and after leaving school in 1902 he went to the University of Vienna, where he studied musicology,

ABOVE: *Anton Webern (1883–1945), a composer of extreme intellectual rigour.*

composition, cello and piano. His early works, including the Piano Quintet (1907) and the Op. 1 Passacaglia for orchestra (1908), are in the Brahmsian tradition.

Between 1904 and 1908 Webern studied privately with Schoenberg. From 1908 onwards he held various conducting posts, and played a leading role in the Society for Private Musical Performances, for which he made many chamber arrangements of pieces by himself and others. In the 1920s and early '30s he conducted many workers' choral societies and symphony concerts, at which he introduced works by Mahler, his fellow pupil Berg, Max Reger and even Charles Ives. From 1927 he was employed as music adviser to Austrian

Radio, but he lost all these jobs under the Nazi regime, when his music was banned. From 1938 onwards he worked as a freelance for his publisher, Universal Edition. He was accidentally shot dead by an American soldier during the last weeks of World War II, while visiting his daughter.

Webern's works up to the late 1920s were atonal in style. From 1928 onwards he adopted serial technique, often using *Klangfarbenmelodie* (timbre melody), in which changes of timbre rather than pitch define the melody. Many of his works are scored for chamber ensembles and use complex structural forms such as canon, palindrome and variation form.

ABOVE: *Anton Webern at the keyboard.*

Life and works

NATIONALITY: Austrian

BORN: Vienna, 1883; **DIED:** Mittersill, near Salzburg, 1945

SPECIALIST GENRES: Chamber and orchestral works.

MAJOR WORKS: Symphony, Op. 21 (1928); Concerto for nine instruments, Op. 24 (1931–4); three cantatas; String Quartet, Op. 28 (1936–8); piano Variations (1935–6); orchestral Variations (1940).

Kurt Weill

I write for today. I don't care about posterity.

WEILL

Kurt Weill was the musical personification of the Weimar Republic. His acidic blend of social realism and jazz reflected the decadent Germany of the 1920s, a time of economic depression, political upheaval and desperate hedonism. Together with his principal collaborator Bertolt Brecht (1898–1956), Weill created a new genre of music theatre, which he later developed on Broadway after his emigration to the USA.

The son of a Jewish cantor in Dessau, Weill studied briefly at the Berlin Hochschule and took masterclasses with Busoni. His first major work, the opera *Der Protagonist*, was performed in Dresden in 1926, and shortly afterwards he was introduced to the left-wing playwright Bertolt Brecht. Among the first fruits

ABOVE: Kurt Weill (1900–50), photographed after his move to the USA.

of the Brecht/Weill collaboration was *Die Dreigroschenoper* (*The Threepenny Opera*), a modern reworking of John Gay's *The Beggar's Opera* (1728), an English ballad opera set in the Soho underworld of thieves and pimps. It was premièred in Berlin in 1928 (with Weill's wife, Lotte Lenya, as Jenny), and scored a huge success with its bitter-sweet jazz idioms and savagely ironic subject. Its central song, "The Ballad of Mack the Knife", became an international hit.

In 1930 the partnership's second opera – *Aufstieg und Fall der Stadt Mahagonny* (*The Rise and Fall of the City of Mahagonny*) – was premièred in Leipzig. By now Weill's music had

been targeted by the emerging forces of fascism, and after the Nazi seizure of power in 1933 Weill fled to France, where his ballet *Die sieben Todesünden* (*The Seven Deadly Sins*), to a scenario by Brecht, was produced in Paris without much success.

In 1935 Weill left France for the USA, where he settled permanently. In 1938 he achieved his first Broadway success with *Knickerbocker Holiday*, which contains the evocative "September Song". He went on to write another ten Broadway shows, of which the best known are *Lady in the Dark* (with Ira Gershwin, 1940), *One Touch of Venus* (1943), *Street Scene* (1946), and *Lost in the Stars* (1949). He also wrote film and radio scores, but all his concert music, which includes a Violin Concerto (1924) and two symphonies, belongs to his "German" period.

Life and works

NATIONALITY: German

BORN: Dessau, 1900;
DIED: New York, 1950

SPECIALIST GENRES:
Theatre music using jazz and cabaret idioms.

MAJOR WORKS:
Die Dreigroschenoper
(1928); *Aufstieg und Fall der Stadt Mahagonny*
(1930).

ABOVE: An album of songs from Weill's famous work, The Threepenny Opera *(1928).*

Francis Poulenc and "Les Six"

Above all do not analyse my music — love it!

POULENC

"Les Six" was the appellation given in 1920 by the French critic Henri Collet to a group of promising young avant-garde composers, who specialized in "shocking the bourgeoisie" along the lines of their mentor, Erik Satie. As a homogeneous group, Les Six — who drew their inspiration from Parisian streetlife, music halls and circus bands — lasted only a few years before going their separate ways.

The most important member was Francis Poulenc, who first attracted attention with his *Rapsodie nègre* for baritone and chamber ensemble (1917). Born into the family of pharmaceutical manufacturers which is now the multinational Rhône-Poulenc company, Poulenc never had to earn a living. He began learning the piano at five, and later studied with the Spanish pianist Ricardo Viñes (1875–1943). In the early 1920s he took private composition lessons, his first major work being settings of Cocteau's *Cocardes*

(1919). Stravinsky recommended Poulenc to the impresario Sergei Diaghilev, who commissioned the ballet with chorus *Les biches* (1923). A sophisticated blend of lyricism with 1920s jazz idioms, the ballet was a great success, but during the 1920s and early '30s Poulenc concentrated on songs — many written for his recital partner, the baritone Pierre Bernac

(1899–1979) — and piano music, including two chamber concertos.

He might have remained an essentially frivolous composer, had not the death of a close friend in a car crash prompted his re-conversion to Catholicism. Poulenc visited the shrine of the Black Virgin at Rocamadour, and the musical result — *Litanies à la vierge noire* (1936) — was the first of a series of fine sacred works. These included the Mass in G (1937), two motets for unaccompanied choir (1941), the Stabat Mater (1950) and the exultant Gloria (1959).

Other important late works include the Sextet and sonatas for cello, violin, flute, clarinet and oboe; the operas *Les mamelles de Tirésias* (*The Breasts of Tirésias*), *Les dialogues des Carmélites*

ABOVE:
Francis Poulenc (1899–1963), photographed in 1949.

LEFT: Parisians enjoying themselves in the 1920s — Dancing at the Moulin Rouge *by Marcel Leprin (1891–1933).*

Life and works

NATIONALITY: French

BORN: Paris, 1899; **DIED:** Paris, 1963

SPECIALIST GENRES: Stage works, concertos, piano music, sacred vocal music.

MAJOR WORKS: Concerto in D minor for two pianos (1932); Organ Concerto (1938); *Les mamelles de Tirésias* (1944); Stabat Mater (1950); *Les dialogues des Carmélites* (1953–6); *La voix humaine* (1958); Gloria (1959).

(the story of a group of nuns during the French Revolution) and *La voix humaine* (*The Human Voice*), the cantata *Figure humaine* (1943), and concertos for organ and piano. All these works allowed Poulenc to develop a naturally lyrical style leavened with wit and irony.

Arthur Honegger

The Swiss composer Honegger (1892–1955) came to fame first with his "dramatic psalm" *Le roi David* (1921), and again three years later with *Pacific 231*, a musical representation of a steam locomotive. A great admirer of Bach, whose influence is evident in his music, Honegger's best-known works are his five symphonies, particularly No. 3, *Liturgique* (1945–6), No. 4, *Deliciae basilienses* (1946), and No. 5, *Di tre re* (*Of the three Ds*, 1950); the *Pastorale d'été* (*Summer Pastoral*, 1920); and the staged oratorio *Jeanne d'Arc au bûcher* (*Joan of Arc at the Stake*, 1934–5), based on a text by Paul Claudel.

ABOVE: Five of "Les Six" with the poet Jean Cocteau, on the viewing platform of the Eiffel Tower in 1921. From left to right: Tailleferre, Poulenc, Honegger, Milhaud, Cocteau and Auric.

Darius Milhaud

Milhaud (1892–1974) studied at the Paris Conservatoire, where he later taught after World War II. The only Jewish member of Les Six, he was forced to leave France in 1940 and settled in the USA, where he taught in California and Colorado. Milhaud (who spent much of his life in a wheelchair due to rheumatoid arthritis) experimented with polytonality. An enormously prolific composer, he is best known for his 1919 jazz and Latin American-influenced ballet score *Le boeuf sur le toit* (*The Ox on the Roof*); the ballet *La création du monde* (1923); and

for the two-piano suite *Scaramouche* (1939). Many of his stage works were based on his friend the poet Paul Claudel's adaptations of Greek myths.

Other members of Les Six

Of the three less well-known members of Les Six, Georges Auric (1899–1983) began as a composer for Diaghilev's Ballets Russes in the 1920s and went on to specialize in film music, writing the scores for the films of Jean Cocteau.

Louis Durey (1888–1979) was only briefly a member of the group. In 1936 he joined the French Communist Party, and after 1945 wrote "music for the masses" in accordance with communist doctrine, setting texts by Mao Zedong and Ho Chi-Minh.

Germaine Tailleferre (1892–1983) was a fine pianist, who wrote over a dozen operas, two ballets, orchestral music including concertos for piano and harp, chamber music including a Pastorale for flute and piano and two violin sonatas, songs, and a few piano pieces. However, her two husbands apparently both discouraged her from composing.

ABOVE: Arthur Honegger (1892–1955).

The French composer Darius Milhaud (1892–1974) conducting.

Aaron Copland

Music that is born complex is not inherently better or worse than music that is born simple.

COPLAND

Copland was the most influential American composer of his time. He strove to create a recognizable "American" idiom, and came to represent the "Establishment" in American music, even though he himself was an outsider, by virtue both of his immigrant background and his homosexuality. Although his life spanned almost the whole of the 20th century, many of his most important works date from the first half of the century.

ABOVE: Aaron Copland (1900–90), the most prominent American composer of the 20th century, still conducting at the age of 81.

Copland's parents were Lithuanian/Russian Jews who had become prosperous Brooklyn storekeepers, and he grew up with a keen interest in music. From 1917 he took composition lessons with the conservative Rubin Goldmark in New York, but when he was 20 he decided to seek more creative stimulation in Paris.

He studied for four years with Nadia Boulanger (1887–1979), one of the most dynamic teachers of her age, and threw himself into the frenzied creative melting-pot of 1920s Paris, absorbing influences from all directions, including Stravinsky and Les Six. In 1925 his Organ Symphony (which he

revised in 1928, without organ, as Symphony No. 1) was performed by Nadia Boulanger on an American tour, eliciting the admiring comment from the conductor Walter Damrosch (1862–1950): "If he can write like that at 23, in five years he'll be ready to commit murder." On his return to New York, Copland divided his time between teaching and composing, joining the League of Composers and — with his fellow composer Roger Sessions (1896–1985) — sponsoring an innovative series of new music concerts in New York.

ABOVE: Eugene Loring as Billy in the original Ballet Caravan production of Copland's Billy the Kid *at the Chicago Opera House, 16 October 1938.*

Life and works

NATIONALITY: American

BORN: New York, 1900;
DIED: New York, 1990

SPECIALIST GENRES: "American" ballet scores, orchestral music.

MAJOR WORKS:
Piano Concerto (1926); *Billy the Kid* (1938); *Fanfare for the Common Man* (1942); *Rodeo* (1942); *Appalachian Spring* (1944); Symphony No. 3 (1944–6).

Popular music

Copland had firm convictions about the role of music in society, and was determined to show that the arts and industry could co-exist on equal terms. His ideas were honed by the Depression and the looming war: he decided that his own music must be, above all, accessible, and he gave it a specifically American sound by incorporating elements of jazz and folk music. Copland's first major hit was the ballet *El salón México* (1936), and from 1938 onwards he produced a series of influential ballets on "American" subjects: *Billy the Kid*, *Rodeo* (for Agnes de Mille) and *Appalachian Spring*. This last, written for Martha Graham's dance company, is a tender portrait of a close-knit pioneering community in the Appalachian mountains, whose aspirations are embodied in the Shaker hymn-tune "Simple Gifts". At the same time he began to write film scores, of which the best-known were for *Of Mice and Men* (1939), *Our Town* (1940), *The Red Pony* (1948) and the Oscar-winning *The Heiress* (1949).

Several other notable works date from this specifically "American" period, including the urban landscape *Quiet City* (1939), *A Lincoln Portrait* for speaker and orchestra (1942), based on Lincoln's speeches; and *Fanfare for the*

ABOVE: A steer wrestler in action at a rodeo in Idaho. Copland's "cowboy ballet" Rodeo celebrates this American tradition.

Common Man, written as an antidote to the usual pompous VIP fanfares. His Piano Variations of 1930 remains his best-known solo work (a Piano Sonata dates from 1939–41, and a Violin Sonata from 1943).

Serialism

Copland's post-war works were more abstract and notably less successful: by then fashions were changing and the fast-paced modern idioms of Leonard Bernstein had overtaken Copland's in the popularity stakes. Among his later works, the beautiful *Twelve Poems of*

Emily Dickinson for voice and piano (1950), the Piano Quartet (1950, which uses 12-note technique), the orchestral *Music for a Great City* (1964), and the *Threnody in memoriam Stravinsky* for flute quartet (1971) are the most memorable. His opera *The Tender Land* (1952–4) was not well received.

From 1940–65 Copland was head of the composition faculty at the Berkshire Music Center at Tanglewood, and also taught at Harvard, where his lectures were published as *Music and Imagination* (1952). He was showered with honours, including a Pulitzer Prize.

ABOVE: A pastoral landscape in the Appalachians, such as inspired Copland's ballet Appalachian Spring *(1944).*

ABOVE: Martha Graham in Appalachian Spring, *seen here with her dance company in 1954.*

George Gershwin

*I don't think there has been such an inspired melodist on this earth since Tchaikovsky...
but if you want to speak of a composer, that's another matter.*

LEONARD BERNSTEIN (1918–90)

Gershwin was one of the most popular composers of the 20th century, and one of history's greatest songwriters. From 1916 until his untimely death from a brain tumour at the age of only 39, he turned out a stream of great melodies which became instant classics. Songs such as "Swanee", "'S Wonderful", "Someone to Watch Over Me", "Embraceable You", "He Loves and She Loves", "I Got Rhythm" (and dozens more) rank with the best of Irving Berlin, Cole Porter and Jerome Kern, but were also much admired by "serious" musicians.

The son of a Russian Jewish immigrant family, Gershwin studied piano, theory and harmony as a child with several distinguished musicians, although he was never good at reading music. In 1914 he went to work for a Tin Pan Alley music publisher and began to write songs for other people's shows. From 1919 onwards he wrote his own Broadway musicals, many in collaboration with his brother Ira

(1896–1983). They included *Lady be Good* (1924), *Oh, Kay!* (1926), *Strike Up the Band* (1927), *Funny Face* (1927), *Girl Crazy* (1930) and *Of Thee I Sing* (1931). From 1931 onwards he also wrote film scores (the songs "Let's Call the Whole Thing Off", "Shall We Dance?" and "They Can't Take That Away From Me"

were written for the 1937 film *Shall We Dance?*).

In 1924 the bandleader Paul Whiteman commissioned Gershwin's famous *Rhapsody in Blue* for piano and jazz ensemble. The story goes that Gershwin did not know he was supposed to write it until he saw an advertisement for Whiteman's forthcoming "Experiment in Modern Music" concert in a newspaper. Ira Gershwin suggested the title, after a painting by Whistler. Its triumphant success led to commissions for the Piano Concerto, the orchestral tone-poem *An American in Paris*, and ultimately to the opera *Porgy and Bess*, set among the black community of the Deep South and using its folk music and rhythms. It is still the only American opera to be performed internationally on a regular basis.

ABOVE: George Gershwin, painted by himself a year before his death from a brain tumour.

LEFT: A poster advertising the 1959 film version of Porgy and Bess.

Life and works

NATIONALITY: American

BORN: Brooklyn, 1898;
DIED: Beverly Hills, 1937

SPECIALIST GENRES:
Popular songs.

MAJOR WORKS: *Rhapsody in Blue* (1924); Piano Concerto in F (1925); Preludes for piano (1926); *An American in Paris* (1928); *Porgy and Bess* (1935).

Samuel Barber

*As to what happens when I compose,
I really haven't the faintest idea.*

BARBER

Samuel Barber's style eschewed the idiomatic "Americanisms" of Copland and looked back to the late-Romantic European tradition. He began to learn the piano at the age of six, and began composing at seven. At 14 he became one of the first students at the Curtis Institute in Philadelphia, where he studied piano, composition, conducting and singing. He nearly became a professional baritone.

Barber's student years at the Curtis Institute produced his first mature compositions, including the popular *Dover Beach* (a setting of a poem by Matthew Arnold for baritone voice and string quartet which Barber himself recorded in 1935), the Serenade for string quartet, and the

ABOVE: The American composer Samuel Barber (1910–81).

Cello Sonata, all of which gave him scope to develop his characteristic lyrical, expressive style. In 1928 he won a travelling scholarship with his Violin Sonata, and another in 1933 for his overture *The School for Scandal*. In the mid 1930s further scholarships, including the American Prix de Rome, enabled him to spend time in Italy. His compositions there included the First Symphony and a String Quartet, the slow movement of which, transcribed for orchestra, became the famous Adagio for strings (first recorded by Toscanini).

From 1939 until 1942 Barber taught at the Curtis Institute, and from 1943

until 1974 he lived in New York State with the Italian composer Gian Carlo Menotti (born 1911), who wrote the libretto for Barber's first opera, *Vanessa*. His Second Symphony (later withdrawn) was written during war service. His post-war works included a fine Cello Concerto (1945), the ballet *Medea* (1946), the Piano Sonata, *Summer Music* for wind quintet (1955), the vocal works *Knoxville: Summer of 1915* (1947), *Hermit Songs* (1952–3), and *Prayers of Kierkegaard* (1954), and three operas, of which *Antony and Cleopatra* (1965–6), based on Franco Zeffirelli's reworking of Shakespeare, was an expensive failure. A post-Romantic, Barber shunned innovation, and continued, as he said, to "go on doing his thing" until the end of his life.

Life and works

NATIONALITY: American

BORN: West Chester, Pennsylvania, 1910; **DIED:** New York, 1981

SPECIALIST GENRES: Orchestral, chamber and operatic works, in neo-Romantic idiom.

MAJOR WORKS: *Dover Beach* (1931); *The School for Scandal* Overture (1933); Adagio for strings (1938); Piano Sonata (1949); opera *Vanessa* (1958); Piano Concerto (1962).

ABOVE: Philadelphia, Pennsylvania, at dusk. Barber studied there at the world-famous Curtis Institute.

Igor Stravinsky

Bach on the wrong notes.

Sergei Prokofiev (1891–1953)

Stravinsky was arguably the greatest – and certainly the most versatile – composer of the 20th century. He was keenly receptive to new trends – from neo-classicism to 12-note music – and perceived the advantages of a protean approach to composition. He also shed his personal skin several times throughout his long life, acquiring two wives and three changes of nationality.

Russian period

The son of an opera singer, Stravinsky went to school in St Petersburg, and began piano lessons when he was nine. On a summer vacation in the country he met Rimsky-Korsakov, who became his teacher and mentor. His early Piano Sonata in F sharp minor was performed at Rimsky-Korsakov's house, and a Symphony in E flat and the orchestral fantasy *Feu d'artifice* (*Fireworks*, strongly influenced

ABOVE: Igor Stravinsky, photographed by Tappe in 1965, while he was writing the Requiem Canticles, *his last major work.*

by Debussy) were largely written under the elder composer's tuition. Stravinsky had no other formal musical education; during this time he spent a couple of years reading law at university, but found it uncongenial. He left in 1905 and the following year he married his cousin Katerina Nossenko, who bore him four children.

Diaghilev's Ballets Russes

In 1909 the *Scherzo fantastique* and *Feu d'artifice* were performed in St Petersburg. In the audience was the impresario Sergei Diaghilev (1872–1929), whose celebrated Ballets Russes employed the dancer Mikhail Fokine and the designers Léon Bakst and Alexandre Benois. Diaghilev lacked a composer for his 1910 Paris season, and he decided to try out the young Stravinsky with a commission for *L'oiseau de feu* (*The Firebird*), based on a Russian folk legend. Stravinsky's brilliant and colourful score – strongly influenced by his Russian forebears including Balakirev, Tchaikovsky and Rimsky-Korsakov – was a huge success.

His next score for Diaghilev began life as a concert piece for piano and orchestra, but then turned into *Petrushka*, based on a grotesque tale of lust and murder in a Russian puppeteer's booth. Another huge success at its Paris première in June 1911, *Petrushka* conjures up a vanishing world of Russian peasant life, complete

ABOVE: A portrait of Stravinsky conducting, by the artist Milein Cosman. Stravinsky conducted recordings of his entire output.

with exotic and exhilarating dances for Cossacks, coachmen, wet-nurses and a host of other characters.

During 1912 Stravinsky worked on his third Diaghilev ballet, *Le sacre du printemps* (*The Rite of Spring*). Its première at the Théâtre des Champs-Elysées on 29 May 1913 caused a riot among its outraged audience. Even now, the primitive violence of Stravinsky's score – especially when coupled with Nijinsky's explicit choreography (the ballet concerns an ancient fertility rite in which a young virgin is selected for ritual sacrifice) – still packs an electrifying punch.

In 1914 Stravinsky's first opera, *Le rossignol* (*The Nightingale*, based on Hans Christian Andersen's fairy-story), was produced under the aegis of the Ballets Russes at the Paris Opéra. (Five years later Stravinsky arranged the music as a symphonic poem, *Le chant du rossignol*, which was choreographed

ABOVE: Stravinsky in his study in later life – a photographic portrait by Karsh of Ottawa.

as a ballet by Leonid Massine with designs by Henri Matisse.)

When war broke out the composer and his family took refuge in Switzerland, where he worked on a new ballet score, *Les noces* (*The Wedding*), scored for four-part chorus,

four soloists, four pianos and percussion ensemble. Stravinsky's researches into Russian folk music for this project also inspired several secondary works, including the burlesque *Renard* (1915–16).

By 1918 Stravinsky had already abandoned the lush orchestral resources of his pre-war ballets in favour of more sparsely scored, chamber-orientated works. These included *L'histoire du soldat* (*The Soldier's Tale*, for three actors, dancer, and small instrumental ensemble) and the ballet *Pulcinella*, based on a *commedia dell'arte* theme with music "arranged" from fragments attributed to Pergolesi, at the suggestion of Diaghilev. *Pulcinella* – which ushered in Stravinsky's absorption in neo-classicism – was first performed at the Paris Opéra on 15 May 1920, with décor and costumes by Picasso. Stravinsky later arranged the music as suites for cello and piano and for violin and piano.

ABOVE: The Moor, the Ballerina and Petrushka – a 1913 illustration by René Bull of the three main characters in Stravinsky's ballet Petrushka.

🎼 Life and works

NATIONALITY: Russian

BORN: Oranienbaum, near St Petersburg, 1882; **DIED:** New York, 1971

SPECIALIST GENRES: Stage works (ballet, opera, oratorios), sacred music.

MAJOR WORKS: *L'oiseau de feu* (1910); *Petrushka* (1911); *Le sacre du printemps* (1912); *L'histoire du soldat* (1918); *Les noces* (1914–23); *Oedipus rex* (1926–7); *Symphony of Psalms* (1930); *Dumbarton Oaks* (1938); Symphony in Three Movements (1942–5); *The Rake's Progress* (1948–51).

ABOVE: Cynthia Harvey and Anthony Dowell as the Firebird and the Prince in the Royal Ballet's production of The Firebird, *Stravinsky's first ballet score for Diaghilev.*

ABOVE: *A scene from Stravinsky's third Diaghilev ballet,* The Rite of Spring.

French period

After the war, Stravinsky decided to make France his home, settling in Paris and Biarritz. The early 1920s saw the composition of several purely instrumental works, including the *Symphonies of Wind Instruments* (1921), dedicated to Debussy's memory, and the Concerto for Piano and Wind (1923–4). He also worked on *Mavra*: a one-act *opera buffa* based on Pushkin, and completed the orchestration of *Les noces*. These two works marked the end of his "Russian" period. At the same time, he began an affair with a married actress, Vera Soudeikine, to whom he dedicated the Octet for wind instruments (1922–3). To his wife Katarina he dedicated the Serenade in A (1925), one of many piano works written in the 1920s which also included the Capriccio for piano and orchestra (1928–9) and the Sonata (1924).

In 1927 Stravinsky celebrated the 20th anniversary of Diaghilev's first Paris season with the opera-oratorio *Oedipus rex*, based on a Latin version of the tragic myth by the poet Jean Cocteau. Neither Diaghilev nor the audience really appreciated this strange hybrid, which is now recognized as a masterpiece. Stravinsky had already begun to cut loose from Diaghilev. His next ballet score, *Apollon musagète* (a title later abbreviated to *Apollo*), was written to a commission from the American patroness Elizabeth Sprague Coolidge, and was the first of Stravinsky's ballets to be choreographed by George Balanchine (1904–83). It was followed by *Le baiser de la fée* (*The Fairy's Kiss*), a Tchaikovskian pastiche, for Ida Rubinstein's rival troupe. Diaghilev had little time to complain: he died in Venice in August 1929. The following year, Stravinsky was commissioned by Serge Koussevitzky (1876–1951) to celebrate the 50th anniversary of the Boston Symphony Orchestra with the *Symphony of Psalms*; and in 1931 he began an association with the violinist Samuel Dushkin, for whom he wrote the Violin Concerto and the Duo Concertante for violin and piano.

In 1934 Stravinsky became a naturalized French citizen. The same year he collaborated with André Gide

ABOVE: *Stravinsky (right), photographed in 1921 with the impressario Sergei Diaghilev, founder of the Ballets Russes.*

ABOVE: *Stravinsky conducting in later life. He moved to the USA in 1939 and remained there for the rest of his life.*

ABOVE: *Stravinsky rehearsing the orchestra of La Scala, Milan, in preparation for the première of his opera* The Rake's Progress.

(1869–1951) on the musical melodrama *Perséphone*, again for Rubinstein, which was coolly received. But by the mid 1930s his main commissions were coming from the other side of the Atlantic. They included the ballet *Jeu de cartes* (*The Card Game*, choreographed by Balanchine in 1937 for the American Ballet), the pseudo-Baroque chamber concerto *Dumbarton Oaks*, and the Symphony in C for the Chicago Symphony Orchestra (1940).

American period

The imminent outbreak of World War II, combined with the deaths of his elder daughter, his wife and his mother, drove Stravinsky to seek sanctuary in the USA. On 9 March 1940 he married Vera Soudeikine, then settled in Hollywood and applied for US citizenship. The early works of his American years include the Symphony in Three Movements, the *Circus Polka* (1942) for dancing elephants in the Barnum and Bailey Circus, *Scènes de ballet* (1944) for a Broadway revue, the *Danses concertantes* (1941–2), and the *Ebony Concerto* for the jazz clarinettist

Woody Herman (1913–87). Stravinsky's last neo-classical work was the opera *The Rake's Progress* (1948–51), inspired by William Hogarth's famous series of etchings, to a libretto by W. H. Auden (1907–73) and Chester Kallman (1921–75). It was premièred in Venice in September 1951.

Last works

After *The Rake's Progress* Stravinsky's style underwent a major change. His meeting in 1948 with the conductor Robert Craft (born 1923), an admirer of Schoenberg, introduced Stravinsky to the music of the Second Viennese School. The first fruit of his own experiments with serial technique was the *Canticum sacrum* (1955), designed for performance in St Mark's, Venice. Two further stage works date from his later years: the ballet *Agon* (1953–4), and the musical play *The Flood*

(1961–2), based on the York and Chester mystery plays and first produced on American television.

Many of Stravinsky's later works, from the 1948 Mass onwards, sprang from religious impulses. They include *Threni* (*Lamentations of the Prophet Jeremiah*) for solo voices, chorus and orchestra (1957–8), the cantata *A Sermon, a Narrative and a Prayer* (1960–1), the "sacred ballad" *Abraham and Isaac* for baritone and chamber orchestra (1962–3), *Introitus* for men's voices and ensemble (1965), and his last major work, the *Requiem Canticles* for soloists, chorus and orchestra (1965–6). One of his last works was the charming setting for voice and piano of Edward Lear's poem "The Owl and the Pussy-Cat" (1966).

In 1969 Stravinsky and his wife moved to New York, where he died two years later. He was buried near Diaghilev in Venice.

ABOVE: The Rake's Progress *is a quasi-Mozartian full-length opera based on an English libretto. This photograh shows a 1952 performance at the Berlin State Opera.*

Sergei Prokofiev

I abhor imitation and I abhor the familiar.

PROKOFIEV

Prokofiev, together with Stravinsky and Shostakovich, belongs to the trio of great Russian composers of the 20th century. Like Stravinsky, he left Russia after the Revolution, settling in America and Paris, but unlike him, Prokofiev then returned in the 1930s, with mixed fortunes. He was a noted composer of stage music, but also – like Shostakovich – made significant contributions to both the symphonic and concerto repertoires.

Prokofiev was the only child of a wealthy and cultured family. He began to compose at five, and studied privately with Reinhold Glière (1875–1956). In September 1904 he entered the St Petersburg Conservatory, where he spent ten years. By the time of his public debut as a composer and pianist on New Year's Eve 1908, he was already an accomplished composer with a reputation for writing astringent, avant-garde music with a tendency to shock.

Prokofiev's life changed dramatically after his father's death in 1910, when he had to start earning a living. His response was to write the first of his five piano concertos, which caused uproar among critics. It was followed by a second (1913), which apparently left its listeners "frozen with fright, hair standing on end". Nevertheless, Prokofiev graduated from the Conservatory in June 1914 with the prestigious Rubinstein Prize.

ABOVE: Sergei Prokofiev, painted in 1934 by Pyotr Konchalovsky (1876–1956).

As a reward, his mother took him to London. There he met Diaghilev, who commissioned a ballet from him. Prokofiev's first attempt was a failure, and his second, *Chout* (*The Buffoon*), remained unperformed until 1921. Meanwhile Prokofiev had returned to a Russia torn by internal political strife and suffering from the deprivations of war. He spent the war years working on his opera *Igrok* (*The Gambler*, 1917, based on Dostoyevsky), the luminous First Violin Concerto (1916–17), and the ebullient, Haydnesque *Classical Symphony*, one of his most popular works. When the political situation deteriorated after Lenin seized power, Prokofiev emigrated to the USA.

America and France

At first, his sensational piano-playing excited the American public, and the Chicago Opera commissioned the opera *The Love for Three Oranges* (which, after initial production problems, eventually became the only one of his ten or so operatic projects to achieve international success in his lifetime). But Prokofiev's performing career had stalled, and in 1922 he left for Paris, where he spent the next 14 years. His works of those years include three ballets, the Third, Fourth and Fifth Piano Concertos (the Fourth, written for Paul Wittgenstein in 1931, for left hand only), the Second Violin Concerto and the First Cello Concerto, and the Second, Third and Fourth Symphonies, as well as piano pieces and songs.

Return to Russia

By 1933 Prokofiev had received many invitations from his homeland, which he revisited several times. His decision to return permanently in 1936 was influenced by the increasing number of Russian commissions he was receiving, including the film music for *Lieutenant Kijé* (1934), and *Romeo and Juliet* for the Bolshoy Ballet (although

ABOVE, FROM LEFT TO RIGHT: *The conductor Ernst Ansermet, Diaghilev, Stravinsky and Prokofiev, c.1921.*

the company initially rejected the score), but he chose an inopportune time to return, just as the Soviet authorities were beginning to interfere in artistic matters.

His first "Russian" works therefore included innocuous pieces, such as the much-loved *Peter and the Wolf* for children; and over the next decade

Prokofiev made a determined attempt to provide "Soviet realist" works which would satisfy Stalinist criteria. But these did not save him from oppression. During World War II his Spanish-born wife Lina was arrested on trumped-up charges of spying and sent to a labour camp under dubious circumstances; by then Prokofiev had formed a liaison with a Communist Party member, Mira Mendelson, with whom he lived until his death. In 1948 Prokofiev was among the composers denounced in the Stalinist press for "formalist perversions".

However, the best works of Prokofiev's "Soviet" period – the film score for Eisenstein's *Alexander Nevsky* (1938), the operas *Obrucheniye v Monastyre* (*The Duenna*, 1940–1, based on Sheridan), and *Voyna i mir* (*War and Peace*, 1941–3, based on Tolstoy), the Second String Quartet (1941), and the Fifth Symphony (1944) – remained true to his own artistic ideals. His last works included another Eisenstein film score, *Ivan the Terrible* (1945–7), the

ABOVE: *Prokofiev at work in the 1930s. He finally returned to Russia in 1936, having been enticed back by promising commissions.*

Sixth and Seventh Symphonies (1945–7), the ballets *Cinderella* (1940–4) and *Kamenniy tsvetok* (*The Tale of the Stone Flower*, 1948–53), and the Symphony-Concerto for cello and orchestra (1950–2), written for Mstislav Rostropovich (born 1927). Prokofiev died of a brain haemorrhage on the same day as Stalin.

🎼 Life and works

NATIONALITY: Russian

BORN: Soutzovka, Ukraine, 1891; **DIED:** Moscow, 1953

SPECIALIST GENRES: Symphonies, concertos, stage works.

MAJOR WORKS: Seven symphonies, including *Classical Symphony* (1917); five piano concertos; two violin concertos; *The Love for Three Oranges* (1919); *Romeo and Juliet* (1935–6); *Peter and the Wolf* (1936); *War and Peace* (1941–3).

ABOVE: *The* pas de deux *from Prokofiev's ballet* Romeo and Juliet *(1935–6), written for the Bolshoy Ballet in Moscow. This performance took place at the Savonlinna Opera Festival in Finland.*

Paul Hindemith

Tell Hindemith that I am extremely pleased with him.

ARNOLD SCHOENBERG (1874–1951), 1924

The German-born composer, conductor, string player and teacher Paul Hindemith spent the early part of his career in Frankfurt, where he was a violinist in the Opera orchestra from 1915 until 1923, and where he studied composition at the Hoch Conservatory until 1917.

In 1921 two one-act operas, *Mörder, Hoffnung der Frauen* (*Murder, Hope of Women*), and *Das Nusch-Nuschi* (based on a play for Burmese marionettes), were performed in Stuttgart, where their scandalous subjects aroused controversy and gained notoriety for Hindemith. At the same time, the Amar Quartet (in which he played viola) was formed by the composer and Licco Amar to première his second String Quartet at the first Donaueschingen Festival, because the ensemble booked to play it had found it too difficult.

Two years later Hindemith was invited to join the festival's committee, and under his guidance it became Germany's leading festival for the promotion of new music. Meanwhile, Hindemith adopted an entirely different style: his series of seven works entitled *Kammermusik* ("chamber music") looked back to Baroque forms and polyphony. During the 1920s he taught at the Berlin Hochschule für Musik, and continued to play viola in the Amar Quartet. In 1929 he appeared at a London Promenade Concert as soloist in William Walton's Viola Concerto.

Although Hindemith was not Jewish, his wife was, and he was attacked by the Nazi party for the unacceptable

ABOVE: The German composer Paul Hindemith (1895–1963).

atonality of his music, and the fact that he openly associated with Jewish musicians. Despite the support of the conductor Wilhelm Furtwängler, who conducted the première of his *Mathis der Maler* Symphony in March 1934, Hindemith found himself on a list of proscribed composers. His opera *Mathis der Maler* (*Mathis the Painter*, based on the life of the 16th-century artist Grünewald), from which he had taken themes for the symphony, was banned by the Nazis and first performed in Switzerland in 1938.

As life in Nazi Germany became impossible, Hindemith joined the general exodus of talent. After some years teaching in Turkey, in 1939 he settled in New York, where he held

several university lectureships and was head of the school of music at Yale. In 1953 he settled in Switzerland. He died of pancreatitis in Frankfurt.

Hindemith was a prolific composer – almost too prolific for his own good. Concerned about the widening gap between the serious composer and the public, he was anxious that his music should be accessible to amateur players as well as professional performers. His works include a great deal of instrumental and educational music written with this in mind, and quantities of chamber music. His best-known works include the ballet *Nobilissima visione* (*Most Exalted Vision*) and the Rilke song-cycle *Das Marienleben* (*Scenes from the Life of Mary*). Many of his works are still neglected.

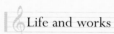

Life and works

NATIONALITY: German

BORN: Hanau, near Frankfurt, 1895; **DIED:** Frankfurt, 1963

SPECIALIST GENRES: Orchestral, chamber and piano music in German neo-classical idiom.

MAJOR WORKS: *Das Marienleben* (*Scenes from the Life of Mary*, 1922–3); operas *Cardillac* (1926) and *Mathis der Maler* (1933–4); *Nobilissima visione* (1938); *Symphonic Metamorphosis on Themes of Carl Maria von Weber* (1943).

William Walton

As a musical joker he is a jewel of the first water.

Ernest Newman (1868–1959), reviewing "Façade"

The son of a Lancashire choirmaster and singing teacher, William Walton became a chorister at Christ Church, Oxford, when he was ten. At the age of 16 he entered Oxford University to read music, leaving two years later without a degree but having acquired a taste for high living. For the next decade he lived as the "adopted brother" of the eccentric Sitwell family in Chelsea and Italy, also spending lengthy periods at the homes of other wealthy admirers – which freed him to compose without the burden of having to earn a living. In 1920s London he associated with the "Fitzrovian" artistic community immortalized in Anthony Powell's series of novels *A Dance to the Music of Time*, which included the composers Lord Berners, Constant

ABOVE: William Walton, photographed towards the end of his life, in 1978. He was knighted in 1951.

Lambert and Peter Warlock. During these bohemian years Walton became keenly interested in jazz, and made his name with the satirical entertainment *Façade*, based on a number of witty poems by Edith Sitwell (1887–1964) and composed when he was only 19. It is still his most popular work.

Larger-scale works followed: the overture *Portsmouth Point* (1925), the Sinfonia Concertante (1926–7), and the Prokofiev-influenced Viola Concerto. In 1931 the oratorio *Belshazzar's Feast* burst upon the English choral scene at the Leeds Festival. Overnight Walton found himself acclaimed as Elgar's successor, a position he consolidated with his First Symphony, the Violin Concerto and the patriotic coronation march *Crown Imperial* (1937).

During the 1940s Walton concentrated on film music, a genre crowned by his three masterly Shakespearean collaborations with Laurence Olivier (*Henry V* in 1944, *Hamlet* in 1947, and *Richard III* in 1955). In 1948 he and his young Argentinian wife Susana Gil abandoned England for the idyllic Mediterranean island of Ischia. The early 1950s were chiefly occupied with his opera *Troilus and Cressida*, but its Covent Garden reception was disappointing. Later works included the Cello Concerto (1956), a Second Symphony (1959–60), and the *Missa brevis* (1966) written for Coventry Cathedral, but few recaptured the sparkle of Walton's earlier years. Knighted in 1951, he died aged 81, a pillar of the musical Establishment.

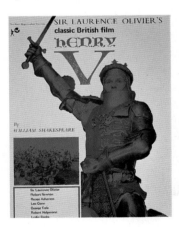

ABOVE: A poster for Laurence Olivier's film version of Shakespeare's Henry V *(1944), for which Walton provided a stirring score.*

Life and works

Nationality: English

Born: Oldham, 1902;
died: Ischia, 1983

Specialist genres:
Orchestral music, film scores, stage music.

Major works:
Façade (1921–2); *Belshazzar's Feast* (1929–31); Symphony No. 1 (1935); Viola Concerto (1929); Violin Concerto (1938–9); *Troilus and Cressida* (1954).

Other Composers of the Era

Tonality is a natural force, like gravity.

PAUL HINDEMITH, "THE CRAFT OF MUSICAL COMPOSITION" (1937)

Spain produced its share of important 20th-century composers. Manuel de Falla (1876–1946) was much influenced by Spanish musical traditions, from Andalucian folk song to 16th-century Spanish polyphony. His one-act opera *La vida breve* (*Life is Short*) won a prize in Madrid in 1905, but was not produced until 1913 (in Nice), by which time Falla had been living in France for six years. In 1915 he wrote the ballet-pantomime *El amor brujo* (*Love the Magician*), but his fame was established in 1919 when Diaghilev produced the ballet *El sombrero de tres picos* (*The Three-cornered Hat*) in London. Falla's other major works include *Noches en los jardines de España* (*Nights in the Gardens of Spain*) for piano and orchestra (1916), the *Fantasia bética* for solo piano (1919), a Harpsichord

ABOVE: *The Spanish composer Manuel de Falla (1876–1946) in 1924 in his studio in Granada, Andalucia.*

ABOVE: *Ottorino Respighi (1879–1936), an Italian composer in the Romantic tradition.*

Concerto (1926) and the chamber opera *El retablo de Maese Pedro* (*Master Peter's Puppet Show*, 1919–22). After the Spanish Civil War he moved to Argentina.

The blind Spanish composer Joaquín Rodrigo (1901–99), who taught music history at Madrid University from 1947 onwards, is chiefly known for two works for guitar and orchestra: the *Concierto de Aranjuez* (1939) and the *Fantasia para un gentilhombre* (1954). His other works, which include concertos for cello, piano, violin, flute, and multiple guitars, are less often performed.

Another popular, middle-of-the-road composer was the Italian Ottorino Respighi (1879–1936), who studied with Rimsky-Korsakov and ended up teaching at the Liceo di Santa Cecilia

in Rome, where he died. His richly scored tone-poems in the Straussian mould have always been popular, especially *Fontane di Roma* (*Fountains of Rome*, 1914–16), *Pini di Roma* (*Pines of Rome*, 1923–4), the *Trittico botticelliano* (*Three Botticelli Pictures*, 1927), *Gli uccelli* (*The Birds*, 1927), and *Feste romane* (*Roman Festivals*, 1928). His ballet *La boutique fantasque* (*The Marvellous Toyshop*, 1919) is based on Rossini transcriptions.

Britain

Walton's English contemporaries included a group of composers based in the Bloomsbury area of London — the "Fitzrovia" of Anthony Powell's novels. Powell's character Morland was based on the composer and conductor Constant Lambert (1905–51), who began his short but brilliant career

ABOVE: *The blind Spanish composer Joaquín Rodrigo (1901–99) playing the piano at his Madrid home, c.1975.*

ABOVE: *The British composer and conductor Constant Lambert (1905–51) in the 1930s.*

with panache when his ballet *Romeo and Juliet* was commissioned by Diaghilev and performed in Monte Carlo in 1926. The next year, Lambert took London by storm with his irresistible, jazz-influenced cantata *The Rio Grande* for piano, chorus and orchestra, based on a poem by Sacheverell Sitwell (1897–1988). From 1941–7 he was music director of Sadler's Wells Ballet, and a one-time lover of the dancer Margot Fonteyn. His second wife

ABOVE: *Aram Khachaturian (1903–78), composer of* Spartacus *(used as theme music for the TV series "The Onedin Line").*

Isabel was a renowned artist and sculptress. Lambert's heavy drinking contributed to his early death. (His son Kit, who also died young, was the manager of the rock group The Who.)

One of Lambert's closest friends was the eccentric composer Philip Heseltine (1894–1930). Heseltine used his own name as an editor of early music, and the pseudonym "Peter Warlock" for performances and publication of his own compositions, which included many folk-song-influenced vocal settings, and the Renaissance-style *Capriol Suite* for string orchestra (1926). Warlock is presumed to have committed suicide.

Another eccentric English composer of the period was Gerald, Lord Berners (1883–1950), an aristocratic painter, author, diplomat and composer with a Satie-esque sense of humour. His best-known work is the ballet *The Triumph of Neptune* (1926), another Diaghilev commission.

Central Europe
The majority of German and Austrian Jewish composers managed to flee Nazism, but a notable group of Czech composers failed to survive the war. Among them was Ervín Schulhoff (1894–1942), who was interned at the Theresienstadt detention camp and then deported to Wülzbourg concentration camp, where he died. His works, which include eight symphonies, two string quartets, a sextet and four piano sonatas, show the influence of jazz and of other new developments.

While composers such as Prokofiev and Shostakovich managed to survive the Stalinist regime but still retain a strong individual voice, others bowed to the political pressure to produce music that the authorities would consider accessible to the masses. The Armenian composer Aram Khachaturian (1903–78) attracted Prokofiev's attention with his Trio for

ABOVE: *Peter Warlock, the pen-name of Philip Heseltine (1894–1930).*

piano, clarinet and violin, and achieved wide success with his First Symphony, his Piano Concerto and the 1942 ballet *Gayané* (which includes the popular "Sabre Dance"). His Second Violin Concerto, however, incurred official displeasure, and he abandoned serious composition in favour of neutral film scores. After Stalin's death he resumed his former career with the ballet *Spartacus*, premièred by the Kirov in 1956.

ABOVE: *The Czech composer Ervín Schulhoff (1894–1942), one of the most prominent musical victims of the Nazis.*

Music

✦ since ✦

World War II

Modern Music

The serial idea is based on a universe that finds itself in perpetual expansion.
PIERRE BOULEZ (BORN 1925)

From the late 20th century, music has become more fragmentary than at any previous historical period. There are no longer "schools" of composition: each composer now strives to find an original and entirely individual voice. If they draw inspiration from other music, it is from the works of individual predecessors rather than from general trends.

Both Shostakovich and Benjamin Britten came into their own after 1945, the year that Britten revitalized British opera with *Peter Grimes*. While Britten's principal importance lies in vocal music, especially his fine sequence of operas, Shostakovich was primarily an instrumental composer. Both were inspired by the playing of the Russian cellist Mstislav Rostropovich, for whom Shostakovich wrote his cello concertos and Britten his Cello Symphony and three solo suites. Both composers worked in an essentially tonal medium, unaffected by avant-garde developments.

Britain has maintained a strong operatic tradition since 1945, in the works of Britten, Michael Tippett, Harrison Birtwistle, Peter Maxwell Davies, and now a younger generation of composers, including Mark-Anthony Turnage and Thomas Adès. In America, Leonard Bernstein revitalized the American musical, especially with his brilliant *West Side Story* (1957), but has proved perhaps more influential as a conductor than as a composer. Meanwhile, Copland (though active up until his death) ceded the mantle of senior American composer to Elliott

ABOVE: VE Day, 8 May 1945. Crowds in Whitehall, London, cheering Prime Minister Winston Churchill and members of the Cabinet after the announcement of Germany's surrender.

ABOVE: The first landing on the Moon — the Apollo 11 mission, 1969.

Carter, whose orchestral and chamber music is characterized by the most rigorous intellectual discipline and formal perfection.

Minimalism
The experiments of John Cage proved a blind alley in themselves (the notorious *4' 33"* took music to its furthest extreme – complete silence), but Cage's ideas have taken root, most obviously in the American minimalist school of Steve Reich, Terry Riley, Philip Glass and John Adams, whose music relies on repetitive rhythmic and melodic *ostinati* for its hypnotic effect. The fact that such music has connections with the harmonic and rhythmic clichés of pop and rock music, as well as with Indian and African music (popular in the West since the 1960s), has contributed to its popularity. The British composer Michael Nyman (born 1944) uses similar techniques in his film scores.

Electronic music
Cage's use of aleatory, or chance, techniques (derived from the Chinese *I-Ching*, or *The Book of Changes*) has been independently adopted and developed to a limited extent by the Polish composer Witold Lutoslawski, and in a more intensely focused way by the Greek composer Iannis Xenakis, many of whose works use electronic tape. The use of electronic instruments, amplification and sampling has become widespread in "serious" music over the last 50 years. Composers who have

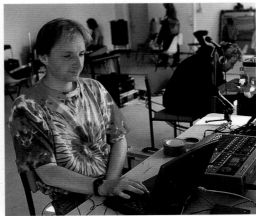

ABOVE: *The American composer Philip Glass (born 1937) rehearsing with musicians in Los Angeles, March 1977.*

ABOVE: *Students using computers on the Electro-Acoustic Composition Course at Dartington, 1999.*

made use of such techniques include the early Franco-American experimenter Edgard Varèse, the Italians Luciano Berio and Bruno Maderna, the British composer Jonathan Harvey, and the German Karlheinz Stockhausen, one of the leaders of the European avant-garde in the 1960s and '70s.

French music in the later 20th century was dominated by two composers. The idiosyncratic style of Olivier Messiaen was influenced by Eastern music, birdsong, the serial technique of Webern – which he refined still further – and his profound Catholic faith. His pupil Pierre Boulez, who founded the major European research centre into modern composing techniques, is a central figure in 20th–21st-century European music. Equally well-known as a conductor, he has helped to co-ordinate the work of composers from many different countries, as well as producing an important and highly original body of work rooted in the French tradition, but cross-fertilized by European avant-garde techniques.

Female composers

One encouraging feature of music in recent years has been the emergence of women composers, and the rediscovery, after centuries of neglect, of the music of talented women of the past, such as Fanny Mendelssohn (1805–47) and Amy Beach (1867–1944). Composers such as Judith Weir (born 1954), Sofia Gubaidulina (born 1931), Elena Firsova (born 1950) and Roxanna Panufnik (born 1968) are now beginning to challenge the traditional male hegemony in composition, as in many other fields, and are proving particularly adept in the developing fields of television and film music.

ABOVE: *Kurt Masur conducting the New York Philharmonic in the Avery Fisher Hall, New York, 1998.*

Dmitri Shostakovich

*The music [Symphony No. 11] to me was self-evidently about
Shostakovich's own experiences in the catastrophe of his life.*

MICHAEL TIPPETT (1905–98)

Together with Stravinsky and Prokofiev, Shostakovich was one of the greatest Russian composers of the 20th century. His 15 symphonies and 15 string quartets are among the finest 20th-century works in those media.

Shostakovich began to learn the piano with his mother, a professional pianist. In 1919, aged only 13, he entered the St Petersburg Conservatory to study piano and composition: his teachers there included Glazunov. A phenomenally gifted student, his First Symphony (written as a diploma exercise) won international acclaim after its premières in Leningrad (1926), Berlin (under Bruno Walter), and Philadelphia (under Leopold Stokowski); a year later Shostakovich received an honourable mention as an entrant in the International Chopin Piano Competition.

During the 1920s Shostakovich – a firm adherent to Socialist ideals – concentrated on stage and film music. An opera, *Nos* (*The Nose*), and two

ABOVE: *Dmitri Shostakovich (1906–75), photographed at the Moscow Conservatory in the early 1960s.*

ballets, *Zolotoy vek* (*The Golden Age*, 1927–30) and *Bolt* (1930–1), showed him developing a brittle, witty and satirical style which owed much to current European avant-garde

influences, and for several years he was regarded as the "great white hope" of Soviet music.

Denunciation

Then came catastrophe. His opera *Lady Macbeth of the Mtsensk District*, a savage tale of adultery, murder and retribution, was produced in Moscow in 1934. At first it won critical acceptance both within Russia and abroad. But Stalin went to see it and was shocked by its graphic portrayal of sex and violence, and by its "advanced" musical idiom. On his orders, Shostakovich was savagely attacked in the press in 1936, in an article entitled "Chaos instead of Music".

Denounced also by his fellow composers, Shostakovich hurriedly withdrew the score of his Fourth Symphony, then in rehearsal, and responded with the more "accessible" Fifth Symphony (1937), which he described as "A Soviet artist's response to just criticism". For a while he

LEFT:
Shostakovich composing at his Moscow flat.

RIGHT:
A view of the Admiralty in St Petersburg, where Shostakovich was born and where he studied.

appeared to have been forgiven: the Fifth Symphony proved popular, his 1940 Piano Quintet received the Stalin Prize, and his Seventh Symphony, written during the German siege of Leningrad in 1941, became an international symbol of heroic resistance (even though its repetitive "invasion" theme was cruelly parodied by Bartók in his Concerto for Orchestra, written in America in 1943).

Shostakovich's next two symphonies were also inspired by the war: the Eighth (1943) by its savagery, and the Ninth (1945) in a spirit of rejoicing at its end. But in 1948 he was once again officially denounced (together with Prokofiev and others), accused of "formalist perversions" and "anti-democratic tendencies in music". Such denunciations, during the Stalinist purges of the late 1940s, were tantamount to a death sentence, and if Shostakovich's posthumously published *Memoirs* are to be believed, from then until Stalin's death in 1953 he lived in fear for his life. He kept his private artistic credo alive with intimate chamber works, while publicly he concentrated on "safe" works based on nationalistic themes.

ABOVE, FROM LEFT TO RIGHT: *The great Russian cellist Mstislav Rostropovich (for whom Shostakovich wrote his cello concertos), Shostakovich, Rostropovich's wife – the soprano Galina Vishnevskaya – and the violinist David Oistrakh.*

The post-Stalin era

After Stalin's death, Shostakovich returned to symphonic writing with the Tenth, Eleventh (*The Year 1905*) and Twelfth (*The Year 1917*) Symphonies. The late 1950s also produced the satirical musical comedy *Cheryomuschki* (*The Cherry Trees Estate*, 1958), a suite, *The Gadfly*, from his film score of 1955, the Second Piano Concerto (written in 1957 for his son Maxim, who became a well-known conductor), the First Cello Concerto (written in 1959 for Rostropovich), and the Seventh and Eighth String Quartets (1960).

In 1962 *Lady Macbeth* was restored to the Russian repertoire (under the new title *Katerina Ismailova*) and hailed as a masterpiece. Shostakovich then produced another controversial work, the Thirteenth Symphony (*Babi Yar*), based on poems by the Jewish writer Yevgeny Yevtushenko (born 1933). Its two successors, particularly the anguished Fourteenth Symphony of 1969 (settings of 11 poems by European writers), are preoccupied with death: the Fifteenth Symphony (1971), with its ironic references to other composers, seems to sum up

Shostakovich's own career. The last decade of his life produced seven more string quartets, sonatas for violin and viola, and a further concerto each for violin and cello.

Towards the end of his life, Shostakovich was allowed to visit the West. He became a friend of Benjamin Britten, to whom the Fourteenth Symphony is dedicated. Like Britten, he died of heart failure in his 60s.

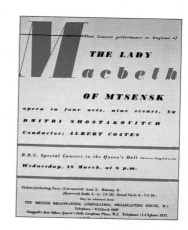

ABOVE: *A programme for the first London concert performance of Shostakovich's opera* Lady Macbeth of Mtsensk, *in 1935.*

Benjamin Britten

If wind and water could write music, it would sound like Ben's.

YEHUDI MENUHIN (1916–99)

Together with Michael Tippett, Britten dominated the British musical scene from the 1930s onwards. His roots lay in the music of Mozart and Verdi, and he never abandoned tonality, but he developed a distinctive style with wide appeal. Much of his music was inspired by specific performers, particularly the tenor voice of his lifelong companion, Peter Pears (1910–86).

Britten was born on St Cecilia's Day, 22 November 1913. He went to boarding school, but studied composition privately with Frank Bridge (1879–1941) in school holidays. In 1930 he entered the Royal College of Music in London, where he studied composition with John Ireland and honed his already formidable skills as a pianist. He wanted to continue his studies in Vienna with Alban Berg,

ABOVE: Benjamin Britten, one of the major British composers of the 20th century.

having heard Berg's opera *Wozzeck* in 1934, but was discouraged by his parents and teachers.

Early works

In 1935, by which time several early works including a Sinfonietta and an Oboe Quartet had already been performed, Britten began to work for the documentary film unit of the General Post Office, where he met the poet W. H. Auden. They shared left-wing political sympathies and collaborated on several works, including the orchestral song-cycle *Our Hunting Fathers* (1936) and the choral work *Ballad of Heroes* (1939). In that year Britten and Peter Pears followed Auden to the USA. By this time Britten's natural predilection for vocal music had already been confirmed with the Rimbaud song-cycle *Les illuminations* (1939), but the

Seven Sonnets of Michelangelo of 1940 was the first of many works which Britten wrote expressly for Pears. Instrumental works of the late 1930s and early '40s included the charming Rossini pastiche *Soirées musicales* (1936), the brilliant *Variations on a Theme of Frank Bridge* for strings (1937), concertos for piano (1938) and violin (1940), and the *Sinfonia da requiem* (1940). From then onwards, Britten wrote few specifically orchestral works. Exceptions were the *Young Person's Guide to the Orchestra* (1946) and the exquisite Serenade for tenor, horn and strings (1943, written

ABOVE: Britten (left) with his lifelong companion Peter Pears in the garden of their house at Aldeburgh, Suffolk. This was one of the last photographs of Britten.

Life and works

NATIONALITY: English

BORN: Lowestoft, 1913;
DIED: Aldeburgh, 1976

SPECIALIST GENRES: Opera and other stage works, vocal music.

MAJOR WORKS: Operas *Peter Grimes* (1944–5), *Billy Budd* (1951), *The Turn of the Screw* (1954), *A Midsummer Night's Dream* (1960) and *Death in Venice* (1973); *War Requiem* (1962); three "church parables"; chamber music and songs, including song-cycles and folk song arrangements.

for Pears and the horn player Dennis Brain), two of his most popular works; the Cello Symphony for Rostropovich (1963); and two "occasional" works written to celebrate the respective openings of the Snape Maltings concert hall and the Queen Elizabeth Hall in London.

Aldeburgh Festival

Britten decided to return home from America in 1942, having by chance read George Crabbe's 19th-century poem *The Borough*, an unflattering portrait of the Suffolk fishing village of Aldeburgh, which inspired his first major opera, *Peter Grimes*. Its première at Sadler's Wells on 7 June 1945 marked a milestone in British music, and in the history of opera. Britten and Pears settled first at Snape, a few miles inland, and then in Aldeburgh itself, where in 1947 they established the annual Aldeburgh Festival. Twenty years later, the festival's main venue moved from Aldeburgh's tiny Jubilee Hall to a converted malthouse at Snape.

Opera and choral works

Three original chamber operas followed *Peter Grimes*: *The Rape of Lucretia* (1946), the comedy *Albert Herring* (1947), both performed at Glyndebourne, and *The Little Sweep* (1949). In 1951, *Billy Budd* (based on Herman Melville's nautical tragedy) was performed at Covent Garden, followed two years later by Britten's one failure, *Gloriana* (intended to celebrate Elizabeth II's accession in 1953): later productions have led to its reassessment. *The Turn of the Screw*, based on Henry James's ghost story, was premièred in Venice, the city which inspired Britten's operatic swansong (and the most direct expression of his love for Pears), *Death in Venice*, based on Thomas Mann's novella. Many people

ABOVE: The Maltings at Snape, converted by Britten's efforts from an abandoned malthouse to a fine concert hall, the major venue for the Aldeburgh Festival.

consider his operatic masterpiece to be the Shakespearean *A Midsummer Night's Dream*.

During the 1960s Britten temporarily eschewed conventional operas in favour of three "church parables" written for performance in Orford Church in Suffolk: *Curlew River* (1964, inspired by Japanese Noh drama), *The Burning Fiery Furnace* (1966) and *The Prodigal Son* (1968). His next opera, *Owen Wingrave*, was written for television in 1970, though it subsequently transferred successfully to the stage. In 1962

his *War Requiem* was performed at the newly opened Coventry Cathedral, with an international cast of soloists, in a spirit of post-war reconciliation. The Requiem text is interwoven with the poetry of Wilfred Owen (1893–1918), and the work is a powerful expression of Britten's pacifism.

Besides composing, Britten was a fine conductor and pianist, and often toured in recital with Pears. In 1973 he had heart surgery, which curtailed his activities, and shortly before his death in 1976 he became the first British composer to be made a life peer.

ABOVE: A scene from the 1995 Covent Garden production of Peter Grimes, *with Bryn Terfel as Captain Balstrode, and Ben Heppner as the fisherman Grimes.*

Michael Tippett

I like to think of composing as a physical business. I compose at the piano and like to feel involved in my work with my hands.

TIPPETT

ABOVE: *For the last two decades of Michael Tippett's life he was the undisputed "Grand Old Man" of British music.*

Like his younger contemporary Benjamin Britten, the English composer Michael Tippett grew up in Suffolk, and studied at the Royal College of Music in London. He left in 1928 and became a schoolteacher and part-time composer. His first mature works were the First String Quartet (1935), the First Piano Sonata (1936–7), and the Concerto for Double String Orchestra (1938–9), which belongs to the early 20th-century British tradition of works for string ensemble.

During the 1930s Tippett became involved in radical politics, organizing the "South London Orchestra of Unemployed Musicians". His passionate antipathy towards the horrors of war, initially aroused by the plight of European Jews, found expression in his deeply moving oratorio based on the true story of a Jewish boy who killed a Nazi diplomat, *A Child of Our Time* (1939–41), which articulates Tippett's lifelong belief in the opposing "dark" and "light" sides of human nature, present in everyone. The oratorio is influenced by Bach's Passions, with negro spirituals replacing Protestant chorales. Tippett was briefly imprisoned for his pacifist beliefs in 1943.

From 1940–51 Tippett was director of music at Morley College in South London. He subsequently became a full-time composer. His first opera, *The Midsummer Marriage*, was produced in 1952, and like each of its successors – *King Priam* (1961), *The Knot Garden* (1970), *The Ice Break* (1976), *New Year* (1989) – it spawned instrumental and vocal works, including an important series of five string quartets, four symphonies, four piano sonatas and the *Songs for Dov* (1969–70) for tenor and chamber orchestra.

In 1995, the year of his 90th birthday, a Tippett Festival at the Barbican in London included the première of his last major work, *The Rose Lake*, a "song without words for orchestra". His last work was "Caliban's Song", part of a *Tempest Suite* commissioned by the BBC to mark the tercentenary of Purcell's death. Renaissance and Baroque music had been a major influence on Tippett's earlier works, including the *Fantasia Concertante on a Theme of Corelli* for strings (1953).

ABOVE: *Tippett composing at the piano in 1992. His sight failed in the last years of his life.*

Life and works

NATIONALITY: English

BORN: London, 1905;
DIED: London, 1998

SPECIALIST GENRES: Opera, symphonies, string quartets.

MAJOR WORKS: Concerto for Double String Orchestra (1938–9); *A Child of Our Time* (1939–41); five operas, including *The Midsummer Marriage* (1952); Piano Concerto (1953–5); *The Vision of St Augustine* (1965); *The Mask of Time* (1980–2); four symphonies; five string quartets.

John Cage

It is better to make a piece of music than to perform one.
CAGE, "SILENCE" (1961)

The American composer John Cage was one of the most interesting experimental artists of his time. He studied with Henry Cowell (1897–1965, himself a noted pioneer of innovative techniques) and with Schoenberg, who called him "an inventor – of genius". From 1937 onwards he developed a strong interest in dance and percussion techniques, and in 1942 he moved from the West Coast to New York, where he began a long association with Merce Cunningham's dance company.

In 1938 he invented the "prepared piano" by inserting small domestic objects such as paperclips and rubber bands between the strings. This instrument, capable of producing extraordinary timbres, was used in Cage's early pieces such as *Sonatas and*

ABOVE: Experimental composer John Cage, more a "musical philosopher" than a composer.

Interludes (1946–8), and *Music for Marcel Duchamp* (1947). *The Wonderful Widow of Eighteen Springs* (1942) is a setting of a poem by James Joyce for voice and closed piano. A devotee of Zen Buddhism (before it became fashionable) and the *I-Ching*, Cage introduced aleatory (chance) techniques into his music, for instance in *Music of Changes* for piano (1951), in which the performance depends on the toss of a coin, and *Cheap Imitation* (1969), an alteration of Satie's *Socrate*, worked out using the *I-Ching*. With these works, he changed the nature of music by removing the necessity of intention from composition.

In 1952, with *Imaginary Landscape V*, Cage began to use electronic tape in his works. In the same year he "wrote" his notorious *4' 33"*, in which the performer sits at a silent piano and is required only to indicate the division

of the work into three movements: the attention of the audience is directed to life (including the chance sounds of the environment) rather than art. Also from 1952 dates *Theater Piece* for Merce Cunningham, the first "musical happening", combining theatre, art and music. From then on Cage used a wide range of electronic media in his works, which are often scored for bizarre combinations. For example, *Imaginary Landscape IV* (1951) is for 12 radios and 24 players, *Speech* (1955) for five radios and newsreader, *HPSCHD* (1967–9) for seven harpsichord soloists and 51 tape machines, and *Postcard from Heaven* (1983) for between one and 20 harpsichords.

Cage was a musical philosopher. He believed that art was whatever the artist said it was: "I have nothing to say, I am saying it, and that is poetry." An avowed anarchist, he followed a strict macrobiotic diet, was a brilliant chess player and an expert on mushrooms.

ABOVE: One of the "instruments" used in the performance by Ensemble Bash of The Art of Concealment *for percussion ensemble.*

Life and works

NATIONALITY: American

BORN: Los Angeles, 1912;
DIED: New York, 1992

SPECIALIST GENRES:
Experimental works for bizarre combinations.

MAJOR WORKS: Numerous works for percussion ensemble, prepared piano and various combinations of instruments and electronic media.

Leonard Bernstein

Any composer's writing is the sum of himself, of all his roots and influences.
BERNSTEIN, "THE JOY OF MUSIC" (1960)

Bernstein was one of the most flamboyant figures of 20th-century music. A talented pianist, composer of both "serious" works and extremely popular Broadway musicals and one of the finest conductors of his age, he excelled in every field he tackled (one of his fellow students remarked that he was "doomed to success").

He studied composition at Harvard University with Walter Piston (1894–1976), and conducting with Fritz Reiner (1888–1963) at the Curtis Institute in Philadelphia; in the early 1940s he attended summer schools at Tanglewood, Massachusetts, where he became Serge Koussevitzsky's assistant. He was then invited to become assistant conductor of the New York Philharmonic Orchestra, and his big break came in November 1943, when he took over a concert at short notice from the indisposed Bruno Walter. This triumphant performance launched his career, helped by his striking good looks and charismatic personality.

From 1946 onwards Bernstein began to conduct opera, beginning with the US première of Britten's *Peter Grimes* at Tanglewood. In 1953 he became the first American to conduct at La Scala in Milan. He made his debut at the Metropolitan Opera House in 1964, and from 1958–69 he was principal conductor of the New York Philharmonic. He also guest-conducted many of the world's great orchestras.

Bernstein's parallel career as a composer began in 1944 with his ballet *Fancy Free* and his musical *On the Town*, which ran for 463 performances on Broadway. An adaptation of Voltaire's *Candide* (1954–6) had a disappointing reception and was later revised, but *West Side Story* (1957) made Bernstein's name. Written in collaboration with Stephen Sondheim (born 1930) and the choreographer Jerome Robbins (born 1918), this brilliant adaptation of the *Romeo and Juliet* story to a modern New York slum setting captured the spirit of the age.

The bisexual Bernstein was married to the Chilean actress Felicia Montealegre Cohn in 1951, and had three children.

ABOVE: *Leonard Bernstein, photographed in the late 1960s.*

LEFT: *The ensemble song "America" from* West Side Story, *as performed at the Prince Edward Theatre in London in 1998.*

 Life and works

NATIONALITY: American

BORN: Lawrence, Massachusetts, 1918; **DIED:** New York, 1990

SPECIALIST GENRES: Populist stage works (ballets and musicals).

MAJOR WORKS: *On the Town* (1944); *Prelude, Fugue and Riffs* for clarinet and jazz ensemble (1949); *Candide* (1956); *West Side Story* (1957); *Chichester Psalms* (1965); *1600 Pennsylvania Avenue* (1976); three symphonies.

Elliott Carter

I am a radical, having a nature that leads me to perpetual revolt.

CARTER, C.1939

After Copland's death in 1990, Elliott Carter assumed the mantle of "Grand Old Man of American Music". But although he too studied with Nadia Boulanger in Paris in the early 1930s, his musical approach (apart from early works such as the First Symphony and the *Holiday Overture*) is very different from Copland's.

On returning to the USA after his Paris studies Carter became a musical director of Ballet Caravan (1936–40), and then began a long and distinguished teaching career in many major American universities and institutions. He has also spent long periods abroad, including fellowships of the American Academy in Rome, where he composed his Variations for Orchestra (1954–5). The Concerto for

Orchestra and the Third String Quartet (1971) were also written in Italy.

Carter's output includes choral music, songs (including "Warble for Lilac Time", 1943, "A Mirror on Which to Dwell", 1975, and "In Sleep, In Thunder", 1981) and incidental music (including the 1937–9 ballet *Pocahontas*). But his most significant works are for orchestra or chamber groups, particularly the five string quartets, which are regarded

as the most important since Bartók's. He is fascinated by the rhythmic and harmonic possibilities inherent in combining ensembles, as in the Symphony of Three Orchestras, the *Penthode* for five instrumental quartets (1984–5), and the Triple Duo (1982–3). The impact of experimental, radical influences on his underlying classical training has resulted in music of apparent complexity, underpinned by an inexorable musical logic of profound simplicity. The fusion of slow-moving formal structures with ebullient momentum gives Carter's work great dramatic power. His later works include an Oboe Concerto (1986–7) and Violin Concerto (1990), *Three Occasions* for orchestra (the third celebrated his own 50th wedding anniversary in 1989); and works for solo instruments, including *Changes* for guitar (1983), *Trilogy* (1992) for oboe and harp, and *Gra* (1993) for clarinet. A quintet for piano and wind, one of his finest later works, dates from 1992.

Life and works

NATIONALITY: American

BORN: New York, 1908

SPECIALIST GENRES: Complex polyrhythmic works.

MAJOR WORKS: Ballets *Pocahontas* (1937–9) and *The Minotaur* (1947); Piano Sonata (1946); Double Concerto for harpsichord and piano (1961); Concerto for Orchestra (1969); Symphony of Three Orchestras (1976–7); five string quartets.

ABOVE:
The American composer Elliott Carter (born 1908).

RIGHT: Carter rehearsing his Triple Duo at the Royal Academy of Music in London.

Witold Lutoslawski

Dissonances are only the more remote consonances.

ARNOLD SCHOENBERG (1874–1951)

Lutoslawski was the major Polish composer of the 20th century. He began to compose at the age of nine, and also studied piano and violin. In 1932 he entered the Warsaw Conservatory, and two years later his Piano Sonata was broadcast on Polish Radio. His Symphonic Variations were performed at the 1939 Krakow Festival.

The war disrupted Lutoslawski's promising career. He was taken prisoner, but escaped and eked out a precarious living playing the piano in Warsaw cafés. Many of his manuscripts disappeared during the wartime devastation: one exception was the *Variations on a Theme of Paganini* for two pianos, which Lutoslawski adapted in 1978 for piano and orchestra. In post-war communist Poland he wrote music for radio, film and television, and folk-based music for children. His First Symphony (1949) was denounced as formalist, and banned for a decade, but his Little Suite for orchestra (1950) and the Concerto for Orchestra (1950–4) – a worthy successor to Bartók's – found acceptance.

In the post-Stalinist thaw, Lutoslawski began to enlarge his harmonic language, exploring different ways of using the notes of the scale. *Funeral Music* (1958), dedicated to Bartók, established his international reputation, and his works of the 1960s, such as *Jeux vénitiens* (*Venetian Games*, 1961), *Trois poèmes d'Henri Michaux* (1963) and the 1964 String Quartet began to experiment with chance elements. His most

important works of the late 1970s include *Paroles tissées* (*Woven Words*, 1965, written for Peter Pears), the Second Symphony (1967), *Livre pour orchestre* (1968), the Cello Concerto (1970, for Rostropovich), Preludes and Fugue for 13 solo strings, *Les espaces du sommeil* (*Sleep's Spaces*, 1975) for baritone and orchestra, and *Mi-parti* (1976).

Many works were commissioned by major artists and ensembles, including the Third Symphony by the Chicago Symphony Orchestra, *Chain I* by the London Sinfonietta, *Chain II* by the violinist Anne-Sophie Mutter (born 1963), and *Chain III* for the San Francisco Symphony Orchestra.

Lutoslawski's last major works included a Piano Concerto (1988), *Interludium* for chamber orchestra (1989) and *Chantefables et chantefleurs* (1990) for soprano and orchestra.

ABOVE: Witold Lutoslawski, the most important Polish composer of his generation.

LEFT: Lutoslawski rehearsing at the Royal Academy of Music in London in 1980.

Life and works

NATIONALITY: Polish

BORN: Warsaw, 1913;
DIED: Warsaw, 1994

SPECIALIST GENRES: Orchestral works.

MAJOR WORKS: Concerto for Orchestra (1954); *Funeral Music* (1958); Cello Concerto (1970); four symphonies; Piano Concerto (1988).

György Ligeti

*It is precisely a dread of deep significance and ideology that makes
any kind of engaged art out of the question for me.*

LIGETI

One of Hungary's most important composers, Ligeti was born in Transylvania of Hungarian Jewish parents, and studied privately during the war in Budapest. After the war he went to the Budapest Academy of Music, where from 1950–6 he was a professor. He left Hungary in 1956, the year of the Soviet invasion, and took up residence in Vienna. He was invited to work at the West German Radio electronic studios in Cologne, and caused a sensation at the 1960 International Society for Contemporary Music Festival with *Apparitions* (1958–9). From 1959 onwards he taught annually on the summer courses for new music at Darmstadt. Ten years later he moved to West Berlin, and from 1973–89 he was professor of composition at the Hamburg Musikhochschule.

ABOVE: The Hungarian composer György Ligeti (1923–2006), photographed in 1993.

his permission – in the score of Stanley Kubrick's 1968 film *2001: A Space Odyssey*. Since the 1960s, Ligeti's most significant works have been *Clocks and Clouds* for 12-voice women's chorus and orchestra, *Melodien* (1971) and *San Francisco Polyphony* (1973–4), both for orchestra, a Double Concerto for flute and oboe (1972), a Piano Concerto (1985–8), a Violin Concerto (1992), a Horn Trio, subtitled "Homage to Brahms" (1982), a set of piano Etudes (1985), and the opera *Le grand macabre*. His individual style, which the composer described as "micropolyphony", is derived from Webern.

Ligeti's early works were influenced by folk song and the music of Bartók. After a few experiments with electronic media in the late 1950s, he began to find an individual style in works such as *Apparitions* and *Atmosphères* for orchestra (1961), *Volumina* for organ (1961–2), and with the two works for solo voices and instruments called *Aventures* and *Nouvelles aventures* (1962–5). His works of the 1960s included a Requiem (1963–5), a Cello Concerto (1966), *Lux aeterna* for 16 solo voices (1966), the orchestral work *Lontano* (1967) and a chamber concerto for 13 instruments (1969–70). Some of his music was used – without

Life and works

NATIONALITY: Hungarian

BORN: Kolozsvár (now Cluj in Romania), 1923

DIED: Vienna, 2006

SPECIALIST GENRES: Orchestral and chamber music.

MAJOR WORKS: *Atmosphères* (1961); *Aventures* (1962); *Le grand macabre* (1976); *Clocks and Clouds* (1972).

ABOVE: "The Horse of the Apocalypse" being prepared in rehearsal for a performance of Ligeti's opera Le grand macabre *at the 1997 Salzburg Festival.*

Olivier Messiaen

One of the most idiosyncratic composers of the 20th century, Messiaen was the son of an English teacher and a poet. He began to compose at the age of seven and, after discovering the music of Debussy, he decided at an early age to become a composer. He studied at the Paris Conservatoire from the age of 11, winning four first prizes in piano, history of music and composition, and during his last years there he wrote his Preludes for piano in the style of Debussy.

After graduating, Messiaen became organist at La Trinité in Paris, where he stayed for over 40 years. He also taught at the Ecole Normale de Musique, the Schola Cantorum, and

ABOVE: *The French composer Olivier Messiaen, photographed in 1937.*

the Paris Conservatoire (where he became professor of composition in 1966). He was a profoundly influential teacher: his pupils included Boulez, Stockhausen, Xenakis and Alexander Goehr (born 1932, who later taught at Cambridge University).

Religious inspiration

Many of Messiaen's compositions celebrate love, both human and divine. The influence of his Catholic faith is omnipresent in his works, many of which take the form of religious "meditations", "homages" or acts of praise. Far from shying away from explicitly religious titles, as other

composers in this predominantly secular age have done, Messiaen made his intention clear, in orchestral pieces such as *Les offrandes oubliées* (*Forgotten offerings*, 1930), *Hymne au Saint Sacrement* (1932), *Et exspecto resurrectionem mortuorum* (*And I Await the Resurrection of the Dead*, 1964) and *Eclairs sur l'au-delà* (*Illuminations of the Beyond*, 1988–92). His early *Quatuor pour la fin du temps* (*Quartet for the End of Time*) for clarinet, violin, cello and piano was written and first performed in a Silesian prison camp where Messiaen was interned by the Germans for two years during World War II. Vocal works on religious themes include the early Mass (1933), *Trois petites liturgies de la présence divine* (1944) and *La transfiguration de Notre Seigneur Jésus-Christ* (1965–9).

Messiaen's keyboard works have also been inspired by his faith, including *Vingt regards sur l'enfant Jésus-Christ* (1944) for piano; and a series of fine organ works including *L'ascension* (1934), *La nativité du Seigneur* (1935), *Méditation sur le mystère de la Sainte Trinité* (1969) and the *Livre du Saint Sacrement* (1984). His only opera, completed in 1983, was based on the life of St Francis of Assisi.

Other influences

While profoundly religious, Messiaen was equally alive to the force of human passion. *Poèmes pour Mi* (1936), for soprano and piano or orchestra, was written in celebration of his marriage to the violinist Claire Delbos. *Harawi* —

ABOVE: *Messiaen with the score of his* Turangalîla-Symphonie *at the Oxford Festival in June 1967.*

ABOVE: Messiaen rehearsing with students at the Royal Academy of Music in London, 1987.

songs of love and death with elements taken from Peruvian folk music – for soprano and piano, *Cinq rechants* (*Five Refrains*) for 12 solo voices, and the massive orchestral *Turangalîla-Symphonie* form a trilogy of works with a powerful erotic charge.

Another major influence was that of birdsong. Messiaen was an expert ornithologist and made a systematic, classified study of all French birds, recording and notating their songs. Their characteristic rhythmic and melodic patterns were transmuted into his own music in specific works such as *Réveil des oiseaux* (*Dawn Chorus*, 1953) and *Oiseaux exotiques* (1955–6) for orchestra, *Catalogue d'oiseaux* (1956–8) and *Petites esquisses d'oiseaux* (*Little Bird Sketches*, 1985) for piano, and *Le merle noir*

(*The Blackbird*, 1951) for flute and piano. Elements of birdsong are found in most of his works.

Messiaen's music

Messiaen's musical language is immensely complex. He set out its principles in his book, *Technique*

de mon langage musical (1944), which analyses the derivations of its rhythmic structures from Hindu and ancient Greek rhythms. His orchestral works are characterized by luscious harmonies and a vast range of timbres, some derived from exotic percussion instruments including the ondes Martenot, an electronic instrument played by Messiaen's second wife, the virtuoso pianist Yvonne Loriod. His fascination with colour and timbre is explored in many works, including *Chronochromie* (*Time-colour*) for orchestra (1960), *Couleurs de la cité céleste* (*Colours of the Celestial City*, 1963), and many of his organ works. His last orchestral work (1989) was entitled *Un sourire* (*A Smile*).

ABOVE: Much of Messiaen's music was influenced by birdsong.

Pierre Boulez

Music should be a collective magic and hysteria.

BOULEZ

Messiaen's most talented pupil was Pierre Boulez, who studied with him at the Paris Conservatoire after moving to Paris in 1942 from his native Montbrison in the Loire region. Boulez was originally destined for a career in engineering, but instead applied his exceptional mathematical brain to musical analysis and composition.

Twelve-note technique, which Boulez studied in the late 1940s with Schoenberg's pupil René Leibowitz (1913–72), influenced his own early works, the Sonatina for flute and piano (1946), the First Piano Sonata (1946), and *Le visage nuptial* (*The Nuptial Countenance*, 1946–7) for chamber ensemble, including two *ondes Martenot*. In 1948 his talent was recognized with the Beethovenian Second Piano Sonata and the cantata *Le soleil des eaux* (*The Sun of the Waters*), based on poems by René Char. The

ABOVE: Pierre Boulez (born 1925), photographed in 1999.

same year he began working on the "multiple choice" collection *Livre pour quatuor* for string quartet, to which he attempted to apply a technique of "total serialization". His most successful essay in this genre was *Structures I* (1952) for two pianos, but he quickly realized its limitations, and during the 1950s abandoned it in favour of freer techniques. He came to international attention in 1954 with *Le marteau sans maître* (*The Hammer without a Master*), settings of René Char poems for contralto and ensemble.

During the late 1950s and '60s Boulez taught at Darmstadt (an important centre of new music), Basle and Harvard. He also established a parallel career as a conductor. He was musical director of the BBC Symphony Orchestra (1971–5) and also of the New York

Philharmonic (1971–8), and was a sought-after guest conductor (he conducted Wagner's *Ring* cycle at Bayreuth in 1976, and the first production of Berg's *Lulu* in Paris). From 1977–92 he was the founder-director of the Institut de Recherche et de Coordination Acoustique/Musique (IRCAM) in Paris, which provides computers and digital facilities for composition.

His most important later compositions – many of which are still being revised – include the Third Piano Sonata (1957), *Pli selon pli* (*Fold upon Fold*) for orchestra, *Eclat/Multiples* for ensemble, *Rituel in memoriam Bruno Maderna* (1974–5), two works called *Dérive* for small ensemble, *Domaines*, for clarinet and 22 instruments (1961–8); ...*explosante-fixe*... (1971–89), and *Répons*, for ensemble including computers and live electronics.

ABOVE: Boulez conducting Stravinsky's The Rite of Spring *in 1963. Boulez never uses a baton to conduct.*

Life and works

NATIONALITY: French

BORN: Montbrison, 1925

SPECIALIST GENRES: Music for various instrumental and vocal ensembles, piano works.

MAJOR WORKS: *Structures I* and *II* (1952–61); *Le marteau sans maître* (1954); *Pli selon pli* (1957–90); *Répons* (1981); three piano sonatas.

Karlheinz Stockhausen

In Stockhausen's good period I came to trust his music more than anything else.

PIERRE BOULEZ (BORN 1925)

When electronic music seemed to represent the future in the 1960s and '70s, Stockhausen was at its cutting edge. He studied at the Cologne Musikhochschule after the war, and then went to Cologne University, where his analytical skills impressed everyone. In 1951 he met Messiaen at the Darmstadt summer school, and went to Paris to study with him; at the same time he made his first experiments with *musique concrète* in the electronic music studios of French radio.

In 1953 Stockhausen went back to Cologne, where he worked in

ABOVE: Karlheinz Stockhausen (1928–2007), one of the most influential German composers of the 20th century.

the electronic music studio of West German Radio (he became its director ten years later), and also studied acoustics at Bonn University. By the late 1950s he was himself a sought-after teacher: he taught at Darmstadt, at various American universities, and at the Cologne Musikhochschule, where he was appointed professor of composition in 1971.

Like many later 20th-century composers, Stockhausen's starting point was the music of Webern. In his own works he attempted a process of

total serialization, of pitch, intensity, duration, timbre, and spatial position. He divided his compositions into "groups" or "moments" (as in *Momente*, 1961–4, for soprano, four chamber groups, and 13 instruments), and then experimented with varying the order of "groups" in performance (as in *Zyklus*, 1959, for percussion, and some of his *Klavierstücke* (*Piano Pieces*).

From the 1970s Stockhausen worked on a huge opera cycle called *Licht* (*Light*), one opera for each day of the week, which spawned a series of related instrumental compositions.

ABOVE: Stockhausen in the recording studio. Many of his compositions use electronic media.

Iannis Xenakis

Mathematics is music for the mind; music is mathematics for the soul.

ANONYMOUS

Iannis Xenakis was born in Romania, but his parents moved back to their native Greece when he was ten. He began studying music from the age of 12, but was trained as an engineer. During the war Xenakis fought in the Greek Resistance, losing an eye and narrowly escaping death. In 1947 he went to Paris, where he studied with Arthur Honegger and Darius Milhaud, and then with Messiaen in the early 1950s.

Between 1947 and 1960 he worked with the French avant-garde architect Le Corbusier (1887–1965), designing the much-admired Philips Pavilion for the 1958 Brussels Exhibition, in which Varèse's specially commissioned *Poème électronique* was played. Xenakis subsequently began to make his name as a composer, and thereafter concentrated on music. He has taught at Indiana University in the USA and also in Paris, where he was professor of music at the Sorbonne from 1972–89.

Xenakis's strong interest in mathematics led him to introduce mathematical concepts and theories into his compositions, some of which are scored for traditional instruments,

others for electronic media. He applied the term "stochastic" to music, relating to the theory of probability, which assumes that a chance sequence of events can reach a predetermined conclusion. In his own works (many of which have Greek titles), the elements of chance are not left to the performer (as in works by Cage or Lutoslawski), but are controlled by the composer, normally by using a computer. Some of his earlier pieces, such as *Nomos gamma* (1967–8) place an orchestra among the audience. His later pieces vary in size from *Okho* (1989) for three players, to *Dox-Orkh* and *Troorkh* (both 1991), respectively for violin and trombone with 89 other players.

ABOVE: The works of Iannis Xenakis (1922–2001) are based on mathematical concepts and theories.

LEFT: Xenakis with one of his scores. He lost his sight in one eye while fighting in the Greek Resistance in 1947.

Life and works

NATIONALITY: Greek

BORN: Braïla, Romania, 1922; **DIED:** Paris, 2001

SPECIALIST GENRES: Compositions based on mathematical concepts.

MAJOR WORKS: *Metastasis* (1953–4); *Oresteia* (1965–6); *Terretektorh* (1965–6); *Persephassa* (1969).

Luciano Berio

Abstract it may be, the human voice...

Together with Bruno Maderna (1920–73), with whom he founded the Studio di Fonologia Musicale at Radiotelevisione Italiana in Milan in 1955, Luciano Berio was one of the most important Italian composers of his generation. He studied at the Milan Conservatory, and has been equally active as both teacher and composer. He has taught composition at Tanglewood; Mills College, California; Harvard University; and the Juilliard School, all in the USA; at Dartington in Britain; and at Darmstadt and Cologne in Germany. In the late 1970s he also worked with Boulez at IRCAM in Paris.

Berio's compositions reflect his fascination with the human voice, intensified by his marriage (1950–66)

ABOVE: Luciano Berio (1925–2003), the major Italian composer of his generation.

Life and works

NATIONALITY: Italian

BORN: Oneglia, 1925

DIED: Rome, 2003

SPECIALIST GENRES: Works for both conventional and electronic media.

MAJOR WORKS: *Epifanie* (1959–61); *Circles* (1960); *Sinfonia* (1968–9); *Coro* (1975–6); *Un re in ascolto* (*King in Waiting*, 1979–83); 11 *Sequenze* (1958–75); four *Chemins* (*Paths*, 1965–75).

to the American singer/actress Cathy Berberian (1925–83). He draws inspiration from the juxtaposition of different musical processes, from Baroque vocal styles to modern techniques of serialism, indeterminacy and the use of electronics and computer technology. His idiomatic use of collage technique is demonstrated in his most popular work, *Sinfonia* for eight voices and orchestra, which quotes from a wide range of sources, including works by Mahler, Wagner, Ravel and Richard Strauss. He has also reworked music by Brahms and Schubert, most recently in *Rendering* (1989), attributed to "Schubert/Berio". Several of his pieces written for Cathy Berberian also use

collage technique, in particular *Recital I (for Cathy)*, for mezzo-soprano and 17 instruments (1972).

Among Berio's best-known works are the *Quattro canzoni popolari* for voice and piano (1946–7); *Circles*, based on poems by e. e. cummings, for female voice, harp and percussion; *O King* (a homage to Martin Luther King), for mezzo and five players (1967); the series of solo works called *Sequenze I–XI* (*No. III*, for voice, was written for Berberian); and a related series called *Chemins* (*Paths*) for solo instrument(s) and ensemble or orchestra. He has written several theatre works, some in collaboration with distinguished writers such as Italo Calvino and Umberto Eco.

ABOVE: Berio rehearsing the BBC Symphony Orchestra in their Maida Vale recording studio in London, February 2000.

Hans Werner Henze

My profession...consists of bringing truths nearer to the point where they explode.

HENZE, "MUSIC AND POLITICS" (1982)

Henze was the eldest of six children of a schoolmaster, who discouraged him from taking up music. He began composing at 12, but received no formal musical training until after the war (during which he had been attached to a unit making Nazi propaganda films). In 1946 he began to study harmony and counterpoint with Wolfgang Fortner (born 1907), and serial techniques with René Leibowitz. In 1953, after finishing his first opera, *Boulevard Solitude*, he settled in Italy.

During the 1960s Henze's music became associated with radical, left-wing politics. He shot to international fame in 1966 when his opera *The Bassarids*, with a libretto by W. H. Auden and Chester Kallman, was produced at the

ABOVE: Hans Werner Henze (born 1926), considered the major German opera composer of his generation.

Salzburg Festival, and his 1968 oratorio *Das Floss der "Medusa"* (*The Raft of the "Medusa"*) – one of his best-known works – was written as a requiem for the guerrilla leader Che Guevara.

Henze also began to work with young musicians, and in 1976 founded the Montepulciano Cantiere in Umbria for communal international music-making. Since 1980 he has taught composition at the Cologne Academy and at the Royal Academy of Music in London, and in 1988 he founded the Munich International Festival of New Music Theatre. He combines composing with conducting, and has been a guest conductor of the Berlin Philharmonic Orchestra.

During the 1970s and '80s Henze collaborated with the British playwright Edward Bond on works such as the "action for music" *We Come to the River*, the ballet *Orpheus* (1979) and the opera *The English Cat* (1980–2). His highly coloured, richly orchestrated works include several operas, of which the early works *Der Prinz vom Homburg* (1958), *Elegy for Young Lovers* (1959–61) and *Der junge Lord* (*The Young Lord*, 1964) are perhaps the best known: the latest is *Venus and Adonis* (1993–5) for singers and dancers. A prolific composer for both instruments and voices, he has also written nine symphonies, two violin concertos, two piano concertos and other concertante works, five string quartets, several ballets, and a great deal of vocal music.

Life and works

NATIONALITY: German

BORN: Gütersloh, Westphalia, 1926

SPECIALIST GENRES: Opera and theatre music.

MAJOR WORKS: *Boulevard Solitude* (1951); *König Hirsch* (*King Stag*, 1956); *The Bassarids* (1966); *Das Floss der "Medusa"* (1968); *We Come to the River* (1976).

ABOVE: Hans Werner Henze at work in 1996.

Other Composers of the Era

It is fortunate that to assert itself in music, a new generation does not need to destroy the works of its ancestors.

Ernst Křenek (1900–91), "Horizons Circled" (1974)

Although the demand for contemporary music is relatively limited compared with that of earlier periods, many talented composers have achieved widespread popularity over the last 50 years.

America

In the USA, a group of so-called "minimalists" came to attention in the 1970s and '80s. Among them is Steve Reich (born 1936), who founded his own ensemble in 1966. He was much influenced by African and Asian drumming techniques, and all his works, which range from vocal and orchestral pieces such as *The Desert Music* (1982–4) for 27 amplified voices and orchestra,

ABOVE: *The American composer Steve Reich (born 1936) introduced the "phasing" technique, whereby instruments play the same patterns at slightly different speeds.*

to the famous *Clapping Music* for two performers (1972), and *Different Trains* for string quartet and tape (1988), deal with *ostinato* patterns subtly altered by variations in time. Similar repetitive techniques govern the work of Terry Riley (born 1935), whose most famous piece is *In C* (1964).

Two other minimalists, Philip Glass (born 1937) and John Adams (born 1946) have developed the technique on a larger scale, including opera. Glass worked with Ravi Shankar (born 1920), and his style was influenced by Indian music. Of his many stage works, *Einstein on the Beach* (1974–5), *Akhnaten* (1980–3)

and *The Making of the Representative for Planet 8* (1988) are the best known; while his orchestral works include *Glassworks* (1981) for chamber orchestra, and a Third Symphony (1994). Adams's style is more eclectic, and he has a substantial international following. The subject-matter of both his operas, *Nixon in China* (1984–7) and *The Death of Klinghoffer* (1990–1), had contemporary resonance; while his *Grand Pianola Music* (1981–2) for two sopranos, two pianos and small orchestra, *The Wound Dresser* (1988–9) for baritone and orchestra, and his 1993 Violin Concerto have become widely known.

ABOVE: *Philip Glass (born 1937), another American minimalist, has been influenced by Indian music.*

ABOVE: *John Adams (born 1947) successfully applied minimalist techniques to opera, including* Nixon in China *(1984–7).*

ABOVE: The Hungarian composer György Kurtág (born 1926) is a highly regarded teacher. His pupils have included the young British composer Thomas Adès.

Central Europe and Russia

The (Romanian-born) Hungarian composer György Kurtág (born 1926), reared in the Bartók-Kodály tradition, has achieved international acclaim for his subtly crafted orchestral and chamber music, often making use of voices and cimbalom. Among his best-known works are *Messages of the Late Miss R.V. Troussova* (1976–80) for soprano and chamber ensemble, *…quasi una fantasia…* for piano and instruments (1987–8), *The Sayings* of *Péter Bornemisza* (1963–8) for soprano and piano, *Hommage à R. Sch.* for clarinet, viola and piano (1990), and the four books of *Games* for piano (1973–6).

The Polish composer Henryk Górecki (born 1933) draws his inspiration from a wide variety of sources: medieval Polish music, Renaissance polyphony, Webernian serialism, and Romantic orchestration. His serenely meditative Third Symphony (*Symphony of Sorrowful Songs*, 1976) was one of the few "classical" pieces to reach the charts.

A similar serenity pervades the sacred choral music of the Estonian composer Arvo Pärt (born 1935), who settled in West Berlin in 1980. His techniques embrace serialism and minimalism, but within an accessible idiom. His works include a St John Passion (1982), and the popular *Cantus in Memory of Benjamin Britten* for strings and bell (1977).

In the former USSR, Alfred Schnittke (born 1934) is held in high regard. His early works were influenced by serialism, and by the avant-garde techniques of Stockhausen and Ligeti, but he has produced a substantial body of work in traditional genres, including symphonies, *concerti grossi*, sonatas, trios and quartets. Together with Schnittke, Sofia Gubaidulina (born 1931) is the most important Russian composer of the present day. Born in Tatar, her work has been influenced by the exotic timbres of Caucasian folk music, and by a sensitive response to words.

Britain

The doyens of British music at the turn of the 21st century are Harrison Birtwistle and Peter Maxwell Davies (both born 1934), original members of the "Manchester School". Both have won wide acclaim, especially for their operas. Birtwistle has assumed the mantle of Britten and Tippett with an original series of theatre works, many inspired by myth. They include *Punch and Judy* (1966–7), *The Mask of Orpheus* (1973–84), *Gawain* (1987–94), *The Second Mrs Kong* (1993–4) and *The Last Supper* (2000), augmented by fine orchestral works including *The Triumph of Time* (1972), *Earth Dances* (1985–6) and *Endless Parade* for solo trumpet and strings (1986–7), written for the Swedish virtuoso Håkan Hardenberger (born 1961).

ABOVE: The recording of Polish composer Henryk Górecki's Third Symphony (1977) was a surprise "hit".

ABOVE: The Russian composer Sofia Gubaidulina (born 1931). Her work is influenced by Caucasian folk music.

ABOVE: *The doyen of contemporary British music – Harrison Birtwistle (born 1934), photographed in Los Angeles in 1994.*

Martyrdom of St Magnus (1976–7), *The Lighthouse* (1979), and a series of *Strathclyde Concertos* for members of the Scottish Chamber Orchestra. He has written a great deal of music for children.

Many of Maxwell Davies' works spring from a religious impulse, as do all the later works of John Tavener (born 1944). Tavener derives his serene, meditative style from his Greek Orthodox faith, and has achieved fame with works such as *Ultimos ritos* (1972), *Resurrection* (1989), *Hymns of Paradise* (1992–3) and particularly *The Protecting Veil* for cello and strings (1987). He first attracted attention in the mid 1960s with his "crossover" cantata *The Whale*.

Several younger British composers promise exciting new developments in the 21st century. Among them are George Benjamin (born 1960), whose *Ringed by the Flat Horizon* (1979–80), *At First Light* (1982), and *A Mind of Winter* (1981) receive international performances. The Scottish composer James Macmillan (born 1959) came to prominence in 1990 with the orchestral work *The Confessions of Isobel Gowdie*, and has since produced an impressive body of work, largely inspired by his Catholicism.

ABOVE: *Peter Maxwell Davies (born 1934). Like Birtwistle, he was a member of the "Manchester School".*

In the 1960s Maxwell Davies founded the contemporary music ensemble The Fires of London (originally The Pierrot Players), for which he wrote theatre pieces such as *Eight Songs for a Mad King* (1969), and vocal and instrumental works such as *Revelation and Fall* for soprano and instruments (1966). The landscape and culture of the Orkney Islands, where he has lived since the 1970s, have inspired many of his later works, including the operas *The*

Mark-Anthony Turnage (born 1960) draws inspiration from many sources including rock and jazz. His operas *Greek* (1986–8), *The Country of the Blind* (1997) and *The Silver Tassie* (2000) have received wide acclaim. Finally, Thomas Adès (born 1971), an extraordinarily talented prodigy, has won international awards for his fluent and characterful orchestral and chamber music. His first opera, *Powder Her Face* (1994–5), is being performed all over the world.

ABOVE: *The British composer John Tavener (born 1944). His works are strongly influenced by the Greek Orthodox tradition.*

ABOVE: *Mark-Anthony Turnage (born 1960), one of the rising stars of the younger generation of British composers.*

ABOVE: *The extraordinarily gifted young British composer Thomas Adès (born 1971) has won international acclaim.*

Glossary

Acoustics: the science of sound.

Aerophone: a wind instrument, such as a flute or trombone.

Air: a simple tune for instrument or voice.

Aleatoric music: music in which random or chance elements are allowed to determine the course of the piece.

Allemand: dance movement in 4/4 time.

Antiphonal singing: when two parts of a choir sing alternately.

Aria: an operatic solo.

Ars antiqua: (old art) style of medieval music based on plainsong and organum.

Ars nova: (new art) musical style of 14th-century France and Italy, less restrictive than *ars antiqua*, introducing new rhythms and more independent parts.

Atonal: having no definite key centre or tonality.

Ballad: a narrative song.

Ballade: (1) a form of medieval poetry and music; (2) an instrumental work suggesting a narrative.

Barcarolle: a boating song (originally of Venetian gondeliers) or a piece of music in the same 6/8 rhythm.

Baroque: the musical period from about 1600–1750.

Basso continuo: ("figured bass") an accompanying bass line for a keyboard instrument, with figures to indicate chords on which the player improvises.

Bel canto: (beautiful singing) Italian style of operatic singing.

Bell: the flared or bulbous end of many aerophones.

Belly: the soundboard of a chordophone.

Blues: a slow, sad musical idiom characterized by the fusion of African and European music.

Body: the soundbox or resonator of a chordophone.

Bridge: a wooden member that is either set loosely or glued to the belly of some chordophones to hold the strings away from the soundboard.

Canon: a composition in which a melody begun in one part is repeated in another part, or parts, before the first has finished.

Cantata: a work for choir and/or solo voice(s), with instrumental accompaniment.

Cantus firmus: a melody borrowed from a religious or secular source, such as a folk song, as the basis for counterpoint from the 14th–17th centuries.

Capo tasto: a movable device tied or clipped to the fingerboard of some chordophones to assist in transposition.

Chanson: a song for several voices current in France from the 14th–16th centuries.

Chanter: the melody pipe of a set of bagpipes.

Chanterelle: the melody string of some members of the lute family of instruments.

Chord: the effect that is produced by sounding two or more notes together.

Chordophone: an instrument with strings, such as the harp and guitar.

Chromatic harmony: harmony that uses numerous chromatic chords (deviating by semitones from typical major or minor chords).

Chromatic scale: a scale ascending or descending by semitones.

Clausula: a cadence in medieval music.

Clef: the sign that fixes the position of a particular note on the staff.

Coda: extra final section of a movement or composition.

Coll'arco: direction to play strings with the bow.

Coloratura: agile, florid singing style, usually soprano.

Compass: the range of a voice or instrument.

Concert pitch: the standard of pitch to which instruments are usually tuned. At present the A above middle C (*a'*) is set at 440 Hertz.

Concerto: a work for solo instrument(s) and orchestra, usually in three movements.

Concerto grosso: instrumental form contrasting a small group of instruments with a larger orchestral group.

Conductus: a medieval secular vocal composition with one given part to which other parts are in counterpoint.

page number footer

Consort: a group of instruments, such as viols.

Coquille: the hole through a valve that allows the passage of air from one side to the other.

Counterpoint: the weaving together of two or more melodic lines to make musical sense, resulting in polyphony.

Courante: a dance in triple time.

Course: two or three strings lying close together, sounded together and tuned to either unison or octave pitch.

Crook: a detachable piece of tubing added to a brass instrument to alter its pitch.

Development: in sonata form, the section of a movement following the initial statement of the themes, in which they are expanded or modified.

Diatonic scale: any one of the major or minor scales of five tones and two semitones.

Drone: a pipe or string that sounds a sustained tone.

Dynamics: variations in loudness and softness.

Electronic music: music whose playing requires electronic means, such as tape, electronic instruments, synthesizers or computers.

Embouchure: in brass and some woodwind playing, the mode of application of the lips.

Equal temperament: a system of tuning by which the octave is divided into a chromatic scale of 12 equal semitones.

Exposition: the first part of sonata form, in which the main themes are stated.

Fantaisie, fantasia: piece of music composed from known tunes, or expressing the free play of the composer's imagination.

Fingerboard: the front of the neck where the strings are stopped by being pressed against the wood.

Frets: fixed or movable divisions of a fingerboard which indicate stopping points.

Frog: the part of the bow used for tightening the hair.

Fugue: contrapuntal work in three or more parts of equal importance, which enter successively in imitation of each other.

Galliard: lively dance, usually in 3/2 time.

Gavotte: old dance in 4/4 time.

Gigue: dance in 6/8 or 12/8 time.

Glissando: a slide up or down, played, for example, by sweeping the hand across harp strings or sliding the finger along a violin string.

Gradual: elaborate plainsong response to passages sung by the priest in a Mass.

Grand opera: 19th-century opera which is all sung, with no spoken dialogue.

Gregorian chant: solo and unison plainsong choral chants associated with Pope Gregory I.

Ground bass: a short bass theme persistently repeated.

Harmonics: the fundamental and overtones of a given tone.

Harmony: the simultanous sounding of notes.

Homophony: music in which the parts move together, presenting a top melody with chords beneath.

Idiophone: an instrument made of naturally sonorous materials, not needing any additional tension as do strings and drumskins.

Impromptu: a short piece of music suggesting improvisation.

Intendant: the administrative director of an opera house.

Isorhythmic: Of motets, having a tenor line in which the rhythm, though not the pitch, is repeated many times.

Jack: a thin strip of wood that carries the plectrum in plucked keyboard instruments.

Janissary music: a style of percussive military music, influenced by Turkish music, popular in 18th-century Europe.

Kapellmeister: the musical director of a private chapel, or of the musical staff at a German court.

Key: the classification of the notes of a scale, determined by the key-note.

Klangfarbenmelodie: a term used by Schoenberg to denote a melody determined by changes in timbre rather than pitch.

Leitmotif: (leading motif) a short theme used repeatedly in a score – especially by Wagner – to denote an object, person or idea.

Libretto: the text of an opera or oratorio.

Liturgy: the written form of religious service.

Madrigal: a contrapuntal setting in several parts of a secular verse.

Maestro di cappella: the musical director of a church, chapel or court in Italy.

Mazurka: a Polish country dance in 3/4 or 3/8.

Melody: a succession of notes of varying pitch with a recognizable musical shape.

Microtone: any interval smaller than a semitone.

Minimalism: term applied to works based on the repetition of very short figures.

Minuet: French rustic dance in triple time adapted to court use in the 17th century, and to symphonic use in the 18th century.

Mode: name for each of the ways of ordering the notes of a scale.

Modulation: key change.

Monody: music on one line, without counter-point or accompanying harmonies.

Motet: Ecclesiastical vocal musical form based on a given melody with other parts in counterpoint.

Motif: a recognizable short group of notes in a work.

Motto theme: a theme that recurs during a piece of music, similar to a *Leitmotif*.

Musique concrète: music created on disc or tape by electronically modifying natural sounds.

Neume: a sign in medieval notation showing the pitch of a syllable of vocal music.

Nocturne: a short lyrical piece, usually for piano, in one movement.

Obbligato: a term used of an instrument having a compulsory or special role.

Opera buffa: comic opera.

Opera seria: serious and formal Italian opera, with heroic or mythological plot.

Oratorio: an extended musical setting of a religious text in semi-dramatic form.

Organum: a medieval form of part-writing based on plainsong harmonized with up to three other parts.

Ornamentation: the insertion of a note or notes additional to the main tune, for decoration.

Ostinato: a persistently repeated musical phrase or rhythm.

Overblowing: the production of overtones on a wind instrument.

Overture: (1) a piece of orchestral music preceding an opera or play; (2) an orchestral work in one movement, usually with a title alluding to a literary or pictorial source.

Palindrome: a piece, usually atonal, which repeats a sequence backwards after a midpoint.

Parody mass: a type of Mass common in the 16th century, based on a melody taken from another work.

Partita: an 18th-century term for a suite.

Pavan: a slow, stately dance.

Pegs: tuning pins used on a stringed instrument.

Pitch: the "height" or "depth" of a note, determined by the frequency of vibrations producing it.

Pizzicato: direction to pluck strings with the fingers.

Plainsong: medieval church music consisting of a single line of unaccompanied music sung in "free" rhythm.

Plectrum: a device used for plucking strings.

Polonaise: a stately Polish dance in 3/4 time.

Polyphony: the simultaneous sounding of different notes, generally in counterpoint.

Polytonality: the simultaneous use of more than one key.

Prelude: a musical introduction, or a short self-contained piece.

Programme music: a piece of music interpreting a picture or story.

Recapitulation: in sonata form, the section of a movement which repeats the original themes after the development.

Recitative: speech-like singing in opera used for dialogue or to precede an aria.

Rib: the side wall of a stringed instrument connecting the soundboard to the back of the body.

Ricercare: contrapuntal instrumental work of 16th–18th centuries, often for keyboard.

Rondeau: a type of medieval French song with a refrain.

Scherzo: (a joke) a lively movement in a symphony developed by Beethoven to replace the minuet and trio.

Score: written or printed ensemble music with all the parts set out one above the other on the page.

Serialism: technique whereby a structural "series" of notes governs the total development of the composition. It led to the 12-note system of composition.

Singspiel: a play with interpolated songs.

Sonata: an instrumental work in three or four movements and for one or two players.

Sonata form: a construction used in the first movement of a sonata or symphony, which is divided into three sections: exposition, development and recapitulation.

Song-cycle: a set of songs grouped by the composer in a particular order for performance, often based on a sequence of poems.

Soundboard: the front of the body of a chordophone that receives the vibrations from the strings and reflects them.

Sound-holes: holes cut in the soundboard to connect the vibrating air inside the instrument with the outside air.

Soundpost: a piece of wood fixed inside a stringed instrument, vertically connecting upper and lower surfaces, thus distributing vibrations over the body of the instrument.

Speaker key: a key that facilitates overblowing on woodwind instruments.

Stochastic: a term denoting a process of which the steps are governed by rules of probability.

Study: an instrumental piece written to improve or demonstrate a particular point of technique.

Suite: an instrumental piece in several movements.

Symphony: a substantial orchestral work, usually in four movements.

Tablature: a system of writing music by indicating the position of the player's fingers, as used for the lute or organ.

Te Deum: a Latin hymn of thanksgiving to God.

Tenor: the highest normal male voice, so called because it held the melody in plainsong.

Tonality: the general key of a piece.

Tone cluster or note cluster: a group of adjacent notes played together.

Tone-poem: a substantial orchestral work intended to interpret a non-musical idea, picture or literary work.

Tone-row or note-row: a sequence of all 12 notes of the octave which forms the basis of a composition in 12-note music.

Tonic: keynote of the diatonic scale, from which the key takes its name.

Transposition: the translation of a piece of music into a key other than that in which it was originally written.

Trio: (1) a combination of three performers; (2) a work for three performers; (3) the centre section of a minuet, traditionally written in three parts.

Troubadour: an itinerant medieval poet/musician of southern France. Their equivalents in Germany were called *Minnesinger* and in England they were called minstrels.

Trouvère: an itinerant medieval poet/musician of northern France.

Twelve-note system: the technique by which all 12 notes within an octave are treated as equal and placed in a particular order (note-row) to form the basis of the composition.

Virelai: medieval French song.

Acknowledgements

The publisher would like to thank the following individuals, manufacturers and music shops for the use of their instruments and facilities for photography.

Felicity Forster (violin), Stuart Hall (*tres*, Cretan *lyra*, *saz* and *kora*), Robert Harbron (English mandolin and concertina), Duncan and Hayley Kerr (bagpipes), Giovanni Sipiano (guitars and percussion instruments).

Folk instruments
Blanks Music Stores Ltd
271–273 Kilburn High Road
London NW6 7JR
Tel: (020) 7624 7777

Strings
David Lipkin and Haim Algranati
L. A. Strings
68 High Street, Barnet
London EN5 5SJ
Tel: (020) 8364 9726

Strings, woodwind and brass
Foote's
10 Golden Square
London W1R 3AF
Tel: (020) 7437 1811

Woodwind
Howarth of London
31–35 Chiltern Street
London W1M 1HG
Tel: (020) 7935 2407

Woodwind and brass
John Myatt Woodwind and Brass
 Instrument Specialists
57 Nightingale Road
Hitchin
Hertfordshire SG5 1RQ
Tel: (01462) 420 057

Percussion
Music Bank (Hire) Limited
100 Clements Road
London SE16 4DG
Tel: (020) 7252 0001

Percussion and computers
Norton York and Colm O'Rourke
The University of Westminster
Harrow Campus
Northwick Park
Harrow HA1 3TP
Tel: (020) 7911 5000

Keyboards and mechanical
 instruments
Finchcocks
Goudhurst
Kent TN17 1HH
Tel: (01580) 211 702

The publisher would also like to thank the following picture libraries for the use of their pictures in the book (l=left, r=right, t=top, b=bottom, u=upper, m=middle). Every effort has been made to acknowledge the pictures properly; however, we apologize if there are any unintentional omissions, which will be corrected in future editions.

AKG, London: 3; 5 (Bach); 16t, bl, br; 17t; 18t, b; 19tl, bl, br; 23br; 32bl; 38bl; 40t, br; 43t; 45bl, br; 47bl; 49tl; 54r; 60t; 63b; 66t, b; 78bl; 81tr; 83bl; 86l, r; 89tl; 108l; 109br; 111b; 114t; 115br; 116br; 133tr; 134b; 135tl, tr; 136bl; 144b; 145tr; 149br; 150b; 154b; 161tr; 172b; 181b; 195tr; 198bl; 203b; 204bl; 208t; 216t; 227br; 229br; 230t; 235bl; 246t; 252–3; 259t; 260t; 266bl; 270t, bl; 272b; 278t; 288b; 290t; 294t; 295t; 296t; 298t; 300t; 303t; 304t, bl, br; 306t, bl, br; 307t, b; 308b; 309tl; 312t; 313t; 314bl; 318t; 320br; 321b; 322t; 323t;

325b; 326t, bl; 328tl, tr, b; 329bl; 330t; 331t; 332t, b; 334bl; 336t; 338t; 342bl, br; 353t; 358bl; 362bl; 374t, br; 377b; 378b; 396b; 397tl; 398–9; 400t; 401t, br; 412b; 413t, 418b; 420b; 433bl; 436t; 469b; *British Library* 254r; *Stefan Diller* 273t; *Marion Kalter* 442b; 489t; 494t, b; *Erich Lessing* 260b; 280b; 288t; 301b; 316–17; 318br; 319t; 325t; 327t; 329t; 335t; 336bl, br; 337b; 341b; 456bl; *Visioars* 334br.

Arena Images Ltd: 7tr, br; 10tr; 34t; 36br; 37tr, br; 38br; 39bl; 41tr; 50b; 55b; 81tl; 96t; 100bl, br; 101t; 109t; 119bl; 121br; 129b; 130bl; 142b; 156b; 161ml; 176tl; 194t, b; 200b; 203m; 206b; 213b; 216b; 217bl; 220b; 221t; 228m; 245m; 246b; *Ron Scherl* 291t; 497br; *Colin Willoughby* 486b.

Art Archive Ltd: 6tr; 8–9; 10bl; 11b; 12br; 17m; 20l, r; 21t, bl; 24t; 27b; 29l; 42r; 46b; 47t; 55tl; 59t, b; 67m, b; 101b; 103br; 111tr; 120tr; 126t; 127l; 129mr; 137b; 147br; 159t; 176tr; 180b; 193tl; 196bl; 200tr; 223b; 227tl; 231r; 233tl; 250l; 259b; 285t; 302b; 334t; 380br; 389t; 419b.

Bridgeman Art Library, London: 6bl, br; 7bl; 14t; 22tl; 23tl; 30t; 33tl, tr; 43b; 56t; 57t; 61tr; 62t; 74bl; 92bl; 104t; 105tr; 109bl; 115t; 118bl, br; 123bl, br; 127r; 128t; 130tl; 132t; 133b; 135b; 138br; 139br; 145l; 149tl; 155t; 160b; 174br; 181tr; 190br; 191br; 192br; 205br; 211m; 218b; 219tl; 223tl; 225l, br; 231l; 244t; 248t; 258; 261b; 262; 264–5; 266t, br; 268–9; 271b; 275t, b; 276t, b; 281b; 283b; 286–7; 289t, b; 290b; 296bl; 297b; 298b; 299tr, b; 310t; 311bl, br; 315tl, br; 318bl; 319b; 327b; 331b; 335bl; 339b; 340b; 341t; 343tl, br; 344–5; 346; 347b; 351t; 356t; 357; 358t; 361t, b; 362t; 363t; 364b; 366t; 367; 368b; 369t; 372–3; 374bl; 375t, b; 383b; 391b; 394t; 395b; 396t; 403b; 408br; 409l; 424t, bl, br; 430–1; 432t, b; 434t, bl, br; 435b; 437tl, b; 438t; 440t; 454t; 460b; 490t; © *Arthur Rackham Estate* 413bl; *Giraudon* 297b; 338b; 370tl; 439t; *Index* 12bl; 30bl; 54l; *David Lees* 290b; *Novosti* 426t; *Peter Willi* 11t.

Camera Press Ltd: 17br; 33br; 58t, b, (all flags); 59 (all flags); 61bl, br; 63tl; 71tr; 72t; 74t; 75tl; 76l, r; 77bl; 80l; 83t; 84l; 93tl, b; 97b; 170t; 171b; 184b; 185m; 211b; 247t; 249bl, br; 251t, m, b; 383tl; 397b; 402br; 419t; 468bl, br; 475bl; 478t, b; 482t; 498t; *Karsh* 459t; 460t; 465t; 467t; *Patraig O'Donnell* 488t.

Christie's Images: 23bl; 103tl; 116t; 126l; 136br; 149m; 153tr.

Eye Ubiquitous: *James Davis* 400b; 480br.

Frank Lane Picture Agency Limited: *H. D. Brandl* 491b; *Roger Wilmshurst* 12t.

gettyone Stone: 23tr; 24br; 31t (3rd from left); 61tl; 68bl, br; 69t; 72b; 94–5; 107t, bl; 110r; 113bl; 119t; 121t, bl; 128br; 131br; 157br; 163t; 164tr; 185t; 189br; 197tr; 201tr; 203t; 209t; 235tl; 241tl; 293t; 404t; 425; 427; 444b; 454bl; 455; 463t, bl; 465b.

Horniman Museum & Gardens: 169t; 178t; 179br; 239t.

Hulton Getty: 463br; 474br; 490b.

Hutchinson Library: 14bl, br; 15t, b; 25t; 111tl; 126b; 151m; 157tr; 166b; 167mr; 173t; 183bl; 185b; 191b; 193b; 207b; 235br; 237tr.

Kobal Collection: 233br.

Lebrecht Collection, London: 13t; 22tr; 24bl; 26l, r; 27tl; 28t, bl, br; 32t; 35tl; 42l; 45t; 46t; 48t, b; 49m, b; 56b; 60b; 62b; 64b; 67t; 69br; 74br; 82l, r; 85bl, br; 89br; 90l; 92br; 102b; 103bl; 106tl; 113t; 114b; 115bl; 122bl, br; 123t; 125br; 129tr; 130tr; 131ml; 132l; 133tl; 145br; 148br; 158bl; 159m, b; 161tl; 163b; 170b; 171t; 172t; 173m; 174bl; 175t, bl, br; 176br; 177l, r; 178b; 179t, bl; 182b; 190bl; 192bl; 211t; 212bl; 219tr, b; 223tr; 225tr; 226b; 227tr; 229bl; 230b; 234bl; 238b; 254l; 255tr, b; 256; 257l, r; 261tl, tr; 267t; 270br; 271t; 274t, bl, br; 277t,

b; 278b; 279t, b; 280t; 281t; 282t, b; 283t; 284t, b; 285bl, br; 291bl, br; 292t; 293b; 294br; 295b; 296br; 297t; 299tl; 300br; 301t; 302t; 303b; 305b; 308t; 309tr; 310bl, br; 314t, br; 315tr, bl; 320t, bl; 321t; 322bl; 324tl, tr, b; 326br; 333; 335br; 337t; 339t; 340tl, tr; 347tl; 348t, b; 349t, bl, br; 350t, b; 351b; 352t, b; 354t; 355; 356bl, br; 358br; 359t, b; 360t, bl, br; 362br; 363b; 364t; 365tl, tr, b; 366br; 368t; 369b; 370tr, b; 371tl, tr, b; 376t, b; 377t; 378b; 379tl, tr, b; 380t, bl; 381t, b; 384t, bl, br; 385; 386; 387bl, br; 388t, bl, br; 389b; 390t, b; 391t; 392t; 393t, b; 394bl; 395tl, tr; 397um, tr; 401bl; 402t, bl; 403t; 404bl, br; 405t, b; 406t, bl; 407b; 408t; 410t, bl, br; 411l, r; 412t; 414t, br; 415t, b; 416t; 418t; 420t; 421t, b; 422t, bl, br; 423t, b; 426bl, br; 428t, bl, br; 429tl, um, tr, br; 433t, br; 435t; 436t; 438bl; 439b; 440t; 441; 442t; 443; 444t; 445; 446t, bl, br; 447b; 448b; 449tl, tr, b; 450t; 451t, b; 452t, b; 453t; 454br; 456t; 457b; 458t, b; 461t, bl, br; 462t, b; 464t, b; 467bl; 469t; 470; 471tl, tr; 472; 473b; 475tl, tr, br; 481t, b; 498bl; *M. Allen* 292b; 304tr; 343tr, bl; 366bl; *Archive Manuel de Falla* 474bl; *Arthur Reynolds Collection* 416b; 417t, b; 429bl; *R. Booth* 134t; 137tl; *Zdenek Chrapek* 56m; *J. M. Cook* 237br; *Milein Cosman* 466b; *N. Dyson* 68t; *Mike Evans* 51t; 229m; 484t, b; *David Farrell* 55tr; 79b; 91tl; 139t; 473t; 486t; 499tr; *Jim Four* 142t; *Betty Freeman* 87m; 479tl; 487t; 499tl; *Joanne Harris* 311t; 450b; *Richard Haughton* 57b; 105tl; *C. R. Henderson* 65t; *Matti Kolho* 409r; 471b; *Kurt Weill Foundation* 459b; *S. Lauterwasser* 49tr; 78t; 88b; 91bl; 413br; *Andre LeCoz* 492b; *Nigel Luckhurst* 247b; 482b; 496b; *Suzie Maeder* 83br; 87t; 487b; 488b; 491t; *Peter Mares* 383tr; *R. Meek* 272t; *B. Morris* 69bl; 347t; 382b; 387t; 394br; *Kate Mount* 51t; 53m; 107br; 221b; 263t;

479tr; 485b; *Odile Noel* 50t; 65b; 143bm; 167tl; 189tl; 247m; *F. Noronha* 38t; 138bl; 197bl; 237tl, bl; *M. Peric* 199b; *Pictorial Press* 63tr; 73tr, b; 75bl; 77br; *Wladimir Polak* 91tr, br; 117b; 147t; 151t; 483b; *Private Collection* 47br; 248b; 313b; 330b; 354b; 447t; 456br; 474t; *Mary Robert* 263bl; *Zsuzsi Roboz* 448t; *Celene Rosen* 255tl; 300bl; *Royal Academy of Music* 80r; 106tr; 125bl; 131t; 312b; 342tl; 392b; 408bl; *G. Salter* 7tl; 34br; 52t, b; 64t; 104bl; 117tl; 137tr; 152br; 153tl; 155br; 161b; 169m; 181tl; 195tl; 198br; 207tl; 208b; 245b; 322br; 323b; 406br; 483t; 489b; *D. Smirnov* 498br; *Richard H. Smith* 492t; 495b; *Chris Stock* 15m; 92t; 100t; 136t; 143br; 152bl; 163b; 166t; 167bl; 168b; 169bl; 174t; 183t; 189tr; 199tr; 207tr; 212tr; 217t; *Horst Tappe* 466t; *Greg Tomin* 480t, bl; *Guy Vivien* 438br; *Toby Wales* 93tr; 479b.

Mary Evans Picture Library: 10br; 13m, b; 17bl; 19tr; 21br; 27tr; 29r; 30br; 33bl; 36t; 44; 84r; 85tr, bl; 124t, b; 125t; 143bl; 188bl; 201bl; 209br; 210b; 222l; 224b; 236b.

Max Wade-Matthews: 169br; 209bl.

Performing Arts Library: 70t; 90r; 437tr; *Clive Barda* 53t, b; 57m; 63m; 78br; 96b; 97t, m; 113br; 151t; 152ml; 153b; 165tr, b; 199tl; 205bl; 228t; 249t; 353b; 457t; 485t; 493t, b; 495t; 496t; 497t, bl; 499bl, br; *Marcelo Benbahan* 202b; *Sisi Burn* 81b; *Ben Christopher* 499bm; *Fritz Curzon* 35b; 263br; 382t; *James McCormick* 146t; *Kate Mount* 210t; *Linda Rich* 22b; 267b; 467br; 468t.

Redferns Music Picture Library: 37tr; 51b; 70bl, br; 71tl, b; 73tl; 75tr, br; 77tl, tr; 79tl, tr; 87b; 89b (all in panel); 105b; 112l; 117tr; 121bur; 139bl; 143t; 157tl, bl; 165tl; 173b; 183br; 191bl; 204br; 205t; 212br; 217br; 226t; 233bl; 240b; 244b; 245t; 250r.

Simon Broughton: 25bl, br; 106b; 196t.

The Stock Market: 453b; 476–7.

Wendy Thompson: 273b; 305tl; *British Library* 329br; *Editions des Musées Nationaux* 294bl; *Harold T. Storey* 407t.

Index